The Dilemmas of Social Democracies

The Dilemmas of Social Democracies

Overcoming Obstacles to a More Just World

Howard Richards and Joanna Swanger

LEXINGTON BOOKS

A division of
ROWMAN & LITTLEFIELD PUBLISHERS, INC.
Lanham • Boulder • New York • Toronto • Oxford

LEXINGTON BOOKS

A division of Rowman & Littlefield Publishers, Inc.
A wholly owned subsidiary of The Rowman & Littlefield Publishing Group, Inc.
4501 Forbes Boulevard, Suite 200
Lanham, MD 20706

PO Box 317
Oxford
OX2 9RU, UK

British Library Cataloguing in Publication Information Available

Library of Congress Cataloging-in-Publication Data

Richards, Howard, 1938–
  The dilemmas of social democracies : overcoming obstacles to a more just world /
Howard Richards and Joanna Swanger.
    p. cm.
  Includes bibliographical references and index.
  ISBN-13: 978-0-7391-0970-0 (cloth : alk. paper)
  ISBN-10: 0-7391-0970-7 (cloth : alk. paper)
  1. Socialism—History. 2. Cooperation and socialism. I. Swanger, Joanna, 1968– II.
Title.
HX21.R596 2006
320.53'15—dc22   2006007713

Printed in the United States of America

♾™ The paper used in this publication meets the minimum requirements of American
National Standard for Information Sciences—Permanence of Paper for Printed Library
Materials, ANSI/NISO Z39.48–1992.

For Caroline, for her love and her teachings; *para los chilenos que en 1970 em-pezaron a construir el camino*; and for all who work for justice and peace at the beginning of the twenty-first century.

Contents

Preface   ix
Acknowledgments   xi

1   On Cooperation and Sharing   1

2   Making Invisible Causes Visible   43

3   The Drama of Spanish Socialism: Tragedy, Farce,
or Conceptual Error? (Part 1)   67

4   The Drama of Spanish Socialism: Tragedy, Farce,
or Conceptual Error? (Part 2)   81

5   A Modest Hypothesis Concerning Swedish
Social Democracy   99

6   Sweden's Rehn-Meidner Model: Too Good to be True,
or, The Stumbling Blocks of Freedom and Property   119

7   The Revenge of the Iron Law of Wages   145

8   Hjalmar Branting's *Uppfostran*   165

9   Karl Popper's Vienna, or, The Straitjacket of Mainstream
Social Science   181

10   Power and Principle in South Africa   207

11   Islam and Economic Rationality in Indonesia   225

12   The Stones that the Builders Rejected   257

13   Middle-Class Values   285

14   The Venezuela That Might Have Been   315

15 Social Democracy on a World Scale: The World Bank
   and the Logic of Love   349

Epilogue   387
Bibliography   391
Index   419
About the Authors   433

Preface

Life would be much easier and happier if individuals and institutions were guided by principles of cooperation and sharing. In saying this we do not mean to express an optimistic view of human nature. That life would be better if people cooperated more is true by definition, whatever human nature may be, and whether or not there is such a thing as human nature, and whether or not the concept "human nature" makes sense. The notion of "cooperation and sharing" *means* working together and facilitating one another's access to resources, and, normally, doing so for some constructive purpose, to meet some need. They thus *mean*, by extension, acting in ways that make life easier and happier. What would happen if people cooperated and shared sets a standard, even though at least part of the road toward moving closer to that standard no doubt goes by way of the intelligent organization of competition and selfishness.

Because doing so would improve the quality of life, it is therefore logical to cooperate and to share. It would be logical for people to help one another, each doing her or his part, to do those things that contribute to making their own and others' lives easier and happier. If ideals of cooperation and sharing guided people to do the things that need to be done, then life would be easier and happier because—and here we insist on the obvious precisely because the significance of the obvious is so often overlooked—because the things that need to be done would be done.

The answers to questions about what is needed, and what is perhaps only wanted but not really needed, are often neither obvious nor uncontroversial. Humans should not postpone cooperation and sharing until the day we reach agreement on those answers; for indeed we believe this day will never come. Helping one another and supporting one another is part of creating a respectful atmosphere in which humanity's endless philosophical conversation about essentially contested concepts, such as "needs," "God," "sex," "art," "democracy," "science," "health," "spirituality," "rights," and so on, can happily continue, and we have a great deal to say concerning the themes of that endless conversation, starting, here, with "needs."

To begin, we believe that what needs to be done to make human life easier and happier is to some extent the same everywhere and not a matter of choice. The human species is subject to attack by bacteria; to viruses; and to pain, accident, and deterioration. The body requires air, water, and food. The soul requires love and appreciation. Nature imposes certain species-wide tasks upon humanity, as species-wide needs.

Human life is, moreover, embedded in the living systems of the biosphere, which include the air, the waters, the sunlight, the soil, and the living plant and animal forms. Making human life easier and happier—indeed making it possible for human life to continue at all—cannot be separated from the care and nurture of the biosphere in which our particular species lives and moves and has its being. Maintaining the health of the earth community is another task nature has set for humanity. It is our task because it is our responsibility, and it is our responsibility because of our power. Today the future of any species other than our own—whether it will go extinct, whether it will be bred along new lines, whether it will multiply and prosper, whether it will be genetically altered—depends far more on its interaction with us than on natural selection.

What needs to be done, however, is not as uniform and largely *is* a matter of choice. Human needs are not just the common needs of all living things, nor are they just the common needs of our species. There are varying needs of people of different cultures and subcultures, and of different temperaments, needs of ethnicities and faiths and groups of different sizes, down to the personally cultivated lifestyle, the unique way of walking and talking, of thinking, of smiling; down to each individual's practice of the art of living. To live, to be, people need, precisely, choices. Without social identity and freedom, the type of life characteristic of our species does not happen.

If individuals and institutions were guided by concepts of cooperation and sharing, then energy and resources would be channeled:

—toward meeting human needs.
—toward living in harmony with the living systems of the earth.
—toward encouraging the free and creative flowering of each kind of person, and of each person.

Life would continue to be, no doubt, hard enough, but it would not be as hard as it is for most people now. Questions about whether people really need God, or sexual satisfaction, or children, or automobiles, or air conditioning, would continue to be as hotly debated as they are now, but the debaters would be happier. And there is nothing at all in the atmosphere of the planet, nothing in the nitrogen, or the oxygen, or the carbon dioxide, or the rare gases, that prevents us human beings from changing our behavior and our institutions in order to make life easier. There is nothing in the waters, either the waters of the seas or the fresh water of lakes and rivers, nothing in the polar ice, or in the clouds, or in the rain, that compels us to refrain from making the world a happier place. There is nothing in the earth, nothing in igneous, sedimentary, or metamorphic rock, that keeps us from cooperating and sharing. There is nothing impeding us in the sunlight, or in the worlds of plants or animals.

There is nothing in all of nature that prevents individuals and institutions from being guided by principles of cooperation and sharing, except: ourselves.

Acknowledgments

The authors wish to thank all who have contributed to the development of the ideas expressed in this book as teachers, students, friends, and colleagues, by offering suggestions or criticisms at one stage or another of their development, including particularly A.J. Ayer, Richard Bernstein, Tony Bing, Alicia Cabezudo, Katie Campbell-Nelson, Len Clark, Jonathan Diskin, Ariel Dorfman, Steve Eskow, Ann Folsom, Roger Folsom, Michael Freeman, Erick García, Juan-Eduardo García Huidobro, Elizabeth Groppe, Ferit Guven, George Guy, Roger Hand, Rom Harre, Caroline Higgins, Catherine Odora Hoppers, Ann Jennings, Kevin Kelly, John King-Farlow, Gil Klose, Rajaram Krishnan, John Manning, JoAnn Martin, Alan Montefiore, John Newman, Brian Nichols, Edmund O'Sullivan, Donald Ranstead, Ken Richards, Richard Rorty, Richard Schmitt, Heather Schwartz, Alexander Sesonske, John Sniegocki, Jeff Streiffer, Peter Suber, Peter Swanger, Anita Swann, Liffey Thorpe, Andres Thomas Conteris, John Townsend, Charles Wilber, Beverly Woodward; and the late and lamented Eric Fromm, Linus Pauling, Yosal Rogat, Dick Spahn, and Paul Wienpaul. These acknowledgments do not imply, of course, that any of the named or unnamed people who over the years have taken the trouble to make perceptive comments on our developing views agree with any or all of them.

Chapter 1

On Cooperation and Sharing

Introduction

Convinced as we are that cooperation and sharing are feasible, we regard the greater part of the suffering we observe as avoidable. This simple and appealing idea is today so distant from the concerns of academic social science that it will take a whole book to make it possible to hope that it might be put on the agenda for serious consideration. Through methods known as "nonviolence" and "cultural action," society could be transformed. We are endlessly frustrated to see that while these methods are misunderstood, rejected, or simply not known, unnecessary suffering continues. We are aghast and amazed that the human family has failed its simplest test: that of assuring that every sister and brother has enough food. From the points of view of agronomy and biochemistry, the test is a no-brainer. Still, humanity flunks it. It also fails to exercise the elementary self-control needed to keep its population within the carrying capacity of the environment. We are aghast and amazed that people do the stupidest things, such as killing other people and destroying habitats.

We do not believe our amazement is due to lack of knowledge of the causes of dysfunctional behavior.[1] Rather we believe that our amazement is due to our having elaborated an especially intense vision of an alternative—a global mosaic of cultures practicing local variations on an ethics of love and responsibility; and to our conceiving an especially clear methodology for putting the alternative into practice. Although the present world crisis may be regarded as a crisis of globalization, or of neoliberalism, or as a security crisis, we think it more accurate to regard it as a continuing crisis of social democracy. The decline of social democracy in the second half of the twentieth century was simultaneously the rise of neoliberalism. It seems more accurate to us to regard humanity's continuing inability to build just societies as the disease, and poverty and war as the consequences of the disease.

Above, in the Preface, we declared true by definition our premise, "that life would be much easier and happier if individuals and institutions were guided by principles of cooperation and sharing." It is to be understood as a tautology: "If people did what needs to be done, then what needs to be done would be done." This is known in Spanish as "a parrot's truth" (*una verdad de perogrullo*). Otherwise viewed, it is a proposed conceptual framework. Readers of Howard Richards' *Letters from Quebec* will recognize the philosophical method we are employing, which may be called a method of metaphysical construction (itself a form of cultural action). There also, Howard Richards laboriously staked out positions that respond to some philosophical objections to this method, such as the objection that the method improperly derives "ought" from "is," or facts from definitions.

The topic of the present book is social democracy, and its purpose is to move forward the construction of social democracy. Our proposal for forms of cultural action toward social democracy rests on our belief that, as Roy Bhaskar writes, "society is at once the ever-present condition and the continually reproduced outcome of human agency."[2] There is no *natural* reason why people cannot cooperate and share; the only barrier to achieving the greater happiness that can arise from increased cooperation and sharing is the way we humans have organized our societies. We believe—and we believe many others believe—that the West European social democracies were, in their heyday from about 1955 to about 1975, humanity's greatest achievement so far in harnessing human energy and mobilizing natural resources and capital in the service of meeting everybody's needs. Therefore, this book analyzes social democracy in principle and worldwide, paying special attention to the historical experience of Western Europe, and within Western Europe, to the experience of Sweden. From studies of their successes and failures, we will draw some conclusions about social democracy's philosophical limitations. We will make some recommendations to activists, particularly to those who are striving to realize the promise of social democracy, while painting it green.

However, before beginning a case-by-case analysis of social democracy, we will give ourselves a running start by mentioning briefly some main ideas of a few of the many thinkers who have advocated cooperation and sharing, namely (in chronological order): Plato, Jesus, Voltaire, Adam Smith, Karl Marx, Mohandas Gandhi, Robert Axelrod, Mother Teresa, and Michael Hardt and Antonio Negri. We must mention a few of the great contributions to the concepts of cooperation and sharing, of which we take social democracy to be the main modern political approximation, in order to give these two concepts more content. Since "cooperation and sharing" will function as a baseline for our study of social democracy, we begin by drawing attention to some of the dimensions that have been contributed to these rich concepts by a few of their main exponents.

Also, we mention some precedents because we do not want to be alone. In our accounts of social democracy we will find ourselves attacking some ideas commonly found in mainstream social science, especially economics and political science. We will be attacking limited historical and evolutionary visions, widely employed root metaphors, and research methodologies that pass as academically respectable. We will also be attacking what passes for common sense in modern western societies. We do not want to appear to be a lone voice in the wilderness denying everything everybody else asserts to be true. In establishing our baseline concept, therefore, we seek to establish also that the idea of cooperating to meet needs has been taken seriously by intelligent people, who really lived, who really meant what they said, and who took important concrete steps to put cooperation into practice.

After getting a running start by citing some of the wisdom of Plato, Jesus, Voltaire, Smith, Marx, Gandhi, Axelrod, Mother Teresa, and Hardt and Negri, we will return periodically to the discussion of alternatives to social scientific orthodoxy—alternatives that take ethics and cooperation seriously. We will be discussing alternative thinkers like, for example, Daniel Quinn, who says, "we need not new programs but new minds," as well as radical critics within the social sciences like Samuel Bowles and Herbert Gintis who provide valuable critical insights from within a worldview too close to that of mainstream social science to fully appreciate modernity's (and social democracy's) limitations.[3] We do not mean to say that we will always be fighting mainstream notions of what social science is all about. We find a great deal of truth, for example, in studies such as Bo Rothstein's study of Swedish social democracy's relative success when it was implemented by "cadres" instead of "bureaucrats," even though the studies rely on methodologies we regard as both typical of contemporary social science and as profoundly mistaken.[4]

On Cooperation and Sharing: A Perspective from Plato

"Is the physician, taken in that strict sense of which you are speaking, a healer of the sick or a maker of money? And remember that I am now speaking of the true physician." "A healer of the sick, he replied." —Plato[5]

Starting with his earliest dialogues, Plato relies on the fact that the specialized knowledge (the characteristic *episteme*) of each profession or art aims at something. The physician aims at health. The pilot aims to guide a ship safely. The farmer aims to produce food. The cobbler produces shoes.

We echo Plato when we teach our children that the postal worker delivers mail, the baker bakes bread, the firefighter puts out fires, the bus driver drives the bus. Howard Richards' four-year-old granddaughter would often ask, "What does he (or she) do?" The answer to her question invariably described a way of serving society.

The specific aim of each *techne* (profession or art) is categorized by Plato in at least four interchangeable ways: it is its good, it is the need it satisfies, it is the interest it serves, it is its use. A recurrent theme in Plato's writings is that although we can state the use of the special knowledge of the carpenter, the potter, the blacksmith, the dentist, and so on, we fall into confusion when we try to state the use of the special knowledge claimed by those who profess to teach virtue, politics, or rhetoric.

Plato's longest dialogue, *The Republic*, begins as an inquiry into virtue, specifically that aspect of virtue known as justice. Plato accepts the idea—a traditional idea at the time he was writing—that virtue has four parts, or aspects: wisdom, temperance (or moderation), courage, and justice. Justice is the topic of *The Republic*, but the other three virtues are also discussed and defined there.

In the first of the ten books of *The Republic*, Socrates, Plato's hero and spokesperson, is frustrated by the superficiality and inconsistency of common notions of justice (i.e., of *dikaiosyne*, also translated as "fairness" or "righteousness"). As is the case with the other virtues, most people think they know what justice is, how to acquire knowledge of it, and what good it does, until they are led into contradictions by a questioner like Socrates who simply asks them to answer simple questions and to state their ideas clearly.

Reading between the lines a bit, one can also discern in Book I of *The Republic* that it is not only most people's confusion that upsets Plato. Plato is also upset by base tendencies toward cynicism and skepticism found in commonsense notions of justice. Reading between the lines a bit one can detect Plato's desire to uplift his readers with his philosophical writings, in order to lead them to ideas of justice that are not only clear and true, but also noble.

Frustrated by an inconclusive, and somewhat degrading, review of common ideas about *dikaiosyne*, Socrates proposes that a better way to approach the topic would be to design an ideal state. What kind of state would we want to live in? What would a good state be like? There, in the image of a utopian vision of a society practicing the good life, it will perhaps be possible to see the true nature of justice, writ large and therefore legible, as a word written in large letters is legible for weak eyes unable to read small letters.

Turning then to the task of designing a state, Plato finds that the true architect of a state (i.e., of a *polis*, a Greek city-state) is the needs of its people. We quote the words Plato ascribes to Socrates at length:

> "A State," I said, "arises, as I conceive, out of the needs of mankind; no one is self sufficing, but all of us have many wants. Can any other origin of a State be imagined?"
>
> "There can be no other." [Adeimantus answers.]
>
> "Then, as we have many wants, and many persons are needed to supply them, one takes a helper for one purpose, and another for another; and when these partners and helpers are gathered together in one habitation the body of inhabitants is termed a State."
>
> "True," he said.
>
> "And they exchange with one another, and one gives, and another receives, under the idea that the exchange will be for their good."
>
> "Very true."

"Then," I said, "let us begin and create in idea a State; and yet the true creator is necessity, who is the mother of our invention."

"Of course," he replied.

"Now the first and greatest of necessities is food, which is the condition of life and existence."

"Certainly."

"The second is a dwelling, and the third clothing and the like."

"True."

"And now let us see how our city will be able to supply this great demand. We may suppose that one man is a husbandman, another a builder, someone else a weaver—shall we add to them a shoemaker, or perhaps some other purveyor to our bodily wants?"

"Quite right."

"The barest notion of a State must include four or five men."

"Clearly."

"And how will they proceed? Will each bring the result of his labours into a common stock? —the individual husbandman, for example, producing for four, and labouring four times as long and as much as he need for the provision of food with which he supplies others as well as himself; or will he have nothing to do with others and not be at the trouble of producing for them but provide for himself alone a fourth of the food in a fourth of the time, and in the remaining three fourths of the time be employed in making a house or a coat or a pair of shoes, having no partnership with others, but supplying himself all his own wants?"

Adeimantus thought he should aim at producing food only and not at producing everything.[6]

Plato thus contributed to civilization two important ideas that support our premise that the lives of human beings would be easier and happier if individuals and institutions were guided by principles of cooperation and sharing:

1) The purpose of each of the various professions and callings followed by the various members of society is to meet people's needs; and

2) The overall design of a good society is a design that will result in the meeting of the needs of its inhabitants.

On Cooperation and Sharing: A Perspective from Jesus

What we wish to demonstrate, or at least briefly illustrate, is that the meanings of "cooperation" and "sharing" (and of similar terms such as "love" and "solidarity") have been indelibly marked by the words of Jesus. When we later argue that social democracy has been an effort to implement solidarity under modern industrial conditions, we will attribute part of the notoriety of some of the images socialism has invoked to Jesus. It is not our aim here to make a case either for Jesus or against Jesus; nor is it our aim to reckon a balance sheet weighing pros against cons to arrive at a sober appreciation of the good and bad aspects of his influence. Our aim is to convey our message in languages that will be widely understood.

To hear echoes of the words of Jesus in the achievements of West European social democracy does not imply attributing to Jesus any originality. The Old Testament, Greek philosophy and religion, oriental sages, contemporary movements and sects in Israel, and the shamans of hunting and gathering peoples can all be cited to prove that many people had the same ideas earlier. A recent and plausible theory about the source of the popularity of the ideas Jesus expressed has been proposed by Riane Eisler.

According to Eisler, cooperation and sharing prevailed in prehistoric times in various cultures at various times and places, and in particular shortly before the dawn of history in Southeast Europe and Asia Minor.[7] The cooperating and sharing "partnership societies," as Eisler calls them, were conquered some time around 2000 B.C. by warlike patriarchal tribes from the north. The results of the conquests were what Eisler, and, following her, Walter Wink, call "dominator societies." The principles of a dominator society include separation, exclusion, force, fear, mutual indifference, and exploitation.[8] Nevertheless, Eisler speculates, the older, gentler values were not extinguished. They were preserved as collective memories, and as alternative practices. People never forgot the old folkways, and people never ceased to respond to the natural tendencies that the old folkways developed. For this reason, Eisler believes, there was an audience ready to listen to the teachings of Jesus. His message was a revival of principles that had been defeated but not lost.[9]

Eisler's theory is, of course, speculative, as is any attempt to reconstruct what the historical Jesus really said. What is not speculative are the words people find on the page when they open a Bible and read it. Whatever the process was through which the words attributed to Jesus have been remembered, written down in Greek in four gospels and in some other books (some of which did and some of which did not make it into the canon), and then translated into English and virtually every other language, the result has been that the Bible is far and away the world's most widely read book. The words of Jesus are the best known of all the words ever written in a book and read by a reader. There is nobody who is a close second. Here are a few of Jesus' best known words, rendered into English by King James's translators:

When the Son of man shall come in his glory, and all the holy angels with him, then shall he sit upon the throne of his glory.

And before him shall be gathered all nations, and he shall separate them one from another, as a shepherd divideth his sheep from the goats.

And he shall set the sheep on his right hand, but the goats on the left.

Then shall the King say unto them on the right hand. "Come, ye blessed of my Father, inherit the kingdom prepared for you from the foundation of the world:

"For I was an hungered and ye gave me meat; I was thirsty and ye gave me drink: I was a stranger, and ye took me in.

"Naked, and ye clothed me: I was sick, and ye visited me: I was in prison, and ye came unto me."

Then shall the righteous answer him, saying, "Lord, when saw we thee an hungered, and fed thee? Or thirsty, and gave thee drink?

"When saw we thee a stranger, and took thee in? or naked, and clothed thee?

"Or when saw we thee sick, or in prison, and came unto thee?"

And the King shall answer, and say unto them. "Verily, I say unto you. Inasmuch as ye have done it unto one of the least of these my brethren, ye have done it unto me."

Then he shall say also unto them on the left hand, "Depart from me, ye cursed, into everlasting fire, prepared for the devil and his angels.

"For I was an hungered and ye gave me no meat: I was thirsty, and ye gave me no drink.

"I was a stranger, and ye took me not in: naked, and ye clothed me not: sick, and in prison, and ye visited me not."

Then shall they also answer him saying, "Lord, when saw we thee hungered, or athirst, or a stranger, or naked, or sick, or in prison, and did not minister unto thee?"

Then shall he answer them, saying, "Verily I say unto you. Inasmuch as ye did it not to one of the least of these, ye did it not to me."

And these shall go away into everlasting punishment: but the righteous into life eternal.[10]

From a different gospel, we read the following well-known words of Jesus:

Abide in me, and I in you. As the branch cannot bear fruit of itself, except it abide in the vine, no more can ye, except ye abide in me.
I am the vine, ye are the branches. He that abideth in me, and I in him, the same bringeth forth much fruit, for without me ye can do nothing.

If a man abide not in me, he is cast forth as a branch and is withered, and men gather them, and cast them into the fire, and they are burned.

If ye abide in me, and my words abide in you, ye shall ask what you will, and it shall be done unto you.

Herein is my father glorified, that ye bear much fruit; so shall ye be my disciples.

As the father hath loved me, so have I loved you: continue ye in my love.
If ye keep my commandments, ye shall abide in my love: even as I have kept my father's commandments, and abide in his love.

These things have I spoken unto you, that my joy might remain in you, and that your joy might be full.

This is my commandment. That ye love one another, as I have loved you.

Greater love hath no man than this, that a man lay down his life for his friends.

Ye are my friends, if ye do whatsoever I command you.

Henceforth, I call you not servants, for the servant knoweth not what his lord doeth: but I have called you friends: for all things that I have heard of my father I have made known unto you.[11]

In these two passages, as in many others, Jesus speaks of "father" (*patros*). As in patriarchy, here *patros* is a principle of authority, but these passages also show some movement away from the coercion associated with patriarchy and toward participation. The believers are like branches of a vine, who are unified by a source of love that comes to all of them through the vine. The principle of authority "abides," dwells, lives, within the soul. The disciples are "friends," not "servants," because they also possess the principle of authority, which is the same thing as the principle of love, within themselves.

The word translated as "love" is *agape*. Outside the New Testament this word is rarely found in ancient Greek texts. To offer an interpretation of the meaning of *agape* it is necessary to rely mainly on the instances where it is used in the New Testament itself. Our interpretation is that *agape* is, besides being Jesus' characteristic qualification of the father principle, an abundant, overflowing, unconditional love that flows from union with the divine. It names the joy of the life of the saved. In one of the rare occurrences of *agape* in Greek literature outside the New Testament, Homer employs the term to name the joy and hospitality with which his family and friends welcomed Odysseus on his return to Ithaca. This suggests that a meaning of *agape* is "welcoming."

Among the many other Biblical passages that could be used to illustrate Jesus' contributions to principles of cooperation and sharing, some of the most significant are the ones where his followers practice sharing. Here is one:

And when they had prayed, the place was shaken where they were assembled together: and they were all filled with the Holy Ghost, and they spake the word of God with boldness.

And the multitude of them that believed were of one heart and of one soul: neither said any of them that ought of the things he possessed was his own; but they had all things common. And with great power gave the apostles witness of the resurrection of the Lord Jesus: and great grace was upon them all.[12]

Although there are many examples of communities that cooperate and share, the example set by the communities of early Christians plays a unique role.[13] Simply because it is recorded in the Bible, the world's all-time bestseller, their example is a guarantee that the possibility of living in joyful and mutually supportive communities cannot be erased from human memory.

Let us suggest that three succinct beliefs about cooperation and sharing can be deduced from the words of Jesus and from the practices of his early followers:

1) The duty to contribute to meeting the needs of others is a peremptory divine command.

2) The transformed individual internalizes the principle of *agape*. Decisions to act from love become, simultaneously, the individual's own free choices and the result of identification with a higher power.

3) Communities practicing cooperation and sharing have existed.

Of these, it seems it is the first that provokes the most bitter opposition. People, on the whole, do not like taking orders, and they especially do not like taking orders, from a God or from humans who claim to be acting in the name of a God, which instruct them to share their property, their time, and their energy. Further, what Jesus commands is so distant from the way most people actually behave that his words seem calculated to make people feel guilty. Because few people pass muster according to Jesus' standards, he can be accused of promoting what Hegel called "the unhappy consciousness." A peremptory divine command that nobody obeys can be called emotional terrorism. There is terror too, in a literal interpretation of images like throwing into eternal hell fire the goats-who-did-not-give-food-to the-hungry-beggars and the withered-branches-cut-off-from-the-vine.

Being controversial, however, does not appear to do anything to silence the voice of Jesus. We suggest that in spite of the harsh judgments that can be made against him, Jesus retains the status of a landmark, or beacon light, with respect to which people take their bearings, regardless of which direction they are traveling. His words are central to language and to culture not just because the Gideons keep putting a copy of the Bible in every hotel room, but also because of the eloquence of the words themselves. Jesus made certain points so clearly and powerfully that, whether or not you agree, it is impossible to misunderstand. "For I was sick, and in prison, and ye visited me not," is not subtle. It is possible to say that such words violate your freedom, that they inhibit your pleasure, or that they attack your self-esteem. Yet it is not possible to say that you did not get the point.

On Cooperation and Sharing: A Perspective from Voltaire

What is virtue? Doing good to one's neighbor. Can I call virtue anything other than what does me good? I am poor, you are liberal; I am in danger, you come to my help; I am deceived, you tell me the truth; I am neglected, you console me; I am ignorant, you instruct me: I do not find it difficult to call you virtuous. –Voltaire[14]

Voltaire can be thought of as a grandfather of social democracy. He was the most prominent writer of the eighteenth-century Enlightenment. The Swedish socialist economist Gunnar Myrdal, for one, who is one of the heroes of this book, took social democracy to be the implementation of the ideals of the Enlightenment.[15]

In one of his early writings, the *Philosophical Letters* of 1733, written in exile in England, Voltaire sought to enlighten the peoples of the world, especially the French, by calling to their attention English civilization's achievements, which he idealized and exaggerated. Among the achievements Voltaire praised were: 1) England's religious diversity and tolerance; 2) the Quakers, whom he took to be simple people devoted to doing good; 3) the scientific worldview of Sir Isaac Newton; 4) empiricist philosophy; and 5) peaceful commerce under the rule of law among people who disagree with one another on religious issues. Voltaire mixes his praise of each one of these with praise of the other four, from which it may be inferred that he regarded them as mutually supportive components of a single admirable culture.

About peaceful commerce under the rule of law, Voltaire wrote:

Take a view of the Royal-Exchange . . . in London, a place more venerable than many courts of justice, where the representatives of all nations meet for the benefit of mankind. There the Jew, the Mahometan, and the Christian transact together as tho' they all professed the same religion, and give the name of Infidel to none but bankrupts. There the Presbyterian confides in the Anabaptist, the Churchman depends on the Quaker's word. At the breaking up of this pacific and free assembly, some withdraw to the synagogue and others to take a glass. This man goes and is baptiz'd in a great tub, in the name of the Father, the Son, and the Holy Ghost; That man has his son's foreskin cut off, whilst a set of Hebrew words . . . are mumbled over his child. Others retire to their churches and there wait for the inspiration of heaven with their hats on, and all are satisfied.[16]

The British thus repeated, in a modern form, an achievement of the ancient Roman Empire: a secular legal system provided a framework in which people belonging to different faith communities could engage in commercial transactions with one another.

At the center of Voltaire's philosophy, and at the center of the Enlightenment, was the principle of tolerance of religious diversity. Coming after centuries of intolerant theology and centuries of wars fought in the name of faith, tolerance was a revolutionary doctrine. Voltaire was persecuted for heresy from time to time throughout his life. Many of his works were published under pseudonyms for this reason.[17]

Voltaire once said that his aim in life was to make his enemies appear ridiculous. His enemies were the pious, pompous, venial, corrupt, militaristic, intolerant aristocrats of Europe, especially those of France. His Catholic enemies and his noble enemies were often the same enemies. The French church was rich. Aristocrats used their influence to get their sons placed in high church offices so they could augment the family fortunes by collecting rents from church lands. The connections between the princes inside the church and the princes outside the church provided Voltaire a great deal of pious pomp, venial corruption, and militaristic intolerance to ridicule.

One of Voltaire's enemies, a young aristocrat named Rohan, was the cause of Voltaire's exile in England. Voltaire was born with the humble name of Francois-Marie Arouet. As a rising star in the literary world of Paris he gave himself the name "Voltaire." One night at the theatre, Rohan approached Voltaire at intermission and accused him of promoting himself socially by changing his name. Voltaire, always a master of repartee, shot back, "Better to start a new name than to disgrace an old one." Rohan responded later by sending out a posse of his lackeys, who tracked down Voltaire and beat him up. Voltaire demanded a duel. Rohan was not about to lower himself by consenting to a duel with a commoner. When Voltaire persisted, Rohan used his influence to have him imprisoned in the Bastille. Voltaire was only allowed to leave jail on condition that he leave France.

In the course of time, Voltaire became a rich commoner. Best-selling books and shrewd investments made him so rich that at age sixty-five he was able to buy the area called Ferney, a part of France on the border with Switzerland. As a major landowner, and as the holder of pensions and titles granted to him by several monarchs, he became an aristocrat himself. Voltaire governed his tiny fiefdom as a model enlightened despot, while his famous friends the absolute monarchs Frederick the Great of Prussia and Catherine the Great of Russia governed their larger territories as despots enlightened by Voltaire. He wrote at the time that "in my villages . . . there is hardly a husbandman without clothes made of good cloth and who is not well shod and well fed."[18] Even though he himself

was a practitioner of the ideals of the Enlightenment, Voltaire was not an advocate of cooperation and sharing. His opinion of human nature was too low. His
outrage against the twisting of the theology of love to mask the practice of greed
was too great. Voltaire could not conceive that better customs could guide worse
natures to follow higher ideals. He wrote:

> Every man is born with a powerful enough desire for domination, wealth, and
> pleasure, and with much taste for idleness. Consequently every man would like
> to have other people's money and wives or women, to be their master, to sub-
> jugate them to all his caprices, and to do nothing, or at least to do only very
> agreeable things. Obviously, having such amiable dispositions, it is as impossi-
> ble for men to be equal as it is impossible for two preachers or two professors
> of theology not to be jealous of one another.
>
> Mankind cannot subsist at all unless there is an infinite number of useful
> men who possess nothing at all. For a prosperous man will certainly not leave
> his land to cultivate yours; and if you need a pair of shoes it is not a judge who
> will make them for you.[19]

Voltaire was, nevertheless, an impassioned advocate of the rights of the poor.
He conceived that his enemies were their enemies. He never doubted that the
cause of religious tolerance and the cause of this-worldly improvement of life
for humanity were the same cause. A few years before his death in 1778 at the
age of eighty-four he wrote the following passage about abbots who enriched
themselves:

> A poor man who has taken a vow of poverty, which leads him to become a
> monarch! It has already been said, it must be repeated a thousand times, that
> this is intolerable. The law complains of this abuse, religion is indignant at it,
> and those who are really poor, without clothes and food, cry to heaven at the
> door of monsieur l'abbe.
>
> But I hear Messieurs l'abbes of Italy, of Germany, of Flanders, of Bur-
> gundy, saying, "Why should we not accumulate possessions and honors? Why
> should we not be princes? After all, bishops are. They were originally poor like
> us, they have enriched themselves, they have elevated themselves. One of them
> has become superior to kings. Allow us to imitate them as much as we can."
>
> You are right, gentlemen, overrun the country; it belongs to the strong or
> the crafty man who seizes it. You have profited from the times of ignorance, of
> superstition, of folly, to despoil us of our heritage and trample us underfoot in
> order to fatten yourselves on the substance of the wretched; tremble lest the day
> of reason arrive.[20]

One of Voltaire's successors in the phase of the construction of modernity usually called the "Enlightenment"—Adam Smith—did his best to help bring about
that arrival of the day of reason.

On Cooperation and Sharing: A Perspective from Adam Smith

The Adam Smith problem is the problem of reconciling Smith's ethics with his economics.[21] His ethics appears to be in substantial conformity with the teachings of the world's great religions, which oblige humans to love and serve one another. His economics, meanwhile, appears to be in substantial conformity with the teachings of egoistic materialist philosophies, according to which humans naturally act from self-interest, and cannot be expected to act otherwise.

One possible solution to the Adam Smith problem is to say that Smith made no substantial departure from the religious and ethical traditions of his part of the world—i.e., the Hebrew-Greek synthesis that defined the ideology of Christendom, and therefore initially that of Europe. In this view, Smith agreed with Plato, Jesus, and others who taught that humans should cooperate and share in order to meet one another's needs. In this view, Smith's discoveries and inventions were simply new means to old ends. We call this the "have your cake and eat it too" interpretation of Smith—and not just of Smith, but of a whole constellation of philosophers who in the seventeenth and eighteenth centuries invented discourses that restructured traditional ethics to fit the needs of the nascent global capitalist economy.

In this "have your cake and eat it too" interpretation, Smith was the advocate of cooperation who had discovered the best way to do it. Certainly Smith was enormously impressed by how weak and helpless a single human being alone is, and by how much each of us depends upon the cooperation of others. In a famous example, Smith shows how even to obtain such a simple thing as a pin to hold up the hem of a garment, a person relies upon the combined efforts of thousands of people, from the one who digs the ore, to the one who smelts it to iron, to the one who draws the metal into wire, down to the one who cuts it, the one who shapes the head of the pin, and the one who transports it to a retail store, and many more besides.

Still developing this "have your cake and eat it too" reading of Smith, we can point to texts where Smith portrays the division of labor as the key to stunningly successful cooperation. If each person does one job and does it well, and learns how to do it faster and with less waste, and thinks about how to improve the process, and acquires equipment with which to do it, the result is that the job is done substantially better. The gains from the division of labor, when compared to an individual trying to be a jack of all trades, allow, on Smith's calculations, a tenfold increase, or a hundred-fold increase, or even a thousand-fold increase in production. The gains from the division of labor are so great that entrepreneurs can afford to pay high wages and still make large profits—a Smithian concept that is still with us today in the form of the idea that wage increases should track productivity increases. Moreover, the expansion of the division of labor to an international level through free trade augments the purchasing power of labor by lowering food prices. Smith observes that even the poorest worker in Scotland or England is incomparably better off than the savage, and he attributes the relative opulence of the British working class to the benefits of the division of labor.[22]

The market economy Smith envisaged allowed, as Smith himself noted, the existence of a small class of wealthy individuals who did not work but lived off the labor of others. Smith acknowledged that their unearned wealth was not a moral merit of the society that bred them, but he considered their existence to be a small price to pay for a system that brought so much welfare to so many. In this respect, on a "have your cake and eat it too" reading, Smith can be regarded as being in substantial conformity with Judeo-Christian ethics, even if not in perfect conformity.

As the division of labor can be viewed as an efficient way to cooperate, similarly exchange can be viewed as an efficient way to share. Following what Smith called the natural human propensity to truck or barter, when a person go to a market to buy or sell, s/he gives something s/he does not need and gets something s/he does need. Exchange is the best way to share. What sharing accomplishes is moving one person's surplus to another person's dinner table. Free exchange in a market could be called the best way to accomplish the purpose of sharing because it is the way that taps the strongest and most reliable motives, the self-interest of the buyer and the self-interest of the seller.

In this "have your cake and eat it too" interpretation, Smith has no quarrel with Jesus or Plato about objectives. Smith is merely the advocate of more effective ways to achieve the same objectives that everyone agrees on. Lines from Smith could be quoted to show that Smith himself says in so many words that the whole purpose of exchange is use, and that if it were not for the value of the uses to which the merchandise exchanged is put, there would be no value in exchange. Smith also says that the whole purpose of agriculture and of manufactures is to supply the wants and conveniences of life.[23]

The "have your cake and eat it too" reading has an important corollary. The merits of the free market are not matters of moral principle. They are empirical findings. The principle is to meet everyone's needs. It is a contingent fact, of which Smith takes large and detailed notice, that markets as he envisaged them work to meet everyone's needs, and work better than any alternative. Yet there is no guarantee that facts Smith described will always be true, and it could well turn out to be the case that at some times and places and to some extent or degree, they might turn out to be false. The corollary is, therefore, that free markets and associated institutions are right to the extent that they in fact end up working, and they are wrong to the extent that they do not work.

What we have called a corollary to a "have your cake and eat it too" interpretation of Smith, was stated in different terms, but with essentially the same meaning, by the twentieth-century Dutch social democratic economist Jan Tinbergen. According to Tinbergen, writing in post-World War II Holland some two hundred years after the publication of *The Wealth of Nations*, there is no significant disagreement between the advocates of capitalism and the advocates of socialism. Capitalists and socialists agree on objectives. They also agree that whatever achieves the objectives most efficiently should be done. Furthermore, they agree on the methodologies to be employed in monitoring economic institutions and measuring their performance. There is therefore nothing left on which to disagree. All that remains is to determine by empirical research whether in any given case it is private enterprise or some form of social enterprise, a free market or some form of regulated market, that performs most effectively to meet any given set of needs.[24] Health care systems, for example, can be studied empirically, using known social science methodologies. The results of studies will show which health care systems produce the best outcomes, i.e., the most health. Capitalists and socialists alike—assuming of course that they consistently accept the consequences of premises they have already endorsed in principle—will agree that in health care the practices that produce the best results define the best ways for humans to cooperate and share to meet one another's needs. And so on in every other field.

We have presented first the simplest solution to the Adam Smith problem, which is to say there is no conflict between his economics and his ethics, and no conflict between his ethics and the ethics of Jesus. We have also mentioned an equally simple corollary, which says that there is in principle no conflict between capitalism and socialism. In reality, the situation is more complex and less harmonious. We move now to an opening discussion of some of the complexities and conflicts.

Although some of Smith's works permit a "have your cake and eat it too" reading, others do not (or at least not on the face of it). Consider the following two passages. The first is taken from Smith's *The Theory of Moral Sentiments*, first published in 1759:

> And hence it is, that to feel much for others and little for ourselves, that to restrain our selfish, and to indulge our benevolent affections, constitutes the perfection of human nature; and alone can produce among mankind that harmony of sentiments and passions in which consists their whole grace and propriety. As to love our neighbour as we love ourselves is the great law of Christianity, so it is the great precept of nature to love ourselves only as we love our neighbour, or what comes to the same thing, as our neighbour is capable of loving us.[25]

The second is a famous passage from *The Wealth of Nations*, first published in 1776:

> It is not from the benevolence of the butcher, the brewer, or the baker, that we expect our dinner, but from their regard to their own interest. We address ourselves, not to their humanity, but to their self-love, and never talk to them of

our own necessities but of their advantages. Nobody but a beggar chuses to
depend chiefly on the benevolence of his fellow-citizens.[26]

The first passage says that solidarity motives are strong, and suggests that we as
a human family should rely on them to assure that everyone is taken care of.
The second passage seems to mock solidarity motives, and to suggest that they
cannot be relied on. Such apparent inconsistencies led Witold von Skarzynski to
propose in 1878 the ingenious hypothesis that during his 1764-66 sojourn in
Paris, Smith had come under the influence of French materialist philosophers,
and had changed his mind.[27] Therefore, *The Wealth of Nations* of 1776 reflects
materialistic egoism, while the earlier book, *The Theory of Moral Sentiments* of
1759 reflects idealistic altruism.

Unfortunately for the change of mind (or *Umschwung*) hypothesis, subsequently discovered notes from the lectures Smith gave as Professor of Moral
Philosophy in the University of Glasgow in the school years 1762-63 and 1763-
64 brought to light that the main ideas of *The Wealth of Nations* had already
been worked out prior to Smith's trip to Paris. Partly in the light of the demise of
the *Umschwung* hypothesis, the editors of a critical edition of Smith's *Theory of
Moral Sentiments* wrote in the introduction:

> There is nothing surprising in Smith's well known statement, "It is not from the
> benevolence of the butcher, the brewer, or the baker, that we expect our dinner,
> but from their regard to their own interests." Who would suppose this to imply
> that Adam Smith had come to disbelieve in the very existence or the moral
> value of benevolence? Nobody with any sense.[28]

At the risk of appearing to fall into the category of those who do not have any
sense, we wish to express the opinion that there is still an Adam Smith problem,
even granted that Smith never ceased to believe in the importance, or even necessity, of benevolence. The problem is that Smith gets more credit than he deserves.

Our formulation of the Adam Smith problem can be made a bit more precise by borrowing a metaphor from Noam Chomsky, in order to distinguish between the surface grammar of Smith's texts and their depth grammar.[29] On the
surface, the drama of Smith's texts is a patient struggle of thoughtful goodness
to overcome the several constraints that retard human progress. The author is
invariably on the side of the generically good: knowledge, sympathy and fellow-
feeling, peace, security, prosperity, enlightenment.

We adopt the notion of "depth grammar" to designate the words and provisions that lawyers sometimes call "operative." These are the rules that determine
the judge's decision in a case or controversy, or what the parties must do to
comply with the terms of a contract, or who gets what property under a will or
trust, or who must pay what tax.[30] As we descend from the dramatic surface to
the operative level, we begin to see divisions in the ranks of the angels. Smith's

market parts company with Plato's *dikaiosyne* (justice), and with Jesus' *agape* (love). Justice and love, as they were understood in the mainstream medieval syntheses of Greek and Hebrew culture, are, in Smith and other philosophers of the early modern epoch, riddled with exceptions, limited, and redefined. We will list some things that happen in Smith's writings at an operative level, which, taken together, substantially undermine cooperation:

1) *Property assumes priority.* The *Wealth of Nations* is an expanded version of the last part of Smith's lectures on jurisprudence, the part concerning the duty of "police" to promote prosperity. But the first duty of police is to establish peace. Peace is established by guaranteeing to every person security in the possession of property. In this and in other ways, the priority of property is presupposed and guaranteed before political economy even begins.

2) *Benevolence becomes voluntary.* Moderns like Smith discard *caritas* as a name for the human duty to cooperate and share with others, and write instead about "benevolence." Benevolence is classified as an "imperfect duty." This means that the beneficiary has no right to enforce performance of the duty; rather, the giver is free to choose whether to comply with the duty of benevolence or not.

3) *Sympathy backs eighteenth-century British common sense.* Sympathy plays a major role in Smith's thought, serving as a touchstone to resolve precise issues in the law of contracts and the law of property rights. Exactly which expectations of the parties are legitimate is determined by reference to the sympathies of a bystander who is not a party. Thus "sympathy," which on the surface appears to be a principle of morals akin to a love ethic, functions on an operative level as an appeal to the common sense norms of a commercial society.

4) *Justice is redefined.* Smith's source for justice is neither Greek nor Hebrew. It is Roman Law. "Justice" means *suum cuique*—"to each his own." And it means *pacta sunt servanda*—"contracts are to be performed."[31]

5) *Love moves to the periphery.* From being, as *caritas*, the main actor, love is demoted to playing bit parts, some of them comic. For example, "Of all the passions, however, which are so extravagantly disproportioned to the value of their objects, love is the only one that appears, even to the weakest minds, to have any thing in it that is either graceful or agreeable."[32]

6) *The natural replaces the divine.* A traditional discourse, such as, for example, that of the prophet Mohammed, would identify that which is good and ought to be with "God's will." Smith helps found modernity by employing "natural" as a buzzword that identifies what ought to be. Conversely, "artificial" becomes a key pejorative label.

7) *Prudence replaces wisdom as the first virtue.* Wisdom (*sofia*) was the first of the classic four Greek virtues. It was also the first of the seven cardinal virtues

of Christendom. It meant the government of life by reason, where the very idea of reason, as reason was in those times conceived, carried overtones of divinity and solidarity. Smith utilizes ideas from Roman stoic philosophy to name the first virtue as "prudence" instead. "Prudence," as Smith and the stoics he cites use the term, carries forward the idea of governing life by reason, but it modifies it in such a way that the first virtue comes to mean, first and foremost, taking care of one's self.

8) *A myth about the history of law shapes civil religion.* The generic struggle of enlightenment against darkness, which we have identified as the dramatic surface of Smith's texts, becomes specific and operational as a creation story about how the legal and ethical framework, which Smith's economics presupposes, came into existence. While eschewing John Locke's myth of the social contract, Smith himself proposes a myth of progress, according to which all societies pass through the same stages of improvement. Private property, as the Scots and English knew it, was not universal. In the eighteenth century it was not yet established among the Arabs, the Tatars, or the Chinese, as Smith recounted in detail in his lectures on the history of law. The legal and ethical framework of the free market was "natural" not because all peoples lived within such a framework, but because the invariant direction of progress in history was such that all peoples were on their way toward it.

Thus, in the end, we propose, there is an Adam Smith problem. Yet it is not just an Adam Smith problem. It is also a David Hume problem, a Frances Hutcheson problem, a Hugo Grotius problem, a Denis Diderot problem, an Immanuel Kant problem. On the surface, the early modern texts are edifying discourses, striving to save society from moral decay by demonstrating a sound basis for ethics, carrying forward the same ages-old good fight for cooperation and sharing that the prophets and philosophers carried on in Biblical times and in ancient Greece. On the operative level, however, a transmutation occurs. Ethics is rewritten to facilitate capitalism.[33] The Adam Smith problem is not what Skarzynski thought it was; it is not that Smith changed his mind after he wrote about sympathy and benevolence and before he wrote about economics. The ethics texts and the economics texts are *indeed* consistent with each other, but the reason why they are consistent is that the ethics texts do not mean what they *seem* to mean. The generous emotions they evoke are not the operative rules that decide cases and establish rights.

The view of the Adam Smith problem we are proposing also serves to show that the market was not anything anybody discovered or invented. A society whose operative rules are those reflected in Roman Law is already a market-oriented society. In such a society one can ask, as an empirical question, what the prices of A, B, or C goods are in a market, but one cannot ask whether there *are* markets, because the basic social structure, the law, the courts, the very language, the very expectations concerning what it means to be a "person," *presuppose* that there are markets. Property, contracts, money, markets are not separate stand-alone institutions, each separately invented, but complementary aspects of the same worldview and framework, an interrelated social structure that evolves over time.

A third consequence of the solution we propose to the Adam Smith problem is that Tinbergen's idea of doing empirical studies to find out what social arrangements work becomes problematic. Our surface/depth metaphor calls attention to powerful but ordinarily unseen (because taken for granted) variables at work in the operative depths of society. One wonders how an empirical study could keep track of the results of social experiments that would run operational concepts of justice through many variations. Yet if one takes seriously the idea of finding out what works by trying out alternatives, then one must be ready to change basic rules. One wonders whether Tinbergen had in mind doing studies that would evaluate twenty-first-century shifts in the meanings of key terms, similar in scope to the conceptual sea change Smith articulated in the eighteenth century, and, if so, what such studies would look like.

On Cooperation and Sharing: A Perspective from Karl Marx

Although social democracy has many roots and precedents, the classical starting point for most social democratic thinking, in Europe and around the world, is the philosophy of Karl Marx. This is not least true when social democracy defines itself by contrasting its tenets with those of Marxism.

Although Marx had many seminal ideas, one of the central ones, which can be taken as a key to what he thought about cooperation and sharing, is the idea that under capitalism there is private appropriation of the products of social cooperation. Collaborative work by many produces the world's goods and services. Yet after the product is produced, the few own the product, and the proceeds from its sale are credited to their account. The few who reap the profits are, of course, the very same few who allowed the production process to start by advancing funds, with the "sly intention" as Marx puts it, of getting back more funds than they advanced. They control the labor process because they start it. If they do not expect it to be profitable, they do not start it, and it does not start. Ownership. Power. What the few accumulate, due to their power, is the surplus created by the labor process. Collective labor causes the outputs to be worth more than the inputs, but the principal benefits of the collective labor go not to the collectivity or to the laborers, but to the owners.

Marx's solution to the problems posed by a cooperative social process skewed by private appropriation of its fruits, is to eliminate the private appropriation. Then there would be real cooperation. There would be social production for social use, establishing a material base for the free and full development of each individual, not just that of the privileged few. On the question of how social cooperation for mutual benefit would be organized after "the expropriators are expropriated," Marx was deliberately vague. At one point he invokes the image of society as one giant collective laborer, who carefully divides up labor time among the various necessary tasks, in order to produce everything the one giant collective laborer needs. At another point Marx contrasts capitalism with the organization of a peasant family, where all the farm tasks are divided among the members of the family, and the family shares the harvest. For the most part, though, Marx thought it best to leave the design of the society of the future to the citizens of the future.

On one occasion, however, Marx had to give some detail about how to organize socialist production in order to reign in some of his over-eager followers. In May of 1875, convened at Gotha as a union of two previously existing organizations, the German Social Democratic Party proposed a program calling for "the cooperative regulation of the total labour with equitable distribution of the proceeds of labour."[34] Marx apparently feared that this language might be taken to mean that instead of dividing the revenue of industry between wages and profit, there would be only wages, no profit, with the share that under capitalism went to the owners being devoted to increase wages. Against any such hare-brained scheme, Marx pointed out that under modern industrial conditions any plan for cooperative working and equitable distribution would have to take into account certain complications, as follows:

Let us take first of all the words "proceeds of labour" in the sense of the product of labour, then the cooperative proceeds of labour are the *total social product.*

From this must now be deducted:

First, cover for replacement of the means of production used up.

Secondly, additional portion for expansion of production.

Thirdly, reserve or insurance fund to provide against accidents, dislocations caused by natural calamities, etc.

These deductions from the "undiminished proceeds of labour" are an economic necessity and their magnitude is to be determined according to available means and forces, and partly by computation of probabilities, but they are in no way calculable by equity.

There remains the other part of the total product, intended to serve as means of consumption.

Before this is divided among the individuals, there has to be deducted again, from it:

First, the general costs of administration not belonging to production.

This part will, from the outset, be very considerably restricted in comparison with present-day society and it diminishes in proportion as the new society develops.

Secondly, that which is intended for the common satisfaction of needs, such as schools, health services, etc.

From the outset this part grows considerably in comparison with present-day society and it grows in proportion as the new society develops.

Thirdly, funds for those unable to work, etc., in short, for what is included under so-called official poor relief today.

> Only now do we come to the "distribution" which the programme, under Lassallean influence, alone has in view in its narrow fashion, namely, to that part of the means of consumption which is divided among the individual producers of the co-operative society.
>
> The "undiminished proceeds of labour" have already unnoticeably become converted into the "diminished" proceeds, although what the producer is deprived of in his capacity as a private individual benefits him directly or indirectly in his capacity as a member of society.[35]

Marx took such exception to the ideas of Lassalle and his followers because plans such as theirs only fueled the argument that the high-minded ideals of socialism such as those we are calling cooperation and sharing were a utopian scheme, doomed to failure. Marx wanted to demonstrate that with careful consideration, cooperation and sharing could indeed be feasible.

On Cooperation and Sharing: A Perspective from Gandhi

In the Western world in the past few centuries ideals of cooperation and sharing have sometimes been in conflict with, and have sometimes coexisted in an uneasy truce with, ideals of property rights and individual freedom. Karl Marx considered the property rights of the owners of the means of production to be a power to exploit workers, and thus to be in conflict with the ideal of cooperation. Adam Smith and others brokered a truce between love and freedom by dropping *caritas* and adopting "benevolence." Benevolence was defined in such a way that it could not conflict with the freedom of the individual because it was, although admirable, purely voluntary.

Mohandas K. Gandhi approached these issues from a non-Western and deeply religious perspective. In place of the ideal of property rights, Gandhi proposed an ideal of trusteeship, extending the meaning of a term borrowed from English common law. He wrote, for example, in 1934:

> Those who own money now are asked to behave like the trustees holding their riches on behalf of the poor. You may say that trusteeship is a legal fiction. But, if people meditate over it constantly and try to act up to it, then life on earth would be governed far more by love than it is at present. Absolute trusteeship is an abstraction like Euclid's definition of a point, and is equally unattainable. But if we strive for it, we shall be able to go further in realizing a state of equality on earth than by any other method.[36]

With respect to freedom, we follow the Gandhi scholar Raghavan Iyer in suggesting that although Gandhi advocated freedom as earnestly as any Westerner, the significance of the word "freedom" in Gandhi's context tilts it away from conflict with cooperation and sharing, not just because (as in Smith) sharing is voluntary, but also because showing love in action is the natural tendency of the free soul.

About freedom Gandhi wrote: "No society can possibly be built on a denial of individual freedom. It is contrary to the very nature of man. Just as a man will not grow horns or a tail, so will he not exist as a man if he has no mind of his own. In reality, even those who do not believe in the liberty of the individual believe in their own."[37] Thus Gandhi identifies being a free individual with having "a mind of [one's] own." Iyer sheds further light on the significance of freedom for Gandhi, and on how he saw the relationship between "freedom and "mind." Iyer writes, "Individual freedom alone, he [Gandhi] argued, can make a man voluntarily surrender himself to the service of society; if freedom is wrested from him, man becomes an automaton and society is ruined."[38]

Here Gandhi is not advocating the kind of individualism that is commonly held up as a Western ideal. Iyer writes, "Whereas Western individualism emerged in modern urban society and is bound up with the doctrine of natural rights, Gandhi's individualism derived from the concept of *dharma* or natural obligations which held together the traditional rural communities of ancient Indian civilization."[39] Iyer further expounds upon this distinction:

> Those who, like Hegel, hold that society and the State are prior to the individual use the word 'individual' in a special sense—to mean a self-conscious moral person. They argue that men become self-conscious and moral only in society, where they can acquire the concepts which enable them to be objects of thought and criticism to themselves. To Gandhi, on the other hand, the human soul is autonomous in society because it is an integral part of the rational and moral order of nature. Traditionally, Vedic thought bequeathed the belief that man lives in a wider society that embraces all the creatures and deities of the universe, and consequently a strong individualism developed in the context of Indian society. There has been a repeated exhortation in the Indian tradition that man should rise above society, and while social virtues are necessary in social life, they must be ultimately transcended by the individual.[40]

The dilemmas of the West thus appear in a considerably different light when seen by Gandhian eyes. Trusteeship and service (sharing and cooperation) come to be seen as the very aims, the manifestations, the results and the essences, of the freedom of the liberated soul.

On Cooperation and Sharing:
A Perspective from Robert Axelrod

Robert Axelrod's *The Evolution of Cooperation* is one of many works that start from the premise that people are self-interested egoists, who seek to find and use the strategies that will most benefit themselves. Axelrod states, "From an individual's point of view, the object is to score as well as possible over a series of interactions with another player who is also trying to score well."[41] Axelrod argues that cooperation among egoists can come about, can become a stable practice, and can resist invasion by non-cooperating "meanies" who might seek to move in and take advantage of the cooperators. If it turns out that in reality people are not complete egoists, then so much the better. Then there will be even more cooperation. But Axelrod is among those who think it important to make a case for cooperation developing even among purely self-interested actors, whose decisions are wholly unaffected by the welfare or the suffering of others.

His argument can be thought of as having two stages, each of which is elaborate. The first stage is a series of computer simulations, in which strategies are tested to see which yields the highest payoff to the player using that strategy. A set of formal assumptions defines the mathematical game being played. The second stage is a series of reports from the real world, with which Axelrod seeks to show that the mathematical results of the computer simulations are consistent with what actually happens in practice.

The formal assumptions that define the mathematical game are, in brief, the following:

1) The game is played round-robin in pairs, with each actor (i.e., each strategy, because the actors are defined by the strategies they employ) facing one opposing party in a match consisting of a series of encounters, or moves.

2) At each encounter, each actor can either cooperate with the other, or defect.

3) At each encounter, each actor decides what to do without knowing what the other will do.

4) However, after the first encounter, each actor knows what his opponent just did, and what the opponent did in all the previous moves of the same match.

5) If you choose to cooperate, and the other defects, then you are a sucker and you get 0 points.

6) If you defect, and the other cooperates, then you win big and get 5 points.

7) If you cooperate, and the other cooperates, then you both win, and each gets 3 points.

8) If you defect, and the other defects, then each gets 1 point.

Within the framework of the formal model some of whose main features we have briefly summarized, experts on game theory were invited to submit strategies, i.e., computer programs defining decision rules that would designate what move an actor would make, never knowing the opponent's current intentions, always knowing the history of the opponent's prior moves in the match. Axelrod then ran a series of computer simulations, in which each strategy took a turn being pitted against each other strategy. The winner was the strategy that garnered the highest number of points overall, i.e., the sum of all the points scored when paired with each of the others.

The winner of the tournament, and also the winner of nearly all of a series of follow up tournaments, was a strategy called Tit For Tat, submitted by Professor Anatol Rapoport of the University of Toronto. The Tit For Tat strategy has the following characteristics:

1) It always cooperates at the first encounter of a match.

2) It is nice. It is never the first to defect.

3) It can be provoked. If the opposing player defects, then it retaliates by defecting on the next move.

4) It is forgiving. If the other player cooperates, then Tit For Tat cooperates on the next move, regardless of what the other player's prior history of defections may have been.

5) It is not envious. It does not seek to best the other player, but rather seeks to maximize its own score.

6) It is simple. It is easy to predict its actions, because it always does whatever the other player did on the immediately preceding move.[42]

Tit For Tat's success as a strategy was amazingly robust. It succeeded in eliciting cooperation from the other party on a regular basis, regardless of what strategy the other party was using. Consequently, it and its opponent each scored three points for cooperation on nearly every move. This did not mean that Tit For Tat bested its immediate opponent, but it did mean that when the tournament scores were added up, Tit For Tat had the highest total score.

The second stage of Axelrod's argument is to bring together empirical evidence from many fields in an attempt to show that the superiority of the Tit For Tat strategy is echoed, if not exactly repeated, in the real world. One of Axelrod's most striking examples is that of Allied soldiers facing German soldiers in the front line trenches in France during World War I. Sociological studies have established that where the same military units faced each other for a long time, they developed a cooperative relationship such that neither shelled the other. He quotes a British soldier, "Mr. Bosche ain't a bad fellow. You leave 'im alone; he'll leave you alone."[43]

Axelrod finds, both in theory and in practice, that a cooperative strategy like Tit For Tat will become generally adopted whenever actors can anticipate frequent future encounters with the same other parties. He states, "The foundation of cooperation is not really trust, but the durability of the relationship."[44] It is therefore desirable, whenever cooperation is desirable, to arrange institutions so that people regularly encounter the same other people. It is also desirable for people to know Axelrod's theory of cooperation, so that by consciously following a strategy like Tit For Tat (with a few amendments for special circumstances) they can accelerate cooperation's evolution.

As a footnote to *The Evolution of Cooperation*, it is worth noting that Professor Anatol Rapoport, who submitted the winning tournament entry, came to believe that world peace and justice could not be achieved solely by strategic thinking of any kind, not even by the relatively benign kind represented by Tit For Tat. Rapoport, who was for many years the world's leading authority on game theory, came to believe that strategic thinking ought to be complemented by thinking more closely identified with dialogue and with normative ideology, which he called "debate."[45]

On Cooperation and Sharing:
A Perspective from Mother Teresa

We feel very close to Mother Teresa. We speak of her in the present tense because her spirit is alive. Her God is our God. Nevertheless, we quarrel with her constantly.

Our quarrel with Mother Teresa has nothing to do with any disapproval of her work. We have nothing but praise for her. What upsets us is our fear that she has a low opinion of us. She writes, "If there are people who feel that God wants them to change the structure of society, that is something between them and their God."[46] We quarrel especially with the phrase "their God." It makes it sound as though social change activists and philosophers have a different God, "their God." We want it to be the same God, "our God." We resist the third person plural and insist on the first person plural.

We quarrel with Mother Teresa when she writes, "I was at a meeting of the Superiors General in Europe. They talked only of changing the structures of society, organizing things in a different way. It all came to nothing. It did not do something for the poor, or preach Christ to those without religion, to those totally ignorant of God."[47] If it were true that nothing has ever come of efforts to achieve structural change, then we would say that we must redouble our efforts. If the principal causes of the misery that the Missionaries of Charity relieve have so far proven to be unmovable, then it is time now to move them. We want to throw in the face of Mother Teresa the words of Hjalmar Branting, the first socialist prime minister of Sweden, who said that if Christians were honest, they would be socialists.[48] But Mother Teresa's remark is not true. It is not true that efforts to remedy the deep structural defects of modern society have always come to nothing. Howard Richards is reminded of the words of a client of his law office who had to undergo expensive spinal surgery, which was paid for out of her deceased husband's pension as a General Motors retiree. She said to him from her hospital bed, "Thank God for the AF of L CIO."

We want to disregard the occasional words found in Mother Teresa's writings that appear to disparage people who work for social change. Perhaps it was a slip of the pen when she wrote "their" and meant "our." Perhaps she was unconsciously defensive, feeling that she needed to defend herself against people who disparage *her* vocation. We want to say that she was more truly herself when she wrote, "It is so beautiful that we complete each other! What we are doing in the slums, maybe you cannot do. What you are doing in the level where you are called—in your family life, in your college life, in your work—we cannot do. But you and we together are doing something beautiful for God."[49]

Our quarrels with Mother Teresa turn on the phrase "the structure of society." The idea of "sharing," on the other hand, is common ground. About sharing she says:

> Share, as the mother of a starving Hindu family did, who, when we took her some food, immediately took half of it to the hungry Muslims next door.[50]

> I did not bring more rice that night because I wanted them to enjoy the joy of giving, the joy of sharing. You should have seen the faces of those little ones! They just understood what their mother did. Their faces were brightened up with smiles. When I came in, they looked hungry, they looked so miserable, but the act of their mother taught them what true love was.[51]

> A gentleman asked me: "What should we do to remove poverty from India?" I answered, "When you and I learn to share with them."[52]

> People are beginning to get more concerned and more anxious to share their help. In Calcutta, for example, we have many more people . . . who come on a regular basis just to do the humble work: to wash, to wash clothes, to cook meals, to feed the people.[53]

Mother Teresa writes few words and speaks mainly with actions. We think it is legitimate to accept some articulations of the principles that guide her actions, found not in Mother Teresa's own words, but in the words of Eileen Egan, one of her biographers. Egan is a person who, as a representative of Catholic Relief Services, brought much of the food which the Missionaries of Charity distributed, a person who spent a great deal of time with Mother Teresa. Egan writes, "Mother Teresa seemed to follow an old maxim that the good that is possible is obligatory. She and her Sisters were obliged to do everything possible for the poorest and weakest; they were not paralyzed by the thought of what they could not do."[54] She also writes, "For Mother Teresa, there was no break between the apprehension of a need and an action to meet that need, however small that action might be."[55]

Back to our quarrel, what is a social structure? It is a rule, otherwise known as a principle, or a norm. The word "structure" is most likely to be used when the rule is a fundamental principle that organizes the life of a society. Mother Teresa does not live according to the rules, the structures, of modern commercial society. She lives according to the principle of love, the rules of cooperation and sharing. Far from being an opponent of structural change, she *is* structural change.

However, as conservative social philosophers like Ludwig von Mises and Friedrich Hayek have emphasized, in the course of making arguments that capital accumulation and therefore capitalism are inevitable and indispensable, and as Marx acknowledged in his *Critique of the Gotha Program*, very often the most efficient way to meet needs is to go *the long way around*.[56] Under modern industrial conditions, the break between the apprehension of the need and the completion of action to meet that need may be years, or even decades. For example, to supply a large city with clean water, or with electricity, it is often necessary to make plans many years in advance, and to carefully calculate the resources required to carry out the project at each stage of its development. Capital investments are often made long before there is any product or payback.

Finding ways to put into practice norms of cooperation and sharing under modern industrial conditions is the challenge of social democracy.

On Cooperation and Sharing:
A Perspective from Hardt and Negri

Empire by Michael Hardt and Antonio Negri brings the theme of cooperation and sharing into the twenty-first century. Its name today is "liberation."[57]

Hardt and Negri take their readers on a dizzying ride on a roller-coaster track, which runs from Imperialism through Empire to the future day when the multitude achieves liberation, which on its course through time runs around and through many of the issues passionately debated today in venues like the World Social Forum, and which is welded together by a coherent argument. How can globalization from above be transformed into globalization from below? Is reversing globalization by promoting localization feasible or desirable? Or is globalization destined to collapse anyway whether people try to reverse it or not? Should progressives push national governments to reassert the power to regulate economic life, or should they celebrate the liquidation of the nation-state by the global market? Could there be global collective bargaining, setting wage levels on a global scale? Is "socialism" still the aim of the world movement for the liberation of the oppressed? Or is socialism so thoroughly discredited that today progressives must imagine a capitalist road to liberation? Is there a third choice? Is it anarchism? Is it Anthony Giddens' "third way"?[58] Is it radicalized democracy? Is the working class still a subject of history? If not, who is? Can anybody speak for anybody else? Are right-wing fundamentalists class enemies, or are they fellow victims of modernity? What should we make today of Marx? Of Foucault? Of identity politics? Of the many writers called "feminist"? Of the many writers called "postmodern"? Hardt and Negri do not name all these passionately debated issues, but they offer breathtaking views on all of them, and they offer the left a proposal for achieving liberation which, if it were accepted, would be the theoretical framework within which these and all other issues debated on the left would be encompassed.

After all of the twists and turns and ups and downs, Hardt and Negri are clear that the destination as and when liberation is achieved will be a world of cooperation and sharing. They write, "[E]very liberatory initiative, from wage struggles to political revolutions, proposes the independence of use value against the world of exchange value."[59] They state furthermore:

> The mode of production of the multitude reappropriates wealth from capital and also constructs a new wealth, articulated with the powers of science and social knowledge through cooperation. Cooperation annuls the titles of property. In modernity, private property was often legitimated by labor, but this equation, if it ever really made sense, today tends to be completely destroyed. Private property of the means of production today, in the era of the hegemony of cooperative and immaterial labor, is only a putrid and tyrannical obsolescence.[60]

The point of departure for Hardt and Negri is a concept of Imperialism that presupposes a Marxist analysis of the instability of the circulation (exchange) of commodities under the rules that govern capitalist markets. They write:

> The wage of the worker (corresponding to necessary labor) must be less than the total value produced by the worker. This surplus value, however, must find an adequate market in order to be realized. Since each worker must produce more than he or she consumes, the demand of the worker as consumer can never be an adequate demand for the surplus value. In a closed system, the capitalist production and exchange process is thus defined as a series of barriers. . . . All these barriers flow from a single barrier defined by the unequal relationship between the worker as producer and the worker as consumer.[61]

The history of capitalism, therefore, is inherently what it is empirically observed to be: a story of "overproduction." (There is said to be "overproduction," e.g., of potatoes, whenever the product cannot be sold, even though, e.g., there may be millions of hungry people who would eat potatoes if they had money to buy them.)

Hardt and Negri discuss theories of Imperialism, relying especially on Rosa Luxemburg's theory, as theories about capitalism's need to colonize non-capitalist societies in a never-ending effort to stabilize itself. Capitalism thirsts insatiably for new space. It needs places to sell produces that cannot be sold in those parts of the world already inside the capitalist orbit. According to Luxemburg, capitalism is continually driven to sell its products to people living in what she called "natural economies," i.e., to people whose way of life is not yet capitalist. Capital needs an "outside" that is not capitalist. That is Imperialism. Or rather, it is the economic dynamic that drives imperialism, shorn of its racism, its militarism, its ideologies, its cultures, and its juridical frameworks.[62]

Yet the drive to accumulate surplus value, buying in order to sell, and then reinvesting the profits in order to buy still more and sell still more, cannot rest content with acquiring colonies and quasi-colonies as markets. It must convert the colonies into places where labor can be exploited. Tribal peoples must become wage earners. Only by establishing relationships of exploitation, in which people produce more value than they are paid, can the potential for profit making be maximized. The consequence is that the outside is continually incorporated, brought inside. Parts of the world that were at first non-capitalist markets for surplus production are eventually transformed into capitalist markets where labor power is bought and sold. There comes a point when the entire world is incorporated into capitalist production relationships.

That is Empire. One system with no outside. It is an empire with no emperor and no Rome, which acts as though there were an emperor at a central capitol sending out decrees that all the world shall conform itself to the requirements of capitalist accumulation at its current stage of historic development. Hence, "[C]onspiracy theories are a crude but effective mechanism for approximating the functioning of the totality. The spectacle of politics functions as if the media, the military, the transnational corporations, the global financial institutions, and so forth were all consciously and explicitly directed by a single power even though in reality they are not."[63]

Capitalism's necessary drive toward expansion is, however, only a part of Hardt and Negri's story about how Empire came into existence in the form it has assumed today. The other part of the story—which takes up most of the book—is about resistance. The particular Empire that exists today is not an Empire that had to come into existence because of capitalism's inherent dynamics. The inherent tendency toward Empire intrinsic to the dynamics of capitalism plays itself out in history as capital responds to challenges. The biggest challenges come from workers who resist being exploited.

Yet "worker" is too narrow a term. The authors broaden the category of "proletariat" to include "all those whose labor is directly or indirectly exploited by and subjected to capitalist norms of production and reproduction."[64] Then they move on to the even broader term "multitude." "Multitude" identifies, in the end, the many human bodies that inhabit the earth. Giving a Foucauldian twist to Marxism, Hardt and Negri portray the human body, subjected to the disciplinary bio-power of modernity, and physically inclined to resist it, as today's great historical opponent of exchange-value. There is now one world-stage and on it two actors: The Empire and The Multitude. The Empire represents exchange-value. The Multitude represents use-value. It stands for "the universality of free and productive practices."[65]

The proposal for the left is clear: organize the multitude on a global scale. "The strategy of local resistance misidentifies, and thus masks the enemy. . . . The enemy, rather, is a specific regime of global relations that we call Empire."[66]

We will not criticize the story told by Hardt and Negri, but in the following pages we will tell a different story. The two stories can be compared by saying that their story is *jenseits* Marx, while our story is *diesseits* Marx. The story about the Empire versus the Multitude is beyond Marx. The story about dilemmas of social democracies is this side of Marx. One can think of the famous passage in Marx's *Capital* where he passes from the analysis of circulation to the analysis of production as marking the boundary between what is *diesseits* Marx and what is properly Marxist. (Borrowing an idea of Louis Althusser, one can say that Marx was not really Marx until he wrote Chapter Seven of *Capital*.) The passage in question states:

> This sphere we are deserting, within whose boundaries the sale and purchase of labour power goes on, is in fact a very Eden of the innate rights of man. There alone rule freedom, equality, property, and Bentham. Freedom, because both buyer and seller of a commodity, say of labour power, are constrained only by their own free will. They contract as free agents, and the agreement they come to is but the form in which they give legal expression to their common will. Equality, because each enters into relation with the other, as with a simple owner of commodities, and they exchange equivalent for equivalent. Property, because each disposes only of what is his own. And Bentham, because each looks only to himself. The only force that brings them together and puts them in relation with each other is the selfishness, the gain, and the private interests of each.[67]

Hardt and Negri follow Marx forward from this passage into the realm of production. They say quite clearly and repeatedly throughout their book that the history of capitalism is to be understood as a history of relations of production. With this premise they build their theory of a paradigm shift from Imperialism to Empire.

We back up from this same passage and—without denying the importance of production and relations of production—we take a close look at the rules that govern the circulation of commodities. Although production relations may well explain, as Marx said, why it is possible to make profits while obeying the rules of circulation, the question remains whether and to what extent the rules of circulation govern in the first place. We remember that in prior pages Marx acknowledged that for thousands of years humans have gone to markets to sell in order to buy. Their aim—the aim ancient philosophers like Aristotle considered natural—was to go to market in order to get something to use, not to accumulate profits. More generally, thousands of human cultures have found ways to organize the exchange of matter and energy with the environment that are substantially different from the folkways of the societies Marx set out to analyze, the ones where wealth appears as "an immense accumulation of commodities."[68] Consequently, the Eden of the innate rights of man, which Marx satirizes, can be deconstructed and reconstructed, not just in one way, but in many ways.

We trace the historical experiences of several socialist movements that have sought in various ways to modify the rules of the commodity exchange game— to conceive freedom, for example, in a context of social accountability; to make equality, for example, less a formal juridical fiction and more a real characteristic of life in a democratic society; to reconstruct property rights, for example, in the light of their social functions and for the purpose of sharing their benefits with more beneficiaries and more owners; to temper self-interest, for example, with an ethic of solidarity and to channel competition in constructive directions. We are interested in social democracy's dilemmas—that is, in its failures, since dilemmas have the characteristic that one horn of the dilemma leads to failure, while the other horn also leads to failure. Our focus is on the systemic, pervasive, and repeated precise reasons for social democracy's failures. Our objective is to show, in detailed discussions of empowering ideas and with concrete examples, that notwithstanding the setbacks suffered by social democracy in the latter years of the twentieth century, there are innumerable ways forward toward liberation. Our insight is that the mechanism that drives the historical dynamics Hardt and Negri describe is *not* a mechanism. It is a cultural structure. Cultural structures do not have dynamics. They have (to use several somewhat overlapping terms) norms, beliefs, roles, customs, practices, and rules, all of which are subject to change.

Notes

1. Having earned four doctorates between us, having studied at a half dozen of the world's prestigious universities (including Stanford, Harvard, Oxford, and Yale), and having concentrated upon and contributed to the unapologetically interdisciplinary field of Peace Studies, it is likely that we have a more comprehensive understanding of the causes of social failure than has the average person.

2. Roy Bhaskar, *Scientific Realism and Human Emancipation* (London: Verso, 1986), 123. See also Anthony Giddens, *New Rules of Sociological Method* (New York: Harper & Row, 1976), 121.

3. Daniel Quinn writes, "If the world is saved, it will not be by old minds with new programs but by new minds with no programs at all. . . . Because where you find people working on programs, you don't find new minds, you find old ones." He clarifies the difference between "old" and "new" minds: when confronting problems of social injustice, old minds ask: how do we stop these bad things from happening? New minds, in contrast, ask: how do we make things the way we want them to be? The problem with "programs," according to Quinn, is that they must always be inadequate precisely because they are, in essence, reactive. Programs, therefore, "can't make good things happen, they only make bad things less bad." Daniel Quinn, *Beyond Civilization: Humanity's Next Great Adventure* (New York: Harmony Books, 1999), 8, 18. One of the most valuable critical insights offered by Bowles and Gintis is that concerning the threat to social democracy posed by capital's power to "exit." See Samuel Bowles and Herbert Gintis, *Democracy and Capitalism: Property, Community, and the Contradictions of Modern Social Thought* (New York: Basic Books, 1986). We also refer the reader's attention to Joseph Collins, *What Difference Could a Revolution Make? Food and Farming in The New Nicaragua* (San Francisco: Institute for Food and Development Policy, 1982). This book offers a succinct statement of precisely the problem we seek to address. During the Nicaraguan Revolution (1979-1990), the Sandinista government, learning from historical experience, sought ways to implement a form of social democracy that would not suffer the economic and other forms of backlash that are "built into the system" as a consequence of the system's mandate for capital accumulation. Collins documents Nicaragua's efforts to address such problems as land hunger and to do so without undermining the productivity of the large landholdings, for the government recognized that to do so would harm all of Nicaraguan society. The Nicaraguan Revolution was constantly under assault by U.S.-funded counter-revolutionaries, and this only exacerbated the problem that despite the Nicaraguan people's best efforts, production did suffer, and shortages did ensue. As a result, the Sandinistas were voted out of office in 1990. This pattern is a concise statement of the dilemmas of social democracies.

4. Bo Rothstein, *Just institutions matter: The moral and political logic of the universal welfare state* (Cambridge; New York; Melbourne: Cambridge University Press, 1998).

5. Plato, *The Republic*, trans. B. Jowett (New York: The Modern Library, 1941), 23-25. Note: This passage comes from Section 341 (S341).

6. Plato, *Republic*, 59-62. This passage is from Sections 369-370.

7. Riane Eisler, *The Chalice and the Blade: Our History, Our Future* (New York: HarperCollins, 1987). Eisler relies on detailed archaeological studies by Marija Gimbutas. Gimbutas concludes her study, *The Gods and Goddesses of Old Europe*, with the following passage: "In Old Europe the world of myth was not polarized into female and

male as it was among the Indo-European and many other nomadic and pastoral peoples of the steppes. Both principles were manifest side by side. . . . Neither is subordinate to the other; by complementing one another, their power is doubled. . . . The role of woman was not subject to that of a man, and much that was created between the inception of the Neolithic and the blossoming of the Minoan civilization was a result of that structure in which all resources of human nature, feminine and masculine, were utilized to the full as a creative force. . . . The study of mythical images provides one of the best proofs that the Old European world was not the proto-Indo-European world and that there was no direct and unobstructed line of development to the modern Europeans. The earliest European civilization was savagely destroyed by the patriarchal element and it never recovered, but its legacy lingered in the substratum which nourished further European cultural developments. The Old European creations were not lost; transformed, they enormously enriched the European psyche." Marija Gimbutas, *The Gods and Goddesses of Old Europe, 7000 to 3500 BC: Myths, Legends and Cult Images* (Berkeley and Los Angeles: University of California Press, 1974), 237-38.

8. Wink defines the "Domination System" as being characterized by "unjust economic relations, oppressive political relations, biased race relations, patriarchal gender relations, hierarchical power relations, and the use of violence to maintain them all." Walter Wink, *The Powers That Be: Theology for a New Millennium* (New York; London; Toronto; Sydney; Auckland: Doubleday, 1998), 39. At the root of the "Domination System," in Wink's assessment, is the fundamental belief that violence must be used to overcome violence. Wink, *Powers That Be*, 91. Wink writes, "Looking back over Jesus' ministry, what emerges with bracing clarity is the *comprehensive* nature of his vision. He was not intent on putting a new patch on an old garment, or new wine in old skins (Mark 2: 21-22). He was not a reformer, bringing alternative, better readings of the law. Nor was he a revolutionary, attempting to replace one oppressive power with another (Mark 12: 13-17). He went beyond revolution. His struggle was against the basic presuppositions and structures of oppression—against the Domination System itself. Violent revolution fails because it is not revolutionary enough. It changes the rulers but not the rules, the ends but not the means. What Jesus envisioned was a world transformed, where both people and Powers are in harmony with the Ultimate and committed to the general welfare—what some prefer to call the 'kingdom' of God. . . . The world, and even the church, had no categories for such fundamental change. It is no wonder that the radicality of Jesus was soon watered down by the church. But his truth has proved to be inextinguishable." Wink, *Powers That Be*, 81. On "dominator societies," see also Walter Wink, *Engaging the Powers: Discernment and Resistance in a World of Domination* (Minneapolis, Minn.: Fortress Press, 1992).

9. Eisler, *Chalice and the Blade*, xvii-xx, 94, 102-03; Wink, *Powers That Be*, 37-111.

10. Matthew 25: 31-46. Note: All passages from the Bible cited in this text derive from the King James Version.

11. John 15: 4-15.

12. Acts of the Apostles 4: 32-34.

13. On cooperation and sharing in early Christian communities, see also David Ganz, "The ideology of sharing: apostolic community and ecclesiastical property in the early middle ages" and the works cited therein, in Wendy Davies and Paul Fouracre, eds., *Property and Power in the Early Middle Ages* (Cambridge; New York; Melbourne: Cambridge University Press, 1995), 17-30.

14. Voltaire, *Philosophical Dictionary*, trans. Theodore Besterman (London: Penguin Books, 1984), 398-99.

15. Gunnar Myrdal, *The Political Element in the Development of Economic Theory*, trans. Paul Streeten (London: Routledge & Kegan Paul, 1953); Gunnar Myrdal, *Beyond the Welfare State: economic planning and its international implications* (New Haven, Conn.: Yale University Press, 1960), 15-16, 163-64; Immanuel Wallerstein, *Unthinking Social Science: The Limits of Nineteenth-Century Paradigms* (Cambridge: Polity Press, 1991), 80-103.

16. Voltaire, *Letters Concerning the English Nation* [also known as *Philosophical Letters*] (Oxford and New York: Oxford University Press, 1994), 30.

17. On his lands at Ferney, true to his own principles, Voltaire, who was a deist, built a Catholic chapel for his Catholic peasants. He hired a priest, one Father Adam, to say mass for them. Father Adam had the honor of mixing socially with the famous Parisian deists, the liberal princes from Germany, the occasional dissident Protestant theologian from Holland, and distinguished intellectuals of all kinds from all parts of the world who made Ferney their Mecca.

18. Voltaire, *Philosophical Dictionary*, 291.

19. Voltaire, *Philosophical Dictionary*, 183.

20. Voltaire, *Philosophical Dictionary*, 15-16.

21. See also James R. Otteson, "The Recurring 'Adam Smith Problem,'" *History of Philosophy Quarterly* 17, no. 1 (January 2000): 51-74.

22. Adam Smith, *An Inquiry into the Nature and Causes of the Wealth of Nations* (New York: The Modern Library, 1937), 3-12, 81, 125. So impressed is Smith with the benefits adhering to the division of labor that the very first sentence of *Wealth of Nations*, Book I, Chapter 1, reads: "The greatest improvement in the productive powers of labour, and the greater part of the skill, dexterity, and judgment with which it is any where directed, or applied, seem to have been the effects of the division of labour." Smith, *Wealth of Nations*, 3. In Smith's view, the colonial relationship was best suited to take advantage of all the benefits of the international division of labor. He writes, "The general advantages which Europe, considered as one great country, has derived from the discovery and colonization of America, consist, first, in the increase of its enjoyments; and secondly, in the augmentation, in the augmentation of its industry." Smith, *Wealth of Nations*, 337. As for the division of labor's promised benefits to the colony, he writes, "The colony of a civilized nation which takes possession, either of a waste country or of one so thinly inhabited, that the natives easily give place to the new settlers, advances more rapidly to wealth and greatness than any other human society. The colonists carry out with them a knowledge of agriculture and of other useful arts, superior to what can grow up of its own accord in the course of many centuries among savage and barbarous nations." Smith, *Wealth of Nations*, 531-32.

23. Smith, *Wealth of Nations*, 6, 650-51.

24. Jan Tinbergen, *Shaping the World Economy: Suggestions for an International Economic Policy* (New York: The Twentieth Century Fund, 1962), 19-39, 101-2. Tinbergen states that the general aims of economic policy in modern times, regardless of the policy makers' principled devotion to free-market capitalism, socialism, communism, or another particular economic system, are the following: 1) maintenance of international peace; 2) maximum real expenditure per capita with "full" employment and monetary equilibrium (i.e., material welfare, as high a rate of employment as possible, and the maintenance of the purchasing power of money for those who are forced to live off sav-

ings and pensions); 3) improvement of distribution of real income or expenditure over social groups and countries; 4) emancipation of under-privileged groups; and 5) as much personal freedom as is compatible with these other four aims. Jan Tinbergen, *Economic Policy: Principles and Design* (Amsterdam: North-Holland Publishing Company, 1966), 15-17. He elaborated these principles partially on the basis of an inquiry conducted by the Netherlands Economic Institute in the period of the late 1950s to early 1960s as to the main characteristics of the economic planning policies in nineteen nation-states whose economies ranged from communist to capitalist. Tinbergen's earlier summary of the main economic goals of nation-states included the following: the increase of national income; the improvement of employment levels; the achievement and maintenance of equilibrium in the balance-of-payments; the achievement and maintenance of price stability; the achievement of a more equal distribution of income among individuals; and the achievement of balanced regional economic development. Jan Tinbergen, *Central Planning* (New Haven, Conn.; and London: Yale University Press, 1964), 32-36. We appreciate Tinbergen's emphasis upon the commonalties in the goals of economic policies and how this emphasis leads him to an uncommon and welcome pragmatism. He writes, "There is a tendency in popular propaganda to speak about the economic and social regimes of the Western countries and the Communist countries as if they were in sharp contrast to each other. The dichotomy is emphasized by labels such as 'free' and 'authoritarian' and 'capitalist' and 'socialist.' There is a danger that top-ranking politicians and diplomats who do not have expert economic knowledge will also think in these black-and-white terms, which are not in conformity with the facts. In other words, there is a danger of doctrinaire thinking which may do great harm to the world. We should be aware of the existence of a whole range of possible systems using institutions and instruments of varying character; our aim must be to find the best system without reference to preconceived ideas. To choose, on doctrinaire grounds, a system which is not optimal would be stupid." Tinbergen, *Shaping the World Economy*, 101-02.

25. Adam Smith, *The Theory of Moral Sentiments*, ed. D.D. Raphael and A.L. Macfie (Oxford: Clarendon Press, 1976), 25.

26. Smith, *Wealth of Nations*, 14.

27. Witold von Skarzynski, *Adam Smith als Moralphilosoph und Schoepfer der Nationaloekonomie* (Berlin: Theobald Grieben, 1878).

28. D.D. Raphael and A.L. Macfie, Introduction to Smith, *Theory of Moral Sentiments*, 20.

29. Noam Chomsky, *Cartesian Linguistics: A Chapter In the History of Rationalist Thought* (New York and London. Harper & Row, 1966), 32-33.

30. Chomsky writes, "[The distinction between deep and surface structure] is often introduced in an attempt to show how certain philosophical positions arise from false grammatical analogies, the surface structure of certain expressions being mistakenly considered to be semantically interpretable by means appropriate only to other, superficially similar sentences." Noam Chomsky, *Aspects of the Theory of Syntax* (Cambridge, Mass.: MIT Press, 1965), 199. Chomsky also delineates the history of the use of this concept, beginning with Wittgenstein, and then further refined by Charles Francis Hockett in 1958 and by Jerrold J. Katz and Paul Martin Postal in 1964. Hockett developed the concepts of "endocentric" and "exocentric" types of syntactical construction Charles Francis Hockett, *A Course in Modern Linguistics* (New York: The Macmillan Company, 1958), 183-98. In a work published the following year, Chomsky offers a further comment on the definition of the concept of "depth grammar," drawing upon the Humboldtian notion of lan-

guage having both "inner" and "outer" forms. He writes, "[L]anguage has an inner and an outer aspect. A sentence can be studied from the point of view of how it expresses a thought or from the point of view of its physical shape, that is, from the point of view of either semantic interpretation or phonetic interpretation. . . . [W]e can distinguish the 'deep structure' of a sentence from its 'surface structure.' The former is the underlying abstract structure that determines its semantic interpretation; the latter, the superficial organization of units which determines the phonetic interpretation and which relates to the physical form of the actual utterance, to its perceived or intended form." Chomsky, *Cartesian Linguistics*, 32-33. The "deep structure," which is a "purely mental" structure, "conveys the semantic content of the sentence." Chomsky, *Cartesian Linguistics*, 35. See also Noam Chomsky, *Language and Responsibility* (New York: Pantheon Books, 1977), especially 169-79.

31. In the sixteenth through nineteenth centuries when lawyers were creating modern private law, building on Roman and other sources, early modern secular philosophers were developing universal ethical theories suitable for commercial Europe. The most influential of the founders of modern liberal ethics was Immanuel Kant. Kant's elaboration of strict moral duties that are owed to others served to bolster these principles of Roman Law. The example Kant uses in his *Foundations of the Metaphysics of Morals* to illustrate strict moral duties to others is that one should never incur a debt without intending to pay it. Having used this example from the field of contracts several times, he remarks toward the end of the second section that he could have made his point even more clearly using as examples attacks on property and freedom. Immanuel Kant, *Foundations of the Metaphysics of Morals*, trans. Lewis White Beck (Indianapolis, Ind.: Bobbs-Merrill, 1976), 48 (first published in German in 1785).

32. Smith, *Theory of Moral Sentiments*, 33.

33. Thus while we appreciate the work of Kenneth Lux, *Adam Smith's Mistake: How a Moral Philosopher Invented Economics and Ended Morality* (Boston and London: Shambhala, 1990), and certainly agree with many of the points made therein, we find that his critique is not deep enough. When Lux explores the famous butcher-baker remark of Smith, he finds a problem that is easily solved. Lux writes, "We . . . should be able to see that Adam Smith left out just one little word—a word which has made a world of difference. . . . That word is *only*. What Adam Smith ought to have said was, 'It is not *only* from the benevolence. . . .'; then everything would have been all right." Lux, *Adam Smith's Mistake*, 87, italics in original. Lux believes that the addition of this word would have helped to prevent "immorality from finding its intellectual and theoretical justification in the name of economics"; and that reinserting principles of honesty, integrity, and fairness into the process of exchange would suffice to solve many of the problems we now face. Lux, *Adam Smith's Mistake*, 88, 90. As we seek to demonstrate in the present work, the operative rules that underlie ethics are themselves part of the problem.

34. Marx quoted in Robert C. Tucker, ed., *The Marx-Engels Reader*, 2nd edition (New York and London: W.W. Norton & Company, 1978), 528. Marx's *Critique of the Gotha Program* was written in response to the leaders of the Eisenach faction of the German Social Democratic movement, who were planning to unite with the Lassallean faction to form a unified German Social Democratic Party. Marx and Friedrich Engels found the Gotha Program "fundamentally flawed by the influence of the ideas of Ferdinand Lassalle." Tucker, *Marx-Engels Reader*, 525. Some of the main points of contention between Marx and Engels on one hand and Lassalle on the other rested on their beliefs that Las-

salle had little depth of understanding of economics, was too interested in political compromise with capitalists, and practiced demagogy.

35. Marx, reprinted in Tucker, *Marx-Engels Reader*, 528-29, italics in original.

36. Mohandas K. Gandhi, *All Men Are Brothers* (New York: Continuum Publishing, 1990), 125.

37. Gandhi quoted in Raghavan Iyer, *The Moral and Political Thought of Mahatma Gandhi* (Oxford: Oxford University Press, 1973), 115.

38. Iyer, *Moral and Political Thought*, 114.

39. Iyer, *Moral and Political Thought*, 115.

40. Iyer, *Moral and Political Thought*, 117. On the same theme of the relationship between the individual and the larger world, Iyer writes, "In traditional Indian thought a distinction was made between two phases of cosmic and human evolution, the phase of *pravrittii,* or involvement, and of *nivriti,* or withdrawal. The ultimate aim, the final human good, is *moksha,* spiritual freedom and redemption. The word *moksha* is derived from the root *muc,* to set free, let go, release, deliver. *Nivriti* means disappearance, completion, repose, discontinuance of worldly acts or emotions. *Tapas* means that which burns up impurities, purificatory action, austerities, penance. The original meaning of the word denotes warmth or heat. Man becomes enslaved by his contact with the sensory world, falls into ignorance and involuntary suffering, is bound down by external forces and conditions. In the end he comes to seek salvation, spiritual autonomy, absolute freedom, transcendental bliss. In the attainment of *moksha* he requires *tapas,* ceaseless self-restraint, an acceptance of suffering, the dispelling of his delusions by a clear vision of his real nature and his essential identity with all other beings. The more he suffers in a conscious and creative manner, the greater is his solidarity with the cosmos, his attunement to the world's misery, and the more intensely he seeks final emancipation and full freedom." Iyer, *Moral and Political Thought*, 235-36.

41. Robert Axelrod, *The Evolution of Cooperation* (New York: Basic Books, 1984), 109. Recent advances in game theory suggest that Axelrod's starting premise, that of humans as self-interested egoists, might be mistaken; but these same advancements offer supportive evidence for the advantages of cooperation. Numerous trials of the Ultimatum Game (devised by game theorist Werner Güth of Humboldt University in Berlin) in various regions of the world reveal that, in sharp contrast to the postulation of neoclassical economics, most people did not act according to the dictates of "rational self-interest." The scenario of the Ultimatum Game is based upon the Prisoner's Dilemma (which we describe below). In the Ultimatum Game, two players, each in separate rooms and without the chance to exchange information, have to decide how to split $100. A coin toss determines which person gets to propose how the money should be divided. The person making the offer can only make a single offer, and the other person has only one chance to accept or reject the proposal. Both people know the rules and the total amount of money at stake. If the proposal is accepted, the deal goes forward as proposed; if the offer is rejected, neither person gets any of the money. In the sample games run by Karl Sigmund, Ernest Fehr, and Martin Nowak, only four percent of players act in the greedy fashion of offering $20 or a smaller amount. Even more interesting is that more than half of players rejected offers that were smaller than $20 as "too small"; whereas neoclassical economic theory holds that rational self-interest would cause a player to accept any offer, since even $1 is better than nothing. Instead, more than two-thirds of players offered between $40 and $50, and the researchers concluded that most people—regardless of age, sex, schooling, numeracy, or cultural background—place high value on outcomes they

consider "fair." Based on this and other research, Sigmund, Fehr, and Nowak propose that there is a kind of "Darwinian generosity" a biologically rooted cross-cultural human trait that allows humans to cooperate with non-relatives and so survive as a species. Karl Sigmund, Ernst Fehr, and Martin A. Nowak, "The Economics of Fair Play," *Scientific American* 286, no. 1 (January 2002): 83-87. See also Martin A. Nowak, Karen M. Page, and Karl Sigmund, "Fairness versus Reason in the Ultimatum Game," *Science* 289 (September 8, 2000): 1773-75; Ernst Fehr and Simon Gächter, "Cooperation and Punishment in Public Goods Experiments," *American Economic Review* 90, no. 4 (September 2000): 980-94; Joseph Henrich, Robert Boyd, Samuel Bowles, Colin Camerer, Ernst Fehr, Herbert Gintis, and Richard McElreath, "In Search of *Homo Economicus*: Behavioral Experiments in 15 Small-Scale Societies," *American Economic Review* 91, no. 2 (May 2001): 73-78; and Bruce M. Knauft, "Culture and Cooperation in Human Evolution," in *The Anthropology of Peace and Nonviolence*, ed. Leslie E. Sponsel and Thomas Gregor (Boulder, Colo.; and London: Lynne Rienner Publishers, 1994), 37-67. Interested readers might also consult works by some of these same researchers and by others that present evidence suggesting how cooperation can evolve and be consolidated through reciprocity. A study by Linnda R. Caporael et al. supports the notion of "Darwinian generosity" with findings that if people are allowed to engage in discussions, most often they will act in individually "irrational" ways for the purpose of promoting group welfare. Linnda R. Caporael, Robyn M. Dawes, John M. Orbell, and Alphons J.C. van de Kragt, "Selfishness Examined: Cooperation in the Absence of Egoistic Incentives," *Behavioral and Brain Sciences* 12 (1989): 683-739. Game theorists Viktor Vanberg and Roger Congleton present evidence to suggest that a "moral program"—in which players in various games mirror one another's strategies within a framework of justice—is a successful strategy, which lends credence to Axelrod's theory of the evolution of cooperation. Viktor J. Vanberg and Roger D. Congleton, "Rationality, Morality, and Exit," *American Political Science Review* 86 (1992): 418-31. Cristina Bicchieri argues that instrumental rationality approaches cannot adequately explain how norms are established and why people adhere to them, and she favors the more comprehensive approach of examining norms in the context of evolution—how they can contribute to a species' survival. She explores the conditions under which cooperation is rational and proposes that cooperation can become well established in small groups and then diffuse—through evolutionary processes—to larger groups. Cristina Bicchieri, "Norms of Cooperation," *Ethics* 100 (1990): 838-61. In addition, there are a number of studies on an elaboration of Axelrod's Tit For Tat in which researchers found that under conditions of uncertainty, generosity proved the consistently most successful strategy, one that could lead to the development of "reciprocal altruism." These researchers distinguish this new strategy with the name "Generous Tit For Tat" (GTFT). See Manfred Milinksi, "Cooperation Wins and Stays," *Nature* 364 (1993): 12-13; Martin A. Nowak and Karl Sigmund, "The Alternating Prisoner's Dilemma," *Journal of Theoretical Biology* 168 (1994): 219-26; Martin A. Nowak and Karl Sigmund, "Tit For Tat in Heterogeneous Populations," *Nature* 355 (1992): 250-53; and Karl Sigmund, *Games of Life: Explorations in Ecology, Evolution, and Behaviour* (Oxford: Oxford University Press, 1993).

42. Anatol Rapoport, *Conflict in Man-Made Environment* (Harmondsworth, U.K.: Penguin, 1974).

43. Axelrod, *Evolution of Cooperation*, 81. The soldiers from the opposing sides developed such a close relationship during the famous spontaneous Christmas truce of 1914 that they refused to begin fighting when the new year started. The only way that the gen-

erals were able to re-initiate warfare on that front following the 1914 truce was to wholly remove these soldiers (on both sides) and replace them with fresh troops who had formed no relationships. See Stanley Weintraub, *Silent Night: The Remarkable 1914 Christmas Truce* (New York: The Free Press, 2001). The author claims that the tenacity of the truce was such that the remainder of World War I could have been avoided entirely.

44. Axelrod, *Evolution of Cooperation*, 182.

45. Rapoport defined "debate" as "a conflict of ideas." Rapoport, *Conflict in Man-Made Environment*, 182. In an earlier work, he writes, "[T]he ramifications of game theory bring to light the purely logical difficulties of dealing with strategy from a supposedly rational point of view." Anatol Rapoport, *Fights, Games, and Debates* (Ann Arbor, Mich.: University of Michigan Press, 1960), 360. Hayward Alker, in a commentary on Axelrod's theory of cooperation, makes a similar point to that of Rapoport: even if game theory allows a solution to the Prisoner's Dilemma, real peace depends on moving away from strategic thinking. Hayward Alker, Jr., *Rediscoveries and Reformulations* (Cambridge: Cambridge University Press, 1996), 320. The Prisoner's Dilemma is a well-known scenario in game theory. Devised in the 1950s by Merrill M. Flood and Melvin Dresher, the basic form of the Prisoner's Dilemma is a scenario in which two individuals are jailed in separate cells on charges of having committed a crime (such as bank robbery) together. The prosecutor meets with each of the prisoners separately and makes each the same offer: each may choose to confess or to remain silent. If one confesses and the other remains silent, all charges against the one confessing will be dropped, and the testimony will be used to ensure a long prison sentence for the one who remained silent. If both confess, the prosecutor will get two convictions but promises early parole for both. If both remain silent, the prosecutor assures them prison time but admits that he would have to convict on a lesser charge (such as possession of firearms), thus resulting in a shorter sentence. The dilemma arises in that whatever the other does, each prisoner is better off confessing than remaining silent; yet at the same time, the resulting outcome when both choose to confess is worse for each of them individually than the outcome that would have resulted had they both chosen to remain silent. The Prisoner's Dilemma is instructive on a number of levels. In one sense, it sheds light on the potential conflict between individual rationality and group rationality, for the Prisoner's Dilemma demonstrates that a group whose members all pursue individual self-interest might end up worse off than a group whose members choose at times to act contrary to individual self-interest. Flood and Dresher originally devised the scenario for the Rand Corporation, which was researching game theory because of its possible applications to nuclear strategy during the Cold War. See Merrill M. Flood, "Some Experimental Games," *Management Science* 5 (1958): 5-26. On the Prisoner's Dilemma, see, in addition to Axelrod, *Evolution of Cooperation*: Anatol Rapoport, *Game Theory as a Theory of Conflict Resolution* (Dordrecht, Neth.: Klüwer, 1974); Lawrence M. Kahn and J. Keith Murnighan, "Conjecture, Uncertainty, and Cooperation in Prisoner's Dilemma Games," *Journal of Economic Behavior and Organization* 22 (1993): 91-117; and William Poundstone, *Prisoner's Dilemma* (New York: Doubleday, 1992).

46. Mother Teresa, *My Life for the Poor*, ed. José Luis González-Balado and Janet N. Playfoot (San Francisco: Harper & Row, 1985), 97.

47. Mother Teresa, *My Life for the Poor*, 31.

48. Branting made this statement originally in an essay entitled "Socialism as a *Weltanschauung*." His words are quoted directly in Tim Tilton, *The Political Theory of*

Swedish Social Democracy: Through the Welfare State to Socialism (Oxford: Clarendon Press, 1990), 33.

49. Mother Teresa, *My Life for the Poor*, 41.

50. Mother Teresa, *My Life for the Poor*, 33-34.

51. Mother Teresa, *My Life for the Poor*, 78.

52. Mother Teresa, *My Life for the Poor*, 54.

53. Mother Teresa, *My Life for the Poor*, 88.

54. Eileen Egan, *Such a Vision of the Street: Mother Teresa—The Spirit and the Work* (New York: Doubleday, 1985), 49.

55. Egan, *Vision of the Street*, 61.

56. Friedrich A. von Hayek, ed., *Collectivist Economic Planning: Critical Studies on the Possibilities of Socialism* (London: Routledge & Kegan Paul, 1935); Friedrich A. von Hayek, *The Road to Serfdom* (Chicago: The University of Chicago Press, 1976 (1944)). On "roundabout methods of production," see Ludwig von Mises, *Socialism: An Economic and Sociological Analysis* (New Haven, Conn.: Yale University Press, 1951), 114-15, 510. Von Mises hails the overall efficiency of these roundabout methods of production for all but the most basic—i.e., hand-to-mouth—"economic systems." We offer further comment on the ideas of both von Mises and von Hayek in succeeding chapters.

57. Like Hardt and Negri, but in contradistinction to Foucault, we believe it is useful and good to speak of "liberation." Foucault writes, "To all those who still wish to talk about man, about his reign or his liberation, to all those who still ask themselves questions about what man is in his essence, to all those who wish to take him as their starting-point, in their attempts to reach the truth, to all those who, on the other hand, refer all knowledge back to the truths of man himself, to all those who refuse to formalize without anthropologizing, who refuse to mythologize without demystifying, who refuse to think without immediately thinking that it is man who is thinking, to all these warped and twisted forms of reflection we can answer only with a philosophical laugh—which means, to a certain extent, a silent one." Michel Foucault, *The Order of Things: An Archaeology of the Human Sciences* (London: Routledge, 2001), 342-43. We reiterate, however, that the present work makes no claim about "human nature" or the "essence" of being human. Our arguments do not depend on any concept of human rights or human liberation that is deduced from a philosophical anthropology—i.e., from a theory of the universal essence of what it is to be human. Instead, our emphasis herein upon "cooperation and sharing" lends itself to a realistic approach that asks fundamental, bread-and-butter questions about whether people get what they need. Thus it is not subject to the charges brought by Foucault against radicals who base their claims for "liberation" on some sort of Kantian imperative that people are supposed to be free because of their rational essences (if indeed there are any radicals of this sort—such radicals are no doubt mainly the creatures of the anti-radicals who invent them in order to refute them).

58. Anthony Giddens advocates a "Third Way," which he considers to be synonymous with "the modernizing left" and "modernizing social democracy," "modernizing" in the sense that the Left and social democrats resolve to accept the reality of global capitalism and to acknowledge the good it has done for the world. For Giddens, third way politics represents the only effective means of pursuing the ideals of social justice and solidarity in the present moment. So insistent is he that the "Third Way" is the only viable path for social democrats that he concludes the preface to his recent work on this subject by stating, "Third Way politics will be the point of view with which others will have to engage." Anthony Giddens, *The Third Way and its Critics* (Cambridge: Polity Press, 2000), vii,

27-29. We therefore intend the present work as a response in part to Giddens. *The Third Way and its Critics* posits three main arguments. First, Giddens argues that the consequences of global capitalism are on the whole good, in spite of serious flaws. The benefits of global capitalism, in Giddens' estimation, include that market exchange is "essentially peaceful"; that market relations "allow free choices to be made by consumers"; and that market relations have the potential to generate "far greater prosperity" than any other system. Giddens identifies the following flaws in capitalism: the potential to "breed a commercialism that threatens other life values"; the lack of limitations on what can be commodified and marketed; and the fact that under capitalism, "ethical standards . . . have to be brought from the outside—from a public ethics, guaranteed in law." Giddens, *The Third Way and its Critics*, 35-36. Second, in conjunction with the first argument, Giddens posits that in any case, global capitalism is inevitable and irreversible. Given these first two arguments, Giddens maintains that the role of "the modernizing left" is limited to correcting the flaws of capitalism. He argues that the rise of neoliberalism and the failure of the old Left's attempts, through organized labor, to shape government policy mean that we must "find ways of taking care of ourselves, because we can't now rely on the big institutions to do so." Giddens, *The Third Way and its Critics*, 2-3, 55-84. Third, Giddens claims that in order for the Democrats (in the U.S.) and the Labour Party (in Britain) to get a hearing with the public, they have speak a new language that the public understands, a language that speaks to the public's current concerns, which are not the concerns of the old industrial proletariat to which the old Left was responding. We wholeheartedly agree with Giddens' third main point—the concerns of the public today are far broader than those of the industrial proletariat taken up by the old Left—and we just as wholeheartedly disagree with his two other main arguments. While Giddens makes some theoretical points that demonstrate how to accomplish transformation, his conclusion with regard to practical politics is, in the main, pessimistic: not much transformation can be accomplished. He writes, "There is a 'big question' that confronts us all today . . . 'how can we combine sustainable prosperity with social solidarity, within institutions that guarantee liberty?' But there is no big answer." Giddens, *The Third Way and its Critics*, 19-20. If Giddens were to take his analysis a level deeper and explore the consequences of, e.g., "liberty" as we currently understand it, and of the "free choices" of consumers, it might become clear that in shifting our understanding of such concepts and thus the ways we put them into practice, big answers to the current dilemmas do indeed come into view. That his analysis does not shine the light on the constitutive rules of capitalism, as the present work seeks to do, is made clear in his general recommendations to social democrats: creating a positive climate for entrepreneurs, "flexible" markets, and the removal of burdensome rules and restrictions placed upon corporations. Such recommendations are certainly neither novel nor, in and of themselves, effectual in achieving the ends Giddens claims to support. Giddens, *The Third Way and its Critics*, 6-7. See also Anthony Giddens, *The Third Way: The Renewal of Social Democracy* (Cambridge: Polity Press, 1998); and Stuart Hall, "The great moving nowhere show," *Marxism Today* (November/December 1998): 9-14.

59. Michael Hardt and Antonio Negri, *Empire* (Cambridge, Mass.: Harvard University Press, 2000), 85.

60. Hardt and Negri, *Empire*, 410-11.

61. Hardt and Negri, *Empire*, 222. They continue, "Certainly, the capitalist class (along with other classes that share in its profits) will consume some of this excess value,

but it cannot consume all of it, because if it did there would be no surplus value left to reinvest." Hardt and Negri, *Empire*, 223.

62. See Rosa Luxemburg, *The Accumulation of Capital*, trans. Agnes Schwarzschild (London: Routledge and Kegan Paul, 1951), especially Chapter 27, "The Struggle Against Natural Economy," 368-85.

63. Hardt and Negri, *Empire*, 323.

64. Hardt and Negri, *Empire*, 52.

65. Hardt and Negri, *Empire*, 316.

66. Hardt and Negri, *Empire*, 45-46.

67. Karl Marx, *Capital: A Critique of Political Economy*, Vol. 50 of Mortimer J. Adler, ed., *Great Books of the Western World* (Chicago: Encyclopedia Britannica, Inc., 1990), 83-84. For additional comments on this passage, see Chapter 6, note 2.

68. Marx, *Capital*, 13.

Chapter 2

Making Invisible Causes Visible

This second chapter will outline the epistemology that will be applied in the subsequent historical studies. Readers not interested in philosophy may prefer to skip this chapter and move on to the historical studies.

One of us taught introductory courses in philosophy to first year college students for twenty-five years, and in the course of doing so became very familiar with the beliefs that:

1) The rich run the world;
2) The rich are up to no good; and
3) Nothing can be done about it.

This philosophy professor proposed for his students' consideration a different set of beliefs:

1) Ideas run the world;
2) The history of humanity is a history of moral progress; and
3) You and I can participate in the ethical construction of a better social reality.

Over the years Howard Richards developed a moderately sophisticated epistemology to support his beliefs. By "epistemology" we mainly mean an account of causality. We take some account of the principle of cause and effect to be central to any epistemology. Richards needed an account of causality because he needed to show that ideas like cooperation and sharing are not only good ideas, but also feasible ideas. This is not to say that epistemology alone can make our case for us by demonstrating the feasibility of cooperation and sharing and the truth of each of the three beliefs stated above. Rather, philosophy (epistemology included) sets the stage. To switch to a chess metaphor, it opens the game. Philosophy makes initial choices about how to go about thinking and talking, which predispose the eventual outcome to come out one way or another.

Richards never explained his epistemology to his first-year students because they would never have understood it. We will explain it now. His starting point is the distinction between brute facts and institutional facts made by John Searle in *Speech Acts*. Searle wrote:

> A marriage ceremony, a baseball game, a trial, and a legislative action involve a variety of physical movements, states, and raw feels, but a specification of one of these events only in such terms is not so far a specification of it as a marriage ceremony, baseball game, a trial, or a legislative action. The physical events and raw feels only count as parts of such events given certain other conditions and against a background of certain kinds of institutions.
>
> Such facts as are recorded in my above group of statements I propose to call *institutional facts*. They are indeed facts; but their existence, unlike the existence of brute facts, presupposes the existence of certain human institutions. It is only given the institution of marriage that certain forms of behavior constitute Mr. Smith's marrying Miss Jones. Similarly, it is only given the institution of baseball that certain movements . . . [by players] constitute the Dodgers' beating the Giants 3 to 2 in eleven innings. And, at even simpler level, it is only given the institution of money that I now have a five dollar bill in my hand. Take away the institution and all I have is a piece of paper with various gray and green markings.
>
> These "institutions" are systems of constitutive rules. Every institutional fact is underlain by a (system of) rule(s) of the form "X counts as Y in context C." Our hypothesis that speaking a language is performing acts according to constitutive rules involves us in the hypothesis that the fact that a man performed a certain speech act, e.g. made a promise, is an institutional fact.[1]

As if in anticipation of the frenzy of postmodern anti-realism that subsequent decades would bring, Searle added in a footnote: "Brute facts, such as, e.g. the fact that I weigh 160 pounds, of course require certain conventions of measuring weight and also require certain linguistic institutions in order to be stated in a language, but the fact stated is nonetheless a brute fact, as opposed to the fact that it was stated, which is an institutional fact."[2]

Now we are willing to admit that there are contexts in which one ought to say that there are facts which are neither brute nor institutional; there are contexts in which facts should be described as at once brute and institutional; there are contexts in which the noun "facts" is misleading and should not be used at all, however qualified. Nevertheless, the contrast between "brute" and "institutional" is illuminating and helpful, for reasons we will now state.

Although the very idea of "brute facts" can be considered a philosophical failure if it is taken as an attempt to salvage empiricism, it must be considered a philosophical success if it is taken as an attempt to score a point in favor of realism. Pointing out that some facts can be called "brute" more properly than others serves as an illuminating and helpful reminder that the interpretation of experience by humans is not all there is. There are facts that would be true even if they were not experienced.[3] There are facts that would be true even if there were no humans at all—as indeed there were not until approximately two hundred thousand years ago.

The word "brute" illuminatingly and helpfully connotes both its etymology and its standard uses. It comes from a Latin root meaning "heavy," "dull," or "irrational." The brutes are distinguished from the humans. The brutal is distinguished from the civilized. The related notion that some facts are relatively more brute than others hearkens back to the ancient metaphysics of Aristotle, a metaphysics of matter and form, in which the lower is more material and the higher more formal. It recalls the age-old human project of building cultures, and building selves, with the raw materials provided by nature.

Qualifying a fact as institutional brings into play the meanings of the noun "institution" and the verb "to institute." The primary meaning of the latter (according to the O.E.D.) is "to set up, to establish." The examples Searle himself gives to show the meaning of the word he has chosen come trailing the clouds of the many times the same word has been chosen by others, among which we beg leave to especially take note of its use by Immanuel Kant in *Perpetual Peace*, where he wrote that since war among humans is natural, peace must be instituted.[4]

That humans are a kind of animal that establishes institutions is related to humans being animals who think—as is shown by, among others, Jean Piaget's studies of the relationships between children's acquisition of the ability to make up games with rules and their ability to perform logical operations.[5] Two thousand three hundred years before Piaget, Plato, in the course of dialogues devoted to making a plan for a just society, identified the agency that could and should establish and implement the laws of a good city as the part of the soul that is *logistikon* as distinct from *alogistikon*—the rational part of the soul.[6] Otherwise translated, we may read Plato's references to the part of the *psuches* that has the *logos* as pertaining to the human capacity to bring motor behavior under verbal control.[7]

Searle's distinction stands in several traditions that distinguish nature from what today we call culture. Nature gives us brutes. Culture gives us institutions. Much as we may love the brutes, and much as we may love our own deep animal impulses, at this stage in history we must confess that there is little we can do to change nature. In an important sense, nature is, by definition, what we cannot change. Therefore the path to a better social reality goes by way of the improvement of culture.[8]

While invoking the larger traditions of the ethical construction of cultural structures, Searle gives us concepts to work with much more specific than the notoriously undefinable concept "culture": "These 'institutions' are systems of constitutive rules. Every institutional fact is underlain by a (system of) rule(s) of the form 'X counts as Y in context C.'"[9] Our project, however, is not so much to contribute to the study of the concept of constitutive rules by deepening understanding of what it is, as it is to contribute to the study of the concept of constitutive rules by broadening understanding of what can be done with it. Much of our inspiration comes from an article published by Charles Taylor.[10]

Taylor shows that it is artificial to distinguish between social reality and the language descriptive of that reality. "The language is constitutive of the reality and is essential to its being the kind of reality it is."[11] He expands the concept of the constitutive. "But just as there are constitutive rules, i.e., rules such that the behavior they govern could not exist without them, and which are in this sense inseparable from that behavior, so I am suggesting that there are constitutive distinctions, constitutive ranges of language, in that certain practices are not without them."[12] Implicit in the practices thus constituted is a certain vision of the agent and the agent's place in society. "The meanings and norms implicit in these practices are not just in the minds of the actors but are out there in the practices themselves, practices which cannot be conceived as a set of individual actions, but which are essentially modes of social relation, of mutual action."[13]

The notion of "modes of social relation" connects Taylor with Karl Marx. As Newton's *Principia Mathematica* is a tale of force (vis) from beginning to end, so Marx's *Capital* is a tale of social relations (*Verhaltnisse*) from beginning to end. We are infinitely grateful to Marx, in spite of the damage done by his mistakes, because he put irrevocably on the agenda for further critical discussion the basic social relations (constitutive rules) of capitalism: freedom, private property, contracts, commodities, production for sale, individual rights. This short list of rules constituting capitalism shows that capitalism is in important ways a great moral advance over previous periods in history. A failure of mainstream social science—especially in economics and in political science—is that it avoids engaging in dialogue on the complex moral issues involved in further moral advance, i.e., advance toward achieving social democracy while avoiding slipping backwards into barbarism. By taking for granted the institutional framework of the behavior it studies, it makes the moral issues posed by capitalism's first premises invisible. Conversely, the work of cultural action is consciousness-raising to make invisible causes visible, in order to change them for the better.[14]

Taylor's extended concept of constitutive rules grounds a critique of mainstream social science. Constitutive practices "do not fit into the categorical grid of mainstream political science."[15] Taylor's concepts speak to the critical omissions as well in the social sciences that have taken the postmodern turn. George Sefa Dei writes, "Social movement politics must not only avoid the schism of the 'self/other,' 'old/new,' 'us/them,' but progressive politics must also critique the 'nostalgic of theory' which confuses ephemeral changes with more fundamental structural transformation. Such politics must guard against the insularity and elitism of academic and discursive practices that fail to recognize heterogeneous, nuanced, complex, contradictory and subjective readings of social reality."[16] A central problem is that the ontology of mainstream social science lacks a concept of collective meaning, community meaning, of the common meanings of a "we"; postmodernism, for all its liberating potential, has only exacerbated this problem. Taylor writes, "The exclusion of this possibility, of the communal, comes once again from the baleful influence of the epistemological tradition for which all knowledge has to be reconstructed from the impressions imprinted on the individual subject."[17] We would add that the rise of the epistemological tradition in question was itself an integral part of the larger historical process of the constitution of the cultural structures of modern capitalist society.[18]

Taylor names modern Anglo-Saxon societies not as capitalism but as interdependent productive and negotiating societies, characterized by bargaining among autonomous agents. Mainstream social science is, of course, aware that core modern Anglo-Saxon institutional facts have not always existed, and aware that its constitutive rules do not govern everywhere. Taylor writes:

> But, of course, such a massive fact does not escape notice. What happens rather is that it is re-interpreted. And what has generally happened is that the interdependent productive and negotiating society has been recognized by political science, but not as one structure of intersubjective meaning among others, rather as the inescapable background of social action as such.[19]

Comparative politics degenerates into the study of the progress of other civilizations toward a correct ("empirical and pragmatic") perception of the political process at the expense of "ideology." At home, social science cannot understand the profound sources of alienation.

Our own project is, like that of Herbert Marcuse, not so much concerned with comparative politics as with possible politics.[20] The blindness of mainstream social science to the constitutive rules of the institutional facts it takes for granted is a problem not so much because it therefore cannot see others, as because it therefore cannot see itself. It cannot subject itself to the negative dialectics needed to make the creative transformation of capitalism a conceivable field of scientific study.

Like Taylor, and like Alasdair MacIntyre who published a similar critique of mainstream social science at about the same time, we are concerned to show that social science does not discover causal laws like those of physics.[21] Unlike them, we are also concerned to show that social science does assert the existence of cause and effect relationships (although they are unlike those discovered by physics). Social science discovers, precisely, effects, which are in large part caused by institutional facts, by constitutive rules. Richards' previous work *Understanding the Global Economy* analyzes the relationships of cause and effect presupposed, postulated, or found by the principal schools of economics. The thesis therein is that causal explanations in economics crucially depend on the constitutive rules of the institutions economists study.[22] The present work is a sequel. It illustrates the thesis with historical examples. The historical examples deal with the much-desired and much-frustrated transition from capitalism to social democracy.

We take the proposition that major causes operating in history are institutional facts, or, more broadly, cultural structures, to be an expanded version of the more colloquial, "ideas run the world." It is not, however, a proposition that supports a philosophy of idealism. We agree with Wittgenstein that ideas are a part of natural life. Ideas are not generically distinct from images, logical operations, and words. These, in turn, are not separable from the activities people perform when they engage in speech acts.[23] As Wittengenstein writes, "Commanding, questioning, recounting, chatting, are as much a part of our natural history as walking, eating, drinking, playing."[24]

To make the approach to social science to be employed in the following historical studies clearer we will now compare and contrast it to some of the views of Jürgen Habermas and Michel Foucault; and to the views expressed in four more recent but less well known works: Nancy Hartsock's *Money, Sex, and Power*, Robert A. Solo's *The Philosophy of Science and Economics*, Bent Flyvbjerg's *Making Social Science Matter*, and Heikki Patomäki's *After International Relations: Critical Realism and the (Re)Construction of World Politics*.[25]

In a well-known text, Habermas divided science into three regions: empirical-analytic science, historical-hermeneutic science, and emancipatory science. "The systematic sciences of social action, that is economics, sociology, and political science, have the goal, as do the empirical-analytic sciences, of producing nomological knowledge."[26] So wrote the Jürgen Habermas of *Knowledge and Human Interests*, which was first published in 1968. A few pages earlier he explained what he meant by "empirical-analytic science" and by nomological (i.e., lawlike) knowledge:

> In the empirical-analytic sciences the frame of reference that prejudges the meaning of possible statements establishes rules both for the construction of the theories and for their critical testing. Theories comprise hypothetico-deductive connections of propositions, which permit the deduction of lawlike hypotheses with empirical content. The latter can be interpreted as statement about covariance of observable events; given a set of initial conditions, they make predictions possible.[27]

Economics, sociology, and political science, together with the empirical-analytic sciences properly so-called, such as physics and chemistry, correspond to a certain kind of human interest, that of producing results, what Habermas calls "the behavioral system of instrumental action." Together they are the same as what Marcuse calls "technological rationality."[28]

As compared and contrasted with Habermas and Marcuse, we wish to emphasize that it makes a great difference that the substance of social science is human action. Whatever the similarities of certain natural sciences and certain social sciences might be at the epistemic level, it is important to stress that they are different at the level of ontology. One is about the institutional world set up by humans; the other is about the physical world. The notions of "instrumental action" and "technological rationality" are systematically misleading, because they tend to make too much of superficial similarities between economics and engineering. In the following chapters we will have several occasions to discuss the importance of emphasizing the differences between the moral substance of economics and the physical substance of engineering.

Seen in historical context, the willingness of Habermas and others to concede in the 1960s that economists had learned to employ "instrumental rationality" (*Zweckrationalitat*) or "technological rationality" in ways that could make a modern economy achieve its objectives (i.e., the *Zweck*) came at a time when Keynesian macroeconomics seemed indeed to have solved the problem of stabilizing capitalism. Economics seemed to have mastered the problem of assuring the constant growth of productive capacity. It appeared that the remaining problems were in the areas of distribution and culture. Today, however, in the wake of the failure of Keynesian macro-management of capitalism, it is much easier to see that the very idea that there is an "instrumental rationality" shared by economists and engineers, applied by both alike to manipulate inputs (independent variables) to produce desired outputs (dependent variables) is and always was an illusion.

As a good Marxist, Habermas was, of course, aware that the economic machine was not a machine. He went on: "A critical social science, however, will not remain satisfied with this [i.e., with establishing lawlike covariance among observable events]. It is concerned with going beyond this goal to determine when theoretical statements grasp invariant regularities of social action as such and when they express ideologically frozen relations of dependence that can in principle be transformed."[29] The latter determination defines a social science whose interest is emancipatory, also sometimes known as critical social science. The ideal of emancipation is Kantian: *mundigkeit*, i.e., autonomy and responsibility. Expressing this Kantian idea, Habermas writes:

> [O]nly in an emancipated society, whose members' autonomy and responsibility had been realized, would communication have developed into the non-authoritarian and universally practiced dialogue from which both our model of reciprocally constituted ego identity and our idea of true consensus [i.e., knowledge, following C.S. Peirce's idea that human inquiry tends in the long run toward consensus, and that the consensus it tends toward is the truth about reality] are always implicitly derived. To this extent the truth of statements is based on anticipating the realization of the good life.[30]

Our concept of the ethical reconstruction of social reality, in contrast, is pre-Kantian and post-Kantian as well as Kantian. The Kantian ideal of autonomy is one, but not the only, ethic invented by *homo sapiens sapiens* in the long march from hunting and gathering societies toward the better society of the future.[31]

In addition to empirical-analytic knowledge, whose interest is technical and instrumental, and in addition to critical knowledge, whose interest is emancipatory, Habermas proposes a third category, the historical-hermeneutic sciences, whose interest is practical. It is practical in the sense that it establishes communication. While the empirical-analytic sciences explain, the historical-hermeneutic sciences understand.

We want to insist that meanings act. Meaningful human activities, employing the languages and other symbols that Habermas and others declare to be the proper objects of hermeneutic (interpretive) study, are causes.[32] They produce real effects in the world. They shape institutions and institutional behavior. In particular, we will show that if explanation is a matter of answering the question "Why?" and if one wants to know why capitalism resists transformation and why social democracy is so hard to achieve, then the place to turn for answers is to the effects of the intersubjective meanings that Taylor (following Wittgenstein) finds to be constitutive of ways of life.

We thus propose to remap the three-region map of knowledge that Habermas provided in *Knowledge and Human Interests*. Economics, sociology, and politics do not belong with engineering. Emancipation is only a part, or aspect, of the ethical reconstruction of society. Meanings are causes.[33]

Michel Foucault famously denies that the study of a society ought to proceed by studying primarily the rules that govern it. He much prefers to work with the category of "power." Power makes rules. Rules do not make power.[34] The bulk of his research traces transitions from older and cruder forms of power to what he chooses to regard not as the taming of power but as subtler, more intrusive, more precise, and more effective modern forms of power. In *Discipline and Punish: The Birth of the Prison*, for example, Foucault weaves into his genealogy of prisons and punishment a description from the early nineteenth century of large quantities of goods from all the world sitting on the docks of the port of London. Too much was stolen. Commerce required protection.[35] Foucault's portrait of goods on the docks illustrates the broader point that the prison (and with it the penal codes that determined who would be incarcerated in it) was born of functional necessity.

In answering the question why goods from all over the world were sitting on the docks of London, tempting thieves, it would be unreasonable to omit institutional facts and constitutive rules from one's etiology. This link in the genealogy of the shift from crude power to precise power is best explained by the expansion of markets and trade. Generally, the context of the rise of bureaucracies is the rise of commerce, on Foucault's account as on Max Weber's account. Economic history, in turn, can be read as the history of the social relations and social practices that constitute markets. It is about rules. Therefore, it is about ethics.

It should also be observed that in much of the social behavior of *homo sapiens sapiens* rules do make power. The working class children of Geneva, whose games were observed by Jean Piaget, normally exercised just as much power as the rules of the games allowed them, no more and no less.[36] Similarly, the president or prime minister of a modern democracy has only the powers that are conferred upon her or him by law, no more and no less. Ethical behavior is not as frequent as it should be, but neither is it nonexistent. It can be thought of as gradually constructed over time, in cultures and in individuals. The endless details of the history of culture enumerated in Foucault's genealogies, concerning the history of punishment, the history of medicine, the history of insanity, the history of science, of schools, of factories, of the military, and of sexuality, do not need to be viewed only through Foucauldian lenses as creeping normalization wrought by ever-more-pervasive power.

The same endless details can also be viewed, instead or in addition, as histories of ethical construction, with setbacks and with advances. Viewed in the latter way, through lenses suggested long ago by Socrates and Plato, these histories show: first, the increasing government of the irrational by the rational, i.e., of impulse by *logos*; second, the ongoing conversation of the species with itself, through which the *logos* is gradually refined and improved; and third, the irrational and yet divine inspiration of platonic love, classically depicted in Plato's *Phaedrus*, through which impulse returns as beauty and joy. Looking at life from this old-fashioned, benign, and optimistic point of view, the following chapters are not genealogies tracing the insidious normalization of individuals to suit the requirements of the modern capitalist state; they are sympathetic accounts of deliberate efforts to improve society by transforming capitalism into social democracy.

Although Richards has written elsewhere about the good spirits needed to fuel and season the good works of a good society, the following pages, admittedly, say little about beauty and joy. Nancy Hartsock says more. For Hartsock, patriarchy is not a parallel form of oppression that accompanies capitalism. It is older and more fundamental. The inhumanity of man to man, that great and tragic puzzle which has baffled sages for centuries, has its deep emotional source in the inhumanity of man to woman. Gender oppression precedes and lays the groundwork for class oppression. At the heart of gender oppression, and thus at the heart of the domination of some people by others generally, lies a necrophilic, hostile deformation of human sexuality which Hartsock names as "the negative erotic."[37]

Under the headings of "exchange theories" and "production as epistemology," Hartsock analyzes in detail the norms we are calling the constitutive rules of capitalism. She finds that they conceal as much as they reveal. She quotes a famous passage from Marx:

> [O]n leaving the sphere of simple circulation or of exchange of commodities

... we can perceive a change in the physiognomy of our *dramatis personae*. He who before was the money-owner, now strides in front as capitalist; the possessor of labour-power follows as his labourer. The one with an air of importance, smirking, intent on business; the other timid and holding back, like one who is bringing his own hide to market and has nothing to expect but—a hiding.[38]

She contributes an analogous thought of her own: "[W]e can now begin to understand the significance of describing contemporary Western social relations as a capitalist patriarchy. Beneath the polite language of sexual reciprocity we have uncovered not only one-sided relations of domination and submission, but also dynamics of hostility, revenge, and a fascination with death."[39]

A hypothetical reader might be tempted to ask, in the light of such considerations, whether it is worthwhile to focus attention on the polite rules of accounting (which ostensibly govern business) and the polite rules of mutual respect (which ostensibly govern social life generally) when the underlying reality is domination, submission, hostility, revenge, and fascination with death. The temptation to ask this question might be strengthened by passages in which Hartsock seems to say that if the dominant class, or dominant sex, really wanted to, it could replace all the constitutive rules with a new and better set of rules.[40]

Inflation, unemployment, capital flight, falling rates of investment, exhausted pension funds, debt, budget deficits, and races to cut costs by cutting wages are—as will be seen in the following chapters—among the typical problems encountered when socialists try to change capitalism. The same hypothetical reader might be tempted to argue—based on the concept of capitalist patriarchy—that all of these economic problems are nothing but consequences of the operation of the rules that the dominant class has imposed on society. And one might be tempted to argue—based on the concept that the dominant class could change the rules if it wanted to—that as soon as a class willing to substitute new rules for old rules comes to power, these economic problems will disappear. Knowing how to solve the problems would be unnecessary. Otherwise put: the solution to all problems is already known: it is liberation from oppression.

Hartsock, we are sure, would not yield to the temptations that we have described as tempting a hypothetical reader. She would say, surely, that all three— the empowerment of the dominated, the transformation of *eros* from negative to positive, and learning how to solve social problems—need to advance together. Building a world that works for everyone without ecological damage clearly requires both wanting to do it and knowing how to do it.

When seen in context, as outcomes of history, as born in and from conflicts and passions, systems of rules will nevertheless be seen to have their own logics, their own consequences. We hope it will make our philosophy clearer to note that our emphasis on the consequences of capitalism's constitutive rules is meant to complement, not to replace, Hartsock's emphasis on the gender-specific roots of ill will.

Our emphasis upon the blindness of mainstream social science to the constitutive rules of capitalism merits a comment upon the particular social science known as economics. When Robert A. Solo was a graduate student in economics at the London School of Economics in the mid-1940s, studying under Karl Popper among others, he learned that the watchword for the science of economics was: Be like physics. Solo writes, "Thus the development of methodology in economics and the development of the modern philosophy of science have followed parallel paths. For both the rule behind the rules has been to BE LIKE PHYSICS."[41]

Many years later, after a distinguished career as an economist, writing as emeritus professor of economics at Michigan State University, Solo took the view that economics being like physics, or trying to be like physics, had never been a good idea. He stated that economics should be a policy science:

> Let the discipline be defined by its problems. . . . Rather than on an established set of assumptions and theories, let it find its continuity in focusing on the same, open-ended set of problem areas, e.g. on the quest for full employment, for price stability, for higher productivity, for a rising real GNP, on the problems of trade imbalance, of resource depletion, of income distribution. Let it find its identity not in the presuppositions and analytic apparatus with which the cohort begins, but in the policy problems on which they vector. And let any statement that is demonstrably relevant to the solution of those problems or to the formation of a policy geared to the solution of those problems be admissible into the discourse.[42]

Solo thus favors neither a pseudo-physics nor a constitutive rules approach to economics, but a wide-open acceptance of whatever proves to be relevant to whatever problem is currently under study. But it would be well to remember a point stressed by Hartsock: that the pseudo-physics of mainstream economics and political science (which she analyzes under the heading "exchange theories") is not simply false. It reflects in economic theory the institutions that structure capitalism in practice. Thus she writes:

> [T]he circularity contained in the concept of rational economic man, the assumption that to be rational is to maximize one's own utilities, can now be recognized as a statement from the perspective of the capitalist that it is inconceivable that one could act in any other way. And of course, it is a materially defining feature of the existence of the capitalist firm that it must seek to maximize utilities (profits) or go out of business. The isolation of individuals from each other in a world structured by institutions can now be understood as rooted in the experience of exchange, and the inadequate account of human community that results from such an understanding must be seen as replicating at the level of theory the real poverty of communities constructed by exchange.[43]

Consequently, in practice, it may not make much difference whether economics calls itself a policy science as Solo recommends, or calls itself social physics. To a considerable extent, the wide-open acceptance of whatever proves to be relevant, may just serve to demonstrate that pseudo-physics was a pretty good approximation to the truth after all because, for example, firms really do have to seek to maximize utilities, or else face going out of business. Calculating the second derivative of a utility function to make it equal to zero is not formally different from doing the same for any function studied by engineers.

What would, however, make a major difference for a policy science would be making it wide-open to consider the restructuring of the institutional structures that at present define the problems. What is it about modern cultural structures that makes unemployment even possible? What sorts of communities have been built, or could be built, mainly around gifts instead of around prices? In what ways are issues that appear on the surface as issues of price stability really questions about what Samuel Bowles and Herbert Gintis have called the exit power of capital—a power conferred on capital by the constitutive rules of the system?[44] What, after all, does the GNP measure, and is it worth measuring?

Making visible the constitutive rules, instead of taking them for granted, would spell the difference between pseudo-pragmatism and real pragmatism, between regarding capitalism as an immutable framework and regarding capitalism as an evolving mutable framework on its way to becoming social democracy.

An ethical construction approach is not in principle opposed to Solo's concept of a policy science defined by its problems and not by its paradigm. Yet it includes the problematique (the set of problems defined by the dominant discourse) among the problems. It recommends thinking of "policy" in an old-fashioned way, as Plato and Aristotle thought of it when in books called "*Peri Politeia*" ("about the *polis*") they engaged in an ongoing search for, and in principle a continual revision of, the great architectonic principles that should structure the lives of people who come together in justice and in friendship to pursue the good of each individual and the good of the community.

Bent Flyvbjerg, in *Making Social Science Matter*, agrees with Solo that social science made a wrong turn when it chose to identify itself as a novice aspiring some day to become a real science like natural science. Flyvbjerg asks the question, "Is theory possible in social science?"[45] In developing an answer to this question, which he takes to be equivalent to the question of whether social science can discover scientific laws like those discovered by natural sciences, he relies on several recent writers, of whom the most prominent are Michel Foucault, Hubert Dreyfus, Anthony Wilden, and Pierre Bourdieu. The answer he gives to his question is, in briefest summary, "No."

What is of particular interest here is the reason Flyvbjerg gives for his negative answer: "The core of their argument is that human activity cannot be reduced to a set of rules, and without rules there can be no theory."[46] He quotes

Pierre Bourdieu: "[P]ractice has a logic which is not that of logic."[47] Flyvbjerg goes on, "The problem in the study of human activity is that every attempt at a context-free definition of an action, that is, a definition based on abstract rules or laws, will not necessarily accord with the pragmatic way an action is defined by the actors in the concrete social situation. . . . Moreover, while context is central for defining what counts as an action, context must nevertheless be excluded in a theory in order for it to be a theory at all."[48] This last point is supposed to be true because a real theory, like the theories of physics and chemistry, is true in all contexts, as there are light waves, silicon, carbon, and other forms of electro-magnetic radiation and other chemical elements on distant planets and stars just as there are on earth.

We and Flyvbjerg appear to be working at cross-purposes. We want to say that there is a logic of exchange built into the constitutive rules of capitalism, and that we need to think about that logic and those rules in order to achieve transitions from capitalism to social democracy. He and others find it important to say that human practices cannot be reduced to rules, or to logics. Agreed, human activity cannot be reduced to a set of rules.

Agreed, without rules there can be no theory. It does not follow, however, that there are no rules, nor does it follow that no useful theory can be built on the rules that there are. The facts are not in dispute—nobody denies the facts about human behavior that Foucault, Dreyfus, Bourdieu and others cite to support their claims. The problem, rather, is to untangle conceptual puzzles and to show the utility of using the ideas of institutional facts, constitutive rules, and ethical con-struction to shed light on the causes and cures of social problems. Rather than making a full-scale attempt to untangle conceptual puzzles, by showing in detail how the same words ("rule" "theory" "science" "logic" "cause") are used in overlapping but not identical ways for overlapping but not identical purposes, it is probably better simply to proceed with our historical studies. They will show that in a series of contexts—Spain, Sweden, Austria, South Africa, Indonesia, Venezuela, in the operations of the World Bank on a global scale, and in other contexts mentioned but not treated in depth—the same constitutive rules of capi-talism pose the same obstacles to the construction of social democracy. Never-theless, before proceeding to the first case study, that of Spain, we will make a few points directly in response to Flyvbjerg.

Among the examples Flyvbjerg gives of practices that depend on tacit skills, expertise, excellence, and virtuosity, which cannot be explained or pre-dicted by rules, are the example of the clever businessperson and that of the in-stinctual financier.[49] They can only be clever and instinctual, however, if they can buy and sell. They can only buy and sell, in turn, if there are rules that constitute and regulate buying and selling. There are such rules. They are not difficult to find. They are found in the law of contracts, which is found in statutes enacted by legislatures and in the reported decisions of judges. Without this background of institutional facts that prescribe the rules of buying and selling, the virtuoso businesspeople and financiers whose conduct cannot be explained by rules would not be able to do their practical wizardry whose logic is not logic.

Flyvbjerg also considers the status of economics. He writes, "What people consider to be money, property, economic behavior (for example, maximization of profits), etc., are taken as given. One thereafter seeks out laws, which relate these socially defined concepts to each other. And so long as there is a degree of constancy in the practices which define the objects and goals for a group of people or a society, economic laws can, in principle, predict just as well as physical laws."[50] On this basis, economics could be considered an historical science, as several prominent economists (including but not only those of the so-called "historical school" active in Germany in the early twentieth century) have considered it to be. Its validity would be bounded by the beginning and the end of the historical period during which the institutional facts it assumes hold true.

Yet Flyvbjerg is not content to recognize the claims of economic theories to be true scientific theories, even if they are admittedly limited to those times and places where the institutional framework they assume is established. He goes on:

> Moreover, as stated, economic theories exist by virtue of the practices by which people define the concepts of money, property, economic behavior, etc., and these can change at any time and thereby undermine the theories' ability to predict. We do not have, and probably never will have, a theory, which can predict the changes in these practices. "An economist," it has therefore been observed jokingly but acutely, "is an expert who will know tomorrow why the things he predicted yesterday did not happen today."[51]

In Flyvbjerg's comments on economics, the possibility that the constitutive rules might change appears as a problem because it shows that economics cannot make reliable predictions. In another light, the possibility that the constitutive rules might change could also appear as a solution because it shows that capitalism might be transformed into social democracy. Seen as a problem, as a decisive reason why economic predictions can never be reliable, it contributes to skepticism about causality.

With respect to the principle of cause and effect, Flyvbjerg and his principal sources can be read as post-positivists. The positivists, named broadly as those "of the positivist temper,"[52] identify causality, or some substitute that does the work of causality, with scientific laws. The post-positivists deny that there are scientific laws in the social sciences. On standard positivist accounts, explanation and prediction are supposed to be symmetrical, so that the same regularities codified in scientific laws (i.e., in equations) both explain the past and predict the future. It follows that if social science cannot make reliable predictions, it cannot discover scientific laws. Accepting the categorical grid implicit in the covering law accounts of causality that they deny, post-positivists deny that the principle of cause and effect operates in the social sciences.

Both positivists and post-positivists can be charged with committing the epistemic fallacy. The question should not be whether the principle of cause and effect operates in the social sciences, but whether it works in the world the social sciences study. Ontology should determine epistemology, but the positivists and post-positivists have it the other way around. They determine what *is* strictly on the basis of what *can be known*. (Or, with much the same result, they ignore ontology altogether, or classify it as a meaningless enterprise.) A case can be made to the contrary: first, a realist ontology should be adopted by the social sciences; and second, causes do produce effects in society, in ways that are not generically different from the way causes produce effects in nature.

That case is made by Heikki Patomäki in *After International Relations: Critical Realism and the (Re)Construction of World Politics*.[53] Society does not invent physical reality. It adjusts to it. Without food a people perishes; if *homo sapiens sapiens* destroys the biosphere, its habitat, it will destroy itself. Society does invent institutions. Institutions have consequences. They produce effects. Admittedly, if causality requires knowledge of constant conjunction of observed regularities, then when knowledge of constant conjunction of observed regularities goes, causality goes. The better philosophies of causality, however, are the critical realist views that do not commit the epistemic fallacy. Whether there are causes does not depend on whether people can know with certainty, or know at all, that there are causes. While Patomäki holds that all beliefs and knowledge claims are socially produced, contextual, and fallible, he also insists that truth-claims have to be about something. It is possible to distinguish those truth-claims that are rational judgments, from those that are not. What truth claims about causes are about is causal powers. Patomäki writes, "[A] realist conception of causality does not equate causality with constant conjunction but with structured powers capable of producing particular, characteristic effects if triggered. In this regard natural and social sciences are similar. There are real causal powers both in natural and in social systems."[54]

The burden of our argument is that constitutive rules are social facts with causal consequences no more and no less real than the consequences of stones or waterfalls or DNA. Moreover, the great ideals that inspire humanity—justice, love, freedom, democracy, peace—are also, like constitutive rules, ideas, forces that act.[55] They do things. The problems of construct validity involved in trying to specify operational definitions of them for purposes of social science research are problems for social science research—but they do not subtract one whit from their causal efficacy as forces at work in the world. Ideals are cultural resources, which, like natural resources, are available for the ethical construction of society. We are impressed by the work of great ideals in history, and we adore the causal powers of working class deities: Krishna born in a jail; Jesus born in a manger; Moses, the Prince of Egypt, who remembered his captive people and led them to freedom; the prophet of Allah walking and leading the camel while his camel driver took his turn riding the camel; the compassionate Buddha declining to enter Nirvana and choosing instead to turn back to earth to cast his lot with suffering humanity.

This chapter has been a concentrated dose of remarks on epistemology. Additional discussions of issues in the philosophy and methodology of science are scattered through the other chapters. An additional point perhaps already evident from the preceding chapter is that we do not think it is necessary to unify discourses into a single meta-discourse. To talk about cooperation and sharing, it is not necessary to agree to define the terms in the same way—as the dialogue among the various participants in Chapter 1 was intended to show. The world is as it is. One planet, many language games. It is true, as Alexander Wendt says, that *homo sapiens sapiens* is an interdependent species which shares a common fate.[56] It is also true, as Wendt says, that to cope successfully with the common challenges of the species there must be ideological labor to facilitate the emergence of ideas that will guide functional behavior; but this does not mean unity at the level of talking alike. It means actions that mesh to solve the problems.[57]

Notes

1. John Searle, *Speech Acts* (Cambridge: Cambridge University Press, 1969), 51-52. Anthony Giddens declines to distinguish constitutive from regulative rules, pointing out that a regulative rule like "don't steal" implies constitutive norms concerning honesty and property rights, while a constitutive rule like "this chess piece is a queen" implies regulative norms about which moves are allowed. True enough, but it is still useful to point out that rules are constitutive of social practices, some more clearly and fundamentally than others, as Giddens' own frequent use of the words "constitutive" and "constitution" attests. See the excerpt from his *Central Problems in Social Theory*, reprinted in Philip Cassell, ed., *The Giddens Reader* (Stanford, Calif.: Stanford University Press, 1993), 119.

2. Searle, *Speech Acts*, 51.

3. Kurt Gödel mathematically proved a corollary to this thought in Gödel's Theorem of Incompleteness (which holds that there are things that remain true although they cannot be proven); but even if he had not, it would remain true. See Ernest Nagel and James R. Newman, *Gödel's Proof* (New York: New York University Press, 1958); and Rudy Rucker, *Infinity and the Mind: The Science and Philosophy of the Infinite* (Princeton, N.J.: Princeton University Press, 2000), 157-70.

4. Immanuel Kant, *Perpetual Peace* (New York: Columbia University Press, 1939), 10.

5. Jean Piaget, *The Moral Judgment of the Child* (London: Trench, Trubner & Co., 1932).

6. See Plato's discussion of the parts of the soul in Book 4 of *The Republic* (various editions).

7. See the interesting discussion of the ideas of Vygotsky and others, and of his own research concerning the genesis of the human capacity to guide action with reason in A.R. Luria, *Language and Cognition* (New York: John Wiley & Sons, 1981), 88 et seq., and Luria's lectures at University College, London, published as *Speech and the Regulation of Behavior* (New York: Liveright, 1961).

8. Readers familiar with the work of Daniel Quinn or Richard Dawkins, upon whom Quinn draws, will recognize our emphasis upon "constitutive rules" throughout this work as similar to the emphasis Quinn places upon "memes." Dawkins coined the term "meme" to designate the cultural equivalent of the gene—i.e., the values, concepts, and rules by which human cultures are replicated one generation to the next. We make the point throughout this work that institutions and their constitutive rules are cultural constructs subject to change by the collective imagination and action of humans. Similarly, Quinn insists that memes be understood as human creations, not as natural forces such as the laws of physics. Quinn, *Beyond Civilization*, 21-32. See also Richard Dawkins, *The Selfish Gene* (Oxford: Oxford University Press, 1989). We insist also that ethically sound human practices such as cooperation and altruism need to be supported and sustained by the institutions we create; many of our extant cultural institutions make cooperation and altruism costly. Jane J. Mansbridge makes a similar argument in "On the Relation of Altruism and Self-Interest," in Jane J. Mansbridge, ed., *Beyond Self-Interest* (Chicago: University of Chicago Press, 1990), 133-43.

9. Searle, *Speech Acts*, 51-52.

10. Charles Taylor, "Interpretation and the Sciences of Man," *Review of Metaphysics* 25 (1971): 3-51. Taylor's article is reprinted in Paul Rabinow and William M. Sullivan, eds., *Interpretive Social Science: A Reader* (Berkeley; Los Angeles; and London: University of California Press, 1979), 25-71.

11. Taylor, "Interpretation and the Sciences," 24.

12. Taylor, "Interpretation and the Sciences," 25.

13. Taylor, "Interpretation and the Sciences," 27. The influences of both Kant and Wittgenstein are apparent here. Kant writes, "In the Transcendental Analytic we have distinguished the dynamical principles of the understanding, as merely regulative principles of intuition, from the mathematical, which, as regards intuition, are constitutive. None the less these dynamical laws are constitutive in respect of experience, since they render the concepts, without which there can be no experience, possible a priori." Immanuel Kant, *Critique of Pure Reason*, trans. Norman Kemp Smith (London: Macmillan, 1964), 546. See also, e.g., Ludwig Wittgenstein, *Philosophical Investigations* (Oxford: Basil Blackwell, 1958), 80-81 (paragraphs 198 through 202). Pierre Bourdieu cites the same passage from Wittgenstein that we cite, apparently—but only apparently—disagreeing with the conclusion we draw from it. We cite Wittgenstein as proof, contra Foucault, that it is possible to treat "rule" as a sophisticated concept, which does not presuppose a world governed by a rule-maker. Bourdieu cites Wittgenstein as proof, contra Lévi-Strauss, that structural anthropology dodges questions about practice that it should answer. But there is no factual disagreement here, only different choices of terminology with different ends in view. We do not deny that habitus (defined as a system of dispositions, and further elaborated in other works by Bourdieu) is a concept useful for answering questions about practice that cannot reasonably be answered in terms of rules or norms. Pierre Bourdieu, *Esquisse d'une theorie de la pratique* (Geneva: Droz, 1972), 172-73, 247.

14. The analysis of constitutive rules complements the idea of doing social analysis by relating history, social structure, and values, with the intention of acting to build a better future, which is advocated by Joe Holland and Peter Henriot, S.J., in Joe Holland, *Social Analysis: Linking Faith with Justice* (Maryknoll, N.Y.: Orbis Books, 1983).

15. Taylor, "Interpretation and the Sciences," 29.

16. George J. Sefa Dei, "Knowledge and Politics of Social Change: the implication of anti-racism," *British Journal of Sociology of Education* 20, no. 3 (1999), 398.

17. Taylor, "Interpretation and the Sciences," 32. George Lipsitz echoes this criticism without direct reference to epistemology and offers a concrete example of the devastating consequences of an epistemology that requires knowledge to be constantly reconstructed from individual experience. Lipsitz contends that in the United States, white people's collective inability to reckon with the reality of institutionalized racism comes not so much from a deliberate unwillingness as from a culture of liberal individualism that makes it nearly impossible to articulate any collective experience. Because the maintenance of institutionalized racism is a collective exercise of power, which, as Lipsitz observes, rarely announces its intent to discriminate against individuals, it does not fit into liberal individualism's narrow definition of what constitutes "racist" behavior. George Lipsitz, *The Possessive Investment in Whiteness: How White People Profit from Identity Politics* (Philadelphia: Temple University Press, 1998), 20. The culture of liberal individualism springs from the faulty epistemology to which Taylor and we are referring; and because it has the effect, in the example offered by Lipsitz, of keeping invisible causes invisible, it thereby serves as an obstacle to dismantling racism.

18. Howard Richards, *Letters from Quebec* (San Francisco and London: International Scholars Press, 1996), 175-85. See also Wallerstein, "Call for a Debate about the Paradigm," in his *Unthinking Social Science*, 237-56.

19. Taylor, "Interpretation and the Sciences," 39.

20. Herbert Marcuse, *One-Dimensional Man: Studies in the Ideology of Advanced Industrial Society* (Boston: Beacon Press, 1964). Also, like the work of Joan Wallach Scott, ours is an expressly political project in which we delve into the study of history not to present a series of givens but rather to open up the possibility of contingencies. Scott is a radical feminist historian who has an interest in the emancipatory potential of history. She describes the problems with the extant women's histories that failed to historicize: "By assuming that women have inherent characteristics and objective identities consistently and predictably different from men's, and that these generate definably female needs and interests, historians imply that sexual difference is a natural rather than a social phenomenon. The search for an analysis of discrimination gets caught by a circular logic in which 'experience' explains gender difference and gender difference explains the asymmetries of male and female 'experience.' Typically the visions of what constitutes male and female experience appeal to or incorporate existing normative definitions. Women's history written from this position, and the politics that follow from it, end up endorsing ideas of unalterable sexual difference that are used to justify discrimination." Joan Wallach Scott, *Gender and the Politics of History* (New York: Columbia University Press, 1988), 4. Just as Scott calls for the historicizing of history, we call for the historicizing of the social sciences and of the present moment. And along with Peter Burke, we welcome the "theoretical turn" on the part of historians and the "historical turn" on the part of theorists. Peter Burke, *History & Social Theory* (Ithaca, N.Y.: Cornell University Press, 1993), 19.

21. Alasdair MacIntyre, *Against the Self-Images of the Age* (New York: Schocken Books, 1971).

22. Howard Richards, *Understanding the Global Economy* (Delhi: Maadhyam Books, 2000).

23. The historiography that acknowledges the need to study ideas as they function in everyday life and not just among elites, begins in the first half of the twentieth century, with the work of Marc Bloch and Lucien Febvre, the founders of the journal *Annales*. Bloch and Febvre developed the concept of *histoire sociale totale*. A key element within this concept, that of *mentalité*, gave rise to the historiography devoted to the history of mentalities, which meant the study of ideas not in narrowly circumscribed "intellectual histories," but in broader and more integrated psychological and anthropological treatments. Carlo Ginzburg, who has contributed to this historiography, nevertheless objects to the narrowness of the approach of Bloch and Febvre on the grounds that a) the concept of *mentalité* can lead to reducing all historical problems to psychological problems; and that b) the historiography embracing the concept of *mentalité* often has a "class-neutral" character that ends up marginalizing the working-class cultures and other cultures of resistance that should share the spotlight in these kinds of histories. The present work should make clear that we would share this criticism of Ginzburg's and seek to analyze the history of ideas in their broadest form. From the Annales school, the historiography moved toward a recognition of the importance of studying "ideology" (this historiographical branch is associated with Althusser) and then toward a recognition of the importance of studying "discourses" (which is associated with Foucault). Still none of these traditions, in our view—with the possible exception of Althusser's insistence upon

the *materiality* of "ideology"—places sufficient emphasis on the *causal* power of ideas. See Peter Schöttler, "Mentalities, Ideologies, Discourses: On the 'Third Level' as a Theme in Socio-Historical Research," in *The History of Everyday Life: Reconstructing Historical Experiences and Ways of Life,* ed. Alf Lüdtke (Princeton, N.J.: Princeton University Press, 1995), 72-115.

24. Wittgenstein, *Philosophical Investigations,* 12.

25. Nancy Hartsock, *Money, Sex, and Power: Toward a Feminist Historical Materialism*(Boston: Northeastern University Press, 1985); Robert A. Solo, *The Philosophy of Science and Economics* (Armonk, N.Y.: M.E. Sharpe, 1991); Bent Flyvbjerg, *Making Social Science Matter: Why social inquiry fails and how it can succeed again,* trans. Steven Sampson (Cambridge and New York: Cambridge University Press, 2001); Heikki Patomäki, *After International Relations: Critical Realism and the (Re)Construction of World Politics* (London: Routledge, 2001).

26. Jürgen Habermas, *Knowledge and Human Interests,* trans. Jeremy J. Shapiro (Boston: Beacon Press, 1971), 310.

27. Habermas, *Knowledge and Human Interests,* 308.

28. Habermas, *Knowledge and Human Interests,* 191; Marcuse, *One-Dimensional Man,* 11, 18, 158-59.

29. Habermas, *Knowledge and Human Interests,* 310.

30. Habermas, *Knowledge and Human Interests,* 314.

31. See the chapters on Kant, Letters 27 through 33 in Richards, *Letters from Quebec,* 211-69.

32. See also Roland Barthes, *Mythologies* (New York: Hill and Wang, 1972), especially 109-45.

33. The germ of each of the points in this remapping can be found in *Knowledge and Human Interests* itself, and to an even greater extent in the later work of Habermas. See, e.g., Jürgen Habermas, *Between Facts and Norms: Contributions to a Discourse Theory of Law and Democracy* (Cambridge, Mass.: MIT Press, 1996). Sociologist Orlando Patterson also makes the case that the social sciences should not seek to imitate or approximate the natural sciences. He writes, "Anxious to achieve the status of economics and the other 'soft sciences,' the gatekeepers of sociology have insisted on a style of research and thinking that focuses on the testing of hypotheses based on data generated by measurements presumed to be valid. This approach works reasonably well for the study of certain subjects like demographics in which there is stability in the variables studied. . . . Unfortunately, for most areas of social life . . . the methods of natural science are not only inappropriate but distorting." Patterson's article is a tribute to David Riesman and to fellow sociologists (such as Erving Goffman) whose subjects and methodologies are now far out of favor in the academy. Patterson writes that these earlier authors "practiced a sociology different in both style and substance from that of today. It was driven first by the significance of the subject and second by an epistemological emphasis on understanding the nature and meaning of social behavior. This is an understanding that can only emerge from the interplay of the author's own views and with those of the people being studied. . . . Today, when mainstream sociologists write about culture they disdain as reactionary any attempt to demonstrate how culture explains behavior." Orlando Patterson, "The Last Sociologist," *New York Times,* 19 May 2002. See also David Riesman, in collaboration with Reuel Denney and Nathan Glazer, *The Lonely Crowd: A Study of the Changing American Character* (New Haven, Conn.: Yale University Press, 1950); and works by Erving Goffman, such as *Behavior in Public Places: Notes on the Social Organization of*

Gatherings (New York: Free Press of Glencoe, 1963); and *Interaction Ritual: Essays on Face-to-Face Behavior* (New York: Doubleday, 1967).

34. Foucault does, however, at least acknowledge that ideas themselves are mechanisms of "power." He writes: "A stupid despot may constrain his slaves with iron chains; but a true politician binds them even more strongly by the chain of their own ideas . . . this link is all the stronger in that we do not know of what it is made and we believe it to be our own work." Michel Foucault, *Discipline and Punish: The Birth of the Prison* (New York: Pantheon Books, 1977), 102-03.

35. Foucault, *Discipline and Punish,* 85-87.

36. Piaget, *Moral Judgment of the Child.*

37. Hartsock, *Money, Sex, and Power,* 155-209. For her analysis of the necrophilia underlying relations of gender as they are currently structured in dominant society, Hartsock relies on the somewhat controversial writings of Robert Stoller. Hartsock acknowledges the objections to Stoller's work, most notably by Andrea Dworkin, and also that Stoller himself would probably not agree with the use Hartsock had made of his arguments; nevertheless, her point is well taken that what is culturally defined as the standard, neutral "sexuality" in the dominant culture is "a masculine sexuality that does not grow from or express the lives of women." Hartsock, *Money, Sex, and Power,* 161. The defining aspects of the "negative erotic" include the following: that fusion with another requires the (usually symbolic) death—or submission—of the other; that bodily feelings must be denied because they are reminders of our own mortality; and that creativity, generation, and reproduction are reformulated—by pornography—in ways that link them with death. Hartsock, *Money, Sex, and Power,* 174. Robert J. Stoller, *Sexual Excitement: Dynamics of Erotic Life* (New York: Pantheon, 1979); Andrea Dworkin, *Pornography: Men Possessing Women* (New York: Perigee Books, 1979).

38. Marx quoted in Hartsock, *Money, Sex, and Power,* 119-20.

39. Hartsock, *Money, Sex, and Power,* 176.

40. Hartsock, *Money, Sex, and Power,* 115, 129, 178.

41. Solo, *Philosophy of Science and Economics,* 38. On the relationship between classical economic thought and the science of physics, see also Israel Kirzner, *The Economic Point of View* (Kansas City: Sheed and Ward, 1960).

42. Solo, *Philosophy of Science and Economics,* 81.

43. Hartsock, *Money, Sex, and Power,* 125-26.

44. Bowles and Gintis, *Democracy and Capitalism.*

45. Flyvbjerg, *Making Social Science Matter,* 25-37.

46. Flyvbjerg, *Making Social Science Matter,* 46.

47. Bourdieu quoted in Flyvbjerg, *Making Social Science Matter,* 48.

48. Flyvbjerg, *Making Social Science Matter,* 42.

49. Flyvbjerg, *Making Social Science Matter,* 34.

50. Flyvbjerg, *Making Social Science Matter,* 44.

51. Flyvbjerg, *Making Social Science Matter,* 44.

52. Richard Bernstein coined the phrase "positivist temper" to name a broad class of writers who share the characteristic tenets of positivism without necessarily identifying themselves or being identified by others as members of a school of philosophy called "positivism" or "logical positivism." He writes, "Basically, the positivist temper recognizes only two models for legitimate knowledge: the empirical or natural sciences, and the formal disciplines such as logic and mathematics. Anything which cannot be reduced to these, or cannot satisfy the severe standards set by these disciplines, is to be viewed

with suspicion." Richard J. Bernstein, *The Restructuring of Social and Political Theory* (New York and London: Harcourt Brace Jovanovich, 1976), 5. Patomäki writes: "By positivism I mean the set of abstract and closely inter-related ideas that causality is about constant conjunctions ('whenever A, B follows'); that the properties of entities are independent; that their relations are external or non-necessary; that the basic things of the world are therefore atomist, or at least constant in their inner structure; and that being can be defined in terms of our perceptions or knowledge of it." Patomäki, *After International Relations*, 3.

53. Patomäki, *After International Relations*.

54. Patomäki, *After International Relations*, 8. See also Mario Bunge, *Causality: The Place of the Causal Principle in Modern Science* (Cleveland, Ohio: World Publishing Co., 1963); Elizabeth Anscombe, *Times, Beginnings, and Causes* (London: Oxford University Press, 1975); Rom Harre and E.H. Madden, *Causal Power: A Theory of Natural Necessity* (Totowa, N.J.: Rowman & Littlefield, 1975).

55. Our view of the cultural constructs of constitutive rules as historical causes, as forces that act, is at once the ultimate recognition of human agency and the long overdue reunification of human agency and "structure" in that most of the systems (e.g., economic) that historians refer to as "structure" (in contradistinction to human agency) are but the congealed results of that human agency. Using the concepts of "state" and "society" in ways similar to the way we are here using "structure" and "agency," respectively, political geographer Joseph Nevins makes the case for realizing the indivisibility of the two. He writes: "As the state socializes individuals through institutions such as schools and militaries, the activities of the state—in terms of law enforcement, for example—increasingly take on an appearance of the normal, and thus, the unproblematic. As a result, the social relations—and their underlying ideologies—that inform state practices are less obvious. This world is one in which there appears to be individuals and their activities, on the one hand and, on the other hand, monolithic and unchanging structures that exist independently of human agency and contain and guide people's lives. . . . It would thus seem that a significant effect of the appearance of a clear division between state and society is the undermining of challenges to the state by making the state seem external to the actions of individuals and, thus, very difficult to influence. At the same time, the state-society divide has served to depoliticize certain phenomena, such as territorial boundaries, associated with the state. As such, certain phenomena seem beyond question, as if their existence were almost natural. In both these regards, the state-society divide facilitates the disempowering of the state's citizenry." Joseph Nevins, *Operation Gatekeeper: The Rise of the "Illegal Alien" and the Making of the U.S.-Mexico Boundary* (New York and London: Routledge, 2002), 160. For works by other theorists who insist upon the recognition of human agents as the creators and active reproducers of culture, see Sherry Ortner, "Anthropological Theory since the Sixties," *Comparative Studies in Society and History* 26, no. 1 (1984): 126-66; Pierre Bourdieu, *Outline of a Theory of Practice*, trans. R. Nice (Cambridge: Cambridge University Press, 1977); William Roseberry, *Anthropologies and Histories: Essays in Culture, History, and Political Economy* (New Brunswick, N.J.: Rutgers University Press, 1989).

56. Alexander Wendt, *Social Theory of International Politics* (Cambridge: Cambridge University Press, 1999).

57. Although this chapter has approached philosophy with a focus on epistemology rather than on ethics, we should add, as Richards argues in detail elsewhere, notably in *Letters from Quebec,* that in the end it makes more sense to read the history of metaphys-

ics, and therefore the history of epistemology, in a manner which makes questions of ethics the central issues. We advocate a love ethic and an earth ethic. We agree with William James and with Emmanuel Levinas that the true can be considered a species of the good, and that truth is found in the ethical relationships among human beings. James writes, "The true is the name of whatever proves itself to be good in the way of belief, and good, too, for definite, assignable reasons." William James, *Essays in Pragmatism* (New York: Hafner Publishing Company, 1948), 155. Levinas writes, "The truth of being is not the image of being, the idea of its nature; it is the being situated in a subjective field which deforms vision, but precisely thus allows exteriority to state itself, entirely command and authority: entirely superiority. This curvature of the subjective space inflects distance into elevation; it does not falsify being, but makes its truth first possible. . . . This 'curvature of space' expresses the relation between human beings." Emmanuel Levinas, *Totality and Infinity* (Pittsburgh: Duquesne University Press, 1969), 291.

Chapter 3

The Drama of Spanish Socialism: Tragedy, Farce, or Conceptual Error? (Part 1)

Maria Victoria López-Cordón has suggested that in the late nineteenth century the main revolutionary ideology of the dispossessed masses of Spain was anarchism, not socialism, for almost accidental reasons. With respect to the years of the liberal revolution and the First Republic (1868-1874), she writes:

> [T]he Congress of Cordoba, celebrated the 25th of December to the [3rd] of January of 1873, adopted a series of resolutions of a character clearly anarchist and insisted on an apolitical posture. Why this preference? In the face of millenaristic or messianic interpretations, especially with respect to the proletariat of Andalucia, today it appears that one should give more weight to the fact that the implanting of a working class ideology depended essentially on whose propaganda got there first. That is to say . . . on the attitude of the intermediaries who linked the local nucleus with the outside world. Let us not forget that we are dealing with a rural society, or with people of a similar mentality, where personal relations play a decisive role.[1]

In favor of the hypothesis that intermediaries whom contemporary social movement theory might call "activist entrepreneurs"[2] made Spain more anarchist than socialist, it can be said that the average peasant or wage laborer might well have been unable to distinguish one group's slogans from another's. The grievances of the suffering masses were the same. The rhetoric employed to channel grievances into organized resistance was similar, whether the organization being built was anarchist or socialist. Therefore, who got to a particular village or worksite first could be decisive.

Nevertheless, it is important to mention some factors that lend credence to the views that López-Cordón corrects. The development of Spanish capitalism was extremely slow in both industry and agriculture. Since Spain was overwhelmingly rural, it was agriculture that counted most. While in England common lands had been enclosed and peasants driven from the land as early as the sixteenth century, for the sake of establishing export-oriented capitalist agriculture, the enclosure of common lands was still going on in Spain in the mid-nineteenth century.[3] In the late nineteenth century the transition from the comparatively easygoing rule of local nobles, who were essentially warrior chieftains, to rule by the merciless logic of profit maximization, was still within living memory. Due to Spain's slow capitalist development, the Spanish peasantry had unusually recent experience with farming for their own consumption and for local markets with comparatively little interference from their overlords. Therefore, although the anarchist ideal of *comunismo libertario* surely strikes the twenty-first-century city-dweller as a utopian pipedream, it could seem like a real possibility to the nineteenth-century Spanish peasant. It took just a little rose-tinting of the memories of grandparents to make *comunismo libertario* an easily imagined modification of rural life in Spain as it had been, and to some extent in some places still was.[4] The overlords might simply go away completely. It is reported that in 1937 and 1938 in areas of Spain controlled by anarchists during the Civil War, the free and cooperative cultivation of land without landlords or bosses was actually practiced.[5] It should be remembered, too, that the workers who swelled the ranks of the anarchist and anarcho-syndicalist industrial unions of Barcelona in the late nineteenth and early twentieth centuries were mainly recent arrivals from the countryside.

In addition, the appeal of anarchism may have been enhanced by a cultural environment receptive to anarchism's generally combative attitudes. Although there were strains of nearly Tolstoyan moral purity and pacifism in Spanish anarchism, its rejection of politics and its reliance on spontaneous action led naturally to the terrorist tactics for which it became famous. The excitement of fighting seems to be an innate source of pleasure for the human species, and to be, in sublimated forms, the source of much of the energy that drives athletics, economics, and politics. In Spain, the land of Don Quixote, a tradition of fighting for high ideals provided cultural reinforcement for this natural tendency. Indeed, the great Spanish poet Antonio Machado was able, in the 1920s, to write with a straight face that Spain, alone among nations, had never gone to war for commercial gain, but had always fought for ideals.[6]

The Spaniards forged their national identity during seven long centuries of struggle against the Moors. When the several warring Christian kingdoms that were to become Spain ceased to fight each other, it was to unite under the banner of a faith against a common enemy with a different faith. The ideals of the knight who fights for the Cross can easily be extended to fighting for secular justice. To this day in the Spanish language members of secular political parties are sometimes called *correligionarios*. A solution acceptable to all, even to those whose normative commitments are in principle opposed, is said to be acceptable *tanto para moros como para cristianos* ("for Moors as well as for Christians"). A solution rejected by all is one not accepted *ni por moros ni por cristianos* ("neither by Moors nor by Christians"). When in 1492 the last emir was driven out of southern Spain, the Spaniards began almost immediately to do to the peoples of vast territories overseas what the Moors had done to the peoples of the Iberian peninsula: to conquer them in the name of God, to plunder their riches, to rule over them as a resident upper class, and to convert them to the one true faith. It is therefore not implausible to suppose that anarchism's combination of a quasi-religious vision of justice on earth with violent revolutionary tactics appealed to knightly traditions that associated glory, honor, faith, and fighting.

In the late nineteenth century, "social democracy" was a generic term that embraced anarchism, socialism, and communism, as well as the currents that eventually became West European social democracy. The party that would evolve to become the Spanish version of West European social democracy was the Socialist Workers Party of Spain, the PSOE (*Partido Socialista Obrero de España*). It was from its founding, on May 2, 1879, a moderating and steadying influence among the impoverished and often desperate working masses. Yet with all of its moderation and steadiness it always defined itself, under its great early leader, Pablo Iglesias, as a revolutionary party that worked to achieve a radical transformation of society's basic structures. Critics on the left and admirers on the right said that whatever its rhetoric might be in any given period, in practice the PSOE was a reformist party, which employed peaceful and legal means to seek modest gains for workers within the framework of capitalism.[7] This, however, was not the party's declared aim; it was not its own interpretation of its historical project.

Pablo Iglesias was more than the PSOE's leader. He was its heart and soul. He was nothing if he was not a man passionately devoted to the ethical construction of a transformed social reality.[8] In his first published writing, written in 1870 when he was nineteen years old, written before he had read Marx, and published in a small and precarious revolutionary workers' weekly called *La Solidaridad*, Iglesias wrote:

> What is war? A crime. If we were deists, if we believed in some of the gods that all the religions harbor in their breasts; if we believed, we repeat again, in some of those idols, we would say that war is a terrible punishment that the gods impose on the peoples of nations for their sins. But, not being like that, not believing in those false divinities, the offsprings of heated brains, the creations of errant imaginations, and being, as we are, rationalists, we know that war is the offspring, and always has been, of a half dozen tyrants, of a half dozen assassins—yes, that is the right name for them—of a half dozen sick and miserable beings, unnatural monstrosities, who, sometimes out of pride, sometimes for mere adventure, sometimes from unbridled ambition, do not doubt, do not even vacillate, in sending their fellow beings, their brothers, to serve as fodder for cannons.[9]

At the age of seventy-five, on his deathbed, in October 1925, at a time when the dictator General Miguel Primo de Rivera had put an end to a period of revolutionary ferment, a few days before Pablo Iglesias lost the ability to put pen to paper and could write no more, he wrote: "Perhaps we will have to endure this regime for a long time; let us use that time to work for ideals, to defend them, so that they will be deeply rooted, so that they will live and make their home in full consciousness."[10]

From a very young age, the events of Pablo Iglesias' life contributed to his deepening understanding of the importance of a culture of solidarity. Upon the death of her husband Pedro Iglesias, who had earned a meager living working for the town of Ferrol, Juana Posse, who could neither read nor write, took her two young boys, Pablo and Manuel, and set out on foot for Madrid, to seek help from an uncle, whom she believed to be employed as a servant in the palace of the Duke of Altamira. When the widow and her two sons arrived, they found that the uncle had died. The two boys were placed in an orphanage, while Juana was left to fend for herself.[11] In the orphanage, Pablo learned the trade of typesetting, which became the material basis of his future. As a working typesetter, he was a member (in fact, a founder) of the typesetters union, and thus a member (in fact, a founder) of the Spanish labor movement. As a typesetter, he was in a position to collaborate in putting out leftist publications, culminating in the newspaper *El Socialista*, of which he was the editor during most of his life. Like many typesetters, he read the books he set into type. He also read novels. Although he had little formal schooling, he took advantage of several educational opportunities open to penniless youth in Madrid in the 1860s and 1870s, and once won a certificate as an outstanding student in French classes. Although, as a class-conscious young worker, he read the works of a number of contemporary European socialist writers, his fundamental intellectual allegiance was to Karl Marx. One of his biographers wrote (with our explanatory remarks in brackets):

> Lafargue [Paul Lafargue, son-in-law of Karl Marx, who came to Spain and helped lay the groundwork for the PSOE] returned to London [in 1873], *La Emancipacion* [a left-wing periodical in which Pablo Iglesias collaborated] continued to appear, now in contact with Engels and Marx, and there was created a rump of the Regional Federation [an early proletarian organization] composed of a handful of sections [a minority that included Iglesias] who did not agree with the criteria of the anarchists.
>
> Lafargue sent a French edition of the *Communist Manifesto*, which was translated into Spanish and published in the periodical, as were single carefully selected chapters of *Capital*. At that time there was appearing the French translation of that book, which was being published a part at a time. Iglesias in Madrid was in charge of receiving them and managing their publication. . . .
>
> And these two fundamental works, read, studied, and meditated upon by Iglesias, gave him clear ideas, which he would never again modify.[12]

What Iglesias learned from Marx confirmed his native bent toward making an ethical critique of capitalism, and toward advocating a transformed society based on better principles, those of solidarity. We believe that a fair sample of the resulting Pablismo is found in the "considerations" which precede the program of the Socialist Workers Party of Spain, drafted mainly by Iglesias, and approved at the party congress in Barcelona in 1888. They are:

> Considering:
> That this society is unjust because it divides its members into two classes unequal and antagonistic: one, the bourgeoisie, which, possessing the instruments of work, is the dominant class; another, the proletariat, which does not possess more than its living energy, is the dominated class;
> That the economic subjection of the proletariat is the first cause of slavery in all its forms: social misery, intellectual mediocrity, and political dependence;
> That the privileges of the bourgeoisie are guaranteed by political Power, which it relies on to dominate the proletariat;
> The Socialist Party declares that it has for aspirations: 1) The possession of political Power by the working class; 2) The transformation of individual and corporate property into property that is collective, social, or common.[13]

Given his premises, Iglesias' entire strategy was: organize the working class! By organizing economically in unions, by organizing politically as a party, the workers would gradually acquire the power to defend the rights they already had, to gain new rights, and to transform society. For this strategy to succeed it was necessary to teach the workers that bourgeois democratic parties did not represent them. The Republicans, the bourgeois proponents of democracy, were in favor of replacing the Spanish monarchy with a republic. They were in favor of the rule of law and of guarantees for basic freedoms. They were in favor of disestablishing the privileges of the church. But they did not represent the economic interests of the working class. Monarchists and Republicans alike represented owners, not workers. From 1909 on Iglesias modified his position and supported a "conjunction" of Socialists and Republicans for the sake of defending the basic freedoms that the workers needed in order to be able to build their organizations.

Against the ideas of the socialists, nineteenth-century conservatives argued, in Spain as in other countries, that what the socialists proposed was impossible; consequently, their efforts to achieve their goals could only lead to illusion and trouble, and not to the achievement of their stated aspirations. Marxist writers have often pointed out that Pablo Iglesias was a public leader, not a theoretician, and that his interpretation of Marx was too simple.

Our own point of view, which we call cultural action or ethical construction, coincides with and overlaps many of the judgments that have already been made about Spanish socialism by its critics and its admirers.[14] We wish to contribute to ongoing conversations by redefining the issues in terms of certain an-

cient and medieval ideals—cooperation and sharing—revalorized in the light of
a realist philosophy of natural science. We believe that such a redefinition or
conceptual shift will invite dialogue with non-western ideologies as well. Non-
western ideologies often enshrine values similar to those of the ancient West,
which the early modern and Enlightenment philosophers undervalued, when
they articulated the ideals of western modernity.[15]

We do not think Pablo Iglesias would disagree with this recasting of the
problem and its solutions. The religious experiences of his early youth were not
lost on him, and even though he lost faith in God, he never lost faith in solidarity, in unity. Nor could he forget the norms that governed his tiny family. Like
so many millions of other poor families, Juana, Pablo, and Manuel cooperated
heroically to support one another in a fragmented world. Iglesias could not have
failed to notice the difference between his family's true social bonding and the
uncaring attitudes of individuals locked in competitive struggles to survive in a
market economy where the poor regularly find that the assets required to satisfy
the needs of daily life all belong to somebody else. Throughout his career, words
denoting kinship ("brothers," "brotherhood") were never far from his lips.

Nor would Marx necessarily disagree with our recasting. In 1896, Bertrand
Russell delivered in London his lectures on German Social Democracy. Social
democracy was then understood in Germany as a movement broadly following
Marx's ideas, although two currents of thought, one mainly inspired by Marx,
and the other mainly inspired by Ferdinand Lassalle, had come together at Gotha
in 1875 to form the German Social Democratic Party (*Sozialdemokratische
Partei Deutschlands* or SPD). Russell explained social democracy's aims:

> For Social Democracy is not a mere political party, nor even a mere economic
> theory; it is a complete self-contained philosophy of the world and of human
> development; it is, in a word, a religion and an ethic. To judge the work of
> Marx, or the aims and beliefs of his followers, from a narrow economic stand-
> point, is to overlook the whole body and spirit of their greatness. I shall en-
> deavour, since this aspect of the movement is easily lost sight of in the details
> of history, to bring it into prominence by a brief preliminary account. Hegel, in
> his "Philosophy of History," endeavoured to exhibit the actual course of the
> world as following the same necessary chain of development which, as it exists
> in thought, forms the subject of his logic. In this development, everything im-
> plies and even tends to become, its opposite, as son implies father; the devel-
> opment of the world therefore proceeds by action and reaction, or, in technical
> language, by thesis and antithesis, and these become reconciled in a higher
> unity, the synthesis of both. Of this process we have an example in Marx's doc-
> trine of the development of production: First, he says, in the savage and the pa-
> triarchal eras, we have production for self; a man's goods and the produce of a
> man's labour are intended solely for his own consumption. Then, in the capital-
> istic era, the age of exchange and commerce, people produce exclusively for
> others; things become commodities, having exchange-value, and destined to be
> used by others than the producers. This is, in technical language, the negation

or antithesis of production for self; the two find their synthesis in the communistic state, in production by society for itself. Here the individual still produces for others, but the community produces explicitly—as in the capitalistic era it produces implicitly—for itself.[16]

Russell may have overstated or distorted the influence of Hegel on Marx, but he is surely correct in identifying exchange-value as the key to Marx's analysis of the capitalist era, and in identifying production by the community to meet the community's needs as what, according to Marx, social democracy is supposed to achieve. Adam Smith, whom Marx greatly respected, had acknowledged that the whole point of economic activity was use, to produce goods and services to supply the necessities and conveniences of life, and that there was no point in exchange for its own sake. Marx showed that a world ruled by the logic of exchange necessarily failed to do what needed to be done: produce the goods, meet the needs. He began *Capital* with an analysis of the exchange of commodities, schematically depicting a contrast between two kinds of exchange:

C—M—C: Commodities—Money—Commodities; and

M—C—M': Money—Commodities—Money

In the first type of exchange, C—M—C, the commodities (the goods, *Waren* in German) are the beginning and end of the process. You have something, but you need something else. You sell what you have for money. With the money you buy what you need.[17] The exchange pattern M—C—M' is in principle different. You have money, and you want more money. You buy commodities with your money, but only with what Marx calls the "sly intention" of getting more money back. This is what Aristotle, whom Marx cites, calls "unnatural" exchange. Goods that people can use, which satisfy some need or provide some pleasure of convenience, are no longer essential to the purpose. The real material use of things only plays a role if, when, and to the extent that it contributes to the increase of money. Money buys a commodity. Consider that, for example, the commodity purchased is, anticipating Marx's analysis later in the book, labor-power. But the commodity purchased is by no means *la chose qu'on aime pour lui-meme* ("the thing one loves for its own sake"). It is only a step on the way to a future sale—for example, the sale of the products created by the labor power. The culmination and purpose of the process is more money.

With his contrast between C—M—C and M—C—M', Marx already established at the beginning of *Capital* an ethical critique of capitalism. Looking backward from the advanced perspective of a better society of the future, capitalism will be seen as a rude and backward stage of civilization—during which society had not yet learned how to produce the goods required to meet its needs. Instead, it produced only a certain subset of those goods, viz. the ones whose production would further the accumulation of capital.

The M—C—M' model also serves to introduce points of supreme importance for any transition from capitalism to socialism. Under socialism, society
works to meet its members' needs. Therefore, by definition, socialism is better
than capitalism. Yet this does not imply that the way to organize society so that
it works to meet its members' needs has been invented. The Islands of the
Blessed are, by definition, better than the earth, but they do not exist. Further, in
this existing capitalist world, money goes forth to earn more money in the expectation that it will succeed in earning more money, and thus complete a cycle
in a chain of accumulation, consisting of links M—C—M', which repeat themselves over and over. In the existing capitalist world, it is expectation of profit
that makes production start. Therefore, any step in a socialist direction that
weakens the expectation of profit will tend to make production stop. Fernando
de los Rios was an early Spanish socialist who made this point well.[18]

The construction of socialism is a moral problem, although not a simple
one. Marx attempted to improve upon the purely moral arguments for socialism
by putting the ideology of the working class on a sound scientific basis. The C—
M—C / M—C—M' contrast was an opening gambit, which led toward more
scientific, less ethical, and ostensibly deeper concepts. For better or worse, Karl
Marx, like many great philosophers before and since, deployed the best and
most up to date science of his day in the service of great ideals that seemed to be
built on sand, only to have it turn out that the ideals outlasted the science.

Pablo Iglesias was a convinced Marxist, but a born moralist. His passions
for truth and rectitude invite comparisons with Socrates and with Gandhi. For
Iglesias it was supremely important to assert the dignity of working people; to
demonstrate that workers are persons, and not zeroes. A few examples: In 1884
he, along with several others, was sentenced to five months in jail, on flimsy
pretexts relating to their having organized a strike of typesetters. Felipe Ducaz-
cal, a personal friend of both Iglesias and the governor, visited him in jail to tell
him that he could obtain a pardon for him. Iglesias would not accept a pardon,
and he served his sentence. His newspaper *El Socialista* refused to be sensa-
tional or sentimental and accepted the consequence that it would not be a paper
with a large circulation. On another of the many occasions when he went to jail
for his beliefs, Iglesias' lawyer sought to defend him by saying that in the rush
of meeting a newspaper deadline he had written things he did not fully mean,
but Iglesias testified that he had thought the matter over carefully and had meant
exactly what he had written. When first elected to public office, as a member of
the Madrid City Council, Iglesias and two other socialists elected with him, became entitled to a share in the spoils system through which council members
recommended candidates for municipal employment. They refused to participate, and instead introduced a resolution (which did not pass) calling for filling
all city posts by open competition according to merit. Their action became a
model for other socialists later elected to municipal offices in Spanish cities.[19]

After Iglesias' death, the socialists actually prospered under the dictatorship of Miguel Primo de Rivera. Primo chose to persecute the anarchists and the communists, while seeking labor peace by negotiating with the socialists. Many labor-management disputes were arbitrated by mixed commissions in which socialist trade unionists spoke for the workers.[20] When Primo finally resigned, in January of 1930, the socialist party and the socialist unions were stronger than ever.[21] Both were flooded with tens of thousands of new members, who expected even greater gains after the restoration of liberty.

It was not to be. The history of Spain from the resignation of Primo de Rivera to March 28, 1939, when General Francisco Franco's troops entered Madrid, is the history of the first great failure of Spanish socialism. "The circumstance that made the civil war in Spain inevitable was the civil war inside the socialist party," wrote the Spanish historian Salvador de Madariaga.[22] The *Pablistas*, led by the philosopher and professor of logic Julian Besteiro, lost control of the party and the trade unions to people who considered themselves more practical, more scientific, more revolutionary, or all three. This contingent ultimately led the PSOE into a disastrous alliance with people the historian Ricardo de la Cierva described as "the chorus of lunatics into which the Spanish Communist Party had degenerated."[23] Madariaga and de la Cierva are two of legions who have at the time and subsequently diagnosed the malady of Spanish socialism in the 1930s. Even now, seventy years later, it is our purpose to offer yet another hypothesis. Spanish socialism in the 1930s failed because it followed an oft-tried and inherently flawed strategy: rather than undertaking the more arduous and more important task of constructing cultural structures of solidarity, the socialists chose to work within existing cultural structures to try to extend greater political and economic power to the rural and urban working classes. This strategy met with a predictable backlash.

The unquestioned strategy of the PSOE from its founding had been to organize the economic power of the working class through a confederation of trade unions, and to organize the political power of the working class through a political party. As the party's 1888 "considerations" state, the bourgeoisie uses political power to back up its economic power. The workers would therefore do the same. The years 1931-32 should have been an ideal time to move this strategy forward. The return of freedom meant that unions could organize. The socialists held several important portfolios in the post-dictatorship government of the Republican Manuel Azana, and they were in a position to use political counter-pressure when owners used political pressure. If the basic PSOE strategy would work at all, it should have worked then.

For an illustration of why it did not work, it is helpful to consider not government, party, or union policy, but instead daily life in a Spanish village in the years 1931-32 and afterwards. In such a village, the socialists used their organized economic power to shift the terms of employment contracts in favor of better wages, hours, and working conditions. In 1932, the government, which formerly could have been counted on to back the owners, appointed a tripartite commission in the village to arbitrate disputes. One member represented Labor. A second represented Property. The third, who turned out to be a local schoolteacher, represented the Government itself. Conditions were ripe for increasingly organized labor to express its collective power, and this is precisely what happened. With the socialists in control, landowners were forced to hire workers to work the land under conditions set by workers themselves and their advocates. Certain results were predictable: farmers lost enthusiasm for farming, and the prices at which crops could be harvested and brought to market were not competitive.[24] On the hypothesis that the crisis in production that afflicted this particular village was general in Spain, it is easy to understand why it is hard to disentangle, among the mixed motives of those who conspired and murdered to defeat and destroy democracy and socialism, the self-interested motives of preserving property and privilege, from the patriotic motives of saving the nation from chaos and collapse.

Yet we are not making an inductive argument based on a single village. We are illustrating a recurrent tendency inherent in the normative structure of capitalist society. It follows from Marx's M—C—M' schema. When the rational expectation of future profits declines, so does production. Further, as Marx pointed out, capitalists compete with each other, and those who cannot "get their labor down" (a phrase of a Connecticut mill owner Marx quoted) are at a competitive disadvantage. Constructing socialism through the economic and political empowerment of workers encounters constraints that are not helpfully articulated in the language of power at all. They are better articulated in terms of cultural structures—normative frameworks that should be improved and transformed.

If it is true that power is deeply embedded in the founding metaphors of modern western thought, then we must expect our thesis that economics and politics are best understood in different terms to fall on deaf ears. Power is not an optional concept. Michel Foucault is not mistaken—even though some of us would say he is limited—when he says, in effect, that we cannot think about power without at the same time thinking in power and with power. Power is, so to speak, written into the software that programs our minds.

We do not rely on a single case in our task of seeking a hearing for a counter-cultural thesis. If we fail to convince anyone that the problem of constructing a new social reality in Spain is best conceived in terms of cultural action to transform normative structures, then the case of Sweden and the other cases we examine provide further evidence. With respect to Spain, however, the 1930s is not the best period for showing the dilemmas of social democracies and how to overcome them—because nobody knows what would have happened in the 1930s if democracy and socialism had not been annihilated by brute violence. Contemporary Spain is a better test case for our hypothesis.

Notes

1. Maria Victoria López-Cordón, *La Revolución de 1868 y la Primera República* (Madrid: Siglo XXI, 1976), 51-52.

2. This concept was originally developed by N. Frolich, J.A. Oppenheimer, and O.R. Young, in *Political Leadership and Collective Goods* (Princeton, N.J.: Princeton University Press, 1971).

3. The tenacity of the commons was particularly strong in the northwestern and northern provinces of Spain such as Galicia, Asturias, León, and the Basque country. Throughout this region, it was not until the 1830s that wealthy landowners began a wholehearted push for the enclosure and privatization of the commons. Raymond Carr, *Spain, 1808-1975* (Oxford: Clarendon Press, 1982), 7. Although we disagree with the terminology employed and the prescriptions offered therein, for a brief summary of the slowness of the development of capitalist agriculture and industry in Spain, see Leandro Prados de la Escosura, "Economic growth and backwardness, 1780-1930," in José Alvarez Junco and Adrian Shubert, eds., *Spanish History Since 1808* (London and New York: Arnold, 2000), 179-90. For a comparison of the cases of England and France, where the enclosure movements had a much longer history, see Eric Kerridge, *The Agricultural Revolution* (London: George Allen & Unwin, 1967); and Marc Bloch, "La lutte pour l'individualisme agraire dans la France du dix-huitieme siecle," *Annales d'histoire économique et sociale* 2 (July 1930): 329-83; and 2 (October 1930): 511-56. For a broad treatment that places Spain's push toward industrialization in a global context, see Joseph Harrison, "Tackling national decadence: economic regenerationism in Spain after the colonial debacle," in Joseph Harrison and Alan Hoyle, eds., *Spain's 1898 Crisis: Regenerationism, modernism, post-colonialism* (Manchester, U.K.; and New York: Manchester University Press, 2000), 55-67.

4. A similar point regarding historical experience making anarchism plausible might be made about the anarchist tendencies of progressive thought in the United States, since well into the nineteenth century the United States was predominantly a nation of largely self-sufficient farmers, who could rather easily imagine that a society could function quite well if there were neither governments nor bosses. Thus Marx wrote of the United States, "There are colonies proper, such as the United States, Australia, etc. Here the mass of the farming colonists, although they bring with them a larger or smaller amount of capital from the motherland, are not capitalists, nor do they carry on capitalist production. They are more or less peasants, who work for themselves and whose main object, in the first place, is to produce their own livelihood." Karl Marx, *Theories of Surplus Value* (New York: International Publishers, 1968), 202.

5. José Peirats, *Los Anarquistas en la crisis política española* (Madrid: Jucar, 1977), 149-68. José Peirats Valls (1908-1989) was a member of the *Confederación Nacional del Trabajo* (CNT) and an anarchist veteran of the Spanish Civil War. He was well known throughout this period for his historical and political analysis, and he served as the editor of anarcho-syndicalist publications *Solidaridad Obrera* and *Ruta*. For other primary accounts and primary documents treating the epoch of anarchist rule in areas of rural Spain during the Civil War, see Gaston Leval (the pseudonym of Pedro Piller), *Collectives in Spain* (London: Freedom Press, 1945), which was reprinted in 1975 by the same press as *Collectives in the Spanish Revolution*; Clara E. Lida, "Agrarian Anarchism in Andalusia:

Documents of the *Mano Negra*," *International Review of Social History* 14 (1969): 315-52; Albert Pérez Baró, *30 meses de colectivismo en Cataluña (1936-1939)* (Barcelona: Editorial Ariel, 1974); and Antonio Rosado, *Tierra y Libertad: memorias de un campesino anarcosindicalista andaluz* (Barcelona: Editorial Crítica, 1979).

6. This sentiment is expressed in several of Machado's poems, and indeed the high ideals of Spain was a common theme among the works of the "Generation of '98." See, e.g., Machado's "Una España joven." See also P. Cerezo Galán, *Palabra en el tiempo: poesía y filosofía en Antonio Machado* (Madrid: Editorial Gredos, 1975), especially 522-63, "El problema de España."

7. Carr, *Spain, 1808-1975*, 717, 737; Donald Share, *Dilemmas of Social Democracy: the Spanish Socialist Workers Party in the 1980s* (New York: Greenwood Press, 1989), 27-31, 40.

8. Pablo Iglesias also served as leader of the UGT (*Unión General de Trabajadores*), which was founded in 1882. Under his leadership, the UGT in that year staged the first effective strike in Restoration Spain. Iglesias was a tireless organizer, and membership in the UGT grew markedly throughout the late nineteenth and early twentieth century, from just over 3,000 members six years after its founding, to over 43,000 by 1904. Carr, *Spain, 1808-1975*, 447, 449.

9. Pablo Iglesias quoted in Juan José Morato, *Pablo Iglesias Posse, Educador de Muchedumbres* (Madrid and Barcelona: Espasa-Calpe, 1931), 40. Translation by Richards and Swanger. Unless otherwise noted, all translations throughout this text are by Richards and Swanger.

10. Iglesias quoted in Morato, *Pablo Iglesias Posse*, 246.

11. Later, Pablo's younger brother Manuel died, and after Pablo left the orphanage, Pablo and Juana shared a small apartment in Madrid for many years.

12. Morato, *Pablo Iglesias Posse*, 51.

13. Program of the PSOE, 1888, reprinted in Enrique Moral Sandoval, *Pablo Iglesias, Escritos y Discursos, Antología Crítica* (Santiago de Compostela, Spain: Ediciones Salvora, 1984), 18-19. The program goes on to state more aspirations, including, already in 1888, the equality of the sexes.

14. For general historical treatments of the PSOE, see Antonio Padilla Bolívar, *El movimiento Socialista Español* (Barcelona: Planeta, 1977); Ricardo de la Cierva, *Historia del socialismo en España, 1879-1983* (Barcelona: Planeta, 1983); and Santos Juliá, ed., *El socialismo en España* (Madrid: Editorial Pablo Iglesias, 1986). On the PSOE in the nineteenth century, see A. Elorza, "Los primeros programas del PSOE (1879-1888)," *Estudios de Historia Social* 8-9 (1979): 143-80. For a treatment of the PSOE during the Second Republic (1931-1936), see Manuel Contreras, *El PSOE en la II República: Organización e ideología* (Madrid: Centro de Investigaciones Sociológicas, 1981).

15. Max Weber acknowledged the similarity of the East and the pre-modern West when he called them both "traditional." Max Weber, *The Protestant Ethic and the Spirit of Capitalism* (Talcott Parsons, transl.) (New York: Charles Scribner's Sons, 1958), 265, 271.

16. Bertrand Russell, *German Social Democracy* (New York: Simon and Schuster, 1965), 1-3. The 1965 publication of Bertrand Russell's *German Social Democracy* is a reprint of lectures originally given in 1896.

17. This type of exchange characterizes what Fernand Braudel calls "material life," in his histories of daily life in Europe; the material processes dominate, and money is used as a convenience to facilitate them. See Fernand Braudel, *Civilization and Capital-*

ism, *15th-18th Century, Vol. 1: The Structures of Everyday Life, The Limits of the Possible* (New York; Cambridge; Hagerstown, Md.; Philadelphia; San Francisco; London; Mexico City; São Paulo; Sydney: Harper & Row Publishers, 1979), especially Chapter 7 on "Money," 436-78.

18. Fernando de los Ríos (1879-1949) discusses the primacy of productivity and the governance of profitability over productivity. He states that it is essential for socialists to understand the implications of the "extraeconomic power" of profitability—or the profit motive—and that it is this extraeconomic power that socialists must find ways to control if production is to be used for the ends of social justice. Fernando de los Ríos, *El sentido humanista del socialismo* (Elías Díaz, ed.) (Madrid: Editorial Castalia, 1976), 223. He also discusses capital flight and the other "anti-social" tendencies of capitalism when it is functioning the way mainstream economists believe it should, as well as the juridical underpinnings of these antisocial tendencies. De los Ríos, *El sentido humanista*, 134-35, 156-60. See also Fernando de los Ríos, *Escritos sobre democracia y socialismo* (Virgilio Zapatero, ed.) (Madrid: Taurus Ediciones, S.A., 1974).

19. Carr, *Spain, 1808-1975*, 450; Morato, *Pablo Iglesias Posse*, 84, 114-16, 166-79.

20. Since 1918, the PSOE had been urging the government to form labor regulation boards with members representing both workers and employers, and Primo found this corporatist system somewhat appealing. Thus, in 1926, he issued a decree-law establishing "*comités paritarios*" (equal committees) on the local level, composed of both workers and employers; "*comisiones mixtas*" (mixed commissions) on the provincial level; and corporation councils on the national level. These bodies were charged with administering a smooth functioning economy for Spain as a whole. Stanley G. Payne, *Fascism in Spain, 1923-1977* (Madison, Wisc.; and London: The University of Wisconsin Press, 1999), 31, 33. As additional evidence of the strength of the PSOE during the Primo de Rivera dictatorship, it should be noted that although real wages for the Spanish working class declined throughout the last half of the 1920s, those of skilled workers in Vizcayan industry who were represented by Socialist and Basque unions in fact rose throughout this period. Payne, *Fascism in Spain*, 33. For an overview of the role of the PSOE during the Primo de Rivera dictatorship, see Enrique Moral Sandoval, "El socialismo y la dictadura de Primo de Rivera," in Santos Juliá, ed., *El socialismo en España*, 192-211.

21. The PSOE formed an alliance with the Republicans and together swept the elections of mid-1931. Payne, *Fascism in Spain*, 44.

22. Salvador de Madariaga.quoted in de la Cierva, *Historia del Socialismo en España*, 173.

23. de la Cierva, *Historia del Socialismo en España*, 109.

24. George A. Collier, *Socialists of Rural Andalusia: Unacknowledged Revolutionaries of the Second Republic* (Stanford: Stanford University Press, 1987), 65-118. The town that Collier treats in his study is a small village in the rugged Sierra de Aracena, located in the in the northern stretch of the southern Spanish province of Huelva. He calls it by the pseudonym "Los Olivos." By the terms of the agrarian decrees issued by the socialists in power, the eight-hour day replaced the traditional *de sol a sol* agricultural working day; employers were required to pay overtime wages; and grounds for employee dismissal were severely restricted. Socialist organizers told workers that they should no longer fear the power of the landowners, and they encouraged workers to demand higher and higher wages. Landowners were forced to absorb the higher labor costs because a depressed market would not bear significantly higher prices for agricultural goods. Other measures specifically restricted landowners' autonomy over managing the land itself: as a

means of addressing the problem of chronic and seasonal underemployment in rural regions, landowners were forced to cultivate fallow land; the use of reaping and threshing machinery was prohibited; and yearlong contracts for a specific number of laborers (depending on the acreage under cultivation) were mandated. Thus, although there were no specific calls for outright land redistribution in this town, workers did issue a radical challenge to the traditional relations of production. For an in-depth treatment of the economic and political consequences of this radical upsurge, see Paul Preston, *The Coming of the Spanish Civil War: Reform, Reaction and Revolution in the Second Republic, 1931-1936* (London: Routledge, 1994); and "The Agrarian War in the South," in Paul Preston, ed., *Revolution and War in Spain, 1931-1939* (London and New York: Methuen, 1984). Preston documents the conservative backlash of employers as they resisted reforms intended to bring about greater social justice and eventually channeled their opposition into a political movement at the national level.

Chapter 4

The Drama of Spanish Socialism:
Tragedy, Farce, or Conceptual Error?
(Part 2)

The Socialist Workers Party of Spain is the party of change. It is also the
party that must assure the tranquility of the Spanish people. Therein lies
the drama of Spanish socialism. —Felipe González[1]

In Spain and in Latin America there have been many violent social conflicts,
most of which the right wing has won. Their history suggests that one need look
no farther for an explanation of continued social inequality than to the ferocity
of property owners and their military backers. Here is a small example, recounted by George Collier, concerning a small village in Spain early in the
1936-39 civil war:

> In Barcelona and Madrid, people were being taken at night from their homes to
> the outskirts to be shot. Militants in Aracena had jailed a number of prominent
> landowners and clergy and threatened worse. A rumor spread among the prop-
> ertied families in Los Olivos that the militants had drawn up a list of rightists to
> eliminate. Meanwhile, insurgent General Queipo de Llano, in a July 25 [1936]
> radio broadcast from Seville, threatened dire reprisals for any action against
> rightists:
> "In various villages of which I have heard, right-wing people are being
> held prisoner and threatened with barbarous fates. I want to make known my
> system with regard to this. For every person killed I shall kill ten and perhaps
> even exceed this proportion. . . . The leaders of these village movements may
> believe they can flee; they are wrong. Even if they hide beneath the earth, I
> shall dig them out; even if they're already dead I shall kill them again."[2]

With a history of social violence to contemplate, it is easy to forget that the
prosaic logic of economics also makes social democracy hard to achieve. The
burden of this chapter will be to illustrate this less dramatic, but ultimately more

important, obstacle. With respect to methodology, this chapter will introduce both a critique and a vindication of rational choice theory—a critique because its schemas do not explain human action, a vindication because it nevertheless describes important mechanisms of economic power that frustrate social democracy.[3]

On October 28, 1982, the Socialist Workers Party of Spain won an overwhelming victory at the polls, electing an absolute majority of the members of the Spanish parliament, and winning 60 percent of the popular vote. The party's First Secretary, Felipe González, became, at age forty, the youngest head of government in Europe. The electoral triumph came 103 years, five months, and twenty-six days after the date when twenty-five young workers met in secret to found what was then a clandestine organization, the PSOE. The socialists would win four successive elections and govern Spain for more than ten years.

Between the death of the winner of the Civil War, the dictator Francisco Franco, in November 1975, and the elections of October 1982, two remarkable processes took place in Spain. First, the authoritarian corporatist state established by Franco and intended by him to last forever, was dismantled and replaced by a constitutional monarchy. Spanish voters approved a new Constitution in 1978. Second, the centrist UCD party (*Unión de Centro Democrático*), which at first was dominant, fell apart and vanished, clearing the way for the left to win the elections of 1982.[4]

On the surface the centrists cratered over social issues, specifically divorce. Spanish women first got the vote in 1933—twelve years earlier than French women. When the *Falange*[5] won the Civil War, however, women lost virtually all rights. Women living under the Franco dictatorship had no right to vote, to divorce, to abortion, to open bank accounts without the husband's permission, to sign contracts without the husband's permission, to travel, or even to be absent from the home more days than the husband allowed.[6] The UCD was a loose coalition whose members ranged from social democrats to recent converts to democracy more or less nostalgic for Franco. When the party leadership proposed to make up for lost time by modernizing Spain's social legislation, it turned out that the members of the party could not agree on divorce. In the ensuing chaos and stalemate, many MPs deserted, a few to the left, most to the right. The UCD collapsed.[7]

Although divorce was the most salient public issue, both the left and the right were working deliberately to destroy the center. The right did not want what appeared to be developing: a future in which Spanish voters would choose at intervals between center and left. The socialist strategy was to eliminate the UCD in order to occupy the center itself. At a multitudinous televised rally at Madrid's main university campus on election eve, Felipe González offered the voters a government that would do what the UCD would not or could not do.[8]

The more significant change leading up to October 28, 1982, was not, however, the dissolution of the center that allowed the socialists to win the election, but rather the dissolution of the dictatorship that allowed the election to be held. Professor Josep Colomer of the Higher Council for Scientific Research in Barcelona has done a valuable study of how Spain was transformed from a dictatorship to a democracy in the years 1975-1981.[9] Understanding this transition to democracy is essential background for discussing what the socialists did during their ten-year reign because democracy is still fragile in Spain and anything a government does there it necessarily does bearing in mind the permanent possibility of a military coup. In discussing at some length Colomer's study of the establishment of democracy in Spain, we want to comment particularly on his methodology.

Colomer studies the demise of dictatorship and the birth of democracy with a method that combines social choice theory and game theory in what he calls a "rational choice approach." He describes it as follows:

> The advantage of the formal, deductive reasoning characteristic of the rational choice approach, is that it permits the identification of those elements which can explain real outcomes in a more accurate and precise manner than the conventional method of inductive generalization from empirical observations. Once a set of alternatives, relevant actors, and preferences has been put forth and the deductive implications of the analysis have been formulated, the contrast between formal results and real outcomes can either confirm the validity of the explanation or suggest a modification or enlargement of the assumptions in order to produce a better fit between the model and reality. In this way, it is possible to purify and refine the explanation, separate what is important from what is superfluous, and to produce real knowledge and understanding.[10]

The first and most important of the assumptions of the approach Colomer uses is "that the decisions of actors can be explained as being derived from rational calculations."[11] This major assumption is surrounded by qualifications. One of them, which bears on the payoffs ("the alternatives") those rational actors are assumed to rationally choose, is: "A regime change is precisely a change of the rules of the game and, logically, the game for changing rules cannot entirely be shaped by the incentives structured by the rules being changed."[12] Colomer offers the following two examples. *Example 1*: The reformers (most famously Adolfo Suárez, head of the UCD) essentially double-crossed the army and the corporatist Council of State inherited from Franco, by breaking their promise that if democracy went forward the Communist Party would continue to be illegal. Once democracy became the new norm, then it seemed rational to legalize all parties. The decision was a rational and legitimate choice given the new rules.[13] *Example 2*: For several hours during the night of February 23-24, 1981, it was not clear whether the rational alternatives—in terms of how what one does now is rewarded later—would be those of constitutional government or military dictatorship. Colonel Tejero of the Civil Guard led three hundred troops into a joint session of the Spanish parliament and held the entire government at gunpoint as part of a planned coup. During those hours the decisions of a rational actor who calculated that democracy would continue would be different from those of one who calculated that the coup would succeed.[14]

We propose to broaden Colomer's rational choice approach by making six methodological comments before going on to apply the resulting modified approach (which might be called a cultural construction approach) to shed light on constraints inherent in the logic of capitalism that made it very difficult, arguably impossible, for the socialists elected in 1982 to carry out their program.

First, we would broaden the idea of "decisions" based on "rational calculations" and speak instead, following Aristotle, of "choices" following "deliberation." Thus the concept of "rational choices" becomes a subset of the wider category of symbolic processes guiding human action, or of discourses that guide practices.

Second, Colomer, like many others, emphasizes that his model need not reflect the actual intellectual, emotional, and moral processes that move human action—as long as its assumptions lead to deductions that are verified by the data.[15] We, also like many others, push instead in a realist direction. We prefer the assumptions to reflect the actual processes that move human action. Consider the following example: We count it as a point in favor of Marx's M—C—M' schema that it is realistic. People really do think in terms of getting more money back when they invest money. The general principles of accounting spell out in great detail how to count money with the intention of ending up with more than you started out with, and these principles are "the language of business." They are rules that *actually* guide life.

Third, Aristotle also observed that people make deliberate choices not on the basis of the facts, but rather on the basis of what they believe to be the facts. In Spain, for example, the military conspirators who took Parliament prisoner on February 23, 1981, made rational calculations that led them to attempt a coup, based on the belief that King Juan Carlos II, who was crowned as king shortly after Franco's death, would support them. What they believed was not a fact. The coup failed when Juan Carlos II spoke on the telephone to each of Spain's eleven regional military commanders, asking them to be loyal to him and to the Constitution, and then shortly afterward sent them telexes with the same message. We are among those who expand nearly to infinity Aristotle's concept that it is beliefs, and not facts, that determine action. The great majority, perhaps all, of the "facts" that guide human decisions are thoroughly embedded in systems of belief. Humans are not animals endowed with direct contact with reality. We live in dreams, and when we are lucky the relationship of our dreams to reality is not completely dysfunctional. We are scientific realists because we believe reality is there, and because we believe that the reason why scientific research has given humans immense power over nature during the past few centuries is that scientific methods succeed in finding out about reality. Yet we are cultural idealists because we believe that we humans live in our imaginations. In this sense we are all like Colonel Tejero when he marched at the head of his troops down the center aisle of the chambers of the Spanish Parliament, and up to the podium, shouting "In the name of the King!"[16]

Fourth, Colomer and game theorists generally focus on "preferences." Colomer explains the motives of the 23 February 1981 conspirators by saying they misunderstood the preferences of the King. Then he maps the preferences of Juan Carlos II, showing why his dominant preference was to be a constitutional monarch.[17] We have already implied that "preferences," whatever they may be, are embedded in belief-systems. Here we must add that decisions based on rational calculations are often not differentiated by preferences at all, but by beliefs about what the facts are, especially by beliefs about the causes that make the world the way it is.

Consider the following example. The preferences of leftist Basque terrorists are similar to the preferences of Pablo Iglesias in that both prefer a classless society and the self-determination of peoples.[18] For Iglesias causal power was to be found in organizing labor unions and political parties. The combination of economic and political power would make a world where socialism could be achieved. Many Spaniards, however, believe that such a causal analysis is incomplete. They speak of the de facto powers (the "*poderes facticos*") and often name them as the Army, the Banks, and the Church. Terrorists take the de facto power thesis a step further by holding that it is productive to attack the de facto powers physically. Thus there is a specious logic behind assassinating army officers, robbing banks, and burning churches. It is a logic that differs from that of Iglesias, and from that of law-abiding citizens generally, not in its preferences, but in its causal analysis of how the world works.

Our fifth methodological comment on Colomer's rational choice approach is that rational choice models have been accused of ethnocentrism. They are said to promote the ideology of *homo economicus* to the status of scientific method.[19] Colomer accommodates this criticism when he acknowledges that of course every rational choice has an institutional context. No great harm is done if in his research he assumes that every decision maker is a rational calculator of alternative payoffs, if we bear in mind that rational choice models are only models, which can be expected to apply, more or less, whenever the institutional context of the research is a context where, in fact, *homo economicus* dwells. Further, the great merit of model building is that by its clarity and specificity it permits tests which measure a model's conformity, or lack of conformity, to reality. If there are people somewhere and sometimes whose decisions cannot be understood with a rational choice approach, then the testing of models will discover their existence in due course. Meanwhile, Colomer's book does show that a rational choice approach does provide explanations of the decisions of political actors in the Spanish transition to democracy from 1975 to 1981.

Fine, but if we want to say that Colomer's book provides "explanations" of decisions as a result of quasi-economic payoff calculations, as distinct from saying that his approach "sheds light" on certain human decisions, then we must be content to use the word "explanations" in a weak sense. There is certainly no Newtonian inevitability in the explanations Colomer's book provides. Quite the contrary. Several times in the course of the book Colomer has occasion to confirm the words of the UCD leader Adolfo Suarez with which the book begins:

> An important lesson which I for one have learned from the Spanish democratic transition, in which I have decisively taken part, is that historical determinism does not exist. In living and making this period of history, I have received the most important ratification of an essential idea: that the future, far from being decided, is always the realm of liberty, open and uncertain, although foreseeable by the analyses of the structural conditions and the operating forces of the society in which we live, the most essential of which is the free will of those men who shape history.[20]

Now, instead of regarding the question as one concerning how to achieve knowledge in the social sciences, let us regard the question as one concerning how to achieve the ethical construction of social democracy. We should be able to accept the observation that the rational choice approach bears a certain ideological affinity to capitalism. However, it seems pointless to say that for the sake of improving society—and not just explaining it—we should advocate irrationality. We should instead advocate deliberation and choice according to a better logic, a logic that embodies higher stages of moral development. Making rational choices according to a better logic does not necessarily mean that the majority of the population has to achieve higher scores on the moral development tests that psychologists have devised. It can mean, instead or in addition, that the normal conventions of society, the ones reflected by the "conventional stage" of the psychologists' tests, evolve to reflect better conventional norms.

Our sixth and final methodological comment is that it is thus advisable to broaden the rational choice approach in two directions: cultural and realist. Culturally, it is wise to remember that rational choice methodology is so thoroughly embedded in historically constructed social institutions that its very terms carry the freight of modern western capitalist metaphysical commitments. To say "preferences," "actor," "decision," "payoff, "rational calculation" is already to enter a discourse with a context. It is not to mirror human nature as it is and always will be. It is to choose a vocabulary. Conversely, the enormous variety of the cultural structures studied by historians, archaeologists, and anthropologists is only a foretaste of the even greater variety of cultural structures that are possible and might be invented. We have more choices than we know we have.

Realistically, there are physical facts that are not institutional facts. One of them is that there could be enough for everybody. With the knowledge that the physical and biological sciences have, or could acquire, all human needs could be met without ecological damage. It is physically possible to implement population policies that would stabilize the earth's population at whatever number is sustainable. It is a physical fact that the long-awaited and often-frustrated civilization of *agape*, where everybody is included and nobody is rejected, is an ever-present possibility.

Let us return now to a consideration of Marx's schema M—C—M'. In the second volume of *Capital*, which is devoted to the circulation of money and capital, Marx gives an expanded version of the M—C—M' schema as follows:

$$M—C—P—C'—M'$$

In this diagram M stands for the money initially invested to buy commodities. The commodities Marx particularly has in mind are the ingredients of production: labor-power, raw materials, and whatever else is needed for production. P stands for production. The key point in the diagram is P, because it is through production that C turns into C'. C' is commodities again, but this time it is commodities with greater value. The increase in value is due to a remarkable quality Marx attributes to labor-power and to nothing else. Labor-power is a commodity that produces value. The value of the commodities the workers produce exceeds the cost of the labor-power that the capitalist purchases. *Voila tout.* The sale of C' (the augmented commodity) yields M', the augmented money, which is what the investor wanted in the first place, and which is the point and purpose of the exercise. By this elaboration Marx subtracts from rather than adds to the realism of the M—C—M' schema.[21] Making money is indeed a conscious intention of investors. It is generally realistic to say that if they did not make money by hiring workers, and by using their labor power to produce more than it cost, then they would not hire them. Marx, however, did not leave it at that. He went on to explain a great mystery, namely, "How is profit possible?" By advancing the plausible theory that it was possible because of the exploitation of labor he added to the scientific prestige of socialism. As plausible as this explanation was, however, over the years it has not withstood scientific scrutiny.[22]

In any case, giving a scientific answer to the question "How is profit possible?" is not really the point. To paraphrase Marx himself, the scientists have only explained the world in various ways. The point, however, is to change it: to achieve, "production by society for itself." And quite apart from the merits (scientific and ethical) of Marx's theory that profit comes from exploitation, his theory does not deny, and indeed it presupposes, that whatever goes on in the sphere of production, the purpose of the process is established by the requirements of circulation. The desired conclusion is always the sale of the product: more money.

Three examples may help to clarify what we mean by the subordination of production to circulation:

Example 1. A sea-going freighter has two sets of officers. The deck officers are in charge of loading and unloading cargo and steering the ship. The engine officers are in charge of keeping the ship going. The captain of the ship is always a deck officer. This is to be expected. A commercial ship is a means for making money. Money is made not inside the ship, but in the ship's transactions with the outside world, as it takes on cargo and puts cargo off.

Example 2. The Chief Executive Officer of a large corporation normally comes from finance or from sales. If, in an unusual case, a production manager advances to CEO, it is not because of his or her skill in producing goods or services, but because of skills more directly related to making the business profitable. The accountants, not the engineers, write the bottom lines.

Example 3. When the striking workers took over Italian automobile factories in Turin in 1921, they found that "possessing the means of production" did not do them any good. They could not buy the raw materials that went into production, and they could not sell the products that came out.

The rule that circulation frames and directs production—represented in the schema M—C—M' in both its short and expanded versions—is not a rule that regulates capitalism. It constitutes capitalism. It constitutes production for exchange, which is not production directly for use, but production for the sake of selling for money. Even if one considers that a proper definition of capitalism must include other elements, the M—C—M' relationship is still constitutive, not merely regulative. It must be implicitly or explicitly part, even if not necessarily all, of a definition of capitalism. It is not a mere rule of the game; rather, it is what creates the game.

Production for exchange is a basic cultural structure. It is "realistic" as an assumption in the social sciences because it is what people really do. It describes a set of working norms that guide human action, rather than being a "factor" derived from the statistical analysis of data, like the "factors" that are said to make up intelligence. But M—C—M' is not "real" in the sense of "physically real independently of human practices." Societies in which the production of commodities for exchange prevails are indeed a minority among the societies known to anthropology and to history. The schema M—C—M' is a socially constructed reality, and it is neither the worst nor the best of the realities humans have constructed. *It can be deconstructed and reconstructed.*

Without being physically real, it is "basic" because it governs what Marx called the metabolism of society, the exchange of matter and energy with the environment, work. When the prerequisites for cycle after cycle of M—C—M' (i.e., "accumulation") are not in place, then, physically, things stop. Factories lie idle. Bread lines form, as well as lines to buy toilet paper, matches, gasoline, diapers, and whatever else turns out to be scarce. This basic cultural structure, situated strategically at the intersection of culture and nature, has ramifications for all aspects of life.

In view of the basic constitutive rules of exchange, one must question whether the program of the PSOE was at all feasible. Nothing jolts investor confidence, and therefore the M—C—M' cycle and the tranquility of a nation, like a proposal to redistribute property, especially if the proposal appears to be accompanied by the power to implement it.

When the PSOE won an absolute majority in Parliament in 1982 it no longer advocated the rapid socialization of the means of production called for by the program adopted in Barcelona in 1888. Nevertheless, even the moderate program on which the party campaigned in 1982 proposed to shift economic power in favor of the organized workers and against owners. The new program called for "socialization" in ways that did not necessarily mean expropriation, but did mean "social control," or "limiting international dependence." They did mean, "penetration of the power of capital through augmenting the power of labor unions, small business supported by the state, cooperatives, and municipal governments."[23] The 1982 PSOE platform called for "real equality" and proposed to remove the obstacles in civil society (in the schools, in labor relations, in consumption, etc.) that impede this "real equality."[24]

Was this too much to ask? As ideology, it was just what candidate and future Prime Minister Felipe González said it was, "the deepening of democracy in every direction."[25] As economics, however, it was a formidable challenge. The challenge was to reshape a society that was already shaped so as to require constant care and feeding to coax investors into initiating the processes that led to the good things everybody wanted: jobs, goods, services, tax revenues. It is not easy to reshape society and maximize incentives for investors simultaneously. The first task requires whittling away at the privileges of property. The second requires catering to its every whim.

Even before the PSOE won the 1982 elections, it had already made a series of compromises with the owners of the means of production by participating in "social pacts" sponsored by the UCD in 1977, 1979, 1980, and 1981. The pacts were comprehensive multi-issue agreements designed, among other things, to achieve labor peace by making limited concessions to workers in return for a no-strike pledge. In the first series of pacts, known as "Moncloa Pacts" because the presidential Moncloa Palace was the place where representatives of the "social partners" sat down to negotiate them, the socialists joined in reassuring business interests that no nationalizations were planned. "They can rest assured," said González.[26]

The Moncloa Pacts and their successors prescribed an austerity program described as uniting the nation behind rational economic measures that would

build a healthy economy for everyone's benefit. The prescribed measures succeeded in reducing inflation slightly, in bringing the Spanish balance of payments back into surplus, and in increasing exports. While wages were kept in
check, the increase in employment that was supposed to follow failed to materi-
alize. Instead, unemployment soared, leaving the Spanish working class to bear
the brunt of the economic crisis.[27]

By the time the PSOE government took office it was not only the working
class who found that the UCD's social pacts were not working. Spain's Gross
Domestic Product was growing at only 1.7 percent per year, which was unfa-
vorably compared to 7.5 percent per year growth from 1960 to 1970 during the
"Spanish economic miracle" under Franco.[28] One logical approach to the perceived failure of the social pacts was to say that although labor had made sacrifices to boost profitability and investor confidence, it had not made enough sacrifices. The working classes would have to sacrifice still more to boost GDP
growth to the desired levels in order indirectly and eventually to achieve its own
goals of lower unemployment and higher wages.

Left-wing elements within the PSOE called for another solution: they
wished to use state investment to expand economic activity, modernize industry
to make it more efficient by means of state-sponsored programs, and ban capital
flight to prevent investors from seeking greener pastures elsewhere.

Was there really a choice? Or was the "expansionary" solution advocated
by the left-wing critics within the PSOE just a pipedream, which, if it had been
tried, would have led to the same dismal results produced by such measures
elsewhere? Adam Przeworski has argued that in such situations social democrats
do not have a real choice, but must bow to reality by doing whatever is necessary to increase the profitability of business:

> Once private property of the means of production was left intact, it became in
> the interest of wage-earners that capitalists appropriate profits. Under capital-
> ism the profits of today are the condition of investment and hence production,
> employment, and consumption in the future. . . . Social democracies protect
> profits from the demands of the masses because radical redistributive policies
> are not in the interest of wage-earners. No one drew the blueprint and yet the
> capitalist system is designed in such a way that if profits are not sufficient, then
> eventually wage rates or employment must fail. Crises of capitalism are in no
> one's mutual interest; they are a threat to wage-earners since capitalism is a
> system in which economic crises must inevitably fall on their shoulders.[29]

We would revise Przeworski's first sentence in the quoted paragraph to read:
"Once private property of the means of production was left intact, and as long as
accumulation is the motor of production, it is in the interest of wage-earners that
capitalists appropriate profits."

Felipe González and the PSOE did what modern European social democrats
normally do, which is what they perceive they have to do: whatever is necessary

to create the conditions under which the M—C—M' cycles of accumulation can move forward. It happened that the PSOE was voted into office at a time when capitalism worldwide found that the type of "regime of accumulation" it required was one that some scholars call "flexible accumulation," i.e., breaking down the "rigidities" that hampered profit-seeking due to labor union power and government social policies during the heyday of the welfare state and Keynesian economics.[30]

Thus the historical role of the PSOE in Spain was to break the social consensus negotiated under the UCD government by imposing policies akin to those of Ronald Reagan in the United States, Margaret Thatcher in the United Kingdom, and Helmut Kohl in West Germany. Such policies included limiting wages; reducing government expenditures; restructuring heavy industry to immediately lay off 65,000 workers and to lay off more in successive waves; devaluing the Spanish *peseta*; raising the prices of electricity, gasoline, and public transportation; cutting pensions; tightening requirements for pension recipients; capping payments to the sick, injured, and elderly; and increasing payroll deductions to fund social security.[31] Prime Minister González admitted on Spanish television: "It is true, as the unions contend, that workers' salaries have risen more slowly than the owners' income. That is the way it is all over Europe, and that is the way it should be in the early stages of recovery. Only this way can profits be invested in productive sectors of the economy."[32]

Consistent with its new-found faith in market-based solutions, and contrary to the platform it ran on in 1982, the PSOE took steps to diminish Spanish self-reliance, which had been carefully nurtured under Franco, and to integrate Spain into global markets. Perhaps the crowning blow came when the French and German governments insisted that free trade in Europe be accompanied by a "social charter" guaranteeing certain basic social rights to workers. The Spanish PSOE government, aware that Spain's comparative advantage in Europe rested on cheap labor, watered down the social charter to make it a matter of national discretion.

Perhaps the most severe challenge faced by the PSOE government, and by its successor, the center-right *Partido Popular*, has been the continual assassinations, robberies, and bombings, carried out by the Basque terrorists. The King's repeated pronouncements that it is illusory to think that a suspension of the Constitution would permit an effective crackdown on terrorists are hardly comforting—since they imply that there are army officers who need to hear the King's message. Like the British in Northern Ireland, and like the United States government trying to combat gangs and drugs in America's inner cities, the Spanish government is engaged in trying to prove that crime does not pay, and that functioning normally as a law-abiding citizen does pay. Again like the British, and like other democratic governments around the world trying to wean defiant ethnic minorities away from violence, the Spanish government finds that the structural limitations on its ability to deliver social justice frustrate its efforts to prove that democracy works while terrorism does not.

We do not mean to imply that an appreciation of the constraints that the basic cultural structures of exchange impose on the achievement of social justice implies that the terrorists have correctly understood power and politics. Cn the contrary. Identifying the problem as cultural and structural strengthens the case for education, and weakens the case for violence.

Nor do we mean to imply that when the socialists wrote their 1982 electoral platform they were lying to the dispossessed classes of Spain by promising them changes they knew they could not deliver. Felipe González, Alfonso Guerra, and the majority faction of the PSOE, which turned out to be the staff of the political administration that brought neoliberalism to Spain, were quite aware in 1982 that "the deepening of democracy in every direction" was hard to achieve, but they specifically mentioned two good reasons for believing that although it was difficult it was not impossible.[33] The good reasons they gave were the examples of Sweden and Austria. Although the constitutive rules of capitalism, diagrammed by Marx as the M—C—M' schema, and summarized by Przeworski's statement of the need to protect profits from mass demands, might seem to imply that we cannot simultaneously administer capitalism and transform it, it seemed that there must be some flaw in any logic requiring that implication. There had to be a flaw, for the Swedes and Austrians had in fact done it. What exists must by definition be possible. In the next chapter we turn to Sweden, one of the alleged living proofs that social democracy can be not just a dream, but a reality.

Notes

1. We dedicate this chapter to Tania Mireles and Bill Shorr as Howard Richards' apology for being unable to attend their marriage ceremony.

2. Collier, *Socialists of Rural Andalusia*, 151.

3. We agree with Bourdieu's scathing attack on rational choice theory, but we do not think his emphasis on habitus provides a fully adequate alternative. It gives to little weight to the constitutive rules of the logic of exchange. Pierre Bourdieu, *The Logic of Practice* (Stanford, Calif.: Stanford University Press, 1990), 47-51, 63-64.

4. In the 1982 election, the PSOE received 10.12 million votes, 4.6 million more than in the previous election. Of these over four million new voters for the PSOE, almost half were new voters, and most of the remainder were voters who had previously voted for either the UCD or the Communists. The UCD's collapse in 1982 was definitive: from receiving almost 35 percent of the vote in the previous election, support for the UCD dropped to seven percent, and the number of seats held by the party dropped from 168 to a mere twelve. In early 1983, the party formally disbanded. Santos Juliá, "The Socialist era, 1982-1996," in *Spanish History Since 1808,* ed. Alvarez Junco and Shubert, 331-32; Share, *Dilemmas of Social Democracy*, 101; Edward Moxon-Browne, *Political Change in Spain* (London and New York: Routledge, 1989), 23.

5. The *Falange* ("Phalanx"), or "*Falange Española*," was founded in the autumn of 1933 by José Antonio Primo de la Rivera, son of the dictator Miguel Primo de la Rivera. At the time of its founding, it was the fifth political party of the radical right wing in Spain, and it soon became the most prominent and deadliest party of the right. On its founding and early history, see the works by Stanley G. Payne, *Falange: A History of Spanish Fascism* (Stanford, Calif.: Stanford University Press, 1961), 38-48; and *Fascism in Spain,* 69-114.

6. This abolition of the civil rights of women was consistent with the fascist doctrine that the primary social function and highest aspiration of women was motherhood. In Spain, the fascists also drew upon an older and particularly Spanish Catholic cultural norm that held that the role of a woman was that of "*perfecta casada*," "the perfect married lady, submissive spouse and mother lovingly devoted to the needs of husband, children and home." Pilar Primo de la Rivera, the leader of the official Francoist women's organization "Sección Femenina," stated that motherhood was a mandate for women, "'a biological, Christian and Spanish function.'" Mary Nash, "Towards a new moral order: National Catholicism, culture and gender," in Alvarez Junco and Shubert, *Spanish History Since 1808,* 296.

7. On the collapse of the UCD, see David Gilmour, *The Transformation of Spain: From Franco to the Constitutional Monarchy* (London; New York; Melbourne: Quartet Books, 1985), 249-68. The internal squabbling over the issue of divorce was the crowning blow that led to the collapse of the UCD, but Gilmour delineates a longer process in the downfall of the UCD, starting with its contradictory stances on the issue of the "state of autonomies" demanded by certain regions within the territorial boundaries of Spain and specifically the UCD's decision to grant elements of autonomy to Galicia, Catalonia, and the Basque country and not to Andalusia.

8. Paul Preston, *The Triumph of Democracy in Spain* (London and New York: Methuen, 1986), 211.

9. Josep M. Colomer, *Game Theory and the Transition to Democracy: The Spanish Model* (Aldershot, U.K.: Edward Elgar Publishing, 1995).

10. Colomer, *Game Theory and the Transition to Democracy*, 4-5.

11. Colomer, *Game Theory and the Transition to Democracy*, 4.

12. Colomer, *Game Theory and the Transition to Democracy*, 6.

13. Colomer, *Game Theory and the Transition to Democracy*, 68-77. Colomer offers details that we omit.

14. Colomer, *Game Theory and the Transition to Democracy*, 113-23.

15. Colomer states that his first assumption is "that the decisions of actors can be explained as being derived from rational calculations." He goes on to state, "This does not mean that the actual intellectual, moral and emotional processes which occurred in the brains and hearts of political activists, professional politicians and members of the military . . . were the graphic schemes, curves and matrices presented herein. Formal tools such as these simply serve to reduce the huge amount of intervening factors in the real world to those which allow the author and the reader to have a clear and parsimonious explanation of the real outcomes. . . . The advantage of the formal, deductive reasoning characteristic of the rational choice approach, is that it permits the identification of those elements which can explain real outcomes in a more accurate and precise manner than the conventional method of inductive generalization from empirical observations. Once a set of alternatives, relevant actors and preferences has been put forth and the deductive implications of the analysis have been formulated, the contrast between formal results and real outcomes can either confirm the validity of the explanation or suggest a modification or enlargement of the assumptions in order to produce a fit between the model and reality." Colomer, *Game Theory and the Transition to Democracy,* 4-5.

16. In her consideration of lying as a component of political discourse, Hannah Arendt offers a comment on the tenacity of human imagination in the face of "facts." She writes, "Lies are often much more plausible, more appealing to reason, than reality, since the liar has the great advantage of knowing beforehand what the audience wishes or expects to hear. He has prepared his story for public consumption with a careful eye to making it credible, whereas reality has the disconcerting habit of confronting us with the unexpected, for which we were not prepared." Hannah Arendt, "Lying in Politics: Reflections on the Pentagon Papers," in *Crises of the Republic* (New York: Harcourt Brace Jovanovich, Inc., 1972), 6-7. Historians have documented numerous instances in which collective imagination—as opposed to "facts"—has had the power to alter the course of history of nation-states. Eric Van Young, for example, documents the notion of "mystical kingship" among working class Mexicans during the battles that would give way to Mexican independence from Spain. Fighting explicitly under the banner of "Our Lady of Guadalupe" and of the deposed King of Spain Ferdinand VII, indigenous and mestizo working class Mexicans acted upon their long-held grievances against *gachupines*, the peninsular-born Spaniards. It was their imagined notion that they were acting on the authority of King Ferdinand that gave them the power to act in such a collective and forceful manner. So fervent was their loyalty to this mythical and completely absent king that throughout the independence struggle, rumors spread throughout the Mexican countryside of sightings of King Ferdinand's coach rolling by. Eric Van Young, "Quetzalcóatl, King Ferdinand, and Ignacio Allende Go to the Seashore; or Messianism and Mystical Kingship in Mexico, 1800-1821," in *The Independence of Mexico and the Creation of the New Nation,* ed. Jaime E. Rodríguez O. (Los Angeles: UCLA Latin American Center Publications, 1989), 109-27; and Eric Van Young, *The Other Rebellion: Popular Violence, Ide-*

ology, and the Mexican Struggle for Independence, 1810-1821 (Stanford, Calif.: Stanford University Press, 2001). Perhaps the best-known work treating the role of human imagination in the rise and maintenance of the historical form of the nation-state is Benedict Anderson's *Imagined Communities: Reflections on the Origin and Spread of Nationalism* (London and New York: Verso, 1983). Anderson defines the nation as "an imagined political community. . . . It is *imagined* because the members of even the smallest nation will never know most of their fellow-members, meet them, or even hear of them, yet in the minds of each lives the image of their communion." Anderson, *Imagined Communities*, 15. For his notion of "imagined communities," Anderson in turn draws upon the ideas of Hugh Seton-Watson. See Hugh Seton-Watson, *Nations and States: An Enquiry into the Origins of Nations and the Politics of Nationalism* (Boulder, Colo.: Westview Press, 1977).

17. Colomer, *Game Theory and the Transition to Democracy* , 116-21.

18. Iglesias showed this latter preference when he opposed Spain's invasion of Morocco, not just because he did not want to see drafted Spanish workers killed in a war from which they would derive no benefit, but also because, to paraphrase Iglesias, the Moroccans are our brothers, entitled to self-determination the same as we are. See Morato, *Pablo Iglesias Posse*, 180-86.

19. Michel Plon, *La théorie des jeux: une politique imaginaire* (Paris: Francois Maspero, 1976), 12-23, 69-100.

20. Adolfo Suarez quoted in Colomer, *Game Theory and the Transition to Democracy*, 1.

21. This elaboration takes place in Volume I of *Capital*, although the schematic diagram we have reproduced here does not appear until Volume II.

22. Joan Robinson, *An Essay on Marxian Economics* (London; Melbourne; Toronto: Macmillan, 1967). Robinson disproves several of Marx's economic theories, but of particular interest to us are her comments on the labor theory of value. Robinson criticizes Marx for constructing a rather murky correspondence between value and price. According to the labor theory of value, only socially necessary labor-time can create value. The difference between this value and price, a difference that comprises surplus-value, determines the rate of exploitation. Robinson states that by his own definition of socially necessary labor-time as the creator of value, Marx should have allowed for greater variations in constructions of what constitutes "socially necessary" on the basis, precisely, of "demand." She states that Marx does not adequately take into account the idea that the scarcity of natural factors of production will increase the labor-time necessary for production and thus also influence price. Thus, argues Robinson, it is too simple for Marx to contend that relative prices correspond directly to relative *values*, for this contention, taken to its logical conclusion, would mean that the rate of exploitation is equal in all industries, which Marx's theory does not in fact hold. Robinson demonstrates that this discrepancy arises from Marx's faulty assumption, tied to the labor theory of value, that there is a uniform rate of exploitation at ground level (i.e., at the level of the generation of surplus-value). Robinson, *An Essay on Marxian Economics*, 14-15. It is important to note that Robinson has no intention of debunking or dismissing Marx, from whom she believes we still have much to learn. In fact, she writes, "[N]o point of substance in Marx's argument depends upon the labor theory of value." Robinson, *An Essay on Marxian Economics*, 22.

23. Platform of the PSOE quoted in Anton Sarasqueta, *De Franco a Felipe* (Barcelona: Plaza & Janes, 1984), 130-34.

24. On the promotion of social equality and other parts of the PSOE platform during the 1982 campaign, see Bruce Young, "The 1982 Elections and the Democratic Transition in Spain," in *Democratic Politics in Spain: Spanish Politics after Franco*, ed. David S. Bell (London: Frances Pinter, 1983), 143-44.

25. Felipe González quoted in Share, *Dilemmas of Social Democracy*, 139.

26. Felipe González, *Socialismo es Libertad* (Barcelona: Galba, 1978), 263. Felipe González made this statement in his speech presenting the Moncloa agreements to parliament. The first round of Moncloa Pacts was signed in October 1977 by representatives of the Spanish government and of all political parties. By the terms of the Moncloa Pacts, the unions accepted a 20 percent limit on wage increases and limits on public spending and agreed to assist in containing worker unrest in return for a promised 22 percent limit on price increases, an expansion of unemployment benefits, the creation of new jobs. The working class and the political left were also assured that in return for their acceptance of the terms of the Moncloa Pacts, the government would undertake educational and syndical reforms that would assist in further consolidating democratic rule in Spain. Share, *Dilemmas of Social Democracy*, 50-51. See this work by Share generally for an account of the PSOE in office.

27. Víctor M. Pérez-Díaz, *The Return of Civil Society: The Emergence of Democratic Spain* (Cambridge, Mass.; and London: Harvard University Press, 1993), 227; Share, *Dilemmas of Social Democracy*, 50-51. Spanish workers suffered the loss of an estimated 1.8 million jobs between 1973 and 1982, with the losses concentrated in the industrial sector. By the mid-1980s, shortly after the PSOE took office, Spain's rate of unemployment, at twenty percent, was the highest among all member nations in the Organization for Economic Cooperation and Development (OECD), and Spain's working population as a percentage of the total Spanish population was one of the lowest, at 48 percent. Pérez-Díaz, *Return of Civil Society*, 227. For an analysis of the Moncloa Pacts specifically, see Curro Ferraro, *Economía y explotación en la democracia Española* (Bilbao, Spain: ZYX, 1978).

28. Joseph Harrison, *The Spanish economy: From the Civil War to the European Community* (Cambridge; New York; and Melbourne: Cambridge University Press, 1995), 13, 18; Pérez-Díaz, *Return of Civil Society*, 216.

29. Adam Przeworski, quoted in Share, *Dilemmas of Social Democracy*, 3. Przeworksi, who advocates socialism as opposed to social democracy, faults social democratic parties for their devotion to Keynesian macroeconomic policies and the welfare state. Such devotion, he asserts, might function effectively to assuage the legitimate grievances of the working class during times of economic growth, but this same devotion leaves social democratic parties little choice but to adopt draconian austerity measures during periods of economic stagnation. In addition, he argues, Keynesian macroeconomic policies only serve to smooth over the inherent contradictions contained within capitalism, and it is only by allowing these contradictions to come to the fore, with all the brutality that implies, that the transition to socialism will be made. Adam Przeworski, *Capitalism and Social Democracy* (Cambridge: Cambridge University Press, 1986), 40-45. See also Charles E. Lindblom, "The Market as Prison," *Journal of Politics* 44, no. 2 (May 1982): 324-36; and Claus Offe, *Strukturprobleme des kapitalistischen Staates* (Frankfurt: Suhrkamp, 1972).

30. David Harvey coined the term "flexible accumulation" to denote the historical period that followed Fordism, which is also known as the historic capital-labor alliance or accord. Fordism is generally recognized by historians to have been in effect from World

War II through approximately 1973. Harvey defines "flexible accumulation" as "[resting] on flexibility with respect to labour processes, labour markets, products, and patterns of consumption" and "characterized by the emergence of entirely new sectors of production, new ways of providing financial services, new markets, and, above all, greatly intensified rates of commercial, technological, and organizational innovation." David Harvey, *The Condition of Postmodernity: an Enquiry into the Origins of Cultural Change* (Oxford and Cambridge: Basil Blackwell, 1989), 147.

31. Pérez-Díaz, *Return of Civil Society*, 91; Share, *Dilemmas of Social Democracy*, 71-79; Moxon-Browne, *Political Change in Spain*, 9.

32. González quoted in Share, *Dilemmas of Social Democracy*, 151.

33. Pedro Calvo Hernando, *Todos me dicen Felipe* (Barcelona: Plaza & Janes, 1987), 239.

Chapter 5

A Modest Hypothesis Concerning
Swedish Social Democracy

Whatever they might have learned from the teachings of Karl Marx in the early years before they became Sweden's perennial ruling party in 1932, the Swedish socialists in office have drawn from Marx very little inspiration. Perhaps it is a generically Marxist idea that workers need to organize politically and economically in order to struggle for their rights, and perhaps in that generic sense they have been good Marxists. On the whole, however, since the Social Democrats initiated their long reign as Sweden's governing party, Swedish social democracy has been guided by its own *sui generis* ideas, formed in the light of Sweden's historical circumstances and in dialogue with mainstream currents of Western academic social science.

In the 1930s the economists of the Stockholm School—Gunnar Myrdal, Erik Lundberg, Dag Hammarskjöld, and others—worried about the same problems John Maynard Keynes was worrying about in England, stimulated by the worldwide Great Depression. They and he contributed to formulating what has become known as macroeconomics.[1] The practical applications of macroeconomics tend toward macro-managing an economy to improve its performance by using policy instruments to affect a few key variables. Swedish social democracy can be viewed to a large extent as an exercise in macroeconomic policy formation, in a country where 90 percent of the workforce is unionized, in a small open economy exporting paper and wood products and other goods to pay for petroleum and other imports, where the culture is permeated by a strong social conscience committed mainly to what Gunnar Myrdal called "the eighteenth century ideals."[2] Liberty. Equality. Fraternity.

At least since the sudden increases in oil prices in 1973, as Sweden and other advanced economies have faltered, confidence in the conceptual framework provided by macroeconomic thinking has waned. In Sweden as elsewhere many economists have been advocating a retreat from the *dirigisme* associated with macroeconomics, and a turn toward leaving social decisions to market forces. Sweden's entrance into the European Union and its increased integration into the global economy have reduced its capacity to implement autonomous social policies at a national level. Many speak of what Erik Lundberg called "the rise and fall of the Swedish model."[3]

In their heyday, the Swedish Social Democrats performed miracles. They achieved the impossible—that is, the impossible according to theories other than their own. On most versions of classical political economy, including most versions of Marxism, an iron law of wages necessarily keeps wages down, but in Sweden—and in other countries that implemented similar ideas—wages rose rather than fell.[4] Many would think it impossible, too, to compel the owners of capital to keep their enterprises in place and running when profits were low, when they could take their capital elsewhere to invest it at a higher rate of return. Yet in Sweden for many years profits were deliberately squeezed between high wages on the one side and high taxes on the other side.[5] Nevertheless, industry kept running. It did not leave. It did not slow down. It grew. Is it possible to squeeze profits and maintain full employment? Sweden showed that it was.

Many think it impossible also to tax the rich heavily without drying up the sources of capital for investment. Yet in the 1960s Sweden had some of the highest and most progressive taxes in the world, and at the same time one of the world's highest rates of capital formation. Some say that success in the global economic race is cumulative, so that poor countries that get behind necessarily stay behind. Yet Sweden, which in the early twentieth century was a poor country from which a quarter of the population emigrated to America to escape misery, under the Social Democrats caught up with and passed nations which had been far richer. To many it seems impossible to practice free trade without dragging down wages to the level of the world's lowest paid workers. Yet Sweden practiced free trade while raising wages to the point where Swedish wages became among the world's highest. It is argued that people will not work when taxes are high, because people will prefer leisure to turning over more than half their income to the government. Yet Sweden has simultaneously had high taxes and one of the world's highest rates of participation in the workforce.

It is said that enormous incentives for executives (such as the huge salaries paid to chief executive officers of U.S. corporations) are necessary to corporate success. Yet tiny Sweden, a nation of merely eight million people, managed to be home to multinational corporations that were global winners, while U.S.-based corporations lost market share in almost every category. It is said that societies cannot involve government bureaucracies and labor unions in business policy decisions without depriving management of the flexibility it needs to adapt to new technologies and changing markets. Yet Swedish exporters have adapted to new technologies and changing markets faster, not slower, than their competitors. According to prominent economic theories it is impossible to compress wage scales in a way that makes wages nearly equal without destroying workers' motivations to perform well and learn new skills. Yet Sweden deliberately adopted a solidaristic wage policy, raising preferentially the wages of the lowest paid, while maintaining and upgrading one of the world's most highly skilled workforces.[6] It is argued that socialist medicine can only demoralize the medical profession and lower the quality of care. Yet objective measures such as life expectancy show that health care in Sweden is better, not worse, than health care in countries that rely on capitalist medicine.

Generally, Swedish social democracy was able to redistribute the benefits of the economy while operating the economy efficiently and productively. Redistribution did not shut down production. We do not want to exaggerate Sweden's achievements: ownership of Swedish industry never ceased to be concentrated in a few families. Nevertheless, the *meaning* of "ownership" was considerably transformed. Sweden has always had its share of complaints, complainers, and things about which to complain. Nevertheless, Sweden became what its great socialist prime minister Per Albin Hansson called a *folkshemmet*, a home for all Swedes.

Even at the height of its glory the Swedish model had its critics. There were always academics, many of them well funded by non-socialist funding agencies, who wrote mathematically elegant empirical studies based on Swedish statistical data, which argued that Sweden would have been even more prosperous than it already was, were it not for the "distortions," "tax wedges," "inefficiencies," "deadweight losses," and "hidden costs" imposed on it by the *dirigisme* of its socialist governments and its strong trade unions.[7] It was argued that the success of the Social Democrats in coping with the Depression of the 1930s was due less to their Keynesian policies than to the stimulation of Swedish exports by Hitler's rearmament program.[8] While Sweden led the world on virtually every measure of social welfare, however, the voices of the critics rang hollow. When the oil price shocks hit an economy that already had structural problems, when the government began to run huge deficits that could only be covered by borrowing abroad, when there were five successive devaluations of the Swedish *krona*, when unemployment began to be a serious problem, when Swedish Gross Domestic Product per capita dropped from the top tier to the middle tier in the ranks of industrialized nations, then the voices of neoliberal critics were heard.

We seek to demonstrate that the resurgence of the influence of conservative economic ideas in Sweden has been due less to their merits than to the exposure of the weaknesses of the quasi-Keynesian Swedish path to socialism.[9] The historical evolution of the Swedish and global economies, which are best understood in the conceptual framework of a philosophy of cultural action, led to a situation where the limitations of what can be done with macroeconomics, which were always clear in theory, became clear in practice.

In 1937, a year after the publication of Keynes' *General Theory*, Erik Lundberg, then one of the younger members of the Stockholm School, published his doctoral dissertation, *Studies in the Theory of Economic Expansion*. In it, he later claimed, he revealed the secret of the instability of a free market economy. When Paul Samuelson wrote his influential *Foundations of Economic Analysis*, he only added mathematical rigor to macroeconomic concepts Lundberg had developed earlier. The cause of the built-in instability of a free market economy, according to Lundberg, was "the combination of the acceleration principle (which determined investment) and the consumption function."[10]

Lundberg was concerned with the same problems that preoccupied Keynes and others at the time. The idea that free markets automatically set the right prices and produced a balanced equilibrium (conceived by analogy with equilibrium in physics) did not seem consistent with the historical experience of people who were living through the Great Depression. The microeconomic approach, which tends to start with the individual economic actor and his, her, or its preferences, was beginning to be questioned by and combined with an approach concerned more with what happens when national accounts, which consider aggregates of all transactions in an economy, are kept.[11]

In the background of macroeconomic thinking is the premise that one person's purchase is another person's sale. Therefore (omitting some complications) when all the purchases and all the sales (including the purchases and sales of labor power for wages) are added up, the two totals must be equal. In the aggregate, total sales equal total purchases. Or, total income equals total expenses.

But people do not spend all their income on making purchases for purposes of consumption. People save some of their incomes. Therefore, in the aggregate, the next time around, there will not be enough money circulating for everyone to have the same income they had the first time around. Unless. Unless the money that was saved somehow gets back into circulation. This would happen if it were all invested. Paul Samuelson in his *Foundations of Economic Analysis* expressed such a situation in the formula: $Y = C + I$. In this formula, Y equals national income at current prices, C equals consumer spending, and I equals investment expenditures. He treats this formula as "clearly" true, abstracting for the moment from sequences as one time follows another, as if taking a still snapshot of an economy.[12]

But in the real world, which is always moving, investment is not necessarily high enough to make aggregate spending high enough to compensate for the gap left by a less-than-total propensity to consume. We want C and I together to be big enough to total a sustainable Y, so that the national accounts will keep balancing, and the system can keep going another time around. We want people to spend enough to sustain everybody's incomes. Purchases by consumers or investments by business people (or both), however, may lag. Therefore, the system is unstable.

Consistent with this thought, there is an observable recurrent tendency to produce more than can be sold of just about everything, with more of just about everything (including labor power) tending to be offered in the market than willing buyers will buy. More people than jobs, too many antique malls for the number of people who want to buy antiques, more apples than apple-buyers, more consultants than people who want to consult them, more lawyers than cases, too many restaurants for the number of diners who eat out, more little boys who want to shine shoes and sell gum than tourists who want shoes shined and gum to chew. On this macroeconomic way of looking at tendencies observed in frequent experience, the standard microeconomic view—that overproduction of something just shows that market signals are telling us that resources should be diverted from producing it to producing something else—is wrong. Overproduction is not just a microeconomic mistake made by apple growers or potato growers or any producers of any particular product (say, to take an even more important example, the parents who produce labor supply by creating babies). A tendency toward "overproduction" is a generic macroeconomic feature of the system as a whole. We put "overproduction" in quotation marks because experience tells us that there may well be not enough food, in the sense that there are people who need food, at the same time there is "overproduction" of food, in the sense that the food already produced cannot be sold for enough money to pay the costs of producing it.

Therefore, an interventionist government, a certain amount of *dirigisme*, is justified for the purpose of implementing policies that will compensate for the system's inherent instability. Gunnar Myrdal argued at the close of World War II that capitalism left to itself was an inherently unstable system, which had only recovered from the Great Depression because of enormous amounts of government spending during the war. Therefore, the Swedish government should continue after the war to play the stabilizing role in the Swedish economy that it had played during the 1930s and during wartime.[13]

Swedish and other Scandinavian economists developed a variation of macroeconomics that distinguished the "tradable" from the "nontradable" sector. For small open economies like theirs, the prices of goods like lumber, which they export, are set by international markets over which they have virtually no influence. The "tradable" sector is the sector where Sweden is a price-taker, accepting whatever international prices might be with no ability to change them. The situation is different with "nontradables," such as, for example, the provision of day care for working parents by Swedish local county governments.[14]

From the time of the formulation of standard components of macroeconomic thinking by the Stockholm School and by Keynes during the 1930s, macroeconomics became a major component of the discourse of social democracy. It provided the vocabulary and the conceptual framework used by the major institutional policy makers. It allowed for a functional working relationship between socialists and big business. Socialists wanted high wages, a welfare state, and democratic control of the economy. Big business wanted an end to the Depression and a return to economic conditions under which it could operate profitably. Macroeconomic theory taught that skillful management of the economy could achieve both what socialists wanted and what business wanted. It also legitimized government intervention in the economy in the form of price supports for farmers, which was important for socialist governments elected with the help of rural votes.

What was "overproduction" of X or Y commodity from a microeconomic point of view, was from a macroeconomic point of view a symptom of a larger and more general underproduction of the necessities of life. Sweden, and indeed the whole world, suffered from the great evils of under-utilized resources and under-employment coexisting with poverty. This was the real inefficiency, and the real objective was to expand the economy on the theory that growth makes it possible for everyone to have more of everything. Macroeconomics provided conceptual tools for calculating ways to get an economy onto a path of sustained growth.

There were four major institutional policy makers during the heyday of Swedish social democracy. They all spoke the same language. Here we offer a brief introduction to each of these four major policy makers.

One of these four was the SAF, the Swedish employers' federation. Many years the SAF insisted upon, and got, nationwide bargaining to establish a frame for wage pacts applicable to all industries. The national bargain included a no-strike pledge, promising an uninterrupted supply of labor. The SAF also insisted upon, and got, assurances that labor would not seek to perform the functions of management.[15]

One might expect Swedish business to be a truculent partner in policy formation, since it confronts a socialist government and strong labor unions. One should bear in mind, however, that the private sector in Sweden has been privileged in at least two respects. First, cartels have been tolerated, and even without cartels the small number of firms per industry made intense price competition of Swedish firms with one another unlikely. At one time the government even kept an official registry of cartels.[16] Second, many businesses have enjoyed generous tax breaks, subsidies, low interest loans, and research and development support. It has been the general policy of social democratic governments in Sweden to assure that private sector corporations, as institutions, have had ample funds. The personal enrichment of individuals has been curtailed, but the operation of business enterprises has been supported.[17]

A second major institutional policy maker within Swedish social democracy was the LO, the federation of blue-collar trade unions. The SAF and the LO insisted together that they should handle wage-setting and many related matters without government participation. In other matters they worked together with government. For example, the decision to bring the wages of women workers equal to the wages of men workers was a parallel and joint commitment of the SAF, the LO, and the government. Policy initiatives tending toward socialism in Sweden typically began in study groups within the LO.[18] After months or years of study a commission report would be approved by delegates representing all of the members of the federated unions (i.e., the majority of the Swedish people). The Social Democratic Party, loosely affiliated with the LO, would then propose a study in Parliament. More months or years of study would often follow, often in a mixed commission appointed by Parliament that included representatives of all major sectors of the population. The SAF and the non-socialist parties in Parliament typically opposed the initiatives that began in the LO, and they usually produced reasons for their views that the socialist members of the mixed commissions ended up agreeing with to some extent. The result was often a unanimous or nearly unanimous report, followed by the actual implementation in a modified form of ideas that had been somewhat radical when they were first proposed to study groups within the LO.

The Swedish model of social democracy, narrowly defined, is sometimes identified with the concepts first advanced by Gösta Rehn and Rudolf Meidner, two staff economists of the LO. They proposed, among other things, to raise wages by encouraging the growth of high wage sectors of the economy. Marginal firms that could not afford to pay high wages were to be allowed to disappear, and their workers were to be retrained and guided toward employment in the internationally successful high-wage sectors of the economy.[19] As time went on, the blue-collar proportion of the work force declined. White-collar workers, including droves of local government employees, had their own unions, which sometimes cooperated with the LO, and sometimes did not.

A third major institutional policy maker was the Swedish government itself. Sweden is a kingdom with a ceremonial king. It has no president. The ministers of the government are charged with implementing laws and policies. The ombudsmen office—*ombuds* is a Scandinavian institution that has now been replicated in other parts of the world—investigates complaints of official misconduct and generally serves an auditing function to assure that ministers and their assistants obey the laws and perform appropriate services in particular cases. The parliament conducts studies and enacts revisions of the legal and policy frameworks within which the organs of government and the nation as a whole carry on their activities. Approving new laws is normally done in the British manner, with the members of parliament belonging to the party or parties which support the current government failing in line to support the positions taken by the Prime Minister.

Swedish social democratic governments have pursued socialism very little by nationalizing industries. Instead they have built a welfare state providing health care, education, job retraining, pensions, and other public services. They have relied little on means-tested programs, available only to those who can prove they are poor. Instead they have made public benefits and facilities available to every citizen, or else tied benefits to working—for example by supporting employment-related retirement plans, sick pay, and unemployment compensation insurance. The private sector has been reshaped, however, by its numerous interactions with a large public sector, and by the detailed provisions of the tax regime used to raise money to pay for the welfare state. Tax incentives channel private behavior in directions thought to be conducive to the public good.

The banking system and particularly the central bank might be included in a short list of major institutional participants in the policymaking processes of Swedish social democracy. The banking system plays key roles in setting interest rates, credit policies, and the rates at which Swedish currency is exchanged for foreign money. In a country where strong unions make cutting wages impossible, and where many of the everyday necessities of life are imported, devaluing the currency by changing the exchange rate is a standard method for lowering the de facto wages of workers. It is a way to make the prices of Swedish exports more competitive in international markets, and a way to discourage Swedes from consuming more than the nation can afford.[20]

One of the burdens of our argument is that policy decisions depend not so much on the identity of the participants in the deliberations as on the underlying logic of the discourse that guides their reasoning, which in turn is embedded in the wider logic of the surrounding culture. In the policy formation processes of Swedish social democracy, the discourse of macroeconomics provided key elements of the conceptual framework.

Swedish statistics are fairly good. The SAF, the LO, the government, the banks, the political parties, the research institutes, and the media all read the same statistics. There was widespread agreement about what to measure and how to measure it. There was also widespread theoretical agreement about what was impossible. The policy puzzle was a fairly well defined game, which consisted of pursuing social objectives subject to constraints that limited what was believed to be possible. Again we do not wish to exaggerate. We do not mean to say that alternative conceptual frameworks were absent but rather that a remarkable degree of consensus concerning the nature of social reality was present.

A first constraint accepted by the consensus was that any viable policy had to stimulate economic growth. Macroeconomics taught that growth was a condition of the stability of capitalism, and the social democrats knew that even though they might in some sense be gradually transforming capitalism, they were for the foreseeable future engaged in administering it. Economic stasis was not an option; the economy would either grow or decline. Growth was also a requirement of Sweden's political compromise. Only if everybody enjoyed more than they previously enjoyed could poverty be eliminated without bitter disputes over the slicing of the economic pie.[21]

A second accepted constraint was that inflation had to be avoided, and since the largest component of prices was wage costs, there had to be at least some degree of constraint in raising wages. Although macroeconomics counseled pump-priming measures to boost aggregate demand, including deficit spending during the 1930s, the glory days of Swedish social democracy came in the period after World War II, when the usual problem to be solved was the "overheated" economy prone to inflationary pressure.

A third constraint upon which the vast majority agreed was that there had to be capital formation. Growth required that savings be put to work in investments, and it also required that there be ample savings to invest. A fourth constraint was acceptance of the notion of "export or die." Sweden had to be competitive in international markets, which meant both staying in the running in many international technological races and keeping Swedish tradable products competitively priced.

Subject to such constraints, the objective was to build a welfare state, a *folkshemmet* that would put into practice the ideals of liberty, equality, and fraternity. Especially in its later phases, its progressive supporters also demanded that Swedish social democracy deliver gender equality and responsible stewardship of the environment.

Presumably there was more than one possible solution to the economic puzzle. Among the several possible solutions some favored the working class more than others. That is why there had to be labor unions and a socialist party. Among the set of possible solutions, the choices had to be narrowed to the subset of solutions that most served the interests of the poor majority—at least that was historically the original concept, even though as time went on the successes of social democracy first made the poor a minority, and then made the poor virtually nonexistent (with the notable exception of considerable numbers of poor undocumented immigrants).

When the Swedish economy began to falter in practice, criticism of the basic premises of its hegemonic discourse mounted. Perhaps Marxism, which Sweden had neglected, had some worthwhile concepts to contribute after all, and perhaps other alternatives to mainstream modern discourse should be pursued. The most prominent dissenting voices came not from the left, however, but from the right, from dissenters more or less in the intellectual traditions of free market liberalism, whose emphases within economics had come to be known as microeconomics. Their mindset made them skeptical of the basic premise that a few big institutional policy makers could and should steer a nation toward the achievement of socially chosen values.

In the mid-1980s when the Brookings Institution sent a team of American economists to study Sweden, the head of the team, Alice Rivlin, described Sweden's then contemporary malaise and the going hypotheses for explaining it as follows:

> By the early 1980s Swedish policy makers understood that the course chosen in the 1970s was not sustainable. They made major efforts to bring the public deficit down by cutting spending, especially industrial subsidies, to reduce foreign borrowing and improve industrial competitiveness. Devaluation improved the trade balance, and the Swedish economy shared in the economic revival of the developed countries.
>
> But inflation remains high in Sweden and is eroding the competitive advantages of devaluation. Productivity growth has not recovered. It seems possible that the current economic recovery is only a temporary respite from more fundamental deterioration in Sweden's competitiveness in world markets and its ability to sustain a rising standard of public and private consumption in the long run.
>
> These concerns have touched off intense scrutiny of Swedish economic policies, scrutiny aimed at fixing blame for past failures and redesigning the nature and mix of economic policies to improve the performance of the economy. Two hypotheses and sets of associated remedies have emerged. One focuses on the impact of microeconomic policy—the influence of wage policy, regulation, taxes, transfers and other subsidies on the decisions of individuals and businesses to work, produce, save, and invest. The hypothesis is that the commitments to equality and full employment have distorted Swedish economic incentives and introduced rigidities that retard adjustment to change. The remedies favor lowering tax rates, reducing transfers and subsidies, and generally eliminating interference with market outcomes.

The other view focuses on macroeconomic policy—the fiscal and monetary instruments that affect the overall level of economic activity, wages, prices, interest rates, and the exchange value of the *krona*. The macroeconomic hypothesis is that whatever the validity of the microeconomic hypothesis Sweden's macroeconomic policies have fostered consumption at the expense of saving and have accelerated domestic inflation to the detriment of the country's ability to compete in world markets. Remedies include retreating from the strong commitment to full employment to reduce the inflationary bias or allowing the exchange rate to adjust to keep exports competitive.[22]

Our hypothesis is that it will be helpful to place both the microeconomics discussion and the macroeconomics discussion in the broader context provided by a philosophy of ethical construction, or, in Paulo Freire's phrase, "cultural action." The concept of ethical construction (or cultural action) is broader and more inclusive than the fundamental concepts of Marxism, microeconomics, and macroeconomics. We hope it will serve to encourage new thinking, or the revival of old thinking, that will show how to achieve what almost everybody wants: eliminating poverty, keeping it eliminated, a social democracy that is financially and ecologically sustainable.

The ethical ideal to be constructed, that of cooperation and sharing, can be thought of as everyone doing what they should do. When everyone does what they should do, then everyone's needs are met without ecological damage.

Indeed, even if some or all people fall short of doing everything they should do, even then all needs may be met, or most needs may be met, provided that the amount of good-doing is sufficient. We are assuming that nature poses no insurmountable obstacles to humans living happily in a sustainable environment. To the extent that insuperable natural obstacles are encountered, as for example, in the inevitability of death itself, then the resulting loss does not count as failure to live up to the ethical ideal, as, for example, in the case of nurses and physicians who do their best to keep a patient alive, but do not succeed.

A free market economy can be thought of as a method humans have devised to realize the ethical ideal. For everyone's needs to be met (in the whole world or in any given area), at least two conditions must be met: 1) People must know what they should do; and 2) they must be motivated to do it. A free market economy uses prices to signal to people what they should do, and it uses monetary rewards to motivate them to do it.

It might be said that it would be sufficient for people to be motivated to act in a pro-social way without knowing what they were doing, but this would conflict with the premise stated above in the preface, according to which we regard human needs as being met only when humans are treated as free and responsible beings, and not as automatons. Without exaggerating the extent to which people understand how their actions fit into the overall pattern of culture and nature, we can still insist that for humans to act as humans they must have a certain degree of self-direction and self-consciousness. A market economy scores high in this respect, since its fundamental unit is the autonomous free individual.

Besides using prices to signal to producers what goods and services they should produce, a market economy brings with it a set of ethical principles in the form of the moral rules of liberal ethics. These include honesty, keeping promises, resolving disputes by legal means rather than by violence, and respect for property rights, all of which can be summed up in the ideal of "integrity." Without a population in which such principles have been instilled, a market economy functions badly or not at all.

A market economy uses monetary rewards to motivate people to work in ways that meet their own and other people's needs, and it does this in a way that in principle respects the freedom and self-determination of each individual. Market culture's combination of price signals, integrity, and monetary rewards is not the only way to organize human conduct so that human needs are met. Its characteristic institutions represent an approach that has important advantages and disadvantages compared to other approaches, and compared to various ways in which market institutions may be combined with non-market institutions.

Among the disadvantages of an unmodified free market is that it implies the iron law of wages. If labor power is sold in a free market, as any other commodity, then it is sold for its market price. Under classic free market conditions, its market price will drift downward to the cost of its production, which is the cost of the subsistence of the worker. This result is not fundamentally changed when workers must be highly trained. In that case, competition drives the price of labor down to the point where its monetary rewards just barely cover the cost of subsistence plus training.

When the problem of eliminating poverty and creating prosperity for the majority of the population, who are waged workers or salaried employees, is viewed from the broader perspective of a philosophy of ethical construction, it can be seen that the iron law of wages is only a part, or a special case, of a wider problem. The market itself is a social institution, which might and might not exist and might and might not function properly. When it does function properly according to its own characteristic norms—freedom, property, setting of wages by contract, and the like—then, even then, there is no necessary reason why any given worker must be employed at all. Beyond the iron law of wages, there is the problem of the marginal population. Marginal people are not in the system at all. They are not employers because they own no businesses and perhaps no property at all, and they are not employees, because nobody has hired them. And even beyond that—that is, beyond the possibility of being part of a floating marginal population cut adrift in a property-owning market society, where other people own property and succeed in selling their services but you do not, there is still the possibility of living in an area where property rights and markets are not well established, but where no other form of cooperative human effort is functioning successfully either. One could be one of the miserable savages Adam Smith imagined and wrote about, condemned to try to subsist alone, without cooperation from other members of the species of any kind.

Keynes discusses four kinds of motives that tend to make a capitalist economy unstable because people keep cash instead of spending it.[23] From the viewpoint of ethical construction there is a more fundamental consideration: the constitutive rules of society set the stage for the social performance called "keeping cash" and they authorize people to keep their cash whenever they want to, for one or more of Keynes' four reasons, or for a fifth or sixth reason he did not consider, or for no reason at all. Failure to perform actions which viewed from a social perspective would contribute to meeting everyone's needs is an ever-present possibility, given human nature, and given the particular set of conventional norms defining human social nature embodied in the constitutive rules of modern economic society.

It may also help to show why we think an ethical perspective is more comprehensive than macroeconomics to comment on a remark by Erik Lundberg. Lundberg wrote, "Savings out of income do not generally constitute a direct demand for capital goods; they can only under certain conditions be transformed into such a demand. It is the investigation of these conditions that constitutes the crux of the theory of capital formation, as well as of any business cycle theory."[24] This remark seems to be true, but the choices of the terms "investigation," "conditions" and "theory" make the problem sound like one in the natural sciences, as if people observed their economies in the way they observe the stars, tracking the wanderings of planets amid fixed constellations. One way to enlarge the formulation of the problem would be to say that the more general problem is to mobilize resources to meet needs, and that turning savings into capital, and smoothing out the ups and downs of business cycles, are just parts of that more general endeavor. Speaking of an economy ethically, as a matter of human action, with goals and a potentially infinite number of creative ways to reach them, also lends itself to recognizing that the stuff an economy is made of is norms, conventions, and rules. Not stars.

From this point of view, both low wages and unemployment can be seen not as economic phenomena to be explained, but as ever-present possibilities, given certain common institutional patterns, and given the human condition. To understand why unemployment exists, it is not necessary to do regressions on variables hypothesized to be the forces that produce that phenomenon. Whenever the socially created rules do not construct institutions that successfully create for people sufficient opportunities to avoid the miserable fate of poverty, then poverty will happen. Poverty is more a default condition that happens when prosperity is not successfully constructed, than a phenomenon that should be regarded as surprising and send us looking for a cause to explain it.

The iron law of wages is a local law that is implied by certain constitutive rules of modern institutions. Those institutions are themselves a subset of the wider set of institutional conditions Anthony Giddens and others call class-divided societies, in which some people control resources and other people are excluded.[25] Class-divided societies, in turn, are themselves a subset of all human societies, and among all societies one must include those societies, several of which have been reported on by anthropologists, where cooperation functions very little or not at all. The "mountain people" studied by Colin Turnbull and the Yanomamo of the Orinoco region of Venezuela are examples of cultures where people do not cooperate much at all, neither through market nor through non-market institutional structures.[26]

The macroeconomic policies that amend free market capitalism have a number of remarkable advantages. Perhaps the greatest of them is that they have contributed to a moral atmosphere in which it now seems natural to measure the "performance" of an economy in terms of, among other things, indicators of social welfare. To many today it seems natural to speak of the "performance" of a national economy for the benefit of its citizens by analogy to speaking of the "performance" of a corporation for the benefit of its shareholders. In this respect almost everybody has become a social democrat. Even those who marshal statistics to prove that labor unions are too powerful and that the welfare programs of the left-of-center political parties do more harm than good, do so on the grounds that the right-of-center policies they advocate will result in superior economic performance, and therefore more welfare for everybody.

The remarkable alliance between economic theory and social democracy that came about in Europe from the 1930s onward was based to a large extent on the premise that the deliberate repeal of the iron law of wages, as an objective of public policy, would not only serve the cause of social justice but would also contribute to the "stability" of capitalism. Allow us here to say a word about the concept of "stability."

Stability is generally considered desirable because the thing people want to be stable is itself desirable. Those who consider something undesirable often want to see that thing be unstable, in order to increase the chances that it will disappear altogether. The goal of making capitalism stable is common to those who think capitalism works well, or can be made to work well, and those who think the best way to transform it into socialism is to build on its successes. Thus the problem to be solved need not be conceived as achieving stability per se, and it might be preferable not to use the word "stable" at all. One could say instead that in some respects capitalism does not "work" well, and that it is prone to periods of time and to regions in space when and where it hardly "works" at all. This way of speaking would have the advantage that it suggests that there is "work" to do—i.e., work to meet human needs and preserve the environment. We suggest this change of terminology because it may serve to make it clearer that the problem of improving the performance of the economy is at root an ethical one.

Speaking of how well the economy is "working" also helps to place the instability of free market economies, of which Erik Lundberg thought he had discovered the secret, in the broader context of the relative success or failure of human cultural structures overall in meeting needs in given environmental and technological settings. Lundberg's view, and economics generally, should be turned inside out, so that "instability," i.e., failure to meet needs, is regarded as the norm, and its correction is conceived more as a human project and less as a quasi-mechanical equilibrium. Human creativity is called upon to construct institutions that will gradually work better and better.

Another remarkable feature of macro-management of the economy, which is at the same time a measure of its conceptual and practical limitations, is that it does not require cultural transformation, central planning, or changes in ownership. It is enough to use "policy instruments" to influence the values of certain key variables: interest rates, public spending, tax rates, exchange rates, and somehow wage levels. It can be accompanied by other policies and programs, and sometimes needs them, but on the whole it is a method to make the economy work better that requires relatively few and small, and therefore relatively achievable, changes. Although some *dirigisme* policies may discourage investors some of the time, on the whole they are usually designed to, and usually do, encourage investors more than they discourage them. The Swedish model was thus of a kind that showed how to do social reconstruction in ways that were achievable, because they worked within the limits of what the capitalist system, as it existed, allowed.

Yet progressive Swedish socialists have always insisted that the Swedish welfare state was not a substitute for radical transformation of the capitalist system, but rather a method for taking achievable steps toward it. It may seem that only a few such steps can be taken, because the decision to work with the system as it is presents would-be transformers with only a few, limited options. It can be argued, however, that there is no reason in principle for supposing that there is only a short list of ways to bend a capitalist economy toward social justice.

It might seem that there is only a short list of ways to bend a capitalist economy toward social justice if one insists on seeing social science as an activity that consists of testing explanatory hypotheses by running statistical tests. There is only a short list of measured variables in Swedish statistical reports to formulate hypotheses about and run tests on. Or, alternatively, it might seem that there is only a short list of options if it is decided in advance to leave the basic rules of the institutional background unchanged.

Yet if one begins with the constitutive rules of the system, as a basis for understanding how it works, and then looks for ways to improve the normative frameworks within which human beings act to meet needs and serve values, then the possibilities for finding creative solutions are limitless.

Capitalism can be viewed (as both Smith and Marx viewed it) as a great series of social inventions, which moved forward the specialization of labor, the organization of tasks, the coordination of production with distribution, the application of science to technology, and the identification of psychological principles that could be relied on to motivate investors, owners, and workers. For the fact that capitalist systems have not worked perfectly, and have at some times and in some respects turned out to be even worse than the traditional ways of life they supplanted, no special explanation is needed. Failure is normal. Undesirable unintended consequences, apathy, indifference to the suffering of others, greed, the attraction of ideas that are simple but wrong, and love of the excitement that goes with violence, are normal too. They should be expected. They are not surprising in the light of what is already known about human behavior.

Looking at capitalism as a partly successful and partly unsuccessful social construction is a way to view its history as a source of ideas and inspiration for continuing the process of social reconstruction. Humanity took a great leap forward when the economists of the 1930s figured out a way to run a mainly capitalist mixed economy on the basis of high wages for the majority of the work force. When World War II ended, partly as a way to fulfill promises made to the masses who had made sacrifices during war time, all the major western nations made a pledge articulated in terms the new economists had created: a pledge to adopt public policies aimed at full employment.[27] The victories of the labor unions and the progressive political parties were facilitated by economists like those of the Stockholm School who showed how what progressives were fighting for could actually be achieved. The result, the relatively prosperous working classes, the welfare state with health care and pensions for all, the middle masses forming a numerical majority of a nation, was a new kind of society. It was something no civilization had ever achieved before.

But the task is hardly begun. Eighty-five percent of humanity, according to Immanuel Wallerstein's estimate, is still in poverty.[28] Building a world that works for everybody, in a responsible partnership with the other living species who share the biosphere with humanity, is a long and difficult task of ethical construction. Before it is completed it will no doubt require the invention of institutional forms that we today have not yet even dreamed of.

In the next chapter we examine the economic strategy of classical Swedish social democracy in greater detail, looking at it through the lenses of the macroeconomic discourse that structured its collective decision making processes, and yet trying to shed light on its successes and failures by holding up its language-games for normative examination against the background of the classical economic theories that macroeconomics criticized.

Notes

1. Bertil Ohlin coined the term "Stockholm School" in 1937. See Bertil Ohlin, "Some Notes on the Stockholm Theory of Savings and Investment—I," *Economic Journal* (March 1937): 53-69; and "Some Notes on the Stockholm Theory of Savings and Investment—II," *Economic Journal* (June 1937): 221-40. The members of the Stockholm School include Erik Lindahl, Gunnar Myrdal, Bertil Ohlin, Dag Hammarskjöld, Alf Johansson, Ingvar Svennilson, and Erik Lundberg. On the Stockholm School generally, see Bo Sandelin, ed., *The History of Swedish Economic Thought* (London and New York: Routledge, 1991). The shift toward macroeconomics was accomplished when those of the Stockholm School undertook the task of understanding how government bodies might make plans to prevent three basic kinds of "disequilibria," and how they might also shift plans to counteract disequilibria not prevented by earlier planning. The three types of disequilibria that drew their attention were the disequilibrium between the actual nominal rate of interest and the "real" rate, or the expected returns on new investment (i.e., how assessment of risk affects price formation); that between savings and investments (i.e., how to balance savings and investment to guarantee economic expansion and without generating rampant inflation); and the disequilibrium in the labor market (i.e., how to sustain decent wage rates and how to combat unemployment at the same time, and to do so during a depression). Erik Filip Lundberg, *The Development of Swedish and Keynesian Macroeconomic Theory and its Impact on Economic Policy* (Cambridge: Cambridge University Press, 1996), 28-33. Lundberg summarizes the view of the opponents of this shift in economic philosophy, those who belonged to the neo-classical school and who sided with microeconomics, as follows: "[They] had complete confidence that a market system would always reach an equilibrium position, if not disturbed by inflexible prices and wages or by government interference. Depressions, as transitional phenomena, had the task of weeding out the investment mistakes made during previous periods of expansion. Artificial injections of purchasing power by governments would merely disturb this equilibrating process and prolong the crisis." Lundberg, *Swedish and Keynesian Macroeconomic Theory,* 71-72. We again draw the reader's attention to the way adherents of both microeconomics and macroeconomics refer to economic "mechanisms" with the same language physicists use.

2. Myrdal, *Political Element,* 118; Myrdal, *Beyond the Welfare State.* Myrdal points to these eighteenth-century ideals as framing his own value premises as well.

3. Erik F. Lundberg, "The rise and fall of the Swedish economic model," *Journal of Economic Literature* 23 (March 1985): 1-36.

4. Lundberg, *Swedish and Keynesian Macroeconomic Theory,* 68; Norman Furniss and Timothy Tilton, *The Case for the Welfare State: From Social Security to Social Equality* (Bloomington, Ind.; and London: Indiana University Press, 1977), 138-39. While neoliberal economists state that the iron law of wages is not valid because the proposition advanced by its earliest exponents—i.e., that wages would sink to the level of subsistence—is not empirically true, and while they are technically correct on this point, we are not interested in the technical controversies concerning the iron law of wages as historically formulated by Ferdinand Lassalle and others. We use the phrase generically as shorthand for the proposition that where labor time is bought and sold in a free market its price will be low and that treating labor-time as a commodity leads to people working

for lower wages than is desirable. For an earlier use of this phrase in the way we are using it, see Section 1, "Scarcity, Violence and Bourgeois Humanism," of Chapter 8, "Class Struggle and Dialectical Reason," in Book II of Jean-Paul Sartre's *Critique of Dialectical Reason* (Alan Sheridan-Smith, transl.; Jonathan Rée, ed.) (London: NLB, 1976), 735-54. The definitive formulation of the "iron law of wages" is usually attributed to David Ricardo (1772-1823), who wrote that "[h]igh wages encourage the [growth of] population; and abundant yields attract foreigners, multiply men; and the multiplication of men in turn makes wages fall, because of the competition amongst them"; and, "From the effect of the principle of population on the increase of mankind, wages of the lowest kind never continue much above that rate which nature and habit demand for the support of the labourers." David Ricardo, *The Principles of Political Economy and Taxation* (London: J.M. Dent & Sons; New York: Dutton, 1965 (1821), 53, 159. Michael Wermel, Joseph Schumpeter, and Pierre-Jean Lancry, however, find an earlier formulation of the "iron law of wages" in the work of Anne-Robert-Jacques Turgot (1727-1781), who was among the first to note the importance of territorial movements of the population as a factor in reducing wages to the minimum means of subsistence. See Michael T. Wermel, *The Evolution of Classical Wage Theory* (New York: Columbia University Press, 1939), 61; Joseph Schumpeter, *History of Economic Analysis* (New York: Oxford University Press, 1954), 266; and Pierre-Jean Lancry, "La conception du salaire chez Turgot," in C. Bordes and J. Morange, eds., *Turgot, Economiste et Administrateur* (Paris: Presses Universitaires de France, 1982), 101-32. Antonella Stirati, on the other hand, points out some careful distinctions in the work of Turgot that indicate that Turgot allowed for the possibility that in an economy with a sufficiently high level of employment in relation to the working population, the normal wage will actually be above the level of subsistence. Stirati writes that "Turgot held that real wages, if disturbed for example by price variations, tend to return towards a level . . . which does not necessarily coincide with the subsistence of the worker and his family, but may be higher." Antonella Stirati, *The Theory of Wages in Classical Economics: A Study of Adam Smith, David Ricardo and Their Contemporaries* (Aldershot, U.K.; and Brookfield, Vt.: Edward Elgar, 1994), 43. Stirati attributes the original formulation of the "iron law of wages" not to Ricardo or to Turgot but instead, in accordance with Marx, to Malthus. Stirati writes: "Malthus identifies the factors that lead to food scarcity as natural phenomena, in particular the limits to the increase of agricultural production. This leads Malthus, unlike the earlier economists and Ricardo, to treat the poverty of the working classes as impossible to modify. Or at least—and this is the main point here—as modifiable not through changes in income distribution, but only through a drop in birth rate and hence population. That is why Marx described Malthus as the inventor of what Lassalle called the 'iron law of wages'. For the predecessors of Malthus . . . the tendency for wages to coincide with the minimum subsistence level rests on considerations different from those that characterize the Malthusian 'iron law'. They saw this tendency as neither immutable nor necessary; they imputed it to specific and economic conditions such as unemployment, or the political and institutional features of the society under observation." Stirati, *Theory of Wages*, 121-22. Therefore, although it was Lassalle who first used the phrase "iron law of wages," Marx writes, "It is well known that nothing of the 'iron law of wages' belongs to Lassalle except the word 'iron' . . . what is [his basis for it]? . . . [I]t is the malthusian theory of population. . . . But if this theory is correct, then again I *cannot* abolish the law even if I abolish wage labour a hundred times over, because the law then governs not only the system of wage labour but *every* social system. Basing themselves directly on this, the economists have proved for fifty years and more that socialism cannot abolish poverty, *which has its basis in nature,* but can only make it *general*, distribute it simultaneously over the whole surface of society!" Karl Marx, *Critique of the Gotha Programme* (originally published in 1875), reprinted in Tucker, *Marx-Engels Reader*, quote at 534-35, italics in original. Although, as the present work makes clear, we are entirely in accordance with Marx in that there is nothing inevitable or natural about poverty, we believe it is important to reckon with the "iron law of wages" as a systemic imperative.

5. Lundberg, *Swedish and Keynesian Macroeconomic Theory*, 56, 68.

6. The goals of Sweden's solidaristic wage policy were 1) to determine wage rates independently of differences in levels of productivity and profitability in different firms and economic sectors; and 2) to minimize wage differentials between "skilled" and "unskilled" workers. Lundberg, *Swedish and Keynesian Macroeconomic Theory*, 79.

7. One of the earliest critics was Eli Heckscher, who maintained that Myrdal's assertion that the government's expansionary fiscal policies during the Depression would become "contractionary" once the Depression had ended was a false assertion. Heckscher believed that in the long run, government expenditures would become such a large and important part of the Swedish economy that the private sector would be "crowded out" and that this would entirely prevent a "free market economy" from functioning. Lundberg considers Heckscher's criticism, made in the first half of the 1930s, to have been prophetic because by the 1970s, Lundberg notes, the only sector with a steady expansion was the public sector, and this did indeed have "a 'crowding out' effect on the supply of labour and finance to the private sector." Lundberg, *Swedish and Keynesian Macroeconomic Theory*, 27, 74. For more recent criticisms of Swedish economic policy, see the periodic reports by the SNS Economic Policy Group. This group was established in the early 1970s by SNS, the Swedish Center for Business and Policy Studies; the authors of these reports are economists, some of whom work closely with the International Monetary Fund.

8. Economic historian Arthur Montgomery was among the first to put forth evidence for this argument. See Arthur Montgomery, *How Sweden Overcame the Depression, 1930-1933* (Stockholm: Alb. Bonniers Boktryckeri, 1938).

9. Therefore, while we appreciate the optimistic answer that Paul Hirst and Grahame Thompson give in their chapter entitled "Can the Welfare State Survive Globalization?" we cannot share in their optimism on this particular count because their solutions to the quandary faced by Sweden and other social democracies arise entirely from within the very premises we find misguided. Paul Hirst and Grahame Thompson, *Globalization in Question: The International Economy and the Possibilities of Governance* (Cambridge: Polity Press, 1999), 163-90.

10. Lundberg, *Swedish and Keynesian Macroeconomic Theory*, 34. See also Erik Lundberg, "A General Formulation Showing the Instability of a Simple Economic System," which is Chapter IV of his *Studies in the Theory of Economic Expansion* (New York: Augustus Kelly, 1964); and Paul A. Samuelson, *Foundations of Economic Analysis* (Cambridge, Mass.; and London: Harvard University Press, 1947).

11. Lundberg, *Swedish and Keynesian Macroeconomic Theory*, 25-26.

12. Samuelson, *Foundations of Economic Analysis*, 1947, 281. See the critical discussion of Samuelson's logic in Johannes J. Klant, *The Rules of the Game: the logical structure of economic theories* (Cambridge: Cambridge University Press, 1984), 144-50.

13. Lundberg, *Swedish and Keynesian Macroeconomic Theory*, 20, 43-44. Gunnar Myrdal was Chairman of the Postwar Planning Commission and served as a member of the Swedish government beginning in the autumn of 1945. He focused his arguments concerning the proven instability of capitalism on three central areas: capitalism's inabil-

ity to guarantee full employment; the uncertainty and downward spiraling tendency of international trade; and the instability of private investment and its role in perpetuating structural imbalances.

14. Lundberg, *Swedish and Keynesian Macroeconomic Theory,* 54-55.

15. In the 1970s the spirit of the historic labor-management pact of 1938 was somewhat violated as labor sought a role in management through representation on corporate boards of directors, stock ownership, and in other ways.

16. Myrdal, however, thought Swedes were ashamed of their cartels, and that some actually disbanded to avoid having to register.

17. Lundberg writes, "The [Swedish] socialist position is that high profits by corporations are acceptable, provided net private income from dividends is kept down and private individuals do not get rich." Lundberg, *Swedish and Keynesian Macroeconomic Theory,* 79.

18. Lundberg, *Swedish and Keynesian Macroeconomic Theory,* 75, 78-82.

19. The position of the LO with regard to the relative merits of the public and the private sector was that the only way to attain and sustain full employment was through expansion of employment in the public sector and the increase of taxes. The LO did not believe the private sector ever would or could guarantee anything remotely resembling full employment. Lundberg, *Swedish and Keynesian Macroeconomic Theory,* 50-52, 75.

20. To this short list of institutional policy makers might be added the political parties, research institutes devoted to studying policy alternatives, the major media, and others.

21. Lundberg, *Swedish and Keynesian Macroeconomic Theory,* 52.

22. Rivlin quoted in Barry Bosworth and Alice Rivlin, eds., *The Swedish Economy* (Washington, D.C.: The Brookings Institution), 1987, 10-11.

23. See Chapter 15 of John Maynard Keynes, *The General Theory of Employment, Interest, and Money* (London: Macmillan, 1954).

24. Lundberg, *Theory of Economic Expansion,* 138.

25. Anthony Giddens, *The Class Structure of the Advanced Societies* (New York; Evanston, Ill.; San Francisco; London: Harper & Row, 1973).

26. The "mountain people" whose culture anthropologist Colin Turnbull studied were the Ik, who, at the time of his study in the late 1960s, lived in the Kidepo Valley in the region where the borders of Sudan, Kenya, and Uganda met. Turnbull writes, "There seemed to be increasingly little among the Ik that could by any stretch of the imagination be called social life, let alone social organization. . . . There is simply no community of interest, familial or economic, social or spiritual. With the Ik the family does not even hold itself together, much less serve as a model for a wider social brotherhood of Ik. Economic interest is centered on as many individual stomachs as there are people, and cooperation is merely a device for furthering an interest that is consciously selfish." Colin M. Turnbull, *The Mountain People* (New York: Simon and Schuster, 1972), 155, 157. Yet as long as they were allowed to roam their hunting grounds, this tribal culture of some 2,000 people flourished. The classic anthropological study of the Yanomamo is that carried out by Napoleon Chagnon, which documents "the importance of aggression" in Yanomamo culture. Napoleon A. Chagnon, *Yanomamo: the Fierce People* (New York: Holt, Rinehart and Winston, 1968), 2. While the Yanomamo did practice meal-sharing and some forms of pacific reciprocity, Chagnon witnessed, in his nineteen months of fieldwork, a great number of incidents of "individual vindictiveness" and "collective bellicosity." Chagnon, *Yanomamo,* 2, 7. Chagnon's study finds that the lack of cooperation among the Yanomamo had given rise to a chronic state of warfare, which permeated Yanomamo cultural mythology and values and was reflected in marriage and settlement patterns and political behavior. Chagnon, *Yanomamo,* 3. Anthopolo-

gist Jacques Lizot offers an alternate view of Yanomamo culture, one that emphasizes cultural structures that are more supportive of social cohesion. Jacques Lizot, "Words in the Night: The Ceremonial Dialogue—One Expression of Peaceful Relationships Among the Yanomami," in Leslie Sponsel and Thomas Gregor, eds., *The Anthropology of Peace and Nonviolence* (Boulder, Colo.; and London: Lynne Rienner Publishers, 1994), 213-40.

27. In 1944, the Swedish social democrats stated that full employment was their paramount policy objective. Within a few years, they decided that they would attempt to achieve a rate of unemployment as low as 2-3 percent. Lundberg, *Swedish and Keynesian Macroeconomic Theory,* 39-40.

28. See Wallerstein, *Unthinking Social Science,* especially Chapter 7, "Development: Lodestar or Illusion?" 104-24. Wallerstein documents the detrimental effects of the widespread acceptance—among both outspoken proponents of capitalism and its ostensible critics—of the ideology of "economic development." He demonstrates how it is *not* in fact a paradox that this widespread acceptance of the ideology of "development" has led to increasing disparities in the global distribution of wealth and attendant standards of living. At the end of the 20th century, an estimated 1.3 billion people—almost one-quarter of the world's population—were classified by the United Nations and the World Bank as living in "absolute poverty," subsisting on less than US $1 per day and most of them suffering malnutrition. United Nations Development Programme, *Human Development Report 1998* (New York: Oxford University Press, 1998), 51; Bread for the World Institute, *Hunger in a Global Economy* (Silver Spring, Md.: Bread for the World Institute, 1997), 3. In the same period, an estimated 3 billion people were living on less than US $2 per day. In third world countries taken together, an estimated 60 percent of the population lacks basic sanitation, 33 percent lacks clean water, and 25 percent lacks adequate housing. United Nations Development Program, *Human Development Report 1998,* 2, 51, 68, 89. Conditions within the United States were not as startlingly different as one might imagine. In 1997, the U.S. Census Bureau declared the poverty rate to be 13.3 percent, meaning that some 35.6 million people in the U.S. were living below the poverty line; and an estimated 30 million people in the U.S. were going hungry for at least a few days each month. United Nations Development Program, *Human Development Report 1998,* 51; John Henry Sniegocki, "Catholic Social Teaching and the Third World" (doctoral dissertation, University of Notre Dame, 1999), 19.

Chapter 6

Sweden's Rehn-Meidner Model: Too Good to be True, or, The Stumbling Blocks of Freedom and Property

Reliably meeting everyone's needs is a goal difficult to achieve in a capitalist society. It is, of course, difficult to meet everyone's needs in any society. We have used the word "capitalist" in order to call attention to certain constitutive rules of the form of society known as capitalism, which create certain formidable and pervasive difficulties. Although "capitalist" is perhaps the most familiar word we could have chosen for the purpose, it is not the most accurate word. Capitalism's inherent structural flaws are due to fundamental normative principles that organize not just "capitalist" society strictly so called, but also any "modern," "economic" or "liberal" society. The basic cultural structures of any such society imply instability and poverty.

We use the word "implies" here not in the strict logical sense in which "if p then q" and "p" imply "q," but in a scientific sense like that in which gravity implies that bodies fall toward the center of the earth. The tendencies toward instability and poverty implicit in modernity's basic cultural structures are like gravity. There are airplanes that defy gravity, and there is Swedish social democracy, which defies the global tendency for most people to be poor most of the time. Nevertheless, falling toward the center of the earth, instability, and poverty are formidable and pervasive tendencies.

It is true that if one had to select, from among all of the societies known to history and to anthropology, those societies that have best succeeded in reliably meeting everyone's basic needs, one would probably select the modern, economic, liberal, quasi-capitalist social democracies of Northwest Europe. Sweden would be at or near the top of the list. Yet this is not necessarily to say that there are no deep-rooted tendencies toward instability and poverty implicit in the basic constitutive rules of even those societies.[1]

Two constitutive principles that organize modern liberal economic society are "freedom" and "property." Freedom implies instability. Property implies exclusion, which in turn implies poverty. Freedom and property together define modern liberal economic society's principal method for organizing work and distributing the products of work: the market. A market is the coming together of owners of property, each of whom is free to choose what to exchange of what she or he owns in order to get something he or she does not own. Free choice. Ownership. Exchange.

Of what he called "the sphere of circulation," i.e., of the market, "a very Eden of the innate rights of man," Karl Marx wrote the famous words:

> There alone rule freedom, equality, property, and Bentham. Freedom, because both buyer and seller of a commodity, say, of labour power, are constrained only by their own free will. They contract as free agents, and the agreement they come to is but the form in which they give legal expression to their common will. Equality, because each enters into relation with the other, as with a simple owner of commodities, and they exchange equivalent for equivalent. Property, because each disposes only of what is his own. And Bentham, because each looks only to himself.[2]

The British economist E.F. Schumacher in *Small is Beautiful* called attention to the expectation that in market exchanges the parties look to their own self interest, and not to the broader interests of other people or of the environment, by writing, "[I]n a sense, the market is the institutionalization of individualism and non-responsibility."[3]

Can this "market" which Marx satirizes and Schumacher criticizes be the same "wonderful bread machine" responsible for the great leaps forward that have made the modern age so much more prosperous and enlightened that any previous age? Can it be the same market that its admirers praise as "natural" and as "efficient," so that any deviation from setting prices by means of markets is called "artificial," and any government action to modify market prices "interference," and so that making decisions "efficiently" is often conceived to be, by definition, calculating costs and benefits at prices that free markets dictate? Can it be the same institution that economists take to be not just an example of efficiency, not just a model of efficiency, but the very *definition* of efficiency, so that any way of making decisions that deviates from the decisions dictated by market prices is by definition "inefficient"? Yes, it can be, the very same. This wonderful institution, the greatest social invention of modernity, has its shadow side. Its shadow goes with it wherever it goes.

Freedom in modernity is an ethical principle that declares that all human persons have a *right* to be free, quite apart from modernity's tendency to endorse metaphysical principles declaring that all human persons are essentially free (or, as Jean-Paul Sartre put it, echoed by more recent anti-essentialists, persons are free just because they have no essences).[4] A metaphysics of freedom declares that humans will be unpredictable no matter what society might do to mold them to follow norms of expected behavior. An *ethics* of freedom adds another dimension, making expectations of stability in human behavior not just necessarily mistaken, but also disrespectful. Commitment is problematic. Within the metaphysics of freedom, using subtle forms of power to make people behave normally—what Michel Foucault calls "normalizing"—is practically necessary, but morally questionable.

This is not the place to discuss ways in which modern civilization has struggled to reconcile an ethic of respect for freedom with the older and still living traditions that tend to be ethics of virtue, or of character. We must note, however, that freedom makes the implementation of macroeconomic policy frustrating. People often do not do what they are expected to do, while the notion of inculcating an ideology of rational solidarity to educate people to live up to the expectations of policy makers runs against the grain of modern civilization. The Italian economist Amedeo Amato gave some good examples of these kinds of frustrations, encountered by Italian policy makers in the 1990s as they attempted to reduce inflation. First, cutting public expenditures was expected to reduce inflation, but the policy failed because legislators and the public would not accept the cuts. Second, reducing the money supply did not work because, contrary to expectations, private lenders increased lending. Third, increasing interest rates did not work because it turned out to produce cost-push inflation, instead of, as expected, reducing demand. Finally, increased taxation of wages would not work because it might lead to wage-push inflation, instead of, as expected, reducing consumer demand.[5]

The best-laid plans of human beings often do go astray. The planets can be relied upon to stay in their orbits, and to do what is expected of them, like clockwork, year after year, always arriving at the places where the astronomers predicted they would be, on time and without excuses. Human behavior, in contrast, is as variable and protean as the AIDS virus. To introduce even a semblance of reliability and stability humans had to invent—or, on Plato's version, the gods had to invent for them—the institution of promise keeping, which Hannah Arendt calls the basic cell of social life.[6] Promises commit the people who make them to resemble planets, to be where they are expected to be, on time, without excuses, and to do what they are expected to do. Max Weber aptly defined traditional societies as societies where rationality consists in following customary norms. Traditional societies elaborate in many ways on pledges and oaths, roles and norms, kinship relationships, sacred duties, myths and ideals and stories, and ceremonies, rituals and prophetic dreams.[7] In this manner, traditional societies create many patterns that define the right way to behave according to the way X, Y or Z culture thinks the world should be. If all goes well, the paradigms of behavior prescribed by a traditional culture's customs produce some tolerably reliable behavior, which in turn produces some tolerably sustainable interaction between humans and the physical environment, so that everyone's needs are met to some tolerable degree.

It remained for modern societies to invent a new variation on the thematic structure of human culture: the anti-norm, *laissez faire*, respect for the freedom of the human person. Henceforth any attempt to pattern behavior in a way that would result in reliably meeting everyone's needs would encounter unavoidable logical difficulties posed by modernity's highest and most treasured value: freedom. Freedom is not just one value among others—as Friedrich Nietzsche, who realized that to be free one must be consistently inconsistent, knew and showed.[8] Freedom authorizes an open-ended critique of all values. When Gunnar Myrdal, always loyal to eighteenth-century European ideals, pronounced himself again and again in favor of freedom, equality, and brotherhood, he must have known that there is something about the very idea of freedom that questions equality and brotherhood. Equality is manifested in patterns of behavior. Brotherhood too shows itself in patterns of behavior. Freedom questions all patterns.

Property rights carry with them, as their shadow side, the right to exclude. Father Bruno Sechi, a social change activist in Brazil, wrote, "The first and greatest violence is the systematic exclusion of people—a great number of people—from society. From this violence other violence directly and indirectly flows. Where you exclude, you must establish instruments to control those who are excluded so that they don't invade the peace of those who have access to opportunities and wealth."[9] As the permanent possibility of irresponsible conduct is the shadow side of freedom, the permanent possibility of the systematic exclusion of people from society is the shadow side of property rights.

In their excellent book *Democracy and Capitalism*, Samuel Bowles and Herbert Gintis cite legal decisions from American courts for the principle that an indispensable part of the meaning of the concept of "property" is the power to exclude. Since in America property rights are constitutionally protected, it follows that the power to exclude others from one's property is constitutionally protected. The constitutive rule of property rights makes it possible to divide society into haves and have-nots. If there were no rules specifying who has a right to be where, and empowering owners to exclude non-owners from places the latter have no right to be, then there could be no class of people who, because they own no space, and have no money to rent space from someone else, are allowed to be only in public spaces, to live in the streets. If there were no rules specifying who owns food, and therefore who has rights to condition providing food to others on being paid, then there could be no class of people who, because they have no money to buy food, go hungry.

It should be clear from this discussion that we believe that the arguments of neoconservative critics who attack people trying to bring about social justice, on the grounds that such efforts undermine "freedom" and "wealth creation," are wholly without merit. One prominent voice making such an attack is that of Michael Novak, who argues that it is neither the wealth of the rich nor capitalism itself that causes poverty, but rather that it is misguided socialist measures that are at fault for the continued existence of poverty. Novak has no patience for ethical critiques of capitalism (such as those issued by the Catholic church) because he believes that these can only lead to the continuation of cultures antithetical to the free-market economy that will surely, if only allowed to flourish unfettered, be the salvation of all.[10] Given that the constitutive rules that provide the philosophical underpinnings for capitalism—the rules of "freedom," "property," and "rights," which Novak hails as the solutions to poverty—have been in place for centuries, the burden of proof is upon Novak to demonstrate that these have succeeded in eradicating poverty wherever capitalism flourishes. It cannot be done.

If the establishment of property rights means exclusion, and if it is only with great difficulty that the implication that some people will therefore be poor can be avoided, then the question how a project for building social democracy will deal with property rights must be asked. Swedish social democracy has had a characteristic perspective on this question.

Swedish social democracy early on, even before the Swedish socialist party came to power, adopted what might be called an "onion" theory of property rights. For Swedish socialist thinkers, Karl Marx was crude when he supposed, in Chapter 32 of *Capital* that at some climactic moment "the expropriators would be expropriated" and thereafter the ownership of the means of production would be transferred to the proletariat, who would then proceed to cooperate to meet all human needs. Marx, and many others, supposed that "property" was a lump, which could be transferred from one social class to another, as a lump of clay is passed from hand to hand. A more sophisticated analysis shows property rights to be very many distinct particular powers, permissions, and even duties, which define how persons relate to things. "Ownership" is like an onion. It breaks down analytically into a large number of privileges, any one of which can be taken away while leaving the onion apparently intact, but in reality a shade smaller. For example, when union members achieve the right to "grieve" by appealing to an established "grievance procedure" in the work place, then the company still "owns" the factory, but since its power to deal with workers arbitrarily and with no accountability has been curtailed, the meaning of "ownership" has shifted. When all the layers of an onion are peeled, it is revealed that there is nothing left, no onion distinct from its peelings. So it is with ownership.

What we are calling the "onion" theory of property partly explains why many Swedish socialists saw no need to choose between reform and revolution. Reform *was* revolution, step by step. It also partly explains why the Swedish socialists have had very little interest in nationalizing industries.[11] Conceptually, there is no need for the state to take property away from its owners, if the bundle of privileges that constitutes ownership can be transformed by careful small steps. Further, conceptually, if it is possible to transform property slowly, layer by layer, then it is better to do it slowly, because, as Rudolf Meidner wrote, piecemeal reform is more likely than wholesale revolution to avoid mistakes, "involving as it does one element [at a time] in a step-by-step policy, where no step is taken into the unknown but each step is taken only when the ground underneath appears firm."[12]

Macroeconomics and an onion theory of property go well together. They are both non-disruptive, overtly nonviolent, gradualist, and scholarly ways to make society better by solving practical problems. While macroeconomics on the whole, like Keynes most of the time, tends to take what Keynes called the "social structure" as given, the concept that property is not a single lump, but a bundle of many privileges, tells us that over time even the most basic constitutive rules of modern society can gradually dissolve, particle by particle, and re-crystallize as something else.

If one sits on a bench at a bus stop for several hours and pretends to be a homeless person, one can achieve a good common sense understanding of the difficulties that stand in the way of reliably meeting everyone's needs in a capitalist society. The passersby may and may not give the person on the bench a break. Somebody might offer money, or a job; or an invitation to sleep indoors on a bed in a room; or an invitation to eat. But maybe not. Maybe nobody will. It is up to them. The passersby are free to choose whether to help or not. No one has a strict obligation to give anything, and therefore the person on the bench has no assurance that s/he will be given anything. If s/he offers to work, someone may hire the person on the bench. But maybe not. It is their decision. The person on the bench has no right to be employed at a living wage, because other people have no such duty to employ people at a living wage. They are free to hire or not, and the wages offered, if any, must be something to which they and the person on the bench both agree. They—the others—are not like the person sitting on the bench. They have houses and cars. They have money. They own things. The actual homeless person sits on a bench because s/he does not own a place where s/he could sleep on a bed in a room, and because s/he does not have enough money to rent a place.

If the person pretending to be homeless then bestirs herself and awakens from her reverie, and walks down the street and enters upon the academic precincts of some secondary school, or college or university, or institute of post-graduate studies; and there enrolls in a course of study in the science of economics; still, by following such a course of study, she will not—such is our thesis—fundamentally improve on the understanding of the root causes of poverty that she acquired sitting on a bench at a bus stop pretending to be a homeless person. Although one would probably never hear it in an economics course, it remains true that the cause of poverty is rights.[13] "The cause of poverty is rights" is among the most telegraphic, provocative, and hermetic phrases we could have chosen to express our concept. Any satisfactory unpacking of its meaning would have to propose the ethical construction of an alternative. It makes no sense to say that rights "cause" poverty if we cannot produce a counterfactual argument that in the absence of the specific interpretation of "rights" we are criticizing, and in the presence of some improved moral order, there would be no poverty. Although we might be permitted to say that prevailing ideas about rights are, in some sense, the cause of poverty, we certainly could not say that the cure for poverty is an absence of rights. The cure must instead be an improved moral theory that would endorse some improved concept of human rights. The improved theory of rights would cleave to the precious concept of the dignity of each human person which modern civilization has laboriously achieved. It would be a call to parents, philosophers, artists and educators to facilitate the continuation and enhancement of the spiritual and moral construction of a world of cooperation and sharing.

In the current setting of our rights-based culture, however, we are left to encounter the stumbling blocks of freedom and property. The right to be free and the right to own property. These constitutive rules of our social order are also axioms and first premises of what is known as "classical" economics, or, alternatively, neo-classical, orthodox, anti-Keynesian, pre-Keynesian, or neoliberal economics.[14]

It might be argued, to the contrary, that the first premises of orthodox economics are not the constitutive rules of modern society, but, instead, universal principles valid at all times and places. Robert Heilbroner, for example, defines economics as the science of setting priorities and making choices when resources are scarce.[15] On his view, economics has existed for as long as humans have existed, because humans have always had to make choices among alternative uses for scarce resources. Those who conceive economics to be a universally valid theory of rational choice take a similar tack. The ancient Chinese, the Incas, the Hopis, and the Hottentots may know nothing of game theory; they may have never heard of the game theory concepts of "maximin" or "minimax"; they may be unable to assign quantitative weights to the values of payoffs, or even unable to rank order their preferences; but nonetheless, it is argued, economic science somehow applies to their lives.

Whatever their merits may be, we regard attempts to construe economics as a universal social science, applicable to all cultures, as universalizing appendices added on later to classical economics, and not as classical economics itself. It is quite clear historically that classical economics arose together with capitalist institutions, as an important part of their ideology. *An Enquiry into the Nature and Causes of the Wealth of Nations*, Adam Smith's founding pioneer document of classical economics, for example, is an expanded version of the last part of his *Lectures on Jurisprudence*, a work which shows Smith's awareness that the ethical premises of economics are not universal.[16] Smith's jurisprudence lectures, given at Glasgow University in 1763-64, contain long passages on the Tatars, the Arabs, and other peoples, who, on Smith's own account, knew nothing of freedom, property, or markets as they were understood in British morals, in British common law and Roman civil law, and in the science Smith was about to found in his concluding lectures. Smith saw himself not as proposing an enlightened theory applicable to any set of institutions whatever, but rather as proposing an enlightened theory applicable to an enlightened set of institutions, namely the institutions of his own time and nation, those of Scotland and England, which he frequently compares favorably to those of other times and nations.

Swedish social democracy, and the macroeconomics of the 1930s generally, arose as a revolt against classical economics. Here are some quotations from a polemical counter-attack directed against John Maynard Keynes by Henry Hazlitt, who declared himself to be a spokesperson for orthodox, classical economics, and an enemy of the "new" economics. "Neo-classical" would probably be a better name for his views, but we have decided to accept his terminology and identify him broadly with a tradition called "classical," represented in our own times by mainstream neoliberal economics. Reading between the lines of these quotations, the reader will fairly easily see that the "causes" and "market forces" whose "results" and "decisions" Hazlitt describes are the actions of free people exercising their property rights. Hazlitt writes:

> Section II of Chapter 2 is notable as the first attempt by Keynes in the *General Theory* to disprove a fundamental proposition of traditional economics—that the most frequent cause of unemployment is excessive wage-rates. This, of course, for "classical" economics, is merely the parallel of the proposition that the most frequent cause for an unsold surplus of a commodity is the refusal of sellers to accept a price that will clear the market.
>   . . . . If our statesmen were *really* educated in the principles of classical economics, they would understand that unemployment is usually the result of union insistence on excessive wage-rates, or some similar price-cost maladjustment.
>   . . . . Whenever men are allowed liberty, and freedom of choice, they will make mistakes. Liberty is not a guarantee of omniscience. But neither are the mistakes of free men a valid excuse to take away their liberty, and impose government controls in its stead, on the ground that all wisdom and disinterestedness resides in the people who are going to do the controlling.
>   . . . . Frozen wage-rates cause frozen unemployment. When wage-rates become fluid again, "full" employment is restored.
>   . . . . In any case, there is the strongest possible presumption in favor of letting free competitive market forces decide the question. When *un*employment exists, it exists because there is *dis*equilibrium somewhere. The most likely place is in the wage-rates of the occupations in which the unemployment exists. This presumption is enormously increased when such wage-rates are arbitrarily held at their existing level by labor-union insistence, which prevents free competitive market forces from operating in those occupations.[17]

Such classical arguments are, on the whole, rather persuasive. Once the constitutive rules of freedom and property are in place, to be thenceforth taken for granted as part of the unseen and unquestioned background, it follows that labor, like anything else, will be purchased only if somebody wants to purchase it. Nobody has to buy anything she or he does not want to buy. If they have no sufficient motivation for hiring workers, employers will not hire. It is plausible to say that on the whole and in general, if labor is to be sold, its price must be low enough to attract buyers.

Similarly, if roundabout means requiring large initial capital investments are the means that bring goods to markets with the required quality and at the required price to make them saleable, then owners of property must be induced to invest, or to rent out, or, in general, to permit the use of their property. To run factories, mines, irrigation projects, research and development laboratories, one must pay for the use of property. Where free owners contract with free owners in markets, then property must have a price, a rent, and the price must be high enough to attract sellers.

Thus, given that the constitutive rules of the capitalist game are taken for granted as part of the unseen and unquestioned background, many of the scientific conclusions of classical economics have the character of descriptions of the inevitable, like descriptions of the orbits of the planets. All of us are familiar with the following dictum: "It does not matter whether you like it, because that is the way it is, whether you like it or not. It is reality. It is what must be. It cannot be changed."

On another level, however, classical economics is more than a dismal report on the hard facts of real life. Hazlitt writes, "Liberty is not a guarantee of omniscience. But neither are the mistakes of free men a valid excuse to take away their liberty, and impose government controls in its stead, on the ground that all wisdom and disinterestedness reside in the people who are going to do the controlling."[18] These words illustrate the second and third of the triple whammy punches of classical economics: not only is it the hard facts of real life, but also 2) this is the way it should be; and 3) the alternative is worse.

The free market should be, because people have a right to be free. The right to be free includes the right to be wrong. It even includes, within ill-defined limits, the right to be bad. Even if we think we know what people ought to do, and what they would do if they were rational and good, we are not authorized to override their freedom in order to force them to do it. Therefore, even when corporations or free individuals damage the environment, create unemployment, or break up communities, they generally have a right to do it. Rights, like gods, make holy demands that sometimes require practical material losses for the sake of loyalty to ideals.

It is also argued that the alternative to letting the market make decisions is worse. If the basic social structure is assumed, and if civil society is assumed to lack any capacity for transforming itself, then the alternative is Government. But power corrupts. Humans are fallible. Officials charged with pursuing other people's welfare will be less zealous than individuals pursuing their own welfare. Therefore, it is said, turning to Government is worse than leaving decisions to the market.

While we generally find the teachings of classical, neo-classical, mainstream, orthodox economics at least partly persuasive, whenever it is allowed to conceal its premises and silently assume them, there is one major point on which it is not at all persuasive. We are not in the least persuaded by the notion that if wage-rates went low enough there would be full employment.

This notion flies in the face of experience. In most of the world most of the time, wages are low and unemployment is high. (Here we are assuming some reasonable measure of unemployment, which includes the discouraged, the depressed, the driven-insane, the informal economies of thieves and street vendors, the landless peasants, the slum-dwellers who live by hustling—and not the rose-colored glasses of official statistics.)[19] In many parts of the world—the Philippines, for example—many people work full time, sometimes twelve hours a day, and still earn too little to buy the necessities of life. And still there is unemployment, even when wages could go no lower and still allow workers to keep body and soul together. In the Dominican Republic, in Uganda, in Zaire, in Bolivia, in India, in Colombia, in Egypt, in all of the territories of the former Soviet Union, in most of the continent of Africa, and now in China, and on and on, there is mass unemployment while wages are low. In abstract classical theory there is Say's Law, which holds that supply creates its own demand, and therefore there is no involuntary unemployment; and there are notions of equilibrium (a metaphor borrowed from physics), which postulate full employment whenever wage rates match the marginal productivity of labor.[20] But no theoretical ingenuity can make credible in the real world the argument that low wages bring full employment.

In Europe in the early 1930s, there was mass unemployment. Millions were hungry and angry. Hitler, Stalin, and Mussolini were on the march. Wages were falling. Orthodox economists tried to explain the situation with their classical theories, and mostly concluded that wages were not falling far enough fast enough.

John Maynard Keynes, a man endowed with a tremendous capacity for work, and a man not convinced by Marxism, which was the main theoretical alternative to classical economics at the time, labored long and hard to prove that classical economics was wrong. In Sweden, the members of the Stockholm School did the same. Dag Hammarskjöld criticized classical theories in a long appendix he wrote for a Swedish Royal Commission appointed to study the problem of unemployment. At the invitation of the socialist finance minister, Ernst Wigforss, Gunnar Myrdal wrote a theoretical appendix to the Swedish government's proposed budget for 1933 in which he argued in favor of active government intervention in the economy. Alf Johansson published a book in 1934 that argued that lowering wages in a depression would most likely make the depression worse. Back in 1929 Erik Lindahl had already made a case for government spending and expansionary tax policies to boost aggregate demand.[21]

One of Keynes' best arguments was the following one, which he made in Chapter 19 of his *General Theory*, published in 1936:

> The demand schedules for particular industries can only be constructed on some fixed assumption as to the nature of the demand and supply schedules of other industries and as to the amount of the aggregate effective demand. It is invalid, therefore, to transfer the argument to industry as a whole unless we also transfer our assumption that the aggregate effective demand is fixed. Yet this assumption reduces the argument to an *ignoratio elenchi*. For, whilst no man would wish to deny the proposition that a reduction in money-wages *accompanied by the same aggregate effective demand as before* will be associated with an increase in employment, the precise question at issue is whether the reduction in money-wages will or will not be accompanied by the same aggregate effective demand as before measured in money, or, at any rate, by an aggregate effective demand which is not reduced in full proportion to the reduction in money-wages.[22]

Here Keynes illustrates the rationale for macroeconomics, as opposed to microeconomics. At a micro level, if one considers one employer and one applicant for employment, one might conclude that the lower the wage the more likely it is that the employer will hire. But at a macro level, if one considers that all industries, taken as a whole, produce in order to sell, and can only sell if there are consumers with money to buy, one might conclude, in certain circumstances, the opposite: the higher the wages, the higher the effective demand for products, and therefore the more employment.

Keynes' prestigious work lent credibility to a vision of a new kind of society, articulated in Sweden in the mid-1940s by the Myrdal Commission, and by a joint committee of the LO and the socialist party. It would be a non-totalitarian society, preserving the essential liberties cherished by modern civilization. It would in general respect the boundaries between the public and the private domains, albeit with some incursions of the public on the private unacceptable to strict libertarians. Most importantly, macroeconomics would be applied to manage the national economy in a way that would benefit the overwhelming majority of Swedes, and arguably all Swedes. Productivity gains would be translated into higher standards of living for workers and larger tax revenues to support government-sponsored health and education programs.[23] The functions of profit would be socially defined and guided: to raise capital for economic growth, to pay pensions, to channel resources in efficient directions.[24] Major long-range capital investments would be coordinated society-wide, in order to avoid the instability Myrdal and others attributed to allowing investment to be governed by calculations of short-term profit. Thus the unrealized potential for meeting everyone's needs created by progress in the natural sciences would be realized because of progress in the social sciences.

Putting macroeconomics into practice was easier to do in Sweden than anywhere else. Macroeconomics theory asks us to consider the aggregate of all industries and the aggregate of all workers. It suggests setting wages, and other key variables, at the levels that will most benefit the society as a whole. In most of the world this theoretical prescription was an academic dream, a speculative theory about what would happen if there were a way to design social policies in a free society in the light of their overall effect on all industries and all workers. But in Sweden all the conditions were ripe. There was one main employers' federation, the SAF. There was one main labor union federation, the LO (later came a second federation, the white-collar TCO). The same political party, the social democrats, stayed in power for decades. The SAF and the LO together set the wage patterns for all industries and all workers, and the government coordinated its policies with theirs.

Looking a little more closely at what Keynes and the diverse contributions of the members of the Stockholm School asserted, it can be seen that most macroeconomics is about *what would happen if certain policies were implemented.* Paraphrasing Keynes in the passage quoted above: Keynes does not say there will be higher wages. He implies that if some measures could be taken to raise wages, then (provided that other conditions are met) there will be more consumer demand, more investment, more production, and more employment. Somewhat similar arguments could be made to assert that other policy goals could be achieved by implementing other policies—perhaps even green policies that would reverse the destruction of the environment.

Keynes successfully shows in passages like the one quoted that Say's Law is mistaken. It is not true that if the unions and the government would only leave the free market alone, then wages would sink to their natural level, and then there would be full employment in the best of all possible worlds.

Yet Keynes does not show that the policies he advocates can successfully be implemented without damaging side effects. Indeed he could not possibly demonstrate in advance that his prescriptions would work. It is one thing to have a model (even a model confirmed by historical data) that says that if X does that and Y does this, then Z will be the result. It is another thing altogether for X to actually do that, and Y to actually do this, and for Z to actually happen.

Keynes attacked classical economics at its weakest point. The strong points of classical economics remained intact. Economic actors throughout the world are still taking their micro-viewpoints. They still act in ways that tend to bid wages down, and overpriced (and even underpriced) labor around the world still tends to remain unsold. Money is still moving into the coffers of people whose economic power enables them to demand rents for their services or for the use of their property. People still show too little inclination to do what they would do if their actions were programmed to act cooperatively for the benefit of all. Mainstream neoliberal economics still tends to describe the world as it is. It predicts that most of the time market incentives will motivate workers and property owners, and that policies that deviate from market pricing will be undermined by the tendencies of human behavior (given prevailing social structures and prevailing cultural norms).

It is only a small exaggeration, and a generalization about many diverse thinkers pardonable under the circumstances, to say that classical economics is an ideology for capitalism built around two main ideas: 1) the idea that if the government and organized labor leave social decisions to be made through prices set in free competitive markets, then the market will take care of us— which is false; and 2) the idea that if the government and organized labor interfere with the free market, in order to set prices and make social decisions according to non-market criteria, then there will be unintended undesirable consequences, and the market will punish us—which is true.

If the constitutive rules of modern society put formidable and pervasive difficulties in the way of building social democracy, which mainstream economics records and reflects, then one would expect, on philosophical as well as on economic grounds, that Swedish social democracy, or any social democracy, would run into trouble—in the form of inflation, falling living standards, stagflation, soaring debt, unemployment, inability to export enough to pay for imports, capital flight, black markets, tax evasion, budget deficits, or in some other form. Trouble is what happened to Sweden in the 1970s. But by the time it finally happened Sweden had already enjoyed several decades of progress toward social justice coupled with miraculous prosperity, and during those decades the Swedish Illusion had become entrenched. Many people, in and out of Sweden, came to believe that Sweden had discovered a theoretically valid approach to macro-managing its economy, which could be expected to succeed indefinitely, delivering more social justice and more prosperity to the Swedish people year after year. Gunnar Myrdal embraced this Swedish Illusion in the Storrs Lectures he gave at Yale Law School in 1958.[25] He was not alone.

The following is a short list of counter-intuitive Swedish achievements in the decades immediately after World War II. Wages consistently rose. Profits were squeezed, but industry, far from shutting down or moving, grew. Full employment was maintained while wages went up and profits were limited. Progressive high taxes went together with high rates of capital formation. Sweden's success in selling its products in export markets exceeded expectations. Free trade did not drag down wages; it helped raise them. Plants were closed as industry adjusted to changing conditions, with very little hardship for workers. The welfare state, with all of its tax burdens, grew at the same time that the economy became more productive and more efficient.

We will focus on just one achievement, which is both representative and key: raising both the wage bite and the tax bite taken out of the revenues of industry (these overlap, because part of the tax bite came out of wages); and at the same time making industry more efficient and more internationally competitive. How did the Swedes do it?

Common experience around the world shows that industry is run for profit, and that when industrialists find that their profits are threatened by labor unions or by socialist governments or by anything, they tend to react by doing any of a number of things to restore and augment the profits that are the sources of their incomes. These reactions range from the routine to the reprehensible, such as: raising prices, keeping inventory off the market until prices go up, laying off workers, cutting wages, shutting down plants or threatening to shut them down unless they get a better deal, diverting new investment to locations where the government is more pro-business, taking their capital and their technologies elsewhere, funding right-wing think tanks that generate pro-profit ideology, bribing (or, more politely, funding) politicians, funding pro-business media to spread pro-profit ideas among the population at large, hiring thugs to beat up labor leaders and left-wing politicians, funding dissident colonels in the armed forces, running right-wing paramilitary death squads, and funding political movements and governments that carry out systematic repression and torture. The economic dislocation and chaos that experience shows to flow from industrialists' responses when their profits are challenged, cause not just the rich to fear socialism. The middle class and even the working class fear socialistic measures too, because they threaten to upset, or to provoke the upset of, the smooth functioning of the economic machine on which everybody depends for their daily bread.

None of this is surprising within a framework that sees the ethical norms that govern society as the economy's constitutive rules. Owners of property are on the whole free to do what they want to do, and they generally want to do what they perceive to be advantageous for themselves.

Compared to the experiences of many countries, the building of Swedish social democracy after World War II was a piece of cake. A first attempt at an explanation might hypothesize that Swedes are unusually nice people. The Swedish socialists had the courtesy and good sense not to threaten the security or comfort of the upper classes. The fifteen or so families who own the bulk of Swedish industry are composed of kindhearted Lutherans; who are pleased to see their fellow citizens get pensions, medical benefits, and unlimited free education; and who do not desire to become wealthier than they already are in order to be able to vie in ostentatious display with rock stars.

The nice folks hypothesis cannot explain very much, however, because in the modern world most business decisions are made not by sentiment, nor even by principle, but by accounting. The directors and officers of a corporation owe shareholders fiduciary duties that require the business to follow generally accepted accounting principles. The managers are obligated by law to be zealous and prudent in building the bottom line, which is profit. Besides, Swedish social democracy was not always nice. It put pressure on weaker firms, which could not afford to pay high wages and high taxes, either to become more efficient or to face bankruptcy. That was part of its strategy for raising wages and government revenues.

A more significant hypothesis is that Swedish social democracy found ways to modify the accounting rules that govern industry, which bent the whole country in the direction of social justice, and at the same time made the books balance, both for the government and for the private sector. It was called the Rehn-Meidner model, named after LO economists Gösta Rehn and Rudolf Meidner, and later merged with the EFO model, named after three economists who produced it for a joint LO-SAF commission: Gösta Edgren, Karl-Olof Faxén, and Clas-Erik Odhner.

A first premise of the Rehn-Meidner model is that the Swedish economy can be divided into two sectors: a competitive sector producing goods tradable in the world market (about a third of the economy) and a sheltered sector of goods produced for home consumption, such as houses and public services (roughly the remaining two-thirds of the economy).[26]

Simplifying a bit, with respect to the tradable sector, Sweden has no considerable influence on prices. Sweden is small, and the world is big. Whatever the selling price is, it is, and Sweden cannot change it. Therefore, if Sweden can produce at lower cost, or produce more goods at the same cost, the result will be pure gain for Sweden. The outside world is regarded for the most part as a giant customer, who sets the price, and who will take any quantity, or at least any quantity tiny Sweden can produce. The key to gains is therefore to produce more at a lower cost. If, by good luck, the prices in the world market of the goods Sweden sells go up, then so much the better.

The Swedish economy was deliberately geared to promote productivity gains. Government, employers, and organized labor worked together toward that end. Each year's productivity gains became a sort of national gain fund, which could then be divided between labor and capital (and directly or indirectly government) through collective bargaining. As the EFO economists put it, "[A] margin for profit and wage increases is created in the competing [i.e., tradable] sector through the rise of productivity in that sector and the influence from price increases in the world market. This margin is distributed between wages and profits through collective negotiations been organizations of employers and employees."[27]

Erik Lundberg calculated the annual productivity gains in the tradable sector to be about 4.2 percent per year during the years 1952-60, and about 8.2 percent per year during the years 1960-68.[28] It should be noted that these gains do not all stem from improved production techniques. They also stem from changing the mix of products to make more of the things Sweden makes best. Thus, real wages in the tradable sector could, in principle, go up 4.2 percent per year during the 1950s, and 8.2 percent per year during the 1960s. This would assume that the productivity gain went to labor and capital equally, payment to each going up by the same percentage.

But what about the two thirds of the economy that is in the sheltered, nontradable sector? There the productivity gains were smaller, and, besides, we are not allowed to make the simplifying assumption that the costs of production and the wages paid to the producers have no effect on demand or on prices.[29] In general, the LO and the SAF implemented a "solidaristic" wage policy. This meant that the wages of those who were lowest paid were raised first. As Meidner put it, everyone should get the same pay for the same work, regardless of whether they happen to work for a highly profitable firm or for an only moderately profitable firm. For this and for other reasons that linked the two sectors, wages tended to go up in the sheltered nontradables sector, moving toward equality of wages nationwide. Freedom. Equality. Brotherhood. Thus the workers in the industries that generated high profits through high productivity gains did not necessarily get the benefit of the highest wage gains. In fact, they were generally last in line to get wage increases, since their wages were high already.

To counter inflationary pressure, i.e., the tendency for prices to go up and up as wages went up and up, Rehn and Meidner recommended that the government follow a tight monetary policy. Taxes were deliberately used to prevent inflation by siphoning away excess revenues, which otherwise might have led to extraordinarily high profits and extraordinarily high wage increases. The tax policies that prevented inflationary pressure by making sure that neither labor nor capital got too much money were also sources of national saving. The public sector became a major source of capital formation in the economy, and a major source of the job training, investment in more up-to-date equipment, and technological research that led to still more productivity gains. Pension funds were another major source of capital formation.

This tight monetary policy, which held down inflation by keeping money scarce, also had the consequence that there would be less overall demand in the economy. The Swedish model was not a crude Keynesian model, which would first fight inflation with taxes, and then build consumer demand up again by lowering interest rates or doing something else to get cash in circulation. No.

Instead, the model targeted islands of unemployment that appeared in the weakest sectors and regions of the economy.

Rehn and Meidner proposed the now-famous "active labor market policy." When islands of unemployment appeared because the weakest firms failed, government programs stepped in to retrain workers.[30] Workers were paid almost as much for being retrained as for working, and since wages were being equalized throughout the economy, their new job would be unlikely to pay less than their old job. The idea was to ease the transition from shrinking sectors of the economy, which were the ones that could not afford to pay high wages and high taxes, to the growing sectors of the economy, which were the ones that could afford to pay high wages and high taxes.

Gösta Rehn in particular managed to sell the idea of using indirect taxes on profits to keep gross profits from being too high as an anti-inflationary measure. His argument was that by preventing business from having excessively high profits, the government could stiffen employer resistance to employee wage demands, since management would know that the firm could not afford to pay higher wages. Management would also have every incentive to invest in new plants embodying more technical progress and using more capital-intensive techniques. What the government took with one hand, it would give back with another, when it was a matter of making Swedish industry more internationally competitive. Marginal plants would be eliminated, thereby raising average productivity. Mergers were also encouraged, in order to achieve economies of scale and other advantages enjoyed by larger firms.

In such a context, Sweden could gain from free trade. It was already operating at or near full employment at high wages. It was geared up to produce goods super-efficiently for export. Bringing in low-priced consumer goods, made in countries with wage-rates far lower than Sweden's, could only raise the standard of living of Swedish consumers. Foreign-made shoes, for example, posed no threat to the Swedish shoe workers, as long as Swedish shoe workers could be retrained to take higher paying jobs making such products as Saab commuter airplanes and Volvo buses.

The question remains, however: how did the Social Democrats sucker the bourgeoisie into accepting this deal? The annual productivity gains were a measure of the fund available for division between labor and capital in collective bargaining. Labor was expected to limit its legitimate demands, on average, to not more than the increase in productivity. Thus, if productivity went up five percent, wages could legitimately go up five percent, and profits could also legitimately go up five percent. In practice, labor tended to demand more, especially in certain sectors and industries, and in practice the debate tended to be not so much over profit share as over whether wage increases were forcing price increases—when wage increases exceeded productivity gains and profits stayed about the same. The unanswered question is why owners acquiesced in not getting more of the productivity gains themselves, as profits.

In the nineteenth century a much different situation obtained in all capitalist countries. Labor was weak, and capital was strong. Technical improvements in factories, and other factors leading to productivity gains, generally resulted in the workers remaining as miserable as ever, while the owners reaped all of the benefits of increased revenues and/or lower costs and amassed colossal fortunes. Surely, if Swedish employers had been united and determined, and had used all the power at their command, they could have driven a bargain that would have given labor less and themselves more. Part of the explanation may be the nice folks hypothesis discussed above. Another part of the explanation is that the Rehn-Meidner model really was rational and well designed to work for the nation's benefit. The conscientious and civilized people who opposed it (like Lundberg) recognized that a democratically elected government had a right to give it a try and to see how long it would work.

But another part of the explanation of the acquiescence of business owners and managers in the implementation of the Rehn-Meidner and EFO models is that it offered wage restraint with respect to the biggest, most profitable, and most dynamic Swedish firms. The solidaristic wage concept, which meant raising the wages of the lowest paid workers first, also meant that the leading firms had to give fewer and smaller wage increases. Big businesses paid less, compared to what they would have had to pay, if they had faced their own unions alone, instead of being part of a national pattern that was part of a national policy. Thus the most powerful employers, who tended to have the most clout within the SAF drew considerable benefit from Rehn-Meidner.[31] Hapless marginal employers, caught between high taxes and high union wage demands and facing bankruptcy, found Big Business, Big Labor, and Big Government, as well as Rehn and Meidner's implacable logic, allied against them.

Nevertheless, as Lundberg noted from the beginning, the Rehn-Meidner model was one that could only work as long as Sweden enjoyed exceptional success in foreign trade, accompanied by exceptionally high annual productivity gains. Absent a miraculous growth of the tradable sector (even beyond the seemingly endless capacity of Swedish social democracy to generate miracles), the discouragement of marginal private-sector employers, combined with a policy of full employment at high wages, could only lead to maintaining full employment by creating a very large public sector, which there would be no way for Sweden alone to pay for. The model would only work as long as the rest of the world provided a steady demand for Swedish products at solid prices. It could work only as long as business management acquiesced in accepting a truce in its formidable and pervasive struggle to raise profits at the expense of wages and taxes. Further, much of its success was due to temporary conditions that made it possible to make large productivity gains by phasing out some industries and expanding others.[32]

As it turned out, the Rehn-Meidner model did prove to be unsustainable, as Lundberg expected, and as one might in any case expect from holding its discourse up for examination against the broader historical and ecological background suggested by the normative principles reflected in classical economics.[33]

As this is written at the beginning of the twenty-first century, what was called the Swedish model is now history in Sweden. Nevertheless, it continues to be of more than academic interest. Its success in its time bred optimism around the world. While Swedish social democracy was still in its heyday, Dag Hammarskjöld moved on to become Secretary-General of the United Nations, and Gunnar Myrdal, together with Alva Myrdal, his wife and lifelong partner in the struggle for social justice, moved on to become the leading exponents of a worldwide anti-poverty program and of what they called a "welfare world."[34] They were three of the Swedish social democrats who spread everywhere the faith that democratic planning could achieve prosperity with justice. Their credibility was enormously enhanced by the fact that in their native land it apparently had done so.

Conversely, the failures of the Swedish model and the exposure of its limitations contributed heavily to worldwide pessimism about social democracy's prospects, and to the worldwide advance of neoliberal economics and philosophy.

We have been contending that modernity's basic cultural structures, freedom and property, make the construction of social democracy difficult. What the Rehn-Meidner model could not transform, and in the end surrendered to, was the basic cultural structure of modern society. In other words, it could not transform economic reality, which constitutes the power of capital. This economic reality, in turn, is rooted in the basic baptism of greed, which modern culture has blessed. We find grounds for a new optimism in today's cultural movements that question the ethical premises of economic society, and seek to build cultures of peace and solidarity; in the cultural action and popular education movements founded by Paulo Freire; in Latin American liberation theology; in similar growth points within Buddhism, Hinduism, and Islam[35]; in the post-materialist counter-cultures of contemporary Western Europe; in deep ecology; in feminism. "Social democracy" remains, however, the best name for aspiring to a culture of cooperation and sharing under modern industrial conditions.[36] By calling attention to the need to critique constitutive rules, we aspire to help social democracy rethink, regroup, and move forward.

Notes

1. It is compatible with saying that inherent difficulties exist and must be contended with, but that especially in the four decades after World War II the social democracies of Northwest Europe succeeded in overcoming those difficulties better than anyone else has so far. Meanwhile, it is also true that modern societies benefit from modern science and technology. The availability of sophisticated technologies for dealing with the problems posed to humanity by physical reality gives modern societies a great margin for error. Even when moral, social, and emotional development lag behind technological development, it is likely—although not inevitable—that prosperity in a modern society will be greater than prosperity in a traditional society.

2. Marx, *Capital*, 83-84. This famous passage is from the end of Chapter 6 of *Capital*, Volume I, "The Buying and Selling of Labour Power." The "Bentham" to which Marx refers is none other than Jeremy Bentham, whose *A Fragment on Government* (1776) and *An Introduction to the Principles of Morals and Legislation* (1789) offered the most systematic elaboration of the hedonistic doctrine that pleasure is the sole ultimate good and pain the sole evil since the original formulations of Epicurus. It seems clear why Marx would be impatient with such a doctrine, but even moreso when taken into consideration the fact that Bentham set forth in his list of "pleasures of sense" not only pleasure of health, of memory, of imagination, and of amity, but also pleasure of wealth and power, and pleasure of malevolence or ill will. Without specific reference to Bentham, Marx offers a scathing critique of "the philosophy of enjoyment" in which he refers to such as "an insipid and hypocritical moral doctrine." See Karl Marx and Friedrich Engels, *The German Ideology, Part One*, ed. C.J. Arthur (New York: International Publishers, 1988), 114-15. Marx also took issue with Bentham because Benthamites extended their philosophical radicalism to almost every social sphere, but based in part on Bentham's shock at the French Revolution, they held private property to be a sacrosanct institution. So important was the institution of property that Bentham even felt compelled to publish a *Defence of Usury* (1787). Myrdal, *Political Element*, 117-18. For a concise introduction to the philosophy of Bentham, see John Dinwiddy, *Bentham* (Oxford and New York: Oxford University Press, 1989).

3. E. F. Schumacher, *Small is Beautiful: Economics as if People Mattered* (London: Blond & Briggs, 1973), 40.

4. Sartre holds that we are "condemned" to be free because we have no essential identity and must forever choose—or make—ourselves. He writes, "[F]reedom can be nothing other than . . . nihilation. It is through this that the for-itself escapes its being as its essence; it is through this that the for-itself is always something other than what can be said of it. For in the final analysis the For-itself is the one which escapes this very denomination, the one which is already beyond the name which is given to it, beyond the property which is recognized in it." Jean-Paul Sartre, *Being and Nothingness: An Essay on Phenomological Ontology*, trans. Hazel E. Barnes (New York: Washington Square Press, 1966), 537. "Nihilation"—from "nihilate" (in French, "*néantir*")—is a term coined by Sartre (and first translated into English by Helmut Kuhn) to designate the process by which consciousness is brought into being; consciousness exists as such only by making a nothingness apart from itself. Sartre, *Being and Nothingness*, 774.

5. Amato cited in Lundberg, *Swedish and Keynesian Macroeconomic Theory*, 111-12.

6. See Hannah Arendt, *The Human Condition* (Chicago: The University of Chicago Press, 1958), especially 188-199, on "The Frailty of Human Affairs" and "The Greek Solution."

7. Modern scholars have charted many of these, and the scholarly literature treating these themes is vast. Here we offer the interested reader only a sampling of recent scholarship on a variety of regions around the world. This is a mix of studies of both historical and contemporary societies, some of which place an emphasis upon traditional cultures as they encounter the encroachment of the cultural constructs we have identified as the "constitutive rules" of modernity. See, for example, Rolf Ziegler, "The Kula: Social Order, Barter, and Ceremonial Exchange," in *Social Institutions: Their Emergence, Maintenance and Effects*, ed. Michael Hechter, Karl-Dieter Opp, and Reinhard Wippler (New York: Aldine de Gruyter, 1990), 141-68; Maria Lepowsky, *Fruit of the Motherland: Gender in an Egalitarian Society* (New York: Columbia University Press, 1993), which treats the Tagula of Papua New Guinea; Marjorie Mandelstam Balzer, ed., *Shamanic Worlds: Rituals and Lore of Siberia and Central Asia* (Armonk, N.Y.; and London: North Castle Books, 1997); Wai-yee Li, "Dreams of Interpretation in Early Chinese Historical and Philosophical Writings," in *Dream Cultures: Explorations in the Comparative History of Dreaming*, ed. David Shulman and Guy G. Stroumsa (New York and Oxford: Oxford University Press, 1999), 17-42; Grant Evans, *The Politics of Ritual and Remembrance: Laos Since 1975* (Honolulu: University of Hawaii Press, 1998); Isaac Jack Lévy and Rosemary Lévy Zumwalt, *Ritual Medical Lore of Sephardic Women: Sweetening the Spirits, Healing the Sick* (Urbana, Ill.; and Chicago: University of Illinois Press, 2002); Galit Hasan-Rokem, "Communication with the Dead in Jewish Dream Culture," in *Dream Cultures*, 213-32; Barbara Tedlock, "Sharing and Interpreting Dreams in Amerindian Nations," in *Dream Cultures*, 87-103; Jeffrey H. Cohen, *Cooperation and Community: Economy and Society in Oaxaca* (Austin, Tex.: University of Texas Press, 1999); Hugo G. Nutini and Betty Bell, *Ritual Kinship: The Structure and Historical Development of the Compadrazgo System in Rural Tlaxcala, Vol. I* (Princeton, N.J.: Princeton University Press, 1980); Marjorie M. Schweitzer, *American Indian Grandmothers: Traditions and Transitions* (Albuquerque, N.Mex.: University of New Mexico Press, 1999); and Catherine Rainwater, *Dreams of Fiery Stars: The Transformations of Native American Fiction* (Philadelphia: University of Pennsylvania Press, 1999).

8. Nietzsche sets forth these ideas on "freedom" most clearly and succinctly in *Twilight of the Idols Or, How to Philosophize With a Hammer*, trans. Richard Polt (Indianapolis, Ind.: Hackett Publishing Co., 1997), especially 48-65. Nietzsche argues that language binds freedom by setting standards of consistency and imposing value judgments.

9. Sechi quoted in Anthony Swift, *Children for Social Change: education for citizenship of street and working children in Brazil* (Nottingham, U.K.: Educational Heretics Press, 1997), 1. In addition to Bruno Sechi's articulation of the concept of "structural violence" or "institutional violence," we also direct the reader's attention to that offered by Johan Galtung. He writes, "[P]roduction has somehow been organized the wrong way. At the fundamental level—enough and varied food, clothes and shelter, a reasonable health level, togetherness, and education—these five needs could have been satisfied for us all. The failure to satisfy them is avoidable, which means that there is violence at work." He elaborates on his definition of "structural violence" when he writes, "Structural violence 'just happens' without any specific actor behind it. The slum child, brain-damaged for life because of protein deficiency, who will have a self-realization level far below any reasonably defined potential, is not necessarily the 'object' of any evil will of any particular 'subject' who has committed the violence. The violence is built into the

structure, usually derived from some fundamental inequity that then generates, and is reinforced by, inequality and injustice." Johan Galtung, *The True Worlds: A Transnational Perspective* (New York: The Free Press, 1980), 21, 68.

10. Novak presents his arguments with great invective in *The Spirit of Democratic Capitalism* (New York: American Enterprise Institute, 1982); and *The Catholic Ethic and the Spirit of Capitalism* (New York: The Free Press, 1993). We find his tone of moral outrage not only disingenuous but also altogether ludicrous. For a systematic critique of Novak's ideas, see Gary Dorrien, *The Neoconservative Mind: Politics, Culture, and the War of Ideology* (Philadelphia: Temple University Press, 1993). In this discussion we should reiterate that the parameters of a debate that holds that ethics is something wholly apart from cause and effect (which arises from a deep built-in Kantian prejudice) are wrongly set. Within these parameters, it is possible to make the misguided argument that once ethics sets our goals, then we need science in order to say how to arrive at those goals. We argue instead that the growth of a culture of solidarity is part and parcel of the building of cooperation and sharing, which *is* how we arrive at our goals.

11. Indeed, what nationalizations there have been in Sweden have mostly been carried out by conservative governments either before 1932, or during times since 1932 when the socialists have been temporarily out of power. In the period from the end of World War II through the 1970s, less than five percent of Swedish industry was nationalized. Eli Schwartz, *Trouble in Eden: A Comparison of the British and Swedish Economies* (New York: Praeger, 1980), 76.

12. Rudolf Meidner, *Employee Investment Funds, an approach to collective capital formation* (London: George Allen & Unwin, 1978), 124.

13. One would have to add, if one were somewhere else, that additional contributing causes of poverty are that there is not enough food, not enough housing, not enough beds in the hospitals, not enough clothing—but these problems, although they are real elsewhere, are real in places many miles away from our bus stop bench.

14. Robert Nozick is an opponent of social democracy who calls attention to inherent conflicts between sharing to advance the welfare of all and rigidly respecting rights as they are embodied and enshrined in capitalist cultures. He writes, for example, "Individual rights are co-possible; each person may exercise his rights as he chooses. The exercise of these rights fixes some features of the world. Within the constraints of these fixed features, a choice can be made by a social choice mechanism based upon a social ordering, if there are any choices left to make! Rights do not determine a social ordering but instead set the constraints within which a social choice is to be made, by excluding certain alternatives, fixing others, and so on." Robert Nozick, *Anarchy, State, and Utopia* (New York: Basic Books, 1974), 165.

15. Robert L. Heilbroner, *The Making of Economic Society* (Englewood Cliffs, N.J.: Prentice-Hall, 1962), 4-5.

16. On the social institution of the contract, for example, which Smith holds as a fundamental ethical premise of both government and economics, he writes: "In the first place the doctrine of an original contract is peculiar to Great Britain, yet government takes place where it was never thought of, which is even the case with the greater part of people in this country. Ask a common porter or day-labourer why he obeys the civil magistrate, he will tell you that it is right to do so, that he sees others do it, that he would be punished if he refused to do it, or perhaps that it is a sin against God not to do it. But you will never hear him mention a contract as the foundation of his obedience. Secondly, when certain powers of government were first entrusted to certain persons upon certain conditions, it is true that the obedience of those who entrusted it might be founded on a

contract, but their posterity have nothing to do with it, they are not conscious of it, and therefore cannot be bound by it. It may indeed be said that by remaining in the country you tacitly consent to the contract and are bound by it. But how can you avoid staying in it? You were not consulted whether you should be born in it or not. And how can you get out of it? Most people know no other language nor country, are poor, and obliged to stay not far from the place where they were born, to labour for a subsistence. They cannot, therefore, be said to consent to a contract, though they may have the strongest sense of obedience. To say that by staying in a country a man agrees to a contract of obedience to government is just the same with carrying a man into a ship and after he is at a distance from land to tell him that by being in the ship he has contracted to obey the master." Adam Smith, *Lectures on Justice, Police, Revenue and Arms* (New York: Augustus M. Kelley, 1964), 11-12. These lectures on jurisprudence were delivered at the University of Glasgow in 1763 and first published in 1896.

17. Henry Hazlitt, *The Failure of the "New Economics": An Analysis of the Keynesian Fallacies* (Princeton, N.J.; Toronto; London; New York: D. Van Nostrand Company, 1959), 17, 152-53, 174, 251, 271; italics in original.

18. Hazlitt, *Failure of the "New Economics,"* 174.

19. In simple terms, official unemployment rates are based on the number of people actively seeking employment divided by the total number of persons in the workforce (or, the total "economically active population," which generally includes people in the age range of 15-65). Most of the industrialized nation-states follow the definitions, guidelines, and methodology of the United Nations' International Labour Organization (ILO) in determining rates of unemployment. In the United States, the national unemployment rate is calculated on the basis of the Current Population Survey (CPS) of 60,000 households, conducted by the Bureau of the Census; the sample sizes in other countries vary by population (in Japan, for example, the sample is 40,000 households). By the ILO definition, an "employed" person is a "paid employed person" who worked, for compensation in wages or salary, a total of at least one hour during the survey period, which is usually one week of a given month. Clearly the use of such a generous definition of "employed" causes most official unemployment rates to be gross underestimates of unemployment. Official unemployment rates do not differentiate between full-time and part-time jobs, cannot take into account the widespread phenomenon of underemployment, nor do they account for people whose search for employment is no longer considered "active."

20. Say's Law (of Markets), formulated by French economist Jean Baptiste Say (1767-1832), holds that an economy based on competitive markets will experience minimal problems with unemployment because supply tends to create its own demand. That is, taking into consideration the limits of labor and natural factors of production, increases in output (supply) will give rise to increases in wages and other forms of income, which will then tend to increase effective demand. The Marginal Productivity of Labor is a tenet within microeconomics, which, taking the individual worker as its basis, offers one measure of labor productivity. Once the productivity of this first worker is calculated, the Marginal Productivity of Labor can be calculated according to how much each additional worker adds to the production process in terms of output. This tenet of microeconomics purports to offer managers a basis for calculating the rate of employment that will guarantee maximum efficiency for a firm.

21. The work by Dag Hammarskjöld, entitled *Utgångspunkter för penningpolitiken efter kriget*, was published in 1944 (cited in Lundberg, *Swedish and Keynesian Macroeconomic Theory*, 41ff). The other cited works are as follows: Gunnar Myrdal, *Konjunk-*

turer och offentlig hushållning (Stockholm: Kooperativa Förbundet, 1933); Alf Johansson, *Löneutvecklingen och arbetslösheten* (Stockholm: Norstedt, 1934); Erik Lindahl, *Penningpolitikens medel* (Lund: Gleerup, 1930), published in English as *Studies in the Theory of Money and Capital* (London: Allen & Unwin, 1939). Reference to all of these works is made in Lundberg, *Swedish and Keynesian Macroeconomic Theory*. Lundberg takes pains to demonstrate that Keynesian thought and the thought of the Stockholm School were formulated independently of each other, but this is not to deny certain parallels and an ideological affinity between the two. Lundberg, *Swedish and Keynesian Macroeconomic Theory*, 19-37.

22. Keynes, *General Theory*, 159-60.

23. A classical source for the idea that systematically increasing productivity makes it possible to raise wages and profits at the same time was the scientific theory of management propounded by Frederick Taylor in 1911, which became known as "Taylorism," and which was praised by, among others, Vladimir Ilich Lenin. Frederick Winslow Taylor, *The Principles of Scientific Management* (New York: Harper & Brothers, 1911). See also Taylor, *Shop Management* (New York: Harper & Brothers, 1903).

24. In the Swedish model, and in other countries that moved toward social democracy after World War II, business was compelled to pay high wages. Consequently, business could only make profits by making the investments needed to increase productivity—investments which were, moreover, encouraged and often guided by tax policies and other government policies. This situation was reflected in mainstream economics in theories that admonished labor to cooperate in raising productivity: it was implied that it was simply a law of nature (e.g., a law of physics), or of logic, that only with productivity growth could wages rise. See, for example, R.B. McKersie and L.C. Hunter, *Pay, Productivity and Collective Bargaining* (London and Basingstoke, U.K.: Macmillan Press, 1973). These authors advocate a system they call "PAR" (for "participation, achievement, and reward") as the best system of "productivity bargaining" for labor; they believe it serves labor's interests best because it offers labor the chance, by placing worker performance directly in the context of wage bargaining, to show management that the workers have taken to heart the best interests of the business. McKersie and Hunter published this work during the time that would soon be recognized as the end of the "historic compromise" between labor and capital; similar advice to labor would soon be in short supply. For an earlier statement of the theory that wages would and could only rise with productivity gains, see Arch R. Dooley et al., *Wage Administration and Worker Productivity* (New York; London; Sydney: John Wiley & Sons, 1964). This work is part of the Casebooks in Production Management series prepared for use in the MBA Program of the Harvard Graduate School of Business Administration. With the decline of social democracy, the formula for making profits (what David Harvey and others call "the regime of accumulation") reverted to its classical form, which includes buying the most and best labor at the lowest possible price. This later situation was reflected in mainstream economics in a vast inconclusive literature attempting to explain the decline in productivity growth, a decline which, unfortunately, according to mainstream theory, implied that wages could no longer rise. Works that take this theory as their point of origin but that were addressed to a broader audience not necessarily versed in the language of economics include Y.K. Shetty and Vernon M. Buehler, eds., *The Quest For Competitiveness: Lessons from America's Productivity and Quality Leaders* (New York; Westport, Conn.; and London: Quorum Books, 1991), which was dedicated to H. Ross Perot; and Edward E. Gordon, *Skill Wars: Winning the Battle for Productivity and Profit* (Boston: Butterworth-Heinemann, 2000). Gordon states in his introduction, "The simple fact is that

America has run out of adequate numbers of well-educated, problem-solving, technically astute workers." Gordon, *Skill Wars*, xvii.

25. See Myrdal, *Beyond the Welfare State*.

26. This premise of the Rehn-Meidner model (which was also a premise of the EFO model), which disaggregated the economy into two sectors differentiated on the basis of productivity growth and price determination, was an analytical device that allowed Swedish economists "surprisingly high returns in terms of the understanding of the economic behaviour of the economy." Lundberg, *Swedish and Keynesian Macroeconomic Theory*, 54. As we will discuss below, however, this model facilitated a narrowing of vision so that the economists' underlying logic remained unquestioned and prevented their understanding of the roots of the crises beginning in the 1970s.

27. Gösta Edgren, Karl-Olof Faxén, and Clas-Erik Odhner, *Wage Formation and the Economy* (London: George Allen and Unwin, 1973), 113. *Wage Formation and the Economy*, first published in Sweden in 1970 (under the title *Lönebildning och Samhällsekonomi*), is the joint work of three staff economists, one from the employers' federation (SAF), one from the blue-collar union confederation (LO), and one from the white-collar union federation (TCO). Erik Lundberg credits Norwegian economist Odd Aukrust with originating the ideas associated with the EFO model.

28. Lundberg, *Swedish and Keynesian Macroeconomic Theory*, 55.

29. Lundberg calculates the annual productivity gains in the sheltered, non-tradable sector as 1.7 in the 1952-60 period and 3.4 in the 1960-68 period, less than half of the gains in the tradable sector in each case. Lundberg, *Swedish and Keynesian Macroeconomic Theory*, 55.

30. The weakest firms failed partly because union and government policies had caused them to fail (first by requiring them to either pay union wages or close their doors, and second by refusing to expand the money supply to bring them more customers).

31. On the weaknesses in the Rehn-Meidner Model's ability to offer its promised benefits and protections to workers, see Peter Aimer, "The Strategy of Gradualism and the Swedish Wage-Earner Funds," *West European Politics* 3 (July 1985): 43-53.

32. Thus Lundberg wrote: "[I]n the 1950s and 1960s, under the favorable conditions provided by a liberal trade policy, Swedish industry did undergo a productivity-raising structural transformation. . . . Relatively high and rapidly rising wage costs had a powerful impact on labour-intensive industries (such as textiles, clothing, and footwear); domestic production was gradually replaced by imports, and new employment was created in the expanding export industries (such as engineering)." Lundberg, *Swedish and Keynesian Macroeconomic Theory*, 51.

33. While Keynes assumes a closed economy, Sweden and indeed most nation-states should be considered "open" economies, subject to exogenous forces. This led the original Swedish School members into extensive discussions regarding how to create an "international space" that would allow the Swedish government to pursue an autonomous expansionary policy. In their view, this primarily entailed finding ways to "loosen" the balance of payments constraint. Because they did not question what we are naming the constitutive rules of capitalist or modern liberal society, initially the only devices they could conceive of by which to achieve their desired results included devaluation, borrowing from foreign sources, higher import duties, and import controls. Lundberg, *Swedish and Keynesian Macroeconomic Theory*, 35. Use of these narrow devices carries with it the potential to unleash upon a given nation-state the "disciplining" effects of neoliberal economic policy. As the faithful disciple of neoliberalism Milton Friedman writes, "[T]he

greater openness of Sweden to international trade enabled competition abroad to discipline governmental control at home." Friedman in Schwartz, *Trouble in Eden*, vii. It should be noted that Friedman cites this as the reason Sweden did not run into trouble *sooner*.

34. See Gunnar Myrdal, *The Challenge of World Poverty, a world anti-poverty program in outline* (New York: Pantheon Books, 1970).

35. Howard Richards' concept of "growth point" corresponds with that which Paulo Freire calls "untested feasibilities" (Paulo Freire, *The Pedagogy of the Oppressed* (New York: Continuum, 1989), 105-06) and to what Jorge Zuleta calls "usable themes" (*temas aprovechables*). People who want to work for structural transformation toward a world in which needs are met and peace is sustainable should identify growth points—i.e., accepted extant cultural practices that already indicate some movement toward greater justice and peace. The growth point is a point where cultural action can be a catalyst that will help the culture to change for the better in a way that it is already inclined to change. To be a "growth point," a given cultural practice must meet four criteria: 1) it must connect strongly with Gramscian "common sense" notions (see Chapter 11, note 21) in that people believe they understand the practice and find it meaningful; 2) it must attract energy from strong and vital basic sources such as the deep-seated human emotions relating to fear, violence, sex, joy, and the like (see below); 3) it must lend itself logically to transformation, such as transforming attachment to and care for "family" into a wider care ethic for "the human family"; and 4) it must lead to positive structural change. Richards in part draws his theories concerning the basic human energies from the work of brain physiologist Paul MacLean. The basic energies—e.g., sex, the joy of play, passion, violence, fear—are those that take form in the parts of the brain that MacLean identifies as the oldest parts of the human brain: those buried deep underneath the neocortex and forming the brain stem and the top of the spine. These are the parts that humans share with our distant relatives, the reptiles, birds, and fish. See Paul D. MacLean, *The Triune Brain in Evolution: Role in Paleocerebral Functions* (New York: Plenum Press, 1990). On Jorge Zuleta, see Howard Richards, *The Evaluation of Cultural Action* (London: Macmillan, 1985), Chapter 15. Readers intrigued by the notion of "growth points" will also be interested in Paulo Freire's discussion of "generative themes." Freire, *Pedagogy of the Oppressed*, 75-118.

36. We place our call for social democracy solidly within the "*economía solidaria*" movement, which has been building networks throughout Latin America (e.g., the Ciudades Educadoras project; the Workgroup on a Solidarity Socio-Economy (WSSE); and work done by the Instituto Políticas Alternativas para el Cono Sur) and which gained a great deal of momentum at the World Social Forum 2003. One of the key writers associated with the *economía solidaria* movement is Marcos Arruda, who explores and seeks ways of implementing the concepts of "participatory democracy," "community-based design," and "participatory development." See Marcos Arruda, "A Creative Approach to Structural Adjustment: Towards a People-centred Development," in *Beyond Bretton Woods: Alternatives to the Global Economic Order*, ed. John Cavanaugh, Daphne Wysham, and Marcos Arruda (London; and Boulder, Colo.: Pluto Press, 1994), 132-44. In a later work, Arruda writes: "[Now is the moment to] remind ourselves of our evolutionary success that has managed to overcome the difficulties inherent in our struggle for survival as individuals, groups and species, by virtue of the sense of co-operation, solidarity and convergence that has endowed mankind with greater strength than all the forces of competition, disaggregation and fragmentation that have pitted us against each other. This is the moment to realise that we must develop, urgently, a new way of seeing the human

race and its existence on this earth, one that awakens us to the awareness that, by natural law, we are interconnected with each other and with the whole cosmos, and that this interconnection is an invitation to link up with others by conscious ties of co-operation, reciprocity, sharing, complementarity and solidarity. This is not just to take an ethical stance, but to opt for what is our natural cause; that is, the only genuinely *rational* course of action open to us. It is time to lay the foundations of a different economy, oriented towards human and social needs, not indifferent to them; an economy that treats each citizen—man and woman—as a subject and at the same time as managers, decision-makers and executors; an economy where finance is harnessed to production; an economy that aims to be only the basis for meeting material needs, capable, by way of technological advances and by democratising productivity gains, of freeing up more and more energy and human labour so that we can concentrate on developing our potential, our attributes and our higher, specifically human, senses." Marcos Arruda, *External Debt: Brazil and the International Financial Crisis*, trans. Peter Lenny (London; and Sterling, Va.: Pluto Press, 2000), 32. A second key writer in the "*economía solidaria*" movement is José Luis Coraggio, who began his work toward developing this movement with an emphasis upon the importance of social pedagogy when undertaking economic reforms to institute greater social justice; the importance of such efforts became clear to him during the Nicaraguan Revolution. See his "Economics and Politics in the Transition to Socialism: Reflections on the Nicaragua Experience," in *Transition and Development: Problems of Third World Socialism*, ed. Richard Fagen, Carmen Diana Deere, and José Luis Coraggio (New York: Monthly Review Press, 1986), 143-70. See also José Luis Coraggio, *Territorios en transición: crítica a la planificación regional en América Latina* (Quito: Ciudad, 1987); and José Luis Coraggio and Carmen Diana Deere, Coordinators, *La transición difícil: la autodeterminación de los pequeños países periféricos* (Mexico City: Siglo Veintiuno, 1986). See also various works by Euclides André Mance, such as *La rivoluzione delle reti: l'economia solidale per un'altra globalizzazione* (Bologna: EMI, 2003). Mance calls for a new philosophical paradigm upon which to base an economy of solidarity among persons, businesses, and political, social, and cultural organizations, an economy that provides each person with the material, political, and educational conditions required for the ethical exercise of her or his freedoms.

Chapter 7

The Revenge of the Iron Law of Wages

In 1967 Frederic Fleisher hailed the miracles embodied in "the new Sweden":

> The new Sweden is the richest country in Europe, with per capita the highest income, the most cars, telephones, television sets, country homes, newspaper print, and wrapping paper. Life expectancy in Sweden is the longest in the world. Though the national income per capita is somewhat higher in the United States as a whole, Swedes are now as well off as Americans. There has been a greater economic leveling out among Swedes, but they also have a rare sense of security. The new Sweden has aimed at developing ways of stimulating incentive, of guaranteeing equal opportunities, and of preventing the partially disabled and the maladjusted from lagging too far behind the general affluence. The new goal is the self-realization of everyone. The citizens are encouraged to develop their creative and productive talents and to experiment with the problems of adjustment in a rapidly changing, highly industrialized society.[1]

A few lines farther on, Fleisher comments on the economic principles that made Swedish affluence possible: "Governmental control of inflation and currency had been practiced in Sweden almost before the ideas of John Maynard Keynes had been formulated and long before Keynesianism was appreciated."[2]

Then he comments on the Swedish philosophy of social change: "Experts and planners can work with a limited number of unknowns and observe the impact of their experiments quickly. If they turn out to be failures the country can afford to scrap them. Changes in Sweden are gradual, but intervals of stagnation are rare. If the effects of pilot projects are encouraging, the course is determined by negotiation and compromise. The results are often far-reaching transformations of sectors of society."[3]

It is not surprising that through the United Nations and other international agencies Sweden became a model of economic and social development for the world, and especially for the poor struggling masses of Asia, Africa, and Latin

America. The illusions of the Swedish model were concealed behind undeniable practical success, macroeconomic concepts that were considered scientifically valid at the time, and a philosophy and methodology of social change that seemed impeccably logical. Thus, worldwide, progress has been blocked by misguided beliefs fortified by the success of Swedish social democracy in the 1950s and 1960s. The purpose of this chapter is to articulate and diagnose some illusions fostered by the Swedish model, for the purpose of helping the world, and especially the poor struggling masses of Asia, Africa, and Latin America, and especially our poor struggling Mother Earth herself, to move forward toward real solutions.

Although the rise of the Swedish model was remarkable, its fall was prosaic. The reasons that led Sweden to give up the policies that had served it so well in the decades immediately after World War II, were the same intractable economic problems that plague most modern countries most of the time. Erik Lundberg described some of them as follows:

> [A] sharp decline in Sweden's share of export and home markets, an extreme profitability crisis and a big decline in industrial investment. . . . Since 1973, a number of industries have been hit by over-capacity breakdowns, coupled with demand failures and profitability crises. This has happened to iron ore, steel, shipyards, textiles, and to some extent to the timber and woodwork industries. We find here a number of inter-related issues: international over-investment during the boom years of the sixties and seventies, stagnating demand development especially in investment branches, keen international competition from newly industrialized countries.[4]

Lundberg notes that Sweden's first response to crisis in the 1970s was to rely on the same Stockholm School and Keynesian policies that had worked for it before. Sweden again turned to active labor market policies aimed at stimulating investment, stabilizing private consumption expenditure, and expanding public works. These measures had proven successful throughout the 1950s and 1960s, allowing Sweden to enjoy balanced growth with full employment, only moderate inflation, and no major balance-of-payments problems. In response to the recession of 1974, therefore, "in accordance with the Keynesian tradition, anti cyclical policies were rapidly and energetically applied."[5] This time, inexplicably within the boundaries of the then dominant Swedish macroeconomic paradigm, the result was "an almost complete policy failure."[6]

Faced with the chronic failure of their planned economy to function as desired, in the 1970s and 1980s the social democrats and the unions were obliged to accept more of the advice of free-market liberals, thus accommodating themselves to the existing ratios of economic power.[7] At the same time, they tried to change the balance of economic power by taking control of capital and capital formation. They tried to vest ownership of major corporations in employees through the acquisition of shares by pension plans and other union-controlled funds. They advocated, and achieved, seats for labor representatives on corporate boards of directors. Meanwhile, the public sector ballooned.[8]

In 1991, after they had already largely abandoned the classic Swedish model of the postwar years, the social democrats were voted out of office. The new conservative government appointed a commission of seven non-socialist economists "to analyze the economic crisis in Sweden and to suggest ways to solve it." Its report was published in English as a book entitled *Turning Sweden Around*, divided into six chapters called respectively "The Swedish Crisis," "Stability," "Efficiency," "Growth," "Democracy," and "Recovery." *Turning Sweden Around* documents the revenge of the iron law of wages. It finds an unemployment rate of 14 percent, public sector spending running at an unsustainable rate of 70 percent of Gross Domestic Product, a fall from arguably first among industrialized nations in GDP per capita to fourteenth, a strong inflation bias, recurrent budget deficits, and severe financial and building crises.[9]

In its six sophisticated, well-written, and mathematically accurate chapters *Turning Sweden Around* repeats again and again one central and pervasive theme: Swedish wages are too high! To compete in international markets, Sweden must produce goods at competitive prices, which means paying less to workers (either directly or indirectly, through taxes).[10]

The main theme of *Turning Sweden Around* is not a surprise. It is common sense. It is the teaching of plain old-fashioned classical microeconomics. It is a conclusion mandated by the constitutive rules of modern society.

That historical experience revealed the limitations of the Swedish model is not a surprise. What is surprising is that in the 1950s and 1960s so many people believed that the Swedish model was sustainable and generalizable to the rest of the world. What needs to be explained, therefore, is the specious credibility of the illusions it engendered.

Please do not misunderstand us. Common sense says that as a general rule, with limited exceptions, high wages cannot be sustained in an open economy because global competition will require producers to cut costs, and therefore wages. We do not, however, side with common sense but instead with the visionaries. We side with R. Buckminster Fuller, who said that what they do not want you to know is: there is enough for everybody.[11] With appropriate technologies and cultures of solidarity there can be work for everyone and prosperity for everyone, without ecological damage, even with ten billion people on the planet. If ten billion is too optimistic a figure, then we will revise our vision to assert: there is no physical reason to prevent humans from reducing natality to bring the population down to five billion, or whatever proves to be the carrying capacity of the planet.

When we say that Swedish social democracy and its international admirers suffered from illusions, we do not mean to say that justice and prosperity for all cannot be sustained. We mean to say that they cannot be sustained without appropriate technologies and cultures of solidarity. It was the marriage of social democracy to Keynesian macroeconomics that had to end in divorce. The illusions of Sweden were illusions about the feasibility of "changing without changing," i.e., of building an ecologically sustainable social democracy on a foundation of modern liberal ethics.

In this chapter we will discuss four kinds of illusions that the revenge of the iron law of wages unmasked: 1) the planning illusion; 2) illusions regarding the functions of profit; 3) an illusion regarding the control of capital; and 4) illusions regarding the mobility of capital.

The Planning Illusion

By "the planning illusion" we mean a certain naïve overconfidence in the ability of modern governments to create distributive justice and general prosperity. The free market illusion is its mirror image. Unfortunate souls unable to penetrate the veils of either illusion go back and forth between planning and the free market, expecting to find in one of them, or in some combination of the two, the key to building a way of life that knows no poverty. The victims of the planning illusion overestimate the power of government. They are not sufficiently aware that humans are governed far more by the laws of nature and by the constitutive rules of society than by any public officers chosen at the polls.

Rather than discuss the planning illusion as a diffuse and generic conceptual malady, we will focus on an articulate and specific theory of planning proposed by Gunnar Myrdal in a work published in 1960.[12] Myrdal's voice carried the enormous prestige of a major architect of the economic policies of a nation that had actually succeeded in creating justice and prosperity. The story he told about planning could not help but appear to be, and surely was in part intended as, a story explaining Sweden's success. It is the centerpiece of Myrdal's proposed world anti-poverty program. It is by and large the doctrine of planning that was adopted after World War II by the United Nations, the World Bank, national governments, and international agencies.[13] When Myrdal gave his series of lectures at Yale Law School in 1958, his topic was "Beyond the Welfare State." A good part of the meaning of "beyond" in the title was that it was time to consider the international implications of the welfare state. As Myrdal developed his theme, it turned out that a central idea running throughout his lectures was "planning."

His audience knew he was from Sweden, but he did not frame his remarks as a report from Sweden. He spoke instead for "the West," and for "the western model of planning." He was able to say with satisfaction that most of the countries of the third world had chosen "the western model of planning" over the Soviet model of planning. Although Myrdal spoke for the West, his examples and concepts came, first and foremost, from Sweden.

One might object that the United States, twenty times larger than Sweden, and at the time the acknowledged leader of what was called the free world, should have been the main source of whatever the West had to teach the rest of the world. Myrdal takes account of the size and importance of the United States, and of its role at the time as the principal source of aid to the developing countries. Nevertheless, he looks upon the USA, and Spain, and even France, as outliers. Social development in the United States was not typical of the main trends after World War II observed in the majority of advanced Western industrial nations, i.e., West Germany, the United Kingdom, the Nordic Countries, the Benelux countries, Switzerland, Austria, and the British dominions of Canada, Australia, and New Zealand.[14] Myrdal spoke of the USA as if it were a somewhat socially retarded but basically well-intentioned Big Brother, immense in size but slower to learn than his precocious siblings. What Sweden had learned about collective bargaining, about social security, about cooperatives, about designing pilot projects, about systematically evaluating social programs, about public housing and public health, Big Brother would eventually learn too. Drawing on Swedish experience to speak for "the West" was thus legitimate for two reasons: first, because Swedish experience was typical of that of the majority of advanced nations; and second, because Sweden was the future. The trend in other countries was to become more like Sweden.

A second objection to the stance taken by Myrdal is that "planning," which he viewed as the key to the West's social progress, was an unpopular idea in the West, especially but not only in the United States. The advocates of the free market outnumbered the advocates of planning, and they tended to identify the latter with the Five-Year Plans of Joseph Stalin, than which there could be nothing worse.

It was not just in Myrdal's mind, however, that in the 1950s, western governments, whose own constituencies were leery of planning, were teaching planning to third world governments. It was really happening. Justifying this practice, Myrdal argued that planning was a practical necessity in the West, and it was a practical necessity to teach it to the East and South.[15] In spite of public opinion, it had to be done, and it had to be taught.

Myrdal took it as a premise of his argument that no nation in the world was willing or able to go back to the old belief in leaving the economy alone, waiting for the free market to work its beneficial magic. That had been the counsel of the *laissez faire* economists. Yet Myrdal maintained that after the two World Wars and the Great Depression of the first half of the twentieth century, and after the invention of tools of macroeconomic management in response to and in conjunction with those historic events, no nation could go back to *laissez faire*. Governments had decided to intervene, and indeed they *had* to intervene.[16]

Specifically, every leading industrial country at the end of World War II had officially pledged to follow a full employment policy. These pledges, enshrined in public documents in every western nation, partly reflected the promise made to the working classes during the war. The working classes had been assured that the democracy they were fighting for, and in many cases dying for, was not merely a formal democracy, but a democratic future in which they would enjoy freedom from want. Governmental commitments to full employment also reflected the conviction—which Myrdal did not question—that since John Maynard Keynes and the rise of the new economics, governments knew how to pursue a full employment policy. Full employment was a promise that could be kept, and, once made, it had to be kept. Thus Myrdal's theory of planning presupposes, as one of its major premises, Keynesian theory and the Stockholm School's theories, which show how to manage the economy to achieve higher levels of employment.

Having established that government intervention in the economy was necessary because keeping the promise to manage the economy to achieve full employment was necessary, Myrdal went on to argue that it was also necessary to coordinate with one another the various specific interventions that governments make at various times and places. Therefore, planning itself was by definition a practical necessity. As Myrdal stated it, "Coordination leads to planning or, rather, it is planning."[17]

If all "planning" amounts to is coordinating the several distinct interventions in the economy that a government makes from time to time, it seems easy enough. It is hard to see how anyone could be against it, except for people who do not want the government to intervene in the economy at all. Myrdal's stance was well suited to allay any fears his American listeners might have that planning was radical and dangerous.

What lends itself to illusion is that Myrdal associates what is difficult with what is easy. It is true that there is a connection between planning and full employment. It is also true that a government committed to full employment must plan. But it is *not* true that planning can bring about full employment. What it really takes to fulfill a government's promise to its working people to provide prosperity with full employment is to deactivate, or seriously modify, market forces firmly rooted in the constitutive rules of society.

The radical consequences of a full employment policy were discussed by Myrdal's fellow Swedish social democrat Gösta Rehn in the following terms:

> If the State has promised to maintain employment at all costs, a group of workers can ignore the fact that their organized wage demands might stamp out a large part of their branch of industry. They can hold that the State must give them employment, if private enterprise does not because of negative profits. In a full-employment society it becomes unnecessary for every trade union to have regard to the financial strength of its employers. Every union can draft a wages policy without concern for the profitability of the work done. The fact that unions in the past did not usually demand wages that would make too many enterprises unprofitable was of course not due to any moral scruples about the right of capitalists to get a fair profit. It was due to the realization that too high wage demands mean unemployment, organized either by employers'

federations (Lockouts) or brought about through the discontinuation of unprofitable firms. By definition a full-employment society is a society where the State always saves those threatened by this sort of unemployment, either through the creation of new jobs or through a monetary policy that allows prices to rise enough to restore profits. Thus no union is any longer compelled to take into consideration the effects of its wages policy on the employment of its members.[18]

Rehn must be right to say that if a government really means to keep a pledge to assure full employment, then it must either provide employment or create employment when markets fail to offer as many jobs as there are workers. Rehn must also be right when he implies that if these things happen, it implies a major shift in the balance of power between workers and employers. Under such conditions, the law of supply and demand, and its corollary, the iron law of wages, are repealed. If it seems fantastic to say "[t]hus no union is any longer compelled to take into consideration the effects of its wage policy on the employment of its members," it should be remembered that for several decades the Swedish government actually did what Rehn said it had promised to do. It offered public employment at high wages when private employment at high wages was not available. Most governments, however, cannot keep such promises even if they make them, and even the ability of the Swedish government to defy (socially created) economic reality proved to have limits.[19]

To say that governments *must* deliver full employment because they have promised to do so implies that they *can*. As a general rule, apart from exceptional circumstances, to say that governments that swim in the constitutive rules of modern western social structures as a fish swims in water *can* deliver full employment is to give more credence to Keynesian macroeconomics than historical experience and the logical analysis of its premises justify.[20]

What really happened in Sweden was not that the government was a pioneer in the post-World War II western model of planning, which decided to plan for full employment, and then brought it to pass. What really happened was that after World War II organized labor in Sweden was in an extraordinarily strong bargaining position. There was a labor shortage. Swedish business was in an extraordinarily strong sales position in export markets, partly because Sweden had been neutral in World War II, partly because Sweden's natural resources (forest products and iron ore) were in high demand, and partly for other reasons. The unions could have used their monopoly of the supply of labor to drive wages through the roof, eventually causing industry to shut down or move elsewhere. Instead, the unions intelligently (but not without employers threatening, and one time actually carrying out, a nationwide lockout) worked together with business and government to maintain the international competitiveness of Swedish industry, cutting a deal in which labor got a major slice of the pie. Another major slice of the pie went to the "social wage" through which taxes paid for benefits for working people. Wages in the particular industries that had become immensely profitable could have raced ahead, leaving the rest of the nation be-hind. Instead, the employers' federation and organized labor worked together to set nationwide wage patterns, which, in principle and to some extent in practice, raised first the wages of the lowest paid.

Labor, business, and government worked together to build the Swedish wel-fare state. If one of the three were to be singled out as having played the leading role, it would have to be organized labor, not government.

Planning, in the sense of learning how to coordinate a government's diverse policies and programs, can easily be taught to graduate students from the third world who come to study at Harvard, Stockholm, London, Stanford, Toronto, Paris, or Syracuse. It can easily be taught on-site to middle-level civil servants at World Bank seminars in Jakarta, Bangkok, Dar-es-Salaam, Dakar, Sao Paulo, or Santiago. Learning how to replicate the conditions that made the success of Swedish social democracy possible, however, is not so easy. Absent extraordi-nary circumstances it is not merely difficult. It is impossible.

In Sweden in the 1970s and the 1980s, the revenge of the iron law of wages showed the limitations of planning. When the Swedish economic crises came, the officers in the ministries of the Swedish government knew perfectly well how to plan. They had long been good at planning.[21] Nevertheless, the experi-ence of having economic crises in spite of excellent planning demonstrated that in earlier, better, times, in the 1950s and 1960s, when Sweden was doing ex-traordinarily well, the mainspring of its success had not been planning.

Illusions Regarding the Functions of Profit

We are suggesting that overconfidence in planning and in the new economics helps explain why the set of policies known as "the Swedish model" seemed to be sustainable. We are also seeking to illustrate a point about the methodology of research in the social sciences.

An "illusion," in an important sense of the word, is a false appearance. If one has an illusion, then one sees what is not there. Or one does not see what is there. Speaking metaphorically, what we see can depend on whether our eyes are open, whether we are wearing glasses, whether the glasses are tinted, how the lenses of the glasses are ground; whether we use a telescope, or a micro-scope, or a magnifying glass; which direction we are looking, how long we wait, whether we have a vivid imagination, and how our nerves interpret the light waves raining down upon the pupils of our eyes.

Less metaphorically, what appears to be real can change as the method changes which is used to ascertain the real. "Reality" can become "illusion" and vice versa. What was taken for granted can become problematic. What was not noticed at all can become the center of attention.

When we write that there is a planning illusion, we are not just saying that certain facts have been overlooked, which, when taken into account, show a certain kind of overconfidence in the powers of governments to be an illusion. We are advocating a shift in point of view and in research methods.

The point about method that we seek to illustrate is that one's understanding of social democracy can be increased by paying attention to modern society's basic cultural structures, its ethical foundations, its constitutive rules. To further illustrate our point about method, and at the same time to begin a discussion of the functions of profit, we will comment on some words of Professor Milton Friedman: "[U]nless the behavior of businessmen in some way or other approximated behavior consistent with the maximization of returns, it seems unlikely that they would remain in business for long."[22]

In our opinion, Friedman's remark is significant and valid, but he has no right to make it. As a confessed positivist, Friedman should, in order to play by his own rules, only accept as scientific laws those generalizations that are built upon empirical foundations. It would not be difficult to gather empirical evidence showing that many firms have not maximized profits, and have stayed in business for a long time.[23] Nevertheless, Friedman's intuition is valid. What makes his intuition valid are the basic ethical and legal norms of freedom and property, which allow, authorize, recommend, and in some cases compel the maximizing of profits.[24] The basic norms of modern society allow people to buy cheap and sell dear, to buy for as little as they have to pay, and to sell for as much as they can get. Business managers are normally authorized and expected to do the best for the owners, which means maximizing profit.

In the competition of capitalists there is an element of compulsion, reflected in Friedman's remark that those who do not maximize profits are unlikely to remain in business for long. If a business does not maximize profits while its competitors do, then the competitors will have access to more retained earnings, with which to keep up with new technologies, advertise, and, generally, to compete. Thus a business that decides to rest content with a moderate profit may find that it is unable to keep up with competitors, and consequently unable to operate at all. Thus, just considering the constitutive rules of markets, one would consider attempts to maximize profits to be very likely, if not inevitable.

Three Swedish authors who influenced and reflected the classical Swedish model of social democracy were the so-called EFO authors, Edgren, Faxén, and Odhner. Although their book *Wage Formation and the Economy* was about wages, it was necessarily also about profits, because how much money goes to wages affects how much money goes to profits.[25] Edgren, Faxén, and Odhner were more consistent positivists than Friedman. Their approach was to use historical data to see how profits and wages varied over the years, and then to explore hypotheses concerning what factors might explain the observed variations. For example, using three different definitions of profit, they show the following figures for Swedish industry for the years 1960-1967.

Table 7. 1. Profits in Swedish Industry, 1960-1967

	1960	1961	1962	1963	1964	1965	1966	1967
Profits (measure 1)	10.7	10.5	9.3	9.2	9.9	9.7	7.9	7.5
Profits (measure 2)	7.8	7.5	6.2	6.1	6.9	6.6	4.7	4.3
Profits (measure 3)	6.4	6.1	4.9	4.8	5.4	5.5	4.0	3.8

Source: Edgren, Gösta, Karl-Olof Faxén, and Clas-Erik Odhner, *Wage Formation and the Economy*, London: George Allen and Unwin, 1973.

Discussing possible explanations of the observed trend, Edgren, Faxén, and Odhner state that the fall in profits is "probably in part to be explained" by rising wages.[26] On the whole, the EFO authors are cautious in interpreting their data. Sometimes the numbers show no discernible pattern. Always more studies are needed.

With respect to the normative question what profits *should* be, the EFO authors are even more reluctant to speak. They appear to accept the positivist doctrine that questions of value have no scientific answers. They write:

> The distribution of income between labour and capital; the allocation between wages and profit, is a question of power and group interests. That cannot be resolved by experts in a volume of this kind, but only by negotiation between the contractual parties, in which their natural opposition of interests finds expression. By threatening strikes and lockouts, and on occasion through strikes and lockouts actually taking place, each party presses its case on the other side.[27]

The EFO authors take the view that within limits determined by what is possible, the rate of profit is determined by a power struggle between capital and labor. But it is not naked power. This is Sweden. The ultimate weapons are the strike and the lockout. There are no streets soaked in blood, no burning buildings, no secret police, no death squads, no civil wars, no political kidnappings, no helicopter gunships attacking civilians, no military checkpoints every few miles on the highways, no torture chambers, no reigns of terror. It is safe to be a positivist in Sweden—because there is no danger that the idea that value judgments have no cognitive significance will be put into practice.

Without surrendering their credentials as technical experts who express no opinions on values, the EFO authors go on to make some murky scientific observations on what is possible and what is not possible that come within an inch of telling union negotiators how they ought to behave at the bargaining table:

An excessively large wage share—a shift in the distribution of income in favour of wage earners at the expense of business firms—has an effect in the first instance on the capacity of enterprises to finance investment for increased productivity and the expansion of capacity. Investment can be financed both through borrowing and through the accumulation of equity capital within enterprises. If the equity/debt ratio . . . of enterprises is not to deteriorate in the long run, however, their capital must grow in step with their total capital stock. Profitability must suffice to permit an increase in own-capital at that rate, both through self-financing and through the general public and the collective savings funds finding it attractive to take up new issues of shares. In other words, these factors limit the extent to which the distribution of income can be shifted in favour of wage earners without leading to consequences which in the long run also operate adversely for wage earners, in the form of a lower rate of economic growth, smaller increases in productivity, a reduced ability to pay wages and a weaker employment position in industry.[28]

The paragraph just quoted is followed by an equally stern admonition to employers, warning them that if they do not concede reasonable wage increases, they will suffer from instability, disorder, wildcat strikes, raises deviating from norms—all of which is summed up in the pejorative phrase "wage drift."

The moral of the studiously amoral story told by the EFO authors is balance and restraint. Aristotle would have loved it. Both sides are admonished, in careful technical prose, to settle somewhere in the middle, without going to extremes. In classical ethics a person of good character is, by definition, a person who has formed the habit of rationally governing the passions, choosing the golden mean, not too much and not too little.

With 20/20 hindsight we can see that the EFO authors, whose book was first published in 1970, wrote at the peak of the prestige of the Swedish model, shortly before its decline began. We can also see why they did not see the decline coming. The lenses of their glasses were ground to keep constitutive rules out of focus.

Profit-seeking, when carried to extremes, is inconsistent with the good faith bargaining that the EFO authors discreetly advocate. It is uncivilized. It violates the spirit of "created harmony" that Myrdal attributed to the modern western welfare state. It is a vice, not a virtue. Medieval moral theology named it "avarice" and counted it among the seven deadly sins.

A major illusion causing the Swedish model to appear to be sustainable was the illusion that privately owned industries, engaging in collective bargaining in the light of the EFO guidelines, could be treated, in effect, as the equivalent of public utilities. Reasonable profits would be fixed at the bargaining table as reasonable utility profits are fixed by public regulatory commissions. Reasonable profits could be regarded as moderate profits calculated to serve socially necessary functions.

In reality, the basic legal and ethical norms of freedom and property allow, authorize, recommend, and in some cases compel the maximizing of profits.

The basic norms of modern society allow people to buy cheap and sell dear, to buy for as little as they have to pay, and to sell for as much as they can get. Business managers are normally expected to do their best for the owners, which means maximizing profits. Maximizing profits is but another name for profit-seeking carried to extremes. One should not have assumed that Volvo, for example, would be content forever with reasonable profits. When tempted by an opportunity to take its technology to a low-wage country, where it could reap even greater profits than those it was already reaping in Sweden, Volvo might choose maximizing over moderation. In fact, it did.

An Illusion Regarding the Control of Capital

The Swedish model required a great deal of capital. The model required capital to keep Sweden ahead, or at least in the running, in several worldwide technology races. The corollary of "Export or die!" was "Obsolete goods cannot be sold!" Even education became a capital-intensive industry, as years of time and large sums of money were spent developing and testing new textbooks, teaching methods, and laboratory exercises.

At the same time, the Swedish model cut profits. Limiting profits was an essential part of its strategy for stabilizing prices, which in turn was essential to remaining competitive in world markets. It was also an essential part of its strategy for raising wages by shifting employment away from less viable marginal firms and toward winning firms.

Consequently, Sweden needed capital at the same time that it was inhibiting the growth of capital. Big business in western capitalist countries has traditionally grown by re-investing its own profits. Retained earnings has been a more important source of capital for expansion than taking out loans, issuing bonds, or selling shares. In any case, the same relatively low profits that diminished retained earnings also diminished the attractiveness of firms to investors.

Sweden compensated for relatively low profits in several ways. Large budget surpluses made the government itself a major source of capital formation (until the ballooning of public expenses drove government budgets into the red). Pension funds were another source. The tax laws peeled some layers off the onion of property rights by telling business it could retain earnings after all, if it would spend them in ways conducive to the welfare of the Swedish people and in ways that enhanced Sweden's competitiveness in world markets.

Reliance on public and quasi-public capital sources turned out, on the whole, to be more an advantage than a disadvantage, partly because these alternative sources of capital were more reliable sources of funds for basic research and development and for implementing projects with a long time horizon. In general, countries like Sweden, Japan, the tigers of Southeast Asia, and Germany, where there is major public participation in long term investment planning, have prospered more than the free-marketeer countries in the highly competitive environment of the global marketplace. (It should be noted that after the crises described in *Turning Sweden Around*, Sweden has bounced back fairly well, although it no longer employs the classical "Swedish model." As of this writing the Social Democrats are back in office, and Sweden is doing as well as any nation-state at balancing social welfare and international competitiveness in the new world of neo-liberalism and globalization.)

In the 1970s, while the Swedish model was doing less well than it had been doing in prior decades, efforts to give organized labor more control over capital intensified. A scheme for employee investment funds was proposed, but not enacted, which would eventually have given the unions control of the major corporations through the gradual acquisition of shares by funds diverted to labor in lieu of excess taxes on profits. Labor influence over capital actually was increased, through pension funds and similar funds, and through employee representation on company boards of directors.

Some of us are looking forward to the day when most corporate shares, and generally most sources of passive investment income, will be owned by institutional investors devoted to worthy causes that promote the people's welfare, such as pensions for the old, workers' rights, medical research, liberal education, habitats for humanity, and cleaning up the environment. Sweden is not the only country that has made a start in this direction. Nevertheless, it should be conceded that there is an illusion, deeply rooted in metaphors that are overused in the social science and in common everyday speech, that lends itself to exaggerating the benefits of putting the supervision of the processes of capital formation and capital investment into the hands of stakeholders and philanthrophists. Rudolf Meidner appeared to be a victim of that illusion when he wrote the following words about the intended goals of employee investment funds:

> What is specific to the employee funds is that they provide a new opportunity for also making more democratic those decisions which are arrived at within enterprises, but which affect a firm's relations with the community as a whole, with consumers, local authorities, the total environment, and so forth. In short, the funds should make it possible to arrive in a democratic manner at those investment decisions which affect what is produced and where. . . .
>
> One might think then that the precise objectives of the employee investment funds could be achieved via labour legislation. But there is an important difference between the right to negotiate and conclude agreements about production decisions on the one hand, and the influence over production which flows from the ownership of capital on the other. He who controls the capital holds the right to initiate and the chance positively to embark on implementing decisions which are thought to be appropriate. In the last resort he who negotiates can only say "No." He cannot press in the same way for particular decisions about proposed ventures if the owner of capital is opposed to committing resources of capital.

This difference, between a positive right to initiate and the possibility of stopping undesirable projects, is illustrated clearly by the fact that the most far-reaching proposal in labour law which has been raised so far concerns a blanket right of veto for the employees, for example over production decisions. . . . But even if a right of this kind were to be introduced, it is obvious that economic democracy could not be said to have become all-pervasive. The right would remain, in fact [in the hands of the capitalists] to take decisions as to the size and nature of investments. Labour legislation cannot therefore be a complete proxy for the power over capital which the employee investment funds would provide.[29]

Before commenting on Meidner's greater good, the positive right to initiate, it is worth noting that even his lesser good, the possibility of stopping undesirable projects, is unattainable for most working people most places most of the time. In most of the world there are ragtag multitudes of people at loose ends, surviving precariously by hook or by crook. They staff restaurants with sparse and seedy diners, sleazy bars with a few lonely drinkers, antique shops full of junk, superfluous travel agencies, barbershops, and beauty salons. They are landless farmers, unemployed prostitutes, sellers of newspapers, telemarketers, door-to-door magazine subscription salespeople, real estate agents, part-time sweepers who sweep up and throw out the trash after laundromats close at midnight, computer amateurs who know just enough to be paid under minimum wage in cash under the table, truck drivers who drive sixteen hours at a stretch and sleep in their cabs, vendors of sundry miracle cancer cures and New Age remedies for anxiety; multi-level marketers selling water purifiers, hand lotions, and expensive shampoos supposed to grow hair on the bald; young men wandering aimlessly from place to place, young women who sell gum, chocolates, and pencils from kiosks. For most people most places most of the time, joining a labor union and going on strike is not an option either because they have no employer, or because their employer is living almost as precariously as they are, or because the ready availability of replacement labor makes a strike an empty threat, or because labor unions are legally and/or illegally suppressed by violence.

Sweden is a tiny little country that is a major source of commodities the rest of the world wants to buy. Most Swedes work in education, in health care, in some other form of government service, or in an industry that produces something buyers really need and want. Instead of having armies of real estate agents desperately trying to make a living by landing sales, the Swedes put ads for available houses in the windows of the same banks that finance the transactions. It makes sense for almost everybody to be in a labor union, because almost everybody works for a viable employer. Pro-labor socialist governments have been in office most of the time for as long as anybody can remember, and since before most people were born. It is in this context that the negative power of giving labor a blanket veto over production decisions can be faulted for failing to make economic democracy all-pervasive. In such a context in the 1970s Swedish labor was not satisfied with mere stop power. It aspired to acquire the go power that was believed to flow from the ownership of capital.

The story of Swedish labor's efforts to take control of capital is a story of disillusionment. Power, like a mirage, vanished as it was approached. By the time the employees' pension money finally made its way into the stock market and started buying shares, it had fallen into the habit of acting like any other money. It made the same investment decisions based on the same criteria. The employee board members turned out not to be radical. They settled down to review accounts and to analyze the options for the future outlined by management much the same as any other directors.

Those who are inclined to do so may exercise their freedom of speech by saying that the Swedish working class was betrayed by its leaders. We think it more pertinent to observe that money has a logic of its own, regardless of whose money it is. And that human life is governed far more by the constitutive rules of society than by who sits in which seats. It only seemed that the Swedish model could be rescued by worker control over capital because people's minds were too clouded by "power" to focus on "rules."

Illusions Regarding the Mobility of Capital

Jonas Pontusson studied the attempts of Swedish labor to gain more control over capital, and concluded that one of the main reasons for its failure was "because the systemic power of capital thwarted the effects of the legislation that labor achieved."[30] Pontusson explains:

> Perhaps the simplest way to think about the systemic power of business is in terms of "exit options." Consider codetermination bargaining. Even if the law prescribed that management must reach an agreement with the unions, capital would still retain the option to exit. If codetermination yielded a bargain that was unfavorable to capital or was perceived as such by management or owners—management would very likely decide to locate new investment in plants with more pliable unions, perhaps abroad.[31]

But to talk of "systemic power" is to name the problem in a way that sheds little light on the nature of "exit options." Once again the ubiquitous notion of "power," which is everywhere in modern thought, clouds a focus on rules. The constitutive rules of modern society prescribe that property owners are free to move their property. Consequently, an attempt to transform society that proposes to change without changing, to achieve social democracy in its classical sense of society producing for itself, producing for the sake of meeting human needs in a harmonious relationship with the earth, while not questioning the basic cultural structure, is based on a philosophy that is not workable.

Similarly, Rudolf Meidner held the unrealistic view that government legislation could somehow prevent multinational firms from investing abroad instead of in Sweden, as is shown in the following passage:

> We discussed . . . the question of multinational firms, which disturbs many of LO's members. We can assume that the community's knowledge of and control over these enterprises will have been considerably improved by the time the introduction of employee funds becomes imminent. Government industrial policy is being steadily strengthened and can be activated in the event of a drop in the private willingness to invest. Tax policy provides a further instrument for influencing the willingness to invest in a positive way. If the decision to introduce employee funds is made in the normal democratic manner, this very fact gives the government a mandate to use appropriate policy measures to ensure that the reform does not lead to an investment strike, reduced capital formation, and a drop in employment. There would undoubtedly be very strong popular support for the idea of taking the necessary countermeasures, should such a situation arise.[32]

Thus Meidner overestimated the sustainability of the Swedish model, and underestimated the ability of capital to move out of Sweden, because he thought the government could exercise "control over these enterprises," that industrial policy could be "strengthened," and that the carrots and sticks of tax policy could "influence" capital to invest "in a positive way."

In our view the "necessary countermeasures" that must be taken to deal with the virtual certainty that the building of social democracy will encounter investment strikes and capital flight include the ethical construction of a culture of solidarity. "Ethical construction" is what Paulo Freire called "cultural action" and not far from what Antonio Gramsci called "cultural hegemony" and "moral and intellectual reform."[33] The next chapter will consider some contributions of two Swedes to the theory and practice of ethical construction: Hjalmar Branting, the first socialist prime minister of Sweden, and the Swedish linguist and anthropologist Helena Norberg-Hodge.

Notes

1. Frederic Fleisher, *The New Sweden: The Challenge of a Disciplined Democracy* (New York: David McKay Company, 1967), vii.

2. Fleisher, *New Sweden*, viii.

3. Fleisher, *New Sweden*, viii.

4. Lundberg in Ralf Dahrendorf, ed., *Europe's Economy in Crisis* (New York: Holmes & Meier, 1982), 198-99. On the economic problems faced by Sweden beginning in the 1970s and increasing in severity throughout the 1980s, see also J. Magnus Ryner, "Maastricht Convergence in the Social Democratic Heartland: Sweden and Germany," *International Journal of Political Economy* 28, no. 2 (1998): 85-123; and Ryner, *Capitalist Restructuring, Globalisation and the Third Way: Lessons from the Swedish Model* (London: Routledge, 2002).

5. Lundberg in Dahrendorf, *Europe's Economy in Crisis,* 198-99.

6. Lundberg in Dahrendorf, *Europe's Economy in Crisis*, 198-99.

7. J. Magnus Ryner asserts that already by the 1970s, Sweden's so-called Third Way was shifting, so that instead of trying to implement a "Third Way" between capitalism and socialism, policymakers had to content themselves with seeking a "Third Way" that was a compromise between neoliberalism and social democracy. J. Magnus Ryner, "Assessing SAP's Economic Policy in the 1980's: The 'Third Way,' the Swedish Model, and the Transition from Fordism to post-Fordism," *Economic and Industrial Democracy* 15, no. 3 (1994), 389, 423.

8. The enormous growth of the public sector was not only, or even primarily, the result of a socialist strategy to exert greater public control over an economy that was failing to respond to traditional Keynesian remedies. It was partly the result of other policies, such as the policy of raising the status of women and making women's pay equal to men's pay, which led to the hiring of many women by county governments to staff day care centers, so that other women could leave their homes to join the wage-labor work force. Perhaps most importantly, the growth of the public sector was a corollary of Sweden's commitment to full employment. Thus Lundberg writes: "Since 1974, the rise of employment in the public sector has absorbed the whole of the increase in the total work force as well as the decline in industrial employment." Lundberg in Dahrendorf, *Europe's Economy in Crisis,* 199.

9. Assar Lindbeck et al., *Turning Sweden Around* (Cambridge, Mass.; and London: MIT Press, 1994), 3-10.

10. The prescriptions offered by these authors with regard to the relationship between wage-rates and the health of the economy overall are familiar. We cite here just a few representative passages: "Competition is severely restricted . . . in the labor and financial markets. In the labor market it is mainly wage formation and the legal rules for hiring and firing of labor, that is, the labor legislation, that is problematic. In particular, wage formation tends to conflict with the need for a flexible labor market, because relative wages have to a large extent become tools for redistributive ambitions. Existing labor legislation springs from a society with less heterogeneous workers and jobs than today, and with less need for flexibility." Lindbeck et al., *Turning Sweden Around*, 7. "The regulations in the labor market may be well intended. Nevertheless, they entail considerable costs—like the regulations in goods markets. In fact, the pervasive role of the labor

market means that these regulations affect the whole economy. . . . It seems clear that some labor market regulations create a conflict between short-term job security for the individual and the need for a well-functioning labor market and flexible firms. It is likely that the negative effects for society as a whole have increased over time, as the need for flexibility in the economy has increased." Lindbeck et al., *Turning Sweden Around*, 90, 92. And: "To mitigate the unemployment effects of wage formation, one may . . . let wage earners and employers themselves bear a larger share of unemployment costs through employer and employee contributions to unemployment insurance. . . . The idea is to increase the resistance among labor market parties to excessive wages by conditioning insurance fees on the risk of unemployment." Lindbeck et al., *Turning Sweden Around*, 38.

11. Buckminster Fuller holds that the ideology of "you or me to the death—on behalf of yours or mine—for there is not enough to sustain us both," an ideology founded upon the beliefs of Malthus, carried forth by Darwin, and replicated in economics, politics, and the form of the modern nation-state, is a fundamental cause of war. R. Buckminster Fuller, *Utopia or Oblivion: The Prospects for Humanity* (Toronto and New York: Bantam Books, 1969), 6, 123-24.

12. Myrdal, *Beyond the Welfare State*. The reader should note that in interpreting Myrdal's text we will be reading between the lines a bit, drawing out thoughts we believe to be alive in the silences of the subtext.

13. On the influence of Gunnar Myrdal upon framing the questions that define the parameters of the post-World War II development paradigm, see "The Myrdal Legacy: Racism and Underdevelopment as Dilemmas," in Wallerstein, *Unthinking Social Science*, 80-103. As the present work makes clear, we are in accord with Wallerstein when he writes, "Myrdal is not, in my view, too harsh on establishment economics, but in his anxiety to gore the ox, he tends to ignore the fact that the folly of establishment economics is merely a *reductio ad absurdum* of a much more widespread malady, the narrow [blinders] that all of the historical social sciences have put upon themselves." Wallerstein, *Unthinking Social Science*, 94.

14. See, e.g., Myrdal, *Beyond the Welfare State*, 53-61, 98-102.

15. Myrdal, *Beyond the Welfare State*, 228-49.

16. Myrdal, *Beyond the Welfare State*, 19-29, 62-64.

17. Myrdal, *Beyond the Welfare State*, 63.

18. Rehn in Erik Lundberg, Rudolf Meidner, Gösta Rehn, and Krister Wickman, *Wages Policy Under Full Employment*, ed. and trans. Ralph Turvey (London: William Hodge and Company, 1952), 39-40.

19. On the difficulties faced by Swedish firms and Swedish unions in keeping wages relatively high and on the rise, see, in addition to sources already cited, Furniss and Tilton, *Case for the Welfare State*, 136-38.

20. Commenting on the somewhat similar decline of British social democracy, Will Hutton writes, "The British State has the form it has because it, too, is the result of the liberal tradition. That the State should stand aside from the economy, that its role is to enforce the rule of law and protect private property, that in the market the public good emerges from the interaction of interests, and that the job of Parliament is to be the forum where those interests interact; the institutions of the British State are built around these fundamental tenets, and it is this that makes attempts to use the State in a different way so ineffectual." Will Hutton, *The revolution that never was: An assessment of Keynesian economics* (London and New York: Longman, 1986), 25.

21. The rationalization of the Swedish bureaucracy has roots back in the days when the Kings of Sweden entrusted the training of their clerks to the Lutheran Church. The government's coordinated responses to hard times made economic reverses much easier for the people to bear than they would have been—and usually are—in less well-organized countries.

22. Milton Friedman, *Essays in Positive Economics* (Chicago: University of Chicago Press, 1964), 22. Friedman goes on to attempt to save his idea that profit maximization is a principle of hard positivist economic science by deducing it from the idea of natural selection. It is, Friedman suggests, what businesses must do to survive; therefore, they must be doing it, whether or not they appear to be doing it, because if they did not do it they would not be surviving. This gambit overlooks two crucial facts. 1) It is notorious that empiricist, positivist, and Popperian philosophers have been embarrassed precisely because they cannot on their principles justify Darwinian or post-Darwinian realism, which is central to all biology. Hence if the truth of the principle of natural selection did imply the truth of the principle of profit maximizing, that would be a point scored by realism, not a point scored by positivism. 2) The selection of successful firms by capitalist competition (or by whatever selects them) does not take place in a natural environment, but in a socially constructed environment. Hence, although it is selection, it is not natural selection.

23. Indeed, Richard M. Cyert and James G. March have done so in *A Behavioral Theory of the Firm* (Englewood Cliffs, N.J.: Prentice-Hall, 1963).

24. Note that throughout this discussion, we believe and are assuming that it makes no difference whether "profit" is defined as operating surplus with or without depreciation, narrowly as return on owners' equity, or broadly to include such things as salaries paid to executives or interest on long term debt.

25. Edgren, Faxén, and Odhner, *Wage Formation and the Economy*.

26. Edgren, Faxén, and Odhner, *Wage Formation and the Economy*, 126.

27. Edgren, Faxén, and Odhner, *Wage Formation and the Economy*, 11.

28. Edgren, Faxén, and Odhner, *Wage Formation and the Economy*, 12-13. That some economists of the LO group made the similar argument that turning profits into collective wage earners' funds would help to make trade unions less militant (see Lundberg, *Swedish and Keynesian Macroeconomic Theory*, 81) indicates that regardless of outward appearance of political difference, all parties involved were trapped by the same logic.

29. Meidner, *Employee Investment Funds*, 77-78, explanation added.

30. Jonas Pontusson, *The Limits of Social Democracy: investment politics in Sweden* (Ithaca, N.Y.; and London: Cornell University Press, 1992), 225.

31. Pontusson, *Limits of Social Democracy*, 233.

32. Meidner, *Employee Investment Funds*, 119.

33. Both Freire and Gramsci are concerned, as we are, with finding nonviolent ways to move the world away from systems of domination and oppression and creating more just and ethical cultures; and both emphasize the importance of using extant common language and establishing new common language in order to carry out the dialogue necessary to such creation. Freire defines "cultural action" as "a systematic and deliberate form of action which operates upon the social structure . . . with the objective of . . . transforming it." Freire, *Pedagogy of the Oppressed*, 180. The aim of "dialogical cultural action," according to Freire, is "surmounting the antagonistic contradictions of the social structure," thereby achieving human liberation. Freire, *Pedagogy of the Oppressed*, 181. Gramsci asserts that moral and intellectual reform must be undertaken in order to create

the "terrain for a subsequent development of the national-popular collective will towards the realisation of a superior, total form of modern civilisation." Antonio Gramsci, *Selections from the Prison Notebooks*, trans. Quintin Hoare and Geoffrey Nowell Smith (New York: International Publishers, 1989), 133. On the process of bringing "cultural hegemony" into being, Gramsci writes, "An historical act can only be performed by 'collective man,' and this presupposes the attainment of a 'cultural-social' unity through which a multiplicity of dispersed wills, with heterogeneous aims, are welded together with a single aim, on the basis of an equal and common conception of the world. . . . Since this is the way things happen, great importance is assumed by the general question of language, that is, the question of collectively attaining a single cultural 'climate.'" Gramsci, *Prison Notebooks*, 349.

Chapter 8

Hjalmar Branting's *Uppfostran*

Regarded from a certain quite respectable point of view, one of the great merits of classical Swedish social democracy was that it was rational, in a sense of the word "rational" approved by Sir Karl Popper. According to Popper, it is rational to change one or a few variables at a time, holding all other factors constant. It is irrational to change society in many ways at once. Multifaceted change is irrational because when many factors affect the achievement of many objectives, there are too many effects to measure, too many independent variables. It becomes impossible to link causes to effects. For this reason, revolutions are always irrational. They change too much, and therefore the consequences of the changes cannot be evaluated.

Swedish social democrats, during the halcyon days of the Swedish model, often thought in patterns Sir Karl Popper would commend. The framework was held constant, while changes were limited and specific. What Rudolf Meidner wrote about proposals for employee investment funds was typical:

> We are conscious of certain conditions which set the scene for us. A number of these are already given and generally accepted, and therefore require no detailed discussion. First and foremost among them there is the demand for full employment, or jobs for everyone. The achievement of this most fundamental of all our aims must not be prejudiced by any reforms in policies toward redistribution.
>
> Closely related to this is the demand for a *high level of capital formation*; indeed, this is an essential condition for high and rising employment. The Swedish economy is very exposed to foreign competition, and a high investment ratio must accordingly be sustained in order to defend our position in foreign markets. Probably few trade movements are as positive as the Swedish one in their attitude to a high level of investment, to the steady expansion and technological regeneration of the apparatus of production. This can be attributed not solely to a ready appreciation of economic relationships but primarily to a successful employment and labour market policy. . . .
>
> Another important stipulation is that any attempts to meet our . . . objectives should be *neutral with respect to costs wages and prices*. A measure of

165

distributive policy which imposed a cost burden on enterprises could conceivably be shifted on to prices and be inflationary without at the same time achieving any real redistributive effect. It also follows that wage policy must not be
prejudiced, and wage bargaining must be assumed to exploit to the full the possibilities for consumption, without being responsible for the relationship between consumption and saving.

Finding an arrangement which reinforces solidarity in wage policy [i.e., a
form of employee ownership of business] must finally satisfy the obvious condition that it does not run counter to the main aim of that policy, which is to
equalise incomes between different groups of employees. This means that any
profit-sharing scheme which gives rise to new disparities in income within the
total aggregate of employees would not be acceptable to the trade union movement.

We have accordingly to conduct our search for solutions to the problems
which we have posed within a fairly narrow framework of specific objectives
and conditions, and this in fact means that the range of choices among various
models for redistribution is a rather limited one.[1]

With the benefit of hindsight, it can be seen that the factors held constant in
the types of macroeconomic discourse characteristic of the Swedish model were
not constant in reality. It is one thing for a model to postulate that government,
or labor, or business, will undertake a small and carefully studied pilot program
and carefully measure its consequences before expanding the application of the
program to a larger scale. It is another thing for history to stand still, allowing a
social experiment to unfold *ceteris paribus*, with all non-experimental factors
remaining equal, frozen in time like mute stone statues, from the moment the
experiment starts until the moment the experiment ends.

As Erik Lundberg noted in a passage cited in the previous chapter, in the
1970s the Swedish government repeated the same Keynesian policies it had applied successfully in the two previous decades. Its model of reality had not
changed. Nevertheless, reality had changed. Indeed, reality had always been
more fluid, more complex, and more subject to variations due to humans not
behaving according to expected patterns, than macroeconomic thinking supposed. It was always a very rough and approximate form of thought, but for two
decades it worked. The reasons why it was working were not necessarily the
same as the reasons why the actors whose actions were guided by it thought it
was working.[2]

We have been saying that classical Swedish social democracy should be
near the top of the list in any ranking of the best cultures that *homo sapiens* has
created so far. This may be a good place to mention two more excellent Swedish
institutions, just to underline how well Sweden has done, before proceeding to
dwell on the Swedish model's limitations. One is "contact days." In Sweden
employers must give parents several days off work each year, in order to enable
the parents to go to school with their children. This keeps the parents in close
contact with the part of their children's lives that is spent in school. A second is
subsidized enterprises for people with handicaps. In a labor market there are

always people who can work, but who cannot work fast enough, or skillfully enough, to make it worth an employer's money to hire them at standard wages. But in Sweden even those with sub-standard speed, strength, or skill can and do work. They even manage their own enterprises. Public institutions are reluctant to treat the handicapped as disabled and to put them on the dole. Instead, they contribute enough to the enterprises of the handicapped to make it possible for them to sell their products at competitive prices on the open market.

We have been showing that Swedish social democracy encountered limitations inherent in the normative framework it took for granted. Maintaining high wages in an intensely competitive global marketplace was one of Sweden's successes that proved to have limits. Now that global markets are even more competitive, and now that Sweden—as a member of the European Union—is even less able to act independently of global markets, those limits can only be more confining. The basic ethical foundations of the market, freedom and property, limit what Sweden can do now even more, now that Sweden is even more dependent on the free play of market forces.

Leaving the constitutive rules of society unquestioned is a great merit from the point of view of the philosophy of social research of Karl Popper. There comes a time, nevertheless, when the possibilities for improvement within a framework of unquestioned premises are exhausted. We should confess, however, before going on, that we have been exaggerating Sweden's allegiance to Popperian rationality. Myrdal, for example, observed that under the social democrats, the Swedish population became more individualistic and more hedonistic, not because anybody intended that result, but because of general historical trends, which were not holding constant while Sweden tinkered with one variable at a time. Many Swedish authors make similar observations about the shift from blue-collar to white-collar employment. Thus Swedes, like everyone else, are quite aware that history is not standing still while social engineers conduct experiments. Nevertheless, the very idea of building socialism by gradual incremental steps tends to assume that society is not rapidly moving in some other direction. Whatever merit confining attention to a few variables at a time may have depends on some degree of faith that the variables regarded as constant are not changing in ways that overwhelm the variables studied. In Sweden, as in other countries, the historical evolution of capitalism changed the context for social democracy.

What we are calling "daring to question the unquestioned" has more than one dimension. We have also been suggesting that the paradigms of social science that regard reality as a set of "variables" or "factors" which have "impacts on" and are "functions of each other" are inadequate paradigms. A distaste for what was perceived as metaphysics led to bad metaphysics. The "impact and function" paradigms of social science do not grasp the main source of law-like regularities in social life, namely, rules. Rules, as the later Wittgenstein pointed out, are not in the end comprehensible in terms of metaphors drawn from the hard sciences at all, but necessarily depend on what he called a *Rechtfertigung*, an appeal to authority. Thus the broadening of horizons we are calling for has three levels: 1) considering alternatives to the premises that social democracy has taken as givens; 2) placing social democracy today in the context of the historical evolution of the global capitalist system; and 3) openness to alternative forms of thought.

French postmodernism and post-structuralism have recently made great contributions to the intellectual task of destabilizing assumptions about the rules of society that economics takes for granted, whether it is the old classical economics, Keynesian economics, or contemporary neoliberal economics. Just a few decades ago, it was possible for Myrdal to describe social democracy as a "created harmony," implicitly contrasting it with *laissez faire* capitalism, which presumably therefore would have to be regarded as something not created, a natural order. That was certainly how the founders of *laissez faire* regarded it. They explicitly put Nature in the place of the Creator, and the principle of contract in the place of the principle of divine command. In Jean-Jacques Rousseau's works on political economy, on education, and on civil government, it is especially clear that there is a systematic shift in discourse, in which the role previously assigned to God, as Creator and source of authority, is assigned to Nature and to human will.[3]

Now that Rousseau's work has been so thoroughly deconstructed by Jacques Derrida, and, in general, the humanism of the eighteenth century has been deconstructed by postmodernists, it is no longer defensible, if it ever was, to regard *laissez faire* capitalism as natural, while treating social democracy as an artificial creation.[4] Similarly, the detailed accounts of the genesis of modern ideas and institutions produced by Michel Foucault, the *Annales* historians, Immanuel Wallerstein, and others remove any plausibility there ever was to treating the normative framework of modern western culture—which is by extension that of the global economy—as natural. It never was plausible to deny that freedom, property, markets, and money are not natural but rather conventional. Now their ideologies have been deconstructed, and their historical origins have been precisely chronicled.

Our ethical construction philosophy, which Howard Richards has developed in detail in other writings, is a way to put a positive spin on postmodernism. What happens in history is that people construct cultures. Even wars construct cultures. Of course, destruction happens too, but it could not happen unless something were constructed first; without construction there would be nothing to destroy. *Homo sapiens sapiens* is an animal whose ecological niche is to be the creator of cultures. The work of constructing cultures is ethical both in that it is about norms ("what should be" or what should be according to some particular culture) and—going to the ancient root of the word "ethical"—in that it is about customs, i.e., conventions.

Modern society, defined by Max Weber as "rational," in contrast to traditional society, which was "customary," is only apparently an exception to the proposition that all cultures are customary.[5] Because rationality itself is a set of customs. Notably, it is conventional, not natural, to call profit maximizing "rational."

We interpret the great thinkers of the past as cultural activists who facilitated the reshaping of norms. Thus we do not look on Jean-Jacques Rousseau as a fool (or charlatan) who imagined (or feigned) illusory conceptual unities, which a smarter (or more honest) philosopher like Jacques Derrida could later deconstruct. We see Rousseau as a creator of culture.

In what follows, we will offer a retracing of a few of the steps by which Swedish social democracy was constructed. At certain stages of its construction, architectural choices were made which allowed some options and ruled out others. The purpose of this retracing of steps is to suggest reconsideration of some options long ago ruled out. No discoveries. Just a thought experiment designed to locate ethical choices most people are already aware of on a conceptual map of a European past imagined as a centuries-long labor of ethical construction.

If we take a short step backward in time from the days when the reign of the Swedish model, narrowly defined, was about to begin, or was just getting underway; to 1948; we find an election that marked an architectural choice. In 1948 the socialists put before the voters a radical program, which would have continued into peacetime some wartime emergency measures, and, generally, extended the economic powers of the government. Whether the conservatives were being accurate or exaggerating, when they called it an attempt to install in Sweden a command economy like that of the Soviet Union, it was true that the socialists proposed a *rapprochement* with the USSR; reducing economic ties to the West, which—Myrdal predicted—would soon relapse into a depression like that of the 1930s; and enhancing ties with the East; balancing the two, not relying too much on one bloc or the other.

Friedrich von Hayek's book *The Road to Serfdom* was influential in Sweden in 1948. Von Hayek cited Hitler and Stalin as two proofs of the same theorem: governments wielding economic power crush individual liberties.[6] The results at the polls showed that his voice had been heard. Although the socialists were not turned out of office, they were warned. The voters of Sweden did not want a command economy.

Retracing Swedish social democracy's steps four more years backward in time, we find another architectural choice made during World War II. Sweden lived under wartime conditions even though it was not formally involved in the war. It had rationing and price controls, and called on its citizens to make sacrifices. As elsewhere, full employment at good wages was achieved for the first time during the war. The maintenance of full employment assumed the status of a right of the working classes, and a duty of the government.

Thus the rules of the game were fixed; the social structure took shape. The options for social democracy were circumscribed. There would not be a command economy. And yet there would be full employment. Given that other options had already been foreclosed by architectural choices made earlier, full employment without a command economy could only mean one thing: booming export sales.

Sales must be expanded to expand the demand for labor. A standard accounting text states the major premise succinctly: "The number of direct labor

employees is a function of the work to be performed, which is a function of materials in inventory, which is a function of the sales forecast."[7] Given that the
employment of labor will be generated by consumer demand (because there will
not be a command economy), full employment can only arise from high demand, which means high sales, and which means, in the case of Sweden, high
sales in foreign markets.

Already in the late 1930s, with the establishment of the system of nationwide collective bargaining, and the historic pacts between capital and labor at
the national level, it had become clear that the tone of the Swedish economy
would be set by the major unions and the major firms—most of which were export-oriented. The radicalism of anti-bigness so common on the American left,
trailing shades of Jeffersonian farmers tilling their own soil, and evoking images
of local self-rule among pioneers on horseback riding the lone prairies of the
New World, was not to be the Swedish way.

The early 1930s was the time of the invention of macroeconomics (although
some say that Knut Wicksell gave Sweden a precocious head start on the rest of
the world by anticipating Keynes' major ideas a generation earlier). The rapid
rise to hegemony of macroeconomics represented an architectural choice, because it meant that the ideas of the Stockholm School, and not Marxism, would
be social democracy's ideological alternative to classical *laissez-faire* capitalist
economics.

The rise of macroeconomics and the eclipse of Marx meant that the ideal of
production for use was off the main agenda, although in Sweden, as elsewhere,
there were persistent, visionary, frustrated souls who continued to dream of it
and to work to put it into practice. Macroeconomics, after all, was about aggregate demand. Increasing aggregate demand meant putting money into people's
pockets so they could spend it; thus generating expectations of profit among
entrepreneurs; thus stimulating investment; and therefore, finally, achieving
what the social democrats wanted, employment. If the only way to boost demand for labor is to boost sales, that is fine with Keynes.

It is not fine with Marx. For Marx what is wrong with capitalism is that it is
production for exchange, not for use; for sale, not for people. The main concepts
in Marx's arsenal flow from his critique of exchange: alienation, commodity,
commodity fetishism, surplus value, accumulation, the exploitation of labor,
private appropriation of the social product, the reserve army of the unemployed,
the holy trinity (profit, interest, and rent), the falling rate of profit, the immisera-
tion of the proletariat. The time of social democracy is, for Marx, by definition,
the time after capitalism when food and other goods will be produced for people,
not for profit.

Hjalmar Branting was the leader of the Swedish social democratic workers
party during most of the early twentieth century. He took the ideal of production
for use seriously. For Branting, the decisive step in the achievement of socialism
was the achievement of universal suffrage. Branting believed that acquiring and
exercising the right to vote was a means for achieving socialism. Socialism was
a rational outcome of the evolution of humanity, which the people would im-

plement when they acquired the authority to name the legislators who would write the laws. Gradually the authority to write the laws would produce a society geared to producing for people not for profit.

In Branting's time the socialist party devoted much effort to preparing the people for their role as rulers of a democratic society. In a speech he gave in 1923, celebrating the twenty-fifth anniversary of the founding of the LO, he said:

> [N]ow as before it is quite simply a matter of our continuing to train our great working people for both political and economic self-government. Now as before we want to win our victories by persuasion, not by force, and to gain an ever stronger position of power in our society for both those great co-operating organizations . . . L.O., whose day we celebrate, and our Swedish Social Democratic Labor party. They both exist not to carry out a fixed plan down to the last detail . . . but as much as they can to lay the foundation for the society that Ibsen dreamed of—where there is room for free and noble men and women, for personalities who in serving their fellow man can realize their own yearning for lofty personal development.[8]

The ABF, the Swedish workers' educational association, sponsored evening classes for working people throughout the nation. There was a proliferation of party and union magazines and newspapers, of union schools and study groups, intended not just to enhance job skills, but to prepare the majority of the people to be the ruling class—a ruling class that would reorganize society according to principles of cooperation and solidarity. The best education of all was, moreover, active participation in the new institutions organized according to non-capitalist principles, which the socialist party was already sponsoring and encouraging: consumer cooperatives, producers' cooperatives, labor unions, innovative forms of local government, burial societies and other mutual aid societies.

Branting's expectation that in the future people would build new institutions, in which production for sale in order to make profit would be replaced by cooperation to meet needs, led him to promote education for citizenship, for participation. Education for social democracy meant education for a world not dominated by exchange. He repeatedly stressed the importance of *uppfostran*, "upbringing" or "character formation," a Swedish word similar to the German word *Bildung*. He declared, "To be able to overthrow the bourgeoisie's domination the working class must therefore raise itself to organizational, intellectual, and moral superiority over its opponents. It must have at its disposal a sum of energy, self-sacrifice, intellectual power, knowledge, and maturity that can only be acquired by unremitting work and schooling in political and union struggles and in the co-operative movement which we have laboriously built up."[9]

Marx was one of the nineteenth-century thinkers who founded social democracy by carrying out what Marx called, in the subtitle to *Capital*, "a critique of political economy." If we trace the steps of the process of social construction even farther back, we come, in the eighteenth century and earlier, to the invention of the object of Marx's critique: political economy. Political economy was capitalism's theory.

As socialism set out not to be capitalism, and as Marx's *Capital* set out to be a critique of political economy, so modern society, which was born in Europe's nascent international capitalist market economy, had its other, which it set out not to be. Medieval Christendom was modernity's other, its first other, the other that created it. Modern thought had its object to critique: the philosophy of the schools, scholasticism, of which the most famous exponent was St. Thomas Aquinas. (Even today, first semester students in economics often learn that St. Thomas's theory of the "just price" is a paradigm of what economics is not.) Later, as the European world economy expanded, as it spread secular modernity around the world, it encountered other others: Islam, Hinduism, Shintoism, Confucianism, Buddhism, and thousands of smaller and less famous cultures and belief-systems.

If one compares what the teachings of traditional religious and spiritual cultures have to say about the topics studied by economists (e.g., "Feed the hungry!"—the first of St. Thomas's seven corporal works of mercy), with the careful and thorough empirical studies prepared by economists, it is hard for some people to resist the conclusion that economists are smarter than God. What, they ask, as a matter of empirical historical fact, has God created? Medieval Europe, also known as Christendom, a cultural region whose peoples acknowledged God as the source of legitimate authority, was marked by poverty, disease, ignorance, short life expectancy, and (in spite of its official *agape* ideology) frequent and commonplace acts of cruelty. India, the cradle of several of the world's great religions, is and was a cradle of misery. In contrast, those societies where the market, and the principles of property rights and freedom of contract, are acknowledged as the sources of legitimate authority, boast the achievements of modern medicine, modern agriculture, and modern sanitation. It is hard to resist giving three cheers for the *paroles* of Jacques Prévert:

> *Notre Père qui êtes aux cieux*
> *Restez-y*
> *Et nous nous resterons sur la terre*
> *Qui est quelquefois si jolie*
> *Avec ses mystères de New York*
> *Et puis ses mystères de Paris*
> (Our Father who art in heaven
> Stay there
> And we will stay on earth
> Which is sometimes so pretty
> With its mysteries of New York
> With its mysteries of Paris.)[10]

Those who cheer asking God to remain in heaven, far away—like the God of the eighteenth-century deists, Who would not think of interfering with the

Laws of Commerce because they were Laws of Nature, and Who, like a clock-maker who had made a clock and then left it to run by itself, would never think of interfering with any Law of Nature—will probably readily agree with us that important architectural choices were made when modern society's foundations emerged from the matrix of medieval Christendom. But it will be another matter to make a plausible case to persuade readers that the choices then made should now be reconsidered.

Medieval Christendom was counted by Max Weber as a member of a large class of "traditional" cultures. By dint of heroic generalizations, Weber charac-terized traditional (as distinct from modern) societies as ones ruled by customs and conventions, by value rationality (*Wertrationalitat*), and by enchantment.[11] Thus he did as good a job as anyone has ever done of summarizing the essential qualities of nearly one hundred thousand years of human experience, on six con-tinents and more than three thousand islands.

If we broaden the question to make it one about all traditional societies, and answer it by asserting that surely somewhere in the many wisdoms of the world's traditional peoples, there must be lessons to be learned about how to cooperate and share to meet needs, which can teach modernity some options worth considering, or reconsidering; then surely no one will deny that our asser-tion, trivial or banal as it may be, is, at least, true. It is evident that when Saint Thomas Aquinas in his *Summa Theologiae* proved that the lower angels can teach nothing to the higher angels, because the higher angels already know eve-rything the lower angels know, that the good saint's vision was blinded by the clarity and consistency of his concepts. It should be equally evident that modern cultures can learn from traditional cultures.

However, we are retracing the steps of the construction of Swedish social democracy, back to the century when economics itself was invented, not in order to prove a general proposition that is self-evident if one thinks about it, but spe-cifically in order to reopen the question of whether economics should have been invented at all. Economics specifically denied the specific principle that unified the ideology of medieval Europe. To reconsider economics, starting at its begin-ning, is to ask whether what economics denied might actually be true.

In a famous and typical remark, Adam Smith stated that he could rely on the self-interest of his baker to get his daily bread, but he could not rely on his baker's benevolence. The word "benevolence" can be divided into two parts, "bene" and "volence," which come from two Latin roots meaning "good" and "will." In other words, Smith denied that he could rely on the good will of his baker to get his daily bread. Similarly, Bernard de Mandeville, in his *Fable of the Bees, or Private vices, Publick Benefits,* originally published in 1714, argued that luxury, selfishness and greed, which were vices according to the teachings of tradition, were sources of material progress. In his book *From Mandeville to Marx: The Genesis and Triumph of Economic Ideology*, Louis Dumont gives many other similar examples. Dumont shows how the early economists were quite aware that they were departing from the ethical norms of medieval Chris-tendom.[12] The economists presumed the existence of a society in which norms of solidarity, expressed in terms of God or kinship or loyalty, no longer reigned. Acting from self-interest, which medieval theology defined as sin, was no longer seen as the problem, but as the solution.

The official constitutive rules of society approved by the church universal of the European Middle Ages were recorded in Saint Thomas's *Summa*. The central organizing idea in that voluminous work is *caritas*. *Caritas* translates the Greek *agape*, which is one of the New Testament's names for God: *ho theon agepen estin* ("God is love."). Another meaning of *agape* in Greek is "welcoming." From *caritas*, the Latin equivalent of *agape*, flowed the accepted rules for the organization of society, as they were articulated and idealized in the reigning ideology: law and justice, the use of property, the rules governing markets and exchanges, just prices, the duties of rulers and ruled, the sharing of goods, the duty to serve others. All norms were derived from *caritas*, directly or indirectly, and all were, finally, judged by *caritas*, the ultimate standard.

The rise of modern society, and its ideology, economics, marked not just an architectural choice, but a change of form of thought, different ways of naming the problems to be solved, different conversations about different topics, discourses governed by different root metaphors.

For the tradition, as it was taught in the schools, it was supremely important to cultivate a good will. Thus a classic of the counter-reformation, the *Spiritual Exercises* of Saint Ignatius Loyola, begins by saying that the purpose of spiritual exercises is to achieve a good will, first to purge the will of disorderly tendencies, then to identify the will with the divine will. There is an important similarity among Ignatius' idea of identification with the divine will, the Marxist idea of de-alienation, and Barbara Marx Hubbard's idea of emerging into essence.[13] In all three cases humans realize who they really are, and find joy, by becoming servant leaders whose being is a being-in-relationship. In Marx's terms, people, who are already human and always have been, become truly human when they realize what he called the *Gattungwesen*, the social essence of the species.

The economists had a better idea. Or, at least, in the 18th century it seemed like a better idea. They believed self-interest more powerful and more reliable than good will. Adam Smith expected his daily bread from his baker's self-interest, not from his benevolence. Therefore, it seemed, if one could construct a science of self-interest, ignoring the educational and spiritual issues that arise when one worries about how to transform wills, one could construct a more powerful and more reliable intellectual engine for the improvement of society.

This story has a moral. If one thinks of social democracy as a social engineering project, then one is likely to treat the constitutive principles that organize society as an unquestioned background while making measured and carefully studied changes. To a considerable extent, this is what Swedish social democracy did. Typically, as is illustrated by the quotation from Rudolf Meidner at the beginning of this chapter, there were only a few options to choose from, in an environment where most parameters were fixed. Looked at from one point of view, this was sound Popperian methodology. Looked at from another point of view, it was a slowly closing trap out of which all the exits were being closed, one by one. In the end, for the classical Swedish model there were no options at all. The number of viable options declined from three to two to one to zero. Then social democratic ideals had to be put on hold. Neoliberal reforms had to be accepted. At that point books were published like *After Social Democracy* by Ralf Dahrendorf, and *The Death Knell of Social Democracy: Sweden's Dream Turns Sour* by Peter Stein and Ingemar Dörfer.[14]

The moral is that there is another way to look at the building of social democracy. If one thinks of history as a process of ethical construction, then one will think about rules, principles, and values. One will ask what principles were laid down when, for what reasons, and with what results. We have been showing how the basic rules of freedom and property, which constitute market culture, laid down long ago, limit what is socially possible. Gunnar Myrdal's dream of building social democracy on the foundation of the ideals of the eighteenth century was not a feasible dream. For the same reasons, by extension, his dream of a world anti-poverty program was not feasible. Meanwhile, since his time, the context has changed. Tendencies inherent in capitalism since its beginnings have been accentuated, namely the tendency toward a global market and the tendency toward a global iron law of wages. The power of any national government to regulate markets and thus buffer its citizens against the blows of market forces has been weakened. As Jacques Derrida has observed, as the power of nations declines, the need to criticize the rules of civil society increases.[15]

Therefore, the movements most likely to make a generalizable contribution to advancing cooperation, sharing, and sustainability are the ones that rest, explicitly or implicitly, on a radical critique of the basic rules of modern society. Fortunately, there are many such movements today. There are many thinkers today who realize that humanity and the planet cannot move forward without reconsidering the eighteenth-century European ideas that provide the ethical framework for the global economy. Some of those to whom we refer are feminists, ecologists, Jungian analysts, theologians, spiritual practitioners, architects, labor union members, innovative economists, students of the psychology of moral development, anthropologists, sociologists, schoolteachers, criminologists, poets, artists of all kinds, lawyers, missionaries and technical experts working in developing countries, medical doctors and medical researchers, historians, industrial designers, sensitive adolescents, and thoughtful parents; as well as philosophers who specialize in ethics and the history of ethics.

One promising movement has been founded by the Swedish anthropologist Helena Norberg-Hodge. She found inspiration for a radical critique of the principles and values of modern society not in Europe's past, but in an ancient Buddhist culture located in the high, barren, and thinly populated Ladakh region of India, in the far north of Kashmir, bounded on three sides by mountainous areas belonging to Pakistan, China, and Tibet. "In Ladakh," she writes, "I have had the privilege to experience another, saner, way of life, and to see my own culture from the outside. I have lived in a society based on fundamentally different principles."[16] Having grown up in Sweden, she came to disagree with a premise that we have been assuming, that Swedish social democracy ranks among the best societies the human species has invented so far. She came to believe that the life of the Buddhists of Ladakh living on the Tibetan Plateau was superior to life in any Western industrialized nation.

Unfortunately, however, we cannot go there to see the ancient culture of Ladakh that Norberg-Hodge praises, because during the sixteen years she was learning from it, Ladakhi culture underwent the process of modernization that is rapidly destroying many cultures around the world. Norberg-Hodge writes, "Increasingly, Western culture is coming to be seen as the normal way, the only way. And as more and more people around the world become competitive, greedy, and egotistical, these traits tend to be attributed to human nature."[17] The cooperation and sharing that existed, the respect for and cooperation with nature that existed, the happiness and love of ceremony that existed, serve as a proof that human nature is not what Adam Smith thought it was, even though they exist now only to the limited extent that Ladakh has been able to resist westernization and modernization.

Norberg-Hodge writes:

> Once I was in the village of Sakti at sowing time. Two households had an arrangement whereby they shared animals, plough, and labor for the few days before sowing could start. Their neighbor, Sonam Tsering, who was not a part of the group, was ploughing his own fields when one of his dzo [draft animal, a cross between a yak and a cow] sat down and refused to work any longer. I thought at first that it was just being stubborn, but Tsering told me that the animal was ill and that he feared it was serious. Just as we were sitting at the edge of the field wondering what to do, the farmer from next door came by and without a moment's hesitation offered his own help as well as the help of others in his lhangsde [work-sharing] group. That evening, after they had finished their own work, they all came over to Tsering's fields with their dzo. As always, they sang as they worked; and long after dark, when I could no longer see them, I could still hear their song.[18]

Ladakh convinced Norberg-Hodge that there are alternatives to modern western ethics. How to put alternative ethics into practice on a large scale is a large question in a world where there are issues such as those concerning capital formation, long-range investment in research and development, the management of pension and retirement funds, working long hours just to pay rent in order to have the right to be somewhere, the division of the revenues of enterprises between capital and labor, a reliance on money and profit which makes effective demand chronically insufficient to keep everyone employed, underutilized resources existing side by side with unmet needs, the exit power of capital, investment strikes, capital flight, tax evasion, structural unemployment, inflation, currency speculation and other forms of profit-making bearing little or no relation to any truly useful purpose, the design of giant systems delivering health care and education in ways that are chronically inadequate, competitive pressures to lower wages and to produce shoddy goods that will soon be thrown away and land-filled, and culture manufactured by the mass media for the sole purpose of selling commodities.

We hope to shed some light on this large question—i.e., the question of how to put alternatives into practice—as we discuss other experiments in social democracy around the world. Meanwhile, let it be noted that increasing numbers of people in Western Europe and in some other parts of the world are taking seriously the concept of living a post-materialist lifestyle, albeit often in small groups and in prototype forms. Concerning Sweden, Norberg-Hodge reports:

> A movement to build eco-villages is sweeping Sweden: two hundred are already planned, all of them based on renewable energy and the recycling of waste. Increasing numbers of people are choosing to buy organic food and are strengthening the local economy by buying from farmers close to home. The government has committed itself to establishing an environmental accounting system in which the destruction of natural resources will be subtracted from the gross national product.
>
> These changes in Sweden reflect a crucial shift in direction. Throughout the industrial world, people are searching for a better balance with nature. In the process, they are starting to mirror traditional cultures. In fields as diverse as hospice care for the dying and mediation as a way of settling disputes, striking parallels are emerging between the most ancient and the most modern cultures. Just as Ladakhi villagers have always done, increasing numbers of people are making the kitchen the center of their household activity, eating whole foods that are grown naturally, and using age-old natural remedies for their health problems. Even in more subtle ways, such as a reawakened interest in storytelling, a renewed appreciation for physical work, and the use of natural materials for clothing and construction, the direction of change is clear. We are spiraling back to an ancient connection between ourselves and the earth.[19]

Notes

1. Meidner, *Employee Investment Funds*, 16-17, explanation added.

2. Myrdal, for example, attributed more efficacy to planning than it actually had. For another example, in the passage just quoted, Meidner attributed more efficacy to the active labor market policy than—according to subsequent studies—it actually had.

3. In the Introduction to his *Discourse on the Origins and the Foundations of Inequality among Men*, published in 1755, Rousseau writes: "I discern two sorts of inequality in the human species: the first I call natural or physical because it is established by nature, and consists of differences in age, health, strength of the body and qualities of the mind or soul; the second we might call moral or political inequality because it derives from a sort of convention, and is established, or at least authorized, by the consent of men. This latter inequality consists of the different privileges which some enjoy to the prejudice of others—such as their being richer, more honoured, more powerful than others, and even getting themselves obeyed by others." Jean-Jacques Rousseau, *A Discourse on Inequality*, trans. Maurice Cranston (Harmondsworth, Middlesex, U.K.: Penguin Books, 1984), 77. In *Emile, or On Education*, published in 1764, he writes: "We are born weak, we need strength; we are born totally unprovided, we need aid; we are born stupid, we need judgment. Everything we do not have at our birth and which we need when we are grown is given us by education. This education comes to us from nature or from men or from things. The internal development of our faculties and our organs is the education of nature. The use we are taught to make of this development is the education of men. And what we acquire from our own experience about the objects which affect us is the education of things." Jean-Jacques Rousseau, *Emile, or On Education*, trans. Allan Bloom (New York: Basic Books, 1979), 38. The same shift in discourse with regard to the role assigned to human will and to Nature replacing that previously assigned to God is, of course, also apparent in *The Social Contract*, published in 1762.

4. For Derrida's commentaries on Rousseau, see "The Linguistic Circle of Geneva," in Jacques Derrida, *Margins of Philosophy*, trans. Alan Bass (Chicago: The University of Chicago Press, 1982), 137-53. This was a lecture given in London in February 1968 under the title, "La linguistique de Rousseau."

5. Max Weber, *The Theory of Social and Economic Organization*, trans. A.M. Henderson and Talcott Parsons (New York: Oxford University Press, 1947); Weber, *Protestant Ethic*.

6. Hayek, *Road to Serfdom*, 24-31, 85-87.

7. Lawrence Tuller, *Finance for Non-Financial Managers* (Holbrook, Mass.: Adams Media Corporation, 1977), 73.

8. Branting quoted in Tilton, *Political Theory*, 36.

9. Branting quoted in Tilton, *Political Theory*, 22.

10. From "Pater Noster," in Jacques Prévert, *Paroles* (Paris: Gallimard, 1949), 58.

11. Weber, *Protestant Ethic*, 26-27.

12. See Bernard de Mandeville, *The Fable of the Bees, or Private Vices, Publick Benefits*, ed. Irwin Primer (New York: Capricorn Books, 1962), especially 74-86. Dumont points out, for example, that the last chapter in Mandeville's *Fable of the Bees* is an anti-Shaftesbury pamphlet. The Earl of Shaftesbury was known as a "rigorist Churchman,"

and he is the only one to whom Mandeville is overtly hostile. Louis Dumont, *From Mandeville to Marx: The Genesis and Triumph of Economic Ideology* (Chicago and London: The University of Chicago Press, 1977), 65. Dumont also discusses Locke's polemics against Robert Filmer in the first of Locke's *Two Treatises of Government*. Filmer had propounded a view of a social order that stemmed from the relationship of God to humans: a kind of hierarchy resembling patriarchal stewardship. With Locke, this kind of subordination of humans is tossed out altogether, along with relations necessitating any form of stewardship among humans and other beings Dumont, From *Mandeville to Marx*, 48-49.

13. See Barbara Marx Hubbard, *The Hunger of Eve* (Harrisburg, Pa.: Stackpole Books, 1976), especially Chapter 4, "Epiphany," and Chapter 5, "Totality," 88-177.

14. Stein and Dörfer do not conceal their delight as they chronicle the problems Sweden faces. They welcome Sweden's fall from its high ideals, which they refer to as Sweden's "moral imperialism." Peter Stein and Ingemar Dörfer, *The Death Knell of Social Democracy: Sweden's Dream Turns Sour* (London: Institute for European Defence and Strategic Studies, 1992). Ralf Dahrendorf, in contrast, is less gleeful, partly because he recognizes that social democracy is—or "has been"—"the great improving force for our age." Ralf Dahrendorf, *After Social Democracy* (London: Liberal Publication Department, for the Unservile State Group [Unservile State Papers, No. 25], 1980), 2. He states that social democracy has "proved the ability of open societies to change without revolution" and that social democracy has been "a force for freedom" but that now social democracy "has begun to produce as many problems as it solves." Dahrendorf, *After Social Democracy*, 1, 2. Our arguments in preceding chapters should make clear our disagreements with him on these points. Certain passages by Dahrendorf, however, lead us to optimism. He writes, for example: "In order to make progress, we have to move sideways and change the subject of concern. Instead of the obsessions of the past—with growth . . . with a scientific-technological world, with more government—we have to seek different horizons of economic, social, cultural and political aspirations. The fact that this will not be the result of deliberate government action, but will require new attitudes on the part of individuals, groups, firms, organization, is itself a part of the change which a new socioeconomic climate requires." Dahrendorf, *After Social Democracy*, 14. We certainly agree with this sentiment. As is so often the case, however, a social scientist will make a radical and provocative statement like this and then follow it, as Dahrendorf does on the next page, by prescribing the now familiar solutions that have proven inadequate many times over: avenues of economic growth must be kept open; "flexibility"; technological progress; "mobility"; an open-market economy.

15. This is a recurring theme throughout much of Derrida's work. See, e.g., Jacques Derrida, *Specters of Marx: The State of the Debt, the Work of Mourning, and the New International* (London: Routledge, 1994).

16. Helena Norberg-Hodge, *Ancient Futures: Learning from Ladakh* (San Francisco: Sierra Club Books, 1992), 1.

17. Norberg-Hodge, *Ancient Futures*, 3.

18. Norberg-Hodge, *Ancient Futures*, 54, explanations added.

19. Norberg-Hodge, *Ancient Futures*, 191.

Chapter 9

Karl Popper's Vienna, or, The Straitjacket of Mainstream Social Science

As this is written (in the year 2001), the social democratic party of Austria (SPO, *Sozialistische Partei Osterreichs*) is more concerned with avoiding moving backward than with moving forward. It is out of office. It is more concerned with defending Austria's social safety net against cuts being made by the governing "blue/black" coalition than with improving the welfare state. Its core electoral constituency, the industrial working class, has shrunk and is still shrinking. The SPO is still tainted by the dramatic exposures of corruption that took place during its years in office. It is still suffering from association with real and alleged inefficiency in government bureaucracies and in state-run enterprises. It has moved from being a working class party, to being a people's party, to appearing to be (in the eyes of its critics) an opportunistic party of the political class. The social democrats have found it hard to convince anyone—least of all the young intellectuals and post-materialists who support the new Green Party—that they can pilot Austria's economy to serve the ends of prosperity, justice, and sustainability in the uncharted waters of globalization. Young workers, who are often the losers, the victims of globalization, have been turning to Jörg Haider's ("blue") xenophobic right-wing populist "Freedom Party"—a depressing reminder of the masses of impoverished and anti-Semitic working people who flocked to the Nazi banners in the 1930s.[1] Pessimists say that in any event it hardly matters what the Austrian social democrats do because whatever they do the future of the working people of Austria is out of their hands, out of Austria's hands, out of the European Union's hands, out of human hands. The future, the pessimists say, will be determined by the impersonal forces of the global market.

181

In the face of this discouraging situation, we offer an encouraging thesis: that a way forward (or, rather, a series of ways forward) can be usefully named by rehabilitating an old principle from social democracy's past: "system-changing reforms." Instead of proceeding directly to elaborate the concept of "system-changing reform," we shall first provide context by discussing some features of Austria's historical experience and some issues concerning the methodology of research in the social sciences.

Our aim is not to suggest an electoral strategy for a party, and our thesis concerns civil society and international organizations as much as the state. Our aim is to advance the ethical construction of social democracy, which we take to include perfecting and supplementing the logic of exchange to make it serve ever better the aims of use, and to include building cultures and societies that are able to employ the profit motive where it is useful, but that are not addicted to it. Societies should be able to live without unhealthy profit-motive dependency, and without suffering severe withdrawal symptoms when the profit motive falters.

We do not aspire to contribute anything to scholarship on Austria, a country about which we have no special expertise. We are using a few reflections on Austrian history to provide a supporting context for a philosophical discussion of basic concepts. We are continuing the discussion of the same issues raised in connection with Spain and Sweden, about which we have no special expertise either. In this chapter, however, we place greater emphasis on what works (or would work) as distinct from what does not work.

Historically, we will focus on the administration of Bruno Kreisky, who was the socialist chancellor of Austria from 1970 to 1986. Our methodological discussion will focus on some key ideas concerning political philosophy and the role of the social sciences, whose most famous and influential formulation is found in *The Open Society and its Enemies* by Karl Popper, written in the years 1941-1942 and first published in 1945.

The Kreisky era (1970-1986) can be considered the high water mark of Austrian socialism. It was the only period in Austrian history in which the socialists won consistent majorities at the polls. They held office without a coalition partner from 1970 to 1983.[2] (However, the pressure for consensus inherent in the post-World War II "Austrian Way" was then still so strong that governing without a coalition partner did not imply, as it might have implied in some other countries, that the government used its majority in parliament to rule unilaterally.) The welfare state was comprehensive and well established, and apparently irreversible. As is typically the case when nations achieve a high level of social justice, crime rates were low. Austrians were proud of living in one of the safest countries of the world, characterized by social partnership, not social conflict.[3] Austria played a conspicuous and constructive role in world politics. It was firmly established among the ten or twelve richest nations in the world, according to the admittedly crude indicator of Gross Domestic Product per capita, along with other West European social democracies like Norway, Sweden, Denmark, Holland, Switzerland, and the Federal Republic of Germany.[4] (Then as now any short list of the world's richest countries in per capita terms will show that many of them have had social democratic parties in office either alone or in coalition with other parties, most, or at least a good part, of the time since World War II. Thus the hypothesis that unfettered free market capitalism leads to maximum peace and prosperity is not empirically confirmed.)

The high water mark can also be regarded as the beginning of the end. By the end of the Kreisky era, the cold winds of the worldwide neo-conservative trend had arrived in Austria, with their well-known tendencies to diminish the role of the state and to accentuate the linking of the fates of nations to the vagaries of the global marketplace. It had become harder to manage the Austrian economy, and harder to deliver prosperity and social justice.[5] The Kreisky government's Austro-Keynesian policy team, which attempted nevertheless, in spite of Austria's decreasing control of its own destiny, to deliver prosperity and social justice both at once through ever-increasing economic growth, could not accommodate at all the vision of a sustainable economy proposed by the new Green Party.

Young Bruno Kreisky, who a quarter century later would be Chancellor Kreisky, spent most of World War II in exile in Stockholm. The Nazis then governed Austria, and they were utilizing Austria's people and its material resources as military assets of their thousand-year Reich. The Austrian social democrats living in exile during World War II had a lot to think about, and several controversial issues to debate. The socialists had held power briefly in Austria when the First Republic emerged in 1918 from the ashes of the defeated Austro-Hungarian Empire.[6] Social democracy was a contender in Austrian politics and master of the municipal government of "Red Vienna" from 1919 until 1934.[7] In 1934 democracy was crushed, and with it social democracy, by an Austrian fascist regime supported by Benito Mussolini's fascist Italy. The anti-socialist majority in interwar Austria had been led by the Christian Social Party (the "blacks") which later became the Fatherland Front of 1934-1938 supporting Austrian fascism, which itself was crushed in 1938 when Hitler annexed Austria to the Reich. In a plebiscite held in April 1938, 99.7 percent of the Austrian people approved union with Germany and accepted Hitler as their leader.[8]

It could be argued, and was argued, that the failure of social democracy to mobilize popular discontent for constructive purposes had led in Austria (and in other countries) to the rise of fascism and Nazism, as it could also be argued that earlier, social democracy's failure to mobilize the masses of Russia had led to the October Revolution and the rise of Communism. The Austrian social democrats in exile debated whether they had been too reformist, or too revolutionary, too wedded to peaceful and democratic means, or not peaceful and democratic enough.[9] It could also be debated whether social democracy had, or had not, in the few times and spaces that history had so far offered it (such as 1919-1934 in

"Red Vienna"), demonstrated a feasible economic alternative, which was neither free market capitalism nor a totalitarian command economy, and which worked.

During his exile years in Sweden, Kreisky was impressed by the leading economists of the Stockholm School, Gunnar and Alva Myrdal, Dag Hammarskjöld, Erik Lundberg, and others; by Sweden's beloved wartime Prime Minister Per Albin Hansson; by the finance minister Ernst Wigforss; and by the social minister and architect of the welfare state Gustav Moller. He was impressed by the "social patriotism" of Swedish workers, who sang songs like "*Sverige för Folket*" ("Sweden of the People"). Songs like "*Sverige för Folket*" associated loyalty to the nation with gratitude for belonging to a nation committed in principle to being a home where all citizens were cared for.[10] Kreisky wrote in his memoirs, published in 1986:

> [O]n the basis of my experience in Sweden, certain political ideas came to appear to me to be much more realistic than I had formerly thought. By this I mean the excellently functioning Swedish democracy, and the successful example of a reformism which had changed the whole structure of Swedish society. In Sweden I learned the Praxis of the difference between what one would later call *system-immanent* and *system-changing* reforms. I have studied this problem and returned again and again to consider it. Now on the basis of the Austrian example I have come to the conclusion—a simple and if you like dialectical conclusion—that through the quantity of reforms the quality of a society changes.[11]

Thus the concept, or at least *a* concept, of "system-changing reform" was very much a part of the thinking of the man who led Austria from 1970 to 1986. If our thesis is valid, and if indeed the Kreisky era was "the beginning of the end," then it follows that the concept of "system-changing reform," as Kreisky understood it and applied it, needs to be reconsidered. We shall suggest that Kreisky's version of system-changing reform tended to overlook, or to consider immutable, a key feature of the system to be changed, namely its dependence on the profit motive. We shall suggest that some creative ways forward were foreign to the worldview of Kreisky's pragmatic and modernizing social democrats. Some such "stones the builders rejected" have been at times characteristic in Austria of the checkered tradition represented today by the conservative People's Party. The "black" People's Party, which today shares the government with the "blue" "Freedom Party" of Jörg Haider, derives from an originally anti-capitalist Catholic social movement of the 1880s, which later as the Christian Social Party became noted for its anti-Semitism, especially under its leader Karl Lueger (mayor of Vienna from 1897 to 1910), and then for its anti-socialism and its support of Austrian fascism, and then still later for its collaboration with the social democrats in the period 1945-1966.[12]

One need not exaggerate the importance of ideas in history to suspect that in Austria the idea of "system-changing reform" needs to be reconsidered in the light of its illusory success. It appeared, in Kreisky's eyes, to have produced a qualitative irreversible change in the character of Austrian society. Yet history is demonstrating that changes are reversible.

While young Bruno Kreisky was living in exile in Sweden, while World War II raged in Europe and Asia, while the Holocaust raged throughout Central Europe, another young Viennese social democrat was living in exile at the opposite end of the earth, in Christchurch, New Zealand, writing *The Open Society and its Enemies*. Karl Popper, like Kreisky, and like countless others, had been shattered by the experience of social democracy's failure in Austria between the two world wars. He too meditated in exile on the collapse of Austria, along with most of the rest of Europe, into an inferno of violence and hatred. Popper, unlike Kreisky, would never return to Austria to live. He returned to Europe to become professor of the logic and methodology of the social sciences at the London School of Economics. Popper's ideas returned to his native land through his contributions to international intellectual currents, which swept over Austria during the Kreisky era, implicitly bearing some key Popperian notions and with them some other internationally accepted ideas, which happened to have originated in Vienna. By 1970 Popper's audience was worldwide. His views were taken for granted by many who had never read him. In neighboring Germany, during the time when Kreisky was chancellor of Austria, the three major political parties, the Social Democrats, the Christian Democrats, and the Liberals, all declared themselves to be adherents of Popper's political philosophy.[13]

Although Popper and his wife Hennie (Josephine Henninger) were members of the Austrian social democratic party, they had not been active members in the years immediately prior to their hasty flight into exile in 1937. Karl and Hennie met when they were both student socialist activists, studying to be teachers at Vienna's Pedagogic Institute. They had been enthusiastic contributors to efforts of the party and of the socialist municipal government to uplift educationally deprived working class youth. As the situation worsened in Austria, they withdrew from politics, partly, Popper later explained, because it was counterproductive for Jews, even assimilated Jews like himself (he was baptized a Lutheran) to be conspicuous socialists. To be an active Jewish socialist would play into the hands of the Nazis, who exploited the anti-Semitic feelings of the masses by identifying social democracy with Jewry. More importantly, Popper believed that Austro-Marxism, which was then the ideology of Austrian socialism, had committed grave theoretical errors. He believed the theoretical errors were responsible for the tragedy he saw unfolding around him, whose terrible outcomes he, more than others, foresaw.[14]

In exile in a small town in New Zealand, he divided his time between his teaching duties as an assistant professor teaching logic and philosophy of science at Canterbury University, desperate attempts to secure visas to help others to immigrate (sixteen of his relatives died in the Holocaust), and writing a political philosophy designed to serve a better future.[15] Hennie typed his manuscripts. The result was a philosophy of "piecemeal social engineering" supporting an "interventionist state."[16] The "interventionist state" should take steps to eliminate concrete evils, such as unemployment and poverty, and should refrain from holistic and utopian visions. It should not seek the overall Good, but remedy the particular and concrete evil. The principle of "love" should be confined to family and friends, since any attempt to apply it on a larger scale was bound to lead to irrational politics and to tyranny. Democracy was to be the only principle socialists would fight for, since only democracy could secure security. All else was to be achieved by persuasion. Although he gave no details, several times in *The Open Society and its Enemies* Popper cited Sweden as an (and he cited no other) example of what an interventionist state should do.[17]

Popper's philosophy is an important systematic defense of certain approaches to social science that have been influential in the post-World War II world. We shall take the liberty of assuming that our readers know roughly, if not precisely, what we mean when we call them "mainstream." There are so many streams in social science that it is necessarily somewhat arbitrary to call one of them main, and perhaps some streams we will characterize as marginal and as needing to be brought more into the mainstream (the psychology of moral development and cultural anthropology) could quite plausibly be declared to be, in their own way, also mainstream. We suspect that it was partly because of the influence of the mainstream ideas we associate with Popper that the Austro-Keynesians of the Kreisky era did not make truly system-changing reforms, but only system-immanent reforms. At the end of the Kreisky era, the system had not changed enough to prevent a second failure of social democracy in Austria, and not enough to prevent a second upsurge of right-wing populism. As Karl Marx once wrote, history repeats itself, the first time as tragedy, the second time as farce. In Austria, Hitler was the tragedy. Haider is the farce.

The genealogy of Haider's "blue" Freedom Party (*Freiheitliche Partei Osterreichs*, FPO) can be traced by lineal descent from the party formed by Austrian ex-Nazis when their political rights were restored, after a period under Allied occupation when they were not allowed to vote. It took Austria fifty-five years, which can roughly be divided into three periods, to go from Hitler to Haider.

Following Hitler's defeat in 1945, the "black/red" period began. This period marks the twenty-five years (1945 to roughly 1970) when Austria was governed by a "Grand Coalition" of its two major parties, representing nearly all of the electorate, the "black" People's Party and the "red" SPO. Together they built the distinctive form of social democracy called the Austrian Model or the Austrian Way. Some of the Austrian Model's characteristics were: consensus seeking and power sharing at every level of society, corporatism, a welfare state, a mixed economy with a large public sector, a social partnership of labor and capital, and neutrality in foreign affairs.[18]

The second period, the sixteen years from 1970 to 1986, was the "red" Kreisky era. It was the high water mark of social democracy. We have somewhat arbitrarily, but for reasons we consider good ones, chosen to call it also "the beginning of the end."

The third period, the fourteen years from 1986 to 2000, can be thought of as "faded red, faded black, a touch of green, and a threat of blue." It was marked by the fading of each and every one of the characteristic features of the Austrian Model. Typically, a laconic report in 1994 stated that the Joint Commission on Wages and Prices, a centerpiece of social partnership, had not held any meetings during that year. Although for the most part a faded black/red coalition continued to hold office, both the People's Party (*Osterreichische Volkspartei*, OVP) and the SPO, under the influence of Popperian social science, had opted for *Versachlichung*, i.e., de-ideologization, or, better put, an anti-ideology ideology. The embrace of *Versachlichung* meant that the Austrian government would make decisions strictly in accordance with the dictates of what they considered to be "objective" and "rational" "laws" of social science. Government officials believed that policy successes were guaranteed once obedience to these "laws" had supplanted actions responding crudely to the fickleness of collective emotion. With *Versachlichung* came: more social science, less politics. More market. Less collective decision making by the state and the corporatist institutions of the social partnership. More foreign ownership of Austrian industry and media. Less security for working people. In the elections of December 2000, Jörg Haider's Freedom Party received more votes than the People's Party. Although the People's Party kept the chancellorship, the Freedom Party became the majority partner in a new blue/black governing coalition.

To say that more market, less security for working people, and the like, came with an anti-ideology ideology is not, of course, to say that they came because of an anti-ideology ideology. We do want to identify *Versachlichung* as a contributing cause, and not just a consequence, of social democracy's decline, but before entering into a methodological discussion that will implicitly suggest some implications concerning the direction of the arrow of causation, we shall review more facts from Austria's past.

Today Austria's social democracy, with its welfare state and its deeply embedded tendencies toward consensus-seeking and power-sharing, still exists, even though it is on the defensive, fading, and perhaps fading away. It is being undermined and eroded by processes and trends whose precise onset cannot be dated, although we have elected to name the Kreisky era "the beginning of the end." Perhaps in some sense the historical forces that are now deconstructing Austrian socialism have "always" existed, being in some periods dominant and in others recessive. Perhaps they have existed for as long as capitalism (some three or four hundred years), or as long as patriarchy (some 3,000 years on Riane Eisler's account, or as long as humanity on other accounts), or as long as *homo sapiens sapiens* (perhaps 200,000 years), or since the beginning of life (perhaps 2.6 billion years), or since logic began to be valid, i.e., since eternity. Assuming that the centrifugal forces that are now disorganizing Austrian social democracy have existed for a long time, they would have to be described as having been recessive and not dominant for at least two decades after 1945.

Austrian socialism was not built by the socialists alone. It was built by a coalition of Catholics and socialists. In 1945, the People's Party (the reorganized Christian Social Party) was still regarded as the political expression of the Vatican's ideology. The People's Party was the majority partner in the black/red alliance. It consistently received more votes than its socialist alliance partner from 1945 until 1970. The office of Chancellor of the Republic of Austria was occupied by the leader of the People's Party from soon after the elections of November 1945, until Bruno Kreisky became chancellor in 1970.

The 1945 election showed that during more than a decade of dictatorship, there had been no major shift in the party preferences of Austrian voters. The People's Party won a narrow victory nationwide. The socialists carried Vienna, and came close to winning nationwide. The Communists had no significant support. The Pan-Germans were not on the ballot.[19]

Yet the post-election process of forming a government signaled an historic break with the confrontational politics of Austria's past. The People's Party and the SPO formed a bipartisan government, representing nearly all the voters. (For a short period the Communists were also included.) Leopold Figl of the People's Party became Chancellor. The ministerial portfolios were divided proportionally between Catholics and socialists. And not just ministerial portfolios. Posts in the civil service, jobs in state run enterprises, academic appointments, judicial appointments, and offices in the many *Bunds* and *Vereins*, which tie together the warp and weft of the fabric of Austrian society, were carefully divided and balanced. Thus was born the principle of *Proporz*, the sharing of power in Austrian society from top to bottom between the adherents of its two main ideological subcultures.[20]

Votes in parliament were often unanimous. The government's programs and policies emphasized humanitarian objectives, concerning which the religious teachings of the Vatican and the secular ideals of social democracy coincided. The two wings of the alliance managed to compromise on divorce, abortion, and parochial schools.

Parallel to and coordinated with the government, there was an elaborate political organization of the private sector. Virtually everyone in business was in some Chamber or other, as virtually everybody who worked was in a union or professional association, which themselves formed Chambers. The business Chambers were generally black, the labor Chambers red, and although there were many complications and exceptions, the net result was always to respect the principle of *Proporz*. Not just wages and labor disputes, but also prices were collectively negotiated. Compared to, for example, the United Kingdom or the United States of America, the number of strikes was insignificant.

Not surprisingly, party membership soared. Already in the 1920s, political and religious affiliations had become a way of life for many Austrians. Vienna, for example, was dotted with coffee houses sponsored by the political parties. Viennese apartment dwellings were notoriously small and crowded, and it was an easy and inexpensive form of social life to go out after a hard day's work and spend the evening in a coffee house sponsored by the Socialist Party, the Christian Social Party, or a Pan-German party (one favoring the union of Austria with Germany), sipping coffee, talking politics, reading the party newspaper and other party literature. After World War II, with most social institutions politicized, the numbers of dues paying party members soared. The People's Party had more dues-paying members than the Christian Democrats of much larger Germany. The SPO had more than the German SPD.

The social democracy created by the black/red coalition after World War II bore a striking similarity to the corporatist state that the Catholics of the Fatherland Front had tried to create by means of the dictatorship of 1934-38, protected and inspired by Mussolini's Italy. The Austrian political scientist Anton Pelinka of the University of Innsbruck recently wrote of it:

> Almost all the People's Party representatives involved in constructing social partnership after 1945 had already had experience in pre-1938 corporatism. Social partnership was and is intended to moderate the main conflict of modern society: the conflict between business and labor, between employers and employees. All three models the pope had in mind—liberalism, socialism, and corporatism—were based on that conflict. All three models agree that this conflict is the primary one and had to be adapted or transformed into a stable political system. The liberal approach tended to declare some basic rights and rules and then abstain from interference. The socialist approach was based on a zero-sum game hypothesis: Nothing but the ultimate victory of socialism would end the contradiction between the classes. The corporatist approach was and is compromise oriented and interventionist. It was not this philosophy that distinguished post-1945 from pre-1938 corporatism. It was the inclusion of the Social Democrats that made all the difference. Pre-1938 corporatism was based on the breakup of the republican constitution and on the defeat of the Social Democratic Party and social democratic labor unions. . . . Post-1945 corporatism had to be based on the Second Republic's consensus, on the historic compromise between the Christian-conservative and the socialist camps.[21]

According to a point of view that we shall ascribe to "the pessimist," the decline of the post-1945 Austrian Model between 1970 and 2001 was inevitable. Although we shall not name any names, we do not regard "the pessimist" as a rare or imaginary creature, but quite to the contrary, as a spokesperson for views that are commonplace and practically orthodox. According to the pessimist, social partnership was possible just after World War II because in those years labor was comparatively strong, while business was comparatively weak. Business participated in the social partnership because it had to. As its power waxed it ceased to participate. Later when business had more power and labor less, social partnership ended, and with it the Austrian Way. Power. Voila tout. Like a Kantian category of the understanding, "power" functions as an explanatory principle that the mind brings to social reality, a condition of the possibility of political science.

One might, to be sure, welcome many of the changes wrought between 1970 and 2001. One might opine that the postwar Austrians who huddled in their parishes and political clubs, gathered in innumerable *Bunds* and *Vereins* for every conceivable purpose from gymnastics to sausage manufacture to chamber music, suffered from groupthink, from which they are now mercifully being liberated by capitalism. But the pessimist's story should not be understood as if it were a story about a voluntary democratic process of amending the Austrian Model to achieve a nicer synthesis of interpersonal bonding and personal individuation. It is a story about historical forces that overwhelm the mind and pre-empt choice.

Against the pessimist, we want to argue the optimistic thesis that the Kreisky administration could have fostered system-changing reforms that would have altered history. It is not too late. History can still be altered now. So far we are in complete agreement with Karl Popper. Popper inveighed against "historicism," the view that history is governed by what Karl Marx called, in a passage Popper frequently cited, "the economic laws of motion of modern society." Popper insisted that humans make social institutions. We and we alone are responsible for their evolution. Rational decision-making, social science, is the way to accept our burden, enduring what Popper called "the strain of civilization," by painstakingly reconstructing society piece by piece, solving its problems one by one. Historicism, the view that history is moving inevitably in a pre-ordained direction is dangerous nonsense. Social science is sober realism.

The pessimist will reply to Popper and to us that in spite of the sober realism of a Bruno Kreisky, who announced that he would govern "not with a wineglass but with a slide rule," in spite of the "modernizing" and "reform" of the "new thinking," in spite of the de-ideologization of the professional social scientists who staffed the Kreisky administration, in spite of the increasing role played by the non-political Council of Economic and Social Advisers, the outcome was nevertheless pre-ordained. Business would have more power. Labor would have less power. Social partnership would end. Apparently, the crux of the matter is power.

Our belief is that in reality the crux of the matter is not so much power as rules. If one thinks in terms of "power," and defines it as "control of resources," then one is likely to overestimate the importance of a shift in control of resources from one group to another. The system is made of rules. It makes little difference who controls resources as long as whoever controls them plays the same game by the same rules, making the same decisions according to the same criteria. We are suggesting that if we think less about power and more about rules, then it will be easier to rehabilitate the idea of system-changing reforms, easier to distinguish reforms that change the system from reforms that do not.

However, for the sake of the argument let us continue for a while to frame the issues as the pessimist frames them, in terms of "power." If one asks why the balance of power shifted in favor of business and against labor, the pessimist will tell a story about the natural evolution of the capitalist system. Profits accumulate. At the end of World War II there was no capital available for rebuilding Austrian industries prostrated by war, and business had to rely on government backing, even on government ownership, and on the United States' Marshall Plan, but as time goes on business becomes more and more able to capitalize itself and to attract foreign investment. Also, as people participate in market behavior year after year, the conventional norms become more and more the norms of market culture. *Homo Economicus*. Buy cheap and sell dear. Material success. As Karl Marx wrote (deliberately oversimplifying, as he himself noted), "The capitalist is but capital personified. His soul is the soul of capital."[22] The moral life of the non-capitalists also is more and more that of buyer and sellers; buying and selling is their norm, their practice, and their discourse too, even though they buy less and have less to sell. The never-ending quest for higher profits and cheaper bargains implies the expansion of the scale of commerce. The market is no longer local; it is Austria; then it is Europe, then it is the Globe; some day it will be inter-planetary, and then inter-galactic. The ability of government to throw its weight into the scales on the side of labor is weakened, because no national government can govern transactions in an international market. Instead, the government's constant preoccupation must be to do what it can to keep profits accumulating, because if profits do not accumulate, the economic process stops, and everybody suffers. Thus the government inevitably becomes an accomplice to the undermining of its own power, and labor's.

The pessimist's account of the inevitable shift in the balance of power in favor of business and against government and labor is a story about the normal evolution of a capitalist system. Yet if the system-changing reforms of the social democrats had really happened, and had really functioned as expected, then Austria would not have had a normally evolving capitalist system. It would have had a different system.

We want to say—and we believe Karl Popper would want to say—that the pessimist's story might be substantially accurate insofar as it is an account of what actually did happen in, or to, Austria. It is an error, however, to say that what did happen had to happen. The Kreisky administration might have carried out its intention to make system-changing reforms more effectively. It could have emphasized a different kind of system-changing reform—a kind that would have altered the rules, the principles, the criteria of action—and Austrian history might have evolved in a different direction between 1970 and 2000.

We must specify, before continuing, that the question is not really whether system-changing alteration of the basic constitutive rules that govern and drive capitalism is possible. The question (to which we give an affirmative answer) is whether alternative rules can be peacefully and democratically instituted that are desirable. Mussolini and Hitler, to name just two, have already demonstrated that running a modern industrial society at full employment according to different rules is possible. Austrian history from 1938 to 1945 (a period most Austrians would prefer to forget) taught that lesson. The Viennese-born economist Peter Drucker, in his book *The End of Economic Man*, published in 1939, described some basic rules of the system imposed on Austria during the Nazi period as follows:

> [I]n a closed economy like the fascist state, which forbids capital exports and enforces compulsory investment, profits are reduced to the status of a book-keeping entry. Instead of abolishing profits in the first place, the government lets them circulate once more through the economic system, only to regain them in the form of taxes and compulsory loans. In addition, profits are so completely subordinated in Germany and Italy to the requirements of a militarily conceived national interest and of full employment that the maintenance of the profit principle is purely theoretical. Profits have lost their autonomy as an independent, not to say the supreme, goal of economic activity. In most cases they have become a substitute for a management fee—with the one qualification, however, that under fascism the owner-manager bears the full risk. There is a definite trend in Italy and Germany to eliminate profit participation and ownership rights of nonmanaging partners and shareholders. The manager of a business, regardless of whether he is the owner or only a paid executive, has been freed from all responsibility toward the outside shareholders, even toward a nonmanaging majority owner. If he does not want to pay dividends though the profits allow it, and prefers to invest in government loans, the government permits him to vote himself a substantial bonus. At the time of writing, a proposal is being discussed in Germany to force the banks to forego their dividend claims "voluntarily" in favor of the government. Since the banks are the largest nonmanaging shareholders in practically all German corporations and are majority owners in more than half, the proposal would effectively abolish the greater part of private corporation profit without touching the abstract principle of private profits at all. . . . Whatever this system is, it is certainly not capitalist.[23]

Thus the question is not really whether social democracy can propose an alternative to a neoliberal juggernaut driven by the logic of profit-seeking and capital accumulation. The question is whether it can propose a remedy that is not worse than the disease it seeks to cure.

If we are correct in believing that the ethical construction of a just, democratic, sustainable, and efficient society requires the modification of the economic mainspring of production and circulation, namely profit accumulation, and the modification of capitalist society's conventional norms, namely those associated with the calculated "rational" behavior assigned to *homo economicus,* then the election of Bruno Kreisky as Chancellor must be regarded as a step backward, a victory of caution over feasibility. Kreisky became the leader of the SPO after the socialists did poorly in the 1966 elections. (They did so poorly that the majority People's Party ended the coalition and governed without the socialists for a few years.) Kreisky ran for party leader in 1967 and for Chancellor in 1970 on a platform that promised a government more pragmatic and less ideological than those that had been led by the black/red Grand Coalition. The Grand Coalition, which governed most of the time from 1945 to 1970, possessed two ideologies, Catholicism and Marxism, each of which, in its own way, provided a philosophical context for a radical critique of capitalism's constitutive rules. The papal encyclicals *Rerum Novarum* and *Quadragesimo Anno* made it crystal clear that the Free Market was not God, Private Property was not God, and Profit Accumulation was not God. Love was God. The Marxist and Lassallean ideals of nineteenth-century social democracy, which twentieth-century Austro-Marxism remembered, called for a society that would produce for itself. They called for the priority of use values over the logic of exchange. Kreisky's candidacy, on the other hand, represented the hope, a tenuous and probably forlorn hope, that system-changing reforms that would make the welfare state irreversible could be enacted within the limitations imposed by the requirements of the logic of exchange.

This is not to say that the way forward for contemporary Austria is to revive Catholicism and Marxism. Austria today may be too secular to take Catholicism seriously. It may be too skeptical to take Marxism seriously. Today it may be the Green Party that can provide a philosophical context for a radical critique of capitalism's constitutive rules. When people are convinced that global warming is not an inevitable process, but a consequence of human behavior and human institutions, they may also be convinced that the globalization of the economy and the erosion of the welfare state are not inevitable processes either. Telling the stories of cultures invented by *homo sapiens sapiens* as part of the larger story of life in the biosphere may help people to see that even the most fundamental norms and assumptions of economics can be changed.[24]

Kreisky's decision to staff his government with more professional social scientists and fewer politicians was not obviously a step forward, and was perhaps a step backward. On the surface, the rise of social science and the increased role of the Council of Economic and Social Advisers represented the definitive triumph of social partnership. The revolution was won. Henceforth, as Marx had prophesied, the governing of people would be replaced by the administering of things. *Versachlichung* (de-ideologization) meant being *sachlich* ("objective"), which meant dealing with *Sachen* ("things"). We repeat: on the surface. However, if it is true, as we suspect but do not know, that the professional social scientists of the Kreisky administration tended to be influenced by currents of mainstream social science that carried an implicit anti-fascist and anti-irrationalist political agenda, then Kreisky's sober pragmatism had to represent some diminution of the spiritual force of the Austrian Model of social partnership. The Austrian version of social democracy was one that reconstructed fascist corporatism (i.e., the *Standestaat*, corporate state, of 1934-38). It relied on irrationalist (i.e., Catholic) allies. Hence it may well be the case that in some ways socialism in Austria was weakened, not strengthened, when the socialists won an absolute majority and were able to govern alone without their Catholic partners—although, to be sure, by the time the socialists won an absolute majority its erstwhile partner, the People's Party, was already drifting away from its confessional base, and toward neoliberalism. (And Catholic social teachings are, of course, only "irrational" when measured against a standard typical of mainstream social science, such as Karl Popper's critical rationalism. When measured against a traditional essentialist rationalism such as, for example, that of Saint Thomas Aquinas, or even against the standards of the twentieth-century theologian Karl Rahner, who was influential in Austria, they are perfectly rational.)

If, as we have been implying, *Versachlichung* or anti-ideology ideology, is part of the problem, not part of the solution, then our views can only be defended if we successfully criticize the case made in its favor by Karl Popper in *The Open Society and its Enemies* and its companion volume, written at about the same time, *The Poverty of Historicism*.

The Open Society and its Enemies was, as it declared itself to be, an antifascist polemic. If there was anything good about fascism, Popper was not going to say so in 1942. In exile in New Zealand, Popper volunteered to join the New Zealand Armed Forces as the Japanese were advancing southward. He was turned down, and he went back to his books to fight the fascists with philosophical arguments. He generalized. Fascism was a contemporary manifestation of a perennial human emotional weakness. Ever since the beginnings in Ancient Greece of science, rationality, and democracy (the three go together), people have been susceptible to being emotionally seduced by political and philosophical doctrines that appeal to their nostalgic yearning for Tribal Unity, for mystical togetherness and for unquestionable certitude. The enemies of the Open Society are the collectivist philosophers—Popper dwells on Plato, Hegel, and Marx, and mentions in passing a host of others—who prey on the anxiety that is the inevitable accompaniment of being a responsible individual in a civilized society. They purvey the spurious spiritual satisfaction of self-surrender to a collective ideal. The enemies of the Open Society short-circuit the critical rational process of learning by trial and error, through which, and through which alone, science and the gradual realization of humanitarian ideals (the two go together) advance.

In Karl Popper's Vienna the Austro-Marxists, the anti-Semitic Christian Social Party, and the Pan-German personality cults that defined the loony Viennese underworld from which Adolf Hitler emerged, all contributed to dulling the faculties of critical reason. All substituted tribal myths of one kind or another for scientific rationality. For the resulting series of social disasters, the Austro-Marxists were more to blame than the others because they were more intelligent and should have known better. In his writings Popper did not attack any Viennese intellectuals or politicians directly, nor did he directly attack the theories espoused by Mussolini or Hitler. Instead he attacked what he took to be their fundamental premises, as they were advanced by great thinkers of the past. He attacked their premises in forms more sophisticated and plausible than the forms they themselves had thought of, or were capable of thinking of. Popper made it a general practice in his writings to compose arguments for his opponents that were stronger than the arguments his opponents had thought of for themselves.

Our first criticism of *The Open Society and its Enemies* is that in its general scope and conception and emphasis it is a serious misreading of history. Our view is that the primary reason why fascists come to power is that social democrats and progressive liberals fail to solve social problems.[25] Mussolini and Hitler are two cases in point. It is significant, for example, that Hitler won the German election of 1932 on a platform that emphasized massive public works to solve the problem of unemployment—a problem that the then-governing Weimar social democrats had failed to solve. Consequently, contrary to what one might be led to believe by a reading of *The Open Society and its Enemies*, the most effective way to fight fascism is to solve social problems. Instead of eschewing appeals to Tribal Unity, hoping to discourage fascism by disagreeing with its philosophical premises, social democrats should utilize such appeals openly and candidly when they contribute to the peaceful and democratic solution of social problems. (Popper was, of course, in favor of solving social problems. Our complaint is that he underestimated, and denigrated, the contributions that collective emotion can make to solving them—no doubt because his experience, and his reading of history, led him to profoundly distrust collective emotion and to regard it as supremely dangerous. Conversely, he overestimated the potential for preventing fascism by adhering to a rigorously non-fascist philosophy.) One can ask, for example, whether a more aggressive, and more emotional, defense of the jobs and wages of Austrian workers left out in the cold by the chill winds of globalization might have prevented their defection from the SPO or the People's Party to the ranks of Jörg Haider's neo-fascist Freedom Party in the elections of December 2000.

We are suggesting that solutions to social problems (such as unemployment and low wages) sometimes require appeals to ideas and emotions that are not characteristic of the modern (capitalist) age. The Austrian Model provides empirical encouragement for this suggestion. It was an unusually successful social democracy, which relied in the process of its construction on ideals and emotions not characteristic of the modern age. If the plausibility of our suggestion is granted, it then becomes an important question how social science can best transcend its historical origins as an ideology (or anti-ideology) of modernity, in order to play a more useful role in solving social problems. We shall suggest that two parts of the answer to that question are for politics and economics to draw more on both the psychology of moral development and on the findings and methods of anthropology. Any such answers, however, will encounter opposition because of the influence of ideas like those found in the philosophy of science of Karl Popper.

Popper's identification of traditional Tribal Unity with the horrors of National Socialism led him to advocate ways of identifying good social science methodology with his own account of good natural science methodology, and both with modernity and democracy and whatever else is good. His methodological stances are political stances. They marginalize, or remove from the conceptual map altogether, solutions to social problems that rely on findings from psychology or on traditional ideals and emotions. As Popper's biographer Malachi Hacohen wrote, "'[E]motional social needs' remained foreign to him, implicated with fascism. When criticism conflicted with traditional life and belief, his stance was clear: Openness and tolerance required that custom and authority give way. He never negotiated between the closed and the Open Society, or showed their possible convergence in the future."[26]

A case in point is Popper's endorsement of what are today called "rational choice models." Popper was so convinced that the advancement of science and the advancement of humanitarian ideals were one and the same that he never doubted that if he could construe social reality in a way that would make society easy to study, he would thereby contribute to improving society. Thus Popper wrote:

> But in fact there are good reasons, not only for the belief that social science is less complicated than physics, but also for the belief that concrete social situations are in general less complicated than concrete physical situations. For in most social situations, if not all, there is an element of rationality. Admittedly, human beings hardly ever act quite rationally (i.e. as they would if they could make the optimal use of all available information for the attainment of whatever end they may have), but they act, none the less, more or less rationally; and this makes it possible to construct comparatively simple models of their actions and inter-actions, and to use these models as approximations.[27]

Popper thus sees the rational actor as an ideal type, to be used as a model to facilitate research, in a light different from the light of ethical construction. For ethical construction any influential model of human action is a product of culture-creating historical processes in which we are still participating today as we engage in the constant reconstruction of social reality. Any model of human action is both descriptive and normative. As descriptive, what it describes is, in Ludwig Wittgenstein's phrase, "language games," i.e., customs, forms of human life. As normative, it influences expectations. Any model of human action publicizes, even if it does not explicitly endorse, a pattern of human behavior to be regarded as normal. Thus social science feeds the imagination of the self-interpreting, socially-defined, self-questioning non-entity, which Martin Heidegger (a philosopher Popper despised and did not try to understand) avoided naming by using the deliberately empty term *Dasein* ("there-being"). The social scientist is inevitably a participant in the social construction of reality.

Popper does not bring into focus the question as to whether it is morally responsible to propose without critical comment a generalized version of *homo economicus* as an ideal type to orient research in the social sciences. His focus is on whether social science can be a scientific success. He believed that physics was already a success, and that experts in physics such as himself (Popper corresponded with Albert Einstein concerning quantum physics and debated the uncertainty principle with Werner Heisenberg) could contribute to the success of the less advanced sciences by showing them the way. We call the passage from the premise that a model makes human behavior easy to study to the conclusion that it is a good model the "ease of study fallacy."

We dwell on "ease of study" and label it a "fallacy" because we believe that something like the opposite is true. It is not necessarily true that when people are easy to study with methods like those of physics they are better. Yet it is necessarily true that when people are easy to study with methods like those of physics they are worse. If it turns out that human behavior ticks along like clockwork so that predictions made by social scientists are exactly correct, when they use rational choice models (or any model with the virtue Popper ascribes to rational choice, i.e., making human behavior predictable in the way that some natural phenomena are predictable); we should not say, "Whoopee! Social science is a success! It can write equations that predict the future!" Instead we should worry. We should worry that people are not engaging in conscientious moral deliberation. If, for example, it can be predicted that between two goods of the same quality, consumers invariably will buy the one that sells for the lower price, then we should worry that consumers do not care whether the goods were made by sweatshop labor, whether the packaging can be recycled, or whether the goods were produced using pesticides that will eventually poison the soil so that future generations will suffer because of today's preference for cheap food.

The reason why we write that it is necessarily true that when people are easy to study with models like those of physics they are worse, is that the methods of physics do not describe human moral deliberation, from which it follows that people who can be easily studied with them do not engage in human moral deliberation.

We are not saying that humans ought to be unpredictable. On the contrary, humans ought to be reliable and trustworthy. We make ourselves reliable by forming the habit of acting according to good norms, such as the norm that promises should be kept. We are saying that the way to understand desirable forms of human predictability is to focus on ethics, not on physics.

Since capitalism is not as much about control of resources as it is about what those who control resources do with them, the construction of social democracy is more about moral development than about transfer of ownership. A rehabilitated concept of system-changing reform requires, to be sure, shifting the control of resources to the nonprofit sector, to the cooperative sector, to munici-palities, to voluntary organizations, to autonomous public corporations, to the public sector, and to the parts of the private sector committed to collective bar-gaining and socially and environmentally responsible management. But it is less important what sector an enterprise belongs to than what criteria are employed to make decisions. If a public enterprise follows the logic of profit maximiza-tion, then the system is not changed. If a private enterprise follows principles of stewardship, trusteeship, or servant leadership, then the system is changed.

The true system-changing reforms are the ones that falsify the premises of the neo-liberal historicists and the Marxist historicists who argue that there is no alternative to mindless profit accumulation driven by the iron law of the accu-mulation of capital. This implies that the government and the public must be sympathetic to the complaints of capitalists who say that they cannot be ex-pected to obey two logics at once, i.e., to maximize their profits and to maximize being socially responsible. It is the competition of capitals that, historicists of all stripes argue, seals the fate of the entrepreneur who does not maximize profits. It follows that to build social democracy the competition of capitals must be re-laxed. The classic reaction to corruption in business and monopoly profiteer-ing—to assert that greed can only be curbed by the discipline of competition in a free market—must be restrained. Society cannot expect business to be socially responsible and at the same time put it in a position where in order to survive it must be socially irresponsible.

All of this implies that psychology and the study of cultural change must play a bigger role. It implies a convergence of the public sector and the private sectors, such that participants in decision-making at all levels in all sectors make conscientious decisions. At this point psychology and the study of culture inter-sect, since research in psychology shows that children develop in such a way that they internalize conventional norms, which vary from culture to culture. A "conscientious" decision, for a normal adult, is one that complies with the con-ventions (otherwise called norms, rules, values, customs, ideals) of the culture. Cultural action, as a form of revolutionary praxis, can be thought of as a method for the transformation of the conventions that govern normal social behavior, such as what people do with their freedom, and what they do with their property. It may appear innocuous, but it changes everything. It dismantles the mechanism that drives the putative "economic laws of motion of modern society."

The crucial test for social democracy is the capital flight test. It is the make or break issue, which decides whether democracy or money will prevail.[28] We are using the phrase "capital flight" to refer broadly to what is sometimes called the systemic power of capital, the power to brake and reverse a movement to-ward distributive justice by moving capital out of a country, or by refusing to make productive use of capital that stays in the country.[29] ("Capital flight" names the phenomenon from the point of view of the country the capital flees from. From the point of view of the country the capital flees to, the phenomenon is called "the race to the bottom." The phrase "the race to the bottom" refers to competition among countries to offer lower wages and lower taxes in order to attract capital.) The question the crucial test for social democracy asks is whether there is a culture of solidarity, in the context of which it will be feasible for the government to take effective measures to curb capital flight. This question tests the conventions that govern normal social behavior. It is a test for civil society more than it is a test for government. Pessimists say there is no possible way to pass it.

We do not believe there is a single example of a social democracy that has passed the capital flight test with flying colors, although some, at some times, have done better than others. In the absence of what we are calling a culture of solidarity, the constitutional structure of a modern democratic state makes it virtually impossible to check capital flight without assuming absolute dictatorial powers, which is neither possible nor desirable, and even with dictatorial powers it is hard to stop capital flight.

A rehabilitated concept of system-changing reform contributes to building the culture of solidarity needed to transcend the systemic power of capital. The rehabilitated concept is derived from the insight that the "power" of capital comes from rules, and rules can be changed. Norms and values can be changed. Restructuring civil society to reduce reliance on the profit motive is the direct route to treating and curing capitalism's addiction to profit, which results in crippling withdrawal systems whenever social reforms limit profits or amend property rights. Such system changing reforms inoculate a society against capital flight because they remove its basis (control of resources) and weaken its motive (profit). Although such reforms may not produce a system completely resistant to capital flight, they may help to limit the damage to a tolerable level. They should at least make the damage less than it otherwise would be.

The gradual reconstruction of the norms of civil society can be called "piecemeal moral improvement." It corrects, or complements, Popper's "piecemeal social engineering." It calls for a greater role for psychology and for anthropology in politics than Popper's philosophy of science admits. Popper advocates the use in social science research of a stylized ideal type of rational actor whose actions are determined by what Popper calls "the logic of the situation." Thus Popper obviates the need to study in detail how people really do reason, and how they really do decide what to do. Open Societies, which practice democracy and support social science research of the kind Popper advocates, are supposed to solve their problems one by one by piecemeal social engineering. There is not supposed to be any need to analyze the basic constitutive rules of modern liberal democracies, or to compare them with the basic constitutive rules of other societies studied by anthropologists. To be sure, thought that deviates from the norm of the rational actor does exist. In Hitler's Germany it was normative. But, in Popper's worldview, whatever psychologists may learn about it has little bearing on the politics or economics of an Open Society.

Popper's motivation for defending logic, and models of human behavior based on logical choices, against what he called "psychologism," and his motivation for criticizing at great length John Stuart Mill's argument that psychology must be the fundamental discipline for all social sciences; and Popper's adherence to a rational and universal cosmopolitan ethics, his intransigent opposition to multiculturalism; can be traced to his reflections on his early experiences in Vienna, as Hacohen shows in his biography.[30] Although we sympathize with Popper's motivations, we cannot agree with the methodology for social science that he derives from his arguments. The psychologists and the anthropologists have the empirical evidence on their side. They are the ones who study what "reason" actually is, in terms of how people really do think, and in terms of the norms that actually govern the many cultures that actually do exist. It is Popper who has reduced "reason" to the logic of a rational actor who is an ideal type which, as he himself admits, corresponds precisely to no empirically existing reality.

The arguments that Popper makes for "reason" and against "irrationality" often suggest that any concession to what he calls "irrationality" will open the floodgates to fascism. In *The Open Society and its Enemies*, Popper posits only two choices: the Open Society, characterized by democracy and critical reason; and the enemies of the Open Society, collectivists who yearn for the mystical certitude of tribal unity. Here are three of the many parades of possible horrors that Popper dwells on in this work:

> It is my firm conviction that this irrational emphasis upon emotion and passion leads ultimately to what I can only describe as crime. One reason for this opinion is that this attitude, which at best is one of resignation towards the irrational nature of human beings, at worst one of scorn for human reason, must lead to an appeal to violence and brutal force as the ultimate arbiter in any dispute. For if a dispute arises, then this means that those more constructive human emotions and passions which might in principle help to get over it, reverence, love, devotion to a common cause etc. have shown themselves incapable of solving the problem. But if that is so, then what is left to the irrationalist except the appeal to other and less constructive human emotions and passions, to fear, hatred, envy, and ultimately, to violence?
>
> . . . . But of all political ideals, that of making the people happy is perhaps the most dangerous one. It leads invariably to the attempt to impose our scale of "higher" values upon others, in order to make them realize what seems to us of greatest importance for their happiness; in order, as it were, to save their souls. It leads to Utopianism and Romanticism. We all feel certain that everybody would be happy in the beautiful, the perfect community of our dreams. And no doubt, there would be heaven on earth if we could all love one another. But, as I have said before (in chapter 9), the attempt to make heaven on earth invariably produces hell.
>
> . . . . This kind of "Christianity" which recommends the creation of myth as a substitute for Christian responsibility is a tribal Christianity. It is a Christianity that refuses to carry the cross of being human. Beware of these false

prophets! What they are after, without being aware of it, is the lost unity of tribalism. And the return to the closed society which they advocate is the return to the cage, and to the beasts.[31]

These three quotations illustrate characteristic Popperian positions. Together with historicism and irrationalism, he includes holism and confidence in utopian social engineering in the general category of beliefs espoused by the enemies of the Open Society. We are suggesting a both/and rather than either/or approach to these beliefs that Popper rejects. We agree with Popper that historicism is mistaken, but it is not entirely mistaken, because the laws of the market (what Marxists call the laws governing the accumulation of surplus value) have such a pronounced tendency to produce what Popper calls "unintended consequences" that the unfolding of their consequences sometimes seems like historical inevitability independent of human will.

However, rather than simply take at face value the requirement (which is both observed and theoretically deduced) that one regime of accumulation or another is necessary to keep capitalism going, we endorse the idea of system-changing reforms.

Although we also, with Popper, prefer rationality to irrationality, we happily concede to irrationalism that the social emotional needs of the human species, which have evolved over many hundreds of thousands of years, are here to stay.

We do not agree with Popper's scientific criticisms of holism. We believe that the ways everything is related to everything else make the whole a unity that is something much more than the sum of independent parts; in particular, we believe that the biosphere is one, and that the global market is one. Although we would concede to Popper that holistic thought provides a metaphorical foothold for totalitarian politics, we do not think the danger is more than metaphorical without a social catastrophe like the Great Depression to provide more concrete motivations for fascist solutions. We also believe that the radical critiques of the liberal capitalist world order made by holistic versions of religion, Marxism, and ecology are invaluable. We do not believe that radical philosophies, which see the root causes clearly, necessarily lead to violence and tyranny. They can be coupled with equally radical commitments to nonviolence and to democracy. A commitment to peaceful persuasion as a means is not a commitment to the status quo as an end; conversely, a commitment to radical transformation as an end is not a commitment to violence as a means. The history of Austria since *The Open Society and its Enemies* was first published in 1945 shows that Popper's opinion that totalizing theories invariably lead to totalitarian politics was mistaken. It was an opinion that appeared to be correct in the light of Austrian history up to 1945. After 1945, however, the Austrian case has been one that demonstrates that people with incompatible holistic philosophies can share commitments to democracy, freedom, consensus-seeking, and power-sharing. The post-1945 Austrian Model is in retreat and on the defensive today, not so much because the irrational passion for collectivist tribal unity, which Popper rightly feared, has returned, as because a more humanistic social science, which Popper wrongly feared, has not yet arrived.

Notes

1. The Freedom Party (*Freiheitliche Partei Osterreichs*, FPO) was formed in 1956 as a reorganization of the League of Independents, which was a party founded in 1949 as a coalition that included monarchists, Liberals, anticlerical conservatives, and former Nazis. Once the party was reorganized as the Freedom Party, under the leadership of Anton Reinthaller and then Friedrich Peter, it became more narrowly rightist. Reinthaller had been a Nazi party member and had served as the minister of agriculture in the cabinet of Arthur Seyss-Inquart after the Anschluss. Peter, a former SS officer, led the party for the twenty years following the death of Reinthaller in 1958. The Freedom Party platform during these years declared that Austria was a German state and portrayed Austrian participation in World War II in a positive light. Barbara Jelavich, *Modern Austria: Empire & Republic, 1815-1986* (Cambridge; London; New York; New Rochelle; Melbourne; Sydney: Cambridge University Press, 1987), 272.

2. Melanie A. Sully, *Continuity and Change in Austrian Socialism: The Eternal Quest for the Third Way* (Boulder, Colo.: East European Monographs; and New York: Columbia University Press, 1982), 201-35; Jelavich, *Modern Austria*, 302, 304-06.

3. From 1970 to 1975, the SPO was able to enhance the Austrian welfare state and improve the quality of life through the following reforms: the extension of benefits to blue-collar and white-collar workers; the adoption of the forty-hour workweek; the legal codification of the equality of women and men; the removal of legal discriminatory barriers against people of homosexual orientation and against children born out of wedlock; the age of majority set at nineteen rather than twenty-one years; the provision of free textbooks and travel for students; the provision of free medical exams for the entire population; and the reduction of military service from nine to six months. Sully, *Continuity and Change*, 202, 207; Jelavich, *Modern Austria*, 303). Throughout the 1970s, unemployment rates remained fairly low, especially relative to rates in surrounding countries (the average rate of unemployment in Austria throughout the 1970s was 1.7 percent, as compared with 3.7 percent in OECD countries taken as a whole), and a social partnership among labor unions, management, and the government meant that a period of industrial peace obtained in Austria, with very little strike activity. Jelavich, *Modern Austria*, 304-05.

4. Sully, *Continuity and Change*, 227.

5. The SPO faced rising budget deficits and was increasingly feeling pressured into reorganizing heavily subsidized nationalized industries and resisting demands for wage increases. Jelavich, *Modern Austria*, 321.

6. When the provisional government was formed in October 1918, the socialists held four of the most powerful positions: chancellor, foreign minister, minister of the interior, and minister of war. Jelavich, *Modern Austria*, 151. The period of the First Republic was 1918 to 1932.

7. Malachi Haim Hacohen explains the origin of the term "Red Vienna": "Excluded from the national government, the socialists focused on building a model community in Vienna. They developed an extensive network of social services: a comprehensive public health system . . .; a comprehensive educational system, including kindergartens, adult education, municipal libraries, and local *Bildungskommissionen*, organizing cultural, sport, and leisure activities; and huge housing projects, financed by heavy income and

property taxes, relieving the city's acute housing shortage. . . . [T]o contemporaries, Red Vienna was a socialist mecca." Malachi Haim Hacohen, *Karl Popper—The Formative Years, 1902-1945: Politics and Philosophy in Interwar Vienna* (Cambridge and New York: Cambridge University Press, 2000), 293.

8. Evan Burr Bukey, *Hitler's Austria: Popular Sentiment in the Nazi Era, 1938-1945* (Chapel Hill, N.C.; and London: The University of North Carolina Press, 2000), 34-38.

9. Sully, *Continuity and Change*, 69-93.

10. Bruno Kreisky, *Zwischen den Zeiten: Erinnerungen aus fünf Jahrzehnten* (Berlin: Siedler Verlag, 1986), 374-78.

11. Kreisky, *Zwischen den Zeiten*, 373-74, emphasis added. In German, the terms Kreisky uses are *"systemimmanente"* and *"systemverändernde."*

12. The nineteenth-century political party known as the Christian Socials strongly criticized *laissez-faire* capitalism and advocated municipal socialism and the creation of a welfare state in which the working class would thrive. Much of the party's membership during this period was composed of peasants, artisans, small manufacturers, and shopkeepers. When the Christian Socials reorganized as the Austrian People's Party (*Osterreichische Volkspartei*, OVP), their constituency was largely composed of peasant-farmers, blue-collar workers, white-collar employees, and businessmen. Jelavich, *Modern Austria*, 86-87, 248.

13. Helmut Spinner, *Popper und die Politik* (Berlin: Dietz, 1987), 44-72.

14. Hacohen, *Karl Popper*, 290-91.

15. Hacohen, *Karl Popper*, 336-37.

16. Hacohen, *Karl Popper*, 46, 486. Popper's stances with regard to "piecemeal social engineering" and the notion of an "interventionist state" were elaborated partially in response to *The Road to Serfdom*, published in 1944, and via intellectual debate with this work's author, Friedrich von Hayek. See Hacohen, *Karl Popper*, 476-86.

17. Karl Popper, *The Open Society and its Enemies* (Princeton, N.J.: Princeton University Press, 1950), 329, 369, 376, 683. For Popper, Sweden offered proof that unemployment might indeed be abolished by piecemeal measures. Other features of Sweden that Popper held in high regard were the Swedish emphasis upon the consumer and the role played by consumer cooperatives, "as opposed to the dogmatic Marxist emphasis upon production" (Popper, *Open Society*, 683); as well as the fact that Sweden was not an imperial power, and the relative prosperity of its working class was not dependent upon the exploitation of colonies (as in, e.g., Holland and Belgium).

18. Social scientists in their respective fields took up the notion of an "Austrian Model." Within economics, J.R. Hicks is largely responsible for the concept of an "Austrian Model" or "Austrian Way" to be held up as an example to be replicated. See J.R. Hicks, "A Neo-Austrian Growth Theory," *Economic Journal* 30, no. 318 (1970): 257-81; and J.R. Hicks, *Capital and Time: A Neo-Austrian Theory* (Oxford: Oxford University Press, 1973). Hicks in turn draws upon and revives the theories of Austrian economist Eugen von Böhm-Bawerk. See Rudolf Hilferding, *Böhm-Bawerk's Criticism of Marx* (New York: A.M. Kelly, 1949).

19. Sully, *Continuity and Change,* 102, 104.

20. Sully, *Continuity and Change*, 102-04; Kreisky, *Zwischen den Zeiten*, 434-38.

21. Anton Pelinka, *Austria, Out of the Shadow of the Past* (Boulder, Colo.: Westview Press, 1998), 140.

22. Marx, *Capital*, 112.

23. Peter F. Drucker, *The End of Economic Man* (New York: The John Day Company, 1939), 149-50.

24. In this sense we share the view of, among others, David C. Korten and Marjorie Kelly, both of whom insist on "changing the story" in order to bring about positive systemic change. Marjorie Kelly, a business ethicist, believes that we are still suffering from aristocratic stories or "myths" that are left over from the feudal era. She lists six principles or cultural values that uphold what she refers to as the economic aristocracy (these are: worldview; privilege; property; governance; liberty; and sovereignty); and she advocates replacing these with principles of economic democracy (enlightenment; equality; public good; democracy; justice; and "(r)Evolution"). Marjorie Kelly, *The Divine Right of Capital: Dethroning the Corporate Aristocracy* (San Francisco: Berrett-Koehler Publishers, 2001), 1-15. Korten draws his inspiration in part from economist and peace theorist and activist Kenneth Boulding and in part from theologian Thomas Berry. Both Boulding and Berry also advocate the importance of story and of imagination in creating meaningful cultural change. Korten names our culture's current prevailing story the "dead-universe story," a story that is entirely linear, recognizes only mechanical causality, and emphasizes boundaries and limitations of all kinds. He writes: "We must take the obvious next step of acknowledging that the dead-universe story deals only with those aspects of our world that can be described in terms of mechanics and the entropic processes of death and decay. It cannot provide satisfactory explanations for the pervasive processes of creation that demonstrably lead not to disorder but to ever more complex levels of organization and capacity for conscious self-direction. Our embrace of the old story's prophecy of death is leading our species inexorably toward self-destruction. The time has come for a story that acknowledges life's creative power and inspires us to strive for new levels of consciousness and function." David C. Korten, *The Post-Corporate World: Life After Capitalism* (San Francisco: Berrett-Koehler Publishers; and West Hartford, Conn.: Kumarian Press, 1999), 3-16 (quote at 11). See also Kenneth E. Boulding, *The Image: Knowledge in Life and Society* (Ann Arbor, Mich.: University of Michigan Press, 1956); Elise Boulding, *Building a Global Civic Culture: Education for an Interdependent World* (New York and London: Teachers College Press, 1988), 95-117; and Brian Swimme and Thomas Berry, *The Universe Story* (New York: HarperCollins, 1994).

25. See "Ginetta and Angeletti," Howard Richards' essay on Italian fascism, in Richards, *Letters from Quebec*, 397-406.

26. Hacohen, *Karl Popper*, 426.

27. Karl Popper, *The Poverty of Historicism* (New York: Harper and Row, 1964), 140-41. Popper dedicated this work to the memory of all those "who fell victims to the fascist and communist belief in Inexorable Laws of Historical Destiny." Popper, *Poverty of Historicism*, iv.

28. Robert Isaak writes, "[I]nstability stimulates the decisive economic fear of the end of the twentieth century: capital flight. Private investors can make a country like Thailand a miracle one day through massive investment, only to break it next day by withdrawing capital overnight if they become disappointed or alarmed—as in the fall of 1997." Robert A. Isaak, *Managing World Economic Change*, third edition (Englewood Cliffs, N.J.: Prentice-Hall, 2000), 12.

29. For a concise explication of the some of the concrete mechanics of the phenomenon of capital flight (especially how the transactions resulting in capital flight were undertaken prior to the 1990s, when computerization greatly increased the ease of financial transactions), see Rudiger Dornbusch, *Latin American Trade Misinvoicing as an Instru-*

ment of Capital Flight and Duty Evasion: Motives, Evidence, and Macroeconomic Impli-cations (Washington, D.C.: Inter-American Development Bank, 1990) (Occasional Paper No. 3). For a study of how capital flight affects communities at the ground level and on a range of responses taken by communities hit by capital flight, see Charles Craypo and Bruce Nissen, eds., *Grand Designs: the Impact of Corporate Strategies on Workers, Un-ions and Communities* (Ithaca, N.Y.: ILR Press, 1993). For an articulation of the "sys-temic power of capital" in the current setting, see Kelly, *Divine Right of Capital*, espe-cially 19-92; and David C. Korten, *When Corporations Rule the World* (San Francisco: Berrett-Koehler Publishers, 1995).

   30. Hacohen, *Karl Popper*, 46-53.

   31. Popper, *Open Society*, 419, 422, 427.

Chapter 10

Power and Principle in South Africa

Chaps, we have to choose. We either keep nationalization, and get no investment, or we modify our own attitude and get investment.–Nelson Mandela, 1992[1]

When put on trial for treason in 1959 by South Africa's white supremacist government, Mandela described himself as attracted by socialism, but not a Communist, and not (at that time) committed to violence. He testified under oath:

> Mandela: My own view is that it is not necessary in this country to employ force and violence in order to bring about either the demands set out in the Freedom Charter, or even to bring about socialism. . . .
> Prosecutor: Do you think it's possible to achieve a transformation to a communist state in this country peacefully?
> Mandela: You keep talking about a communist state; I talk about a socialist state.[2]

The Freedom Charter, to which Mandela alluded in his testimony, was adopted in 1955 as the common program of the party to which Mandela belonged, the African National Congress (ANC) and other groups allied with it in the struggle against apartheid. Apartheid was a system of strict racial segregation, which denied people of color practically all rights. It was gradually implanted in South Africa after the National Party, dominated by Afrikaner descendants of Dutch Boer settlers, won the elections of 1948.

In 1956, three years before he was tried for treason, Mandela, writing in the left wing South African magazine *Liberation*, had denied that the Freedom Charter was, strictly speaking, socialist. Mandela wrote:

> Whilst the Charter proclaims changes of a far-reaching nature, it is by no means a blueprint for a socialist state but a programme for the unification of various classes and groupings amongst the people on a democratic basis. Under social-

ism the workers hold state power. They and the peasants own the means of production, the land, the factories, and the mills. All production is for use and not for profit. The Charter does not contemplate such profound economic and political changes. Its declaration "The People Shall Govern" visualizes the transfer of power not to any single social class, but to all the people of the country, be they workers, peasants, professional men or petty-bourgeoisie.[3]

Mandela could hardly deny, however, that if the Freedom Charter did not call for socialism in a narrow sense of the term, it did call for social democracy in a wide sense of the term. Some of its clauses were as follows:

THE PEOPLE SHALL SHARE IN THE COUNTRY'S WEALTH!

The national wealth of our country, the heritage of all South Africans, shall be restored to the people;
The mineral wealth beneath the soil, the banks, and monopoly industry shall be transferred to the ownership of the people as a whole;
All other industry and trade shall be controlled to assist the well-being of the people;
All people shall have equal rights to trade where they choose, to manufacture, and to enter all trades, crafts and professions.

THE LAND SHALL BE SHARED AMONG THOSE WHO WORK IT!

Restriction of land ownership on a racial basis shall be ended, and all the land redivided amongst those who work it, to banish famine and land hunger;
The State shall help the peasants with implements, seed, tractors, and dams to save the soil and assist the tillers;
Freedom of movement shall be guaranteed to all who work on the land;
All shall have the right to occupy land wherever they choose;
People shall not be robbed of their cattle, and forced labour and farm prisons shall be abolished.

THERE SHALL BE WORK AND SECURITY!

All who work shall be free to form trade unions, to elect their officers, and to make wage agreements with their employers;
The State shall recognize the right and duty of all to work, and to draw full unemployment benefits;
Men and women of all races shall receive equal pay for equal work;
There shall be a forty hour working week, a national minimum wage, paid annual leave, and sick leave for all workers, and maternity leave on full pay for all working mothers;
Miners, domestic workers, farm workers and civil servants shall have the same rights as all others who work;
Child labour, compound labor, the tot system and contract labour shall be abolished.

THERE SHALL BE HOUSES, SECURITY AND COMFORT!

All people shall have the right to live where they choose, to be decently housed, and to bring up their families in comfort and security;
Unused housing space shall be made available to the people;
Rent and prices shall be lowered, food plentiful, and no one shall go hungry;
A preventive health scheme shall be run by the State;
Free medical care and hospitalization shall be provided for all, with special care for mothers and young children.[4]

The Freedom Charter concluded: "Let all who love their people and their country now say, as we say here: THESE FREEDOMS WE WILL FIGHT FOR, SIDE BY SIDE, THROUGHOUT OUR LIVES, UNTIL WE HAVE WON OUR LIBERTY."

When Nelson Mandela emerged from twenty-seven years in prison, in February of 1990, he immediately assured the African National Congress, in his first speech, which he addressed to the multitudes who welcomed him in downtown Cape Town, that he was still a loyal party member; his program was still the ANC program as it had been declared in the Freedom Charter of 1955. The changing of Mandela's mind, to the point at which he could say in 1992 that he and his ANC colleagues should "modify our own attitude and get investment," was rapid. According to his authorized biographer, Anthony Sampson, Nelson Mandela changed his mind on nationalization in February of 1992, two years after his release from prison, and approximately two years before he was elected President of the Republic of South Africa.[5] Before discussing the immediate occasion of Mandela's change of mind, three points should be made about the historical context at that time.

First, to a considerable extent, by 1992, South African industry had already been nationalized or placed under government control by the Afrikaners of the National Party. Prior to 1948, the Anglos had dominated the economy. The National Party made the public sector mainly an Afrikaner preserve, and enlarged the public sector. It was widely assumed that blacks in power would do what the Afrikaners in power had done, i.e., promote their ethnic interests by strengthening their own role in the state and strengthening the state's role in the economy.[6]

Second, the ANC had only limited success fighting apartheid with electoral politics, with challenges to apartheid in the courts, with mass demonstrations, with strikes. It failed with nonviolence and it failed with violence until—if we may be allowed to exaggerate to make the point—investment in South Africa faltered. When investment faltered, the previously apparently invincible white supremacist police state began to dissolve. Investments faltered partly because of sanctions (boycotts and the like) and partly because investors lost confidence. (One reason why the statement that prior efforts of the ANC got nowhere is an exaggeration is that those prior efforts helped to bring about the imposition of sanctions and the loss of investor confidence. Another reason is that the ANC's emphasis on nonviolence for many years, combined with its long history of willingness to work with anti-apartheid whites, contributed to the moral atmosphere that eventually made a peaceful transition possible.) Influential members of the business community pinned their hopes on a Mandela-led ANC government as a political solution to the country's social problems—a solution that would reverse, not accelerate, the trends that had made South Africa unattractive to investors.

Third, Anthony Sampson writes that when Mandela was released from prison:

> [He] still believed in a classless society, while "painfully aware" of the opposite trend. He looked for ways to reduce inequality. In September 1991 he told businessmen that only nationalization could redress the imbalances, though he would welcome an alternative. The confusing signals reflected arguments within the ANC which were more extreme than those that had raged through the socialist parties of Europe; for South Africa had long been an extreme case, both of inequality and of dependence on international capital.[7]

Thus the problem Mandela faced was—in addition to, and intertwined with, the problems of building a non-racial and non-sexist society—the problem of how to build a classless society in a country whose economy was highly dependent on foreign investment capital.

The immediate occasion of Mandela's change of mind was a meeting of the World Economic Forum held at Davos, Switzerland, in February of 1992. About the sponsoring organization Richard Falk has written, "Without any formal authorization, the World Economic Council at Davos that brings together mega-capitalists on an annual basis has virtually displaced the United Nations as a source of guidance on global issues."[8] As a probable future President of the Republic of South Africa, a man who had just a few years previously been breaking rocks on Robben Island under the blinding sun and under the watchful eyes of sometimes sadistic Boer guards had been invited to Davos. Sampson recounts the occasion of Mandela's changing his mind:

> He was lionized by the world's bankers and industrialists at lunches and dinners. He argued with them that other industrial countries, including Britain, Germany, and Japan, had needed nationalized industries to restore their economies after world wars. "We are going through a traumatic experience of war against the people," he explained, "and therefore we need nationalization." . . . .
> He was finally turned by three sympathetic delegates from the left. The Dutch Minister of Industry was sisterly and understanding, but smashed his argument. "Look, that's what we understood then," she explained, "but now the economies of the world are interdependent. The process of globalization is taking root. No economy can develop separately from the economies of other countries." Leaders from two Asian socialist countries—China and Vietnam—told

him how they had accepted private enterprise, particularly after the Soviet Union collapsed. "They changed my views altogether," recalled Mandela. "I came home to say, 'Chaps, we have to choose. We either keep nationalization and get no investment, or we modify our own attitude and get investment.'"[9]

The story might have continued from here in several different ways. It might have been that after Mandela, the revolutionary guerrilla leader released from prison, had sold his revolutionary soul, the devil dutifully kept his part of the bargain by delivering major foreign direct investment to South Africa. Or, it might have happened that after Mandela had proved himself not to be what Margaret Thatcher feared he might be, "just another half-baked Marxist,"[10] he proved himself to be instead a realistic economist, or at least a statesman who knew enough to appoint realistic economists to advise him, and the result of the realism and the economics might have been creeks and rivers of capital flowing into South Africa.

What actually happened was less dramatic and more painful. South Africa under the ANC adopted grow-and-share policies similar to those of other left-leaning democracies. First they were called Reconstruction and Development, and then later Growth, Employment and Redistribution, GEAR for short. Economic growth was supposed to create jobs and build the tax revenue base. Growth and shifts in priorities were supposed to pay for massive low cost housing construction, better schools, more health care, and the like. To make the growth happen, a campaign was launched to entice more foreign capital to come to South Africa. Some progress was made, but on the whole the results were disappointing:

> The target of a million new houses in five years could not be reached, and the promises of more jobs proved hollow. . . . Mandela faced some disillusion. He had seen how foreign businessmen had piled into the apartheid boom in the sixties while he was in jail, when labor was cheap and the price of gold was shooting up. Now gold was slumping and labor was more expensive, and Africa was shunned by investors, who were racing into the miracle economies of Southeast Asia. He tried to attract investors by reducing exchange controls, preparing to privatize and confronting the unions; but in the end they put their money elsewhere anyway.[11]

The ANC was thus left in the position of people who sacrifice long-held principles to please their lovers, only to find that in spite of their moral sacrifices, and in spite of their efforts to make themselves attractive, their lovers prefer others, do not come, and do not stay.

In 1998, after nearly four years of Mandela's presidency, a South African businessman named Anthony Ginsberg wrote a book entitled *South Africa's Future* in which he argued that major changes were needed. Something had to be done. The population was growing, while the economy was shrinking. Of people leaving school and entering the job market, only one in fourteen (7 percent) was able to find a job. Fifty percent of blacks ages 18 to 35 were unemployed. Seventy percent of South Africans, including ten percent of whites and the great majority of blacks, lived in conditions classified as poor. Inequality was extreme: 53 percent of total consumption of goods and services was enjoyed by ten percent of the population, while the bottom forty percent of the population accounted for only ten percent of consumption. Gross Domestic Product per capita, adjusted for inflation, fell from 8,380 rands in 1995, to 7700 in 1996, to 7192 in 1997, to 6932 in 1998. According to Ginsberg, there was "a need to generate 425,000 new jobs per year, in order to just absorb the annual number of new entrants into the labour market, let alone make any dent in the unemployment statistics. In 1997 and 1998 [the South African] formal sector contracted by an average of 100,000 jobs."[12]

Something had to be done. With nearly half the young population forced to subsist without jobs, crime rates soared. Johannesburg set global records for crime, with more murders and rapes per capita than any other city in the world. South Africa as a whole had a murder rate seven times that of the United States and ten times the world average. Ginsberg describes the desperation of the situation in 1998:

> Millions of innocent South Africans now effectively live jailed inside their houses, surrounded by their own barbed-wire fences and walls. Meanwhile, criminals rule the streets. How healthy is such a society to be bringing up our children in? .... The continued increase in crime has led to a renewed wave of emigration out of South Africa, made up primarily of those with the skills necessary to be able to secure good employment prospects abroad. As *The Star* newspaper has said, whether your name is Domingo, De Beer, or Dlamini the fact is that you could be the next victim of rape, torture or hijacking, or just as likely, murder.[13]

Ginsberg does not blame President Mandela for any of this. He portrays Mandela as the true father of the nation, who brokered a peaceful transition in a situation that might have led to a tragic civil war. He blames the economic and social policies of the preceding white supremacist governments as much or more than he blames the ANC. Nevertheless, he insists that something must be done. Soon.

Something must be done. But what? *South Africa's Future* tells the reader exactly what. Ginsberg is not plagued by self-doubt. Nor is he a lone voice in the wilderness. He purports to know what "tough decisions" need to be made and to echo the voices of rational and well-informed leaders of the private sector, of academia, and of enlightened segments of the public sector. Although he makes a large number of proposals, each of which deserves to be considered separately on its own merits, the centerpiece and main thrust of his argument is plain and clear: Attract more foreign investment!

Ginsberg recognizes that the South African government is already trying to attract foreign investment, but he believes it is not trying hard enough. To be sure, South Africa has established permanent trade missions dedicated to wooing capitalists in the principal places where capitalists are found, including the United States. But there is no permanent South African trade mission in California. How can South Africa be serious about attracting investment, Ginsberg asks, if it has no trade mission in California, or in any of the ten western states of the United States? To be sure, there are government agencies charged with trying to find investors and bring them to South Africa. But there is no cabinet-level ministry devoted to bringing in foreign capital. Ginsberg gives a list of thirty countries that now have cabinet-level ministries for promoting investment. When will South Africa wake up, smell the coffee, and get in step with its competitors? To be sure, South Africa is offering tax breaks to investors and exporters. But what South Africa needs is a thorough overhaul of its taxation policies and a new tax system, one that will shift the bulk of the burden of taxation from investors to consumers. To be sure, the government has curbed labor union demands. But when will South Africa realize that workers are better off with jobs than unemployed, even if the jobs are at low wage rates? There are more than 300 Export Processing Zones (EPZs) around the world where multinationals can run manufacturing operations while paying no duties and no taxes at all to the host governments. When will South Africa get on board and create EPZs?[14]

The outlook for social democracy appears to be bleak. When Nelson Mandela reluctantly gave up nationalization, he intended to keep his ideals and to pursue them by other means. In the light of the logic of global competition that proved to be inherent in the pursuit of investment capital, it appears that essential parts of Mandela's ideals must be abandoned or indefinitely postponed. Whether any alternative to a neo-liberal agenda like the one Ginsberg advocates is viable depends on whether there are any chinks in its logical armor. It depends on whether Ginsberg is talking about reality or "reality." Ginsberg's case that his foreign-investment-driven plan for South Africa is a (and the only) solution to the nation's problems rests on two kinds of arguments, which can be called empirical arguments and rational model arguments.

His empirical arguments are, in brief: There is no need for South Africa to reinvent the wheel. The solution to its problems is known. It can be learned by studying the experiences of countries that have already solved their problems by successfully attracting international investment. Ginsberg cites Costa Rica, the Ivory Coast, the Dominican Republic, Malaysia, Malta, Mauritius, the Philippines, Mexico, China, Thailand, Singapore, Chile, Brazil, and the Czech Republic as empirical proof of his theses. He even cites Russia as a bright example of a country that has privatized industry faster than South Africa (although he also cites Russia as a bad example of a country unable to collect taxes, and as a bad example, like Colombia and South Africa, of a country where crime is out of control).[15]

Although *South Africa's Future* was published only a few years ago, already some of the stars in Ginsberg's firmament have dimmed. The notion that foreign-investment-led development was moving society in the direction of solving deep problems of poverty and inequality has lost credibility, even among those who might formerly have given it credence. International capital is a fickle lover; or, to change the metaphor, the flow of money around the globe does not crest and fall regularly as the tides rise and ebb under the regular influence of our moon's gravity; rather it lurches unpredictably from shore to shore under the influence of unknown moons economists pretend to understand but which astronomers have never detected, whose gravitational pulls are as erratic as they are powerful. Yet the decline of some of yesteryear's high growth economies once temporarily favored by international capital is not the only or even the most important objection to Ginsberg's evidence.

A more important argument is that a tax haven, even in its bright heyday, is never empirical evidence that counts in favor of the thesis to be proved. The thesis is that South Africa, or any country, can do what tax havens do and get the results they get. Tax havens, however (and similar environments that make themselves "business friendly" by weakening government and labor), are, by definition, places that acquire an advantage by offering lower taxes than their competitors in the race to attract capital. "Lower than" implies that some countries have to have higher taxes to preserve the differential that gives the tax haven its advantage. To say that every country could be a tax haven if only it would wise up and understand economics, is like saying that better coaching could improve the present dismal record of the world's basketball teams, which, on average, lose 50 percent of their games. Countries that succeed in becoming magnets for capital provide evidence for the proposition that incentives for business attract business. They do not provide evidence for the proposition that if every country followed suit, all countries would prosper.

So much for the empirical evidence. What we will call rational model arguments, i.e., arguments based on the inherent logic of the market rather than on empirical case studies, provide stronger support for neoliberalism. The rational model arguments are compatible with the neoliberal admitting that there is no guarantee that any given nation will win in the intensely competitive race for investment capital—but saying that nevertheless, every well-advised nation will play the game as best it can, because there is no other game to play. Ginsberg writes:

> In many ways, international capital markets have more power to affect our economy and the future policies we will need to adopt, than anything our own policy-makers may be dreaming up. We have to understand the way markets work—what drives them up or down. The world has changed and we must appease our new masters if all our citizens are to enjoy an improved quality of life. Every day the capital markets are deciding which countries of the world are worth investing in, and which are ready for the trash heap, or have a long

way to go before they, the markets, will reward such countries with a signal to buy. Today the bond markets of London, New York, and Tokyo decide whether South Africa or Argentina is the country to invest in. We cannot afford to thumb our nose at these powerful market forces.[16]

We recognize that advocates of neoliberal solutions have a right to speak for themselves. Nonetheless, we will now formulate for them eight of what we believe to be their implicit premises, using the case of South Africa as an example. Of course, anyone who disagrees or feels misrepresented is free to reply.

Premise 1. The only way to overcome poverty is for poor people to get money with which to buy housing, food, medical care, and other necessities and conveniences.

Premise 2. The only way (at least the only desirable way) for a poor person to get money is for that person to find a job.

Premise 3. Jobs come into existence only when investors create jobs.

Premise 4. All human beings, including investors, seek to maximize the satisfaction of their preferences.

Premise 5. In the case of investors, Premise 4 mainly means maximizing some combination of high earnings and low risks (greater risks being acceptable when the expected earnings are higher).

Premise 6. South Africa does not have enough domestic capital to create jobs fast enough to absorb unemployment and keep pace with the growth of the population.

Premise 7. Therefore, to overcome poverty, South Africa must seek foreign capital.

Premise 8. Following from Premise 5, foreign investors will invest only on terms they accept, and these will be terms that maximize their confidence that they will achieve their investment objectives.

Conclusion. Consequently, to overcome poverty, South Africa must remold itself in order to become—insofar as it possibly can become—an environment where potential investors will feel confident that they will achieve high rates of return and/or run low risks.

If all eight premises and the conclusion following from them are true, then neoliberals like Ginsberg correctly state some things that must be done (whatever else is done). Their plans for remolding South Africa may not be optimal, and in particular they may have no convincing reasons for their belief that growing wealth in the country will trickle down to the poor. Nevertheless, if the above premises are true, there is no alternative to the main thrust of what they propose. Consequently, if there is an alternative, it must be because one or more of the premises stated above is not true.

Our opinion is that all eight premises are false, and that the conclusion is therefore also false. Although not everyone will share this opinion, most people will probably find one or more of the eight premises to be at least dubious. The reason why such ideas are taken for granted is that they float in the vague fuzzy background of neoliberal discourse, not stated and therefore not examined.

In particular, Premise 4, which amounts to saying that all people are selfish, is not true. It can be made true by definition in abstract economic theory, but it is not true in any substantive sense. Mohandas K. Gandhi and Mother Teresa are extreme counterexamples, but they are not unique. Nelson Mandela has not lived for personal gain, but to serve the public good, and so have thousands of his comrades. Gandhi, Teresa, and Mandela, and the millions who have been inspired to emulate them and others like them, are not legends. They are flesh and blood, anatomically identical to the rest of the species. The very large class of unselfish people includes many who are called Christians or Muslims or Jews or Buddhists, many who are called socialists, many who are called mother or father, and many more who go by other names, including some who go by the names "capitalist," and "investor." It includes a fifth column of advocates for justice found even on Wall Street and even on the campuses of expensive private liberal arts colleges. It is partly because of the fifth column's work for socially responsible investment policies that the ANC partisans on the front lines were able to bring down apartheid. Today, there are idealists interested in promoting the common good of the world's peoples, who are working to bring global capital flows under the control of a democratic system of world governance. Psychological studies show that most normal adults want to be good, and that there is a natural developmental progression toward principled behavior.[17] Omitting unselfish behavior from economic theory is a scientific error. Overlooking the need to nurture and encourage unselfish behavior is a policy error.

Given that one or more of the premises from which neoliberal prescriptions can be deduced is false, it follows that there might be an alternative. It also follows that whatever alternatives there are must be ones that contradict one or more of the premises from which neoliberal conclusions ineluctably follow. It remains to move on from saying that it is not necessarily true that there is no alternative, to saying that there are alternatives.

From an empirically existing alternative, the work of organizations in the nonprofit and cooperative sectors, we will draw some principles for an alternative rational model. In making our description concrete by referring to an institution that actually exists, we will necessarily refer to an institution with blemishes, and our example, Habitat for Humanity, is meant to be an example of a self-critical organization struggling with its own limitations, as well as an example showing principles common to many nonprofit organizations, which, if extended, would make possible the realization of the goals of the Freedom Charter.

One of the issues Habitat struggles with is the tension between the ethic of giving, which is demanded by the ancient scriptures that define its normative framework, and the modern world where cooperation and sharing are organized (imperfectly, one might politely say) by money. This tension appears in the following words published in Habitat's international magazine:

> Habitat for Humanity affiliates walk a fine line between ministry and accountability when it comes to the issue of mortgage payments. On one side is founder and president Millard Fuller's challenging dictum: "If you've got ten homeowner families and you have no payment problems, you've selected the wrong ten families." In other words, affiliates may not be taking enough risks. His words are undergirded by Jesus' message of forgiveness: "Give to those who ask of you;" and "Forgive us our debts as we forgive our debtors." Through mercy, relationships are redeemed and new life is born. Yet on the other side of the line is a legitimate need to responsibly run a business, handle money, administer mortgages and bring reality to the concept of "home ownership." Affiliates are called to be faithful stewards of the "Fund for Humanity" so a healthy revolving fund will continue to finance the construction of more houses.[18]

The same source indicates that as of January 2000, total foreclosures for non-repayment in the United States were less than two percent of the houses Habitat built.

Although a repayment failure rate under two percent perhaps represents a valid balance between giving and stewardship, the failure rate is much higher in, for example, Guatemala. This suggests that for some areas more giving is needed. Further, the fact that reimbursement of part of the costs of construction is required at all implies that the model does not work in a subsistence economy where money is little used. Cooperative building of homes should not be a wedge that forces people into a money economy when, on the whole, they would be better off in their immediate future remaining in a subsistence economy. One might also complain that Habitat has not done enough to promote the new green sustainable housing technologies.

Blemishes aside, the work of Habitat and other non-governmental organizations suggests five alternative principles for managing resources to meet needs, which might be called principles for cooperation and sharing:

> *Principle 1: The principle of production for use* (Marx's principle). People work on constructing houses, for the purpose of producing houses for people to use. The logic of exchange and the profit motive, with their endless complications and cruelties, are bypassed.

Principle 2: The principle of trusteeship (Gandhi's principle). Those who possess resources do not possess them for their own benefit, but as trustees for the benefit of the poor.

Principle 3: The principle of volunteerism (The unity principle taught by the world's major religions). People volunteer of their own free will to work on houses that other people will live in. This principle is not always practiced, since sometimes people stop work when their own houses are completed and do not contribute labor to the construction of other people's houses. But this is not a shortcoming of the principle, but a sign of the lack of a culture of solidarity, or, in religious language, of conversion.

Principle 4: The principle of the revolving fund (Ecology's principle). People are expected to put back in what they take out. Instead of the money—commodity—money sequence, in which investors put in funds for the purpose of producing commodities, which are then sold so that the investors can accumulate more money, there is a cycle of resource use. What is consumed is put back for the benefit of future beneficiaries.

Principle 5: The principle of local initiative (Helena Norberg-Hodge's principle). Although Habitat for Humanity is a global network, and although there is transfer of resources from rich areas to poor areas, projects are locally initiated and controlled and are carried out with local resources insofar as possible.

We do not want to insist on these particular principles, nor do we want to exaggerate the benefits to be derived from the activities of non-profit organizations. Yet we do want to insist that the general sort of thing these principles exemplify is a strategy, a key, a turning point, a conceptual divide. We have responded to the challenge of presenting an alternative to neoliberal premises by giving an example of radically different principles that demonstrably work in practice, because houses get built and people who formerly had no houses and could not afford to buy houses now live in them. Yet having felt a need to be rather concrete and specific to respond to that challenge, and having articulated some principles not out of thin air but out of functioning practices, we now feel a need to say that we do not have a patent on the one right way to do things.[19] There are many ways to overcome poverty by organizing a community to meet needs. Many social logics. Some are new, and some are, as Latin American popular educators say, *de rescate*; that is, they are old traditions of indigenous peoples that could and should be revived. Nelson Mandela has said that one of the reasons why he was attracted to socialism was its similarity to the traditional Xhosa tribal practices he knew as a youth.[20] Many different cultural structures have mobilized resources to meet needs, during many thousands of years of history and prehistory.

Now that we have made it clear that we do not advocate replacing a single global system (the global economy ruled by the people and principles Ginsberg calls "our new masters") with another single global system (one ruled by the five principles we have suggested), we want to insist, nevertheless, that there is a single central issue, and that with respect to it, the principles that guide nonprofits and cooperatives at their best are key, crucial, strategic, a turning point, a conceptual divide. We want to insist that neoliberalism must be taken seriously. Its prescriptions are unavoidable, given its premises. It is of no use trying out this or that economic policy or political strategy within a conceptual framework that accepts the same premises, vainly hoping to do better than neoliberalism while accepting the same assumptions about human nature, and the same assumptions about the constitutive rules of society.

This is a short chapter, and it is no substitute for the many books and articles written about South Africa every year. South Africa has problems A, B, and C, not mentioned in this chapter. The solutions are D, E, and F, not mentioned in this chapter. Our claim is a bold one concerning a central issue. It is that whatever else may be done to diagnose and cure South Africa's problems, neoliberalism will continue to be valid; and the remedies that it prescribes will continue to require the sacrifice of the ideals of the Freedom Charter, until different principles, providing in one way or another for cooperation and sharing, play a larger role.

Albert Luthuli, who was president of the ANC from 1952 until his death in 1967, stated the central issue clearly in the following words:

> I do not find myself among those people who tend to reduce all human affairs to questions of economics and economic pressures. None the less, the basic point at issue in South Africa is the question of ownership. Because the races inhabiting the country disagree fundamentally on the answer to this question, the whole controversy is hopelessly tangled with racial factors, and on both sides these racial distinctions have become an unavoidable part of the struggle. One cannot separate the issue of race from the argument about ownership at present, because one race insists on exclusive ownership. Who owns South Africa?[21]

The expectation was that the abolition of apartheid would bring true democracy, and with it popular sovereignty and therefore a people's government. The people's government would rewrite the rules governing property relationships along the lines envisioned in the Freedom Charter. The premise would be that South Africa belonged to all its citizens, and that its resources should be put to work to meet the needs of all of its citizens.

That did not happen. It is not hard to understand why it did not happen.[22] What is hard to understand is what the ANC can do now, lacking the means to achieve the goals of the Freedom Charter, having tried to run a grow-and-share economy without much support from international capital and without much success, now facing demands to give up more and more of its ideals in order to make South Africa attractive to investors.

It is in this context that we suggest that principles illustrated by the work of nonprofit organizations are strategic, key, crucial, and significant as a conceptual break with the mainstream principles that govern the global economy. Whatever their confessional affiliations, or lack of confessional affiliations, the projects of nonprofit and cooperative organizations can model what Nelson Mandela and the ANC would have done if they had dared, and would have done if they had had the power to do it. Nonprofits can be the moral equivalent of guerrilla warfare, opening pockets of resistance ruled by responsible stewardship of resources, in a world ruled by greed, waste, and apathy. Unlike guerrilla warriors, the nonprofits are fighting not as much for power as for principles. The wider application of principles of cooperation and sharing already used by nonprofits is not just reform. It is system-changing reform.

Since we believe that the building of social democracy is not as much a struggle for power as it is a struggle for principles, we might be accused of ignoring the struggle for power, as if it did not matter. It is true that we do not believe in a dictatorship of the proletariat, or in any dictatorship. It is true that we do not believe that the consent of the governed obtained by violence or fraud has any legitimacy. It is true that we consider nationalization to be in most (but not all) instances a crude and ineffective way to transform property rights for the purpose of channeling resources in useful directions. It is also true that we regard "power" as an overused word, which tends to lump together and obscure facts that should be separated and illumined.

Nevertheless, power does matter, and the danger that nonprofits will function to mask and preserve domination by existing power structures is a real danger. On the positive side, some contributions that the work of nonprofits and cooperatives can make to democratic power sharing in society are: first, by facilitating the growth of the skills and the cohesion needed to manage resources, they can increase the probability that the people will acquire resources to manage; and second, to the extent that mobilization of community resources at the grassroots level actually increases a nation's self-reliance, it enables a nation's leaders to negotiate with the outside world, including international investors, from a position of dignity. Dignity requires a capacity to be loyal to principles, and some degree of autonomy. Third, nonprofits can engage in a whole series of practices that go under the names of "empowerment" and "consciousness-raising." Fourth, nonprofits can keep alive ideals that can set a standard for the rest of society.

Supporting, encouraging, or even allowing NGOs (non-governmental organizations) to facilitate self-help among the urban poor and the rural poor requires some unselfishness on the part of the state, its officials, and its civil servants. The state often favors the formal economy based on capital investment and wage labor because it can easily be taxed. Supporting the work of tax-exempt organizations among people forced to subsist in the shadows of informal economies is in some important ways contrary to the self-interest of the military, the police, the judiciary, the members of parliament, and all whose salaries are paid from taxes. Similarly, self-reliance in the countryside and in the slums and townships offers less to the staff of the state apparatus than international trade. International trade moves through ports and airports, and it is fairly easy to skim off a percentage for whoever controls the ports and the airports. Emphasizing overcoming poverty with what a nation has, as distinct from what it might import or export is in this respect contrary to the self-interest of the state officials who control the interface between the nation and the outside world. In this respect public servants like Mandela, who did not enrich himself while in office and who gave a substantial portion of his salary as president as donations to nonprofits, set an important precedent, which needs to be expanded to the level of a certain degree of self denial on the part of the entire state apparatus if development is to be inward-oriented rather than outward-oriented.

To the extent that our suggestions on how to keep Nelson Mandela's ideals alive tend toward encouraging inward-oriented development, they may conjure up visions of Johan Galtung's advice to developing nations to "decouple" themselves from the global economy, of Juan Perón's efforts to keep Argentina out of the International Monetary Fund and the World Bank, of Julius Nyerere's "Ujamaa" in Tanzania, of Sarvodaya Shramadana's building of self-reliant rural communities in Sri Lanka and East Africa.[23] Our comment on these visions of self-sufficiency is that it is not necessary to go to extremes. Anthony Ginsberg may be right when he says that his country cannot afford to thumb its nose at international capital markets. But to do what one can to be able to approach international capital markets from a position of strength and dignity is not the same as thumbing one's nose at them. To propose that normative frameworks illustrated by the best work of nonprofits can help keep Nelson Mandela's ideals alive by practicing social democracy at a grassroots level, is not to propose self reliance as the answer to all questions.

Concerning Nelson Mandela's central question, as we have formulated it—how to build a classless society in a nation heavily dependent upon foreign investment—we have proposed an answer, or at least the beginning of an answer, based on what many nonprofit and cooperative organizations are already doing. It is to put his ideals into practice where it is possible to do so.

Notes

1. Nelson Mandela, quoted by his authorized biographer Anthony Sampson, in *Mandela: the Authorized Biography* (New York: Alfred A. Knopf, 1999), 429.

2. Mandela's testimony at the 1959 trial, quoted in Martin Meredith, *Nelson Mandela: a Biography* (New York: St. Martin's Press, 1998), 184.

3. Mandela quoted in Meredith, *Nelson Mandela*, 138-39.

4. The Freedom Charter of 1955, reprinted as Appendix B to Albert Luthuli, *Let My People Go* (New York: American Library, 1962).

5. Sampson, *Mandela*, 427-28.

6. Robert M. Price, *The Apartheid State in Crisis: Political Transformation in South Africa, 1975-1990* (New York and Oxford: Oxford University Press, 1991), 287. Price, whose work treats the period just before the collapse of apartheid, states that the Mass Democratic Movement showed a clear preference for the English Westminster model of democracy, a system characterized by "parliamentary sovereignty," which allows the governing party "unfettered latitude" in policymaking as long as that party maintains a parliamentary majority. It was precisely because the Westminster model offered no constitutional proscriptions or structural constraints that would inhibit the government from pursuing redistributive goals that the National Party—once faced with the prospect of black South Africans with the franchise—quickly changed its stance and began to favor constitutional mechanisms that would place constraints on government action. Price notes that South Africa's ruling National Party offered no criticism of the Westminster model inherited from British colonialism as long as black South Africans remained disenfranchised. He states, "Indeed, it was the power available in the Westminster parliamentary system that gave the National Party the opportunity to elevate Afrikaners through statist economic policies of regulation, allocation, and public ownership. The extent of state intervention was such that the South African economy was characterized by one expert as 'about as interventionist and centrally directed a policy regime as could be found in the world.'" Price, *Apartheid State in Crisis*, 286-87.

7. Sampson, *Mandela*, 428.

8. Falk in Joseph A. Camilleri, Kamal Malhotra, and Majid Tehranian, eds., *Reimagining the Future* (Bundoora Victoria, Australia: Politics Department, La Trobe University, 2000), xii.

9. Sampson, *Mandela*, 429.

10. Thatcher quoted in Sampson, *Mandela*, 412.

11. Sampson, *Mandela*, 507.

12. Anthony Ginsberg, *South Africa's Future: From Crisis to Prosperity* (London: Macmillan, 1998), 10.

13. Ginsberg, *South Africa's Future*, 39, 41.

14. Ginsberg, *South Africa's Future*, 137-220.

15. Ginsberg, *South Africa's Future*, 43, 63-64, 153, 164-82.

16. Ginsberg, *South Africa's Future*, 138.

17. See, for example, Thomas Lickona, ed., *Moral Development and Behavior: Theory, Research, and Social Issues* (New York: Holt, Rinehart, and Winston, 1976), and the sources cited in the articles contained therein. Moral development is a vast field with an

extensive literature and several specialized journals and professional associations, but the interested reader should start with the work of Lawrence Kohlberg, who developed the theory of the stages of moral development. See, e.g., Lawrence Kohlberg, "Stage and sequence: The cognitive-developmental approach to socialization," in D.A. Goslin, ed., *Handbook of socialization theory and research* (Chicago: Rand McNally, 1969), 347-480, in which Kohlberg presents evidence from six cultures to demonstrate the cross-cultural validity of his theory of the stages of moral development. Kohlberg's most famous critic is Carol Gilligan, who challenges Kohlberg's formulation of his theory of stages on the grounds that it is biased against people who were not included in Kohlberg's research. Kohlberg's theory is based on his study of eighty-four males over the course of twenty years, and Gilligan notes that people not included in this sample, most notably girls and women, seem to fall most commonly in Stage 3 of Kohlberg's stages, in which morality is conceived in interpersonal terms and goodness is equated with helping and pleasing others. Yet Gilligan's arguments only serve to bolster the point we are making here because she shows that whole categories of people, not accounted for in Kohlberg's work, also have the desire to be good and demonstrate principled behavior. In the higher stages in Kohlberg's schema, relationships are subordinated to rules, and Gilligan faults Kohlberg for choosing to consider a "morality of rights" as more valid than a "morality of relationships" because she finds that this latter form of morality is often the guiding form for women. Gilligan writes, "[H]erein lies a paradox, for the very traits that traditionally have defined the 'goodness' of women, their care for and sensitivity to the needs of others, are those that mark them as deficient in moral development [according to Kohlberg]." Carol Gilligan, *In a Different Voice: Psychological Theory and Women's Development* (Cambridge, Mass.; and London: Harvard University Press, 1982), 18-19. Furthermore, in addition to psychological research demonstrating a developmental progression toward principled behavior, research in conflict resolution and peace studies indicates that although normative behavior such as acting according to a moral code is not necessary to sustain cooperation among humans, moral behavior can serve as the catalyst that transforms noncooperation into cooperation. Tetsuo Kondo, "Some Notes on Rational Behavior, Normative Behavior, Moral Behavior, and Cooperation," *Journal of Conflict Resolution* 34 (1990): 495-530.

18. Joe Gatlin, "Ministry vs. Fiscal Responsibility," *Habitat World*, April/May 2001, 2.

19. In fact, we agree with Daniel Quinn that if all humans began to live in the very same way, even if this single way of living were on its face less destructive and wasteful than the ways many of us are currently living, it would likely be disastrous in the long run. The reason is that it is not ecologically sound. As Quinn notes, "Macaws have a good life, but their habitats would fail if all birds lived like macaws. Giraffes have a good life, but their habitats would fail if all mammals lived like giraffes. Beavers have a good life, but their habitats would fail if all rodents lived like beavers. *Diversity, not uniformity, is what works.*" Quinn, *Beyond Civilization*, 97, emphasis added.

20. The amaXhosa, or Xhosa people, are those who speak the Xhosa language, which is part of the Bantu family of languages. The groups who speak Xhosa include the Xhosa (both Gcaleka and Rharhabe), Thembu, Xesibe, Bomvana, Mpondomise, and Mpondo. For a history of the Xhosa people, see J.B. Peires, *The House of Phalo: A History of the Xhosa People in the Days of Their Independence* (Berkeley; Los Angeles; London: University of California Press, 1982). For a more thorough explication of Xhosa cultural constructs, see Jeff Opland, *Xhosa Oral Poetry: Aspects of a black South African*

tradition (Cambridge; London; New York; New Rochelle; Melbourne; Sydney: Cambridge University Press, 1983). Opland offers some discussion of Xhosa traditions of cooperative labor, sharing, and a cultural respect for individuals co-existing with a cultural condemnation of individualism when it is asserted in ways contrary to the common good.

21. Luthuli, *Let My People Go*, 86-87.

22. If the constitutive rules of a commercial society go far to explain why South Africa failed to achieve the ideals of the Freedom Charter, then similar failures to move from dependent capitalism to social democracy in other countries might be easier to explain than has often been thought. Roger Bartra argues that it is a first priority political necessity to understand the Mexican national character in order to explain the Mexican Revolution's failure, "given the extreme precariousness of projects or models of development (which are usually no more than a posteriori justifications of the course followed by capitalist accumulation)." Roger Bartra, *La Jaula de la melancolia; identidad y metamorfosis del mexicano* (Mexico: Grijalbo, 1987), 188. But it does not follow from the superficiality of models of development that national character (important as it is) needs to be invoked to explain the failures of transitions to socialism. The requirements of capitalist accumulation themselves make capitalism hard to change.

23. In 1945, when Tanganyika (later to become Tanzania) was a part of German East Africa under British Mandate, schoolteacher Julius Nyerere founded the Tanganyika African National Union (TANU). TANU quickly gained a large popular following and grew into an independence movement, and Tanganyika gained independence in 1961. Ujamaa ("Togetherness") was the program launched in 1967 to create rapid and socially equitable economic development. The program nationalized banking, finance, industry, and large-scale trade; reorganized land tenure to favor communal village settlements; and channeled resources to make major improvements in education and health care. See Randal Sadleir, *Tanzania, Journey to Republic* (London and New York: The Radcliffe Press, 1999), especially 212-51; and Susan Geiger, *TANU Women: Gender and Culture in the Making of Tanganyikan Nationalism, 1955-1965* (Portsmouth, N.H.: Heinemann; Oxford: James Currey; Nairobi: E.A.E.P.; Dar es Salaam: Mkuki Na Nyota, 1997). The Sarvodaya Shramadana movement was founded by schoolteacher A.T. Ariyaratne in 1958. This movement made use of the cultural resource of Buddhist values and ideals in order to improve living conditions in rural villages. The Buddhist concept of "*Sarvodaya*" ("awakening of all"), or individual and community enlightenment, is achieved through "*Shramadana*," the selfless sharing of one's labor. The movement began as an educational/work-camp movement for students and gradually grew to become a village self-help economic development movement with the launch in 1967 of the "Hundred Villages Development Scheme." This was a project to establish village "reawakening" (*gramodaya*) in one hundred villages. On the Sarvodaya Shramadana movement, see George D. Bond, *The Buddhist Revival in Sri Lanka: Religious Tradition, Reinterpretation, and Response* (Columbia, S.C.: University of South Carolina Press, 1988); Joanna Macy, "In Indra's Net: Sarvodaya and Our Mutual Efforts for Peace," in Fred Eppsteiner, ed., *The Path of Compassion: Writings on Socially Engaged Buddhism* (Berkeley: Parallax Press, 1988), 170-81; and J.R. Williams, "Religion, Ethics, and Development: An Analysis of the Sarvodaya Shramadana Movement of Sri Lanka," *Canadian Journal of Development Studies* 5, no. 1 (1984): 157-67.

Chapter 11

Islam and Economic Rationality
in Indonesia

This chapter will demonstrate a point already implicit in previous chapters: answers to crucial questions in ethics and politics turn on answers to questions in the philosophy of science. What causes what? On what grounds does one attribute an effect to its alleged cause? What is possible and what is impossible? Why? Why not? In particular, what are the causes of poverty? What are the causes of prosperity and economic security? Much turns on whether it is recognized that the norms that guide human action are causes that explain them.[1]

A guiding principle of social democracy, from its earliest days, has been the idea, expressed in various ways, that the progress of the human species requires a critique and a transformation of the constitutive rules that govern life in a capitalist society. The constitutive rules to be criticized and transformed include the moral and legal norms governing freedom, property, contracts, sales, credit, and competition. These rules constitute markets and provide the ethical framework for market behavior.

The historical movements that have inscribed social democracy's name on their banners can be regarded as movements seeking a higher level of ethical life. Narrow economic rationality, which tends to be defined in terms of calculating optima, where it is deemed optimal to buy as cheap as possible and to sell as dear as possible, is to be broadened by considering other criteria, which also contribute to defining good and bad, just and unjust, right and wrong.

Social democracy means, first, that the rational criteria used to arrive at social decisions are improved by incorporating principles of welfare and justice, and in recent decades, principles of ecology, into decision-making processes. It means, secondly, giving weight to the voices of common people, and empowering those who labor. The institutionalization of processes for making social decisions fair and responsible corresponds to the capacity to discern the good, which on the level of the individual is called "conscience." The second, the institutionalization of shared governance and democratic participation by citizens and workers in decisions that affect their lives, the shifting of the social balance of power in favor of the power of the people, corresponds to the steadfast will to do the good, which on the level of the individual person is called "character."

The persisting underlying tendency of social democracy is to improve capitalism and to transform it, until it actually accomplishes the purposes that advocates of capitalism have always ascribed to it—the prosperity and security of everyone. When such a transformation has been achieved it matters little whether the end result is called democratic socialism or enlightened capitalism. It benefits individuals and social systems.

As Christian social democrats we identify with early twentieth-century thinkers such as Karl Polanyi, Sir Stafford Cripps, Heinrich Pesch, S.J., and Hilaire Belloc[2]; with more recent Christian writers on economics and development such as Charles K. Wilber, Kenneth P. Jameson and Denis Goulet of Notre Dame[3]; and with the doctrinal statements on peace and social justice of the Catholic and Protestant churches.[4] From such a point of view it is tempting to regard the ethical achievements of twentieth-century social democracy as a resumption of the gradual moral progress of Christendom, which was to a considerable extent interrupted for three hundred years by a suspension of social and moral accountability.

Pre-twentieth-century *laissez faire* capitalism tended to conceive the market as a natural reality that neither could nor should be made answerable to conscience. Misplaced metaphors—forces as metaphors for patterns of human conduct—disguised the fallacious attribution of consequences of deliberate human action to nature. The self-interest of privileged beneficiaries of capitalism, and the intellectual prestige economics acquired by imitating natural science, allowed the metaphors to remain misplaced until they were challenged by the social democracies of the twentieth century that built the welfare states of Western Europe and inspired a global movement for social justice with democracy.

Nobody would say, however, that in terms of some measure of moral progress—if such a measure could be imagined—humanity, or Europe, got steadily better from the dawn of history until the beginning of capitalism, and then declined until it began to improve again because of twentieth-century social democracy. Moral progress often takes two steps forward and one step back, and sometimes one step forward and two steps back. It is complicated by the fact that what counts as "progress" includes both greater compliance with existing standards and the elevation of standards. It is further complicated by the fact that there are honest differences of opinion concerning which direction is progress and which direction is regress.

Moreover, nobody would ignore the respects in which it is precisely modernity—and not the revitalizing of ancient and traditional ideals of social solidarity—which defines the ideals of socialism. Ernesto Laclau and Chantal Mouffe in *Hegemony and Socialist Strategy* define the ethical ideology of socialism as a set of chains of equivalence, political democracy, economic democracy, democracy in the family, democracy in schools . . . which add up to a radicalized liberalism. As they see it, social democracy is a higher form of ethical life because it seizes the best that capitalist modernity has to offer, purifies it, generalizes it, and makes it consistent.[5]

Credit must be given to the moral advances represented by the liberal ideologies that have accompanied the growth of capitalism in Europe. Nevertheless, the views of thinkers like Polanyi, who find ideals for democratic socialism not just in radicalized liberalism but also in democratized conservatism, cannot be ignored. If the rules of liberal ethics function as we have portrayed them in our accounts of social democracy in Sweden and in Austria, then Laclau and Mouffe's radical liberalism is neither workable nor attainable. Its ethical framework leaves governments and peoples powerless to prevent capital flight. Capital flight implies the erosion of wages and the erosion of the welfare state. An ethical framework which puts more emphasis on virtue, on loyalty, and on duties to society and to other people, in other words a conservative ethical framework, is needed to make it feasible to carry out the social planning of saving and investment.

It is true that capitalism is ideologically vulnerable because it contradicts itself when it promises more freedom, more rights, and more equality than it delivers. Yet it is not true that a workable alternative to capitalism can be constructed just by criticizing capitalism's hypocrisy and demanding that it transform itself to conform to its own ideals. Social obligations, duties, and the functional differentiation of roles are also needed.

Thus the achievement of social democracy in the West—where social democracy is built on a liberal heritage—calls for an *Aufhebung* in which the liberal ideals of the past few centuries are valued and preserved at the same time that the older ideals, the conservative ideals identified with spirituality and community and family, are reaffirmed, detached from their unholy alliance with free market economics, and synthesized with liberal ideals. Such a program for a social democratic cultural politics is consistent with the findings of research in the psychology of moral development that show that at higher stages of moral maturity subjects show *both* greater respect for individual autonomy *and* greater solidarity with others.[6] It is consistent, too, with reading the history of European modernity *both* as the history of the growth of humanitarian ideals, democracy, and the rule of law, *and* as a relative eclipse of customary virtues of traditional peoples. In Max Weber's terms, modernity moved humanity both forward and backward when it replaced custom by economic rationality. In Sir Henry Maine's terms, there was both gain and loss when status was replaced by contract.[7] Whatever security, whatever sense of duty and identity, was derived from custom and from status, tended to dissolve as human connections became merely market transactions—a consequence especially disastrous for those who had no money.

The respects in which capitalism has been a step backward in the moral history of the human species form an indispensable part of the picture, even though they are not the whole picture. Some of them are underlined by the Catholic social philosopher Hilaire Belloc in these terms:

> With all these influences increasing throughout three hundred years and becoming riotous today—that is, increasingly feverishly—we have come to the end of a process whereby in the loss of Status and the replacement of it by Contract we have found chaos: a society without bond or cement. We have further produced an economic state of affairs in which the condition of the mass of men deprived of Status is desperate. That is why in their persistent efforts to reestablish security and sufficiency for themselves, the modern proletariat is really expressing and apparently beginning to satisfy an appetite for Status.[8]

Belloc is at one with many Islamic social philosophers in his conviction that the economic rationality of self-interested individuals is no fit basis for a social order. Like Mohamed Aboulkhair Zaki Badawi, Abdullahi Ahmed An-Nalim, Isma'il R. al-Faruqui, Ayatullah Mahmud Taliqani, Khurshid Ahmad, M. 'Umar Chapra, Abulhasan Bani-Sadr, and others, Belloc regards liberal individualism as an error into which much of humanity has fallen during the past few centuries.[9] In some better future age, humanity will outgrow the liberal ethics of modernity. Although one cannot yet say whether their views will prove to be true about the future, one can say that they are right about the past.

For Plato, for Aristotle, for Augustine, for Aquinas, and for the great majority of major pre-modern European thinkers, as for the great thinkers of Islam and Asia, the improvement of a nation was indistinguishable from the moral improvement of its people. "Development" in the sense in which post-World War II thinkers regard "economic development" as coming first, and something called "social development" as trailing it, was inconceivable. Aristotle is a good example. His ideas were influential in Islam through Avicenna and Averroes, as well as being, through Aquinas, orthodox in the West.[10] Aristotle thought of politics as an extension of ethics, and of a better *polis* as one characterized by more virtue and less vice. Better government traditionally meant better character formation among the governing and among the governed, and better character formation meant more virtue, more solidarity, more devotion to the common good, more stewardship of resources, and less unaccountable exercise of property rights.

For centuries it seemed to be self-evident that the more people valued their souls over their bodies, and the more they followed divine injunctions to devote their lives to service and good works, the better off the political community would be. When Adam Smith declared that the human desire to do good works was a weak and unreliable motive, and that the prosperity of a commonwealth could and should be built on the strong and reliable foundation of self-interest, he represented the interruption of a long tradition that had assumed, as a premise hardly requiring proof, that the task of politics was moral education. And that the way to produce a republic that would achieve the common good was to produce citizens who desired to contribute to achieving the common good. It is true that Plato took considerable pains to refute Gorgias and others who argued that an individual could find personal happiness by pursuing self-interest without caring about the good of others or the good of the state. But it never occurred to Plato, as it occurred to Smith, that an individual could best contribute to the good of others and to the good of the state by pursuing personal self-interest.

Ancient ideologies of solidarity, in both East and West—the Hinduized dynasties of Java, and the Merovingian dynasties of France are two examples—went together, to be sure, with the widespread practice of violence, cruelty, and indifference. Service often meant military service to the king or emperor, which meant killing someone else for the glory and enrichment of one's earthly lord, and for a share of the spoils. Religion and conquest competed and blended as sources of authority, but religion was never merely a consequence of conquest, with no causal efficacy of its own.[11] (The Qur'an, by the way, specifically states that there is to be no compulsion in matters of religion.) Although history does tend to show that social cohesion provided by religion works in favor of military success, it does not support a vulgar Marxist or vulgar Foucauldian reductionism, which would hold that religion and ethics are nothing but manifestations of non-religious and non-ethical power. Pre-capitalist religious sages around the world anticipated the cosmopolitan ideals of universal benevolence that would later be articulated in secular forms by the ethical philosophers of the seventeenth and eighteenth centuries. The Qur'an, for example, repeatedly names Allah as "the merciful, the compassionate." What pre-capitalist sages did not anticipate, and what the modern West discovered, was that a secular ideology advocating the systematic pursuit of individual self-interest could be the basis for an enduring if not entirely viable social order.

Seen from the perspective of the common tendencies of the world's great pre-capitalist belief systems, the human solidarity advocated by social democrats is not a new idea, and not a local idea. It is the pretension of economics to be a globally applicable social science, which takes human nature as given, and which does not take the perfecting of human nature through spiritual discipline and the cultivation of ethical ideals to be the central problem of social philosophy, that is a new idea. It is a new idea that has become credible because of the miraculous practical achievements made under the aegis of economics' theoretical premises.

Assuming that one could somehow disentangle the myriad causal threads that tie modern technology and modern economics to each other, and to attribute historical effects to capitalism itself, as distinct from the growth of scientific knowledge that has accompanied it, then, it seems fair to say, that even leaving out of the equation the miracles due to modern science, that the modern capitalist market has performed miracles that ancient philosophers would not have considered possible. Plato, for example, proposed an ideal Republic in which every craft worker contributed to the good of the whole by pursuing the specialty he or she was best suited for, under the guidance of the wisdom provided by philosophical guardians (*archai*). The guardians' supervisory task was to assure the harmonious dovetailing of each person's work with each other person's work, so that the overall result would serve the good of the whole. Other ancient sages had similar ideas about how to organize the performance of complementary tasks.

It was not until modern times, however, that scholars came to appreciate the amazing capacity of markets to coordinate human cooperation. And the tendency to equate "rationality" with "economic rationality," and "economic rationality" with "reliance on free markets" is a modern tendency.[12] In a famous example, Adam Smith points out that thousands of people cooperate to make a pin, without knowing one another, without having any moral obligations to contribute to one another's welfare, without needing to know anything about how to make a pin except for knowing how to perform one's own bit part, without having any common superior who knows what they all do, and without sharing a common belief system that defines their roles and tasks. The same market mechanism, illustrated by Smith with the example of pin-making, now structures the global economy—pin-making writ large. Causes produce effects. The constitutive rules that create the market, as causes, produce the wondrous phenomena of modern capitalism, as effects.

Humanity is on the road to becoming a company of strangers. Each one of more than six billion people increasingly relies on all the others for the necessities of life without knowing most of them or caring about them. Each is connected to all the others through markets, through trillions of purchases and sales.

Social democracy since its inception, and through the thousands of historical successes and thousands of historical failures which it has now registered, has always been a counter-current to a narrow economic rationality that would define the good as acquiescence in market outcomes, given the status quo distribution of property and talents. Social democracy has always represented a critique of what economists call Pareto optimality, i.e., of the idea that outcomes produced by a free market under ideal market conditions are, by definition, good outcomes.[13] Social democracy has always represented a consciousness-raising effort designed to make people aware that economic reality is not physical reality. In this respect the opposite of democratic socialism is not capitalism; it is naturalism. Its opposite is the idea deeply embedded in economic discourse that the legal and moral norms of property and contract, which establish and constitute markets, are laws of *nature*. Unlike vulgar Marxists and vulgar Foucauldians, social democrats believe that ethical ideologies can reshape economic relationships. This is true whether the ethical ideology is radicalized liberalism, as in the cases of Laclau and Mouffe's or Bowles and Gintis's arguments for economic democracy; or social gospel, as in the cases of Latin American liberation theology, contemporary progressive Islamic writers, or arguments inspired by

Karl Polanyi for "re-embedding" economic relationships in social relationships.[14]

Unfortunately, social democracy—especially those forms of it which recognize the impossibility of arriving at socialism by generalizing the ideals of capitalism—suffers from a philosophical weakness. The philosophical weakness leads to paralysis in practice. It makes ethical socialism incredible to sophisticated minds. The weakness is that social democracy's ideals appear to represent parochial, discredited, outmoded, and inoperative traditional religious and philosophical belief systems. Capitalism, in contrast, appears to be scientific and up-to-date. It appears to stand for a cosmopolitan economic rationality, valid everywhere and for everybody.

In Indonesia, the fourth most populous country in the world, there are 250 million people, most of them poor and poorly educated, inhabiting a vast equatorial archipelago, speaking hundreds of languages and dialects, practicing innumerable versions of the majority religion (Islam) and the four other officially recognized religions (Hinduism, Buddhism, Catholicism, Protestantism) and, in secret, many religions and cults that are not recognized. The economists who arrive from Berkeley, from Harvard, from Canberra, and from IMF and World Bank headquarters in Washington, and the local economists who were mostly trained in the same places the foreign economists come from, appear on the scene as incarnations of a universalistic rationality in a society which threatens to dissolve at any moment into a particularistic chaos. Throughout the world, not just in Indonesia, ethics and religion seem to be based on local myths. Capitalism seems to be based on universal science. Thus social democracy, conceived as an aspiration to a higher ethical life, suffers from the philosophical weakness from which Karl Marx tried to rescue it in the nineteenth century when he tried to replace socialism's reliance on ethical appeals with a political program based on a rigorous scientific critique of capitalist political economy.

There is another way to look at ethics and religion, and another way to look at economics. It is not necessary to perceive ethical codes and religious beliefs as local, customary, sectarian, pre-scientific belief systems, which can and should be superseded by modernity, where modernity is equivalent to capitalism, and where capitalism owns "economic rationality." It is not necessary to view the intellectual framework of capitalism as universal, rational, cosmopolitan science. Instead, one can view humanity's social nature as universal. As Thomas Berry has said, humans are biologically coded to be culturally coded.[15] Humans form social relationships. Humans invent norms and beliefs to govern social relationships. Humans everywhere internalize conventional group norms. They renegotiate them and play with them every day. Seen in this light it is the capacity of *homo sapiens* to be a creator of culture that is universal. It is economics that is local and customary, having governed some of humanity some of the time for the past few centuries.

Whether economics is sectarian depends on which economists one reads. As Amartya Sen notes, "[E]conomics has had two rather different origins, both related to politics, but related in rather different ways, concerned respectively with ethics, on the one hand, and with what may be called 'engineering' on the other."[16] Economics can be conceived either as a branch of ethics, in dialogue with the other branches of ethics, or as a branch of engineering.

Seeing the human capacity to create culture as universal and economics as a particular set of cultural phenomena, strengthens social democracy against the criticism that its ideal of solidarity is an ethnocentric prejudice. Granted, conceiving an ethic of social responsibility as the implementation under modern industrial conditions of the ideals of West European Greek and Judeo-Christian traditions is clearly parochial. For Indonesia, where 90 percent of the people identify themselves as Muslims, while perhaps as many identify as Buddhists or Hindus as identify as Christians, an ideal of social unity derived from the Greek *polis*, the Hebrew *shalom*, or the Christian *agape*, might seem to have little relevance. Yet this is not a reason for dismissing Judeo-Christian or ancient Greek ideals. From an ethically constructive viewpoint, consigning Greek and Judeo-Christian ideals to the ashcan would do nothing to further ideals like the Islamic *zakat*, the Hindu *moksha*, and the Buddhist *sangha*.[17] Not only would the denigration of Christianity not further the ideals of non-Christian religions; it would cheapen them. It would imply that they, also, are nothing but old-fashioned local pre-scientific ideals.

If we shift the focus of our conceptual lenses so that we see the spiritual treasures of the world's civilizations as gifts of God to humanity, then instead of worrying that the uniqueness of each spiritual message impairs its universal validity, we will honor historically existing cultural forms as sources of constructive contributions to the common task of an interdependent species whose members share a common fate. We have suggested naming this common task "cooperation and sharing." Antonio Gramsci named the common task as "intellectual and moral reform" to be "tied to a programme of economic reform."[18]

There is no lack of texts in the world's sacred scriptures to support the idea that people with diverse beliefs should focus on constructive contributions to the common good, and not on quarreling with one another. For example, in the Holy Qur'an it is written:

> And to you We have revealed the Book containing the truth, confirming the earlier revelations, and preserving them (from change and corruption). So judge between them by what has been revealed by God, and do not follow their whims, side-stepping the truth that has reached you. To each of you we have given a law and a way and a pattern of life. If God had pleased He could surely have made you one people (professing one faith). But He wished to try and test you by that which He gave you. So try to excel in good deeds. To Him will you all return in the end, when He will tell you of what you were in variance.[19]

Nor is there any lack of ancient texts to provide counterweights and fine-tuning to modernity's emphases on freedom, property, contracts, sales, credit, competition, and markets. Freedom is tempered by numerous commands to obey God by doing good works, throughout the Qur'an, throughout the Bible, and throughout other sacred texts. Property rights are tempered by numerous assertions that humans hold whatever they possess only as stewards.

The ancient texts do not, however, provide much guidance for solving characteristically modern problems: the ethical use of science and technology, the planning of long-term capital investments, sharing the benefits of economies of scale, the functions of prices and profits as signals for choosing what goods and services to produce, the motives and sources of savings and their channeling into productive uses, the organization of pension plans and health plans for millions of beneficiaries, the lifelong education and the continual upgrading of skill levels throughout the population, and the like. Modern production is, as Ludwig von Mises said, "round-about production."[20] It is capital-intensive. It is information-intensive. It requires sophisticated technical knowledge, the well-timed commitment of resources over periods measured in years, and the systematically organized teamwork of many individuals. These combine to create production processes much more powerful than anything ancient peoples knew. Without them today's large human populations could not exist.

One can say that the ancient texts provide ethical norms for "direct" alleviation of poverty, for example by requiring believers to share wealth. In modern times humanity is challenged to develop norms for the "indirect" alleviation of poverty through the ethical governance of the processes of research and development, savings, investment, income distribution, and operation of enterprises.

Social democracy is about solving modern problems ethically. Stated in a very general form, the problem of constructing social democracy can be divided into two stages, or aspects: 1) socialization, so that human impulses—which so often tend toward violence greed, apathy, lying, lust, grand tyranny, petty tyranny, and evasion—are brought under the guidance of cultural norms; and 2) transformation, so that the cultural norms move from dysfunctional to functional. The critique implicit in the idea of "transformation" is that the conventional norms of modern society stand in need of improvement, even when well-intentioned and well-socialized people follow the "rules of the game." Conventional market norms are not equal to the task of providing ethical governance of a complex modern economy. They are, in the idiom of structural-functionalist sociologists, "dysfunctional." Marxists call them "contradictory." Amartya Sen has suggested that they are an "irrational rationality." In Gramscian terms, 1) socialization into conventional norms could be called "acquiring common sense," while 2) transformation could be called "moving from common sense to good sense."[21]

To apply and to elucidate the general ideas sketched above, in the specific case of Indonesia, we shall attempt to make a brief sketch of what might be called an inventory of Indonesian cultural resources. By calling it an "inventory" we do not mean that it will be a complete list of all Indonesia's cultural resources; we simply wish to highlight aspects of Indonesian culture from which the rest of the world has something to learn.

We mean the phrase "cultural resources" as an exact parallel with "natural resources." A resource is something that can be used to meet a need. The rich volcanic soil of central Java, for example, is a resource that can be used to grow rice, which can be made available for food, thus meeting a human need. In exactly the same sense, duties imposed by kinship ties, for example the duty to share food with kin, are a resource that can operate to assure that rice is shared. Kinship implies that rice will be provided, for example, to a sick relative, or to whoever in the family might need food. A cultural resource enables the social side of a system for meeting needs to function, as a natural resource enables the technical side of the same system to function.[22]

What makes a resource "cultural," as distinct from physical or natural is that it guides human behavior by symbolic means. (Or, alternatively, by means of "signs," if one adopts C.S. Peirce's terminology.) It is learned as distinct from genetically inherited. It depends on cohesive interpersonal relationships, as distinct from individual physical acts. Although many counter-examples could be given, where symbols, learning, and cohesion have been used to exclude, exploit, and dominate the weak, culture has a tendency—and it has a realizable potential—to establish the strength of the weak. A cultural resource is able to guide impulse and brute force in ways that work toward building a socially created reality that works for everyone.

1) Economic Rationality

"Economic rationality" is first on our list of cultural resources of Indonesia. It has been systematically developed there from the beginning of the Republic in 1949, and the foundation of the School of Economics at the University of Indonesia in 1950. Although economic rationality is sometimes contrasted with cultural values, it is better thought of as itself a cultural value. The rational choice of an economic actor is not made on impulse, but guided by symbolic practices, usually by numerical calculations. The habit of thinking before acting is a good habit, a virtue. It is learned. Making rational economic choices only makes sense in a culturally defined institutional context, a market, where there are enforceable rights.

It is true that there is sometimes a thin line to be drawn between greed, considered as an anti-social vice, and a problem in linear algebra which consists in calculating the maximum profit, subject to given conditions and constraints. It is a thin line worth drawing. Although the latter might be regarded as the former quantified, the former is nevertheless a character fault, a passion out of control, while the latter is an intellectual exercise, a reasoning process. The general principles of accounting, and the mathematical techniques of business and public sector planning are intellectual disciplines. They may and may not coincide in their results with anti-social vices. In social democracies they do not.

"Economic rationality," like its companions "economic development" and "stability," is an essentially contested concept. Nobody (with a few exceptions) is against it. Almost everyone wants to define it so that it supports his or her conclusions. Thus like "scientific" and many other essentially contested concepts it is not a concept with a definite meaning. It is a trophy. Contestants vie to prove that they are "rational," and their opponents "irrational." It is an expandable concept. The hyper-individualism the anthropologist Clifford Geertz found in his study of bazaar traders in a small Indonesian town is a very narrow kind of economic rationality, concerned with maximizing money profits in the short run.[23] The versions of economic rationality promoted in the infinite pages of the reports published by the International Monetary Fund are somewhat broader but still narrow. They tend to identify rational choice with choosing what sells, or with what would sell in a truly free market.

Indonesia's National Development Planning Board (known as *Bappenas—Badan Perencanaan Pembangunan Nasional*) has generally followed the definitions of economic rationality required by the IMF whenever Indonesia has desperately needed to borrow money from it. But in the late 1970s and early 1980s, and again in the early 1990s, when the Indonesian government as lessor of the nation's oilfields was awash in petrodollars because of high world oil prices, Indonesia could afford to disagree with the IMF. *Bappenas* then defined "economic rationality" more broadly, putting more emphasis on national self-reliance and less emphasis on selling Indonesian products in the global marketplace—the former emphasis being, according to the IMF, irrational, and the latter emphasis, according to the IMF, rational.

For a somewhat enlightened World Bank president like Robert McNamara, "economic rationality" takes on a wider meaning. It includes criteria which on a narrower view would be "social goals" to be traded off against, rather than identified with, "economic rationality." Indonesia's ideological dance with the World Bank has generally followed the steps of its dance with the IMF. Sometimes important circles inside the World Bank have defined meeting the basic needs of people as economically rational, and important people in Indonesia have taken the same view, including (when she was in opposition) Indonesia's current president, Megawati Sukarnoputri. At this time, however, Indonesia is deeply in debt to foreign creditors. It must earn dollars to service the debt. Megawati is under pressure to pretend to agree with IMF doctrine about economic rationality, both to get short-term relief from the IMF and to establish and make credible policies that bring in the needed dollars. This implies using Indonesia's comparative advantage as a low-wage country by keeping wages low, and emphasizing making shoes, textiles and other labor- intensive products for export.

Professor Habibie, on the other hand, who was president of Indonesia for part of 1998 and part of 1999, believes it is economically rational for Indonesia to use government subsidies to develop high-technology capital-intensive industries, such as aircraft manufacture.[24] The economists at the Jakarta thinktank called the Center for Strategic and International Studies do not agree with the IMF either. They think economic rationality for Indonesia consists less in following the price signals transmitted by global markets, and more in adopting deliberate and coordinated long-term national strategies. They find inspiration in Meiji Japan, and advocate more reliance for foreign funding on the Japanese government and to Japanese investors.[25]

Since independence, the Republic of Indonesia has steadily achieved increasing capacities to plan the use of resources "rationally," whatever "rationality" might mean or might come to mean. The lack of a single agreed upon definition of "economic rationality" should not be viewed as a problem. If it were a problem, somebody might solve it. That would be worse.

One might think, however, that such an expandable, hospitable concept, which anybody can construe as the name of the most efficient way to achieve the objectives she or he values, would play no role in political controversies. One might think the phrase "economic rationality" would disappear from public debate, since it is agreed that whatever it is, it is a good thing, while the agenda to be debated concerns what is possible and what is impossible, and within the limits of the possible what objectives to pursue, at what cost, at whose cost, with what sources of funding. Not so.

2) Indonesia's Social Democratic Constitution

Indonesia, like many other nations emerging from colonialism, declared social democratic principles in its constitution. According to its constitution, written in 1945 and in force today, Indonesia is a social democracy. If it is not the best social democratic constitution in the world, it is not because it is not socialist enough, but because it is not democratic enough. Every citizen has a constitutional right to an education and to a good job. The Constitution provides for a large public sector, and actuality complies with the Constitution. There is to be a large cooperative sector. Moreover, Article 33 provides that the entire economy is to be a "joint endeavor" (*usaha bersama*). The government has sweeping powers to direct all economic activity.

Given the principles of its anti-liberal (anti-capitalist) constitution, it was a question in the early days of the Republic whether private enterprise was to be allowed in Indonesia at all. This question was analyzed at a public symposium in 1955 by Widjojo Nitisastro, a young economist who would later become the director of *Bappenas*, and a leading light of the school of thought known as "the technocrats." The technocrats have been important for many reasons, partly as go-betweens who gave the authoritarian government of General Suharto (from 1966 to 1998) credibility with international agencies such as the IMF, the World Bank, and the IGGI (Inter-Governmental Group on Indonesia, a consortium of aid donors). Western governments gave huge amounts of aid to Indonesia during Suharto's reign (sometimes 25 percent of the total national budget, and more than half the budget when combined with fees paid by foreign oil companies for the right to extract petroleum from Indonesian territory. In Indonesia the capacity of the government to collect taxes from its own citizens has been shaky). Western donors justified giving so much money to a government with a dismal human rights record partly because they considered aid to be a way of increasing the influence of people like Nitisastro, who were looked upon as counterweights to military and crony influence.

Early in his analysis, Nitisastro, who was destined to play such a key role in Indonesia's history, observed that "the forms of enterprise are not the fundamental issue. The basic question to be considered in the study of any economic system is that of the operation of the economic process within the framework of the given system."[26]

Indonesia would later provide many examples of the truth of Nitisastro's observation. When Dutch assets were seized in 1957, many of them were taken over and run by and for the benefit of military units, creating an economic sector unique to Indonesia, the military sector. One of the reforms that foreign donors have urged, via the conduit of the technocrats, has been transparency in the public sector and in the quasi-public military sector, so that planners would at least know where public money was coming from and where it was going. As Nitisastro's distinction between "form" and "operation" implies, there is no guarantee that an enterprise nominally in the public sector will act for the benefit of the public.

Nitisastro's main point in his analysis of the Constitution, however, was not that public enterprises do not necessarily operate for the common good, but rather that private enterprises can—and under the provisions of the Constitution will—operate for the common good. The key is planning. The constitutional scheme provides that the government's policy instruments are to be used to guide the ensemble of national economic effort toward the benefit of all. Nitisastro stated:

> [T]he unit which is to be characterized by joint efforts for the good of all members and by an equitable distribution of the results of these efforts among all the members is not a unit in the sense of an enterprise or a firm but rather the entity of the community as a whole.
>
> When the provisions of these three paragraphs of Article 38 are considered together it is obvious that the state occupies a leading position in the entity that comprises the community as a whole, the state being the directing agency guid-

ing the joint efforts toward raising the level and the equitable distribution of the
returns from these efforts. Thus . . . [t]he economic system shall be based on
the joint efforts of the entire community, the objective being the raising of the
level of living of the community (the increase of *per capita* income) and the
equitable distribution of the returns derived from these joint efforts (the equitable distribution of income), with the state playing an active role in guiding and
implementing economic development.[27]

    With such words, partly implying and partly asserting that the humanitarian
principles of the Indonesian Constitution are best implemented through the rational and scientific management of the entire nation by professional economists, Nitisastro set the stage back in 1955 for enacting in Indonesia a version of
one of the dramatic dilemmas of social democracy. Although the Constitution
gives every Indonesian the right to a good job, the good jobs will not exist until
there is a large increase in per capita income. Such an increase will not happen,
so the argument runs, until there is something named "economic development,"
which requires Indonesia to exploit its comparative advantage as a low-wage
nation, with wage levels even lower than those of Thailand and Malaysia.

    That the development of the country must happen at the cost of keeping
wages low and of allowing unchecked exploitation of natural resources does not
seem to be intuitively valid from the viewpoint of common sense norms. The
ordinary people who are told by professional economic experts that "development" must happen before they get the social justice promised to them surely
feel cheated. They know about corruption. Everybody in Indonesia knows about
corruption. Everybody knows that people use, or buy, political power for the
sake of economic advantage. Everybody sees the lifestyles of people who have
money, who are usually the same as the people who have, or buy, political influence. Although the rational argument for keeping wages low may be, or may
appear to be, logically compelling, it is also an argument that functions as a justification, or rationalization, of an unfair distribution of wealth and income.

    There is an upside. The technocrats do not admit that they are not trying.
They officially agree with the Constitution's objectives. Indonesia is supposed
to be a social democracy in which the economy is a joint endeavor whose fruits
are equitably shared. If it were not so, they would not claim, as they do, that
Indonesia at times has done better at alleviating absolute poverty than Nigeria,
than India, than Brazil, and in general better than comparable third world and
OPEC nations. They claim that their advice, when it has been followed, has on
the whole worked for the benefit of the poor, and they claim that the poor have
suffered when technocratic advice has been ignored. If they did not see their
economic theories as being a means toward, as distinct from being a substitute
for, social justice, they would not be making such claims.

    Consequently, if anybody could demonstrate that the suffering of the poor is
not as necessary as versions of economic rationality such as those sponsored by

the IMF imply, then the Indonesian technocrats should rejoice and happily agree.

The Qur'an is open to the existence of more than one good faith belief about how to end poverty. It does not condemn those who fail to find the solution to the problem, but rather those who do not try and do not care. It states, for example, "Have you seen him who denies the Day of Judgment? It is he who pushes the orphan away, [a]nd does not induce others to feed the needy. Woe to those who pray [b]ut who are oblivious of their moral duties, [w]ho dissimulate [a]nd withhold things of common use (from others)."[28]

3) Family Ties

In his recent study of life in Bima, a district occupying the eastern peninsula of the island of Sumbawa, in eastern Indonesia, the British anthropologist Michael Hitchcock mentions several ways in which family ties contribute to mobilizing resources to meet needs. Concerning housing, relying in part on an unpublished earlier study by J.D. Brewer, Hitchcock writes:

> Men say they prefer to have their sons live near them and it is customary for a father to provide each son with a house. Fathers like to build their sons' houses next door; but, given the shortage of land near Bima Bay, this may be impossible, and parents have to contend with any available plot. Since married couples are expected to own their own homes, fathers struggle to provide the basic amenities, and only the poorest members of society continue to live with their parents after marriage. If a man is sufficiently wealthy to take a second wife he is obliged, in accordance with Islamic law, to provide his new spouse with her own home: wives expect equal treatment.
>
> The ideal is for a man to begin constructing his son's home when the boy reaches adolescence. As the structure becomes habitable the boy starts to sleep there and gradually it becomes his permanent sleeping quarters. The eldest son often shares the building with his younger brothers until they move into dwellings of their own. The younger sons are expected to vacate the building on the marriage of the oldest brother. From the moment a boy moves into his new home it is known as a *ruka*; but it becomes a complete household, *uma*, when his bride takes up residence.[29]

Housing norms in a precinct of Bima are a small sample among many.

The world over, multitudes of ethical frameworks define kinship. They guide cooperation and sharing. The meanings of the vital basic words "good" and "bad" flow partly from their employment to judge performance in kinship. The verdict "good" or "bad," is often decided conclusively by what a person does or does not do to meet the needs of family members. There is generally no appeal—no opportunity to reverse the judgment by changing the definitions of the terms. A good son takes care of his mother in her old age. A mother who neglects her children is a bad mother. A good husband repairs the chicken coop, plants a garden (unless it is a culture where only women plant gardens), and—with the help of good brothers and good cousins—digs a well. A bad husband squanders the family's food money on alcohol and other women. Good parents take care of their children when they are young, while good children take care of their parents when they are old. Family ties are cultural resources. So it goes in diverse contexts for many forms of kinship, including some relationships that have no English names, which are defined in other languages.

Seeing the imperative to motivate the satisfactory performance of conventional social roles, and seeing the correlative imperative to forbid anti-social vices, leads to understanding why religion is an integral part of so many of the survival strategies of the poor, and why it is often closely related to kinship. God is not useless.

Not surprisingly, resistance to life in the jungle of modern market culture has everywhere relied on invoking older pre-modern ideals, almost always including the invocation of the older ideals of kinship. The Left calls for brotherhood, sisterhood, *fraternite*, and sometimes invokes an ideal entity named the family of man or the human family. To help his readers imagine an alternative to capitalism, Karl Marx described a family:

> For an example of labor in common, or directly associated labor, we have no occasion to go back to that spontaneously developed form which we find on the threshold of the history of all civilized races. We have one close at hand in the patriarchal industries of a peasant family that produces corn, cattle, yarn, linen and clothing for home use. These different articles are, as regards the family, so many products of its labor, but as between themselves, they are not commodities. The different kinds of labor, such as tillage, cattle tending, spinning, weaving various products, are in themselves, and such as they are, direct social functions, because functions of the family, which, just as much as a society based on the production of commodities, possesses a spontaneously developed system of division of labor.[30]

Although the ideal of universal brotherhood and sisterhood, and the simile of a whole nation acting economically like a single family, is a common one, Indonesia has actually made it a constitutional principle. Paragraph I of Article 33 of the Constitution of Indonesia states: "The economy shall be organized as a joint endeavor based on the principle of the family relationship."[31] Widjojo Nitisastro, the prominent Indonesian economist already quoted above, interpreted this clause of the Constitution in the following words:

> In my opinion this term must be understood as indicating that the economic process will take place in one or more units, which embody features characteristic of the family relationship. Among the characteristic elements of the family relationship there is the element of living together, the element of joint effort by the members for the common good of the entire family, and the element of dis-

tribution of acquired advantages among the individual members according to the needs of each member. Thus the economic unit or units, within which the economic process is to take place according to the principle of family relationship, are to be characterized by the fact of joint efforts to raise the level of living of all members of the unit and by an equitable distribution among all members of the benefits derived from these joint efforts, and not by a distribution which benefits certain individuals or groups only.[32]

Nitisastro's gloss on the Constitution fits perfectly the definition of social democracy, "society producing for itself," given by Bertrand Russell in his lectures on German social democracy in 1896. Nitisastro goes on to explain how the anti-liberal (anti-capitalist) economy prescribed by the Indonesian Constitution will work in practice. Its three sectors—public, cooperative, and private—will operate within a legal framework shaped by the nation's public policies. Thus Indonesia will be faithful to ideals of kinship, at the level of the nation as a whole. Nitisastro writes:

Various forms of control can be exercised: controls in the field of fiscal policy, budgetary policy, balance of payments policy, price and wage policy, and so on. Moreover, it is possible to use direct methods to crush the forces of monopoly and oligopoly.[33]

The level of income is a matter of output, which is a function of investment.[34]

The existence of collective and cooperative enterprises constitutes one of the factors of utmost importance, especially in strengthening the bargaining position of the small producers in relation to the middlemen, so that the former are assured of securing a just return. Moreover, these collective and cooperative enterprises are institutions for mobilizing savings for investment purposes.[35]

An economic system based on anti-liberalism is one which ensures structural change in our economy, and which directs the appropriate volume and flow of investment to those sectors which ensure an increase in output, and consequently an increase in the level of income.[36]

In effect, Nitisastro proposes standard social democratic macroeconomic policies, as they have developed in Western Europe and the United States, with an Indonesian twist. The Indonesian twist is that the family principle, cooperation, is taken to be the basis of it all. Indonesia is supposed to save as if it were one big family. Of course some saving will be public, some private, some cooperative, and some done by foreigners—but that is a matter of form. Nitisastro assures us that what matters is not form, but how the economy operates, and how the economy operates will be guided by public policy. Similarly Indonesia, following the family principle, is supposed to *invest*, which will produce increased *output* resulting in more income. "Most important, however, is the fact that, in an economic system of this character, the state is obligated and empowered to play an active role in pursuing an equitable distribution of income for all members of the community."[37]

Nitisastro in power, or close to power, from 1966 to 1997, had the opportunity to put his vision of paragraph 1 of Article 33 of the Constitution into practice. Officially he and his fellow technocrats were the economic team making policy during most of that period. It should be mentioned, however, that regardless of the merits of Nitisastro's vision of orthodox macroeconomic rationality harnessed to social justice goals, it was an uphill battle against corruption to pursue any rational policy. For example, President Suharto, a virtual dictator clothed in a thin veneer of democratic legitimacy, engaged in nepotism, using his office to channel economic benefits of political power to members of his own family—a mockery of the "family principle" of the Constitution. In Gramscian terms, regardless of the presence or absence of "good sense," there was a great lack of "common sense."

By any standard, success was modest, even disregarding the denouement in the crash of 1997, from which Indonesia still has not recovered. In 1994, according to World Bank figures, per capita Gross Domestic Product was still under $700 per year. Average life expectancy was age sixty, the lowest in the region, even lower than the Philippines and Viet Nam. The empirical results have been thoroughly examined by a number of scholars, including two Australians, Hal Hill, who emphasizes the successes, and Richard Robison, who emphasizes the failures.[38]

We will not focus on the empirical record, but on a conceptual difficulty. The conceptual difficulty raises the question whether what Nitisastro proposed is possible. If what he proposed—macroeconomic management that approximates on a large scale what family solidarity achieves on a small scale—is in principle impossible, then Nitisastro's technocratic vision needs to be modified, quite apart from what can be learned from the empirical study of the historical circumstances that partly assisted and partly obstructed its implementation.

The conceptual difficulty is that seeking to achieve the equivalent of family ties through macroeconomic management collides with the constitutive rules of modern social order. There is a mismatch. There is a questionable attempt to connect fragments drawn from two disparate realms of discourse.

The incongruity of the mismatch should not be surprising. The modern social order was invented in Europe. From there it expanded to shape today's global economy. Its basic normative principles were formulated in the early days of capitalism by reviving the principles of Roman Law—most famously in the Napoleonic codes, Blackstone's *Laws of England*, and—most directly relevant to Indonesia—Roman-Dutch law. The Romans deliberately created their *jus gentium*, the progenitor of modern commercial law, to be a normative framework governing market transactions among people not obligated to each other by kinship ties or common religious faith. *Pacta sunt servanda. Suum cuique. Honeste vivere.* The three Latin phrases just quoted, which Roman Law takes as its three basic postulates, can be glossed: 1) Respect contracts; 2) Respect property; and 3) Respect persons.[39] A normative framework for a culture of solidarity it is not.[40]

In a modern framework the state, through its National Development Planning Board (*Bappenas* in Indonesia) and its other agencies, is not in the position of a patriarchal *paterfamilias* who is able, like Marx's imaginary collective laborer, to step into the shoes of the head of a peasant family, assign tasks, allocate labor time, and distribute benefits. The state can, to be sure, grant what in Indonesia are called "facilities." It can require licenses. It can refuse to grant a license unless there is a convincing feasibility study. It can grant a monopoly, a subsidy, or a tax exemption. It can require that investment funds be deposited in state banks. It can require hiring Indonesian engineers instead of expatriates. It can require any number of permits. Nevertheless, nothing will happen until investors and lenders decide to call it a go. They will sit on their property rights and exercise their economic power to do nothing until they are satisfied that the end result will be to obtain for themselves whatever *they* want. *Suum cuique.* Normally they want high profit and low risk. Charles Lindblom made a similar point when he wrote that "although governments can forbid certain kinds of economic activity, they cannot command business to perform. They must induce rather than command."[41]

Consequently, in practice, setting macroeconomic policies for Indonesia is only partly a matter of establishing an ethically valid management of savings, investments, outputs, and incomes. It is only partly conscientious deliberation among persons acknowledging mutual kinship obligations as members of the same extended family, the family of Indonesians, or the family of humans. It is largely a matter of making arms-length commercial deals. The investors and the lenders do not necessarily have to be given everything they want, but they have to be given enough to motivate them to say yes and sign the contract. What Indonesia has to sell—cheap labor, oil, nickel, gold, copper, cloves, vanilla, nutmeg, tamarind, hardwoods—has to be marketed by playing off potential buyers against each other. What Indonesia makes for home consumption—rice, beer, cigarettes, cement—has to be coaxed out of the owners of the means of production by creating stable conditions under which they can expect the same high profits and low risks that foreigners are in a position to demand. (Indeed, in the case of Indonesia, the major players in the domestic market can play the same cards foreigners can play, because they already do business in several countries and they decide from day to day how much business to do in Indonesia and how much business to do elsewhere.) The powers-that-be in Indonesia have to be given a cut in any major deal, since they have the power to stop others from getting what they want. That is what it means to be a power-that-is. There will be no deals, though, and consequently no cuts, unless the owners of property decide to call it a go. *Pacta sunt servanda. Suum cuique. Honeste vivere.* They have no moral duty to call it a "go," and they will do so only if they choose to.[42]

Structuring macroeconomic policy to offer attractive terms to owners of property so that there will be deals, is sometimes called "pragmatism." Refusing to give investors what they want is sometimes called "being an ideologue." These phrases name two horns of a dilemma. "Pragmatism" falls far short of conducting economic policy in a way that realizes the ideals of the Constitution. But the most readily apparent alternative, "being an ideologue," falls short even farther, because it produces no tangible benefits for anyone.

An unfortunate consequence of pragmatically paying what the market requires for the use of savings and other resources is that when it comes time to distribute the increased income resulting from investments and increased output, the ordinary citizen of Indonesia, whose only moral claim on the proceeds is that of a person with needs, that of a member of the family, is last in line. The investors and the lenders are first in line because they hold contracts saying so. That was the deal. If they had not been given enforceable rights to a future income stream they never would have consented to the use of their property for the project. *Pacta sunt servanda*. The market is constituted by rights. At payoff time rights to payment come first, leaving social justice behind.

There is *no way* to avoid this conclusion without moving the basic parameters that establish its premises. There are ways to avoid this conclusion *by* moving the basic parameters that establish its premises. When Lindblom, quoted above, writes about what governments "must" do, it is a soft "must," a "must" deduced from a socially constructed context, not a "must" deduced from hard laws of physical reality.

It is true that physical reality, not just social customs, decree that it is impossible to have investment without savings. Although the extent to which the relief of poverty depends upon investment is commonly exaggerated by those who see the world through the lenses of economic theory, it is nonetheless the case that it is impossible to solve the problem of poverty without investment. "A technology that will raise man-hour productivity without net investment has yet to be discovered."[43] It is in general impossible to raise outputs, and therefore impossible in general to raise incomes, without investments. This is true even if it is granted that a good deal of investment heretofore has been humanly and ecologically short-sighted—even if it is granted that the investments really needed are in sustainable technologies and in human resources to facilitate grassroots community building.

Other impossibilities, however, are produced by social structures, not natural structures: It is impossible to redistribute wealth and income in ways that do not paralyze wealth and income creation. It is impossible for a nation dependent on foreign capital to obtain the money it needs on terms not acceptable to foreign owners of money. It is impossible to pay debts without earning money with which to pay debts.

All of the above are impossible, given the basic cultural structure of the modern world-system. All is not lost, however, for it is quite possible to extend the limits of the possible. It is possible to modify the causes of these impossibilities. Their causes are chiefly (even though not entirely) socially constructed normative structures. Socially constructed normative structures can be reconstructed to make the impossible possible.

Nitisastro's interpretation of paragraph I of Article 33 of the Constitution represents a real possibility to the extent that Indonesia's cultural resources enable its implementation. A culture of solidarity is required. There must be some flexibility, some bending, on the issue of property rights, some acknowledgment of a duty to use property for the common good. More stewardship. More accountability. More social obligation and less private privilege. More fiduciary duty and less plenipotentiary right. There need to be more debt forgiveness and less speculation in land values and financial instruments. More coordination of human action in the pursuit of common purposes and less maximization of individual self-interest. More long-term wisdom measured in ecological terms, and fewer short term fixes. More physical improvement of land and soil and less paper profit. More accumulation of usable capital equipment, and less whisking off of cash profits to secret accounts in foreign banks. This paragraph is not meant to be just a list of *desiderata*; it is meant to be a list of *desiderata* whose achievement requires a process of intellectual and moral reform that embraces a revision of the constitutive rules that govern life in a capitalist society.

The program that Nitisastro envisioned as a young man appears to be impossible because constitutive rules defining contractual obligations and property rights appear to be laws of nature. But it is not truly impossible, because constitutive rules are not laws of nature and therefore can be socially reconstructed.

To the extent that savings and investment become capable of going forward without contractual obligations forcing delivery of the bulk of their benefits to property owners, the limits of the possible are extended. Social justice becomes more possible. Similarly, to the extent that enterprises can succeed by meeting real human and environmental needs, without necessarily making a profit by selling products for which there is effective demand (i.e., people with money who will buy them), the limits of the possible are extended.

It is clear, however, that many uncertainties must be favorably resolved before the indirect path to poverty relief through savings, investment, and increased output can result in the desired equitable distribution of increased income. Therefore, it would seem wise to put more emphasis on direct relief. Sharing resources with those who need them is called "*zakat*" in Islam. It is also prescribed by the scriptures of Indonesia's minority religions. The direct path cannot replace the indirect path, because the population is too large to survive without technologies that require investments, but it can contribute to building the culture of solidarity required to open the indirect path.

In the next chapter we will continue inventory of Indonesia's cultural resources. Norms are causes. Norms can change.

Notes

1. Some scholars will argue that the concept of "cause and effect" is outdated, and that it must now be replaced by some more sophisticated concept, such as functional dependence (a la Russell), or genealogy (a la Foucault), or *archi-ecriture* (a la Derrida). We do not believe that such potential objections weaken our point, since we believe that it could be reformulated in terms of any proposed replacement for "cause and effect."

2. Heinrich Pesch (1854-1926) was a German Jesuit scholar trained in law, philosophy, theology, and economics. He traveled to England around the same time as Marx and was equally shocked by the plight of the English working class. He developed the concepts of "solidarism" and "the solidaristic system of human work." Pesch writes, "Considered in the broadest terms possible, the essential meaning of the solidarist system is to be found in complementing and regulating power by binding people together in solidarity, while exercising mutual consideration and concern in accordance with the demands of justice and charity, by a well-ordered cooperation and reciprocity within the various forms of natural and free, public and private communities, and in accordance with their natural and historical peculiarities, toward the goal of securing the true welfare of all involved. In others [*sic*] words, it is the sense of community without exaggeration, which shows due regard for the rights of the individual person, but at the same time of the social community, for freedom as well as for order, for individual autonomy as well as for social responsibility." Heinrich Pesch, *Heinrich Pesch on Solidarist Economics: Excerpts from the Lehrbuch der Nationalökonomie*, trans. Rupert J. Ederer (Lanham, Md.; New York; Oxford: University Press of America, 1984), 68. The solidaristic system of human work emphasizes the social aspect of work. Pesch writes, "We are stressing as emphatically as possible the *community* as opposed to its atomistic dissolution, and the *sense of obligation to the community* as opposed to the individualistic cry for freedom." Pesch, *Solidarist Economics*, 113, italics in original. French-born poet, novelist, historian and social commentator Hilaire Belloc (1870-1953) was a devout Roman Catholic who wrote numerous works advocating the reform of capitalism as a Christian duty. Writing in the midst of the Great Depression, when the failings of capitalism were becoming clear to the multitudes, Belloc was one of the clearest and most vocal critics of capitalism. He states, "Indeed, the chief mark of those societies in which freedom is restricted by Capitalism— that is, by the ownership of a few and the dispossession of the many—is the way in which human dignity and the whole life of the soul, of which human dignity is the expression, is degraded." Hilaire Belloc, *The Catholic Church and the Principle of Private Property* (London: Catholic Truth Society, 1933), 23. He concludes his treatise against the degradations of capitalism by calling for humans to undertake the measures needed to correct the social injustices that were fueling the desire for more radical solutions by stating, "There is one remedy for the abominations of Industrial Capitalism. . . . This remedy is the better distribution of property and the working for as large a proportion of families as possible to be possessed of their share in machinery and in land, both inalienable and alienable, until the number so enfranchised determines the character of the whole State." Belloc, *Catholic Church*, 24. See also Hilaire Belloc, *The Crisis of Civilization* (New York: Fordham University, 1937). Sir Richard Stafford Cripps (1889-1952) was a British statesman who spent most of his career as a member of the Labour Party. Although he is perhaps best known for the partition of India and the creation of Pakistan, which fuels

grievances to this day, we direct the reader's attention to his writings on peace and Christian democracy. In *The Struggle For Peace*, published in 1936, he wrote that in each case the measure of justice must be the good of humanity, "and not the good of this or that section, class, or nation," and he stressed that "[m]ankind has other capacities [other than resorting to violence] for solving problems of development . . . and it is these capacities which distinguish him, or should distinguish him, from the brute beast." Stafford Cripps, *The Struggle For Peace* (London: Victor Gollancz, 1936), 11-12. Although we would extend his measure of justice to include a larger ecology than just humanity, we wholeheartedly agree with these sentiments. In a later work, Sir Stafford Cripps recognized that society was organized on the basis of encouraging fear as a driving force for individual action and called for a reorganization of society. He wanted to encourage the surge of unselfishness and the subordination of personal desires in favor of the collective good that he had witnessed on a large scale during World War II, and he called for the recognition of the redemptive power of love as a motivating force. Stafford Cripps, *Towards Christian Democracy* (New York: Philosophical Library, 1946), 73-76. He writes, "If we are to carry out the general desires which have been expressed in a multitude of different ways for a better Britain, or a fairer and happier world, we shall have to substitute a cooperative and more selfless attitude for this acquisitive individualistic approach to life. We must replace the competitive fear, the negative impulse, by the positive power of love and brotherhood." Cripps, *Towards Christian Democracy*, 76-77. The economist and social philosopher Karl Polanyi (1886-1964) spent his early years in Vienna and Budapest and emigrated to London in 1933, where he participated in the Christian Left Group. In an essay entitled "Our Obsolete Market Mentality," originally published in 1947, Polanyi writes, "We find ourselves stultified by the legacy of a market-economy which bequeathed us oversimplified views of the function and role of the economic system in society. If the crisis is to be overcome, we must recapture a more realistic vision of the human world and shape our common purpose in light of that recognition." Polanyi in George Dalton, ed., *Primitive, Archaic and Modern Economies: Essays of Karl Polanyi* (Boston: Beacon Press, 1968), 60. Polanyi emphasizes the fiction of transforming land and labor into commodities and the fallacy of the concept of "economic motives," with "economic" being as vested with meaning as the truly human realms of aesthetic, religious, and sexual need. Polanyi in Dalton, *Primitive, Archaic and Modern Economies*, 61-63. In concluding his essay, he writes, "I plead for the restoration of that unity of motives which should inform man in his everyday activity as a producer, for the reabsorption of the economic system in society, for the creative adaptation of our ways of life to an industrial environment. . . . [L]aissez-faire philosophy, with its corollary of a marketing society, falls to the ground. It is responsible for the splitting up of man's vital unity into 'real' man, bent on material values, and his 'ideal' better self." Polanyi in Dalton, *Primitive, Archaic and Modern Economies*, 72-73. See also John Lewis, Karl Polanyi, and Donald K. Kitchin, eds., *Christianity and the Social Revolution* (London: Victor Gollancz, 1935); Karl Polanyi, *The Great Transformation* (New York and Toronto: Rinehart & Company, 1944); and Karl Polanyi, "The Economy as Instituted Process," reprinted in *The Sociology of Economic Life*, ed. Mark Granovetter and Richard Swedberg (Boulder, Colo.; and Oxford: Westview Press, 1992), 29-53.

    3. Charles K. Wilber and Kenneth P. Jameson advocate cooperative behavior through cooperative institutions as a fulfilling—or in our terminology, "de-alienating"—way to dampen the detrimental effects of capitalism and reform it in a positive way. They write that a well functioning economy requires "a shared conception of the moral base of the

economy." Charles K. Wilber and Kenneth P. Jameson, *Beyond Reaganomics: A Further Inquiry into the Poverty of Economics* (Notre Dame, Ind.; and London: University of Notre Dame Press, 1990), 10. They believe that the legitimate goals to be met by a well functioning economy include 1) life-sustenance—i.e., meeting the physiological needs of all people; 2) a sense of belonging and fellowship for everyone; and 3) freedom, which they define as full consumer sovereignty, full worker sovereignty, and full citizen sovereignty. Wilber and Jameson, *Beyond Reaganomics*, 11-14. Self-described "philosopher of development" Denis Goulet writes that in the process of development, it is necessary to nurture cultural and ecological diversity and to create new solidarities that extend to the entire world. According to Goulet, the ultimate goals of development "are those of existence itself: to provide all [humans] with the opportunity to live full human lives. Thus understood, development is the ascent of all [humans] and societies in their total humanity." Denis Goulet, *The Cruel Choice: A New Concept in the Theory of Development* (New York: Atheneum, 1971), x. Goulet believes that the processes of development are best understood by examining the value conflicts they pose. Denis Goulet, *The Uncertain Promise: Value Conflicts in Technology Transfer* (New York: IDOC/North America, 1977), 5. See also Denis Goulet, *Etica del desarrollo* (Montevideo: Instituto de Estudios Políticos para América Latina, 1965); and *A New Moral Order: Development Ethics and Liberation Theology* (Maryknoll, N.Y.: Orbis Books, 1974).

4. The Catholic Church has issued numerous doctrinal statements on peace and social justice beginning in the late nineteenth century and continuing throughout the twentieth century, and here we can only highlight a few of them. John Sniegocki dates the inception of modern Catholic Social Teaching in 1891, with Pope Leo XIII's issuance of *Rerum Novarum*. In this encyclical, Pope Leo XIII, while castigating socialism on a number of grounds, discusses at length the ways capitalism should be reformed so as to engender greater social justice. The pope advocates limits on working hours, the abolition of child labor, and the institution of "just wages" (which, states Pope Leo XIII, are not set simply by contract or the laws of supply and demand). Sniegocki, "Catholic Social Teaching and the Third World," 153-55. The second major papal encyclical within the tradition of Catholic Social Teaching is *Quadragesimo Anno*, issued in 1931 by Pope Pius XI. Sniegocki notes that while this encyclical was in large measure a reaffirmation of ideas presented in *Rerum Novarum*, the language criticizing capitalism had, in the midst of the Great Depression, become much stronger. Sniegocki writes, "Pope Pius argues that unregulated competition has in fact led over time to 'economic dictatorship,' to 'immense power and despotic economic domination concentrated in the hands of a few' while, at the same time, the many suffer. 'The whole economic life,' he says, 'has become hard, cruel, and relentless in a ghastly measure.' Singled out for special criticism as a cause of current problems are modern corporations and the legal framework supporting them." Sniegocki, "Catholic Social Teaching," 158-59. Pope Pius XI advocates reorganizing the economy toward the ends of the common good. Sniegocki, "Catholic Social Teaching," 162. In *Mater et Magistra*, issued in 1961, Pope John XXIII states, "The economic prosperity of any people is to be assessed not so much from the sum total of goods and wealth possessed as from the distribution of goods according to norms of justice"; and "If the organization and structure of economic life be such that the human dignity of workers is compromised . . . then we judge such an economic order to be unjust, even though it produces a vast amount of goods whose distribution conforms to the norms of justice and equity." *Mater et Magistra* quoted in Sniegocki, "Catholic Social Teaching," 169. *Pacem in Terris* (1963) calls for broadly instituted social justice as a basis for lasting world

peace. Statements made in *Gaudium et Spes*, issued by the Second Vatican Council in 1965, argue along the same lines as the statements made by Islamic social philosophers we cite below (note 9). Vatican II castigated "excessive inequalities" and insisted that the goods of creation were intended by God to be shared equitably by all persons, which meant that limits should be placed upon the institution of private property. Sniegocki, "Catholic Social Teaching," 179. And the 1968 Medellín Conference, Latin American bishops undertook even more fundamental critiques of "structural injustice" and "institutionalized violence," opening the way for the development of Liberation Theology. Sniegocki, "Catholic Social Teaching," 189. See also Michael Schuck, *That They Be One: The Social Teachings of the Papal Encyclicals, 1740-1989* (Washington, D.C.: Georgetown University Press, 1991); and Donal Dorr, *Option for the Poor: A Hundred Years of Vatican Social Teaching* (Maryknoll, N.Y.: Orbis, 1992). In recent decades the Roman Catholic Church has been especially active in articulating the relationship between ancient ideals and economic rationality in modern times. See, for example, United States Catholic Conference, *A Justice Prayer Book with Biblical Reflections* (Washington, D.C.: United States Catholic Conference, 1998); Fred Kammer, *Doing Faith Justice: An Introduction to Catholic Social Thought* (New York: Paulist Press, 1991); and Michael Walsh and Brian Davies, eds., *Proclaiming Justice and Peace: Papal Documents from Rerum Novarum through Centessimus Annus* (Mystic, Conn.: Twenty Third Publications, 1991). Although not solely comprising Protestant churches, the World Council of Churches is a good starting point for Protestant statements on peace and social justice. Since the late 1970s, the World Council of Churches has sponsored projects and conferences on social justice issues under the title Justice, Peace, and the Integrity of Creation (JPIC). The National Council of Churches has its own Eco-Justice Working Group, which has published numerous documents. See Robert Booth Fowler, *The Greening of Protestant Thought* (Chapel Hill, N.C.; and London: The University of North Carolina Press, 1995); and Frederick W. Krueger, ed., *Christian Ecology, Being an Environmental Ethic for the Twenty-First Century: The Proceedings from the First North American Conference on Christianity and Ecology* (San Francisco: Conference on Christianity and Ecology, 1988). For doctrinal statements on peace, see the documents by the three "historic peace churches" in the Protestant tradition: the Mennonite Church, the Church of the Brethren, and the Society of Friends (Quakers).

5. Ernesto Laclau and Chantal Mouffe, *Hegemony and Socialist Strategy: Towards a Radical Democratic Politics* (London: Verso, 1985), 176-94. Laclau and Mouffe write, "*The task of the Left . . . cannot be to renounce liberal-democratic ideology, but on the contrary, to deepen and expand it in the direction of a radical and plural democracy.*" Laclau and Mouffe, *Hegemony and Socialist Strategy*, 176, italics in original.

6. See, e.g., Lawrence Kohlberg, "Continuities and Discontinuities in Childhood and Adult Moral Development Revisited," in Kohlberg, *Collected Papers on Moral Development and Moral Education* (Cambridge, Mass.: Moral Education Research Foundation, Harvard University, 1973), 29-30.

7. Weber, *Protestant Ethic*. Sir Henry Maine elaborates the shift from status rights—rights claimed on the basis of, for example, a person's sex or position within the family—to contractual rights arising from negotiation between individuals in his *Ancient Law* (London: Murray, 1861), especially Chapter 5. On Sir Henry Maine, see R.C.J. Cocks, *Sir Henry Maine: A Study in Victorian Jurisprudence* (Cambridge; New York; New Rochelle; Melbourne; Sydney: Cambridge University Press, 1988). Cocks writes that Maine was "particularly worried at the idea that his theory of contract flew in the face of modern

ethical beliefs. He believed that a society based on contract was a society in which, of necessity, individuals had come to adopt high moral standards, and these standards, he believed, enabled them to trust each other in the course of commercial and other dealings." Cocks, *Sir Henry Maine*, 61. Yet Maine witnessed fraud all around him. Cocks, *Sir Henry Maine*, 62. For one account of the constitution of patterns of economic behavior through the imposition of modern Western property and contract law on traditional peoples, see Gunnar Myrdal, *Asian Drama, Volume 2* (New York: Twentieth Century Fund and Pantheon Books, 1968), 1029-1139, especially 1031-47.

8. Belloc, *Crisis of Civilization*, 140.

9. Isma'il R. al-Faruqui would consider liberal individualism a component of "secularist metaphysics," which he holds in great disregard. He calls for a metaphysics that integrates faith and rational thinking. Isma'il R. al-Faruqui and Abdullah Omar Nasseef, eds., *Social and Natural Sciences: The Islamic Perspective* (Jeddah, Saudi Arabia: Hodder and Stoughton for King Abdulaziz University, 1981), v. 3. Al-Faruqui refers to the Islamic principle of ummatism (from *umma*, "the community of believers") and states, "This principle holds that no value, hence, no imperative, is merely personal, pertinent to the individual alone. Neither value-perception nor value-realization pertains to consciousness in its personal moment. . . . Islam affirms that God's commandment, or the moral imperative, is necessarily societary." Al-Faruqui and Nasseef, eds., *Social and Natural Sciences*, 14. Abulhasan Bani-Sadr discusses monotheistic unity (or *"towhid"*) as a basic principle underlying the way an Islamic government is realized. He states that monotheistic unity depends on dismantling the thought structures based on dualism, which is the underpinning of liberal individualism, in which the self can be thought of as separate from the whole. Abulhasan Bani-Sadr, *The Fundamental Principles and Precepts of Islamic Government*, trans. Mohammad R. Ghanoonparvar (Lexington, Ky.: Mazda Publishers, 1981), 14-19. Bani-Sadr states also that humans should take as the basis for all other relations their relationship to the divine. When the proper relationship with the divine is undertaken, no other relations can be based on force or compulsion. Abulhasan Bani-Sadr, *Work and the Worker in Islam*, trans. Hasan Mashhadi (Tehran: The Hamdami Foundation, 1981), iv. M. 'Umar Chapra notes that if individual self-interest is to be fostered, it must be within a social context, and it must not violate the Islamic goals of social and economic justice and the equitable distribution of income and wealth. M. 'Umar Chapra, *The Economic System of Islam* (Karachi, Pakistan: Department of Publications, University of Karachi, Pakistan: 1971), 26. Khurshid Ahmad writes, "The Islamic vision of a just and prosperous society is one of an enterprising and sharing community which values increase in virtue and equity more than mere increase in the flow of goods and commodities." In al-Shaykh-al-Imam Taqui al-Din Ahmad Ibn-Taymiya, *Public Duties in Islam: The Institution of the Hisba*, ed. Khurshid Ahmad (Leicester, U.K.: The Islamic Foundation, 1982), 6-7. See also John L. Esposito and John O. Voll, "Khurshid Ahmad: Muslim Activist-Economist," reprinted in *Islamic Resurgence: Challenges, Directions and Future Perspectives, A Roundtable with Prof. Khurshid Ahmad* , ed. Ibrahim M. Abu-Rabi (Islamabad, Pakistan: Institute of Policy Studies, 1995), 33-54; and Abdullahi Ahmed An-Nalim, ed., *Human Rights in Cross-Cultural Perspective: A Quest for Consensus* (Philadelphia: University of Pennsylvania Press, 1992).

10. The Arabian physician and philosopher known in Latin as "Avicenna" (980-1027) was accomplished in the fields of physics, mathematics, logic, and metaphysics, and his numerous writings reveal him as a faithful student of Aristotle. Avicenna spread to the Muslim world Aristotelian ideas concerning definition, the logic of representation, and

the classification of sciences. The Arabian philosopher and astronomer known in Latin as "Averroes" (1126-1198), who spent most of his life in Spain under Moorish dominion and in Morocco, offered numerous Aristotelian treatises, commentaries, and writings on jurisprudence. So influential were his "Commentaries" on Aristotle that he was often referred to simply as "the Commentator."

11. Patrick J. Geary, *Before France and Germany: The Creation and Transformation of the Merovingian World* (New York and Oxford: Oxford University Press, 1988), 95-116; Ian Wood, "Teutsind, Witlaic and the history of the Merovingian *precaria*," in Davies and Fouracre, eds., *Property and Power*, 31-52; Theodoor Pigeaud, *Java in the 14th Century* (5 volumes) (The Hague: Martinus Nijoff, 1960-1963). The Merovingian dynasties ruled the Frankish kingdom from 481 to 751, beginning with the rule of Clovis I. In addition to the work by Geary, see Wood, "Teutsind, Witlaic and the history of the Merovingian *precaria*," on the theme of Merovingian kings releasing ownership of land to petitioners in the form of land grants. For a political history of the Merovingian dynasties, see Ian Wood, *The Merovingian Kingdoms, 450-751* (London and New York: Longman Group, 1994). In Javanese tradition the sacred and the secular were not clearly distinguished; castes were supposed to be functional and to owe reciprocal duties to one another; rituals led by royalty were supposed to assure order, prosperity, and fertility for all. See Pigeaud, *Java in the 14th Century*.

12. The writings of Ludwig von Mises serve as a succinct statement of the view that associates roundabout production with a "rationality" that refers specifically to "economic rationality" and in turn with "reliance on free markets." When human societies live in the simple manner of hand-to-mouth "economic production," he states, calculations of "rationality" do not need to be made. He continues, "But to choose whether we shall use a waterfall to produce electricity or extend coal-mining and better utilize the energy contained in coal, is quite another matter. Here the processes of production are so many and so long, the conditions necessary to the success of the undertaking so multitudinous, that we can never be content with vague ideas. To decide whether an undertaking is sound we must calculate carefully." He goes on to state that the unit of calculation should and indeed *must* be the objective exchange-value of commodities, which is expressed as a money calculation. To those who would object that this is far too narrow a means for assessing the wisdom of a wide range of possible human actions, von Mises is prepared to respond. He is willing to admit that *even though* they do not enter into exchange relations, such non-economic considerations as aesthetics, health, and ethical constructs like honor should still be considered "just as much motives of rational action" as economic motives; nevertheless, these cannot enter into money calculations. Having said this, von Mises returns to affirm the primacy of "rational calculations" over these "non-economic" considerations, and he falls back into reification to avoid having to answer for the damages that arise from this construction. He writes, "That [these non-economic factors] cannot enter into money calculations arises from the very nature of these calculations. But this does not in the least lessen the value of money calculations in ordinary economic matters. . . . If we know precisely how much we have to pay for beauty, health, honour, pride, and the like, nothing need hinder us from giving them due consideration. Sensitive people may be pained to have to choose between the ideal and the material. But that is not the fault of a money economy. It is in the nature of things." Von Mises is explicitly advocating a "free-market" system because in his estimation, socialist systems lack "the ability to calculate, and therefore to proceed rationally." "Once this has been generally recognized," von Mises assures himself as much as his readers, "all socialist ideas must

vanish from the minds of reasonable human beings." Von Mises, *Socialism*, 114, 115, 116, 510.

13. Pareto optimality refers to a condition of perfect competitive equilibrium, in which firms maximize their profits at the same time that consumers maximize their utility-functions (i.e., act in ways that enhance their general well-being and meet their personal preferences). The theory of Pareto optimality (or "Pareto efficiency") holds that an economic allocation is inefficient if some alternative allocation would improve the standing of all firms and all consumers at the same time. Therefore, in the state of Pareto optimality, no one's standing can be improved without worsening the standing of another. For Pareto's definition of the theory in his own words, as well as objections to the theory, see Maurice Godelier, *Rationality and Irrationality in Economics* (New York and London: Monthly Review Press, 1972), 42, 50-51.

14. On Latin American liberation theology, see Gustavo Gutiérrez, *A Theology of Liberation: History, Politics, and Salvation*, ed. and trans. Sister Caridad Inda and John Eagleson (Maryknoll, N.Y.: Orbis Books, 1973; Gustavo Gutiérrez, *The Truth Shall Make You Free: Confrontations*, trans. Matthew J. O'Connell (Maryknoll, N.Y.: Orbis Books, 1990); Leonardo Boff, *Eclesiogénesis: Las comunidades de base reinventan la Iglesia* (Santander, Spain: Editorial Sal Terrae, 1986). Khurshid Ahmad and M. 'Umar Chapra are among the progressive Islamic writers calling for the ethical reshaping of economic relationships. Ahmad writes that Islam emphasizes "the optimal utilisation of resources that God has endowed to man and his physical environment . . . [and] their equitable use and distribution and promotion of all human relationships on the basis of Right and Justice." Khurshid Ahmad, ed., *Studies in Islamic Economics* (Delhi: Amar Prakashan, 1983), 180. He states that economic development should be understood as merely a part of a larger and more important process of human development, both within (i.e., spiritual) and without (i.e., physical, social, cultural). Ahmad lists among the principal tenets of a development policy suited to the ethics of Islam the following: 1) the character development and education that can lead to "a new structure of relationships based on co-operation, co-sharing, and co-participation"; 2) the expansion of production based on use-value ("Production would not mean production of anything and everything which may have a demand or which the rich may be able to buy; production would be concerned with things which are useful for man in the light of the value-pattern of Islam and the general experience of mankind"); and 3) the improvement of the quality of life, including employment opportunities, a broad-based system of social security based on the principle of *zakat* (the duty to share resources with those in need), and the equitable distribution of income and wealth. Ahmad, ed., *Islamic Economics*, 180-81. M. 'Umar Chapra's *The Economic System of Islam* is the best short summary of the Muslim stance on various economic concepts held dear within capitalism (e.g., contracts, freedom of enterprise, investment, landholdings, profit, property as trust, taxation, etc.). In this work he notes that while profit is not prohibited within the tenets of Islam, there is a common understanding that holds that when the profit motive is converted from an instrument used to spur production into a primary goal, many social ills arise. Islam calls for the placing of "certain moral restraints" upon the profit motive, so that production is established for the ends of social harmony. Chapra, *Economic System of Islam*, 26. See also the numerous writings by Sheik Mohamed Aboulkhair Zaki Badawi on banking, finance, and business ethics; as well as writings by Sayyid Muhammad Baqir Sadr and Ayatollah Sayyid Mahmud Taliqani on Islamic economic theories and practices. On Karl Polanyi, see Polanyi in Dalton, *Primitive, Archaic and Modern Economies*, 70.

15. Thomas Berry, *The Dream of the Earth* (San Francisco: Sierra Club Books, 1988), 92- 93. Berry writes that in other beings, genetic coding provides sufficient guidance for the necessary activities of life with only minimal teaching required after birth; in humans, however, our genetic coding "establishes only certain directions and the freedom and intelligence needed to activate these other realms of accomplishment." He states that education is the passing of cultural coding from one generation to the next. Berry, *Dream of the Earth*, 93.

16. Amartya K. Sen, *On Ethics and Economics* (Oxford: Basil Blackwell, 1987), 2.

17. "*Zakat*" is the duty within Islam to share resources with those in need. "*Moksha*" is the term in Hinduism for "spiritual release." "*Sangha*" is a Buddhist term meaning "community of practitioners."

18. Antonio Gramsci, *The Modern Prince and Other Writings* (New York: International Publishers, 1959), 140.

19. Qur'an 5:48. Note: All passages from the Qur'an cited in this text derive from following version: *Sacred Writings: The Qur'an*, trans. Ahmed Ali (Princeton, N.J.: Princeton University Press), 1988.

20. Von Mises, *Socialism*, 114, 510.

21. Antonio Gramsci defines "common sense" as "the traditional popular conception of the world." Gramsci, *Prison Notebooks*, 199. As he defines it, "common sense" is the rather fragmented understanding of the world that dissuades us—or prevents us out-right—from engaging in the kinds of critical reflection necessary to develop a coherent conception of the world, which in turn would allow us to make good and meaningful transformations in the world. "Good sense," in contrast, is "the healthy nucleus that exists in 'common sense,'" and it is a unitary and coherent conception of the world that gives our actions conscious direction. Through engaging in a philosophy of praxis, Gramsci asserts, we can increasingly make the transition from "common sense" to "good sense" understandings. Gramsci, *Prison Notebooks*, 326, 328.

22. Our concept of cultural resources is similar to the combination of products, forms of political and social organization, values and norms, spaces and contexts, be-haviors and attitudes which Manfred Max-Neef articulates as the means for achieving the end of satisfying basic human needs. Manfred Max-Neef, "Development and Human Needs," in Paul Ekins and Manfred Max-Neef, *Real-life Economics: Understanding Wealth Creation* (London and New York: Routledge, 1992), 197-214.

23. Clifford Geertz, *Agricultural Involution, the process of ecological change in Indonesia* (Berkeley: University of California Press, 1963), 40-46.

24. Richard Robison, "Indonesia: Crisis, Oligarchy, and Reform," in Garry Rodan, Kevin Hewison, and Richard Robison, eds., *The Political Economy of South-East Asia: Conflicts, Crises, and Change* (Melbourne; Oxford; New York: Oxford University Press, 2001), 118. On the policies of the Habibie administration generally, see Bilveer Singh, *Succession Politics in Indonesia: The 1998 Presidential Elections and the Fall of Suharto* (Houndmills, Basingstoke, Hampshire, U.K.; and London: Macmillan Press, 2000; and New York: St. Martin's Press, 2000), 155-261.

25. Adam Schwarz, *A Nation in Waiting: Indonesia in the 1990s* (Boulder, Colo.; and San Francisco: Westview Press, 1994), 255.

26. Widjojo Nitisastro, *The Socio-Economic Basis of the Indonesian State* (Ithaca, N.Y.: Modern Indonesia Project, Southeast Asia Program, Department of Far East Studies, Cornell University, 1959), 17.

27. Nitisastro, *Socio-Economic Basis of the Indonesian State*, 18-19.

28. Qur'an 107: 1-7. We also acknowledge that one can, of course, cite Islamic scripture in support of a rigid defense of strict private property rights.

29. Michael Hitchcock, *Islam and Identity in Eastern Indonesia* (Hull, U.K.: University of Hull Press, 1996), 100-01.

30. Marx, *Capital*, 34.

31. Quoted by Nitisastro, *Socio-Economic Basis of the Indonesian State*, 16.

32. Nitisastro, *Socio-Economic Basis of the Indonesian State*, 16-17.

33. Nitisastro, *Socio-Economic Basis of the Indonesian State*, 18-19.

34. Nitisastro, *Socio-Economic Basis of the Indonesian State*, 19.

35. Nitisastro, *Socio-Economic Basis of the Indonesian State*, 19.

36. Nitisastro, *Socio-Economic Basis of the Indonesian State*, 19.

37. Nitisastro, *Socio-Economic Basis of the Indonesian State*, 19. While president of Indonesia, Sukarno had sought to put the Indonesian family principle into practice as well. He referred to himself as *"Bapak Pembangunan"* (the Father of Development), always addressed his audience as "Brothers and Sisters," and in his speeches made frequent reference to Article 33 of the Indonesian Constitution. In one of his annual speeches commemorating Indonesian independence, Sukarno stated, "How can we possibly build a society of social justice, if individualism rules as it wants in our heart? Therefore, it is very necessary that we now make a social re-ordering in order that there can be put into practice what is meant in the 1945 Constitution, Article 33, that the economy shall be organized as *a joint effort based on the family principle.*" Sukarno, *Toward Freedom and the Dignity of Man: A Collection of Five Speeches by President Sukarno of The Republic of Indonesia* (Djakarta: Department of Foreign Affairs, 1961), 59, emphasis in original.

38. See Hal Hill, *The Indonesian Economy* (Cambridge: Cambridge University Press, 2000); Richard Robison, *Indonesia: The Rise of Capital* (Sydney: Allen and Unwin, 1986); and Richard Robison, "Politics and Markets in Indonesia's Post-oil Era," in Richard Robison et al., eds., *The Political Economy of South-East Asia: An Introduction* (Melbourne: Oxford University Press, 1997). For a more qualitative approach to understanding the severity of the Indonesian economic crisis, with a particular emphasis upon the rural areas of Java, see Jan Breman and Gunawan Wiradi, *Good Times and Bad Times in Java: Socio-economic dynamics in two villages towards the end of the 20th century* (Leiden, Neth.: KITLV Press, 2002).

39. We offer these three famous phrases from Roman Law as a convenient way to bring to mind some principal features of the legal framework of capitalism, often called "private law." They are similar but not identical to the three commandments of the law stated at the beginning of *Justinian's Institutes*: *honeste vivere, alterum non laedere, suum cuique tribuere* (live honorably, do not injure others, give to each his own). *Justinian's Institutes*, trans. Peter Birks and Grant McLeod, with the Latin text of Paul Krueger (Ithaca, N.Y.: Cornell University Press, 1987), 37. Although *alterum non laedere* (do not injure others) also supports the general point we are making, namely that the legal framework of the global economy provides a minimal morality that needs to be revised to call for higher ethical standards in order to advance social democracy, we think another famous legal principle, *pacta sunt servanda* (agreements are to be kept), the principle of human relationships governed by contract, is even more central to private law as it has evolved since Roman times, and to the understanding of the obstacles that stand in the way of transforming capitalism. For a collection of texts from Roman authorities on the law of *pacta*, see *Justinian's Digest*, Book 2, sections 14, 15, and 18. Alan Watson, ed.,

The Digest of Justinian (Philadelphia: University of Pennsylvania Press, 1985). The Roman sources of legal ideas fundamental to the market economy—including respect for property rights, the ordering of human relationships by contract, and the freedom of individuals to make economic choices—turned out to be seminal, not so much because they were uppermost in the minds of Roman jurists, as because they turned out to be what future ages needed. In Franz Wieacker's phrase, key Roman legal ideas were influential "because they matched later social structures rather than those of their own day." Franz Wieacker, *A History of Private Law in Europe* (Oxford: Clarendon Press, 1995), 7. There were features of Roman Law which made it particularly suitable to be the seedbed from which grew the legal framework of global commerce. For reasons too complex to mention here, Roman Law was, in contrast to Islamic Law, Hindu Law, and several other traditional legal systems, from early times secular, separated from religion. See Alan Watson, *The Spirit of Roman Law* (Athens, Ga.; and London: University of Georgia Press, 1995). Its early manner of growth was not religious teaching, but rather announcements ("edicts") by magistrates at the beginnings of their terms concerning what kinds of cases they would hear, which wrongs they would grant remedies for. Thus, again in contrast to other legal systems, to behave legally was to stay within the bounds of a clearly marked subset of the broader category of behaving according to accepted social norms. For example, one of the principles recorded in *Justinian's Digest* is: "Not everything which is lawful is honorable." *Justinian's Digest,* Book 50, part 17, rule 144. This limited, rather than expansive, concept of law prepared the way for the Kantian idea of freedom within a legal framework which is today the philosophical framework of the market culture expressed in the global economy: "law . . . empowers the individual to be independently ethical, but does not force him to be so; the individual's rights [are conceived of] as the space in which he is free to act consistently with the freedom of others; legal transaction and contractual intention as the action-space of the autonomous personality." Wieacker, *History of Private Law*, 315. Although we do not entirely disagree with Wieacker when he suggests that even if ancient Rome had not existed at all, model commercial society would have devised similar legal principles to the ones it has, we would also suggest that the availability of the Roman Law tradition as a source of rules for commercial transactions provides part of the answer to Immanuel Wallerstein's question: why it was Europe and not China which proved to be the nucleus which expanded to become today's global economy. Immanuel Wallerstein, *The Modern World System, Vols. 1-3* (San Diego, Calif.: Academic Press, 1989). There is considerable plausibility in the pronouncement by the nineteenth century German legal historian Friedrich Karl von Savigny, concerning the subsequent influence of Roman Law that "it took the organic adoption of Roman law to maintain the healthy parallel development of culture and law; for the whole culture of modern peoples is and has been international." Cited in Wiecker, *History of Private Law*, 312, interpolations by Wieacker omitted. Savigny's pronouncement is plausible because the peoples Savigny calls "modern" live in capitalist cultures engaged in international commerce, and the Roman tradition provides the seeds of a suitable legal framework for such a culture. The work of Savigny and others deriving modern private and commercial law from Roman sources also demonstrates that there are no major contradictions between Roman principles and those of modern law's more or less non-Roman sources, whose histories have been more or less intertwined with the history of the influence of the Roman Law tradition, such as social contract theory, the natural law of reason philosophy of the Enlightenment, and the rules embedded in the cases and statutes of the English common law.

40. Although the point that the Roman Law tradition nurtured modern ideas of freedom could be illustrated by citing any of many maxims of Roman Law, we associate freedom with "live honorably" (*honeste vivere*) by the following three-step identification: 1) "Honorably" means "with dignity." For the Romans, "dignity" implied rank. Different forms of honor were appropriate depending on who was being honored, or who was being honorable. For example, in *Justinian's Institutes*, different damages were awarded to compensate for offenses, depending on the rank of the person offended: "The valuation of contempts rises and falls according to the victim's social standing and honor. . . . A contempt to a senator or to a parent or to a patron is differently valued from one committed against an outsider or a person of low degree." *Justinian's Institutes*, Book IV, Section 4.4, 127. 2) With Luther, Kant, and modernity generally, dignity was democratized. Today, "human dignity" in principle belongs to everyone. 3) Human dignity, according to its most influential and cogent exponent, Kant, is just human autonomy: freedom. Thus a lineal descendant of the Roman "live honorably" is "live free," i.e., insist on your autonomy, and respect the autonomy of others.

41. Charles Lindblom, *Politics and Markets* (New York: Basic Books, 1977), 173.

42. Gunnar Myrdal illustrates the importance of granting recognition to "*pacta sunt servanda*" as a critical issue when he writes: "Generally speaking, the less privileged groups in democratic society, as they become aware of their interests and their political power, will be found to press for more and more state intervention in practically all fields. Their interest clearly lies in having individual contracts subordinated as much as possible to general norms, laid down in laws, regulations, administrative dispositions, and semi-voluntary agreements between apparently private, but in reality, quasi-public organizations [e.g., wage agreements between Swedish unions and employers' confederations, and their counterparts in other countries]." Myrdal, *Beyond the Welfare State*, 38.

43. Nitisastro, *Socio-Economic Basis of the Indonesian State*, 19.

Chapter 12

The Stones that the Builders Rejected

I. The Locational Revolution

In the conclusions of his excellent book *Power in Motion: Capital Mobility and the Indonesian State*, Jeffrey Winters states that for labor the party is over. The poor will stay poor. Low wages will stay low. High wages will fall. The pessimistic conclusions of Winters' book are not only about Indonesia. Indonesia provides local data to prove a global thesis.[1]

Winters' theory is that capital mobility causes nation-states to offer low wages, and other incentives such as low taxes and lax environmental standards, in order to attract investors. His theory is about the entire global economy. The nations of the world (and within the nations the regions) are in a race to the bottom.[2] The jurisdictions whose laws favor capital over labor tend to win the race to attract investors, but in the process of winning the race to attract investors they also participate in a race to lower standards. Competitors on the verge of losing the race to attract investors shift their policies so that they favor capital over labor still more, and still more, and still more.

Indonesia is a test case, from which Winters draws confirmation of his theory. Winters' data show not only that the Indonesian government bent its policies to favor capital, but that it bent its policies the most to favor the most mobile capital, and bent them the least to favor the least mobile capital. Thus he is able to construct a proof of the form John Stuart Mill in his *Logic* called "induction by concomitant variation."[3] The mobility of capital must be the cause explaining why governments grant favors to investors, because the more mobile the capital is, the more favors the investors who own it get. The less mobile capital is, the fewer favors its owners get.

Important parts of Winters' argument are summarized in the following passage from Richard Robbins' own excellent recent book, *Global Problems and the Culture of Capitalism*:

257

The case of Indonesia offers a good example of what countries need to do to attract capital (Winters 1996). Indonesia fought for and gained independence from the Dutch in 1949. After a period of intense regional competition, President Sukarno, the victor in the competition, instituted a policy to free the country from foreign influence, carefully trying to balance power between the army and a strong Communist Party. Among his actions, he began nationalizing foreign firms. With their property at risk, and no longer guaranteed by the state, companies and investors began to pull their money out of the country. Consequently, the economy collapsed. Then in 1965 the military, under General Suharto, put down an alleged coup by the PKI, the Indonesian communist party. The subsequent blood bath led to the slaughter of hundreds of thousands of Indonesians believed to be sympathetic to or members of the Communist Party and removal of Sukarno from power.

With little money, the new ruler, President Suharto, faced the problem of rebuilding an economy in ruins. To solve the problem Suharto turned to economics professors at the University of [Indonesia at] Jakarta and assigned them the task of designing a policy to attract foreign investors. The first thing they did was to send signals through the press that they were changing economic policies and appointing people to government offices known to be friendly to foreign investors. Next, they applied for loans from multilateral institutions such as the World Bank and the IMF, hoping their approval would build the confidence of foreign investors in their country. Then, to assure capital controllers that their country was politically stable, the government suppressed all political dissent and limited the power of workers to mobilize unions. The result was that foreign capital began to flow into the country, and in the late 1960s and early 1970s the Indonesian economy began to thrive.

But the story did not end there; what happened next illustrates how the power of capital controllers to create conditions favorable for investment is not absolute. Indonesia has large oil reserves, and when in the early 1970s oil revenue increased, Indonesia's need for foreign investment decreased. Since it had another source of money, the country became less friendly to foreign investors: taxes increased, preference was shown to domestic industries, and bureaucratic procedures became more cumbersome for foreigners wanting to do business in Indonesia. As a result, foreign investments decreased dramatically. As long as oil revenues were stable, Indonesia had no problem. But in the early 1980s, oil prices plunged, and once again the Indonesian economy was close to ruin. Once again, in response to domestic political pressure from those who were suffering from economic decline, the government, still under the control of President Suharto, found itself instituting the measures outlined above to attract capital investors once again.

Foreign investment did return to Indonesia, particularly in the growth of assembly plants; thus until late 1997, the economy was doing well. However the collapse of the value of Asian currencies in late 1997 left the Indonesian economy once again in ruin, its currency plummeting in value, unemployment spreading, and social unrest increasing. The government responded with greater social and political repression but ultimately Suharto resigned.[4]

Although the case Winters uses to test his theory is Indonesia, he also comments on events in a number of other countries. He finds that humanity is now experiencing a Locational Revolution, whose eventual consequences will be as profound as those of the Industrial Revolution. The comfortable middle masses of the First World, who enjoyed the benefits of high wages and generous government programs in the middle decades of the twentieth century, have only begun to feel the effects of the Locational Revolution that happened as the century closed.[5] Structural forces that are now at work are bringing most people lower wages and fewer government benefits. Governments are inexorably led to adopt measures favoring capital against labor.

In the light of Winters' extremely gloomy prognosis (which nobody will deny has a great deal of truth in it, even if it is not the whole truth) the diagnosis of the problem, and the prescription of the cure, if any cure is possible, become extremely urgent. The tragedy of the situation is heightened by the somber reflection that there is no natural reason for poverty.[6] The natural sciences stand ready to provide appropriate technologies, which could be used to meet the basic needs of all human beings, within the limits of presently existing resources, without damage to the environment.

The tragedy of the situation is mitigated, however, by the reflection that there has always been poverty. In some periods of history it has been worse than it is now, and perhaps it once was even worse than it will have become when the full impact of the Locational Revolution is felt. Indonesia is not as poor as most of Africa. How bad poverty seems to be (from the points of view of onlookers who are not themselves poor) depends on the criterion for badness—whether the situation here and now is compared with what might be, or with some other time, or with some other place.

We believe that the appropriate criterion is what might be, insofar as *it would be if we (i.e., responsible human actors) took steps to make it be. We are the cause of the suffering that exists because of our actions, and because of our inaction.*

The first step, and in many ways the hardest step, is to undertake a never-ending process of thinking about the causes of poverty. Actions without concepts are blind. The thesis of this book is that the causes of poverty are to be found primarily in the constitutive rules of capitalism. Otherwise put, its causes lie in the failure of human beings to construct the constitutive rules of a poverty-free social order.

II. Sources of Despair in the Age of Globalization

What drives us to despair, in our more pessimistic moments, is not the inherent hopelessness of the situation of the majority of humanity, nor is it the spin-offs of the majority's poverty, which make the biosphere insecure for all of humanity, including the wealthy. The situation is not inherently hopeless. What drives us to despair is that humanity sometimes seems to be incapable of thinking solutions to the problem. What drives us to despair are the power paradigms and exchange paradigms that make the cultural resources that could solve the problem entirely invisible to social scientists. What drives us to despair are the clueless activists who protest the Locational Revolution with no concept whatever of its cause or its cure. What drives us to despair are the mainstream economists who implement short-term fixes that instead of solving the problem make it worse—as an addict's fix makes the addiction worse. What drives us to despair are the social democratic true believers (known in the United States as "liberals") who still expect the angels on horseback of human rights, compassionate welfare states, and collective bargaining to be the saviors of every proletariat in distress.

In defense of the somewhat abrasive tone of the preceding paragraph, we would plead that although we usually try to make it a practice to refrain from insulting people, nonetheless, with respect to the causes and cures of the Locational Revolution, it is so important to foment debate on vital issues that, all things considered, we have come to believe that it is appropriate to feign a certain degree of hostility and intolerance. Much as we would prefer a dispassionate and impersonal analysis, we have regretfully come to believe that to get attention amidst the cacophony of voices sounding as brass in the maelstrom of today's accelerated world, we should try to make a deliberate effort to be rude. We hope that someone will feel sufficiently offended to defend the ideas we are attacking, and then, the debate once joined, the corrosive acids of free speech will, in the fullness of time, separate gold from dross, truth from error. There is, of course, no a priori reason why the opinions of those whom we have pejoratively characterized as blind, clueless, shortsighted, and outdated are wrong, while ours are right. In the following pages although we shall heap scorn upon mainstream political scientists, many anti-globalization activists, most mainstream economists, and many progressive political leaders, it is not because we are certain that our views are right and theirs wrong.

Poverty: A Class Struggle Lost, or an Unsolved Social Problem?

We could criticize mainstream political science for the treatment its practitioners have meted out to General Ibnu Sutowo, who retired in disgrace from his post as chief of Indonesia's government-owned oil monopoly Pertamina, after it ran up short-term debt that it could not possibly pay. Sutowo treated Pertamina as a source of quick money for worthy projects. In his own words, "I helped all the military people with their projects, and you can't find a single road or school or hospital that wasn't at least partly funded by the money I borrowed through Pertamina."[7] Political scientists have uniformly looked at Sutowo through the lens of patron-client power politics. He has been categorized as a power-holder building his power-base by dispensing patronage. Were there, somewhere in rural Indonesia, military officers and their wives civic-minded enough to want a hospital built as a contribution to the common good, then they too would be as invisible when viewed through the lens of a power paradigm as the man of good intentions Sutowo thought he was. Or we could criticize exchange models a la Gary Becker, hardly better than, and hardly different from, power models.[8] But we will not. Instead, we will focus a critique of power paradigms on the idea of "class struggle." Since the concept of history as class struggle is a specific form of the larger concept of history as power struggle, our comments on class struggle may have some bearing on the larger concept of the course of history being determined by power, in one or more of the many senses of that ubiquitous word.

Neither Winters nor Robbins employs the phrase "class struggle," perhaps because using it would divert attention from broader issues to narrower issues raised by images of narrow-minded radicals bent on violence. "Class struggle" is, nevertheless, an unavoidable topic in the discussions they pursue, since the struggle between capital seeking to raise profits and labor trying to raise wages is at the heart of the dynamic which propels capital around the globe in quest of ever more favorable legal frameworks in which to do business.

"Class struggle" is, moreover, a major species in the genus "power politics," which is a central object of study in the academic discipline of political science, Marxist or not. Thus when Anthony Giddens wrote a book to refute Marxism, what he argued was that not all power politics is between classes narrowly conceived as economic interest groups—some struggle is about military security, or control of territory, or religion, or prestige; and in some struggles the state itself, not the state as the instrument and representative of a class apart from the state's own apparatus, is the principal protagonist. Giddens, and non-Marxist social scientists generally, tend to reject a narrow concept of "class struggle" only in favor of what could fairly be called, "class struggle broadly and loosely defined."[9] For those of us who regard the ethical construction of social institutions as a vital force in history, therefore, it is convenient, as well as necessary, to demur to the claim that class struggle is the motor of history—not just to refute the few who still maintain a narrow Marxist doctrine of class struggle, but also to introduce into the debate considerations which, while they serve to refute narrow Marxism (which is not to be confused with intelligent Marxism), also refute mainstream social science.

It is almost an unconscious reflex, rather than a deliberate mental choice, for a modern mind to construe the facts adduced by Winters and Robbins in agonistic categories: Capital won. Labor lost. Can labor fight back? Or is the victory of capital decisive and permanent?

A moment's reflection, a pause designed to convert reflex to choice, will show that the proposition that the defeat of the poor in the class struggle explains poverty is not obviously true. The bourgeoisie is not struggling to achieve the poverty of the masses. Poverty's continuing persistence is not an intentional objective pursued by rich people. It is certainly true that Shell Oil Company has committed and continues to commit numerous bad acts, not all of which are strictly required by the structural features of capitalism. The same is true of individual executives employed by Shell.[10] Nevertheless, it is difficult to imagine that the investors and executives of Shell Oil Company, which reaps large profits from exploiting Nigeria's oil reserves, are rejoicing because they have won a class struggle against Nigeria's poor. Do they keep golden telescopes in the windows of the upper stories of glass and steel office towers in Lagos, so that they can enjoy their triumph over the poor by peering from a distance into the squalor of the slums? When they sight a baby dying of diarrhea do they toast each other with martinis and send up a shout, "Hip Hip Hooray! We won the class struggle!" Do they measure pain and suffering, and then count high scores as the trophies and proofs of their victory? Not bloody likely.

The argument that the bourgeoisie will inevitably fight to keep in place a system that gives them privileges and keeps the poor poor—from which it is deduced that the cause of poverty is a class struggle that the poor have so far not won—is further weakened by the fact that mass poverty takes away from the rich the one thing that neo-Hobbesian mainstream political science postulates that all political actors want: power. Given the proclivity of the disinherited of the earth to enforce the sharing of the wealth by private and public violence, by knife-point in dark alleys, and by riots in public streets, the existence of millions of impoverished fellow citizens obliges the rich to pay for protection. The more desperately poor people there are, the more the rich must pay for security, and the less security they get for their money.[11]

Adam Smith thought it was a law of history that whenever people hire other people to do their fighting for them, they end up dominated by their defenders. Smith could have produced no better example to illustrate his law than Indonesia. Most of Indonesia's private wealth is held by a small ethnic Chinese minority. It is normal in Indonesia for TNI, the Indonesian armed forces (formerly known as ABRI), to be all-powerful or nearly so, while the wealthy Chinese minority, lacking political power of its own, pays handsomely for favors from those who do have political power. The vulnerability of the rich is demonstrated when the forces of order either lose control, or choose not to exercise control, or divide, as periodically happens. Mobs kill Chinese men, rape Chinese women, burn the buildings of Chinese businesses, and burn their cars. Although the July 2001 transfer of presidential power from Wahid to Megawati proved to be fairly peaceful, thousands of Chinese left the country anyway as a precaution, fearing the repetition of the violence of the dispossessed typical of moments of political tension in Indonesia.

That the existence of mass poverty brings fear and expense into the lives of the privileged, and power into the hands of the military, is illustrated at the level of the United States of America, the world's global superpower, in the 1998 report entitled "Vision for 2020," issued by the United States Space Command, which states that because of the corporate "globalization of the world economy," there will be a widening gap between the "haves and have nots." The U.S. Space Command intends to "control and dominate" space in order to protect U.S. "interests and investments."[12] The conclusion of this line of thought is that the bourgeoisie can enjoy political power, peace, tranquility, human rights, and democratic governance only when social tensions are reduced.

Thus the concept of "class struggle" is a misleading concept, and the broader concepts of the power paradigms of mainstream political science are hardly less misleading. Worse: the power paradigms of mainstream political science tend to make invisible and therefore unimaginable the intelligent options that sane rich people, as well as enlightened poor people, would choose if they could see them and imagine them, and if they could see and imagine the means to make them real.

It is true that the revenue of a firm can be divided only once—what goes to pay wages is not available to disburse as profit, and what goes to profits is not available to disburse as wages. It is true that many business people have grown rich by paying low wages, while many businesses have failed because they could not meet payroll. It is true that generals and colonels have carried out military coups around the world at the behest of property-owners, for the immediate purpose of crushing labor unions and socialist political parties, and for the ultimate purpose of restoring conditions under which profits could be accumulated. But it is not true that under capitalism the rich have plenipotentiary power and can do as they please. And it is not true that it is in the interest of the rich for the existing capitalist global economy to continue as it is. Any sane rich person offered a choice between living in a world with mass poverty, and living in a world without mass poverty, would choose the latter. Giving up some privileges for the sake of cooperating in the ethical construction of a better world is an intelligent choice.

Post-Seattle Global Activism

The world changed at Seattle. Prior to December of 1999, when the protests in Seattle's streets led to the cancellation of top-level meetings of the World Trade Organization, there was no visible worldwide grassroots anti-globalization movement. Since Seattle, wherever capitalism's top brass convene to press further the advantages that the Locational Revolution has given capital over labor and big business over small business, it is predictable that they will be confronted by thousands of activists, ready and willing to play bit parts on the stage of history, whether the venue be Prague, Genoa, or Göteborg; Quebec, Washington, or Mexico City. United by the internet, by a common enemy, and by a common cause, the world's social activists have become the visible opposition to the world's economic system.

The actions of the violent fringe of protest against the world's economic system confirm the sad truth that even when grave issues are at stake, even when the future of life hangs in the balance, young males are prone to imagine themselves as knights in shining armor when they are really only crackpots. Many imagine themselves to be the contemporary voices of the philosophies of Peter Kropotkin or Rosa Luxemburg, while what they do contradicts their ostensible purposes. They smash the windowpanes of small businesses for the ostensible purpose of protecting small business against big business. They impose on the local governments of host cities millions of added police and security expense, for the ostensible purpose of empowering local institutions to resist being engulfed by the tidal waves of globalization. Through the media they telecast to all the world a picture of the anti-globalization movement as irresponsible and irrational, for the purpose of convincing the public that the cause of economic justice is the cause of wisdom.

Meanwhile, the peaceful majority accumulates grievances against the police. The great majority of the demonstrators desire only to communicate their message, and in many cases to employ nonviolent self-suffering, as Gandhi did, to demonstrate the sincerity of their convictions. Sometimes the police are unable to distinguish the legitimate activists from those drawn to the dangerously false romantic image of revolutionary violence. Sometimes police officers lose it. Sometimes they have orders to intimidate the opposition. Sooner or later, citizens who have assembled peacefully to petition for the redress of their grievances are bludgeoned on the head with a police truncheon. At that point whatever the issues had been, the issues immediately become human rights and freedom of speech—whether the demonstrators have the right to express their ideas. But what are their ideas?

Several methodologies might be employed to identify the ideas animating today's worldwide anti-systemic activism. Since we ourselves have participated in some of the protests, we might use introspection. It would be more scientific to interview a random sample of protest organizers—the moderators of the websites, the nonviolence trainers, the inventors of creative tactics, the facilitators of affinity groups, the captains of medical and legal support teams, the coordinators of logistics—in order to identify the principles that prescribe for the protagonists the point and purpose of protest. Instead, for better or worse, our method will be to comment on the ideas found in one well-chosen book, *Globalization from Below*, by Jeremy Brecher, Tim Costello, and Brendan Smith.[13]

The back cover of *Globalization from Below* quotes *Newsweek*: "There are now two visions of globalization on offer, one led by commerce, one led by social activism." *Globalization from Below* is a strategy proposal for the second vision, the vision of humanity's future offered by the social activists. The authors write, "The argument of this book is that people can indeed exercise power over globalization, but only by means of a solidarity that crosses the boundaries of nations, identities, and narrow interests. A corporate-driven, top-down globalization can only by effectively countered by globalization from below."[14]

The argument of the book is incomplete and flawed. If it is true that "people" can exercise "power" over "globalization," then the first things "people" need to know, in order to guide their actions intelligently, are the causes of globalization. And even before explaining the phenomena over which it is proposed that "people" should exercise "power," one ought to justify naming them "globalization" when a greater practical and intellectual heritage could be identified by naming the problem as "capitalism."

Globalization from Below does not make, or cite as its theoretical premise, any argument about the dynamics of capitalism, either in general, or in its current phase. Instead of an account of the causes of "globalization," it reports on the genesis of a global coalition of social activists. *Globalization from Below* does, to be sure, successfully name some of the key problems that appear on the surface of our suffering world, such as: "global competition to lower labor, environmental, and social costs (the global race to the bottom); the power of highly mobile capital to pour into a country, create an economic bubble, and then devastate it by withdrawing [Indonesia in 1997 was a prime example]; the bargaining power of corporations vis-a-vis governments; the power concentrated in the nexus that links the US Treasury, corporations, and global institutions such as the WTO, IMF, and World Bank."[15]

Instead of an account of the constitutive rules that produce the key problems it names, however, and instead of a method for transforming the cultural structures that cement the problems in place, *Globalization from Below* reports on the genesis of a worldwide multi-issue activist coalition. The women's movement has become aware that most women are poor, that the majority of women live in Asia, and that the workers exploited in third world sweatshops are mainly women. It has dawned on environmentalists that the environment is being destroyed for the sake of profit. People of conscience, in churches and out, have noticed that the Locational Revolution undermines social justice. Small farmers around the world, who are losing their lands and their livelihoods, have realized that global free trade gives the upper hand to big farmers. Labor has learned from experience that the promised benefits of free trade do not accrue to labor. Human rights activists have documented many cases of abusive practices that are part and parcel of economic development strategies designed to attract investment. The story of the building of a coalition is one thing; an analysis of the causes of the problems is another.

Lacking a diagnosis, *Globalization from Below* prescribes a cure. The cure is not a treatment the movement will administer; it is the movement itself. This surprising conclusion, that the very social movement whose genesis *Globalization from Below* reports is itself the solution to the world's principal problems, is deduced from Gene Sharp's theory of power, which the authors of *Globalization from Below* endorse. According to Sharp, people have power because other people consent to their having power.[16] Consequently, power disappears when there is withdrawal of consent. If one adds as a surreptitious *petitio principii* a causal diagnosis that is operative even though it is unstated, namely that the cause of the world's problems named as "globalization from above" is that the multinational corporations, the IMF, and the World Bank have too much power, and therefore the solution of the world's problems is to take power away from them; one can then move on to the further results: 1) that withdrawal of consent causes the world's problems to disappear; and 2) the movement in itself simply is the solution to those problems because it is withdrawal of consent.[17]

Globalization from Below quotes Gene Sharp: "[T]he exercise of power depends on the consent of the ruled who, by withdrawing their consent, can control and even destroy the power of their opponent."[18] What the movement is doing is "utilizing the hidden power of social movements—the dependence of all power centers on the consent of the people—to force institutions to comply with global norms." "By such means do the people of the world withdraw their consent from globalization from above and impose their own norms on the global economy."[19]

The title of the concluding chapter, Chapter 9, summarizes the cure as "Fix It or Nix It." The paradigm for "fix it or nix it" is the strike. A caricature carrying the same logic farther will make clear its limitations: If the world's agriculture and food distribution systems are working so badly that half of humanity is going hungry, then "fix it or nix it" implies that everybody should threaten to withdraw their consent to the established institutions. Everybody should demand that somebody "fix it," i.e., make it work for everyone, or else they should "nix it," i.e., shut it down. As the capitalists wield power not by producing goods, but by refusing permission to use their property until their terms are met, so globalization from below will change the world by organized inaction, "for example, by blocking roads, occupying buildings, or demonstrating in violation of injunctions and police orders."[20] Roland Barthes has observed that a strike is always a scandal because it always injures the innocents, the general public.[21] Its asymptote is paralysis, which is intolerable. We would add that the reliance of labor and social activism on slowdown and stoppage is not as much the key to structural change as it is evidence of the need for structural change. It is a structural trap. The cultural structure is such that what appears to be a general means for changing it, and which is indeed at some times and places appropriate and useful, slowdown and stoppage, is a boomerang. The power to shut down is necessarily the power to make oneself unpopular.

Globalization from Below is a symptom and a representative sample of ideas which, if they are not the only ones that animate today's global social activism, are widely believed and acted on. Its authors have made other major contributions to the movement literature, including *Global Village or Global Pillage* and *Strike!*[22] Its quotes and notes parade a Who's Who of voices activists listen to, such as Vandana Shiva and Walden Bello. Other writers whose opinions carry weight in the movement have endorsed *Globalization from Below*, including Medea Benjamin, Susan George, Saskia Sassen, and Frances Fox Piven. Much of the book summarizes pronouncements of NGOs and coalitions of NGOs which, like *Globalization from Below* itself, deplore injustice more than they analyze its causes, while threatening that they will "nix it" if they are unable to persuade other people, whom they think have power, to "fix it." The ideas in *Globalization from Below* are not a sneeze; they are an epidemic. Worse, they are symptoms of deeply entrenched patterns of thought, which make it difficult to imagine and to implement constructive solutions to social problems.

The Dismal Science

As this is written, the world's mainstream press is praising Megawati, Indonesia's president, for appointing a cabinet dominated by non-political economists, known in Indonesia as "technocrats," or "the Berkeley mafia." The saddest news is that the mainstream media are probably right. Given the existing practical limitations on what is thinkable and on what is doable, she probably made a correct decision.

Everybody knows what the technocrats will do. They will restore investor confidence in Indonesia. They will make Indonesian policy conform to the demands of the International Monetary Fund. They will declare that it is their professional opinion, supported by the weight of hundreds of well-funded and highly quantitative studies, that people who propose to redistribute wealth, in any form, are no friends of the poor. As IMF orthodoxy asserts, the free market is the true friend of the poor, as it is the friend of all. The IMF will release a five-billion-dollar loan, which Indonesia desperately needs, which it has frozen until Indonesia falls into line with the teachings of orthodox mainstream economics.

The economists in Indonesia's cabinet will administer a quick fix. They will cement ever more solidly into place the structural traps that keep most of humanity poor, and almost all Indonesians poor, in a world where natural science stands ready to provide technologies that can meet everybody's needs with existing resources. The nation will become even more addicted to profit, while labor will become even more powerless. The economists will do these things blindly, without seeing what they are doing. They will do them not because they are uneducated, but because they are highly educated. They see the facts through the lenses of the concepts they learned at Berkeley.

There is an extensive literature carefully dissecting the conceptual errors of mainstream economics.[23] We will not say anything new. We will not add another voice to the already redundant chorus of proofs that the discourses and practices of mainstream economics are historically limited and valid only when confined to certain institutional settings. Our aim is not to discredit economics, but to contribute to building something better which will embrace its findings and methods in a wider synthesis. If not economics, what?

We will be brief. We will not bore people who are already familiar with the anti-economics literature, but instead we will make a slightly novel point not previously mooted in it. For people not familiar with the anti-economics literature, who, perhaps, if left to themselves, would see no alternative to the common sense of everyday life under capitalism, and, therefore, no alternative to economics, we will try to show that, yes, conceiving of society as an ethical construction is a real possibility. Our slightly novel point will serve our immediate purpose, which is to show that as humanity tries to cope with the so-called Locational Revolution, mainstream economics is a source of despair. It will also serve our larger purpose, which is to contribute to building social democracy. To make our slightly novel point, we change our metaphor from "seeing" to "speaking." After saying that economics is "blind" and that mainstream economists cannot "see," we switch to asking, "What is the language of economics?" "What can economists say?" "What can economists not say?"

We begin our discussion with quotes from two writers who laid foundation stones for the building of modern society: Rene Descartes and Jean-Jacques Rousseau.

From Descartes' *Discourse on Method*, originally published in 1637: "I took pleasure more than anything else in Mathematics, because of the certainty and clarity of its reasoning, but I did not yet discern its true use, and thinking that it served only the mechanical arts, I was astonished that on foundations so firm and so solid nothing higher had been built."[24] Descartes, the inventor of analytic geometry, was not a single isolated individual, who happened by chance to hit on great ideas, which happened by chance to become influential. He was a child of nascent capitalism in Europe. He was a part of the invisible college, the Republic of Letters, including both rationalists and empiricists, who, together, as Richard Rorty has observed, labored to create a modern secular worldview as an alternative to the traditional religious worldviews which had, thitherto, been the only worldviews.[25]

If anyone has fulfilled Descartes' dream of building something higher than mechanics on the foundations of mathematics, it has been the economists. Economics is nothing if not Cartesian. From beginning to end it consists of graphs drawn on Cartesian planes. It is made of functions, defined as sets of Cartesian ordered pairs. Demand curves and supply curves move up or down, left or right, slope backward or slope forward, in Cartesian space.

Less obviously, but with profound and powerful ramifications, there is a parallel between a basic distinction of economics, the distinction between exchange-value and use-value, and the distinction drawn by the early modern philosophers between primary and secondary qualities. Descartes complained that the ancient and medieval philosophers had speculated endlessly about the virtues and the passions, without coming to any solid conclusions. He proposed that science be built anew, on solid foundations, starting with the clear and distinct ideas of mathematics. It was but a hop, skip, and a jump from this proposal to the conclusion that *what is expressed in mathematics—because it can be known—is what is real.* The colors, sights, and sounds of life were deemed to be mere secondary qualities. When Descartes analyzed a piece of wax, and concluded that its substantial reality was not in what could be felt, but in what could be measured, he started the tradition in which economists stand when they focus their attention on money. Money, the medium of exchange, is pure quantity. Anybody can use it to buy anything. The only thing that matters about it is how much of it there is. Thus exchange-value abstracts from all qualities, ignoring them all in favor of one summary measure: the price. It is part and parcel of a worldview that identifies what is clear and distinct and measurable with what is real and operative and worthy of consideration.

From Jean-Jacques Rousseau's *La Nouvelle Heloise*, originally published circa 1755: "Love is mere illusion. It invents, so to speak, another universe; it surrounds itself with objects that do not exist or to which only love itself has given life. Since it expresses all its feelings by means of images it speaks only in figures (*"comme il rend tous ses sentiments en images, son langage est toujours figure"*)."[26]

Mere illusion? No. Of "love" it could be said, as Gandhi said of "God," that it is one of the richest words in language, and that a lifetime is not long enough to plumb the depths of its meaning. Nonetheless, Rousseau's brilliant remark illuminates not just love but all the virtues. Love is a virtue (the greatest of the seven cardinal virtues), and like the other virtues it surrounds itself with invented objects, it gives life, it speaks in images. Its language is not found in the lexicon of mechanics. Love talk is soul talk.

"Soul," another ancient idea, whose history has been interwoven with the history of "love" at least since Plato defined lovers as soul-mates, is classically defined as an inner source and principle of motion. Humans, like dogs but unlike stones, have souls. Economics is inaccurate when it employs mechanical principles of cause and effect—independent variables as causes, dependent variables as effects—because humans are more like dogs than like stones. If one kicks a stone, it will move in a direction and with a velocity given by the parallelogram law, the first corollary to Newton's three laws of motion. If one knows the independent variables, the vector force of the kick and the mass of the stone, one can calculate the dependent variable, where the stone will go and how fast. But if one kicks a dog, there is no telling what will happen. A dog is an "animal"—a word that originally meant something with an *anima* (Latin for "soul"), i.e., something animated, something that moves of its own accord. Humans, being more like dogs than like stones, have especially well-developed imaginations, and especially well-developed voices. We have what Plato called a *logistiche psuche*, a rational (word-guided) soul. Human action is characterized by deliberation, and by acting on the basis of what one *believes* to be true.[27] It is governed, for those who are properly socialized, by moral habits, also known as character, formed by acting and talking in interaction with other people, crystallized as stable virtues and as adherence to social norms.

Descartes complained that the philosophies of virtue and social norms (*moeurs*), which had been elaborated in philosophical discussions by the Greeks and the Romans, were indefinite and variable, built, as he put it, on sand and mud, sable and bone. He argued that the right way to build society was to build it on solid foundations, as mechanics had been built, with the tools provided by the clear and distinct ideas of mathematics. The opposite is true. Because humans have souls, socialization and social reform are accomplished precisely by the method of Socrates, by dialogue.

Cartesians to the core, mainstream economists advance a number of excuses for ignoring the details of how humans actually make decisions. Some say that economics is concerned only with human behavior in the aggregate, and that in the aggregate individual psychology does not matter. Some say that as long as an economic model yields correct predictions, it does not matter whether its assumptions are realistic. Some say that whatever their initial errors may be, over time their science is self-correcting, since an infinite series of empirical tests of well-defined hypotheses will confirm or disconfirm their economic theories, and thus systematically improve them, regardless of which first principles they start out with. Some say that empirical evidence confirms that people are in fact materialistic, calculating, payoff-maximizing creatures, just as economic theory postulates. Some say that economic theory is true a priori by definition, and need not rely on facts at all, since it is necessarily true that debits equal credits as A equals A, income equals consumption plus investment, total sales equal total purchases, maximum welfare equals maximum satisfaction of revealed preferences, net investment cannot exceed net savings. Some say that pure economics is a theory of rational choice, not an empirical study of the actual choices that flesh and blood human beings make. Some say that economics, as it was elaborated by Ludwig von Mises and the Austrian school, already possesses an adequate philosophy of human action, or that economics has nothing to learn from ethics because the principles of ethics and the principles of markets are the same. Some say that economics has more to teach psychology than to learn from it, as is evident when psychologists use exchange models and reinforcement schedules in their research. Some say that they find words like "soul" unintelligible, and that until someone can clearly explain to them what such words mean, they will assume that they mean nothing. Some say that although it may be true that somebody should study the details of how humans actually make decisions, such studies fall in someone else's field, not in economics.

Whatever may be the merit, or lack of merit, of such defenses of mainstream economics, what is at stake in the debates is more than its scientific credentials. What is at stake is the relationship of economic science to social change. The central question is whether economists are going to participate, along with people of good will of every calling, in the reconstruction of social reality.

If our neo-Aristotelian philosophy of human action is valid, then people act (at least to a large extent) on the basis of what they believe to be true. If, then, economists, or their successors who practice a more comprehensive social science, are obliged to study the real causes of human action, they will be obliged to study beliefs. They will be obliged to acknowledge that belief-systems are embedded in the contexts of the cultural systems studied by anthropologists, sociologists, and historians. They will come to recognize that the language of desire, the operative language of the dreams and passions that move people to action, is more like the *langue* figure of Rousseau than it is like the *idees nettes et claires* of Descartes.

Mainstream economics, wedded as it is to mechanical causality, is worse than inaccurate. It is demoralizing. Its discourse excludes the edifying dialogues and inspiring images that are the lifeblood of a culture of solidarity, the air it breathes, the stuff of its dreams, and the causes of its effects.

Human Rights, Compassionate Welfare States, Collective Bargaining: Will they survive the Locational Revolution?

No discussion of the sources of despair in the age of globalization would be complete without mentioning the social democratic true believers (known in the United States as "liberals") who still expect the angels on horseback of human rights, compassionate welfare states, and collective bargaining to be the saviors of every proletariat in distress.

Instead of naming names and quoting texts, we will tell a story. It is a story whose characters are widely believed ideas, so superficial and so tempting, which give the democratic left today its vision. The ideas in this story are, in our opinion, often believed but rarely examined. They lie in a half-conscious penumbra. Our story aims to make them more conscious, and therefore more open to criticism and improvement.

The story goes like this: *"Once upon a time, before globalization, the citizens of the developed industrial democracies decided, and enshrined as principles of their constitutions and laws, that certain things were too important to be left to the mercy of the forces of the marketplace. The developed industrial democracies were, in those days, regarded as examples of the future which the rest of the world would eventually enjoy, after the third world was developed, and after the second world was liberated, and so their ideals were, in important ways, all the world's ideals.*

"The citizens believed in the ideal articulated by the eighteenth-century German philosopher Immanuel Kant, who taught that everything has either a

price or a dignity. What has a price can be bought and sold on the market. The human person has dignity (Wurde), *which is beyond all price. For this reason, human rights, which are nothing other than respect for the dignity of the human person, are absolute, not to be bought or sold, and always to be honored, regardless of what the market may say. The citizens agreed with this philosophy, and voted it into law.*

"Similarly, the citizens of the democracies believed that there ought to be a social safety net, entitlements, which guaranteed that everyone, regardless of means, would have enough to eat, basic medical care, schooling, a pension in old age, and a decent burial. Because they believed that wealth and income determined by the market should not govern access to necessities, they voted for the laws that established the welfare state.

"The citizens also adopted the philosophy that human labor is not a commodity. The price of labor should not, in principle, be determined by the laws of supply and demand that govern the price of eggs and the price of cheese, because humans are, unlike commodities, the very purpose and end of society. The market is an instrument, a means; the human is an end. Therefore minimum wages, worker rights, and collective bargaining were made the law of the land, and the principle that wages were not to be determined by the market was officially declared—for example in the Clayton Act and Wagner Act in the USA, in the Constitutions of Italy and the Federal Republic of Germany, and in the concepts stated by John Ruskin in Unto this Last, *which were endorsed by the Labour Party of Great Britain.*[28]

"Mindful that efficiency and democracy are not best served when collective ownership is extended to all of the means of production, the democracies opted for mixed economies, where a great variety of types of firms, some cooperative, some municipal, some non-profit, some small, some large, some public, some private, some employee-owned, some financed by debt, some supported by grants and subsidies, some supported by donations and bequests, some financed by equity, some financed by rents and royalties, and some financed mainly by retained earnings, performed a great variety of functions, all within the framework of the rule of law, which was the rule of democracy.

"Thus democracy hedged around the market with non-market principles: human rights, the welfare state, collective bargaining, and the regulation of business for the common good. Social democracy had its ups and downs, but, on the whole, it made satisfactory progress in the advanced nations in the decades immediately after World War II, and its ideals were also those of the developing nations, who hoped some day to enjoy social democracy too.

"Then something went wrong.

"Free market capitalism, which had been considered an obsolete nineteenth-century ideology, made a comeback. Public sectors were privatized. Real wages fell. Holes appeared in the social safety net. Homelessness exploded. Gangs of criminal youths, rejected by economies characterized by the perma-

nent unemployment of an underclass, roamed the streets of first world cities. And then, suddenly, in June and July of 2001, in Göteborg, Sweden, and Genoa, Italy, respectively, it was revealed that the citizens of first world countries could no longer count on their governments respecting the fundamental human rights of peaceful assembly and free speech. The third world had invaded the first world.

"Why did it happen? There were many causes, but fundamentally there were two. First, the corporations bought the governments. Money learned how to buy the technologies that shape public opinion, learning how to sell candidates, laws, and economic theories as it had previously learned how to sell soap and automobiles. Second, business made an end run around democracy. If capital could not get what it wanted from the voters, it would leave. By leaving and threatening to leave, capital taught the voters of the first world what the dictators of the third world had long known: you do not write laws to govern capital, you write laws to attract capital.

"The remedy follows from the diagnosis. Grassroots citizens' movements must take political power back from the corporations. Global democratic solidarity must counter global capitalism. The world needs worldwide standards for corporate behavior. It needs global labor solidarity. It needs international enforcement of human rights. Global democracy will leave capital with no place to go, and no alternative but to play the game according to fair rules. The measures taken in the best of the industrial democracies to hedge around the market with non-market ethical principles, must now be repeated on a global scale."

"P.S. The big story is illustrated with encouraging small anecdotes, like: jailed Indonesian labor leader is saved from torture and death, because of pressure brought by Japanese, U.S., and European unions; and like: Monsanto cancels its plans to sell seeds that do not reproduce, thus moving toward a monopoly of the genetic codes of life, because of pressure from a coalition of international non-governmental organizations."

We hope that this little story serves to bring to greater awareness ideas that many well-intentioned people hold half-consciously. It seems unnecessary to comment that the remedy proposed is not likely to work, at least not without some extra missing ingredient absent from the analysis and the prescription. It seems unnecessary to insist on the obvious, that it is wishful thinking to expect an expanded version of yesterday's strategies to replicate on a global scale the degree of democratic control over market forces that was achieved in the best of the social democracies after World War II.

We believe that the ideas we have expressed in our story are widely held, and that many people of good will are acting on them. Rather than criticize these people, we wish to focus on the missing ingredient that will make the ideals for which they are striving realizable. The missing ingredient that will make social democracy work is a love ethic.[29] The several forms it takes are that which we call "cultural resources."

III. Sources of Hope in the Age of Globalization

We are of the school of thought that regards the so-called Locational Revolution as a part of the history of capitalism. It is a continuation of tendencies capitalism has manifested since it began. We are also of the school of thought that says the same of the Industrial Revolution. Immanuel Wallerstein points out that it was not technical inventions that made the Industrial Revolution. It was the readiness of the market for the inventions. The steam engine, for example, had been invented before, and in several places. Only when commerce had a great need for what it could do, and not before, the steam engine transformed industry.[30] In general, the market drives technology more than technology drives the market.

If the Locational Revolution is conceived by analogy with the Industrial Revolution, then it should be observed that both happened when capitalism needed them. As David Harvey has shown, what is called "globalization" (which Harvey subsumes under the larger category "flexible accumulation") came about primarily because of the unsustainability of the Keynesian welfare state.[31] The social democracies were not working. They could no longer sustain their debt burdens, and they could not keep profits high enough to generate the growth needed to sustain full employment.

Contrary to the little story told above, it was not that the greedy corporations destroyed social democracies that were idyllic and would have remained idyllic if only the wrong people had not grabbed power. The system itself was in crisis. It was driven to lower wages, by going global and in other ways, by its inherent need to create profitable opportunities for capital accumulation. Globalization happened because capitalism—and the social democracies retained capitalism even while they ameliorated it and tried to transform it—at a certain stage of its history required it.

It follows that social democracy's strategy for coping with the Locational Revolution has to be a strategy for continuing its efforts to ameliorate and transform capitalism, under adverse conditions that result in part from the failure of the Keynesian welfare states that social democracy constructed. Globalization happened because social democracy did not work; and it is therefore misguided to think that the cure for globalization is either 1) to return to yesterday's national welfare states, or 2) to transpose yesterday's social democracy to a higher level by establishing the same model on a global scale.

It is crucial to remember also that the Keynesian welfare states, even at their best, even if they had proven to be sustainable (which they certainly did not) were able to deliver full employment and high wages *only* through ever increasing economic growth. They were systems that could only stabilize themselves by resorting to the processes that lead to insane consumerism and ecological disaster.

If a positive future for humanity means transforming capitalism in ways that hitherto existing democratic socialist movements have not been able to achieve, it must be asked why they failed even before globalization, as well as why the reforms they did achieve are being reversed by globalization. The theories that hold that the market, not the steam engine, created the Industrial Revolution, also imply views (sometimes called "circulationist") that show that socialism was misled by Karl Marx's distinction between the sphere of circulation and the sphere of production. Marx believed, and led many others to believe, that nothing of great consequence could be determined at the level of what he took to be the mere surface of society, the market, the exchange of commodities, the sphere of circulation. For change to be meaningful, it had to occur at a level he thought was deeper: the level of production. For Marx, the main motive forces of history were to be found in the technology of production, and in the ownership of the means of production.

Experience has shown what could have been demonstrated in theory even without experience (and what Jürgen Habermas actually did demonstrate in theory in a long footnote in *Knowledge and Human Interests*): that the contrary is true, that circulation controls production.[32]

Consequently, coping with capitalism, and transforming it, is primarily a matter of transforming the circulation of goods and services. It is phenomena at the level of circulation—markets, recession, depression, inflation, capital flight, the collapse of markets—that block the transformation of the ownership of the means of production into more ethical and sustainable forms. Mixed economies with substantial public sectors would have triumphed worldwide long ago had not market forces—i.e., phenomena of circulation—consistently undermined them.

Perhaps better put: it is the interface between circulation and production that is crucial. The general form of the problem of ethically constructing society is: How can we mobilize resources to meet needs, and do so sustainably? If circulation is defined as production for exchange, i.e., for sale, then the problems become: 1) How can we produce only for the market, in a way that meets needs sustainably? and 2) (the same problem stated differently) How can we organize processes consisting entirely of exchange to reliably serve the ends of use? The answer to both questions is: We cannot. The goals are simply not the same, even though they overlap. Even though it is true, as Adam Smith said, that the whole point of exchange is use, if we make exchange the end-in-itself, the *chose qu'on aime pour lui-meme*, we will, by definition, *never* make meeting needs sustainably the end in itself.

It follows that circulation should not be defined as exchange—i.e., as something that will occur only in order to realize the exchange-value of commodities. Circulation has to happen, i.e., people have to decide to do things that meet their own and others' needs, for reasons other than making a profit on the sale of the product. We have been calling these reasons for doing things in order to meet needs "cultural resources."

The concept of "cultural resources" is not meant to exclude meeting needs through markets, nor is it meant to exclude production for profit. It is meant to include them *as* cultural resources, among other cultural resources. What the concept is designed to exclude, however, is addiction to markets and profits, which makes a society so dependent on them that it lacks capacity for autonomy and integrity and ethical judgment because it is driven by forces beyond the control of conscience to get a fix to satisfy its uncontrollable dependency.

The idea of "cultural resources" is inclusive. It reflects a leap to a higher level of abstraction like those that Gaston Bachelard identifies with major breakthroughs in science.[33] As Einstein's physics is more general than Newton's, and recognizes Newton's as a special case, so "cultural resources" is a concept more general than "production for exchange," which is a particular kind of cultural resource. Continuing with the inventory of Indonesian cultural resources we began in the previous chapter, we offer the following further examples, starting with the fourth item in our list.[34]

4) Rice Stories

According to the ancient myths of Java, which were told and retold before Hindu and Buddhist ideas arrived from India, before the coming of Islam, before Christianity, and long before Economics, the first human beings cultivated rice. The *slametan*, the versatile ritual meal that is the traditional centerpiece of the spiritual life of the majority of Indonesians, features rice in several forms, as do Indonesian birth celebrations, circumcisions, weddings, and funerals. A wedding feast, for example, is likely to feature a layer of yellow rice on top of a layer of white rice, in each person's banana-leaf dish, the yellow rice standing for love and the white rice for purity.

The technocratic economic planning teams of the post-1945 Republic, in spite of their expensive training in western graduate schools, never even tried to subject rice, the sacred grain, to the impersonal forces of the market. Radius Prawiro, a key policy-maker, explains:

> So central is rice that it is conceptually interchangeable with "food." Rice is more than the basis of Indonesian agriculture, it is the centre of most important social intercourse. It is eaten for breakfast, lunch, and dinner. Typically, when people work together, it is over rice. When a serious communal conflict is resolved, reconciliation is frequently over rice. When they celebrate together, mourn together, or simply come together, as family and friends, rice is the constant that is at the centre of many daily human interactions, rituals, and rites of passage in Indonesia's traditional life. . . . For these reasons, whenever rice is

scarce, it is a profoundly troubling experience for Indonesians. It portends that the world, in some way, is falling apart.[35]

When Indonesia fell heir to the unexpected windfall of massive increases in oil revenues in the 1970s and 1980s, the dictator Suharto himself ordered the recycling of petrodollars to subsidize rice production. Huge sums were invested in new agricultural technologies, and, above all, huge sums were invested in producing fertilizers, which were distributed below cost to farmers. In 1985, Indonesia became self-sufficient in rice, an achievement that has kindled national pride ever since. General Suharto made a trip to Rome to receive a special award from the Food and Agriculture Organization of the United Nations.

Thus Indonesia hit on a sub-optimal but nevertheless roughly functional solution to one of the dilemmas posed by the Locational Revolution. Indonesian firms could export labor-intensive products at competitive prices by keeping Indonesian wages low. But the wages of Indonesian workers were not as low as they seemed, because workers were able to buy subsidized rice. They also enjoyed other subsidies. The rice subsidies expressed the principle that the rents paid by foreigners for the extraction of Indonesia's natural resources belonged to all the citizens of Indonesia. They should be spent to meet the basic needs of all citizens. Oil royalties bought fertilizers, which were distributed at bargain prices. Cheap fertilizers produced cheap rice for the people. A national agency, Bulog, has long been charged with assuring that there will always be enough rice for everybody. Prawiro states, "Bulog was deliberately created to distort the price mechanism for rice. It violated a basic economic tenet held dear by all the country's economic policymakers, that is, that the markets themselves should be free to set prices."[36]

Indonesian populists have been handicapped in their decades-long ideological tug-of-war with the IMF and allied agencies over subsidies. Selling rice for less than it costs to produce it is a no-no from the point of view of narrow-minded free market theory. Further, production costs for rice in Indonesia have been driven to above-market levels because an Integrated Pest Management policy has been adopted for ecological reasons, in place of using straight pesticides, which would be cheaper. Producing at higher-than-market costs and selling at lower-than-market prices is a double no-no. Further, any IMF economist can produce a mathematical proof that "Indonesia" (which we place in quotes because the word purports to name a unified entity that is not in fact unified) would be better off being less self-reliant, producing less rice for home consumption, exporting more and paying for imported rice with the profits from the increased exports. And, as if all these handicaps were not enough, those who argue for legitimate subsidies bear the burden of proving that the subsidies they advocate are different from corruption, and different from handing out government largesse to special interest groups. Nevertheless, in spite of all this ideological heavy artillery arrayed against them, Bulog and rice subsidies have survived.

In the decades long tug-of-war between the Indonesian populists, who pull for subsidies, and the IMF and its allies, who pull against them, rice stories weigh in on the side of the populists. The social status of rice, as fuel and symbol of life, is a cultural resource that mobilizes resources to meet needs.

5) Volunteering

One of the best examples of volunteering in Indonesia has been in family planning programs designed to slow the rate of population growth. Many thousands of volunteers have worked without pay, giving their time to share information and supplies, sister to sister, brother to brother.

6) The Pancasila Ideology

Since the first days of the Republic, Indonesia has had a five point official ideology, known as *Pancasila* or the "five principles." It has had a checkered career. Often it has been more a source of pretexts for suppressing independent thinking than a source of constructive ideas for solving problems. The five principles and their interpretation have been elaborated in voluminous writings. In brief English translation[37] they are:

   a) A belief in one supreme being.
   b) A just and civilized humanitarianism. Less literally: internationalism.
   c) The unity of Indonesia.
   d) A people led or governed by wise policies arrived at through a process of consultation and consensus.
   e) Social justice for all the Indonesian people.

7) Pre-Capitalist Forms of Cooperation and Sharing

The human species flourished on the planet earth for several hundred thousand years before capitalism. It invented innumerable ways to mobilize resources to meet needs. The surviving remnants of pre-capitalist practices and discourses can be regarded as the cultural equivalent of a gene pool, from which organizing codes can be drawn as needed to further improve modern improved varieties, and to make them disease-resistant.

For example, the anthropologist Clifford Geertz reports on the *seka*, a pre-capitalist institution found in the Indonesian province of Bali:

> The general organization of the Balinese village, and hence of its economy—for the two cannot be sharply differentiated—is perhaps best seen as a set of the overlapping and intersecting corporate associations the Balinese call *seka* (literally: "to be as one"; "to be unified"). A *seka* is a social group, formed on the basis of a single and exclusive criterion of membership, and dedicated to a particular and usually rather narrowly specified social end. . . . Every Balinese belongs to from three or four up to nearly a dozen of these groups, and the value of *seka* loyalty, putting the needs of one's group above one's own, is . . . a central value in Balinese social life. . . . [F]ield-crop cultivation is carried on within the general framework of a separate and independent *seka*-type organization specifically devoted to it and usually referred to in English as an "irrigation society." . . . The members of an irrigation society consist of all those individuals who own riceland which is irrigated from a single watercourse—a single dam and canal running from dam to fields.[38]

Geertz borrows from Karl Polanyi the term "embedded" to describe Balinese economic life as embedded in a network of social relations. But for Polanyi, the Christian democratic socialist, the "disembedding" of economics from society that happened in what he called "the great transformation," the emergence of modern society in which the market became a law unto itself, was in many ways unfortunate. The Notre Dame economists Charles Wilber and Kenneth Jameson, inspired by Polanyi, advocate a "moral economics" in which markets will be once again "re-embedded" into a framework of ethical values. Geertz, in contrast, sees the "embedded" economy of the *seka* as an obstacle to progress. Although Geertz may have changed his mind later in his career as an anthropologist, at the time he described the Balinese *seka* he was so convinced that Indonesia needed personalities similar to those of the protestant entrepreneurs Max Weber had described in *The Protestant Ethic and the Spirit of Capitalism* in order carry out "savings and investment" leading to "takeoff" as described by Walt Rostow in *The Stages of Economic Growth*, that he frankly advocated "disembedding" as a process that had to happen for the sake of Indonesia's "economic development."[39]

A philosophical regrinding of conceptual lenses makes it possible to see pre-capitalist forms of cooperation and sharing, like the Balinese *seka*, not as obstacles to progress but as cultural resources *for* progress.

Notes

1. Jeffrey A. Winters, *Power in Motion: Capital Mobility and the Indonesian State* (Ithaca, N.Y.: Cornell University Press, 1996).

2. The "race-to-the-bottom" thesis is a common one in the literature treating "globalization." See also, e.g., William Greider, *One World Ready or Not: The Manic Logic of Global Capitalism* (New York: Simon and Schuster, 1997); and Hans-Peter Martin and Harald Schumann, *The Global Trap: Globalization and the Assault on Democracy and Prosperity* (London: Zed Books, 1997).

3. For Mill's explication of the objections to the Method of Concomitant Variations, see John Stuart Mill, *The Logic of the Moral Sciences* (London: Gerald Duckworth & Co., 1987), 70-71.

4. Richard Robbins, *Global Problems and the Culture of Capitalism* (Boston: Allyn and Bacon, 1999), 110-11.

5. Winters uses the term "Locational Revolution" because he believes that the relative mobility of capital is becoming a better predictor of the interests and leverage of investors than is its nationality. According to Winters, the question is less whether capital is foreign or domestic than whether it is mobile or immobile. The "Locational Revolution" thus refers to the changes brought about when capital is able to shift locations quickly.

6. We do recognize, of course, that natural phenomena such as droughts can be a contributing cause to poverty. Those living in Timor, for example, have known droughts for centuries, and their language even includes terms for "big famine" and "little famine" brought about by droughts. Nevertheless, we believe that in most circumstances, human action—especially in the forms of technologies and a culture of solidarity—can substantially alleviate such problems.

7. Interview with General Ibnu Sutowo, quoted in Winters, *Power in Motion*, 84.

8. The Royal Swedish Academy of Sciences awarded Gary Becker the Nobel Prize in Economics in 1992 for "having extended the domain of microeconomic analysis to a wide range of human behaviour and interaction, including non-market behaviour." Becker universally applies the exchange paradigm to even the most intimate of human relationships, such as that between a nursing mother and child.

9. In his thorough study of historical materialism, Anthony Giddens argued that conceiving of history as economic class struggle was inadequate mainly because it underestimated the importance of political power, both in traditional class-divided societies and in modern societies where information, surveillance, and sophisticated means of violence confer power. Thus: "I think it fair to say that Marx anticipated fierce class struggles and dramatic processes of revolutionary change—in which he was not wrong—but not the appalling violence that has in fact characterized the present century." Anthony Giddens, *The Nation-State and Violence* (Volume 2 of *A Contemporary Critique of Historical Materialism*) (Berkeley: University of California Press, 1981), 3. In other works Giddens develops a theory of social structure that considers the interplay between constitutive rules and power. He elaborates on social structure as rules and resources, where control of resources is a major form of power, which is itself sometimes determined by rules. Anthony Giddens, *The Constitution of Society: outline of a theory of structuration* (Berkeley: University of California Press, 1984). For a critique of Giddens that argues that a focus on "relations" (as in Marx's *Verhaltnisse*) provides an even better way to

think about rules, social structure, and power, see Patomäki, *After International Relations*, 114-21.

10. Shell Oil denies that it has caused the environmental devastation in the Ogoni region of Nigeria, but years of oil-drilling and flaring gas have released millions of tons of methane and carbon dioxide and caused severe air pollution, and toxic by-products have contributed as well to soil and water pollution in this once fertile land. The ecological damage is beginning to manifest in a range of human health problems such as asthma, bronchitis, cancer, miscarriages, and skin diseases. All of these health problems have an incidence rate significantly higher in Nigeria's oil regions than in its non-oil regions. In addition, Shell Oil collaborated with the regime of Nigerian military dictator General Sani Abacha in the perpetration of other human rights abuses. In the late 1990s, human rights groups uncovered a memorandum written by a Nigerian military official stating: 'Shell operations still impossible unless ruthless military operations are undertaken for smooth economic activities to commence.' Quoted in David A. Love, "Shell Oil disregards human rights in Nigeria," *The Progressive*, 25 June 1998, 2. Fearing that local protests would interfere with its operations, Shell asked for assistance from the military dictatorship; Shell admits this. Human rights watchdog groups also indict Shell for failing to intervene on behalf of nine activists who were executed on trumped-up charges of murder. Activist-playwright Ken Saro-Wiwa and eight others had been pushing for the Ogoni people to receive a greater share of oil revenues and for Shell to clean up hundreds of spills throughout the Ogoni region. They were hanged in November 1995. The response of Shell Oil to most of these accusations is to hide for cover in the generous split between ethics and legality allowed by the constitutive rules. Shell asserts that it does not have legal responsibility over its Nigerian operations because it is a mere holding company, a conglomerate of independent subsidiaries and diversified investments. Love, "Shell Oil disregards human rights," 1-2. Lest the reader think that we are singling out Shell Oil, we can assure the reader that ChevronTexaco has also committed its share of bad acts in Nigeria (see below), and indeed, we are confident that corporations all over the world have committed and are continuing to commit misdeeds that are not strictly required by the structural mandates of capitalism. One of the best ways for interested readers to stay abreast of this issue is to read the reports issued in the journal *Multinational Monitor*.

11. The case is illustrated by recent events at the ChevronTexaco oil production terminal in the Niger Delta. The terminal, which is the size of 583 football fields, is protected by the company's private security force, as well as the Nigerian police, the paramilitary mobile police, the Nigerian Army, and the Nigerian Navy. It is also surrounded by barbed-wire fences and moatlike waterways, which are supposed to separate it and thus protect it from the surrounding community of tens of thousands of impoverished Nigerians. Still, in December 2002, hundreds of Nigerian women "commandeered a boat and infiltrated the terminal, fanning out across the docks and the airstrip, entering office buildings where Chevron managers worked and homes where they slept." The shock of the event drew a quick response from Chevron: "Word of the women's raid quickly spread from this remote village to London, where Chevron executives cut short a management meeting to rush to Nigeria." The women staged a peaceful occupation of the terminal for ten days, demanding that Chevron respond positively to their long list of grievances. It is the tremendous and visible disparities in wealth that primarily fueled their rage. Within the fences of the terminal, Chevron executives never want for electricity, air conditioning, or any of the expensive conveniences they provide themselves with the profits they derive from the extraction of Nigerian oil. Meanwhile, the residents of the

surrounding villages live in very spare conditions. Chevron hires very few of them (and nearly all of those hired are men) and pays its Nigerian employees quite meager amounts. Since the arrival of the U.S. companies in the 1960s, sources of employment for women have been reduced dramatically, and now prostitution is one of the few means of survival. The women also accused Chevron of allowing run-off to pollute and erode the creek that runs near a cemetery, threatening to destroy their burial grounds. Norimitsu Onishi, "As Oil Riches Flow, Poor Village Cries Out," *New York Times*, 22 Dec. 2002, 1, 14-15.

12. U.S. Space Command, "Vision for 2020," quoted in Carah Ong, "Ballistic Missile Defense: Shield or Sword," *Waging Peace: Newsletter of the Nuclear Age Peace Foundation* 11, no. 2 (Summer 2001): 6.

13. Jeremy Brecher, Tim Costello, and Brendan Smith, *Globalization from Below* (Cambridge, Mass.: South End Press, 2000).

14. Brecher, Costello, and Smith, *Globalization from Below*, x.

15. Brecher, Costello, and Smith, *Globalization from Below*, 35-36.

16. Gene Sharp, *The Politics of Nonviolent Action* (Boston: Porter Sargent, 1973).

17. Indeed, the authors of *Globalization from Below* write, "Social movements can be understood as the collective withdrawal of consent to established institutions. The movement against globalization from above can be understood as the withdrawal of consent from such globalization." Brecher, Costello, and Smith, *Globalization from Below*, 21.

18. Sharp, *Politics of Nonviolent Action*, 4.

19. Brecher, Costello, and Smith, *Globalization from Below*, 121, 120.

20. Brecher, Costello, and Smith, *Globalization from Below*, 113.

21. Barthes, *Mythologies*, 39. A longer statement of this notion can be found in "L'usager de la greve," in the 1957 French edition of *Mythologies* (Paris: Editions du Seuill).

22. Jeremy Brecher and Tim Costello, *Global Village or Global Pillage: Economic Reconstruction from the Bottom Up* (Boston: South End Press, 1994); Barbara Corcoran, *Strike!* (New York: Atheneum, 1983).

23. For refutations of mainstream economic theory, see Martin Hollis and Edward Nell, *Rational Economic Man* (London: Cambridge University Press, 1975); Amartya K. Sen, "Rational Fools: a Critique of the Behavioral Foundations of Economic Theory," *Philosophy and Public Affairs* 6 (1977): 317-44; Janos Kornai, *Anti-Equilibrium* (Amsterdam: North Holland Publishing Co., 1971); Charles K. Wilber and Kenneth Jameson, *An Inquiry into The Poverty of Economics* (Notre Dame: Notre Dame University Press, 1983); and Richards, *Understanding the Global Economy*.

24. Rene Descartes, *Discours de la Methode pour bien conduire la raison et chercher la verite dans les sciences* (Paris: Fayard, 1986), 16.

25. Richard Rorty, *Essays on Heidegger and others: Philosophical papers, Vol. 2* (Cambridge; New York; Port Chester; Melbourne; Sydney: Cambridge University Press, 1991), 155-57, 172. There were some exceptions among the ancients; they were, however, separated from Descartes by the intervening "Dark Ages."

26. Jean-Jacques Rousseau, *La Nouvelle Héloïse, Lettres de deux amants*, in *Oeuvres Completes, Vol. II* (Paris: Gallimard (Biblioteque de la Pleiade), 1961), 15.

27. Here we follow the ancient account of it given in the *Nichomachean Ethics*, which has now been updated and essentially confirmed by contemporary philosophies of human action and by cognitive-developmental psychology. Aristotle, *Nichomachean Ethics*, trans. Martin Ostwald (Indianapolis, Ind.: Bobbs-Merrill Educational Publishing, 1962).

28. On the influence of John Ruskin upon the Labour Party, John Rosenberg writes, "Clement Atlee, who was converted to socialism after reading the works of Ruskin and his disciple William Morris, dates the birth of the Labour Party in 1906, when twenty-nine independent Labourites were returned to the House of Commons; according to a questionnaire circulated among them, the book which most profoundly influenced their thought was *Unto this Last* [by Ruskin]." John D. Rosenberg, ed., *The Genius of John Ruskin: Selections from His Writings* (New York: George Braziller, 1963), 220.

29. For many the contrast between the minimal morality of private law and a love ethic appears as a contrast between scientific or formal law and attempts by legislators and judges to achieve substantive justice or solidarity. See, e.g., Roberto Mangabeira Unger, *Law in Modern Society: Toward a Criticism of Social Theory* (New York: The Free Press, 1976), 206-09.

30. Wallerstein, *Unthinking Social Science*, 41-50.

31. Harvey, *Condition of Postmodernity*.

32. See Habermas, *Knowledge and Human Interests*, footnote 14 to the third chapter. In his terminology, it is "social preconditions of production" that govern, more than they are governed by, "production relations."

33. Gaston Bachelard, *The New Scientific Spirit*, trans. Arthur Goldhammer (Boston: Beacon Press, 1984). On Gaston Bachelard, see also Mary McAllester Jones, *Gaston Bachelard, Subversive Humanist: Texts and Readings* (Madison, Wisc.; and London: University of Wisconsin Press, 1991), especially 39-60.

34. The list of examples starts with number four, because the first three items in this inventory were already given in Chapter 11.

35. Radius Prawiro, *Indonesia's Struggle for Economic Development* (Kuala Lumpur: Oxford University Press, 1998), 131-32.

36. Prawiro, *Indonesia's Struggle*, 133.

37. We are following the suggestions for translating the five *silas* into English given by Michael Morfit in "Pancasila Orthodoxy," a chapter in Colin MacAndrews, ed., *Central Government and Local Development in Indonesia* (Singapore: Oxford University Press, 1986).

38. Clifford Geertz, *Peddlers and Princes: Social Change and Economic Modernization in Two Indonesian Towns* (Chicago: The University of Chicago Press, 1963), 83-84, 90.

39. Walt Whitman Rostow, *The Stages of Economic Growth: A Noncommunist Manifesto* (New York: Cambridge University Press, 1990).

Chapter 13

Middle-Class Values

In our opinion, the major tragedies of the twentieth century happened not because of bad people but because of good people with limited understanding. We use the phrase "middle-class values" to describe the values of good people who do not understand the limitations of capitalism. Capitalism is a system and way of life that we believe to be seriously inadequate and incomplete. In this chapter we will share more of our views on the causes and cures of historical tragedies, of endemic violence and poverty.[1] We shall continue to draw our historical illustrations from the history of Indonesia.

The idea of "middle-class values" became a focal point for our musings about a year ago as a result of a conversation with the young principal of an elementary school in a small city in Indiana in the U.S. Midwest.[2] She lamented the disorderly conduct of some of her third graders, second graders, first graders, and even kindergartners. They had no interest in books, and would rather tear them up than learn to read them. They flew into uncontrollable rages and attacked other students and sometimes the teacher. They sometimes ran away, and sometimes they were found sneaking into someone's house to steal. They were shameless liars, sexually precocious, insolent and indolent—although sometimes they broke out crying and wailing, wanting to be comforted. She did not remember any children so difficult to deal with from her own school days, and took their presence in her school as a sign that society was deteriorating.

She identified the problem children with problem parents—drugs, alcoholism, single mothers with a series of boyfriends, fathers in jail, unsteady employment or none, wife-beating. The good children, on the other hand, took music lessons, played Little League baseball, did their homework. They wanted to please their teacher as they wanted to please their parents. They came from good, solid middle-class homes. They had middle-class values.

Somewhere, maybe in college, this young school principal had encountered somebody who had asserted that it was ethnocentric and undemocratic to believe that middle-class values are better than other values. Middle-class as opposed to what? The "others" who lack middle-class values are presumably those many people refer to as the lower class and the upper class, which we prefer to refer to as the working class and the leisure class. Whoever it was who had asserted that there was nothing special about the middle class was somebody she was eager to refute. "Middle-class values are just values that work," she said. "All children should learn middle-class values because that is what they need to succeed in life." She argued that it was the right and the duty of the schools to reinforce middle-class values in the children who already had them, and to instill them in children who did not have them yet.

Her philosophy neatly sidestepped the issue of race. African-Americans and the many Spanish-speaking immigrants now arriving in Indiana can never be White Anglo-Saxon Protestants, but they can be middle class. White Anglo-Saxon Protestants can be poor, or, even if they have middle-class incomes, they can fail to have middle-class values. By making class the issue, the principal made race irrelevant. At the same time, since the criterion was not class per se, but the values attributed to a class, she allowed for the possibility that even the poorest of the poor, and even the richest of the rich, could redeem themselves by adopting the solid, practical values of the middle class.

Introductory Philosophical Remarks

Having thus discovered the idea of "middle-class values" while doing anthropological research among the Hoosiers in central Indiana, Howard Richards asked himself whether this concept, which his informant found so persuasive and so vital, could open a path leading through Indonesian history to a general philosophy of social reality.

The general philosophy we have in mind is roughly this: Throughout the history of the human species, cultures have socialized the young to internalize conventional norms, also known as ethics, morals, values, rules, or customs. The norms have on the whole gradually improved over time in the sense that they have generally led to more functional behavior. We call this gradual process of improvement, "the ethical construction of social reality" (a phrase we also apply to the more conscious and less gradual improvement we believe is needed today). There was a break in the continuity of ethical development at the beginning of capitalism. Part of the break was the splitting off from ethics of economics. Economics became a realm regarded as quasi-nature, studied by a quasi-science. This split is a conceptual error. Economics is best regarded as part of ethics. Its subject matter consists of deliberate action guided by conventional norms. It is an error that has consequences for the progress of social democracy, which has been first slowed down and then reversed in the second half of the twentieth century by structural impediments which appear to be "human nature" or "economics" but which are in fact *cultural* structures. We regard the progress of social democracy as virtually equivalent to the progress of peace and justice. We believe that the further progress of social democracy would be facilitated by seeing through, as opposed to seeing with, economics.

"Middle-class values" appears to be a popular name for some important contemporary conventional norms. We believe that conventional norms are deep causes that explain historical events. We shall use the phrase "middle-class values" as a bridge to connect Indonesian history to a general philosophy of social change.

Basic Problems

First we will repeat, by restating in slightly different terms, some of the bold general claims that frame the context for this chapter.

> 1) Little can be accomplished in the construction of peace and social justice in the world without finding solutions to two fundamental problems:
>
>> a) How to pay high wages, given today's competitive global markets, given factor mobility, and given that worldwide labor supply greatly exceeds labor demand at nearly all skill levels; and
>>
>> b) How to provide access to the basic requirements of a decent life for the millions, nay billions, who are now excluded, lacking prosperity and security.
>
> 2) The above (1) must be accomplished simultaneously with a reorientation of the human relationship to the earth, from exploitation of nature to cooperation with nature.
>
> 3) The above (1 and 2) require new thinking. They cannot be accomplished by relying on the cure-all prescribed by Keynesian and mainstream economics, namely "growth"; nor by relying simply on shifting government budget priorities from armaments to social programs.
>
> 4) Conceptual reform is needed because mainstream social science is not now capable of showing how to accomplish the above (1, 2, and 3), not because it has not studied the problems long enough, and not for lack of data, but because its characteristic methods and worldviews are fundamentally flawed.
>
> 5) Nevertheless, the above (1, 2, 3, and 4) can be accomplished. There are no inherent obstacles in nature or in human nature that make it impossible to construct a sustainable world that works for everyone.

This chapter is intended as a contribution to the "conceptual reform" called for in (4) above. Perhaps it would be better to say, following Antonio Gramsci, "moral and intellectual reform," in order to emphasize that the concepts to be reformed are at once practical and theoretical. They are *idees-forces*, principles that guide action, normative structures, rules, ideas and ideals that shape practice. Following Gramsci again, one might call a move from "middle-class values" to "human values" a move from "common sense" to "good sense."

We suggest that when social science makes the post-Wittgensteinian move from mechanical models to rule-based normative understanding, the distinction between the social sciences and the humanities dissolves. The distinction between economic base and cultural superstructure disappears because the causal mechanisms economics uses to explain phenomena are seen to be pseudo-mechanisms made of rules.[3] Consequently, science rejoins the world of values. It rejoins the world of *les moeurs*, from which Descartes separated it, and to which Wilhelm Dilthey and many others have already sought to reconnect it.[4] Findings in the fields of religion, literature, philosophy, history, and art are then every whit as capable of being causal explanations of human behavior as findings in sociology, political science, economics, and psychology.

Historical events can be better explained if they are seen as largely caused by, and in any event conditioned by, conventional cultural norms. Some norms are more basic than others, in various senses of the word "basic," including the sense that a norm is basic when it governs the acquisition of the necessities of life, such as food. The critique of neoliberalism and the renewal of the progress of social democracy can be better accomplished if basic conventional norms (especially constitutive rules) are brought into focus under a bright light that makes it clear that there could be other, modified, and different norms.

The idea of ethical construction of social reality leads to a benign and optimistic philosophy. It agrees with Plato that knowledge of the good provides a motive to do the good. Evil results more from ignorance than from ill will. The disasters of the twentieth century—Hitler, Stalin, Pol Pot, the World Wars, the Great Depression of the 1930s, terrorism, and our other major disasters—were caused, in a reconstructed sense of the term "cause," by incomplete ethical construction. They were caused by failure to build a world that works for everybody without ecological damage. Tragedy is not inevitable. The disasters of the twentieth century need not be repeated.

We certainly do not mean to say that the ethical construction of social reality is easy, to be accomplished simply by correcting conceptual errors. It is the real work of the world. It is the slow and laborious improvement of human institutions.

We will be examining two tragedies that befell Indonesia in the second half of the twentieth century: 1) the dashing of hopes for social democracy in the first two decades after independence from the Dutch, culminating first in the abolition of democracy by President Sukarno, and second in a reign of terror marked by the mass murder of hundreds of thousands of Indonesians upon the fall of Sukarno; and 2) the ongoing intolerable poverty of the Indonesian masses, exacerbated by the economic collapse of 1997 and the subsequent economic stagnation.

A first reading the history of Indonesia in 1965-66 lends credence to a philosophical view that we hold to be false, namely the view that tragedy is inevitable. Reading about Indonesia during that period is like reading a Greek tragedy in which the tension that Sophocles packed into intimate relationships is magnified to grip a nation. It is also like reading about Chile in 1972-73 or Spain in 1937-38. Amid all the lies and confusion, amid everything accidental, there is an implacable military power in operation, which is stronger than anything else, which can—and when the time comes will—massacre the left. The military machine of the right wing is irresistible. Whatever the progressive and democratic forces say or do, whatever anybody says or does, there is going to be a bloodbath. There is going to be a reign of terror. The people who have joined and supported left-wing political parties and labor unions are going to be the victims.

Somewhat similarly, reading the history of Indonesia in 1997 is like reading the history of the bursting of any economic bubble. The biggest one was the worldwide depression of the 1930s. After 1997 Indonesia is like many other so-called depressed areas. All the elements required to establish a system for meeting human needs are there, but they do not come together to function. Unemployed people, unused resources, and unmet needs coexist in gridlock.

We will approach these topics in Indonesian history using "middle-class values" as a starting point.

More on Middle-Class Values

"Middle-class values" is a rich phrase with many connotations. We believe that the phrase can properly and usefully be applied to name great traditional and popular values East and West, in a truncated form that separates ethics from economics. The middle class needs and espouses the great values of which civilizations are built, but it also needs to adjust to capitalism and to live in it.[5] It accomplishes the required adjustment partly by regarding economic calculations as similar to physical calculations. Economists are commercial engineers. Business is nature. An accountant is a professional person in the same sense that a dentist is a professional person, although the accountant works with money and the dentist works with teeth.

If the ethical critique of economics is beyond the middle-class horizon as what it does not see, concern about base instincts getting out of hand is at center stage, as what it does see. The middle class is the class that is not vulgar. The idea of middle-class values thus brings into play the theory that civilization is built on the repression of instincts. This Freudian theory combines neatly with the Whig doctrine that the middle class is the civilizing element in political society. The middle class is, par excellence, the class that sublimates.

Freud deduced a brilliant theoretical insight from his humble empirical observation that poor people like to talk dirty. (He apparently did not make any observations of the poor people who join puritanical religions.) For Freud the proclivity he observed among members of the working class of Vienna to banter about sex and other forbidden subjects was a symptom of rebellion and rejection. The working classes reject the bargain society offers them. Society demands the repression and sublimation of the basic instincts (*Trieben*), especially sex. In return for hard work and clean living, society offers the joys and comforts of middle-class life.[6] "There is nothing in it for us," say the people in the working classes, and they opt for the direct satisfaction of instincts. Their speech reflects their rebellion, or, to update Freud's language to make it post-Foucauldian, their resistance.[7]

Building on Freud, our Hoosier informant, the young elementary school principal mentioned earlier, could have said that middle-class values are by definition pro-social, since they grow from the sublimation of instincts and the redirection of natural energies into channels prescribed by society. Working-class values, she could have argued, are anti-social because they express unsublimated instincts.

She could also have built on the thinking of Emile Durkheim to argue that leisure-class values are anti-social. Durkheim found that rich people suffered from the affliction of easy lives. They could become playboys, or playgirls. They are free of many of the limits that structure the lives of ordinary people. He called the social disease the rich were likely to suffer from "*anomie*," which is usually translated "normlessness," which we take to be roughly equivalent to being anti-social.[8]

Another, somewhat similar, experience in Indiana reinforced the salience of the theme of middle-class values. Again it was a matter of coping with the anti-social behavior of rebellious young people. The occasion was a planning meeting of a group of self-selected volunteers, who had come together to implement in an Indiana county what is called the "Assets" program. "Assets" is based on research painstakingly assembled at a Lutheran-sponsored thinktank in Minnesota called The Search Institute, and published in a book by Peter Benson entitled *All Kids are Our Kids: What Communities Must Do to Raise Caring and Responsible Children and Adolescents*.[9] The research team reduced what is known about the factors that are correlated with children turning out well (as measured by a series of indicators) to a list of forty "Assets" (for example, the availability of healthy forms of recreation). Children who live in families and towns that possess and provide the forty assets turn out well. Community action guided by these research findings is now underway in several hundred places across the United States and is being undertaken statewide in Kansas.

As Howard Richards sat in a high school cafeteria in Indiana with a volunteer group assembled to be "boosters" for "Assets" in their county, he asked himself, "Who are these people? Who are these people who voluntarily give their time and treasure for the good of the community?" As people introduced themselves one by one, and as he became better acquainted with them, he learned that almost all of them were members of mainline Protestant churches: Methodist, Presbyterian, Lutheran, Anglican, Baptist. A disproportionate number were related to law-enforcement officers. To the best of his knowledge, none of the boosters had high incomes or personal wealth. Nevertheless, in the event the group proved itself able to support its programs by mobilizing resources to meet needs—cash, volunteer time, use of equipment, use of space, donated food, and the like. The resources came from diverse sources—local government, local foundations, schools, individuals, churches, and local businesses.

The youth boosters displayed themes in U.S. culture that are analyzed in *Habits of the Heart*, a sociological study of America by Robert Bellah, et al.[10] Bellah and his co-authors find to be deeply ingrained in the United States values and "languages" like those of John Wesley, Jean Calvin, Martin Luther, *The Book of Common Prayer*, and Roger Williams. Well-remembered languages, which are older than today's prevailing idioms of business and therapy, are available to express sub-dominant alternative worldviews. They can nudge communities toward the practice of more cooperative and less individualistic norms.

The youth boosters were one of many groups we have known which have led us to ask the question, "If there is so much good will in the world, why is the world so messed up?" This book suggests an answer to that question: Because of conceptual errors.

Long before his recent close encounters with the middle-aged middle class in a mid-sized midwestern city, Richards learned in literature classes in school that in eighteenth-century England, the novels of Henry Fielding expressed the values of the traditional aristocratic ruling classes, while the values of the rising middle classes were expressed in the novels of Samuel Richardson. Richardson was born into a Whig and Protestant family in middling circumstances. Like Benjamin Franklin, he was apprenticed to a printer. Later he set up his own printing business. He prospered. He attributed his prosperity to hard work and strict rectitude. Although money could not buy him admittance to upper-class English society, he acquired his own circle of admirers among those who appreciated his literary talent and shared his values.

Richardson's literary works are all about marriage. The moral of his stories is that the reader should be punctiliously good in every way, if s/he wants to be rewarded by winning the hand in marriage of a being who is, also, punctiliously good in every way. The critic Samuel Johnson described Richardson's work as "placing the passions under the command of virtue."[11] The first volume of his *Pamela, or Virtue Rewarded* concludes with these memorable lines:

I will allow you two hundred pounds a year, which Longman shall constantly pay you, at fifty pounds per quarter, for your own use, and of which I expect no account; . . . . And, added the dear generous man, if this be pleasing to you, let it, since you say you want words, be signified by such a sweet kiss as you gave me yesterday. I hesitated not a moment to comply with these obliging terms, and threw my arms about his dear neck, though in the chariot, and blessed his goodness to me. But, indeed sir, said I, I cannot bear this generous treatment! He was pleased to say, Don't be uneasy, my dear, about these trifles: God has blessed me with a very good estate, and all of it in a prosperous condition, and generally well tenanted. I lay up money every year, and have, besides, large sums in government and other securities; so that you will find, what I have hitherto promised, is very short of that proportion of my substance, which, as my dearest wife, you have a right to.

In this sweet manner did we pass our time till evening, when the chariot brought us home; and then our supper succeeded in the same agreeable manner. And thus, in a rapturous circle, the time moves on; every hour bringing with it something more delightful than the past! Surely nobody was ever so blest as I![12]

Significantly, in the passage quoted, whether it was proper for a lady to kiss a gentleman in a chariot *was* an issue, while whether it was proper for the dear generous man to become wealthy by collecting rent and interest was *not* an issue.

Much water has passed under the bridge since the eighteenth century. Humanity has experienced the rise of consumer society, and then the spectacle society; the rise of the mass media and mass popular culture; the prosperity and then the decline of unionized labor and the middle masses; the rise and decline of Keynesian economics; and now neoliberalism, globalization, and the race to the bottom. Nevertheless, even today some of Richardson's eighteenth-century puritanical middle-class ideas live on in certain minds and hearts. Among them are the work ethic, and the idea that in the natural and just and normal course of events, those who are good are rewarded with prosperity, leadership positions in the community, and happy marriages.

We will now elaborate a bit more on the meaning of "middle-class values." We take the phrase to reflect a human universal: namely, the need to socialize youth to internalize the values of society, any society. More particularly, in the West, middle-class values are a modern version of ancient Western values, those of the tradition that was formed by synthesizing Greek, Roman, and Judeo-Christian ethics, and then transformed by the Protestant Reformation and the Catholic Counter-Reformation, and then transformed again by the Enlightenment. Middle-class values are adaptations of ancient religious ideals, philosophical ideals, and folk ideals to the practical needs of life in the new worlds created by capitalism. They are virtue truncated—truncated because they accept the economic structure of the world as it is now. It is a structure much different from the world as it was back in the ancient days when the ancient ideals were first formulated, and presumably also much different from the world as it will be in some future happy day when peace, economic justice, and a sustainable relationship to the environment are achieved. Middle-class values are the great values of the distant past: honesty, self-discipline, wisdom, courage, justice, faith, hope, charity—adjusted and modified to become the values of the most influential class in a society based on private property, money, and "free" (i.e., somewhat managed) markets.

Constitutive Rules and the Failure of Indonesian Social Democracy

Fifty years earlier than the described encounters in Indiana, and two hundred years later than the publication of Richardson's novels in England, in 1945, the Republic of Indonesia declared its independence. What the Republic began with was not, properly speaking, either capitalism or socialism. When the Dutch left, the capitalists left, and to the extent that they could, they took their capital with them. Indonesia as a newly independent nation emerged from the ravages of the Depression of the 1930s, the ravages of Japanese occupation in World War II, and the ravages of a prolonged struggle with the departing Dutch. What might be constructed from the shambles that remained was an open question.

We have been saying that an economy is a cultural structure. It follows that the project of building some sort of viable economy in the midst of the shambles that remained in Indonesia when the Dutch finally agreed to leave in 1949 was a project of cultural construction. The need for cultural construction was recognized, in its own way, by American social scientists funded by generous grants from the Rockefeller Foundation and the Ford Foundation, who sought to make comprehensive studies of what might be done by the young Indonesian Republic. They generally realized that middle-class values and capitalism go together. One does not function without the other. Capitalism needs honest and dependable people who will dutifully perform the roles of buyer and seller, employer and worker, investor and entrepreneur. Clifford Geertz, the lead anthropologist for the Indonesian teams of the Massachusetts Institute of Technology and the University of Chicago "new nations" research projects, arrived in Indonesia with the explicit purpose of studying the conventional norms operating in everyday life, in search of the cultural values required for economic takeoff. The result was a classic series of studies of everyday life in Indonesia during the early independence period.[13]

Geertz's conclusions were, on the whole, pessimistic. Disregarding the smaller ethnic groups, he classified the Muslim majority in three divisions: the *abangans*, the majority, who tended to mix Islam with older and looser spiritual traditions; the *santri*, more strict and businesslike; and the *priyayi*, the aristo-cratic and civil servant class, also inclined to syncretism, and especially inclined to estheticism. It was among the *santri* that Geertz found the best hope for the emergence of an Indonesian analogue of the Calvinist entrepreneurs, celebrated by Max Weber, whose middle-class values facilitated the rise of capitalism in Europe.[14]

Somewhat at cross purposes with the plans that the U.S. foundations and universities had for their country, the intellectuals and political leaders of newly independent Indonesia, did not want a capitalist takeoff at all, but rather an autochthonous version of social democracy. A synthesis of European social de-mocracy and Indonesian (mainly Javanese) cultural reality had been the ideal envisioned by Indonesia's nationalist intellectuals during their decades-long resistance struggle against Dutch colonialism, as is touchingly recounted in a series of historical novels set in the period, written by the great Indonesian nov-elist Pramoedya Ananta Toer.[15] Now, the promised time had come. Once liber-ated from the Dutch, it was time for Indonesians to realize the ideal.

The building of a uniquely Indonesian form of social democracy was the will of the Indonesian people after independence according to all available means of ascertaining the people's will—the results of the single free national election held in 1955, the platforms of the major and minor political parties, and the texts of the several draft constitutions that were composed and discussed. The early governments of the Republic actually made some progress toward social democracy, including setting up a vast system of cooperatives, and orga-nizing some major enterprises in the public sector. Parts of the private sector too made some progress after Independence, and in the years from 1950 to 1953 rice production increased by 22 percent.[16] But social democracy was not to be.

During the early days of independence in the early 1950s, under what is called the Old Order, Indonesia was favored with high export earnings because of the Korean War. Moderate leaders such as Mohammad Hatta and the social-ists grouped in the Indonesian Socialist Party (PSI) favored a version of social democracy that encouraged foreign investment and a strong private sector within a framework of long range national planning. As time went by, their efforts were frustrated, and they lost influence. With the confidence of the major foreign and domestic investors flagging, the shattered Indonesian economy remained shat-tered. President Sukarno's solidarity-building rhetoric tried to compensate for the cooling of standard profit motives by igniting the fires of traditional commu-nal values of *gotong royong* ("mutual aid"), and by fanning the flames of patri-otism. Efforts toward building solidarity, however, were dampened by ethnic rivalries and by every other kind of rivalry known to humankind. The stirring speeches of the president faded away into mists of illusion. In his 1960 Inde-pendence Day address President Sukarno declared to the nation:

> [F]or those who join in that mighty current of the Revolution, the dynamic of
> the Revolution becomes a Romanticism arousing a passionate spirit—drawing,

binding with spiritual longing, inspiring, fascinating. Frankly, I tell you: I belong to the group of people who are bound in spiritual longing by the romanticism of Revolution. I am inspired by it, I am fascinated by it, I am completely absorbed by it, I am crazed, I am obsessed by the romanticism of Revolution. And for this I give utter thanks to God who commands all nature![17]

Mass mobilizations of the dispossessed and occupations of land by squatters achieved paralysis, but did not achieve transformation. Efforts to implement a Lenin-style New Economic Policy that would harness old-fashioned profit incentives within the broad framework of socialist policy floundered in a morass of corruption. For example, when the government tried to incubate a new class of small entrepreneurs among the Malay majority (the *pribumi*) by granting them licenses and contracts, many of the *pribumi* simply turned around and assigned them to established ethnic Chinese entrepreneurs. They used political connections to derive a quick profit from government favors, without doing any work, and without starting any businesses. The Chinese, in turn, reportedly stashed their profits in foreign banks. When the bloodbath and reign of terror began in October of 1965, the Indonesian economy was, on the whole, still a shambles, back at Square One, where it had been when the Republic commenced.[18]

A focus on constitutive rules makes it easy to see why the newly independent Republic's attempt to build social democracy had to fail. It had to fail because it could neither generate enough investor confidence nor could it find any substitute to replace private investment for profit as a motivational system for mobilizing resources to meet needs. There was no way to stimulate and organize the pro-social functional behavior required to meet the needs of the people. Otherwise put, conventional behavior, governed by the main conventional norms operating in post-colonial Indonesia, would only mobilize resources to meet needs to the extent that the conventional expectation that a business would show a profit was satisfied. The rules set up the system in such a way that it either worked because people had confidence in it and decided to invest their talent and treasure, or else it did not work. Given that the rules were the rules, the only way to discourage the profit motive and simultaneously increase production and make distribution more equitable would have been to transform social conventions and personal motivational patterns. Given the utter impracticality of doing the latter rapidly, a practical solution might have been what moderates like Hatta had proposed in the beginning, to encourage normal profit incentives, while transforming society slowly, at a viable pace, carefully building on the cooperative traditions that already existed in Indonesia.

President Sukarno understood well enough that middle-class values could not be counted on to function in post-Independence Indonesia, and that even if they could, what he needed to build revolutionary socialism was not a limited and prudent virtue like that of a Whig middle class, but unity and solidarity, of the type he attributed to idealized native Indonesian traditions. He understood the problem well enough, but it was a problem he was unable to solve. It will never be known what might have happened if the Sukarno regime had enjoyed, instead of the hostility of Western governments, the unstinting largesse of Western foreign aid donors of the kind that poured forth soon after his fall. Nor will it be known what would have happened if a Communist coup had succeeded and been followed by a full-on effort to build an Indonesian command economy. No doubt if those or any number of other things had happened, there would have been a somewhat different story to tell. Nevertheless, in the context of what actually happened, the basic structure—the constitutive rules—of the system Sukarno was trying to transform made his strategy for transforming it unworkable.

Values and the Seizure of Power by the Indonesian Military Elite

Middle-class values, the conventional social norms conducive to the functioning of capitalism, cannot be regarded as the cause of Indonesia's inability to construct social democracy between 1945 and 1965, since we have the testimony of Geertz and others that such values were lacking. Nevertheless, our broader claim that historical tragedies are less due to bad people than to good people with limited understanding can be illustrated by the Sukarno epoch. *Gotong royong* and revolutionary romanticism, for example, do not count as middle-class values, but they do count as good intentions. It was a conceptual error to suppose that the political program associated with those good intentions was feasible.

The construction of capitalism in Indonesia commenced, or recommenced where the Dutch had left off, after a hiatus of several decades, when the military took over the government in 1965.[19] The soldiers were supported by mass demonstrations of university students. The citizenry had already lost its right to hold the government accountable by the ballot box, since President Sukarno had already, six years earlier, replaced democracy with a bogus "Guided Democracy."[20] He had arranged to have himself designated president for life. Many were more than happy to give up what little freedom they had left in exchange for the reforms they expected from the army. Indonesian capitalism was, nevertheless, a camouflaged capitalism, which remained, and still remains to this day, formally within the framework of the social democratic constitution of 1945.

The official story told by the Indonesian armed forces is that the downfall of Sukarno and the Old Order was precipitated when the Communists unsuccessfully attempted a coup d'etat, designed to eliminate anti-Communist military officers and clear the way for bringing Indonesia within the Communist orbit. One established fact is that in the early morning hours of September 30, 1965, six important anti-Communist generals were assassinated. Although it is probably impossible to know exactly what happened; although in the midst of chaos and violence, with almost everyone trying to deceive almost everyone else, with fortuitous accidents having great consequences, with no one sure of anyone else's intentions, it is doubtful that even the principal actors themselves knew exactly what they were doing and why; and although an early study by two Cornell scholars cast doubt on the army's official story; recent scholarship tends to confirm that the army's official story is substantially correct.[21] It is probably true that there was a leftist coup attempt, and it is probably true that it almost succeeded.

It was the social democrats themselves, the intellectuals in and around the Indonesian Socialist Party (*Partai Socialis Indonesia*, or PSI), who drew the logical conclusion that post-Sukarno Indonesia would have to embrace the capitalist logic of economic orthodoxy. The elections of 1955 had shown that the PSI had very little popular support, less than two percent. By the time Sukarno fell, the PSI had long been a part of the anti-Sukarno opposition. It had been banned. It had opposed Sukarno's abolition of democracy, his Jakarta-Peking axis in foreign policy, his refusal to grant any degree of autonomy to Indonesia's regions, and his declaration of war against Malaysia. Although small, the PSI continued to be important in university circles, often in conjunction with religiously oriented parties, Catholic and Muslim, with larger memberships.[22] It was from the milieu in and around the PSI that the non-party technocrats emerged, who would be the managers of Indonesia for three decades under General Suharto's New Order, and now, again, under Megawati.

While the blood was still wet on the corpses of the slain, General Nasution, the chief of the army (who had narrowly escaped assassination the morning of September 30, 1965, eluding his captors by jumping over a wall to seek refuge in the Iraqi Embassy), was instrumental in convening a seminar of economic experts at the University of Indonesia. Indonesia's president-to-be, General Suharto, also spoke at the seminar. Nasution, who took the lead in the army's formulation of an economic policy to "win the peace," was a somewhat puritanical *santri* Muslim, very politically astute, very highly regarded in military circles. It had long been his opinion, and for the most part the army's opinion, that politicians should leave economics alone. It had been Nasution's constant theme, as the spokesperson for the army at the highest levels of government, that civilian politicians should not meddle in internal military affairs. These were technical matters, to be decided by technical criteria. They were beyond the competence of the non-specialist. By a parity of reasoning, economics was another technical specialty, concerning which non-specialists should have neither voice nor vote.

The Indonesian military elite, and the civilian supporters who helped it to establish the New Order in 1965-66, embraced a value system that affirmed the core characteristics of western middle-class values. Truth, justice, goodness, and love were its ideals, as they are the ideals of most civilized people in most places. The people it declared to be its enemies—the Communists and the radical Muslims—it also declared to be enemies of truth, justice, goodness, and love. As the New Order took form over the years, it increasingly made its ideals concrete in the theory and practice of *pembangunan*, development. The army set out to modernize the country, and that meant to develop it.[23] *Pembangunan* was serious truth, measurable in concrete terms. More and more Indonesians came to enjoy the conveniences of modern life. It was a form of justice that brought real increases in the living standards of the poor, as contrasted with the empty promises of the Sukarno era. It was rice. It was schools. It was the promise and partial attainment of the good life enjoyed by the middle classes of the developed countries, as shown in Indonesia on television and in movies. It was patriotic and charitable love, the love of the country and its people.

The hypothesis that Suharto and the military and civilian elites supporting him really believed in the values they said they believed in, is supported by their plausibility. Almost thirty years of substantial, albeit limited, economic progress seemed to confirm that they were right to put *pembangunan* first, ahead of democracy and human rights. Virtue had to be truncated to fit the requirements of Indonesia's technocratic capitalist development model. Sound and serious economic science prescribed providing guarantees of political stability and guarantees of a docile workforce to attract investors. Therefore, middle-class values implied that good people supported autocracy.

So far we have been writing as if the middle-class values in New Order Indonesia after 1965 were similar to middle-class values in the West—solid, traditional virtues, adjusted to fit the requirements of capitalism. Yet we must offer reply to the many writers who portray Indonesian autocracy in the much different light provided by cultural diversity theories. For them the good burgers of Indonesia are not at all like the good burgers of the West. For them the constitutive rules that require stability and low wages to attract investment are not at all what explains New Order autocracy.

Cultural diversity explanations liken Sukarno and Suharto to traditional Javanese rulers who claimed to have—and were believed by their subjects to have—mystical power and divine authority. They point to consensus, deference to authority, and communalism as Javanese values that contradict western ideals of freedom. They conclude that democracy and human rights are unsuitable to the Indonesian temperament. The regimes of Sukarno and Suharto are explained psychologically, as responses to the deep need of the Indonesian soul to be dominated by an autocrat.[24] Our first response is that while the cultural diversity explanation might be somewhat plausible in the case of Sukarno, it is probably not plausible in the case of Suharto and definitely not so in the case of the three presidents after Suharto: Habibie, Wahid, and Megawati.

Our second response is to present a list of reasons why the cultural diversity explanation of Indonesian autocracy is not plausible, while the rules of capitalism explanation is plausible:

1) Indonesia's predominantly Muslim culture is not generically different from Western culture:

> a) Islam is a Western religion, not an Eastern one. Its heritage includes the Old Testament and New Testament, as well as the Qur'an.

> b) Islam shares with Christianity and Judaism the heritage of the Greek philosophers, who were read and commented on by Arab scholars before they were rediscovered by Europe.

> c) The classic ideals of "virtue" and "character" come from ancient Greece, and are the common heritage of Islam, Judaism, Christianity, and secular humanist traditions.

2) Today all over the world people watch the same television programs, see the same movies, and use the same Internet.

3) The advisers to Suharto, the alleged Javanese mystical ruler, were overwhelmingly either from the United States or trained in the United States.

4) Many Indonesians are Christian. Middle-class ethnic Chinese are especially likely to be Catholic and to be educated in Jesuit schools. What could be more Western than that?

5) For better or worse, U.S.-trained economic technocrats under Suharto succeeded in modernizing and monetizing the Indonesian countryside, thus destroying most of what was left of the traditional peasant cultures associated with subsistence economies.

6) Several scholars[25] find that there has been a progressive "santrification" of Indonesia, which suggests that the class of Muslims Geertz found to be most like the Protestant entrepreneurs of early capitalist Europe has been gaining influence.

7) If it were true, as the cultural diversity school claims, that the Indonesian people crave a Javanese king, who will rule over a "just and prosperous kingdom," then Indonesia would be back under dictatorial rule by now since more than four years of democracy have brought no prosperity. There is plenty of evidence that Indonesians treasure their freedom even in times of economic adversity.

8) Organizations that protest human rights abuses are as active in Indonesia as anywhere. Although there is evidence that during the New Order many were convinced by the argument that human rights violations were a necessary cost of economic progress, there is not a shred of evidence that the majority of the people of Indonesia do not want human rights.

We conclude that the ethical basis of Suharto's New Order dictatorship was mainly what General Suharto said it was: *pembangunan*. The function of the New Order's appeals to its conservative interpretation of *Pancasila* and to traditional anti-liberal values was more to keep wages down and labor disorganized than to promote Javanese mysticism for its own sake.

Middle-Class Values and the Crisis of Mainstream Economics

When the Indonesian economy collapsed in 1997, it revealed that middle-class values dwell in a house built on sand. The values and norms that constitute capitalist society conceal a yawning chasm. At their heart is the ever-present possibility that people may not buy. Since the value of anything is given by what it can be sold for, the value of anything falls when, for whatever reason, people do not want to buy it. The economic security of the middle class hangs by the fragile thread of human freedom. Whenever people choose not to buy what the middle classes have to sell, their assets become valueless. The constitutive rules of the system aim to produce stability, but instead they produce instability. They are designed for the ostensible purpose of guaranteeing security, but instead they produce an omnipresent insecurity. For those readers who think the collapse of the house of cards that was the Indonesian economy is a special case, not relevant to the future of wiser and more advanced nations, we remind them of what Karl Marx said to his German friends who complained that his research at the British Museum on the history of the English economy was not relevant to Germany: *De te fabula narratur* ("The story is about you.").[26]

Although we claim that the crash in 1997 in Indonesia is one of numerous historical tragedies that demonstrate that the very constitutive rules of commodity exchange make capitalism inherently unstable, we do not expect that mainstream economists will hear this claim, for our claim amounts to telling them that their science is based on fundamental conceptual errors. It amounts to asking them to shift paradigms.

As Thomas Kuhn recounts in *The Structure of Scientific Revolutions*, the Ptolemaic astronomers could not be refuted by empirical observations. They could always employ their theory to "explain" the facts without giving up their worldview, according to which the sun revolved around the earth.[27]

Today's most exasperating flat-earthers are the mainstream and neoliberal economists, who stubbornly refuse to recognize that mass unemployment, underemployment, marginalization, and poverty are structural features of the capitalist global economy. They make endless calculations about imperfect labor markets, as yesterday's flat-earthers made endless calculations about epicycles within epicycles to "explain" the movements of the planets among the stars.

The case of the collapse of the Indonesian economy in 1997 can be compared to the astronomical observations of Tycho Brahe in the late sixteenth century.[28] It would be hard to find a clearer empirical demonstration that mainstream economics proceeds from false premises. Nevertheless, as in Brahe's case four centuries earlier, ingenious ways of saving the theory from the facts may last well into another generation before it is finally acknowledged that the paradigm needs to shift.

Three circumstances combine to make Indonesia in 1997 an especially difficult case for economic orthodoxy to explain away. The first is that mainstream economics was imposed on Indonesia for thirty years by the all-powerful ABRI, the Indonesian armed forces. Dissenters were jailed, tortured, exiled, and killed. They were lucky if they were merely silenced. Economists can often explain away the failure of policies based on their recommendations with the excuse that politicians were unwilling to make the "hard choices" and "difficult decisions" required to please investors for fear of losing votes. They blame democracy. No such excuse was available in Indonesia in 1997. The hard choices were made by force.

Secondly, for the same thirty years, the Indonesian government had an open checkbook it could use to purchase the services of the best economists in the world. The heavy hitters in the academic literature were at its beck and call. Whatever Berkeley, Harvard, Oxford, or the World Bank knew, Indonesia knew. Sometimes mainstream economists can escape acknowledging that there are fundamental flaws in their discipline's characteristic methods and worldviews, by claiming that the paradigm is right, but it was wrongly implemented. They blame incompetence, or lack of sufficient technical expertise. That excuse was not available in Indonesia in 1997 either.

Third, the mainstream economists were surprised by the crash. Hal Hill, author of *The Indonesian Economy* and an editor of *The Bulletin of Indonesian Economic Studies* wrote: "I did not foresee the set of events which unfolded after mid-1997. It may be something of a consolation to observe that I am not aware of anyone else who did."[29] If economics were a science, it would be able to predict events, as well as to explain them after they happen. The fact that mainstream economics was caught off guard by events in Indonesia in 1997 is evidence that it is not a science.

Constitutive rules simplify the explanation of the crash at least as much as the heliocentric theory simplified astronomy. The basic rules of the game prescribe that people may choose to invest in Indonesia, or they may choose not to invest in Indonesia. Sooner or later, for whatever reason or reasons, or for no discernible reason, many people will simultaneously choose not to invest (or not to continue investments previously made). This simple explanation does not explain why 1997 was the year. It does, however, explain why crashes can be expected to happen. It explains that middle-class values, which are famously identified with the passion of the bourgeoisie for stability, are built on instability.

With 20/20 hindsight, embarrassed mainstream economists have written many articles and books that attempt treat explaining the debacle of Indonesia in 1997 as what Kuhn calls puzzle-solving within normal science, without altering their worldviews. We will not refute them. The ones that were written soon after the event have already been reviewed and refuted by Paul Burkett and Martin Hart-Landsberg in their excellent article, "East Asia and the Crisis in Development Theory."[30] We agree with Burkett and Hart-Landsberg that in 1997 orthodox economic theory did not just stumble. It fell. What we wish to add, however, is that when mainstream economics fell, Indonesian middle-class values fell with it. Many good virtuous citizens had reluctantly accepted police brutality against labor as unfortunate collateral damage. The physical repression of the working class, and the psychological repression of the conscience of the middle class, were moral sacrifices made for the sake of the greater good. The greater good was the scientific path to modernization and economic development chosen by General Suharto, the military elite, the technocrats, and the foreign advisers and donors. The economic stagnation of Indonesia since 1997 has demonstrated that the bloody moral bloody sacrifices made on the altar of *pembangunan* were made in vain. The devil did not keep his promises.

The death of *pembangunan* was not just the death of an economic theory. It was also the death of an ethics which was built around and which depended on an economic theory. The lessons to be drawn do not apply only to Indonesia. They apply to any technocracy anywhere that sets to one side its culture's traditional virtues of solidarity, drawing a bright line to separate the province of ethics from the province of economic science. The way forward is to refine and improve traditional cultures and modern institutions together. Separating economics from culture leads to a dead end. It leads to a dead end because at the heart of economics itself stand the constitutive rules of modern society. Cultural resources are needed to supplement them. Left to themselves, they allow (among other things) crashes like the Southeast Asian crash of 1997.

Burkett and Hart-Landsberg come out in favor of alternative, socialist development visions based on community empowerment and sustainability. Reading between the lines of their review and critique of the mainstream's attempts to explain away the collapse of an economy it had long lauded as its most exemplary tutee, one finds the implicit message that the time has come to acknowledge that Karl Marx was right after all. Capitalism really does have inherent contradictions. Not even the technical ingenuity of the world's most brilliant economists, backed by the irresistible force of ABRI, can make its contradictions go away. The next step, if the message of Burkett and Hart-Landsberg's subtext is correct, is to specifically identify the contradiction Marx long ago detected, the contradiction that ineluctably leads to instability. Our opinion is that the contradiction is, at bottom, that between exchange-value and use-value. (We could make this opinion more explicit by unpacking the idea of "exchange-value" to depict it as a proxy for the constitutive rules of the circulation of commodities.) Consequently, the solution to the contradiction is, in our opinion, for humanity to learn to produce goods and services for use, because they are needed.

In one sense middle-class values are the problem, because they are truncated values. Their ethical critique stops where economics begins. Their virtue contributes to the functioning of capitalism, but refrains from judging it. In another sense, middle-class values are the solution, because they are the modern representatives of the ancient ideals of virtue and good character, which can in principle by expanded and perfected to serve the good more effectively.

Summary and Conclusions

This chapter has essayed to trace a path through Indonesian history, leading to a general philosophy of social reality. As a bridge connecting the tragedies that have befallen Indonesia to a general philosophy of social change, it has employed the idea of "middle-class values."

"Middle-class values" is not a precise operationally defined concept. We hope, however, that what it lacks in precision, it makes up for in resonance, as an historically existing *idee force*, a normative structure, a source of principles and ideals that guide action. While its denotation is variable and expandable, it has acquired some significant characteristic connotations. Middle-class values are the values of children who want to please their teachers, who take music lessons, who prefer team sports to fighting. They are the values of people who sublimate their animal impulses to form what Freud called the *geistliche Schatzen* ("spiritual treasures") of civilization. They are the Whig values for which participation in politics is the practice of civic virtue. Middle-class values are contrasted with those of the riff raff, the drug addicts, the criminals; the Communist labor agitators, the radical Muslim terrorists; and the dissolute rich, including the entertainment celebrities whose scandalous lives fill the tabloids.

The closest we can come to defining the ideology of the middle class is to identify it with its blindness. What the middle class does not see is that certain conventional norms it dutifully follows—respect for private property, balancing the checkbook, keeping accurate financial accounts—are norms that exclude the poor. What is experienced as honest and correct by the middle class, is experienced as rejection and indifference by the dispossessed. It is precisely this rift between the haves and have-nots that enables profit-making, otherwise known as capital accumulation, to go forward smoothly. Property multiplies as profits, interest, and rent are reckoned to the accounts of property-owners; and are reinvested to yield still more profits. Nothing is reckoned to the accounts of the poor but the proceeds of the sale of their labor, and sometimes they cannot sell even that.[31] The formation of a set of middle-class values, such as those of Golkar, the state-sponsored political party that supplied a thin veneer of democratic legitimacy for Indonesia's New Order dictatorship, is the formation of a belief-system that shapes traditional virtues to support the existing model of capital accumulation. In Indonesia that model was *pembangunan*. Middle-class values were norms that made *pembangunan* work.

It remains to assess what, if anything, we have accomplished by weaving an account of Indonesian history around the theme of middle-class values. We might have discussed the failure to build social democracy; the fall of Sukarno and the ensuing genocide in Central and East Java, Bali, and Sumatra; the formation of the beliefs and values of the military and civilian elites of the New Order; the collapse of the economy in 1997 and the consequent fall of General Suharto and the New Order in 1998—all without mentioning the middle class. We might have made the point that the constitutive rules of society are deep causes of historical events without mentioning middle-class values.

We hope, however, that in offering the historical account in this manner, we have accomplished an advance toward demonstrating, or at least suggesting for the reader's consideration: a) that the normative structures just beyond the conceptual horizon, and therefore invisible, for the middle classes, are the same as the normative structures that are deep causes of the historical events that unfold in a capitalist world; b) that the values of the middle class are capable of transformation; and c) that transformation of values amounts to a change in conventional norms, which amounts to a change in social structure. Such a change can remove impediments to the solution of the Basic Problems stated at the beginning of this chapter, i.e., how to have high wages, how to include everyone in the benefits of society, how to live in harmony with the environment.

Points (a) (b) and (c) may be made clearer by further comments on the contradiction between use-value and exchange-value—a concept we introduced above in offering a structural explanation of why the Indonesian economy suddenly collapsed. We will use capital letters A, B, and C to make our respective comments on points (a) (b) and (c).

A) Adam Smith (from whom Karl Marx got the use-value/exchange-value distinction) was quite clear that the whole point of economic activity was use. The purpose, he said, was to provide the "necessaries, conveniences, and amusements of human life." Exchange was not an end in itself, but a means to an end. Smith believed that an invisible hand would guide exchange so that everybody's needs would be met. We now know that he was wrong. It should be acknowledged that he had the best of intentions: to harness the powerful motive of self-interest, and the immense efficiency made possible by the specialization of labor, to build a society in which everybody's needs would be met. Smith did not foresee a situation like the one in which Megawati's Indonesia finds itself today. He did not imagine that a government would be powerless to activate the economy because of a lack of sufficient numbers of people, with enough money and enough motivation, to make the investments-with-the-expectation-of-profit apparently required to sop up unemployment and get the economy going again.

There was never any fiendish grand design or conspiracy to create a world where governments are constrained in the policies they adopt by the overwhelming need to create a favorable environment for profit accumulation—and where they sometimes fail to do so in spite of their best efforts. Yet that is the way history has turned out, and that is the way the world is. The middle class does not see that there is an ethical issue here. It accepts the economy as quasi-natural and economics as quasi-science. The root of the problem and what the middle class does not see are one and the same.

B) The transformation of middle-class values is not mysterious or far-fetched. Use-value itself, the idea that something should be produced for use because it is needed, provides a viable growth point. It is a simple concept. The homeless need homes. The hungry need food. The sick need doctors, nurses, and hospital beds. Muslims and Christians, and everybody in one idiom or another, have inherited from the distant past the language of *zakat* and *agape*, which mean inclusion. The excluded, the rejected, ought to be included. Direct action to meet needs is a logical extension of existing values. It is also what is needed to overcome the constraint that hogties governments: namely, that they can find no way to meet the basic needs of their peoples without first establishing the conditions that will attract investment and create jobs.

By "direct action" we mean seeing a need and acting to meet the need. Direct action implements a "care ethic" as Carol Gilligan once defined "care ethic": i.e., "attending to and responding to needs."[32] It means volunteering, organizing charities, non-profit foundations, land trusts, cooperatives, self-help groups, intentional communities, government programs, labor union programs, worker-owned enterprises, family farms, farmers' markets, shared housing, mutual aid, municipal enterprises, traditional tribal forms of cooperation and sharing, faith-based communities, microcredit programs like the Grameen Bank, nonprofit hospitals and schools, access to tools for self-reliance, gleaning from the fields, sharing with neighbors . . . it means whatever works. Although the reason for using the phrase "direct action" is to say there are alternatives to meeting needs by creating the conditions under which capitalists will create jobs and produce commodities, direct action does not imply ruling out private business. Sometimes markets work well. Sometimes private ownership works well. In the situations where capitalism is working well, there is no need to fix it. The problem is to find ways to include and meet the needs of the billions for whom capitalism is not working well.

Thus, to quote from the title of Peter Benson's book, the goal of middle-class parents, namely to raise caring and responsible children, is in accord with the broader goal of building a caring and responsible economy.

C) Neoliberal economists will object that large amounts of direct action to mobilize resources to meet needs, based on the principle of use-value ("for people and not for profit") will "crowd out" private investment. To the extent that human needs are met by government programs, the nonprofit sector, and cooperatives, there are fewer opportunities for profit. Thus direct action interferes with the overriding imperative of neoliberal public policy: to create conditions favorable to capital accumulation. Much ink has been spilled to try to prove that the net result of "crowding out" is to do more harm than good. Here we are taking another point of view: a change in values, a care ethic, amounts to a change in social structure, which liberates government, labor, and everyone from the overriding imperative to create conditions favorable to capital accumulation. It is true that the neoliberal drive to privatize everything and to let markets determine all prices is frustrated by direct action, but that is only a negative result if one thinks that economic science has already discovered the definition of the ideal world, and that the definition is private property plus free markets. If one believes that democratic polities should be able to choose mixed economies, freed from the constraint of having to subordinate everything else to the imperative of attracting investors, then one sees the ideal differently. A better ideal would be a worldwide mosaic of cultures in harmony with nature, within which many different sets of norms mobilize resources to meet needs.

Neoliberals are wont to reply that history is over, that history has proven that only capitalism works, and that there is no empirical evidence that socialism works. We reply that any short list of the nations whose living standards are highest will show that a majority of them are nations which have had social democratic parties in power, either alone or in coalitions, for major parts of the second half of the twentieth century. We refer to the painstaking statistical work by Amartya Sen, Richard G. Wilkinson, and others, which has shown that, measured by objective standards, the most successful societies are the ones which have managed to reduce gross inequalities of wealth and income.[33] Limiting attention to the immediate vicinity of Indonesia, the three nearby societies that work the best appear to be Australia, New Zealand, and Singapore, all three of which can lay claim to being social democracies and welfare states, albeit with significant blemishes. We would add, furthermore, that throughout the world, even in the United States, wherever ordinary people have attained high wages, pensions, the rule of law in the workplace, health care, and education, it has been through the enactment of measures typical of the social democracies of Western Europe. What more empirical evidence do you want?

In our long and fascinating conversations with neoliberal economists, we sometimes suspect that they assume that there is no empirical evidence to support our views because it seems to them that a radical philosophical critique of the foundations of capitalism implies advocacy of something bizarre that has never been tried. Like a high-tech economy based entirely on barter. Or forcing everybody to live on rural communes. Because we write about unavoidable problems inherent in money, in freedom, in markets, in the profit motive, and in private property, some neoliberals apparently assume that we must advocate a society with no money, no freedom, no markets, no profit motive, and no private property. They accuse us of being hypocrites if we carry a wallet, shop in a store, or own a bicycle.

Our emphasis on the structural impediments to economic transformation is not meant to be an argument for something that has never existed and never could exist. Today social democracy is everywhere in retreat, and everywhere struggling to conserve its past achievements. Our focus on structural impediments is for the purpose of showing ways to overcome them. We wish to make a small contribution to piloting the democratic left through the current storms into smooth sailing that resumes social democracy's steady progress toward a world that works for everyone.

We regard the argument of this chapter as support for those promoters of middle-class values who are taking a step forward from the private to the public. They are encouraging people who aspire to be good in their private lives also to engage social issues constructively, from an ethical point of view. Psychologists and therapists, schoolteachers, preachers, and youth group leaders, who are showing young people and adults how to live value-centered lives, should have the courage of their convictions. They should dare to challenge the economists and the politicians. Economics and politics should be conceived as value-centered too, not just because such a concept would be edifying, but also because norms are the very stuff of which economic and political institutions are made.

Post-Script: Answer to an Objection

It can be objected that Indonesia under Suharto cannot be evidence for any claims about middle-class values because of the government's legendary levels of corruption. If honesty is one of the main middle-class values, then, one might argue, no account of events in Indonesia (under Suharto, or, perhaps, during any time period) explains anything about what happens in a society with middle-class values. Our reply to this objection is as follows.

As a preliminary, it should be noted that the relationship between mainstream economic theory and the kleptocratic character of the Indonesian government was different before and after the crash of 1997-98. Before the crash, a major reason given by foreign aid donors for supporting the technocrats was that the alternative was even more corruption. Clear technical reasons for policies, which kept policy-making out of politics, somewhat limited the opportunities for corruption. After the crash, the mainstream economics establishment had to explain why a nation that had been their star example of the benefits of following mainstream advice, had relapsed into economic paralysis. The high level of corruption then served as one of several post hoc explanations of the disaster.

Whichever spin is given to the corruption factor, it does not refute our claim that the failure of mainstream economic theory implies the failure of middle-class values. Although its middle-class values were sullied by flagrant dishonesty, Indonesia under Suharto did have middle-class values. We define middle-class values as the traditional and perennial virtues found in the main religious and philosophical traditions of humanity, truncated to subtract out economics as a quasi-natural realm where science replaces ethics. Middle-class values is an adaptation of ethics to modernity. In Indonesia that adaptation posited development as the supreme value, to which other values had to be sacrificed, and it posited mainstream economic theory as the science which prescribed the means to attain development.

When the science proved to be false, its associated ethics lost one of the essential premises from which it was deduced, and therefore it proved to be false as well.

It might be replied that the science did not after all prove to be false, precisely because the corruption factor explains its failure to predict as due to an oversight by mainstream economic theorists, who did not realize that corruption would wreck capitalism in Indonesia before the crash, but do realize it now. Admittedly the corruption factor, as well as some other post hoc explanations of the 1997-98 crash adduced by apologists for mainstream economics, introduces some fog into the proof that mainstream economics does not do what it purports to do, namely explain and predict the phenomena it studies. Conceivably the theory might be saved by regarding it as true again once it is patched up by taking corruption more completely into account.

But this sort of patching up is far-fetched. And whatever persuasive power it might have to lead the reader to think that our constitutive rules approach is wrong, and that mainstream economics is right (after it too is patched up) should be dispelled by the other case studies we present, of other nations, where the fog factors have been different, but the dilemmas of social democracy, given the constitutive rules of modern economic society, have been the same.

Notes

1. An earlier version of this chapter has previously been published in the journal of the Gandhi Peace Foundation, *Gandhi Marg* 24, no. 4 (January-March 2003): 389-400.

2. Although the conversation to which we refer was one that took place between Howard Richards and this particular principal, note that Joanna Swanger, while living in El Paso, Texas, in the Mexico-U.S. border region, has had numerous conversations that replicate this one in its basic contours. Indeed we are certain that many readers, particularly in the United States, will recognize this conversation as a familiar one.

3. See the detailed discussion of causal explanation in economics in Richards, *Understanding the Global Economy*.

4. Wilhelm Dilthey's epistemological stance is that presumed objectivity is a dream. We are all steeped in worldviews—*Weltanschauungen*—that form the basis for why we believe what we believe. He writes that although the natural and social sciences presume themselves valueless and ascribe to themselves and to the knowledge they produce a kind of metaphysical status, this is actually impossible. Knowledge must be grounded, and we must examine its context; it is here that values enter in. Wilhelm Dilthey, *Introduction to the Human Sciences: An Attempt to Lay a Foundation for the Study of Society and History*, trans. Ramon J. Betanzos (Detroit, Mich.: Wayne State University Press, 1988), 309-19. Dilthey writes, "It is inherent in the unity of human consciousness that experiences it contains are conditioned by the context in which they appear. From this ensues the *universal law of relativity which governs our experiences of external reality.*" Dilthey, *Introduction to the Human Sciences*, 309, italics in original.

5. Robert Putnam, professor of public policy at Harvard, is a leading advocate of what we are calling "middle-class values." See Robert Putnam, *Bowling Alone: The Collapse and Revival of American Community* (New York: Simon & Schuster, 2000). Putnam documents and deplores a decline in the United States of what he calls "social capital," which he defines as closely related to what others call "civic virtue," while calling attention to the fact that civic virtue is most powerful when embedded in a dense network of reciprocal social relations. Putnam, *Bowling Alone*, 19. "Social capital" is conceived by analogy with economic capital, and like middle-class values, is supposed to facilitate the smooth working of the economy without questioning its ethical foundations. See also, along similar lines, the works of William J. Bennett and of Stephen L. Carter. William J. Bennett, *The Book of Virtues: A Treasury of Great Moral Stories* (New York: Simon & Schuster, 2000), which uses the stories of Aesop, Charles Dickens, and William Shakespeare, among others, to virtues such as compassion, courage, honesty, friendship, and faith; and William J. Bennett, John J. DiIulio, Jr., and John P. Walters, *Body Count: Moral Poverty . . . and How to Win America's War Against Crime and Drugs* (New York: Simon & Schuster, 1996). Conservative commentator Bennett excoriates the erosion of values we are calling "middle-class values," and this erosion he attributes in large part to liberal social and economic policies that he considers misguided, the results of which, in his estimation, manifested most clearly in the social upheaval of the late 1960s and early 1970s, an historical epoch for which he has not a whit of nostalgia. Bennett and his co-authors write, "[W]e Americans now clearly place less value on what we owe others as a matter of moral obligation; less value on sacrifice as a moral good, on social conformity, respectability, and *observing the rules*; less value on correctness and restraint

in matters of physical pleasure and sexuality; and correspondingly greater value on things like self-expression, individualism, self-realization, and personal choice." Bennett, DiIulio, and Walters, *Body Count*, 197, emphasis added. Bennett has great faith, however, that "middle-class values" can be resurrected, which will be for the social and economic good of all. Of works by Stephen L. Carter, we draw the reader's attention to the following in particular: *Integrity* (New York: HarperPerennial, 1997); and *Civility: Manners, Morals, and the Etiquette of Democracy* (New York: HarperCollins, 1999). Carter's approach differs somewhat from those of Putnam and Bennett et al. in that he does recognize that the ethical improvement of economic relationships is part and parcel of ethical improvement generally. In the works cited, he states this frequently; however, he does not elaborate. Francis Fukuyama is explicit in making virtue a means to success in the competitive capitalist world economy. Francis Fukuyama, *Trust: The Social Virtues and the Creation of Prosperity* (New York: The Free Press, 1995), especially 43-48 and 349-62. There is indeed a vast literature consisting of empirical studies demonstrating a positive relationship between what we call "middle-class values" and economic success. See, e.g., Partha Desgupta and Ismail Serageldin, eds., *Social Capital and Poor Communities* (Washington, D.C.: World Bank, 2000). Similarly, theologian Hans Kung advocates improved ethical standards to facilitate the smooth functioning of global capitalism. Hans Kung, ed., *Yes to a Global Ethic* (New York: Continuum, 1996); and Parliament of the World's Religions, Karl-Josef Kuschel, and Hans Kung, eds., *A Global Ethic: The Declaration of the Parliament of the World's Religions* (New York: Continuum, 1994).

6. A tragic irony—one among many—is that the economic institutions that middle-class values falsely attribute to nature are themselves among the causes of behavior that the middle class typically deplores and which it ascribes to the working class. Friedrich Engels, with his publication of *The Condition of the Working Class in England* in 1844, was a pioneer in the study of what today are called cultures of poverty. See Steven Marcus, *Engels, Manchester, and the Working Class* (New York: Norton, 1985). We must emphasize, however, that the work of Engels stands apart from the widely discredited work of the modern founder of the "culture of poverty" thesis, Oscar Lewis. The work of Lewis is rightly criticized for failing to make any link between economic institutions and the cultures the author was observing and for failing to offer any kind of structural analysis whatsoever. The early research of Engels, in contrast, dramatically demonstrated links between economic structures and such behavioral patterns as lack of planning for the future, alcohol abuse, and sexual irresponsibility. Oscar Lewis, *La Vida: A Puerto Rican Family in the Culture of Poverty—San Juan and New York* (New York: Random House, 1966). For a critique of the work of Lewis, see Carmen Teresa Whalen, *From Puerto Rico to Philadelphia: Puerto Rican Workers and Postwar Economics* (Philadelphia: Temple University Press, 2001), especially 183-241.

7. See, e.g., Sigmund Freud, *Jokes and Their Relation to the Unconscious* (New York: Norton, 1960), 100, 110. Freud writes, "We can observe how men of a higher class are induced, when they are in the company of girls of an inferior class, to reduce their smutty jokes to the level of simple smut." Freud, *Jokes*, 101.

8. Durkheim writes, "Wealth . . . by the power it bestows, deceives us into believing that we depend on ourselves only. Reducing the resistance we encounter from objects, it suggests the possibility of unlimited success against them. The less limited one feels, the more intolerable all limitation appears. Not without reason, therefore, have so many religions dwelt on the advantages and moral value of poverty. Forcing us to constant self-discipline, it prepares us to accept collective discipline with equanimity, while wealth,

exalting the individual, may always arouse the spirit of rebellion which is the very source of immorality." Emile Durkheim, *Suicide, a study in sociology* (Glencoe, Ill.: Free Press, 1951), 254. Durkheim introduced the concept of "*anomie*" in his first work, *The Division of Labor in Society*, originally published in 1893. Durkheim regarded the state of "*anomie*" as having arisen from society's failure to allow sufficient contact between all of its members; this failure in turn arose because of the division of labor. It was not until his work on suicide, though, that the concept of anomie would begin to take on its eventual theoretical significance.

9. Peter L. Benson, *All Kids are Our Kids: What Communities Must Do to Raise Caring and Responsible Children and Adolescents* (San Francisco: Jossey-Bass, 1997).

10. Robert N. Bellah, Richard Madsen, William M. Sullivan, Ann Swidler, and Steven M. Tipton, *Habits of the Heart: Individualism and Commitment in American Life* (Berkeley; Los Angeles; London: University of California Press, 1985).

11. Samuel Johnson, quoted in the introduction by Leslie Stephen to *The Works of Samuel Richardson* (London: Henry Sotheran Co., 1933), xxviii.

12. Richardson, *The Works of Samuel Richardson*, Volume 1, 420.

13. See the works by Clifford Geertz: *The Religion of Java* (Glencoe, Illinois: Free Press, 1960); *Peddlers and Princes*; and, stretching back earlier to consider in more detail the heritage of Dutch colonialism, *Agricultural Involution*; and *The Social History of an Indonesian Town* (Cambridge, Mass.: MIT Press, 1965).

14. The *santri* are "pious or thorough-going Muslims." Herbert Feith and Lance Castles, eds., *Indonesian Political Thinking, 1945-1965* (Ithaca, N.Y.: Cornell University Press, 1970), 8.

15. See Pramoedya Ananta Toer, *The Fugitive* (New York: W. Morrow & Co., 1990); *Child of All Nations* (New York: W. Morrow & Co., 1993); and *House of Glass* (New York: W. Morrow & Co., 1996).

16. Pierre van der Eng, *Agricultural Growth in Indonesia: Productivity Change and Policy Impact since 1880* (New York: St. Martin's Press, 1996), 89, 134-35.

17. Sukarno, "The Dynamism of Revolution" (extract from the 1960 Independence Day message entitled "Like an Angel that Strikes from the Sky: The March of our Revolution"), reprinted in Feith and Castles, eds., *Indonesian Political Thinking*, 113.

18. Anne Booth and Peter McCawley, eds., *The Indonesian Economy during the Soeharto Era* (Kuala Lumpur; Oxford; New York; Melbourne: Oxford University Press, 1981), 1, 91-93. Booth and McCawley's study finds that by the mid-1960s, production and investment in most key sectors in Indonesia had declined since 1950. According to these authors, manufacturing accounted for less than 10 percent of Gross Domestic Product; budget deficits had reached 50 percent of total government expenditures; export earnings had slumped considerably; inflation had given way to hyperinflation; and in 1966, real per capita income was probably below that if 1938. Booth and McCawley, eds., *Indonesian Economy*, 1.

19. Readers interested in Indonesia's New Order period should see David Bourchier and Vedi Hadiz, eds., *Indonesian Politics and Society: A Reader* (London: Routledge, 2002); this authoritative work presents a comprehensive treatment of this period of Indonesian history based on primary documents.

20. "Guided Democracy" ("*Demokrasi Terpimpin*") was the official name for the political system that operated in Indonesia from 1959 to 1965. When he introduced the concept, President Sukarno contrasted this political system with the rather dry and empty interpretation of democracy as simply "one person—one vote." As outlined by Sukarno

in a speech in August 1959, the concept of "Guided Democracy" emphasizes that "a) every individual has the obligation of serving the *public* interest, serving society, serving the Nation, serving the State;" and "b) every individual has the right to a proper living in Society, the Nation and the State." President Sukarno, "The Rediscovery of Our Revolution," Speech delivered August 17, 1959, reprinted in Sukarno, *Toward Freedom and the Dignity of Man*, 58, emphasis in original. On Guided Democracy generally, see Baladas Ghoshal, *Indonesian Politics 1955-59: The Emergence of Guided Democracy* (Calcutta; New Delhi: K.P. Bagchi & Company, 1982). Ghoshal states that Guided Democracy could be characterized as the antithesis of liberal democracy; although meant to be a political philosophy based on the recognition that a just and prosperous society requires systematic guidance and planning, Indonesian Guided Democracy was suffocatingly paternalistic, if not dictatorial. Ghoshal, *Indonesian Politics*, vii, 230. In a similar vein, Adam Schwarz considers Guided Democracy reminiscent of Javanese feudalism. Schwarz, *Nation in Waiting*, 16.

21. Feith and Castles, eds., *Indonesian Political Thinking*, 17, 412-13; Schwarz, *Nation in Waiting*, 19. On the coup and its aftermath, see Harold Crouch, *The Army and Politics in Indonesia* (Ithaca, N.Y. and London: Cornell University Press, revised edition 1988).

22. M.C. Ricklefs, *A History of Modern Indonesia since c. 1200* (Houndmills, Basingstoke, Hampshire, U.K.: Palgrave, 2001), 304; Herbert Feith, *The Decline of Constitutional Democracy in Indonesia* (Ithaca, N.Y.: Cornell University Press, 1962), 129-31.

23. See, e.g., Booth and McCawley, eds., *Indonesian Economy*, 1-20.

24. See, e.g., Bernhard Dahm, *Sukarno and the Struggle for Indonesian Independence*, trans. Mary F. Somers (Ithaca, N.Y. and London: Cornell University Press, 1969). Dahm emphasizes Sukarno's deep-seated "Javanism," or his belief in a cyclical movement of history in which foreign colonial powers would be brought to their demise by the hand of *Ratu Adil* ("Just Savior"). In his Foreword to Dahm's study, Harry J. Benda notes that in the author's treatment, Javanism was also responsible for "Sukarno's inveterate tendency to combine, synthesize, and submerge divergent, even opposite, trends and groups into a spurious unity of his own making. Such disavowal of conflict, such eagerness to reduce opposites to a common denominator are deeply embedded in Javanese thought." Benda in Dahm, *Sukarno and the Struggle*, vii.

25. See, e.g., Greg Barton, "Islam in opposition? It's not that simple," *Inside Indonesia*, no. 52 (Oct.-Dec. 1997), 1-3; Bahtiar Effendy, *Islam and the State: The transformation of Islamic political ideas and practices in Indonesia* (Singapore: Institute of Southeast Asian Studies, 2002); and Donald Porter, *Managing Politics and Islam in Indonesia* (London: Routledge-Curzon, 2002). Barton discusses the growth of the mass-based Muslim organization Nahdatul Ulama (NU), popular especially among rural and working-class sectors of Indonesia, and Muhammadiyah, a Muslim mass organization comprising mostly urban and middle-class members. In late 1997 NU claimed a membership of more than 30 million and offered its members a grassroots, village-based system of traditional religious schools, or *pesantren*. Muhammadiyah, claiming tens of millions of members as of 1997, also has an elaborate network of social services, including schools, universities, hospitals, orphanages, and other charitable institutions. Effendy's work treats the formation of close to 200 new political parties in Indonesia following Suharto's departure; Islam provides the ideological basis for and the symbolism used by many of these parties. Porter offers an extensive analysis of the rise of these mass organizations and the ways

that the Indonesian government has tried to channel the "santrification" movement in directions other than opposition to the government.

26. Marx, *Capital*, 6. Marx writes that if the German reader "shrugs his shoulders at the condition of the English industrial and agricultural labourers, or in an optimistic fashion comforts himself with the thought that in Germany things are not nearly so bad; I must plainly tell him, '*De te fabula narratur*.'" In a post-Cold War "globalized" world in which capitalism is no longer impeded by spheres of socialism, lessons from all parts of the world have even more relevance to the audience in the rest of the world.

27. Thomas Kuhn, *The Structure of Scientific Revolutions* (Chicago: University of Chicago Press, 1970), 68-69, 154.

28. Although Copernicus elaborated proof for a heliocentric system in 1543, the preferred worldview during the lifetime of Danish astronomer Tycho Brahe (1546-1601) remained the Aristotelian-Ptolemaic geocentric system. According to the geocentric worldview, the Earth was the center of the universe, and the moon, sun, and planets were attached to crystal spheres that revolved around the Earth, with all motions being perfectly circular; the phenomenon of gravitation applied to the Earth only and was held to be a manifestation of things in the universe seeking their rightful place. The planetary motions as observed by Tycho Brahe did not appear to fit with the geocentric worldview; nevertheless, although his observations could have been explained through use of the Copernican model, Tycho Brahe held fast to his earlier worldview and merely devised his own system that would not have to depart from this worldview in order to incorporate the facts. According to his new system, the Earth remained in the center of the universe, but there were no crystal spheres, and some of the planets were allowed to orbit the sun rather than the Earth.

29. Hill, *The Indonesian Economy*, xiv.

30. Paul Burkett and Martin Hart-Landsberg, "East Asia and the Crisis in Development Theory," *Journal of Contemporary Asia* 28, no. 4 (1998): 435-56.

31. On the specific question of the social costs of the accounting system as currently devised, see the following works by Ralph W. Estes: *Accounting and Society* (Los Angeles: Melville Publishing Co., 1973); and *Tyranny of the Bottom Line: Why Corporations Make Good People Do Bad Things* (San Francisco: Berrett-Koehler Publishers; Emeryville, Calif.: Publishers Group West, 1996).

32. Dr. Gilligan gave this particular definition of "care ethic" in a lecture Howard Richards attended at the Ontario Institute for Studies in Education at the University of Toronto; unfortunately, he does not recall the date or the title of the event. In her well-known *In a Different Voice*, Gilligan refers to the "care ethic" as resting on "the vision that everyone will be responded to and included, that no one will be left alone or hurt." Gilligan, *In a Different Voice*, 63. Throughout *In a Different Voice*, Gilligan relates an ethic of care to a network or web of relationships—as opposed to hierarchy.

33. Amartya K. Sen, *On Economic Inequality* (Oxford: Clarendon Press, 1997); Richard G. Wilkinson, *Unhealthy Societies: the Afflictions of Inequality* (London: Routledge, 1996).

Chapter 14

The Venezuela That Might Have Been

This chapter will suggest, and seek to put on the agenda for further discussion, a way to advance the construction of social democracy. It would have been especially effective in Venezuela in the middle of the 1970s, when that country enjoyed a bonanza in oil revenue. Like Norway, Venezuela has had unusual opportunities to build social democracy because of oil. No matter how much international competition pushes wages down, rents derived from the extraction of a natural resource, in this case oil, are still available to subsidize social improvements. Much depends on which improvements are deemed to be worthy of being subsidized. Budget becomes philosophy.[1]

Based on the same ideas advanced in other chapters, we will propose an answer to the question concerning what most deserves to be subsidized. Borrowing a phrase from Ernest Mandel, we will call our suggestion "subsidizing progressive de-alienation." It could also be regarded as an augmentation and improvement of the idea of "integrated development."[2]

To make "subsidizing progressive de-alienation" plausible we will again try to facilitate a conceptual shift toward thinking of society in terms of cultural structures. We will be comparing de-alienation to other social change strategies on the basis of the ways they address both production and circulation. De-alienation differs from most other social change strategies in that it changes the control of the means of production and the norms that govern circulation (the distribution of goods and services) simultaneously, rather than one before the other. With the process of de-alienation, ownership and the market change together. (Hence "integrated development.") The conceptual shift toward seeing conventional cultural norms as causes of historical events will contribute to showing why such an integrated strategy for change is both necessary and possible.

We have been insisting that there is no way for social democracy to avoid dealing with the radical critiques of capitalism made by Karl Marx and others.

315

Poverty, and therefore violence, are simply not going to go away until the contradictions of commodity exchange as a way of life are successfully resolved.
One name, perhaps the best name, for these fundamental contradictions is
"alienation." "Subsidizing progressive de-alienation" is therefore intended as a
name for a practical way to deal with and overcome the systemic obstacles to
change that radical critiques expose.

Some Practical Conclusions Drawn From
Radical Critiques of Capitalism

Since we will be endorsing a practical approach to social change that follows
logically from a radical critique of capitalism, it is helpful to begin by reviewing
briefly some of the main practical conclusions that others have drawn from radical social analysis. This review does not bear directly on our constructive argument, which will take the form of an outline of a version of a concept of alienation, from which practical ideas concerning what to do to achieve de-alienation
will follow. We review briefly other practical programs derived from radical
critiques of the basic structure of the global capitalist system mainly because
people who advocate them sometimes think that the view they hold is obviously
correct. By pointing out that it is only one view among an array of possibilities,
we hope to encourage the consideration of alternatives, and, specifically, the sort
of alternative we are naming "subsidizing progressive de-alienation."

"Social democracy" is sometimes excluded from the list of programs derived from radical social analysis, and defined as a confession that democratic
governments cannot transform society. Social democracy is identified with accepting the anti-revolutionary practical conclusion that the best a "socialist" or
"labor" government can do is to successfully manage capitalism. At most, a social democratic party in power cuts a better deal for workers than a frankly conservative government would cut.[3] Such a surrender of socialist ideals is often attributed (understandably but mistakenly) to AD, *Acción Democrática*, which is a
member of the Socialist International and which has been the largest party in
Venezuela most of the time since the inception of that country's democratic period began after the fall of the Pérez Jimenez dictatorship in 1958.[4]

"Democratic socialism," in contrast, is a phrase sometimes reserved to
name the movements that still aspire to achieve radical social transformation by
democratic means. In Venezuela this term more or less describes MAS,
Movimiento al Socialismo, the largest of Venezuela's small parties and the one
that has had the most influence among students and in the universities during the
democratic period.[5]

The social democrats are commonly said to have either forgotten entirely
Marx's radical analysis which calls for a de-alienated society, in which the purpose of producing goods and services would be to meet human needs, or else to

have given up any pretense of trying to create such a society, relegating the memory of movements for social transformation to the dusty shelves of historical nostalgia. Democratic socialists keep alive the ideal, but they are commonly said to be a minority who have never had power and never will.

We are opting to use the phrase "social democracy" generically, not distinguishing it from "democratic socialism," seeking to keep alive the ideals that presided over the origins of both in the nineteenth century.[6] We will argue that even AD, and even COPEI (*Comité de Organización Política Electoral Independiente*), Venezuela's Christian Democratic Party, are heirs to intellectual traditions that contain the seeds of real change.[7]

Among those who, unlike AD and COPEI, are less often accused of having simply abandoned radical social analysis and accepted capitalism, one might list the following:

Those for whom radicalism implies violence. It is supposed that if one believes that one social class has power over the means of production, and another does not, then, given that "no social class has ever given up power voluntarily" the only way to achieve the fulfillment of the founding ideals of social democracy is by force. In Venezuela such ideas have sometimes been associated with the concept that it is fruitless for the working class to form anti-imperialist electoral alliances with a national bourgeoisie, in part because according to the argument, no national bourgeoisie exists. Venezuela is thoroughly integrated into the global capitalist system.[8]

Those for whom radicalism implies class-identification with workers and/or the marginalized unemployed or underemployed. The measure of radicalism becomes the extent of commitment to solidarity with the victims of the system. Sometimes too, such "radicals" are those particularly unwilling to form alliances or to compromise.[9]

Those for whom radicalism is mainly anti-imperialism. It is supposed that at this stage in history, the CIA, the American military machine, and the transnational businesses it protects, are the concrete embodiments of global class rule. The political goals of the impoverished masses become identified with the goals of third world nationalism.

Opponents of modernity. Radicals are identified, (often actually more by their critics than by themselves) with admiration for pre-capitalist and non-capitalist cultures. They are supposed to desire complete, rather than partial, abolition of the characteristic institutions of modern society.

Those for whom radicalism is an academic stance. Intellectuals may be concerned to demonstrate that class analysis has more explanatory power than mainstream social science, or that critical pedagogy is a superior way to help students make sense of the world.

What Really Follows from a Radical Critique of Capitalism

The above short list of practical conclusions drawn from radical social analysis omits some radicals, describes others more than once, and describes nobody perfectly. Whatever else might be said about radical social analysis, we believe that it must be said that its premises are true. It is certainly true, for example, that there are obstacles preventing the elimination of poverty that are systemic, or, to use another term, "structural." It is also certainly true that in a world where technology is capable of meeting everybody's basic needs, the achievement of a world that works for everybody without ecological damage is frustrated by the most basic conventional norms that govern life under capitalism. An economic system whose motivating dynamic is the accumulation of capital is inherently unstable and unjust.

Although Karl Marx was among those who called attention to the inherent instability and injustice of capitalism, some of his further characterizations of the nature of its contradictions are inaccurate and misleading. It is true that in a world where every firm makes investments in the expectation of profit, every firm operates on the expectation that its receivables will exceed its payables. Since one firm's receivable is necessarily another firm's payable, however, it is impossible for all firms to have more receivables than payables. The instability inherent in the impossibility of satisfying the accounting expectations that move economic activity is a reflection of a more general problem. The constitutive rules of the system are such that satisfying human needs, the quest for "value in use," as Adam Smith called it, does not in itself mobilize resources to get economic activity going. Actors are free to act to meet the needs of others or not, and they may or may not choose to do so.

Although these facts that Marx pointed out, or at least alluded to, are true, his claim that production relations determine distribution relations is only half true. The other half of the truth is that distribution relations determine production relations. Further, it is not true, as Joan Robinson and others have shown, that Marx discovered the secret of profit making by using the labor theory of value to demonstrate that all profit comes from the exploitation of workers. Venezuela is a good example showing that Robinson is right and Marx is wrong on this point.[10] Virtually all of the nation's discretionary income comes from the oil industry, which employs only two percent of the workforce. Far from being the exploited two percent, from whom surplus value is appropriated to create the nation's wealth, the two percent are privileged inhabitants of the *país petrolero* surrounded by many underprivileged inhabitants of the rest of the country, sometimes called the *país nacional*. Most oil revenue is rent derived from owning a natural resource, not surplus value derived from the exploitation of the workers who extract the petroleum.

If one regards the core of the problem as "alienation," and the core of the solution as "de-alienation," then it is possible to see how social democracy can solve the problems that structural obstacles make it hard to solve—while agreeing with Karl Popper that the only legitimate use of violence is to use it to defend democracy and the rule of law, i.e., to defend nonviolence; while promoting a program of social peace, justice, and sustainability that actually serves the long-term best interests of the rich, even though the principal impetus for it can be expected to come from the poor, who would be its principal beneficiaries; while identifying the world's principal problems as systemic (as caused, as Emile Durkheim would say, by institutions in which conventional roles persist while the persons who fill them come and go)[11] without blaming the problems on CIA agents, Americans, managers of corporations, military officers, terrorists, or any other persons or groups of persons; and while appreciating without exaggerating the positive contributions of religions and other pre-modern and non-modern belief systems.

What actually follows from a radical analysis is that society ought to be changed. The most valid conclusion to draw is an ethical one. Needs, by definition, ought to be met. Therefore, poverty ought to be eradicated. The systemic and structural obstacles that prevent the eradication of poverty (or, to be more precise, permit it only under unusual circumstances such as those prevailing in Western Europe right after World War II, or in unusual locations such as Singapore) should be removed. Those obstacles are, as we have sought to demonstrate in these chapters, conventional norms. Cultural norms are the stuff to be transformed. In Aristotelian and biblical terms, they are the *hyle* to undergo *metanoia*.

Radical critiques of modern society could be made, as Martin Heidegger and many others have made them, starting with Greek philosophy; or like Jacques Maritain and Emmanuel Mounier, one could start with medieval philosophy; or with one or another non-western philosophy. One could start with ecology or with theology, or with Paulo Freire's (or another's) theory of education.[12] However, we do not believe that anybody has done a better job of analyzing the shortcomings of the basic cultural structures that govern modern society than Karl Marx. Our starting point will draw from and build upon his concept of "alienation" (*Entfremdung*). Later in this chapter we will also draw upon the ideas of a Venezuelan writer whose tradition is that of Christian humanism.

The Concept of Alienation

Marx wrote:

> The product appropriated by the capitalist is a use-value, as yarn, for example, or boots. But, although boots are, in one sense, the basis of all social progress,

and our capitalist is a decided "progressist," yet he does not manufacture boots for their own sake. Use-value is, by no means, the thing *qu'on aime pour lui-meme* in the production of commodities. Use-values are only produced by capitalists, because, and in so far as, they are the material substratum, the depositaries of exchange-value. Our capitalist has two decided objects in view: in the first place, he wants to produce a use-value that has a value in exchange, that is to say, an article destined to be sold, a commodity; and, secondly, he desires to produce a commodity whose value shall be greater than the sum of the values of the commodities used in production, that is, of the means of production and the labour power, that he purchased with his good money in the open market. His aim is to produce not only a use-value, but value; not only value, but at the same time surplus value.[13]

Concerning this passage from Marx, we would like to make four observations.

First, at the risk of making it appear that our guiding aim is to determine exactly what Marx meant, rather than, as is in fact the case, to use cultural resources drawn from Marxist traditions to improve society, we would like to observe that the passage quoted is not unusual or isolated. It is representative of many similar and related passages found throughout Marx's writings. It is from *Capital*, one of Marx's later works. It is from the first volume, edited by Marx himself and not prepared for publication by Friedrich Engels or Karl Kautsky. It cannot be dismissed as expressing an opinion of the young Marx, which the mature Marx outgrew. It was not written by the person Althusserians call the pre-Marxist Marx, the Marx not yet sufficiently freed from the illusions of bourgeois ideology to be a Marxist.[14]

Second, the passage quoted is about alienation even though the word "alienation" does not appear in it. As Bertell Ollman has shown, the key social relations that Marx describes define and imply each other.[15] The social reality Marx describes in the passage quoted is the same social reality that appears, when regarded from another perspective, or with a focus on another facet, as "alienation."

Third, the quoted passage implies, as several commentators have already noticed and many commentators have deliberately and sometimes elaborately not noticed, that working to meet human needs ought to be the *chose qu'on aime pour lui-meme*, the goal. In Plato's terms, people having boots to wear is the *agathon*, the good, at which the *techne*, the craft, of the boot-maker aims. Use-value is the true, the ethically valid, aim of economic activity. Gandhi was right: life ought to be regarded as a series of opportunities to serve others; property ownership ought to be stewardship. Thrasymachus, Callicles, Gorgias, and all of Socrates' interlocutors who advocated selfishness, the maximization of private pleasures, and practicing as much injustice as one can get away with, were wrong. Of course, Adam Smith, who was himself a supporter of using use-value as a measuring stick to evaluate economic institutions, was also right when he pointed out that love for other people is often a weaker and less reliable motive than self-interest. Although working to meet the needs of others is what people should do, it is frequently not what they do do. Political economy therefore wisely advises policies that encourage the natural tendency to truck or barter, through which each person gives up something unwanted, or less wanted, in exchange for something wanted, or more wanted. When a market works well, it rewards people for acting as they should act, namely, for acting in ways that make other people happy. But Smith's policies are wise precisely *because*, and *in so far as*, they deliver the boots: dry boots to keep the children from catching cold and flu on rainy days, warm boots to keep grandma's feet from freezing in the snowy Andes, work boots for fisherfolk, elegant boots for parades and ceremonial dances.[16]

Fourth, Marx accurately represents the problem as that of a society organized in such a way that making the things people need, so that they can use them, is not the purpose of human effort. Instead, the purpose of human effort in such a poorly organized society is the accumulation of money. Producing and distributing what is needed is not the *chose qu'on aime pour lui-meme*, although it should be.

Alienation as Separation

The connection between the basic conventional norms, or constitutive rules, which frame and define capitalism, as Marx elaborates upon them in *Capital*, and the term "alienation," which Marx uses in *Capital*, but discusses more thoroughly in his earlier works, notably the *Economic and Philosophical Manuscripts of 1844*, can be clearly seen in this additional typical passage which we quote from *Capital*:

> The labour process, turned into the process by which the capitalist consumes labour power, exhibits two characteristic phenomena. First, the labourer works under the control of the capitalist to whom his labour belongs; the capitalist taking good care that the work is done in a proper manner, and that the means of production are used with intelligence, so that there is no unnecessary waste of raw material, and no wear and tear of the implements beyond what is necessarily caused by the work.
>
> Secondly, the product is the property of the capitalist and not that of the labourer, its immediate producer. Suppose that a capitalist pays for a day's labour power at its value; then the right to use that labour power for that day belongs to him, just as much as the right to use any other commodity, such as a horse that he has hired for that day. To the purchaser of a commodity belongs its use, and the seller of labour power does no more, in reality, than part with the use-value that he has sold. From the instant that he steps into the workshop, the use-value of his labour-power, which is labour, belongs to the capitalist. By the purchase of labour power the capitalist incorporates labour, as a living ferment, with the lifeless constituents of the product. From his point of view, the

labour process is nothing more than the consumption of the commodity purchased, i.e. of labour power; but this consumption cannot be effected except by
supplying the labour power with the means of production. The labour process is
a process between things that the capitalist has purchased, things that have become his property. The product of this process belongs, therefore, to him, just
as much as the wine which is the product of a process of fermentation completed in his cellar.[17]

Quoting this passage affords us the opportunity to explain further our use, at the
beginning of this chapter, of the phrase "conceptual shift." The conceptual shift
we are proposing is moving away from conceiving modern society as natural
and toward conceiving it as an ethical construction.

What is at stake in the passage quoted above are the ethical principles that
construct the relationship between capitalist and worker, and between both of
them and the larger society. Pace Althusser, pace Ollman, and pace many others,
there is present here a clearly identifiable concept of cause and effect. What relates causes to effects is the conventional norm, here specifically the norm that
the worker works under the control of the capitalist, and the norm that the product belongs to the capitalist. As is typical of Marx, he shows here how relationships among persons become disguised as relationships among things. As natural. Social-convention-as-cause becomes disguised as thing-as-cause. The rules
and norms of capitalist institutions become disguised as the quasi-laws of a
quasi-natural science.[18]

This passage also shows the inextricable mixture of what Marx calls the
"sphere of simple circulation or of exchange of commodities," with what he
calls the "sphere of production." It was perhaps Marx himself who, enthusiasti-
cally believing that he had explained the secret of profit-making by leaving the
surface and going down to the deeper level of production relationships, inadver-
tently allowed people to mislead themselves into thinking that once the ownership of the means of production had passed from the bourgeoisie to the proletariat everything would be smooth sailing from then on out. The passage just
quoted shows, however, that a production process in which a worker's time is
bought as one might rent a horse is inextricably related to a circulation process
in which money is advanced to buy commodities for the purpose of using them,
in turn, to make more commodities, which will be sold for more money. The
passage suggests—although it does not spell out in any detail—that any feasible
project for transforming such a system would have to simultaneously transform
the norms relating to ownership and the norms relating to markets.

The passage also shows how "alienation" begins with "separation." "Separation" is one of the words sometimes used as a synonym for "alienation." The
worker under capitalism, unlike a craft worker, no longer owns tools, but works
under the control of the capitalist. The worker is separated from the raw material, from the tools, and from the product, by the norms of commodity exchange
that govern the relations of production.

The use of the term "progressive," to indicate that a de-alienating cultural process proceeds gradually and requires patience, is made more plausible by the passage just quoted, when one reflects that the passage is an analysis of the common sense of people who live in capitalist societies. Marx reveals in the mirror of art what is normally concealed. It is so taken for granted that it is not seen. It is not reasonable to expect that people will easily and rapidly change attitudes that they are not even aware they have, and norms that are nowadays so much second nature that people are not even aware that they follow them.

Degrees of Alienation

At another point in *Capital* Marx wrote:

> [I]n any given economic formation of society, where not the exchange value but the use value of the product predominates, surplus labour will be limited by a given set of wants which may be greater or less, and that here no boundless thirst for surplus labour arises from the nature of the production itself. Hence, in antiquity overwork becomes horrible only when the object is to obtain exchange value in its specific independent money form; in the production of gold and silver. Compulsory working to death is here the recognized form of overwork. Only read Diodorus Siculus. Still, these are exceptions in antiquity. But as soon as people, whose production still moves within the lower forms of slave labour, corvee labour etc. are drawn into the whirlpool of an international market, dominated by the capitalistic mode of production, the sale of their products for export becoming their principal interest, the civilized horrors of overwork are grafted onto the barbaric horrors of slavery, serfdom, etc. Hence the negro labour in the Southern States of the American Union preserved something of a patriarchal character, so long as production was directed chiefly to immediate local consumption. But in proportion, as the export of cotton became of vital interest to these states, the overworking of the negro and sometimes the using up of his life in seven years of labour became a factor in a calculated and calculating system. It was no longer a question of obtaining from him a certain quantity of useful products.[19]

The moral we draw from this last passage is that there are degrees of alienation. An environment can range anywhere from complete alienation to no alienation. It can be wholly hostile to the needs, interests, and feelings of people; it can be one where, in violation of Kant's categorical imperative, humans are treated entirely as means. As Marx elsewhere puts it, "It is now no longer the labourer that employs the means of production, but the means of production that employs the labourer."[20] At the other extreme, there are friendly pro-social work environments, where there is little or no alienation. Fast-forwarding from Marx's contrast of relatively humane ancient with comparatively inhumane early modern practices, one can imagine a business in a contemporary democracy where the workers do an honest day's work for an honest day's pay and are decently treated. The company provides a good and useful service for its customers, is a responsible contributor to the wider community, and is ecologically conscientious. The workers may have a good union, or feel they do not need a union but could form one if they chose to, and they may have paid vacations and health benefits. This hypothetical non-alienated firm might have hands-on owners who earn a reasonable profit putting their own sweat equity into the business, or its shares might be held by pension funds or by foundations devoted to medical research.

A litmus test for distinguishing alienation from non-alienation is the absence or presence of consent. Time and again Marx characterizes alienation as a situation where workers are virtually enslaved, living lives they do not control or choose. Our story about the un-alienated small business in a contemporary democracy, in contrast, is a story about people who have choices in a society that offers choices; it is about workers who may, under the circumstances, choose to be workers and to go home at 5 p.m. after an 8-hour day to relax, engage in do-it-yourself projects around the house, garden, or work out at the gym; it is about workers who might not want to be capitalist entrepreneurs who have to file five or six tax returns instead of one, worry 24 hours a day about meeting payroll and servicing commercial debt, and about keeping up with competitors in a fast-changing market. It is about a society in which, as John Rawls proposes, there is a commitment to an ideal of equality of opportunity in which every role is in principle open to every citizen, and where the legal framework within which people play their diverse roles is in principle established by legislators freely elected by all of the people.[21]

Democracy is a step toward de-alienation because it establishes the principle that the laws are made by and for the people. The quasi-mechanical implacable laws of economics are ameliorated in principle by the prospect of humanitarian amendment. According to the strict rules of capitalism, if you are in the unfortunate position of being a person who has no goods or services to sell that anybody wants to buy, and if you have no investments producing income for you, then you lose. You lose, you are on the street, and nobody has a duty to give you a break. But according to the principle that it is the people's representatives who make the laws, when there are too many losers, it is time to change the rules of the game.

The Core of Alienation

In the earlier *1844 Manuscripts*, the only place where Marx devotes several paragraphs to explicating the meaning of the word "alienation," Marx describes "alienation" as "not being at home."[22] To be de-alienated is to be "at home." The German word translated as "alienation" is *Entfremdung*, which comes from the adjective *fremd* meaning "strange" or "foreign." The core of the idea of *Entfremdung* is in the center of the word, *fremd*. Alienation is the process of becoming a stranger, a rejected foreigner, unwelcome. In its English and Spanish versions, both drawn from French, the core of "alienation" and *alienación* can be found in *lien*, which means "attachment." Alienation is the process of losing attachments, losing connections, losing bonds. Besides "separation," "objectification," "fetishism" and "commodification" can be used as equivalents to "alienation."[23] They express the idea of inhumanity, of the displacement of the personal and the humane by the impersonal and the thing-like.

Ollman points out two other words, which Marx uses as practically equivalent to the word *fremd*, which is at the core of *Entfremdung*: *ausser* (outside) and *unabhangig* (independent).[24] The significance of the latter is that the product, and, on a larger scale, the economy, assume powers independent of the humans who make them.

Thus to be alienated is to confront inhuman objects alone. It is to be a stranger, to be in a foreign land, in hostile territory. Per Albin Hansson must have had such an idea in mind when he said that social democracy would make Sweden "home" for its people. Marx contrasts the savage, who is at home anywhere, with the "civilized" worker, who must pay rent in order to have a place to call home, who can be thrown out onto the street whenever the cash needed to pay the landlord is not available. In several passages where Marx wants to contrast capitalism with something else he gives examples of peasant families or peasant villages where resources are shared and where it is the business of all to meet the needs of each.[25] In briefest summary, as Ollman concludes in his book on Marx's concept of alienation, alienation is disunity. De-alienation is unity.[26]

As an example of extreme alienation imagine a poor laborer in Venezuela who finds in one place a rice or cacao plantation, fenced with barbed wire, where he or she is not welcome; in another place a petrochemical complex, guarded by armed guards, where she is not welcome either; in other places freeways and modern buildings which are not for him; who among all the spaces on this earth is only legally allowed to locate her body sometimes in a shabby rented room, sometimes on public streets, in either case in danger of being attacked, sometimes by criminals, sometimes by the police; a person who finds no place on earth a safe spot that is home; who finds no family, no clan, no labor union, no political party or church, which will take him in and welcome her as one of their own.

Our example of extreme alienation brings out a point not much emphasized by Marx, namely that a person who is unemployed and homeless can be just as alienated as a poorly paid worker who functions as a cog in a machine calculated to maximize someone else's profits. However, our example fails to bring out a point that Marx (like Paulo Freire) does emphasize, namely that under capitalism, the capitalist, ostensibly privileged, is also alienated.[27] Ollman writes, paraphrasing Marx, "The capitalist's relation to the product of the proletariat's labor likewise places him in a state of alienation. For him, the object of another man's life activity is only something to sell, something to make a profit with. He is as indifferent to what it is actually used for and who will eventually use it as he is to the process by which it came into being."[28]

Criticisms of the Concept of Alienation

We believe that the version of the concept of "alienation" that we are developing is immune to some of the main attacks made against such concepts.[29] One kind of attack is made by Marcuse. It is that "alienation" becomes a questionable concept in advanced industrial societies where individuals identify themselves by the existence which is imposed on them by mass culture. They identify with their Corvette automobile, or their designer clothes. The logic behind this criticism of the concept of alienation seems to be this: According to Marx, a) there is an essence of humanity, a social species-being, *Gattungwesen*, which everybody really is; b) under capitalism, people are alienated from their true selves, and cease to be who they really are, really human; c) alienated people are unhappy. But in advanced industrial societies, people are alienated from what Marx would call their true selves, inasmuch as they identify with consumer goods and mass culture, with things more than with social relationships, but they are not unhappy. Marx's concept of alienation appears to become unusable when faced with the counter-example of happy alienation. Marcuse goes on to say that nevertheless, the life of a well-paid working class in a consumer society shows a deeper form of alienation, not envisaged by Marx. It is a form of alienation that, unfortunately for the revolution, the masses do not seem to be inclined to revolt against.[30]

From the point of view proposed here, these arguments are neither here nor there. There may and may not be a social essence to human nature. We are proposing ways to use "alienation" and "de-alienation," mostly drawn from Marx, as terms that do not refer to an essence of human nature, neither to say that there is or is not such an essence.

A second line of attack on the idea of "alienation" characterizes philosophies of alienation as about subjectivity. They depend on the illusion that the bourgeois sense of self as a juridical subject reflects universal human nature. They make "self" and "subject" into philosophical categories untainted by history.[31] We do not think this sort of objection applies to "alienation" as we have discussed it either. We have here tried to avoid participating in nineteenth- and twentieth-century European philosophical debates, and to ground "alienation" in the practical reality that people are separated from food, from housing, from friendly human companionship, and from cooperative material assistance in meeting the needs of life.

Alienation and Christian Humanism

The idea that the ethical norms of everyday life have to change if the structure of society is going to change is not a new idea. It is not an idea confined to humanistic and Gramscian Marxists. Christian Democrats have thought of it too. It is a frequent theme in the social teachings of the church. In an important sense, the core Christian idea of *agape* is logically equivalent to the idea of alienation that we have constructed mainly by following some of Marx's insights. *Agape* means love for everybody, welcoming, inclusion. Alienation means hostility for everybody, rejection, exclusion. Being in favor of *agape* and being against alienation are, in set-theoretic language, co-extensional. To include everybody means the same thing as to exclude nobody.

Most of the founders of COPEI, the Venezuelan Christian Democratic Party, were formed as activists and organizers in study circles devoted to Catholic social doctrine, led by Manuel Aguirre, S.J. Padre Aguirre described Christian social teaching as equidistant from free-market liberalism and Marxist socialism, and castigated equally the errors of each.[32] Marx's views on "alienation," however, were not among his targets; and indeed Padre Aguirre's own words were often similar to Marx's on this point, for example when he wrote: "The Manchester School in its doctrine of the labor contract degenerated to the point where it arrived at the concept of *homo economicus*, considering labor as an article of commerce, as a commodity; and the worker as a machine."[33] He frequently quoted typical Christian language calling for the solution of social problems through the consistent application of the principle of *agape*, as, for example, these words from *Quadragesimo anno*: "The true union of all for the sake of the common good will only be achieved when all parts of society feel intimately that they are part of one great family and children of the same heavenly Father; and further, are one body in Christ, being all members of one another, so that if one member of society suffers, all of the others suffer sympathetically ["*compadecen*"]."[34]

The concept of alienation, *Entfremdung*, built around the adjective *fremd*, names a complex of unfortunate limitations of the characteristic basic cultural structures of modern society. It echoes similar critiques of modernity made by people who in other respects disagree with Marxism—Christians, Muslims, Buddhists, Hindus, romantic philosophers and poets. Modernity is impersonal. People are treated like things. As Max Weber wrote, it is disenchanted.[35] Our emphasis, however, is on another familiar critique of modernity: it does not work. It fails to deliver the goods. We are proposing "de-alienation" as a strategy for building a world that is more personal, more human, more charming and enchanting, and also more functional.

De-Alienation

There is an irreducible romantic element in the idea of de-alienation. If humans are alienated, it is because they are separated from some bonds and connections they might have had. Syntactically, they are bonds and connections they did have at some earlier time before the process of estrangement set in. Yesteryear is bathed in a golden light in spite of evidence that yesteryear was, for the most part, worse than the current year. The Hobson's Choice between *Gemeinschaft* (traditional community) with solidarity but without plumbing, and *Gesellschaft* (modern society) without solidarity but with plumbing, is biased in favor of the former. The challenge and the goal of democratic socialism, however, is to avoid this Hobson's Choice: to achieve solidarity along *with* advanced technology, freedom *with* community. The idea of "de-alienation" must therefore be handled gingerly, to give it a content somewhat at odds with its etymology, to make it name a future better than the past.

In our experience, many activists who are working with the poor to overcome poverty are already working along the lines that a de-alienation strategy would suggest. What we are proposing is more support for much of the anti-poverty work that is already underway. Examples of the sorts of de-alienating activism already underway in many places around the world can be drawn from several community development programs carried out in the early 1980s in the Orinoco River Basin in southern Venezuela, in the towns of Pariaguan, San Diego de Cabrutica, and Mapire.[36] The programs were subsidized by MARAVEN, one of the four operating subsidiaries of the nationalized Venezuelan petroleum industry.[37]

The fact that MARAVEN put up the money to subsidize de-alienation is itself de-alienating. It signals that the oil wealth of the Venezuelan nation is not separated from its people. The oil is owned by the people. Oil wealth under the stewardship of its managers is being used for the people's benefit. Similarly, the democratic context of MARAVEN's decisions signals de-alienation. In Venezuela in the 1980s, in principle, the laws governing property rights and those creating parastatal semi-autonomous entities like MARAVEN were laws created by and for the people.[38] Property did not confront the propertyless as an alien force, but rather provided a practical legal framework for living, designed to serve the common good, enacted by representatives the people had elected.

It is not an objection to the de-alienating ideals stated in the preceding paragraph that the motives of the MARAVEN executives were impure. (They wanted to gain public support for their presence in the Orinoco Valley, and to avoid being confined to operating solely in western Venezuela around Lake Maracaibo.)[39] Nor is it an objection that Venezuelan democracy was and is imperfect. (Every democracy has been and is.) These are not objections because the only possible way to move in the direction of de-alienation is to start by taking advantage of the motives and practices that exist, which are, inevitably, mixed and flawed. As anthropologists have consistently found, in any culture there is a difference between the ideal norms that are professed, and the actual norms that are practiced, and yet the former are not irrelevant to the latter. Articulating ideals and keeping them alive in an impure and imperfect world is not describing the facts; it is making an effort to encourage improvement. It is a political commitment.

MARAVEN money was used to hire a team of community development facilitators from the Institute for Cultural Affairs (ICA), headquartered in Chicago, and a team of social scientists from the University of Venezuela's Center for Development Studies (CENDES). ICA, which already in the 1980s had thirty years experience in participatory grassroots problem solving in many countries around the world, is an offshoot of Saul Alinsky's Industrial Areas Foundation. Its approach to building the power of the people is considered less confrontational than Alinsky's original version. The scholars from CENDES were mainly associated with MAS, *Movimiento al Socialismo*, and other parties that advocate democratic socialism.[40]

What the facilitators did was to facilitate dialogue, which is another step toward de-alienation. From the times of Socrates and the compassionate Buddha to the times of Lawrence Kohlberg and Paulo Freire, the simple practice of coming together to engage in conversations about matters of common concern has been recognized as a key to achieving a higher level of moral consciousness and more intelligent concerted action.[41] Everybody in town (the total population of San Diego de Cabrutica was only 2,000) was invited to share ideas on the problems of the town and how to solve them. Nobody was excluded. Sometimes the conversations went on all night.[42]

Jürgen Habermas has convincingly argued in *Communication and the Evolution of Society* that the simple act of engaging in conversation brings into play certain minimum norms of cooperation and honesty.[43] Surely the commitment to cooperation and honesty is still greater when one voluntarily attends a meeting with one's fellow citizens to discuss the problems of one's town or neighborhood. If everyone is invited to say what they think the problems are, then there is an implicit commitment to the norm that people ought to care about the problems. The notion that the people are powerless to do anything to solve their problems is implicitly denied. The notion that all resources are under the control of hostile strangers, and will not be available to meet the needs of the members of the community, is implicitly denied as well. Skilled community organizers have developed methods for building on these almost inevitable consequences of people coming together to discuss common problems. They catalyze bringing out people's capacities to join in creating solutions.

Even if one's participation in small group discussions and larger plenary sessions consists entirely of complaining, the possibility that one might volunteer to do something to help the community solve the problems that everybody complains about is always implicitly on the agenda. Volunteering comes in many kinds and degrees. It may be a matter of earning merits as a member of a political party or other organization, or of getting experience, or building a network of contacts, any or all of which may eventually lead to paid work. Volunteering may carry privileged access to sacks of flour and powdered milk that are sent to Venezuela by foreign aid donors. It may be involuntary volunteerism, as when local customs require that twice a year everybody turn out to clean up the public streets and parks. Volunteering may be sweat equity put into building homes, which contributes to one's own family getting a house to live in.[44] It may take the form of putting time into organizing a local for-profit business, or cooperative, or municipal service. It may take the form of gleaning food left to rot in the fields because it makes no commercial sense to pay people to harvest it (because it would not sell for a high enough price to cover the costs) and storing it to feed hungry people in hard times.

Whatever form it takes, volunteering often shifts the locus of control; the paymaster controls the workers, but the volunteer coordinator can only persuade people to do what they want to do and what makes sense to them. The efficiency of the delivery of public services increases, in the sense that more work gets done for less money, at the same time that local institutions acquire more cohesion and authority, and hence more power to demand a larger share of national resources. Thus, in many ways, people coming together can meet needs by mobilizing resources that would not have been mobilized if people had remained isolated from one another, waiting for someone to come to create a job for them by making an investment.

The physical accomplishments of MARAVEN-sponsored projects in the Orinoco Valley in the 1980s included the installation of systems for collecting clean rainwater from roofs, improving docks at ports on the Orinoco River, building roads, several measures to promote local food self-sufficiency, and a series of projects providing technical assistance for small farmers, including the reintroduction of cotton cultivation in the area.[45] An additional accomplishment flowed from another consequence of de-alienating the people. When the people participate, there is greater transparency in the use of public funds; more eyes watch those who handle them. One interesting fallout of projects sponsored by the nationalized oil industry was public discovery of a scandal that led to the arrest of the former head of a government-owned bank on charges of using public funds to profit from land speculation.[46]

De-alienation as a People-Oriented form of Integrated Development

The social scientists from the University of Venezuela used the Orinoco Valley experiences to elaborate, in the unusual circumstances of Venezuela in the 1970s and 1980s, a people-oriented theory of integrated development. They challenged the *desarrollista* (developmentalist) theories that have been, on the whole, dominant in Venezuela, and in the rest of the world.[47] The unusual circumstances were high oil prices and an increased role for the Venezuelan state in the oil industry. In 1973, following the Arab-Israeli war, the Organization of Petroleum Exporting Countries, of which Venezuela was a founding member, increased the price of a barrel of oil from $1.76 to $10.31. In 1976 the Venezuelan oil industry was nationalized. Everybody knew that the high oil prices would not last forever, and that some day the wells would run dry. There was a national consensus that it was necessary to *sembrar el petroleo* ("sow the petroleum").[48] Venezuelans considered that the windfall, which nearly tripled the income of the Venezuelan government, ought to be used to build a Venezuela that would be viable when the windfall ended.[49] It was in this context that CENDES challenged the *desarrollistas*.

To little avail. In spite of the efforts of its best dissenting intellectuals, for the most part Venezuela in the 1970s and 1980s, under AD and COPEI governments, accepted the illusory theory that there is a social process called "development," leading from the "undeveloped" or "developing" nation-state to the "developed" nation-state displayed by the social democracies of Western Europe. We have already shown the futility of this illusion, particularly in the four preceding chapters on Sweden. Instead of people-oriented integrated development, the oil bonanza mainly brought "heightened competition among capitalists for access to state projects and funds and, ultimately, for position within the entrepreneurial state."[50] The most influential technocrats were the ones who subscribed to an orthodox developmentism. We have already shown the futility of such developmentalist and technocratic illusions, particularly in the three proceeding chapters on Indonesia. Quite predictably, when oil prices fell, as everybody knew they would, the impoverished masses of Venezuela found themselves as impoverished as ever.[51]

Today, more than ever, in the endless slums around Caracas one sees children sniffing glue, young men and women already accustomed to lives of crime and prostitution, old men drinking, sick old women watching Mexican soap operas on TV in shacks while patiently waiting for a son or daughter to bring them a banana or a cup of weak tea. If one gazes on such sights through the lenses now fashionable in contemporary academic writing, one will see the resiliency and creativity of people who are able to find ways to survive and to enjoy life under adverse circumstances. If one gazes upon the slums, instead, through the eyes of the modernizing developmentalist theories that were in vogue in the decades immediately after World War II, what one will see is a problem called "lack of development" for which the solution is "development." If, instead, one makes the conceptual shift we are suggesting—to a philosophy of ethical construction of social reality—one will see "alienation," for which the solution is "de-alienation."[52]

Judging from their fervent support for Venezuela's president, Hugo Chávez, the slum-dwellers of Caracas do not agree either with current academic fashions in the human sciences, or with *desarrollismo*, or with a theory of progressive de-alienation or cultural action. They appear to want an old-fashioned revolution in which the poor take power from the rich.

History is repeating itself. As has happened in so many countries, the business and political elite of Venezuela, advised by technocrats, tried to use the resources available, in Venezuela's case the oil windfall of the mid-1970s, to achieve a "development" that would end poverty. They failed. When oil prices fell, the AD and COPEI governments, which had been populist governments distributing a considerable amount of largesse to the masses, stiffened. They imposed the austerity measures that economic orthodoxy prescribed, and which the IMF required.[53] In 1992, a left wing army officer, paratrooper Hugo Chávez Frías, attempted a coup d'état and earned a two year prison sentence for his pains. He became the symbol of the demands of the masses for revolutionary change.[54]

Forming his own party outside the traditional parties, Hugo Chávez ran for president and was elected in December 1998. He received 59 percent of the vote and was granted extraordinary powers.[55] The measures he took to favor the poor spooked investors. The economy got worse, and, consequently, so did unemployment, and, consequently, so did crime. Business leaders called for Chávez's resignation. It would be contrary to the lessons of all known historical precedents to believe that the business leaders do not have the covert support of sectors of the military and of plotters in high places in Washington, D.C. The press and the traditional parties, almost unanimously, have denounced Chávez too, although some think he should be given a chance to mend his ways before being forced to resign. President Chávez, defiant and combative, has taken to making long rambling speeches on Venezuelan television. He compares himself to Chile's elected democratic socialist president Salvador Allende. Chile's revolution failed, Chávez says, because it was a revolution disarmed. Venezuela's revolution will succeed, because it is a revolution armed. To drive his point home he has the joint chiefs of staff solemnly declare in public that the armed forces are solidly behind the elected president. To make his point even clearer, he sends squadrons of air force jets thundering across the sky over Caracas.

He forgets that Juan Domingo Perón in Argentina also had the solid support of the armed forces, as did Juan Velasco Alvarado in Peru. But neither of them could withstand the corrosive power of the constitutive rules of modern society. Neither succeeded in mobilizing the resources of the nation to meet the needs of its people. It is not possible to foresee how this unfortunate confrontation will end, but it seems quite likely that it will end in violence, loss of civil liberties, and a rightwing government that will impose "economic rationality" by force.[56] If Venezuela had followed—if political reality had allowed it to follow—the concepts of integrated development elaborated at the Center for Development

Studies of the University of Venezuela in 1981, it would have been facing brighter prospects in 2002.[57]

Criticisms of the Concept of De-Alienation

A criticism can be made of de-alienation, from the point of view of better-known strategies for social change, such as carrying out a revolution to seize control of the means of production, or patiently building a welfare state by extending government programs and citizen entitlements, on the grounds that de-alienation is a relative newcomer, untried, with relatively little historical experience behind it. De-alienation can reply that it is precisely historical experience that has shown the shortcomings of the main transformation strategies attempted so far, and the need to make changes at the deeper level of basic cultural norms.

De-alienation is a humanistic approach to social change. It is roughly similar to the ideas of integrated development that Venezuelan intellectuals have elaborated but have, so far, been unable to implement on a large scale. It is different from most older and better known challenges to capitalism. Most alternatives to straight capitalism focus on either production or distribution.

The best known challenge to capitalist economics focuses on production. Its classical statement is in Chapter 32 of Marx's *Capital*, where Marx prophesies that at some point in history "the expropriators will be expropriated." The working class will seize the means of production. Experience with worker seizures of factories in Russia, Italy, and other countries quickly taught that when workers seized and held a single isolated factory, they could do nothing with it. The practical version of seizure by the proletariat became identified as nationalization of industry.

But if alienation is the problem, then nationalizing industries is not in itself the solution. A nationalized industry can pursue profit maximization as the bottom line the same as a privately owned one. As General Alfonzo Ravard, the first president of the government-owned Venezuelan Petroleum Company, stated during the nationalization process, the Venezuelan Petroleum Company, "has been structured and operates as a commercial company . . . which seeks to obtain maximum economic benefit for its sole shareholder, the Venezuelan State."[58] Fortunately for the Orinoco Valley, at least one of its operating subsidiaries, MARAVEN, took the position that nationalized industries should serve the people's welfare by more direct means.

Similar considerations apply if instead of nationalization, a nation fosters forms of social ownership such as cooperatives, worker-owned enterprises, *kibbutzim*, *ejidos*, municipal corporations, and the like. Whatever the form of ownership, the enterprise will be to a considerable extent constrained by markets to act selfishly.[59]

The existence of a large and varied public sector, and of social sectors composed of cooperatives, nonprofit hospitals and schools, scientific research foundations, artists' collectives, small family farms, and many diverse forms of non-capitalist production, is desirable and important for many reasons. Yet it does not in itself deliver the goods. Carrying it to its logical extreme by eliminating private enterprises will not deliver the goods either, and will make the situation worse instead of better. If mobilizing resources to meet needs is the problem, then finding an optimum mix of forms of ownership for productive enterprises is only a part of the solution.

The second best known challenge to straight capitalism is Western European social democracy, of which Sweden is a good example. Here the focus is on distribution. The private sector is not nationalized, but it is regulated with a series of complex carrots and sticks, whose final objective is to secure the social use of the social product. West European citizens enjoy a series of entitlements: free health care, free education, free housing if they need it, guaranteed pensions. Nobody goes hungry. Large tranches of what Smith called "value in use" are de-commodified, taken out of the market, and made available as a matter of right to all citizens. Entitlements change distribution.

A standard problem with entitlements is that they are similar to high wages. Indeed, they are sometimes called a "social wage," or "fringe benefits" added to wages. Like high wages, they drive production to other locations. A poor country struggling to attract investments generally cannot afford to raise taxes to pay for more entitlements. (Indeed, most poor countries cannot even afford to enforce the tax laws, the environmental regulations, and the other disincentives to profit-making, that are already on the books.) Precisely because of the struggle to attract investments, the current worldwide trend, neoliberalism, is in the opposite direction: every day there are fewer free medical benefits and more charges, more toll roads, more fees to use public parks, less good public water and more need to buy bottled water from private firms, less good free public education, more user fees to use public libraries, and so on. There is a reason for the pressures worldwide that are behind this unfortunate trend. The reason is that social democracy did not succeed in making changes in distribution compatible with providing adequate motivation for production.

Subsidizing de-alienation is neither of the above. It changes the control of the means of production and the norms that govern circulation (the distribution of goods and services) simultaneously, rather than one before the other. Ownership and the market change together. (Hence "integrated development.") It aspires to a level of reconstruction of conventional ethical norms to which neither nationalization nor entitlement aspires. It does not flatly deny that Adam Smith was right when he attributed more power to self-interest than to benevolence, but it does demonstrate—in practice and not just in theory—that Adam Smith lacked imagination when he failed to consider all the ways in which self-interest and benevolence can be blended. It proposes to use rents to subsidize the dissolution of the structural obstacles to social change.

Another criticism of de-alienation flows from the idea of competition of capitals. It flows from Marx's own analysis of competition of capitals, and is eagerly embraced by conservative economists like Milton Friedman, who argue that corporations (public, private, or parastatal) neither can nor should make grants for such things as community development.[60] It envisages a world of fierce competition, where corporations need every dime they have to finance keeping up with new technologies and new marketing techniques. Or else. Or else their competitors will drive them to the wall. The typical firm cannot afford to raise wages; it cannot afford to lower prices to consumers; it cannot afford to make gifts to charity; it cannot afford environmental cleanup costs; it is stifled by the taxes it already pays and cannot afford to pay more. The MARAVENs of this world, it can be argued, are few and far between, and not sufficient to fund social transformation.

There is certainly a lot to be said for the argument that most firms are not free to be socially responsible, even if they want to be. But the argument is neither here nor there with respect to our proposal for funding progressive de-alienation, since the proposal is not to fund from the precarious earnings of entrepreneurs, but to fund from rents.

The economic idea of "rents" has its classical source in the early nineteenth-century writings of David Ricardo. He defined rent as the increased production from good land, as differentiated from production derived from the worst land still good enough to be worth cultivating.[61] The same labor goes into good land and bad land. Seeds cost the same. The owner of the good land is able to collect rent not because the farmer who farms it farms it better, but because the land itself is better. Generalizing: any resource—farmland, iron mines, timber, center city real estate, petroleum deposits—yields rent. The extra income it makes possible is due to it, not to the people using it.

Thus the rentier, the person or institution that lives from rents, is to a considerable extent above the fray. Cutthroat competition may be keeping entrepreneurs on their toes, and in constant danger of being driven out of business, but the rentier, the owner of a resource, to a considerable extent can continue to collect rent as entrepreneurs come and go. Business entities can go through bankruptcy, disappear, and be reorganized under another name; debts can be forgiven and economic life can start over again, as in the ancient Hebrews' years of jubilee, but still rents are collected. The rentiers can afford to be generous. The point is general. The example above is about an oil-rich rentier named MARAVEN, a parastatal semi-autonomous entity created by the Venezuelan state, which voluntarily supported de-alienation. But rents can be collected by many forms of entities: parastatal, governmental, private, or other. Once rents are collected, channeling them to subsidize social improvements can be voluntary or involuntary. Much depends on which improvements are deemed to be most worthy of being subsidized. A philosophy of de-alienation gives priority to using subsidies to multiply the benefits of the self-help projects organized by the poor themselves, and by the good citizen volunteers, poor or not, who want to contribute to improving society.

Another criticism of de-alienation is: de-alienation yes, but not yet. Karl Marx, the classic source of the idea of alienation, is also the classic source of this argument against de-alienation. In his *Critique of the Gotha Program*, he endorses *agape*, the logical equivalent of de-alienation, as it is expressed in the biblical maxim, from the Acts of the Apostles, "from each according to his ability, to each according to his needs." But not yet. Before de-alienation there must come a long period in which first the bourgeoisie, and then the proletarian state develop the productive powers of society. Marx is seconded on this point by John Maynard Keynes, who recognizes that the vice of self-interest rules society now, but declares that the world is not yet ready for virtue.[62] Virtue must wait. When vice has done the work of making society wealthy, then it will be time for virtue to do the work of sharing the wealth with the poor.

A cruel joke. The so-called "development of the wealth of society," in the absence of social democracy, in practice does nothing for society. The "wealth" is accumulated by private individuals, who mainly keep it in Swiss banks, Miami real estate, and other safe places. It is a metaphysical prejudice of economists, accustomed to think in numbers, to suppose that "wealth" is a fungible entity, which, once it exists, can be divided and shared. In fact, accumulated automobiles, factories for making deviled ham, dude ranches for the horsey set, and spa resorts that feature facials with aromatherapy and full-body mud wraps, even if they are located in Venezuela, can only with great difficulty be turned into rice, beans, fresh vegetables, and flu vaccine to meet the needs of the poor. It is easier to plant a beanfield in the first place than to first build a golf course, and then change it into a beanfield years later. Perhaps in Marx's time, when the leading industry was textile manufacturing, and when science and engineering had hardly begun to develop the technological capacities that today make it feasible to meet everybody's needs without ecological damage, it might have seemed that more factories had to be built before there would be enough cloth to go around. Today it is clear that to wait until enough wealth and productive power is accumulated before direct action is taken to meet the needs of the poor is not a necessary first phase. It is a delay.

In favor of encouraging virtue now, and not later, pace Keynes, one can cite the experience of Venezuelan agriculture. By devoting enormous amounts of oil-money to agricultural improvements, Venezuela, in spite of its generally poor tropical soils, has managed to achieve increases in agricultural production just barely ahead of increases in population growth. But, frustratingly, Venezuela's dependence on food imports has grown, even though agricultural production has kept pace with population growth. The reason is that the prosperous classes have changed their eating habits, and now eat more meat. There is more grain, but it becomes feed-grain to feed animals for the rich to eat, leaving less grain for the poor to eat.[63] Alienated, accustomed to commodity exchange as a way of life, the rich consider it natural, and not to be a matter of cultural convention, that if they have enough *bolivares* to buy steak, it is their right and privilege to eat steak every day. If they did not feel separated from the poor, but felt a sense of unity with their poor brethren, they might reconsider. But it is not reasonable to expect that people will easily and rapidly change attitudes that they are not even aware they have. Change will require time and patience, which is a reason for starting sooner rather than later. Thus the practice of relying on vice to build the wealth of society, as Keynes recommends, makes the feeding of Venezuela precarious, liable to fail whenever the price of oil falls. Vice builds, physically, feedlots and slaughterhouses, which do not lend themselves to realizing the eventual goal of sustainable development for the benefit of all the people.

A related argument against de-alienation, and against democracy, is that the power of the people will favor today's consumption over saving for investments needed in the long run, such as building dams for irrigation and hydroelectric power. Expressed more technically, the marginal propensity to save is said to be lower in the working classes, and higher in the wealthy classes, for which reason it is said to be advisable for the sake of a nation's future development to skew the distribution of income in favor of the wealthy classes. It follows from this specious argument that poor countries are not yet ready for democracy, since democracy is likely to lead to a redistribution of income inimical to meeting long-term needs. This is an argument, however, that West European social democracy has already answered in practice: funding for long range investments, and for servicing the debt on loans taken out to pay for long range investments, does not in fact come from individuals in the wealthier classes. It comes from the retained earnings of public, private, and parastatal business entities. Experience shows that electorates are able to understand the need for retained earnings to finance long term investments. The most relevant question to ensure financing for long run investment is not whether an empowered populace will insist on eating the seeds needed for planting next year's crop, but rather the one often put to incumbents in Venezuelan electoral campaigns: *¿Donde están los reales?* (What happened to the money?) With respect to this question, the really relevant one, it can be answered that greater participation by the people can only lead to more transparency, and to more honest use of funds.

Much more can be said for and against subsidizing progressive de-alienation. We hope these words are sufficient to suggest the idea and to put it on the agenda for further discussion.

Notes

1. The reader will note that our approach contrasts with those for whom "rent-seeking" is a pejorative term. Some imply that utopia would be a world in which all prices were set by competitive markets with no rents. One of the best exemplars of this point of view is the collection edited by Charles K. Rowley, Robert D. Tollison, and Gordon Tullock, *The Political Economy of Rent-Seeking* (Boston; Dordrecht, Neth.; and Lancaster, U.K.: Kluwer Academic Publishers, 1988), which the authors dedicate to "all those entrepreneurs whose profit-seeking contributions have outperformed rent-seeking waste and have thus provided ongoing contributions to the wealth of nations." Rowley, Tollison, and Tullock, *Political Economy of Rent-Seeking*, v. Gordon Tullock was the first to devise the concept of rent-seeking in his article, "The Welfare Costs of Tariffs, Monopolies and Theft," *Western Economic Journal* 5 (1967): 224-32; although it was Anne Krueger who coined the term, in "The Political Economy of the Rent-Seeking Society," *American Economic Review* 64 (June 1974): 291-303. The corruption that often exists within countries with large rents from oil in particular has also been much studied. For a recent such case study, see Bradford L. Dillman, *State and Private Sector in Algeria: The Politics of Rent-seeking and Failed Development* (Boulder, Colo.; and Oxford: Westview Press, 2000); and for the case of Venezuela specifically, see Terry Lynn Karl, *The Paradox of Plenty: Oil Booms and Petro-States* (Berkeley: University of California Press, 1997). Our proposal is not to try to create a world without rents, but to channel rents to socially beneficial uses. In this sense, our work is meant to be a contribution to a growing movement, spearheaded by such organizations as the Lincoln Institute of Land Policy, that seeks ways for communities, regions, and nation-states to capture rents and surplus-value in ways that do not necessarily spur capital flight or incur insurmountable reprisals. As used by the Lincoln Institute and others, the concept of "value capture" refers to the process by which increments in land value attributed to "community interventions" instead of land-owner actions (i.e., "unearned increments") are recouped by the public sector—either indirectly through conversion into public revenues as fees, exactions, taxes, or other fiscal means, or indirectly through on-site improvements to benefit the community at large. See, for example, Alfonso X. Iracheta Cenecorta and Martim Smolka, eds., *Los pobres de la ciudad y la tierra* (Zinacantepec, Mexico: El Colegio Mexiquense, 2000); and Martim Smolka and Fernanda Furtado, eds., *Recuperación de plusvalías en América Latina: alternativas para el desarrollo urbano* (Cambridge, Mass.: Lincoln Institute of Land Policy; and Santiago, Chile: Pontificia Universidad Católica de Chile, 2001). The first of these two works is a collection of essays and case studies presented at a seminar co-sponsored by the Lincoln Institute and El Colegio Mexiquense in March 1999, entitled "Value Capture Policies to Provide Land for the Urban Poor." It offers a discussion of how, in general, to capture surplus-value in land values, and, more specifically, of fiscal and regulatory instruments for mobilization of land value increments for the provision of urban services and infrastructure. The latter work explores the dramatic social inequities present in many urban centers throughout Latin America, which are expressed in formidable urban land price differentials associated with the process through which land value increments are generated, appropriated, and used. Its authors demonstrate not only that value capture policies are theoretically feasible, but also that legislation and other tools

for their implementation are already in place in many nation-states. An additional point of interest related to this discussion is that in the context of the British administration of India in the nineteenth century, James Mill argued that the state should be the ultimate recipient of land rents and should use the revenue from rents to advance the welfare of the people. See Eric Stokes, *The English Utilitarians and India* (Oxford: Clarendon Press, 1959). A similar idea is the basis of the single tax theory of Henry George. See Henry George, *Progress and Poverty* (New York: D. Appleton & Co., Inc., 1881).

2. The concept of "integrated development" we refer to comes from CENDES, to be elaborated below.

3. A summary of this argument concerning social democracy is found in Tony Wright, *Socialisms: Old and New* (London and New York: Routledge, 1996). Wright delineates the criticism of social democratic "substitutism" for substituting the nebulous notion of "the people" for a more appropriate and purposeful *class* analysis. In instances when this kind of substitution took place, states Wright, "the casualty seemed to some to be not merely one kind of socialism but *any* kind of serious socialism." Wright, *Socialisms*, 102-3, italics in original.

4. Until 1989, AD held the greatest number of seats in Congress and won every presidential election except for two; it did share power, though, with other parties, especially with COPEI. Miriam Kornblith and Daniel Levine, "Venezuela: The Life and Times of the Party System," in Scott Mainwaring and Timothy Scully, eds., *Building Democratic Institutions: Party Systems in Latin America* (Stanford, Calif.: Stanford University Press, 1995), 45. For a thorough treatment of the early history of *Acción Democrática*, see John D. Martz, *Acción Democrática: Evolution of a Modern Political Party in Venezuela* (Princeton: Princeton University Press, 1966).

5. On the rise of MAS and its influence among various segments of the Venezuelan population, see Steve Ellner, *From Guerrilla Defeat to Innovative Politics: Venezuela's Movimiento al Socialismo* (Durham, N.C.: Duke University Press, 1988).

6. For a succinct explication of the reasons for the "divorce between socialism and democracy" in the twentieth century, see the Introduction to Carollee Bengelsdorf's *The Problem of Democracy in Cuba: Between Vision & Reality* (New York and Oxford: Oxford University Press, 1994), 3-11. Bengelsdorf makes the point that radical critiques of capitalism that trace their origins to Marxian analysis are "infused with a profoundly emancipatory vision, based on the dis-alienation of human beings in every arena of their existence and activity." Bengelsdorf's "dis-alienation" is complementary to the concept of "de-alienation" we are putting forth. Bengelsdorf's "dis-alienation" is an expansion of the formal definition of democracy, "in its understanding of the people as subject rather than subjected, as the determining rather than the determined element, as the authors of their own histories." Bengelsdorf, *Problem of Democracy*, 3. This is akin to our insistence upon human agency—primarily through the construction, re-creation, and change of cultural norms—as historical cause.

7. AD and COPEI are the two Venezuelan political parties that had the broadest popular support throughout the latter portion of the twentieth century. Together they received approximately 60 percent of votes cast in presidential elections until 1973 and more than 85 percent in the period from 1973 to 1988. Kornblith and Levine, "Venezuela: The Life and Times," 49.

8. Expressions of this idea can be found in some of the literature produced by Causa R, Venezuela's strongest leftist political party.

9. We believe, in contradistinction to this presumption that refusal to enter alliance constitutes "radicalism," that, as Bernice Johnson Reagon stated, if one is too comfortable in the movement, it is a sure sign that the movement is not radical enough—in that it is not inclusive enough. We must recognize the necessity of coalition politics; and also that the diversity that coalition politics demands rarely allows participants to feel altogether comfortable. Still, as important as separatism can be, especially for movements in their early stages, we believe that far more and far better things can be accomplished through coalition politics than through separatism. Bernice Johnson Reagon, "Coalition Politics: Turning the Century," in Barbara Smith, ed., *Home Girls: A Black Feminist Anthology* (New York: Kitchen Table, Women of Color Press, 1983), 356-68. See also bell hooks, *Ain't I A Woman: black women and feminism* (Boston: South End Press, 1981), 157-58.

10. For the marginalist economists, it was important to prove that Marx was wrong to say that all value is produced by labor. They argued that land and capital also contribute to the production of value; hence, when the worker is paid wages at a market rate, she is not being exploited but is instead being paid her proportionate share of the value of the product, corresponding to her proportionate contribution to producing it. We argue that what follows from this now mainstream critique of Marx is that the non-labor proportionate shares of the revenue, corresponding to the proportionate contributions to the product of land and capital (which Marx called, respectively, "gifts of nature" and "gifts of history") ought to be administered responsibly for the common good. Joan Robinson would agree with us on this point. She writes, "It is more cogent to say that capital, and the application of science to industry, are immensely productive, and that the institutions of private property, developing into monopoly, are deleterious precisely because they prevent us from having as much capital, and the kind of capital, that we need." She also argues that rent, as well as capital, represents productive capacity (because the land produces a surplus), which implies that the right of the rentier to private appropriation of rents is morally questionable. Robinson, *Essay on Marxian Economics*, 19, 52ff.

11. See Emile Durkheim, *The Division of Labor in Society*, trans. George Simpson (New York: Macmillan, 1933), especially chapters 3 and 6.

12. See Jacques Maritain, *The Degrees of Knowledge* (South Bend, Ind.: The University of Notre Dame Press, 1995); Jacques Maritain, *The Person and the Common Good* (South Bend, Ind.: The University of Notre Dame Press, 1973); Emmanuel Mounier, *Personalism* (South Bend, Ind.: The University of Notre Dame Press, 1979); Freire, *Pedagogy of the Oppressed*; Paulo Freire, *Cultural Action for Freedom* (Cambridge, Mass.: Harvard Educational Review, 1988).

13. Marx, *Capital*, 89.

14. See Louis Althusser, *For Marx* (New York: Verso, 1996), especially Part Two, "On the Young Marx," 51-86. This work was originally published in Paris in 1965 as *Pour Marx*.

15. Bertell Ollman, *Alienation* (Cambridge: Cambridge University Press, 1971).

16. The aim of use-value is now so far removed from the current workings of our economic institutions that economics does not even recognize the concept of "need." Economist William Allen writes, "In economics, 'need' is a non-word. Economics can say much which is useful about desires, preferences, and demands. But 'need' presumably is a moral, psychological, or physical imperative which brooks no compromise or adjustment—or analysis. If we 'need' something, we must have it: there is literally no alternative of either substitution or abstinence. But the assertion of absolute economic 'need'—

in contrast to desire, preference, and demand—is nonsense." William R. Allen, *Midnight Economist: Broadcast Essays III* (Los Angeles, Calif.: International Institute for Economic Research, 1982), 23.

17. Marx, *Capital*, 89.

18. This attribution of *natural* properties to human-created institutions is considered a form of alienation so severe that it has its own designation in Marxist terminology: reification. Gajo Petrovic offers the following concise definition of "reification": "The act (or result of the act) of transforming human properties, relations and actions into properties, relations and actions of [hu]man-produced things which have become independent (*and which are imagined as originally independent*) of man and govern his life." In *A Dictionary of Marxist Thought*, ed. Tom Bottomore, Laurence Harries, V.G. Kiernan, and Ralph Miliband (Cambridge, Mass.: Harvard University Press, 1983), 411, emphasis added. Listening to the ways in which not only economists but also people in general often speak of "the economy" or "the market"—as if these are entirely beyond human control—provides a general example of reification in action. A specific example occurs whenever the U.S. Congress debates the issue of raising the minimum wage and Republicans oppose the measure on the grounds that doing so will cause unemployment to rise, as if the process to which they refer were an immutable and inevitable law of physics.

19. Marx, *Capital*, 113-14.

20. Marx, *Capital*, 150.

21. John Rawls, *A Theory of Justice* (Cambridge, Mass.: The Belknap Press of Harvard University Press, 1971), 84, 87, 205-21.

22. Karl Marx, *Economic and Philosophical Manuscripts of 1844* (Moscow: Progress Publishers, 1959), 72.

23. For use of the term "fetishism" in a way both synonymous with the definition of "reification" outlined above and expressive of the concept of alienation, we turn to Bertell Ollman, who writes: "Fetishism runs rampant. People do not recognize their laws, constitutions, queens, gods, customs, moral codes, academic prizes, etc., as their own creations; instead they offer allegiance and allow themselves to be dominated by them. An individual who sees through this cobweb is little better off, for he remains captive of the relations in which the actions and delusions of others have left him. The ultimate degradation, vicarious living through the royal family, movie stars, football players and assorted Beatles has never been so widespread." Ollman, *Alienation*, 245.

24. Ollman, *Alienation*, 288n.

25. Not a few have found models for de-alienation in cultures in place in Latin America prior to the European Conquest. Aníbal Quijano writes of the "seminal contribution of Andean rationality to the new European imaginary, which was then constituted by the discovery of Andean social institutions established on the basis of reciprocity, solidarity, the control of arbitrariness, and on an intersubjectivity founded on the joy of collective work and a vital communion with the world—or, in European terms, nothing short of the unity of the Tree of Life." In Quijano's estimation, Marx and other Europeans were able to imagine a future de-alienated society because Europeans had encountered de-alienated societies in America. Aníbal Quijano, "Modernidad, identidad y utopia en América Latina," in *Modernidad y Universalismo,* ed. Edgardo Lander (Caracas: Editorial Nueva Sociedad, 1991), 29.

26. Ollman writes, "The whole has broken up into numerous parts whose interrelation in the whole can no longer be ascertained. This is the essence of alienation, whether the part under examination is man, his activity, his product, or his ideas. The same separation

and distortion is evident in each." Ollman, *Alienation*, 135. Jurgen Moltmann offers another concise description of what the terms "alienation" and "de-alienation" connote for us. He writes, "The ideology that 'there is never enough for everyone' makes people lonely. It isolates them and robs them of relationships. The opposite of poverty isn't property. The opposite of both poverty and property is community. For in community we become rich: rich in friends, in neighbors, in colleagues, in comrades, in brothers and sisters. Together, as a community, we can help ourselves in most of our difficulties." Jurgen Moltmann, *The Source of Life* (Philadelphia: Fortress Press, 1997), 109.

27. Freire writes, "The oppressors do not perceive their monopoly on *having more* as a privilege which dehumanizes others and themselves. They cannot see that, in the egoistic pursuit of *having* as a possessing class, they suffocate in their own possessions and no longer *are*; they merely *have*." Freire, *Pedagogy of the Oppressed*, 45, italics in original. Although we make no claims regarding the essence of human nature, because the Freirean conception of alienation emphasizes dehumanization, it might be appropriate here to quote the words of Edward Soja, who implies that moving toward de-alienation is an essentially human act. He states, "To be human is not only to create distances [between subject and object] but to attempt to cross them, to transform primal distance through intentionality, emotion, involvement, [and] attachment." Edward Soja, *Postmodern Geographies: The Reassertion of Space in Social Theory* (London: Verso, 1989), 132.

28. Ollman, *Alienation*, 155.

29. One sort of attack, which complains that the concept is too vague to be scientifically useful, we will not reply to. Instead we refer the reader to the replies to that sort of attack already made by Bertell Ollman and by Marcuse in *One-Dimensional Man*.

30. Marcuse, *One-Dimensional Man*, 56-83. Marcuse discusses at length the state of alienation that he names "Happy Consciousness." Of this state, he writes, "It reflects the belief that the real is rational, and that the established system, in spite of everything, delivers the goods. The people are led to find in the productive apparatus the effective agent of thought and action to which their personal thought and action can and must be surrendered. . . . Conscience is absolved by reification, by the general necessity of things." Marcuse, *One-Dimensional Man*, 79.

31. See, e.g., Nicole-Edith Thevenin, *Revisionnisme et philosophie de l'alienation* (Paris: Christian Bourgeois, 1977).

32. Manuel Aguirre, *Esquema de la Doctrina Social Católica* (Caracas: Ediciones SIC, 1940).

33. Aguirre, *Doctrina Social Católica*, 32.

34. Quoted in Aguirre, *Doctrina Social Católica*, 132. *Quadragesimo anno* was a papal encyclical issued in 1931.

35. See Talcott Parsons' introduction to Weber's *Theory of Social and Economic Organization*, especially 56-86.

36. Among many other sources of practical ideas for accomplishing goals that can be called de-alienation are Richards, *Evaluation of Cultural Action*; and Howard Richards' Nehru Lectures given at Baroda University in India, available on the Internet at www.howardri.org. Both of these suggest research methods for evaluating projects to determine to what extent there is a change in cultural values.

37. As the nationalized oil industry was organized during the first administration of Carlos Andrés Pérez, PDVSA (Venezuela Oil, Inc.) acted as a holding company for three oil companies owned by Venezuela: MARAVEN, LAGOVEN, and CORPOVEN.

In a subsequent reorganization, MENEVEN joined these three to comprise the four operating subsidiaries of Venezuela's nationalized petroleum industry. Maria Victoria Murillo, *Labor Unions, Partisan Coalitions, and Market Reforms in Latin America* (New York and Cambridge: Cambridge University Press, 2001), 73.

38. John D. Martz and David J. Myers, eds., *Venezuela: The Democratic Experience* (New York and London: Praeger Publishers, 1986), 250. The oil company's sole goal at that time was profit for its single shareholder, the Venezuelan government. From the end of World War II to the end of the twentieth century, oil exports accounted for approximately two-thirds of government revenue and more than ninety percent of Venezuela's foreign exchange earnings. Oil revenues allowed the expansion of state-owned enterprises and allowed Venezuela to follow the development strategy known as import-substitution industrialization. The subsidies generated as a result of high taxes and royalties on oil profits and production were distributed in such a way as to enhance democratic stability in Venezuela. Jeffry Frieden, "Invested Interests: The Politics of National Economic Policies in a World of Global Finance," *International Organization* 45, no. 4 (Fall 1991), 184; Miguel Rodríguez, "Public Sector Behavior in Venezuela," in *The Public Sector and the Latin American Crisis*, ed. Felipe Larraín and Marcelo Selowsky (San Francisco: ICS Press, 1991), 238-41; and Terry Lynn Karl, "Petroleum and Political Pacts: The Transition to Democracy in Venezuela," in *Transitions from Authoritarian Rule: Latin America*, ed. Guillermo O'Donnell, Phillipe Schmitter, and Laurence Whitehead (Baltimore, Md.: Johns Hopkins University Press, 1986), 210-12; Dorothea Mommer, *El Estado Venezolano y la Industria Petrolera* (Caracas: Universidad Central de Venezuela, Facultad de Ciencias Económicas y Sociales, 1974). For the best statement of the reasons behind the Venezuelan oil nationalization, see Rómulo Betancourt, *Venezuela: Política y Petróleo* (Barcelona; Caracas; México; Editorial Seix Barral, 1979), originally published in 1956. Betancourt was the leader of organized labor in Venezuela whose decades-long campaign for nationalization brought him to the national stage and brought the nationalization to fruition. He is also credited with taking the initial steps in the formation of the Oil Producing and Exporting Countries cartel.

39. Laura Randall, *The Political Economy of Venezuelan Oil* (New York; Westport, Conn.; London: Praeger Publishers, 1987), 144-47. On the geological differences between these two regions, see Luis Vallenilla, *Oil: The Making of a New Economic Order, Venezuelan Oil and OPEC* (New York: McGraw-Hill Book Company, 1975), 198-99.

40. Martz and Myers, eds., *Venezuela: the Democratic Experience*, 278, 287, 289.

41. In his political history of Venezuela, Diego Bautista Urbaneja argues that it was precisely through this kind of grassroots-level political dialogue that the AD was able to achieve its early its early strength. The AD utilized a system of dense networks of social contacts, which Bautista Urbaneja labels "*el sistema conversacional venezolano*" ("the Venezuelan conversational system") or "*ideología del agasajo*" ("ideology of the banquet"); arising from these grassroots-level networks were the social compacts made among sectors of civil society and various party affiliates. According to Bautista Urbaneja, all of Venezuela's major political parties practiced this utilization of direct channels to the electorate (although the AD was perhaps the most skillful in this regard), and their emphasis upon consensus and social negotiation succeeded in suppressing the kind of overt disorder that has historically been used as pretext for coup d'etat by Latin American militaries. Diego Bautista Urbaneja, *Pueblo y petróleo en la política venezolana del siglo XX* (Caracas: CEPET, 1992).

42. A better known example of the general idea of community meetings to set goals for using public funds is the participatory budget process used in Porto Alegre and other cities. See Rebecca Abers, "Learning Democratic Practice: Distributing Government Resources through Popular Participation in Porto Alegre, Brazil," in M. Douglass and J. Friedmann, eds., *Cities for Citizens: planning and the rise of civil society in a global age* (Chichester, U.K.; and New York: J. Wiley, 1998), 39-66. See also Rebecca Abers, *Inventing Local Democracy: grassroots politics in Brazil* (Boulder, Colo.: Lynne Rienner Publishers, 2000).

43. Jürgen Habermas, *Communication and the Evolution of Society* (Boston: Beacon Press, 1979).

44. On sweat equity projects for home construction in Venezuela specifically, see Donald L. Herman, *Christian Democracy in Venezuela* (Chapel Hill, N.C.: University of North Carolina Press, 1980), 169.

45. Randall, *Political Economy*, 164-66.

46. These events occurred in the MENEVEN-dominated community of El Tigre; the former president of the bankrupt Banco de Trabajadores de Venezuela (BTV) was arrested and detained in 1984. Martz and Myers, eds., *Venezuela: the Democratic Experience*, 289.

47. See Centro de Estudios del Desarrollo (CENDES), *Estudio de diagnóstico para el plan maestro de ordenamiento territorial del area de la Faja Petrolifera de Orinoco* (Caracas: University of Venezuela, 1976). In the interest of academic honesty, we should point out that some scholars have raised objections to studies issued by CENDES, most notably the political scientist Daniel H. Levine. He criticizes CENDES studies for being too consensus-oriented, too willing to ignore and even trample cultural heterogeneity, and for merging explanation with prescription. Daniel H. Levine, *Conflict and Political Change in Venezuela* (Princeton, N.J.: Princeton University Press, 1973), 243-53. Although we cannot condone the trampling of cultural heterogeneity, our own writing should make clear that we consider Levine's other two criticisms less valid. Regardless, Levine's criticisms focus on the potential dangers of relying upon CENDES reports for assessing the political climate in Venezuela at the time he was writing and do not bear on our reliance upon such sources for our present purposes.

48. "*Sembrar el petróleo*" is a commonly used phrase in Venezuelan political discourse. It was popularized by Arturo Uslar Pietri in *De una a otra Venezuela* (Caracas: Monte Avila Editores, 1972), first published in 1946.

49. A good summary of the development of Venezuelan oil policy is offered in Franklin Tugwell, "Petroleum Policy and the Political Process," in Martz and Myers, eds., *Venezuela: the Democratic Experience*. For economic histories that treat the role of oil in the Venezuelan national economy and the use of oil in projects of "economic development," see Edwin Lieuwen, "The Politics of Energy in Venezuela," in *Latin American Oil Companies and the Politics of Energy*, ed. John D. Wirth (Lincoln, Neb.: University of Nebraska Press, 1985); and Jorge Salazar-Carrillo, *Oil in the Economic Development of Venezuela* (New York: Praeger Publishers, 1976). Both of these treatments corroborate our assessment of the basic trends in the twentieth-century economic history of Venezuela. Lieuwen and Salazar-Carrillo, however, would disagree with our assessment of the causes for the recent failures of Venezuelan attempts to use oil to fund the project of social democracy. This disagreement stems from these authors' acceptance of tenets that we call into question. Because Lieuwen and Salazar-Carrillo do not historicize the concept of "economic rationality," they find historical causality only within the

mechanisms of capitalist economic rationality. Therefore, Lieuwen places substantial blame upon the exclusive role of the state, which, in his estimation, crowded out the private sector, with attendant repercussions for the Venezuelan economy as a whole. Salazar-Carrillo places blame in part upon deterioration of terms of trade; poor handling of balance-of-payments problems; and the fact that contrary to the hopes of Venezuelan policy-makers, economics does not posit a positive correlation between a just income-distribution and "economic growth."

50. Fernando Coronil, *The Magical State* (Chicago: University of Chicago Press, 1997), 247. On the implosion of the oil bonanza, see also Karl, *Paradox of Plenty.* In trying to explain why so many of the oil-producing nation-states cannot seem to achieve satisfactory levels of "development," she finds that "a common condition reduces the range of decision-making, rewards some decisions and forms of behavior more than others, and shapes the preferences of officials in a manner that is not conducive to successful development." Karl, *Paradox of Plenty,* xvi. She explains further, "frameworks for decision-making, that is, the incentive structures embedded in the institutions of a particular political economy, hold the key to understanding different development trajectories. Above all else, these incentives are the reflection and product of power relations . . . at a given point in time; they cannot be attributed primarily to either belief systems or preferences, although both may play a role. They tend to persist even when power relations and their accompanying ideologies have begun to change, and they cannot be changed at will—even when there is widespread understanding that they are sub-optimal or outright should be altered." Karl, *Paradox of Plenty,* xvi. Although these cited passages should make clear that we strongly disagree with several key points in her analysis, we are sympathetic to Karl's identification of *institutions* as holding the key to understanding what has gone awry in Venezuela and indeed in the world as a whole. We also believe that had Karl analyzed these institutions not only in the realms of politics and economics but also at the epistemological level, she might have altered her conclusion as to whether these institutions can be "changed at will."

51. See Hans-Peter Nissen and Bernard Mommer, *Adiós a la bonanza, crisis de la distribución del ingreso en Venezuela* (Caracas: ILDIS-CENDES, Editorial Nueva Sociedad, 1989); and Ricardo Hausmann, "Sobre la crisis económica venezolana," in *América Latina, alternativas para la democracia,* ed. Juan Carlos Rey, Julia Barragán, and Ricardo Hausmann (Caracas: Monte Avila Editores, 1992), 87-113.

52. For a vision of alienation and poverty in today's Venezuela, see the film written by Nestor Caballero and Elia Schneider, *Huelepega, ley de la calle* ("Glue-sniffing, the Law of the Street"), directed by Elia Schneider (Caracas: Venezuela Unity Films, 1999).

53. From 1983 to 1993, Venezuela was racked by a number of severe economic and political crises and violent upheavals. On February 18, 1983 (so-called Black Friday), the currency collapsed. This collapse was followed by years of economic stagnation and inflation. The next major catastrophe was the Venezuelan government's adoption of IMF structural adjustment policies. President Carlos Andrés Pérez had previously characterized the IMF as "assassins in the service of economic totalitarianism"; by the time he surrendered to the wishes of the IMF in 1989, he claimed that he was not a neoliberal but "a true social democrat with no alternatives." Murillo, *Labor Unions,* 56. The adoption of IMF policies was met with a wave of urban riots beginning on February 27, 1989 (this day is commonly referred to as "27-F" by Venezuelans). The year 1992 saw two coup attempts, on February 4 ("4-F") and on November 27 ("27-N"). Yet another crisis of political legitimacy came with the impeachment of President Carlos Andrés Pérez in May

1993, on charges of corruption. An account of the structural problems and social tensions that would give way to these events is offered in Jennifer McCoy, "The Politics of Adjustment: Labor and the Venezuelan Debt Crisis," *Journal of Interamerican Studies and World Affairs* 28 (Winter 1986-87): 103-38.

54. Venezuelans across the political spectrum were exhibiting growing frustrations with neoliberal economic policies during the administration of President Carlos Andrés Pérez (1989-1993) and that of his successor, President Rafael Caldera (1994-1999). See Steve Ellner, "The Politics of Privatization," *NACLA Report on the Americas* 31, no. 3 (Nov.-Dec. 1997), 6-9. For a critique of neoliberalism by a member of the Venezuelan Left, see Fred Rosen's February 1997 interview with Pablo Medina, a founder of *La Causa R* (Radical Cause). *La Causa R* was founded by union leaders; although it was quite small at the time of its founding, this leftist party grew to have nationwide support and strength because of its opposition to the neoliberal reforms carried out by the Pérez administration. At the time of Rosen's interview with Pablo Medina, *La Causa R* was preparing to take action to right the economic injustices facing Venezuela by bringing the issue of the Venezuelan foreign debt before the International Court of Justice. *NACLA Report on the Americas* 31, no. 1 (July-Aug. 1997): 55-56. The failure of the privatization schemes and other neoliberal measures imposed during the Caldera administration, in accordance with the dictates of the IMF, was borne out in drastically declining living standards in the latter half of this administration. By June 1997, unemployment rates were running high; the historically low-paying informal economy was in rapid expansion; an estimated 45 percent of Venezuelan households lacked sufficient income to meet basic needs; and nearly one-fifth of households were unable to meet minimal dietary requirements. Margarita López-Maya and Luis E. Lander, "A Military Populist Takes Venezuela," *NACLA Report on the Americas* 32, no. 5 (March-April 1999), 12. That Chávez and his attempted coup became symbols around which the popular classes rallied is expressed clearly in Angela Zago, *La rebelión de Los Angeles* (Caracas: Fuentes Editores, 1992).

55. In the election for a Constituent Assembly held July 25, 1999, voters gave an overwhelming majority to the coalition of Hugo Chávez, the Patriotic Pole (PP). Candidates of the PP won 123 out of 131 seats. The newly elected legislative body was charged with drafting a new constitution, which was drawn largely from a proposal written by Chávez himself. Measures Chávez put forward in favor of the popular classes included guaranteeing the right to plebiscites, referenda, and popular "consultations"; the direct popular election of judges; and a guaranteed right to health care. Gregory Wilpert, "Venezuelans Give Chávez Control of Constituent Assembly," *NACLA Report on the Americas* 33, no. 2 (Sept.-Oct. 1999): 45-46.

56. Indeed, according to the U.S. media, President Chávez "resigned" from power on April 12, 2002, only to return to power two days later, on April 14. The consensus that emerged in the weeks following, however, holds that this was not in fact a resignation but rather a coup d'état that failed. During the brief time of this ouster of Chávez, the acting president was Pedro Carmona Estanga, the head of the Venezuelan Chamber of Commerce (technically known as the Federation of Chambers and Associations of Commerce and Production, or FEDECAMARAS). Carmona Estanga had the support of the Bush administration in the U.S. During his brief time in power, Carmona Estanga dissolved the Venezuelan National Assembly and Supreme Court and fired all the mayors and governors throughout the nation. He also announced the immediate termination of Venezuelan oil sales to Cuba. "Bush Officials Met With Venezuelans Who Ousted Leader," *New*

York Times, 16 April 2002; Christopher Marquis, "U.S. Revises Report of Venezuela Contacts," *New York Times*, 18 April 2002; Ginger Thompson, "Behind the Upheaval in Venezuela," *New York Times*, 18 April 2002. See also the coverage by Maximilien Arvelaiz, Temir Porras Ponceleon, and Alexander Main in the Spring 2002 issue of *Covert Action Quarterly*. This journal carried an article by the first two of these three authors outlining the shifts taking place in Venezuela in March 2002 that seemed to indicate an imminent coup attempt. As the journal went to press with this article predicting an attempted coup to overthrow Chávez, the predicted events occurred, and the journal included a firsthand account written by these three authors, who were present in Caracas. See Alexander Main, Maximilien Arvelaiz, and Temir Porras-Ponceleon, "Virtual Reality: Real Coup," *Covert Action Quarterly*, no. 72 (Spring 2002): inside cover, 5, 34, 40; and Maximilien Arvelaiz and Temir Porras Ponceleon, "U.S. Pushing for a Coup d'Etat: Venezuela, Target of Opportunity," *Covert Action Quarterly*, no. 72 (Spring 2002): 12-17. Another eyewitness account of the events of April 2002 is presented by Gregory Wilpert, "Coup and Countercoup: An Eyewitness Account," *NACLA Report on the Americas* 35, no. 6 (May/June 2002): 2, 6, 55. As the finishing touches were being put on this chapter, the Venezuelan economy was being shaken and Venezuelan society rent asunder by a weeks-long general strike instigated by oil workers opposed to the Chavez administration.

57. Academics from CENDES are advising Chávez. See Teodoro Petkoff, *Una Segunda Opinión* (Caracas: Grijalbo, 2000). This does not change our opinion that if more of the humanistic integrated development ideas associated with CENDES had been applied earlier, Venezuela would be better off now. Prophetically, a CENDES report stated in 1976: "[W]ithout actions based on timely foresight, the beginning of the 21st century may find a Venezuela where the phenomena of marginalization of the population, of the destruction of the environment, and the deterioration of the quality of life will not only have deepened, but will have become much more widespread." CENDES, *Estudio de diagnóstico*, 2.

58. General Alfonzo Ravard quoted in Martz and Myers, eds., *Venezuela: the Democratic Experience*, 250. Nationalization as a measure taken to bring about greater social justice typically fails because it occurs strictly within the constitutive rules of modern society, and within these rules are mechanisms that serve to punish nation-states that undertake nationalization. Paul Sigmund attests to this when he writes of the Chilean copper nationalization that occurred during the Allende administration: "The Chilean experience seems to indicate that—in the absence of authoritarian economic controls, an explicit commitment to egalitarianism, and external financial support as in Cuba—nationalization may actually be counterproductive to the goal of creating social justice because it adversely affects productivity, investment, and prices." Paul E. Sigmund, *Multinationals in Latin America: The Politics of Nationalization* (Madison, Wisc.: University of Wisconsin Press, 1980), 168. For a lengthy study focused on the inherent weakness of nationalization (and by extension, other efforts at social change that focus solely on the sphere of production), see Joanna B. Swanger, "Workers' Control and the Structural Trap of the Chilean Copper Nationalization, 1955-1973" (master's thesis, University of Texas at Austin, 1993).

59. Leaving aside the question of ownership for a moment, history demonstrates that even efforts to assert minimal forms of increased worker *control* over production can have boomerang effects. An oft-repeated example of this is that unionization and union activism can result indirectly in workers finding their circumstances worse than before

such efforts when corporations simply relocate production to avoid worker demands and leave an area sorely lacking in jobs. One of the best recent treatments of this phenomenon is Jefferson Cowie, *Capital Moves: RCA's 70-Year Quest for Cheap Labor* (Ithaca, N.Y. and London: Cornell University Press, 1999). Cowie follows RCA's moves as it shifted production from the heavily industrialized (and unionized) northeastern United States (Camden, New Jersey); to Bloomington, Indiana; to the "right-to-work" U.S. South (Memphis, Tennessee); and finally "offshore" to Ciudad Juárez, Mexico. He focuses on the demands pressed by workers in each community and upon the eventual consequences for these communities after RCA left. See also Andrew Herod, ed., *Organizing the Landscape: Geographical Perspectives on Labor Unionism* (Minneapolis, Minn.: University of Minnesota Press, 1998); and Doreen Massey, *Spatial Divisions of Labour: Social Structures and the Geography of Production* (London: Macmillan, 1984).

60. Milton Friedman (with the Assistance of Rose D. Friedman), *Capitalism and Freedom* (Chicago and London: University of Chicago Press, 1962), 31-36.

61. Ricardo, *Principles of Political Economy*, 275.

62. John Maynard Keynes, *The End of Laissez-Faire* (London: The Hogarth Press, 1926), 39-40, 50-54.

63. See George W. Schuyler, *Hunger in a Land of Plenty* (Cambridge, Mass.: Schenkman Publishing Company, 1980). The trends upon which Schuyler reports only continued. By the late 1980s, Venezuela was one of the top five markets for semi-processed foods imported from the U.S. Maury E. Brendahl, Philip C. Abbott, and Michael R. Reed, eds., *Competitiveness in International Food Markets* (Boulder, Colo.; San Francisco; Oxford: Westview Press, 1994), 86.

Chapter 15

Social Democracy on a World Scale: The World Bank and The Logic of Love

Why De-Alienation is a Solution to the Problem of Poverty

It is not obviously true that de-alienation, as we have adapted the concept, names practices that would solve the problems of poverty. Yet it is true. The reasons why it is not obvious do not stem from lack of empirical data. The factual premise needed to prove that de-alienation would end poverty is, although not well known, in plain sight for all to see and not in doubt. The lack of obviousness of the conclusion is due to the difficulty of explaining the meaning of the concept. Once the concept is understood, it becomes obvious that if it were put into practice there would be no poverty.

The factual premise is that there is no natural obstacle to eliminating poverty. Many of the relevant facts are documented in *Food First* by Frances Moore Lappé and Joseph Collins, which demonstrates that there would be no hunger if there were democratic control of resources.[1] Other relevant facts are documented in *Food Resources, Conventional and Novel* by N.W. Pirie, a biochemist at Rothamstead Laboratories in England, who shows that as a matter of biochemistry, the problem of transforming the earth's resources into adequate nutrition for all is easily solved.[2] R. Buckminster Fuller summed up the matter when he wrote, "We now know scientifically that for the first time in history there can be enough to support continually all of expanding humanity at previously undreamed-of and ever-advancing standards of living and intellectual satisfaction in effective participation in the evolutionary processes."[3]

Alienation means separation. De-alienation means unity. If people were de-alienated, they would work together in unity. Since there is no natural obstacle to eliminating poverty, it follows that if people worked together in unity to eliminate it, it would be eliminated. Thus the proposition that de-alienation would end poverty is very nearly a tautology. The proposition does not say, however, how to persuade and guide people to work together in unity. It opens a space for two crucial questions which it asks but leaves unanswered: 1) where are people going to get the motivation to do the things that must be done to meet other people's needs, and thus to eliminate poverty? And 2) assuming that they are motivated, how are people going to be guided so that they will know what to do to meet other people's needs?

Nevertheless, the near-tautology that de-alienation would end poverty is significant, because it throws into relief the fact that if people would and could work together to end poverty, it would end. It makes it clear that when and if answers to the two questions stated above are found and implemented, there will be no poverty.

Conceptualizing the problem of poverty in this way makes it easy to see two further points, which may be loosely termed corollaries:

> *Corollary 1.* Expecting people to be motivated to act to meet other people's needs by a desire for economic gain or profit is only a partial answer to the problem of motivation, not the whole answer.

> *Corollary 2.* Expecting the price-signals generated by supply and demand in markets to tell people how to act to meet other people's needs is only a partial answer to the problem of guidance, not the whole answer.

Conceptualizing the problem in this way, and noticing that markets and market-like institutions are prominent among economic arrangements world-wide, also makes it easy to see what can be called a "corollary" of the "corollaries," which has been corroborated many times by bitter experience:

> *Corollary 3.* To the extent that a society depends for meeting people's needs on profit motives and price-signals, measures designed to alleviate poverty, which weaken profit motives and/or distort price-signals, are likely to backfire.

Thus the proposition that de-alienation will end poverty, although it relies on confidence in findings of the natural sciences for its optimism, is not so much a prescription for ending poverty as a frame of reference for thinking about what would be required to end poverty.

Similar points can be made about other concepts we have proposed or discussed as frameworks for thinking about how to end poverty: Adam Smith's concept of value-in-use, cultural resources, stewardship, trusteeship, volunteering, putting back into nature what you take out, local self-reliance, society producing for itself, Islamic social principles, Buddhist ideas of community and of right livelihood, and others.

The Logic of Love as Another Framework for Thinking about Poverty

In this chapter we are going to work with yet another concept, which is also a near tautology. It is also true by definition once some factual premises that are not in doubt are acknowledged. It can also be accepted or rejected as a useful way to think about how to eliminate poverty. By introducing now in this last chapter still another concept of social democracy, i.e., social democracy as a logic of love, we do not want to be understood as dropping one subject and taking up another. Rather we are continuing to practice the philosophical strategy that we endeavored to demonstrate in Chapter 1, and to articulate in Chapter 2.

Our shifting from one concept to another and our reliance upon diverse traditions is not simply an assertion that everybody is right and nobody is wrong. Rather, our catholicity and conceptual flexibility pursue a vision of human language and thought in which questions about who is right and who is wrong fade into the background. Judging logic, which Aristotle defined as sets of rules for the conduct of arguments, according to its own rules, is comparatively unimportant, compared to the more important task of judging logic according to whether it functions (or fails to function) to facilitate the delivery of the goods: the food, the clothing, the housing, the health, the happiness.

Viewed in the manner we recommend, social democracy does not require any single ideology. At any given time and place, it requires some ideology, because people have to share a code to communicate, and people have to communicate to cooperate. But it does not depend for its success on universal agreement. On the contrary: it depends for its success on the celebration of diversity.[4]

When we introduce still another way of talking about the limitations of economics and the construction of social democracy, it is not because we have changed our minds, now dropping the idea of de-alienation and taking up instead the idea of the logic of love. It is because we continue to believe that there are any number of different sets of conventional cultural norms, and any number of patterns-of-talk, which can function to facilitate cooperation to meet needs. Unfortunately, there are also any number of character flaws, and any number of conceptual errors, that function to frustrate cooperation and sharing.

To begin our discussion of the World Bank and the logic of love, we repeat an assessment made in the previous chapter: "Poverty, and therefore violence, are just not going to go away until the contradictions of commodity exchange as a way of life are successfully resolved."[5] Commodity exchange as a way of life can be called non-love as a way of life. This is because the extant institution of commodity exchange perpetuates the structural contradictions that make the elimination of poverty on a world scale an impossible task until those contradictions are resolved (even though it is possible to eliminate poverty locally in open economies that benefit from favorable terms of trade with the rest of the world, such as Holland and Singapore).

The basic rules of the game of modern society can be called rules of non-love. Rules for deals. The logic of exchange. The worker says to the employer, "I will work for you, but only if you pay me." The employer says to the worker, "I will pay you, but only if you work." The property owner says to the tenant, "I will share my property, but only if I am paid." The customer says to the merchant, "I will give you money, but only if you give me what I want to buy." The merchant says to the customer, "I will give you what you need, your daily bread, your prescription medicine, or whatever it may be, but only if you pay my price." The investor says, "I want the maximum return on my investment consistent with safety. If the needs of others are met by my investment, that is okay, but my purpose is to make money, not to meet needs." Thus accumulation of profit becomes the motor that moves society, and when that motor falters, society falters.

The rules of the logic of exchange are so basic, so much a part of modern common sense, that it is assumed that they reflect human nature, the way humans are and always will be. Economics, for its part, building a social science from the material offered by the institutions it observes, takes pride in distinguishing itself from the pre-economic notions, like the "just price" of St. Thomas Aquinas, in terms of which traditional societies understood themselves. It has been the pride of economics that, like God, it accepts people just as they are, just as it observes them to be in the societies it studies. Unlike God, it does not try to change them. Adam Smith's friend David Hume held that any plan for the reform of society that relied on the improvement of manners and morals was wholly imaginary. Smith agreed with Hume, and the economists following him have dedicated themselves to squaring the circle: manipulating the rules of non-love to maximize welfare.

The logic of love is more comprehensive. In its basic form it is simpler than the logic of exchange. Early cultures discovered it long before economics was invented. The logic of love says that we ought to act to meet another person's needs because of what the other person needs, not because of what we ourselves will get out of the deal. Given, however, that exchange may actually work to everyone's benefit, we can think of exchange itself as a sort of friendly game we play with each other, in which, at least some of the time, everybody wins. Competition thus might be love in disguise. It might be what Hegel called a "ruse of reason" in which what appears to be action from self-interest turns out, in general and in the long run, to be a practical form of love.

A moment's reflection will show that Gandhi was quite correct to maintain that without the logic of love, which he called "the law of love," the human species would have perished long ago.[6] The logic of non-love works, to the extent that it works at all, only in the middle years of life. The very young and the very old are smelly and unproductive. They are non-starters in games played according to the logic of commodity exchange. They do not produce anything of value to sell in a market. If they are going to have their needs met at all, it will be because they are loved unconditionally. (It is true that in modern society, by the legal fiction of property ownership, there are times when we say that a very old person, even one bed-ridden and demented, is "paying" for board and care, out of earnings from prior years deposited in a bank. This is a fiction because all they have to offer today in exchange for their care is money saved from work they did in the past, which is theirs because the law says it is theirs. Since they produce nothing now, they could confer a net benefit on the rest of the world by dying and letting someone else inherit their savings. In any case, whatever one thinks of the legal fiction of property ownership, the majority of very old persons exhaust their savings before they die, and rely for their care during their last years on inter-generational solidarity.)

A further moment's reflection will show that even in the middle years of life there is no necessary reason to suppose that a person's needs will be met by the logic of exchange. There is no necessary reason to suppose that each person in society will have something to sell, some marketable skill or valuable service to provide. There is no necessary reason to suppose that each person in society is in a position to earn enough to be able to strike deals to obtain from willing sellers her or his food, clothing, shelter, and other necessities. Thus the very basic rules that constitute society produce what Viviane Forrester has aptly called "the economic horror."[7] The horror of economics is that everybody is presumed capable of earning enough on the open market to get by, but it is not true. Those who do not earn enough to get by are told that it is their own fault. As *homo economicus* they fail, and where being human is defined in terms of *homo economicus*, they fail as humans. And Forrester's examples are drawn mainly from France—a country in the first world, the developed world. She does not even consider the greater economic horrors found in the third world.

Although ancient peoples knew many horrors, the horror of being rejected by the labor market as an unsalable commodity is a modern invention. Nobody doubts, nonetheless, that the modern world is on the whole better. What some people doubt is whether it can be improved to eliminate its principal horrors, or whether its basic structure makes its horrors insuperable. Rephrased, the question is whether capitalism is tough love, or not love at all. One alternative, which we will call the Tough Love Worldview, conceives of today's global capitalist economy as the current phase in humanity's ethical construction of its social reality. It regards capitalism as a servant of a transcendent ideal. Its logic, the logic of exchange, can in principle be held accountable to, and transformed by, a standard higher than itself. The rules of non-love can be thought of as practical concessions to human nature, whose great merit is that some of the time they produce indirectly what love would have produced directly. The other alternative we will call the Immutable Framework Worldview: capitalism is not love at all. This view holds that the nations of the world whose attempts to create social democracy within their borders have been frustrated by the requirements of the global marketplace have encountered an insuperable obstacle, a global quasi-physical reality that neither should nor can be transformed. The logic of exchange rules humanity, and not vice-versa; it is just what it is, by natural right, objective fact, cruel fate.

Our argument will be that the history of the World Bank supports reasons for choosing the first of these two alternatives. With all due respect for those who advocate framing the problem in a different way, and with sympathy for those who fear that we may just further muddy already muddy waters by analyzing multifaceted issues in a dualistic framework, we will proceed according to the heuristic hypothesis that the contrast between Tough Love and Immutable Framework is illuminating and useful.

The Birth of a Moral Orphan: the World Bank

The World Bank, together with its sibling, the International Monetary Fund, was born at Bretton Woods, New Hampshire, in the second week of July of 1944. It was born an orphan; its natural parents, the U.S. Department of the Treasury and the British Exchequer, abandoned it immediately, insisting that from the moment of its birth it be autonomous. The closest thing it had to a moral compass was Article III, section 4 (vii) of its founding charter as stated in its Articles of Agreement, which provided, "Loans made or guaranteed by the Bank shall, except in special circumstances, be for specific projects of reconstruction or development." Although "World Bank" is its commonly used nickname, the official name given to it at Bretton Woods was "International Bank for Reconstruction and Development." Much turned on the word "development," especially since the other alternative, "reconstruction" ceased to be pursued a few years after World War II was over. For what purpose there was supposed to be "development" was not stated or known. The World Bank was born with no religion, no cosmology, no philosophy, and no democratic process for validating its rules and actions by the consent of the world's peoples.

Its early years were dominated by a single imperative: to gain the confidence of Wall Street's institutional investors. (Wealthy private individuals have never been a significant source of funds for the World Bank.) To do anything, the Bank needed to raise capital, and right after World War II there was only one significant capital market in the world, the United States capital market. The people in that market to whom the Bank had to sell itself were directors of life insurance companies, directors of mutual savings banks, trustees of large charities, trust companies, trustees of educational institutions, and the state legislators in the several states who determined which securities were eligible for purchase by managers holdings funds in a fiduciary capacity. Most of them had been stung before. In the 1920s Americans had bought large quantities of foreign bonds, only to see many of them go into default in the 1930s. Now, beginning in the 1940s, the World Bank was offering them a new deal that was a sweet deal: supposedly no-risk bonds, guaranteed by the capital subscriptions and the credit of the governments which had signed the Articles of Agreement of the World Bank. Only the United States government guarantee was considered to be worth anything, and after Franklin Roosevelt's holiday on foreclosures and other populist shenanigans, even the U.S. guarantee was imperfect. Thus the World Bank, regardless of what it might mean to be a "development bank" with the welfare of the world's peoples somehow at heart (as distinct from just being a plain bank) believed that it had to start by gaining the confidence of American institutional investors.

In this atmosphere, the provisions of the United Nations charter, which provided that the Bank would be a specialized agency of the United Nations responsible to the General Assembly, quickly became dead letters. The Bank had to be an autonomous agency, above politics, above international law as expressed in the UN Charter, above democracy, above morals, above love, above God, above reason, above ecology, above sentiment, above humanitarian ideals—for the sake of one high standard at least temporarily more important than all else: to assure trustees and directors in charge of investing other people's money that the funds advanced to the Bank would be repaid, on time, and with interest. That capitalism was immutable, that no government and especially no revolutionary or reformist third world government had any right to change it, that it was answerable to no authority higher than its own rules, was not deduced from philosophy or theology. The Immutable Framework Worldview appeared at the time to be an obligatory ideology, imposed by facts, since it appeared that if the Bank could not gain the confidence of investors, it could not do anything else.

Clinging to the Idea of "Development" for Lack of a Moral Compass

The period dominated by establishing the credibility of the Bank as a borrower coincided roughly with the period when the Bank made reconstruction loans to Western Europe. Thereafter, in the early 1950s, the Bank began what would prove to be its main activity: making development loans in the impoverished nations of the third world. Humanitarians in and around the Bank clung to the word "development" because it was the only major value-laden word that suggested normative standards, including some sort of concern with meeting the needs of people. The alternatives to "development" were value-laden words like "sound," "competent," and "creditworthy" that suggested approving only low-risk loan applications, and then efficiently collecting principal and interest payments, with no goal more heroic than milking the third world to produce a steady flow of unearned income to bondholders. Similarly, humanitarians often clung to the twin disciplines of competitive markets and technical rate-of-return calculations because the alternatives were corruption, sloth, and nepotism. Any port in a storm.

In spite of the role that the idea of "being a development bank" played in keeping alive the idea that the Bank had some sort of mission to alleviate the plight of the world's poor in some way, the idea of "development," especially as the Bank interpreted it in its early years, was an inherently dysfunctional concept. The Colombian scholar Arturo Escobar, in his book *Encountering Development*, has admirably charted the rise of development ideology after World War II under the aegis of agencies like the World Bank.[8] His excellent account is enriched by his own experience as a participant in dysfunctional efforts to "develop" Colombia. Without presuming to add anything to Escobar's account, we will make three brief points about what is wrong with the very idea of "development."

First, with respect to the role of "development" as a concept organizing the space of the world, "development" divides the globe geographically into two parts: the "developed" countries, and the others, which are classified as "underdeveloped" or "developing." This way of organizing space overlooks and obscures the more important division of humanity between the rich, whose needs are met, and the poor, whose needs are not met. Rich and poor are found in every country.

Second, with respect to the role of "development" as a concept organizing time, the very idea postulates that the "developing" countries are moving from a past in which human needs were not met, toward a developed future in which human needs will be met.[9] The images of a "developed" society that typify the end goal to which "development" is supposed to lead have been drawn mainly from the social democracies. As we have shown in detail in the four chapters on Sweden, however, although it is possible under exceptional circumstances to pay for a welfare state with revenues derived from export-led growth, it is not possible for all countries simultaneously to be "developed," in this sense (i.e., the sense in which Sweden and others typify "development"). The constitutive rules of capitalism imply that the future promised to "developing" countries by the concept of "development" is a utopia that will never come.

Third, with respect to the role of "development" as a concept identifying the causes and dynamic forces which have led to the relative prosperity of the first world, and which supposedly could, in principle, lead to a similar prosperity of the third world, World Bank ideas of "development" center on the Bank's role in contributing to meeting the "capital needs" of developing countries. The Bank "finances" development, as one might "finance" a business to enable it to invest and thereafter to turn the investment into a profitable enterprise. Development is conceived as economic growth, which means capital accumulation—not to be sure, simply as accumulating money, but as accumulating physically usable capital goods. This view of historical causality overlooks and obscures the fact that insofar as the working classes of the social democracies achieved high wages, health benefits, pensions, and safe working conditions, their success was not caused by unfettered capital accumulation, but by a prolonged struggle by the democratic elements of society to win a larger share of the social product for the people. The very idea of "development" as the World Bank has employed the term, connotes a kind of capital accumulation in the third world that organized labor did not let capital get away with in the first world.[10]

The inherently dysfunctional categories for thought provided by mainstream ideas of "development" have led humanitarians to improve the concept by advocating revisions such as integrated development, balanced development, integral development, constructive development, and sustainable development.[11] Others, such as the Peruvian theologian Gustavo Gutierrez, have argued that people of good will should not speak of "development" at all but instead of "liberation."[12] We are introducing into these terminological debates another way to distinguish a better from a worse category of thought, which is to contrast a narrow logic of exchange with a broad logic of love. The narrow worldview we are calling Immutable Framework, and the broad worldview Tough Love.

We are proposing as an alternative to the categories derived from the logic of exchange and accumulation that are embedded in mainstream ideas of "development," categories derived from what Gandhi called "the law of love." We will suggest that over time, and in the light of experience, the World Bank, and the international community generally, have been moving toward a love ethic. Our proposal draws on an idea expressed by Martin Luther King, Jr., in his doctoral dissertation: Justice has no ontological reality independent of love. "Justice is dependent on love. It is a part of love's activity."[13] It is not that there are no rules of justice—for example, the rule so important to the logic of exchange and so important to the Bank that debts ought to be paid—but that those rules are meant to serve a higher purpose. We are supporting the idea of *caritas* as the general form of the virtues that should guide life that was systematically developed by St. Thomas Aquinas in the Middle Ages.[14]

But before developing further the idea of the logic of love as an alternative to, or more comprehensive form of, the idea of development, it is necessary to say a few words about the ambiguous status of humanitarian ideals in the early history of the Bank. We have analyzed the Bank's idea of "development" as dysfunctional in the light of the presumed purpose of eliminating poverty, but it is by no means clear that the Bank in its early days had any such purpose.

The early memoranda by Harry Dexter White, the United States Treasury Department official whose proposals eventually took the form of the Articles of Agreement that chartered the World Bank, do not say anything about great humanitarian ideals. The problem as White saw it was that normal commerce had been disrupted by World War II, and even before World War II normal commerce had been disrupted by defaults and nationalizations that made investors in the rich countries unwilling to risk their capital in the poor countries. White's proposal for a World Bank was a scheme for shoring up capitalist normality.[15] John Maynard Keynes, who chaired the committee at Bretton Woods that prepared and presented the final draft of the Articles of Agreement, stated that a principal function of the Bank would be to develop the productive capacities of the world.[16] He may have intended to imply that increased productive capacity would in itself relieve the suffering of the poor, in which case what he intended to imply was false. Or he may have had in mind that parallel to the Bank's work in financing the increase of productive capacity there would be the sort of Keynesian macromanaging of the economy that would feature raising wages to create more aggregate demand for industry's products.[17] It is true that the speech of U.S. Treasury Secretary Henry Morgenthau at Bretton Woods spoke in glowing terms of the benefits to humanity to be expected from the IMF and World Bank, but it remained unclear whether this meant that eliminating poverty was to be in itself an explicit goal of the Bank's operations, or simply a consequence attributed by mainstream economic theory to the normal processes of capital accumulation.[18]

In the early years of the World Bank (until Robert McNamara's speech as its president in Nairobi in 1973), it remained ambiguous whether contributing to ending poverty was the Bank's goal, and whether it would measure its success by what it did to end poverty. During thirteen of its early years the Bank's President was Eugene Black. He was credited with having done more than anyone else to make the Bank credible as an issuer of bonds on Wall Street—where he himself had worked for Chase Bank before he moved from New York to Washington to join the World Bank. Black said that the Bank was setting out to prove to the world that private enterprise works.[19] Perhaps he meant that the once-profitable business of private investment in the third world could be revived with the help of World Bank loans guaranteed by the commitments of first world governments to make their taxpayers cover any defaults. But perhaps he meant instead, or also, that private enterprise would solve the problems of the poor by creating general abundance in which the poor would share.

Another Approach: the Logic of Love as a Real Moral Compass

Suppose we wipe the slate clean, state frankly and unambiguously that eliminating poverty and meeting human needs is our goal, and forget, at least temporarily, the whole idea of "development." One of the first things we will notice if we mingle with the impoverished masses of the world and observe their lives, is that the logic of exchange is not working for them. They do not have enough money. They do not have enough to sell, either as services or as goods, to get enough money. Unable to meet their needs relying only on Adam Smith's famous "natural tendency to truck or barter," they are finding other ways to pursue happiness.

Some of the alternatives to the logic of commodity exchange are versions of the logic of love, and some are not. Millions are turning to fundamentalist religions, finding that pre-modern rules for living grounded in precepts such as those of the Holy Qur'an work for them. They give their lives meaning and hold together the families and clans on which they depend for mutual aid. Millions are turning to crime, finding that what they cannot get on the free market by voluntary exchange where buyer and seller consent, they can get by involuntary exchange, enforced by violence or concealed by stealth. Large numbers, especially in Africa, have turned to civil war as a way of life; even children arm themselves and live by plunder in the service of a warlord or political cause. Millions more have turned to begging. What they cannot get by offering equivalent value in return, they get by appealing to the hearts of passersby. Millions more live on relief supplies provided by charitable organizations, while additional millions live on welfare payments provided by governments. Millions more scavenge on the streets, picking up and using the trash that others have discarded. Millions more are in prison, living at public expense as officially certified enemies of society—while other millions also live at public expense as their guards. Many others in the ghettos of this world elect to detach subjective reality from objective reality. Not being served by any of the cultural logics humans have invented to make life work, they escape into altered states of consciousness. Some drink themselves to death, some hurl insane curses at imaginary interlocutors, some cling to a studied apathy while they wait to die.

The evident inability of the logic of exchange and of capital accumulation to provide the motivation and guidance needed to meet the needs of the people of the world, does not imply that there is no role for the logic of exchange. Indeed, some of the most successful movements for alleviating poverty have consisted of the imaginative use of the logic of exchange combined with a healthy dose of the logic of love. For example, love is built into the ideology of the Grameen Bank in Bangladesh, which has been copied more or less faithfully in many countries. The Grameen Bank loans small sums to five-member groups of poor people to empower them to make a living. Muhammad Yunus, the founder of Grameen Bank, describes as follows part of the pre-loan training given to borrowers:

> We repeat the following advice many times to them so that they will remember it when the occasion arises: "Please never get angry with the person who cannot pay the installment. Please don't put pressure on her to make her pay. Be a good friend, don't turn into an enemy. As a good friend, your first response should be, 'Oh, my God, she is in trouble, we must go and help her out.'" We advise them, "First find out the story behind the non-repayment. From our experience we can tell you that most often there is a sad story behind each case of non-repayment. When you get the full story, you'll find out how stupid it

would have been to twist her arm to get the money. She can't pay because her husband ran away with the money. As a good friend your responsibility will be to go and find her husband and bring him back, hopefully, with the money. It may also happen that your friend could not pay the installments because the cow that she bought with the loan money died. As good friends, you should promptly stand by her side, give her consolation and courage at this disaster. She is totally shaken by the shock of the event. You should cheer her up and help her to pull herself together. Ask Grameen to give her another loan, and re-schedule and convert the previous loan into a long-term loan."[20]

Starting with the principle that meeting needs is the goal, one can propose a logic of love as a viewpoint including, but more comprehensive than, the early World Bank's concept of "development." Three basic tenets of a logic of love are the following:

Tenet 1. With respect to organizing the space of the world, it is useful to think of the world as divided into "ghettos" and "suburbs." By "ghetto" we do not mean a racially or ethnically segregated area, but a place where poor people live, such as the inner city of an American metropolis. The ghetto can be thought of as a place where there is no major investment. It is a low-profit high-risk area, and therefore not attractive to investors.[21] Consequently the people there must live in some way other than by earning money through a job created by an investor—by government subsidy, by crime, or in some other way. In this sense, most of Africa, most of the Middle East, most of the former Soviet Union and Eastern Europe, much of Asia, much of Latin America, as well as the inner cities of the United States are ghettos.

Tenet 2. With respect to periodization, the way we conceptually organize time, history might be divided into three periods: a pre-economic past, prior to the time when humanity learned to benefit from the worldwide specialization of labor and the coordination of the self-interested activities of millions of people through markets; an economic present; and a post-economic future in which humanity does not forget what it learned from economics but at the same time learns to broaden the scope and variety of motivational and guidance systems used to mobilize resources to meet needs.

Tenet 3. With respect to the dynamic principles of cause and effect that operate in the world, the emphasis should be on the logics, the conventional norms guiding practice, that govern institutions. Cultural structures are causes. People have souls; they deliberate; they accompany and sometimes guide their acting with thinking. For *homo sapiens sapiens* practice and discourse are inseparable. Humans follow, and sometimes violate, or renegotiate, social rules.

If we define the problem as how to meet people's needs, it is evident that the logic of exchange, a discourse and a set of social rules which guides many practices today, solves only part of the problem. It does not adequately motivate people and guide people so that needs are met without damage to the environment. Therefore, the dynamic problem to be solved can be thought of as: 1) how to improve the functioning of the logic of exchange, so that it works to meet the needs of more people; and 2) how to limit and complement the logic of exchange with other desirable logics.

The History of the World Bank Interpreted as a Series of Stages of Moral Progress

By and large and in the main, as stated above, the World Bank has been guided by an ideal of "development" conceived as "economic growth." It has evaluated the "performance" of borrowing countries by indicators of growth. As a history of the Bank published by the Brookings Institution states:

> The development indicators commonly taken into account in Bank analysis include various measures of (a) the rate of growth of national and per capita income, (b) rates of growth of factor inputs, particularly domestic savings rates and public sector savings rates, (c) rates of growth of output and investment in various sectors, (d) putative measures of efficiency of resource use, such as sectoral and aggregate capital-output ratios, and (e) various measures of external viability.[22]

Nevertheless, the history of the Bank's development loans has been the history of a learning process. The progress of the Bank's learning has been in the direction of a logic of love, although sometimes it has taken one step forward and two steps back. That history can be summarized as eleven somewhat overlapping stages.

Stage One: The Early Port, Railway, and Electric Power Loans

The constitutive rules of modern society provide that sales are consensual transactions between buyers and sellers. They provide that owners may and may not choose to let others use their property, and owners may and may not dedicate their property to productive purposes. Owners of money may and may not decide to invest it, and if they do invest, it is up to them to decide where. There is no reason to suppose that in general there will be enough investment to create enough jobs to pay the entire worldwide working class adequate wages. Hence there is no reason to suppose that the world's poor will thus be enabled to engage in sales transactions in which willing sellers will sell them the food, clothing, housing, and medical care they need.

Although President Black wanted the World Bank to prove that private enterprise works, its very existence was proof that although private enterprise might work some places some of the time, it does not work in all places all of the time. The poor areas of the world, the areas Bank ideology calls "developing," and which our ideology calls "ghettos," are low-profit high-risk areas for investors. The probability that investment funds will spontaneously flow into them in sufficient quantity to employ all willing workers at wages sufficient to meet their basic needs is zero. The reason why a government-sponsored international development bank was proposed in the first place was that private investors did not want to invest in the third world.

The Bank's initial responses to third world reality conceived of private investment as normal, and its own activity as a government-sponsored facilitator of investment as abnormal. It was in the anomalous position of being a public agency that (at first) only made loans to governments, which, nevertheless, endorsed an ideology strongly supportive of private enterprise. The Bank looked for ways to help governments prime the pump for, or, to vary the metaphor, to jump-start, the flow of private capital. Some thought of the World Bank as a transitory institution, which would shut up shop and dissolve itself when the world became normal, as was expected to happen soon. It was reasoned that two things were needed to jump-start private investment in the third world: infrastructure, and government policies designed to create a favorable investment climate. The Bank as a lender started out making loans for infrastructure, for port facilities, railways, and above all for electric power generation, mostly in Mexico, Brazil, and India.[23] The bank as an adviser encouraged governments to make the "tough decisions" (i.e., low wages, low taxes, unrestricted repatriation of profits) that would attract private investors. The roles of lender and adviser coalesced when the Bank insisted that the borrowing countries raise prices. When persuasion proved to be ineffective, the Bank began to condition its loans on "rate covenants" requiring borrowing governments to charge higher fees for the use of port facilities, higher railway fares, and higher electric rates.[24] Since the loans were made to public utilities that were monopolies, there was nothing the citizens could do but pay the higher rates. The hands of their own governments were tied by covenants with the force of international law.

In order to prove that private enterprise worked the early loans were nonstarters. What the Bank proved was that low-profit high-risk investments can be turned into high-profit low-risk investments when an international quasi-governmental agency (the World Bank) sells gilt-edged bonds through Morgan Stanley and First Boston Corporation, and then uses the proceeds of bond sales to make loans at close-to-commercial rates to third world utility monopolies, whose rates are set by governments; and when the governments are required to raise the rates. The Bank rationalized this outcome by reasoning that sound business practice required a company to charge enough for its products to acquire an adequate reserve to be sure its debts would be paid, and to be sure it could retain enough earnings to finance its own future expansion. Of course, sound business practice, so defined, cannot be generalized. If all firms in Mexico, Brazil, and India, had similarly raised their prices, the result would have been inflated prices with nobody better off than before. The effect of the World Bank's rate covenants was that certain firms, the ones the Bank lent to, were allowed and required to raise their prices, thus guaranteeing high profits for a privileged sector and no risk for the buyers of World Bank bonds.

Stage Two: Expanded Lending to Carefully Selected Borrowers

The Bank never admitted that a large part of the world is not a promising field for the establishment of profitable businesses. Arturo Escobar illustrates the Bank's dysfunctional blindness in this respect with his thorough account of the efforts of the Bank and associated agencies in Colombia, which never acknowledged the basic fact that producing food to sell to people who have no money is not profitable. Instead of acknowledging the reality imposed by the very constitutive rules of modern society, which is that the limited number of profitable businesses investors will set up voluntarily is bound to be insufficient to produce and distribute enough to meet everybody's needs, the Bank interpreted the problem as a lack of technical managerial skill in third world countries. The poor countries lacked the technical skills needed to prepare loan applications to the Bank. They did not know how to write business plans and how to project financial rates of return.[25] The Bank insisted that there was no lack of funds for making loans. That part was true. As long as it could sell government-guaranteed bonds on the bond market, and as long as it could make selective loans to carefully studied borrowers, and as long as it could require governments to allow its borrowers to charge high prices for their products, World Bank bonds would be blue chips.

Acting on the basis of what it believed to be true, the Bank undertook to train potential third world borrowers in the skills needed to make loan applications to itself. Soon it found itself reviewing for approval loan applications where it had itself been involved in every phase of the application process, starting with identifying promising projects, and selecting which ones deserved priority.[26] Since priority was determined largely by calculating opportunity costs (i.e., by comparing how profitable the proposed investment would be compared to other uses of the same money) the Bank had no trouble equating what was good for its bondholders (i.e., being sure they would be promptly repaid with interest), with what was good for the borrowing country. As Escobar recounts, the third world soon acquired a class of highly paid technical experts in development, whose role was to facilitate the funding of foreign aid projects financed by the World Bank and other agencies. Some of the most successful of them joined the headquarters staff of the World Bank in Washington.[27]

Expanded lending was accompanied by the continuation and expansion of the World Bank's role as adviser to third world governments. Governments were encouraged to adopt policies that would raise profits high enough to attract private investment, both their own local domestic private investment and international investment. They were required to put in place whatever policies were called for in order to ensure that Bank-financed projects would be profitable. The Bank was able to boast in its early years that it had selected and planned its loans so carefully that it had never suffered a default.[28]

Given the basic cultural structures of the modern world, the expanded lending of the Bank and other agencies working along similar lines, often in tandem with the Bank, could in the course of time only lead where it did lead, namely: 1) to the rich getting richer, while the poor on the whole stagnated or got poorer; 2) to the countries of the third world assuming debt obligations which they could repay only at great human sacrifice, or not at all; and 3) to the flooding of the first world by cheap-labor goods from the newly industrialized third world, thus undermining the relatively high wage and benefit levels in the first world that had been achieved with so much pain and suffering during the previous century.

Stage Three: The Opening of the Soft Loan Window

Although the United Nations had effectively been barred from any decision-making role at the World Bank, several United Nations agencies, and a number of third world countries using the UN as a forum, notably India and Chile, doggedly insisted that there had to be a serious global effort to end world poverty. It was obvious that the World Bank's development loans at close to commercial rates were not going to accomplish that goal. To make a clean break with poverty, there had to be a clean break with the logic of exchange. The haves of the world had to take responsibility for sharing and cooperating with the have-nots. A number of independent commissions, one of them headed by the philanthropist and sometime New York governor Nelson Rockefeller, came to the same conclusions.[29]

As a cumulative result of many conscientious efforts, the World Bank opened its soft loan window in 1960. It is called the International Development Association, but it has the same staff and same president as the Bank. The European contributors to the soft loan fund were inclined to use the money to make *grants* for development, not loans. In deference to what was believed to be the attitude of the United States Congress and the American people, however, it was decided that the new window would not give money away, but would loan it on terms so favorable that the terms would almost amount to gifts. The soft loan window began making loans to be repaid in fifty years with no interest, with only a small service charge, and sometimes with a long moratorium period with no payments due at all. On the basis of using a standard discount rate to calculate the present value of the stream of payments that would flow back into the Bank to repay the soft loans, the soft loans were often 80 percent to 90 percent gifts. Unlike the Bank's hard loans, funds to make soft loans did not come from selling bonds. The soft loan funds have been donated by the governments of the rich countries of the world.[30] They are gifts from first world taxpayers.

Another source of funds for soft loans has been the World Bank itself. Since the Bank charges higher rates of interest on its hard loans than the rates it pays to its bondholders, the Bank has been a profitable institution. Only so much can be spent on the Bank's own staff and on expanding its formidable research capabilities. When Poland withdrew from membership in the World Bank, it took with it not only a withdrawal of its initial capital subscription, but also its share of the profits the Bank had earned so far. The Bank's Governors and staff did not want that to happen again the next time a country withdrew.[31] A much better use for the Bank's profits, one much more consonant with its ideals, was to donate the profits from the hard loan window to the soft loan window.

With regard to the Bank's proud track record of never having suffered a default on a loan, the soft loan window opened just in the nick of time. Already in 1960 India and Pakistan had borrowed more than they could possibly repay. Their hungry masses were already groaning under the burden of debt repayment. The soft loan window quickly bailed out India and Pakistan, and thus, indirectly, bailed out the hard loan window.[32]

The soft loan window is an ethical milestone. It is a recognition that giving is a normal part of human life. It is a recognition that the needs of everyone on the planet are not going to be met solely through any practice of the logic of exchange, however sophisticated.

As the World Bank has handled it, the soft loan window is an intelligent form of giving. A major objection to gifts sent to the third world from the first world is that they have a "crowding out" effect. When free food from first world donors is available, an unintended result can be that third world farmers lose customers. Food that might have been grown locally is not grown; the farmers become dispirited and dependent. An area that might have produced its own food may become permanently dependent on free or subsidized imports. A misguided version of the logic of love crowds out the logic of exchange.

Intelligent giving requires achieving a "crowding in" effect. The objective is to meet more needs, not just to meet the same needs in a different way. On the positive side of the ledger, the World Bank has been careful to use soft funds in ways that complement hard funds to produce a higher total net benefit. On the negative side of the ledger, loan agreements, however generous, which tie third world borrowers to the tutelage of the World Bank for fifty years, are less beneficial than forms of aid that entail greater respect for the autonomy of the peoples of the third world, and greater liberty for them to seek their own tutors in the marketplace of ideas.

Stage Four: Funding Social Projects Without Reference to the Profit Motive

When the Philippines applied to the soft loan window for funds to build roads, the World Bank turned it down. The reason for denying the soft loan was that the Philippine economy at the time was growing fast enough to enable the Philippines to make payments on a hard loan.[33] Unlike the hard loan window, which always has more funds to lend than it has qualified loan applicants, the soft loan window has too little money to fund all the worthy projects brought to it. Therefore, the Philippines should apply for a hard loan.

There was a catch. The Philippine government was not talking about toll roads. They were proposing a project that was not going to make any money. It was going to provide needed infrastructure for the benefit of the people, at government expense. Up until that time, the Bank had lent money only for self-liquidating projects, for enterprises that were expected to generate the profits from which repayment of the loans would be made. It had not made loans to be repaid from future tax revenues.

Considering the matter carefully, in the light of its experience and its growing sense of itself as a benevolent organization, the World Bank decided that it made no sense to fund non-profit projects out of its soft loan window, and then to refuse to fund non-profit projects out of the hard loan window for countries that were too rich to meet the strict demands of the means-test used at the soft loan window. Since the early 1960s, the Bank has made loans for social projects that do not generate any profits, including population control projects, nutrition projects, many health sector loans in cooperation with the World Health Organization, and many education loans in cooperation with UNESCO.

Stage Five: Legitimating the Public Sector

In 1968 the World Bank passed another milestone when it decided that it would no longer refuse to make loans to support business enterprises located in the public sector. It soon found itself making the majority of its loans to government-owned and autonomous public entities in the third world.

The presence of the World Bank in the public sector has been a mixed blessing. It has tended to insist that public enterprises operate for profit the same as private enterprises, thus nullifying the prospects for managing a public enterprise to make it socially responsible with respect to a gamut of objectives, among which earning a decent profit for its owner, the state, would be only one. The Bank has also insisted that government-owned recipients of its loans have independent boards of directors, responsible to no political authority, and indeed, like the Bank itself, not effectively responsible to anyone at all. The result has been to encourage independent economic fiefdoms. They are clothed with public authority They often possess monopolies, tax exemptions, and privileged access to natural resources. But they are not accountable to the people directly or indirectly.[34]

Also, although the Bank has accepted public ownership as a legitimate form of ownership, it still favors private profit. It appears to take the view that private investment for profit is the norm, to be relied on wherever possible, and that public investment is an inferior form of investment to which recourse must be had when profits are too low, or the risks too great, to attract private capital. Thus the Bank has participated in, and has done little or nothing to discourage, partnerships of public and private capital in which public money has been used to make low-interest loans to projects whose profits go to private enterprises. The government puts up enough cheap public money to make the enterprise attractive to a private partner.[35]

Stage Six: Concern for the Good of the Whole

In its early days the Bank's reviews of loan applications concentrated on the financial rate of return. The leading question was whether the borrower would make a large profit with the money borrowed. Later the Bank added to its loan approval analysis the concept of "economic rate of return." The question shifted from whether the particular project to be funded would make money, to the question whether the loan would benefit the economy as a whole.[36] The classic case in which the Bank saw a major difference between the financial rate of return and the economic rate of return was the case in which the borrower planned to make large profits in a protected market. Its earnings projections counted on selling its products not at world market prices, but at higher prices created by protective tariffs and import restrictions. In such cases, the Bank reasoned, a particular proposed borrower would win, but the nation's consumers and the nation as a whole would lose. Therefore, the loan application should not be approved.[37]

Our opinion, on the contrary, is that most nations most of the time are better off choosing greater national and local self-reliance, even when it means making purchases at higher than world market prices. Of course, our opinion does not count for much compared to the World Bank's opinion. We are, however, persuaded by Jürgen Habermas and others who have advanced weighty arguments in favor of democracy.[38] They imply that the decision concerning how to handle the trade-off between the advantages of trusting one's own resources and the advantages of purchasing less expensive goods on the world market should be made by the people of a nation, not by us, and not by the World Bank.

The principles of democracy, that there should be government of, by, and for the people, are not arbitrary principles. In addition to the weighty arguments in their favor, there is the weighty experience of history, which teaches that although democracies have many failings, and real democracies always have more failings than ideal democracies, the alternatives are worse. There should be open public debate on issues important to the people's welfare, such as how much to import and how much to produce at home. There should be transparent processes of policy formation. We know that elites will always govern one way or another, but we are nonetheless grateful, and we believe everybody should be grateful, when elites are constrained by norms that require them to obtain the consent of the governed in some form, when they are in some way accountable to laws and to constituencies.

The idea of "economic rate of return" is only meaningful, in the last analysis, if someone identifies what outcomes are desired. If it is the political will of a nation that what is desired is greater local self-reliance, then an economic rate of return, properly calculated, will show that the nation gains, and does not lose, when it becomes more self-sufficient. It is the considered judgment of many thoughtful people in the third world, and often a majority opinion, that the policies that would be in the best interests of their nation are not the policies that the World Bank thinks are in the best interests of their nation.[39]

The general concept of considering the good of the whole nation, as distinct from considering the expected financial rate of return of a particular project, was a step forward for the Bank. The principal *application* of the concept, which consisted of substituting economic theories endorsed by the Bank for the consent of the governed, was a step backward.

Stage Seven: The Elimination of Poverty as the Bank's Mission

In 1973 the Bank passed another ethical milestone. World Bank President Robert McNamara declared: "We should strive to eradicate absolute poverty by the end of this century. That means in practice the elimination of malnutrition and illiteracy, the reduction of infant mortality, and the raising of life-expectancy standards to those of the developed nations."[40] Thus ended almost two decades of uncertainty concerning the purpose of the Bank, as the Bank itself announced the standard by which its performance should be judged.

McNamara's clarification of the Bank's purpose came with an important admission. He admitted that he personally, and the World Bank in general, did not know how to solve the problem of world poverty. His admission implied that economic growth was not the solution to the problem of world poverty. The World Bank had identified its mission as "development," and it had identified development with economic growth. If economic growth were the solution to the problem of world poverty, the World Bank would have known the solution all along. McNamara explicitly recognized the need to redefine "development," to make it more than just economic growth.

Under McNamara the Bank made important commitments. If it did not know how to end world poverty, it would use its formidable research capabilities to find out. If economic growth was not the answer, it would find out what was the answer and pursue whatever that answer was. If the Bank could not do it alone, it would partner with other agencies committed to the same goal.

President Black, in 1962, had declared that the only way the Bank was able to "get away with" what it was doing was to put forward its economic calculations as "morally antiseptic," as if economic forecasts were, like weather forecasts, predictions of natural events.[41] His wordview was that of the Immutable Framework. President McNamara, in contrast, in 1973 and many times afterward, spoke with the moral passion of a crusader against poverty. In the end, nevertheless, despite his good intentions, McNamara did more damage than Black.[42] By enormously expanding the Bank's activities, he made poverty worse. Bruce Rich, of the Environmental Defense Fund, explains why:

> Although population growth and poverty are often blamed for the growing masses of uprooted people in the developing world, in many countries economic development as it has been practiced is as much a cause of such poverty as a solution. . . . A disproportionate number of these "development refugees," as anthropologist Thayer Scudder calls them, come from the marginalized peoples of the earth: tribal and indigenous groups, the *harijans* (outcastes) in India, the landless and homeless—all those who increasingly fall outside the mainstream of the modern market economy. Jacques Attali's vision of a planet overrun by hordes of global nomads is no mere nightmare, but one possible outcome of the historical project of Western development.[43]

Stage Eight: The Bank as Intellectual Leader of the Finance Community

Stage Eight refers not so much to a step in the evolution of prevailing thinking at the World Bank (from the logic of exchange to the logic of love), as to a step in the evolution of the influence of the World Bank, as its model of thought became the accepted model for the world finance community at large. Starting from the early days when it undertook to train third world technical experts in how to prepare loan applications, the Bank found that it had a potent source of intellectual influence in its ability to combine seminars with top-flight economists with the concrete rewards that went with loan approval.

It later learned that it could do more to induce thinking it regarded as sensible if it joined forces with other aid agencies. Once a consortium of aid agencies, all of them more or less committed to mainstream capitalist economics, reached consensus on what was best for a third world nation, there was little anybody could do to stop their intellectual consensus from becoming policy. The nation itself usually had little or no discretionary capital to invest, and was therefore inclined to make its policies conform to advice that came with money. Private sector investors were generally unwilling to move without guarantees from governments. There were occasional breaks in the ranks, as when the government of the Netherlands withdrew from the consortium that coordinated development policy for Indonesia, because it could no longer stomach the human rights abuses of General Suharto's dictatorship.[44] By and large, however, cooperation among the major players engaged in conceptualizing, funding, and guaranteeing third world development has produced the closest thing to a de facto world government the world has yet known. The de facto world government has been strengthened by clauses in treaties associated with the World Trade Organization that explicitly curtail the powers of national governments.

It was natural that the World Bank, and to a lesser extent its sister institution the International Monetary Fund, should become the intellectual leader of the international consensus of the world's major aid and finance institutions. It was not because the World Bank put up the lion's share of the funds for most international projects. Indeed, since the mid-1980s, private commercial bank loans, guaranteed but not funded by governments, have become the major source of capital flows to the third world. The World Bank has taken the intellectual leading role because it has more information than anyone else. Its highly profitable operations have enabled it to hire a large research staff and to produce vast quantities of high quality well documented publications. Its practice of meticulously studying every loan application, every loan applicant, and every national economy made it the brain of the global economy.

As the World Bank became the leading intellectual center for the study of development, it also became home to a number of diverse currents of thought within its own staff, as well as a venue where visiting lecturers, often with views at odds with the Bank's views, came to participate in ongoing dialogues concerning development policy. Questions about the importance of family planning to the future of Malaysia are hotly debated in the corridors of the headquarters of the World Bank at 1818 H Street in Washington, D.C. These debates among people from diverse regions of the world would set the stage for the World Bank to reach additional ethical milestones as time went by.

Stage Nine: The Structural Adjustment Programs

In the historic race between education and catastrophe, catastrophe pulled ahead in the 1980s, as it became apparent that the nations of the third world could not repay their loans. As John Maynard Keynes had candidly observed in 1944, speaking at the time mostly to deaf ears, the only way to maintain most third world loans as performing loans was to roll them over at maturity into new loans. Many nations needed continuous injections of new loans in order to stay current on payments on the old loans. These nations were, as Cheryl Payer wrote and extensively documented, caught in a debt trap.[45] In the early 1980s, certain triggers proximately caused first Mexico, and then other major borrowers, to threaten to stop payments not just on World Bank loans but on foreign loans in general. The triggers were: 1) the second big OPEC raising of oil prices in 1979; and 2) the decision of the United States Federal Reserve Board to raise interest rates, which raised interest rates all over the world. But these were only the triggers: underlying the newly manifested economic problems was the fact that Keynes had been basically correct in the first place.

In spite of the progress World Bank thinking had made in discarding one by one the premises of the notion that the logic of exchange, if only it is intelligently administered, will function to meet the needs of the world's people, it and the IMF were not ready to admit—and perhaps could not admit—that their basic ideology, the Immutable Framework posited by mainstream economics, was wrong. Instead of moving forward intellectually to acknowledge that doctrinaire free market capitalism was irreconcilable with reality, the World Bank and IMF moved backward to insist ever more strenuously that the nations of the third world abide by the rules of games at which they could only lose. Like a prairie dog who hears a vehicle coming down the road, instead of running out into the unknown for safety, they sought safety by returning to the known. The prairie dog, racing to its hole, must cross the road and risk getting run over. The World Bank and the IMF raced back to free market orthodoxy, which requires drastic cuts in the living standards of the poor people of the world—the very people the Bank was committed to lifting out of poverty.

It was at this point that the World Bank, together with the IMF, became the world's most hated institution. As a small sample of the vast literature attacking the Bank, we will quote the following words written by Davison Budhoo, an economist from the small third world nation of Grenada, who created an international sensation when he resigned from the IMF staff in 1988 in protest against what he called "its increasingly genocidal policies." Budhoo states:

> 1994 marks the fiftieth anniversary of the founding of the World Bank and the International Monetary Fund at Bretton Woods, New Hampshire.
>
> But as the North congratulates itself and celebrates, the South and its three billion poor will tear out their hair in rage. For the operations of these agencies there have been catastrophic. Instead of development and favorable adjustment, the Third World today is in an accelerating spiral of economic and social decline. That decline is linked directly to the World Bank and the International Monetary Fund.
>
> IMF-World Bank structural adjustment programs (SAPs) are designed to reduce consumption in developing countries and to redirect resources to manufacturing exports for the repayment of debt. This has caused overproduction of primary products and a precipitous fall in their prices. It has also led to the devastation of traditional agriculture and to the emergence of hordes of landless farmers in virtually every country in which the World Bank and IMF operate. Food security has dramatically declined in all Third World regions, but in Af-

rica in particular. Growing dependence on food imports, which is the lot of sub-Saharan Africa, places these countries in an extremely vulnerable position. They simply do not have the foreign exchange to import enough food, given the fall in export prices and the need to repay debt.

Basic conditionalities of the IMF-World Bank include drastic cuts in social expenditures, especially health and education. According to the UN Commission for Africa, expenditures on health in IMF-World Bank programmed countries declined by 50 percent during the 1980s, and spending on education by 25 percent. Similar trends are evident in all Southern regions.

. . . Using figures provided by the United Nations Childrens Fund (UNICEF) and the UN Economic Commission for Africa, it has been estimated that at least six million children under five years of age have died each year since 1982 in Africa, Asia and Latin America because of the anti-people, even genocidal, focus of IMF-World Bank SAPs.[46]

Budhoo and other critics of the World Bank often do not clearly state whether a cultural transformation from a narrow logic of exchange to a logic of love is needed to end world poverty. Sometimes they seem to say that the circle could be squared: that somehow production for profit could become production to meet needs if only the World Bank and the IMF did their jobs right, instead of doing them wrong. We would say—probably restating what Budhoo and others mean—that the structural adjustment catastrophes were not the result of the Bank's incompetence. No bank has ever been more competent. They were the result of the general concept of trying to force third world countries to pay debts that could be paid only with tragic sacrifice, or could not be paid at all.[47] They were the result of the lack of an essential component of the logic of love, the logic of forgiveness.

As John Cobb, Jr., has noted, it is a mistake to think that Structural Adjustment Policies were just policies the IMF and the Bank adopted at a certain point in history, because "the same policies follow from standard economic thinking in general."[48] It is the paradigm itself that is the problem, not the agency.

We would add, further, that by the time catastrophe hit, the World Bank had already repented of the idolatrous worship of the legal foundations of capitalism. It had already acknowledged that private enterprise alone is not enough. It had already accepted that the haves should share with the have-nots because of the needs of the have-nots, and not because a market bargain could be struck according to the logic of exchange. It had already decided to count not-for-profit projects as equally meritorious with for-profit projects. It already recognized that the true bottom line is physically measured, by ecology and natural science, and not measured in dollars or other artificial units established by social convention. Under Robert McNamara it had already adopted the philosophy that human economic arrangements, and by extension the legal rules of property and contract, are meant to serve a purpose, the purpose of mobilizing resources to meet the needs of the needy. Therefore, by implication, they ought to be modified as and when necessary in order better to achieve their purpose. The Bank had already admitted that economic growth would not solve the problem of poverty. If the Bank in the 1980s had not learned enough to respond creatively and humanely to the debt crisis, it was not because it was not learning anything; but rather because in the face of crisis, the Bank panicked and momentarily tossed aside its new knowledge, hurriedly retreating to older forms of "knowledge" that did not in fact square with empirical reality.

Stage Ten: Cooperating with Non-Governmental Organizations and with Stakeholders

Non-governmental organizations (NGOs) became more significant as the debt crisis, brutally confronted with Structural Adjustment Programs, worsened. Many of the NGOs were church-related charitable agencies, which were left to pick up the pieces of the lives of the poor when the public sector was forced to cut back services because of conditions imposed on governments by the IMF and the World Bank. The NGOs became, in many cases, both the partners of the World Bank, because of necessity, and the critics of the World Bank, because of conscience. Already in 1982 the World Bank set up a special NGO-World Bank coordinating committee.

As time went on the NGOs began to hold their own international summits, at which they gradually put together a series of socially-conscious alternatives to the Bank's top-down mainstream economism. They particularly devoted themselves to confronting the Bank on its funding of huge mega-dam projects, such as the Sardar Sarovar Dam Project in India, which wrought havoc with the environment and flooded the former homes of 90,000 people, most of them tribal.[49] Dialogue with outside critics from the NGOs became a principal source of transformative ideas inside the Bank.[50] Some of these ideas flowed from the offices of the Sustainable Development Division, which was established within the Bank in 1991.

A 1996 World Bank publication stated: "While only six percent of all Bank-financed projects in the period 1973-1988 included provisions for some form of involvement by NGOs, NGOs were to be involved in about 30 percent of all bank-financed projects in FY 93, and between 40 and 50 percent of projects approved in FY94 and 95. . . . The Bank is striving to increase both the quantity and the quality of NGO involvement in Bank-financed projects."[51]

In the same year, 1996, James D. Wolfensohn, who became President of the Bank in 1995, declared to the Bank's Board of Governors:

> The lesson is clear: for economic advance, you need social advance—and without social development, economic development cannot take root. For the Bank, this means that we need to make sure that the programs and projects we support have adequate social foundations:

—By designing more participatory country strategies and programs—reflecting discussions not only with governments but also with community groups, NGOs, and private businesses

—By putting more emphasis on social, cultural, and institutional issues, and their interplay with economic issues, in our project and analytical work

—By learning more about how the changing dynamics between public institutions, markets, and civil society affect social and economic development.[52]

Environmentalist and communitarian professions of faith have proliferated at the Bank since the early 1990s. Paradoxically, now that neoliberalism is becoming ever more dominant worldwide in practice, ecology and solidarity are becoming ever more popular in theory. The premises required to limit and complement the logic of exchange with other desirable logics have been proclaimed, and are available. Nevertheless, the Bank, along with the rest of the world's major financial players, now more than ever takes as its primary operating rule the simple version of exchange logic that was articulated in 1994 by the Bank's former chief economist Lawrence Summers when he declared his first principle to be: "Markets work. Capital responds to incentives."[53]

Stage Eleven: Accepting the Inevitability of Massive Loan Defaults

In its early years the World Bank was run by people who were unreconstructed fundamentalists on the issue of debt repayment. Its loans were made to governments, and it would not loan to a government that was in default on any of its past debts. The Bank refused to make any loans to Guatemala, for example, until Guatemala satisfied debt obligations it had incurred in 1829. By the mid-twentieth century, of course, 1829 Guatemalan government bonds were collector's items. They had already passed through the hands of a series of speculators who had bought them up at small fractions of their face values.

What the Bank demanded, as a condition of making new loans to countries that had defaulted in the past, was not full payment of the old loan with accumulated interest. It demanded making a settlement with the bondholders. The bondholders were willing to compromise. After all, they had thought they were holding worthless pieces of paper until they learned that the economic muscle of the World Bank was on their side.

Through the end of the 1970s the Bank maintained that it had not only persuaded third world countries to cure their old defaults, but also that it had itself never suffered any defaults on its new loans. The latter was a fiction, as noted above, because the Bank used soft loans to bail out hard loans. It was an obligatory fiction for those who dealt with the Bank. Like a hospitalized psychotic who succeeds in making others on the ward buy into his or her way of looking at the world, the Bank succeeded in creating a socially constructed reality in which nobody defaulted. It stood foursquare and blind for the principle that loans are always repaid—in a world where insolvency and bankruptcy were already standard parts of the professional practice of the average accountant and average lawyer, in a world where non-performing loans were part of the daily experience of ordinary bankers, in a world where the tax laws of every nation allowed lenders to write off debts that would never be paid.

During the 1980s and 1990s the fiction was gradually abandoned. In 1981 alone thirteen Bank loans had to be rescheduled to permit repayment on easier terms. The World Bank participated along with other major lenders in rewriting third world debt, sometimes on soft terms, sometimes with debt cancellation. Social change activists took up the cause of debt relief. They advocated the release of the third world from debt bondage, as three centuries earlier English debtors had been released from prison after Parliament passed the first Bankruptcy Act. The Vatican declared the year 2000 to be a Year of Jubilee. The Pope reminded the world that according to the Old Testament, the ancient Hebrews periodically declared a Year of Jubilee in which all debts were forgiven.[54]

As this is written, in 2002, the World Bank and the IMF appear to be accepting the inevitability of massive defaults. They appear to be drawing the wise conclusion that the smooth functioning of the global economy requires an orderly process for handling the bankruptcies of nations that should no longer be required to pay their debts. They should be forgiven, and helped to get off to a good fresh start.

A Higher Form of Pragmatism

The incomplete moral evolution of the World Bank, which we have just briefly interpreted and summarized as taking place in eleven stages, gives a new meaning to the word "pragmatism." "Pragmatism" as a philosophy was articulated by the American philosopher C.S. Peirce in 1878 in the following terms: "Consider what effects, that might conceivably have practical bearings, we conceive the object of our conception to have. Then, our conception of these effects is the whole of our conception of the object."[55] William James picked up Peirce's idea twenty years later, named it "pragmatism," and took a somewhat different view. James's philosophy of "pragmatism" made the true a species of the good. James writes, "The true is the name of whatever proves itself to be good in the way of belief, and good, too, for definite, assignable reasons."[56]

The term "pragmatism" in development economics has been associated with following eclectic policies, doing "what works." This has meant, for the most part, accepting the fact that in the world as it exists, measures must be taken to make a country attractive to investors. It means accepting the fact that since the logic of exchange dominates the world, decisions must be made according to the logic of exchange. Singapore is an authoritarian welfare state which calls itself a social democracy, and which attributes its success to "pragmatism." Two observers of Singapore's economic miracle wrote of the ideology of that country's political elite: "[P]ragmatism has become equated with rationality. If it works, use it; if it doesn't work, discard it and try one of the alternatives."[57]

The principles that limit and complement the logic of exchange, which the World Bank has adopted, and to some extent practiced, give a new meaning to the word "pragmatism." Whereas in development circles, "pragmatism" has meant doing what the logic of exchange requires, now it can mean modifying the logic of exchange in order to do "what works" in a larger sense—"what *really* works."[58] "Pragmatism" can mean doing whatever works to meet needs and to eliminate poverty. It can mean moving beyond the Immutable Framework, and working pragmatically with a moving and evolving Mutable Framework.

In this broad sense, the pragmatism sometimes shown by the World Bank—in response to many pressures, in the light of many experiences, after too many all-too-avoidable catastrophes—contributes to answering the question posed at the beginning of this chapter. The principles of capitalism (which are the principles of common sense of the modern world, and which are the principles framing modern legal systems) are best conceived as intended to be principles of Tough Love. The other alternative posed above—that they are simply facts about the way things are, natural and immutable, cruel fate—does not square with the evolving practice of the World Bank. At its inception the Bank was an institutional citadel of doctrinaire free-market ideology. It has not changed because of its own inherent biases, but because reality made it change. Its institutional evolution has dismantled the Immutable logic of exchange and accumulation Framework it began with. If the claim that the commodity exchange as a way of life is obligatory for human beings was ever believable, it is not believable now. Its most powerful and most influential believer has recanted, principle by principle, step by step.

For the purpose of carrying out the good intentions we should ascribe to it, capitalism should evolve in the direction of social democracy. With respect to whether what should happen will happen, the history of the World Bank provides qualified good news. The principles required to move from a narrow logic of exchange to a broad logic of love have been articulated. They have been officially endorsed, and are now legitimate.[59] They license NGOs and people of good will generally to criticize economic actors in public and private fora. They can be used to drive home the truth that the World Bank and other major players on the world economic scene are not living up to ideals they publicly profess. Although the logic of love is not, for the most part, operational, the news is still qualified good news. It is better for the Tough Love Worldview to be non-operational and legitimate, than for it to be non-operational and illegitimate.

Notes

1. Frances Moore Lappé and Joseph Collins, *Food First: Beyond the Myth of Scarcity* (New York: Ballantine Books, 1977).

2. N.W. Pirie, *Food Resources, Conventional and Novel* (Baltimore, Md.: Penguin Books, 1969).

3. Fuller, *Utopia or Oblivion*, 151. The work of architect William McDonough and chemist Michael Braungart should assure the reader that the historical moment of which Fuller spoke in 1969 has not definitively passed and that even with the population growth of the last thirty years, human creativity still has much to contribute to improving living standards in responsible and sustainable ways the world over. See William McDonough and Michael Braungart, *From Cradle to Cradle: Remaking the Way We Make Things* (San Francisco: Northpoint Press, 2002). McDonough insists upon "changing the story"—or cultural codes—in order to resolve many of the problems in today's world. As an architect and an advocate of democratic design, he suggests that we practice the intellectual exercise of imagining ourselves (as indeed we are) as designers of the world; then to ask ourselves what are the steps we would take to design by intention a world with the degree of alienation we experience in our current world. Doing so, he believes, can help us to imagine the precise nature of the steps needed to construct a more loving and viable world.

4. We agree with legal theorist Seyla Benhabib, who writes that because "communities tend to constitute themselves by excluding difference, the task of a philosophical politics is to conceptualize new forms of association which let the different appear in their midst." Seyla Benhabib, "Democracy and Difference: Reflections on Rationality, Democracy, and Postmodernism," unpublished manuscript, 1994, 30, quoted in Cowie, *Capital Moves*, 194. See also Nicola Lacey, "Community in Legal Theory: Idea, Ideal, or Ideology?" *Studies in Law, Politics, and Society* 15 (1995): 105-46.

5. Any reader who does not understand this assessment, or who thinks it has been proven false by the success in eliminating poverty of Sweden and other social democracies of Western Europe, should go back to Chapter 1 and start over.

6. Gandhi, *All Men Are Brothers*, 78-9, 91.

7. Viviane Forrester, *L'Horreur Economique* (Paris: Fayard, 1996).

8. Arturo Escobar, *Encountering Development: the Making and Unmaking of the Third World* (Princeton, N.J.: Princeton University Press, 1995).

9. The classic articulation of the concept of "development" as a certain standard of living that any nation-state can achieve if only it follows the prescriptions derived from studying the economic histories of the North Atlantic nation-states is Walt Whitman Rostow's *The Stages of Economic Growth*. Immanuel Wallerstein's world-systems analysis offers a concise rebuttal of the tenets underlying the concept of development presented by Rostow and other development economists. See "Development: Lodestar or Illusion?" in Wallerstein, *Unthinking Social Science*, 104-24. For an expansive historical treatment of the institution of structural inequalities—the constitutive rules of capitalism—that mitigate against the possibility of following Rostow's development prescriptions with the success he implicitly promises, see Wallerstein, *Modern World System*.

10. See Deepak Lal, "The Misconceptions of 'Development Economics,'" *Finance and Development* 22 (June 1985), 10-13; Gérard Destanne de Bernis, "Development or Pauperization," in Paul-Marc Henry, ed., *Poverty, Progress, and Development* (London: Kegan Paul, 1991), 86n. There is an extensive literature documenting the history of resistance to unfettered capital accumulation by the working class in the first world. For an historical treatment of this process in the United States, and of how gains made by the working class were gradually incorporated into government policies, see, e.g., Herbert G. Gutman, *Work, Culture & Society in Industrializing America: Essays in American Working-Class and Social History* (New York: Vintage Books, 1977); David Brody, *Workers in Industrial America: Essays on the 20th Century Struggle* (New York and Oxford: Oxford University Press, 1980); Christopher L. Tomlins, *The State and the Unions: Labor Relations, Law, and the Organized Labor Movement in America, 1880-1960* (Cambridge; London; New York; New Rochelle; Melbourne; Sydney: Cambridge University Press, 1985); David Montgomery, *The Fall of the House of Labor: The workplace, the state, and American labor activism, 1865-1925* (Cambridge: Cambridge University Press, 1987); Gary Gerstle, *Working-class Americanism: The politics of labor in a textile city, 1914-1960* (Cambridge; New York; Port Chester; Melbourne; Sydney: Cambridge University Press, 1989); Alan Dawley, "Workers, Capital, and the State in the Twentieth Century," in J. Carroll Moody and Alice Kessler-Harris, eds., *Perspectives on American Labor History: The Problems of Synthesis* (DeKalb, Ill.: Northern Illinois University Press, 1989), 152-202; Lizabeth Cohen, *Making a New Deal: Industrial Workers in Chicago, 1919-1939* (Cambridge; New York; Port Chester; Melbourne; Sydney: Cambridge University Press, 1990); David Brody, *In Labor's Cause: Main Themes on the History of the American Worker* (New York and Oxford: Oxford University Press, 1993); Melvyn Dubofsky, *The State and Labor in Modern America* (Chapel Hill, N.C.; and London: The University of North Carolina Press, 1994); and Kevin Kenny, *Making Sense of the Molly Maguires* (New York and Oxford: Oxford University Press, 1998).

11. The critiques of the concept of "development" are quite varied and too numerous to name. The writing of Gary Gereffi offers an example of a critique that does not depart substantially from the tradition of developmentalist theory but seeks to broaden it. Gereffi notes the very limited conceptions of "development" that have arisen from generalizing based on analyses narrowly focused at the national level. He calls for an integration of the global, national, and local levels of analysis and states that such integrated analysis will necessarily indicate a number of alternative paths toward national development. Gary Gereffi, "Rethinking Development Theory: Insights from East Asia and Latin America," in A. Douglas Kincaid and Alejandro Portes, eds., *Comparative National Development: Society and Economy in the New Global Order* (Chapel Hill, N.C.; and London: The University of North Carolina Press, 1994), 26-56. For one of the earliest calls for a radical redefinition of "development," see Galtung, *True Worlds*, especially 55-65, 149-68. In Galtung's redefinition, "development" means the realization of ten normative goals: personal growth, socioeconomic growth, equity, solidarity, diversity, equality, autonomy, participation, social justice, and ecological balance. For more recent, post-Cold War radical reformulations of "development," see Herman E. Daly, *Beyond Growth: The Economics of Sustainable Development* (Boston: Beacon, 1996); and Brian Milani, *Designing the Green Economy: The Postindustrial Alternative to Corporate Globalization* (Lanham, Md.; Boulder, Colo.; New York; and Oxford: Rowman & Littlefield, 2000). As for the concept of "sustainable development," the first use of this term by an international institution was in 1972 at the United Nations conference in Stockholm. The term gained wide

acceptance in government and NGO circles alike following its endorsement by the World Commission on Environment and Development (WCED) in 1987. For a comprehensive overview of the debate surrounding "sustainable development" during this initial period of the term's widespread use, see Michael Redclift, *Sustainable Development: Examining the Contradictions* (London: Methuen & Co., 1987). For the state of the debate on this term in the present moment, see Neil Middleton and Phil O'Keefe, *Redefining Sustainable Development* (London: Pluto Press, 2001). The authors put forth a critique of the concept similar to critiques of "development" put forth by Galtung and others. They argue, furthermore, that the dominant discourse of "sustainable development" merely contributes to the perpetuation of capitalism and that it is therefore, in the final analysis, entirely detrimental. We respectfully disagree with this assessment, on the basis that seemingly small changes in the dominant cultural codes—in this case the specific code of "developmentalism"—have the capacity to engender deeper and more meaningful (and therefore enduring) systemic changes.

12. Gutierrez, *Theology of Liberation.*

13. Martin Luther King, Jr., "A Comparison of the Conceptions of God in the Thinking of Paul Tillich and Henry Nelson Wieman" (doctoral dissertation, Boston University, 1955), 147. King drew on the ideas expressed in Paul Tillich, *Love, Power, and Justice* (New York: Oxford University Press, 1960). See also Martin Luther King, Jr., *Where Do We Go From Here: Chaos or Community?* (New York: Harper and Row, 1967).

14. The general structure of the second part of the second part of Aquinas' *Summa Theologiae* (the part on moral theology) makes *caritas* ("love" or "charity") a consequence of faith and justice a consequence of *caritas*. Justice, in turn, provides the outline for rights and laws. Both justice and love are described as, in a sense, synonymous with virtue in general. "For as charity (*caritas*) may be called a general virtue because it sets the activities of all the virtues toward the divine good, so it is with legal or general justice which sets them toward the common good." St. Thomas Aquinas, *Summa Theologiae* (London: Blackfriars, 1975), Vol. 37, 37 (2a 2ae 58, 6). "It must be said that charity is the form, mover, and the root of the virtues." St. Thomas Aquinas, *St. Thomas Aquinas on Charity* (Milwaukee, Wisc.: Marquette University Press, 1960), 35.

15. Edward S. Mason and Robert E. Asher, *The World Bank Since Bretton Woods* (Washington, D.C.: The Brookings Institution, 1973), 13-16, 20-21. White's introduction to his "Proposal for a United Nations Stabilization Fund and a Bank for Reconstruction and Development of the United and Associated Nations," issued in April 1942, reads in part: "No matter how long the war lasts nor how it is won, we shall be faced with three inescapable problems: to prevent the disruption of foreign exchanges and the collapse of monetary and credit systems; to assure the restoration of foreign trade; and to supply the huge volume of capital that will be needed virtually throughout the world for reconstruction, for relief, and for economic recovery. Clearly the task can be successfully handled only through international action." Quoted in Mason and Asher, *World Bank*, 15.

16. Mason and Asher, *World Bank*, 1-2.

17. For an historical treatment of the development of the ideas of John Maynard Keynes with regard to national macroeconomic policy in an increasingly volatile world economy, see Robert Skidelsky, *John Maynard Keynes, Vol. 2: The Economist as Saviour, 1920-1939* (London: Macmillan, 1992).

18. Armand van Dormael, *Bretton Woods: Birth of a Monetary System* (New York: Holmes & Meier Publications, 1978), 172-73.

19. Mason and Asher, *World Bank*, 62.

20. Muhammad Yunus, "Redefining Development," in Kevin Danaher, ed., *50 Years is Enough: The Case Against the World Bank and the International Monetary Fund* (Boston: South End Press, 1994), xii.

21. We extend our gratitude to our colleague Jonathan Diskin, professor of economics at Earlham College, for offering this definition of "ghetto." Diskin's conception of the ghetto, in turn, draws upon the works of several authors. See, e.g., David Rusk, *Inside Game/Outside Game: Winning Strategies for Saving Urban America* (Washington, D.C.: The Brookings Institution, 1999); William Julius Wilson, *When Work Disappears: The World of the New Urban Poor* (New York: Knopf, 1996); Richard D. Bingham, ed., *Managing Local Government: Public Administration in Practice* (Newbury Park, Calif.: Sage Publications, 1991); and W. Dennis Keating, "The Dilemma of Old Urban Neighborhoods," *Washington University Journal of Law and Policy* 3 (2000): 699-708. See also Jane Jacobs, *The Death and Life of Great American Cities* (New York: Random House, 1961) and Mike Davis, *City of Quartz: Excavating the Future in Los Angeles* (New York: Vintage Books, 1992), on alienating and de-alienating urban designs.

22. Mason and Asher, *World Bank*, 443. "External viability" basically refers to whether the country can pay its foreign debts.

23. Mason and Asher, *World Bank*, 160-61, 197, 233, 707, 715-16.

24. Mason and Asher, *World Bank*, 237-29.

25. Escobar, *Encountering Development*, 73-85. Escobar documents the process of "infantilization" of the third world carried out by the early development economists, which is especially clear in their prescriptions concerning technology. With regard to the literature written by development economists promoting the so-called "Green Revolution," for example, Escobar notes that it was "full of cultural assumptions regarding science, progress, and the economy, in which one can discern the authorial stances of a father/savior talking with selfless condescension to the child/native." Escobar, *Encountering Development*, 159. See also 29-30.

26. Escobar, *Encountering Development*, 164-67.

27. Escobar, *Encountering Development*, 35-39, 44-47.

28. The World Bank publicly continued to maintain the fiction of its default-free record long past the time when it ceased to be true. In 1978, a spokesperson for the World Bank commented: "We have not had any losses on loans. We have never had a write-off of a loan. We have never had a nonaccruing loan. We have a firm policy against debt rescheduling. We do not tolerate late payments. There are substantial pragmatic reasons why borrowers do not default on World Bank loans. In the event of a default, no further disbursement would be made on that loan or any other loan we had outstanding in the country. . . . Borrowers know our policies in this regard, and given the substantial amount of our undisbursed loans, I suggest they would be extremely reluctant to take steps to jeopardize the transfer of future resources." Quoted in Cheryl Payer, *The World Bank: A Critical Analysis* (New York: Monthly Review Press, 1982), 46. Payer goes on to demonstrate the hyperbole of this statement. Our discussion of the World Bank's "soft loan window" further demonstrates the statement's inaccuracy.

29. The commission headed by Rockefeller, the U.S. International Development Advisory Board, issued a report in March 1951 that called for the creation of an international finance corporation, which would be an affiliate of the World Bank, with the authority to make loans to private enterprise "without the requirement of government guarantees." Mason and Asher, *World Bank*, 347. This commission found that there were "many projects of basic importance to the development of underdeveloped countries that

cannot be financed entirely on a loan basis.'" Quoted in Mason and Asher, *World Bank*, 384.

30. Payer, *World Bank*, 33; Mason and Asher, *World Bank*, 222.

31. Mason and Asher, *World Bank*, 120.

32. Mason and Asher, *World Bank*, 399-403.

33. Mason and Asher, *World Bank*, 400.

34. One example of the World Bank's lack of accountability comes from Brazil, one of the places the World Bank got involved in very early in its history. Fátima Vianna Mello writes: "[T]he World Bank invested more than US $500 million over the course of the 1980s to support the Brazilian government's Polonoroeste project in Rondonia, which has been called the greatest ecological disaster ever funded by the Bank. This megaproject was supposed to rationalize the colonization [i.e., settlement] process, provide local infrastructure, and protect indigenous areas in the Amazon. Hundreds of indigenous peoples, rural workers and rubber-tappers were expelled from their lands after a road to the interior was paved, yet they had no say in the project's design at all. Acknowledging its part in that debacle, the Bank is now investing US $167 million in a new project called Planafloro, which is supposed to reflect a more sustainable approach to development in the area affected by the previous project. Although good in intention, Planafloro was not designed with the involvement of local communities either. The Bank only initiated the process of consultation after being pressured by Northern environmental groups." Fátima Vianna Mello, "Making the World Bank More Accountable: Activism in the South," *NACLA Report on the Americas* 29, no. 6 (May-June 1996), 20. On the Polonoroeste project, see also Payer, *World Bank*, 345-51. One of the best known cases of transnational financial institutions allowing the development of private economic fiefdoms in borrower nations is the case of IMF involvement in Zaire/Congo during the increasingly dictatorial regime of Mobutu Sese Seko. This case is well documented in Michela Wrong, *In the Footsteps of Mr. Kurtz: Living on the Brink of Disaster in Mobutu's Congo* (New York: HarperCollins, 2001). See especially 195-215.

35. See, e.g., Payer, *World Bank*, 135-56.

36. Making decisions for the good of the whole as distinct from maximizing benefit to some person or entity is related to topics discussed under the headings of public goods, or making public decisions. See, e.g. Inge Kaul, Isabelle Grunberg, and Marc Stern, eds., *Global Public Goods: Global Cooperation in the 21st Century* (New York and Oxford: Oxford University Press [published for UNDP], 1999); and John S. Dryzek, *Rational Ecology: Environment and Political Economy* (Oxford and New York: Basil Blackwell, 1987). Such discussions usually make a stated or unstated assumption that the constitutive rules of capitalism are in place and are not going to be modified.

37. Mason and Asher, *World Bank*, 247-54.

38. Habermas offers the *locus classicus* of philosophical arguments in favor of democracy in *Between Facts and Norms*. Others who advocate democracy proffer arguments ranging from that which holds that "democracy" or the liberal nation-state is the best guarantor of a stable and peaceful world to a philosophy of radical egalitarianism to arguments concerning the devastating material consequences that occur when democracy is betrayed or otherwise deterred. See Kant, *Perpetual Peace*; Gramsci, *Prison Notebooks*; Chantal Mouffe, ed., *Dimensions of Radical Democracy: Pluralism, Citizenship, Community* (London: Verso, 1992); William K. Greider, *Who Will Tell the People: The Betrayal of American Democracy* (New York: Touchstone Books, 1993; and Noam Chomsky, *Deterring Democracy* (London: Verso, 1991).

39. The literature criticizing World Bank and International Monetary Fund policies that has been produced by people who are originally from third world countries or who have spent a good deal of their professional lives in third world countries is an extensive literature that has been growing exponentially since the mid-1990s. A good starting point for the reader interested in third world critiques of these international institutions would be the following works: Arjun Makhijani, *From Global Capitalism to Economic Justice* (London: Zed Books, 1991); Peter Gibbon, Yusuf Bangura, and Arve Ofstad, *Authoritarianism, Democracy, and Adjustment: The Politics of Economic Reform in Africa* (Uppsala, Sweden: Scandinavian Institute of African Studies, 1992); Bright Erakpoweri Okogu, *Africa and Economic Structural Adjustment: Case Studies of Ghana, Nigeria and Zambia* (Vienna: OPEC Fund for International Development, 1992); Chakravarthi Raghavan, *Recolonization: GATT, the Uruguay Round, and the Third World* (Penang, Malaysia: Third World Network, 1990); Vandana Shiva, *Staying Alive: Women, Ecology and Survival in India* (New York: St. Martin's Press, 1989); and Vandana Shiva, *Stolen Harvest: The Hijacking of the Global Food Supply* (Boston: South End Press, 1999). These works contain several concrete historical case studies and offer the principal points of contention with the policies of the World Bank and the IMF and the climate they have created to allow greater corporate hegemony. See also the works listed below, in note 47.

40. Address of Robert McNamara, President, to the Board of Governors, Nairobi, Kenya, September 24, 1973, reprinted in Robert S. McNamara, *The McNamara Years at the World Bank: Major Policy Addresses of Robert S. McNamara, 1968-1981* (Baltimore and London: The Johns Hopkins University Press, 1981), 233-63 (quote at 259). McNamara thought it was beyond the Bank's power to eliminate poverty in general, and he proposed only to eliminate the worst poverty, absolute poverty.

41. Eugene Black, quoted in Bruce Rich, *Mortgaging the Earth: The World Bank, Environmental Impoverishment, and the Crisis of Development* (Boston: Beacon Press, 1994), 63.

42. The moral gains of Stage Seven have recently been experiencing a resurgence. The starkest indication of this was the publication in 2000 of *Voices of the Poor: Crying Out for Change*. This book was the result of a study commissioned by the World Bank in preparation for its *World Development Report 2000/01: Attacking Poverty*. The introduction states that the origins of the study lay "in the conviction that at the start of the 21st century any policy document on poverty should be based on the experiences, reflections, aspirations and priorities of poor people themselves." Deepa Narayan, Robert Chambers, Meera K. Shah, and Patti Petesch, *Voices of the Poor: Crying Out for Change* (Oxford and New York: Oxford University Press, 2000), 3. The book is published for the World Bank and carries the Bank's current slogan, "Our dream is a world free of poverty." This study offers a wide range of policy prescriptions based directly on the testimony of people living in poverty in twenty-three countries around the world, and its scope of inquiry focused on four main themes: wellbeing and "illbeing"; the identification of problems and priorities and how these had changed; the role of institutions; and gender relations. Narayan et al., *Voices of the Poor*, 4-5. The emphasis upon ways that people living in poverty want institutions to change and become more responsive is particularly important. In the concluding section, "Agenda for Change," the authors state: "[Poor people] call for systemic change. They want more government, not less—government on which they have influence and with which they can partner in different ways. They look to government to provide services fundamental to their wellbeing. Poor people's problems cut

across sectoral divides. They challenge us to think and plan beyond narrow disciplinary boundaries while still remaining responsive to local realities. This requires institutions that are more decentralized, facilitative and accountable to poor women and men." Narayan et al., *Voices of the Poor*, 266. See also 267-89.

43. Rich, *Mortgaging the Earth*, 155-56.

44. In 1967, following the seizure of power by Suharto, the Netherlands took the leading role in the formation of the Intergovernmental Group on Indonesia, with the hope of preventing the outright collapse of the Indonesian economy. Mason and Asher, *World Bank*, 526.

45. Cheryl Payer, *The Debt Trap: the IMF and the Third World* (New York: Monthly Review Press, 1975). See also Cheryl Payer, *Lent and Lost: Foreign Credit and Third World Development* (London and New Jersey: Zed Books, 1991).

46. Davison Budhoo, "IMF/World Bank Wreak Havoc on Third World," in Danaher, *50 Years is Enough*, 20-21.

47. See Carlos M. Vilas, "Neoliberal Social Policy: Managing Poverty (Somehow)," *NACLA Report on the Americas* 29, no. 6 (May-June 1996): 16-25; Carlos M. Vilas, "Economic Restructuring, Neoliberal Reforms, and the Working Class in Latin America," in *Capital, Power and Inequality in Latin America*, ed. Sandor Halebsky and Richard Harris (Boulder, Colo.: Westview Press, 1995); Duncan Green, *Silent Revolution: The Rise of Market Economics in Latin America* (New York: Monthly Review Press, 1996); Howard Handelman and Werner Baer, eds., *Paying the Costs of Austerity in Latin America* (Boulder, Colo.; and London: Westview Press, 1989); E. Wayne Nafziger, *The Debt Crisis in Africa* (Baltimore, Md.; and London: The Johns Hopkins University Press, 1993); Christopher L. Delgado and Sidi Jammeh, eds., *The Political Economy of Senegal under Structural Adjustment* (New York Praeger Publishers, 1991); Dharam Ghai, ed., *The IMF and the South: The Social Impact of Crisis and Adjustment* (London: Zed Books, 1991); and Bade Onimode, ed., *The IMF, the World, and the African Debt*, Vol. 1 (London: Zed Books, 1989).

48. John B. Cobb, Jr., *The Earthist Challenge to Economism* (New York: St. Martin's Press, 1999), 93.

49. J. Magot, "New Report Slams Bank Dam Record," *BankCheck Quarterly* 10 (December 1994): 12.

50. See "A Coherent Opposition," Chapter 7, 108, of Cobb, *Earthist Challenge to Economism*. It is conceivable that input from NGOs, with their extensive experience in the field, could eventually break the stranglehold that persons trained as professional economists have had on the issuance of political and economic advice throughout the twentieth century. The early history of this particular stranglehold is well documented in Paul W. Drake, *The Money Doctor in the Andes: The Kemmerer Missions, 1923-1933* (Durham, N.C.: Duke University Press, 1989). See also Paul Drake, "The Money Doctors: Foreign Advisers and Foreign Debts in Latin America," *NACLA Report on the Americas* 31 (Nov.-Dec. 1997): 32-36. The World Bank's *Voices of the Poor* study offers evidence that this stranglehold is beginning to dissolve. The very first paragraph of the book states: "There are 2.8 billion poverty experts, the poor themselves. Yet the development discourse about poverty has been dominated by the perspectives and expertise of those who are not poor—professionals, politicians and agency officials. This book seeks to reverse this imbalance by focusing directly on the perspectives and expertise of poor people." Narayan et al., *Voices of the Poor*, 2. Another promising development with regard to Stage Ten is the creation of the World Bank's Global Development Network

(GDN). This network encourages collaboration among NGOs and other workers at the grassroots level and think tanks in all regions of the world and is based on the premise that "local knowledges" are crucial in the consensus-building process. On the Global Development Network, see Diane Stone, ed., *Banking on Knowledge: The Genesis of the Global Development Network* (London: Routledge, 2000). This work contains contributions by many of the participants in the conference in Bonn in 1999, which launched the creation of the GDN.

51. Claudia Fumo, *The World Bank's Partnership with Nongovernmental Organizations* (Washington, D.C.: World Bank, 1996), 5.

52. James D. Wolfensohn, "People and Development" (Annual Meetings Address to the Board of Governors of the World Bank, Washington, D.C.), 1 October 1996. Although the World Bank has recently strengthened its commitment in principle to neoliberalism, the Bank has begun to propagate institutions that spring from its acknowledgment of the need for greater local participation and more emphasis on social development. One such institution is the Social Investment Fund (SIF), which the World Bank conceives of as a mechanism for mitigating some of the harsh effects of the structural adjustment programs. The stated priorities of the SIFs, which now operate in most countries that underwent structural adjustment, are social assistance programs (e.g., food aid), emergency (short-term) employment programs, and longer-term employment programs aimed at promoting "productivity" (e.g., worker training and microcredit programs that assist small businesses). The SIFs can be criticized for helping to legitimize neoliberal economic policies that have already proven disastrous. Nevertheless, the existence of the institution of the Social Investment Funds has created apertures for governments in borrowing countries to mold these SIFs to their needs. One shining example of a success in this regard is the Chilean Solidarity and Social Investment Fund (FOSIS), instituted in 1990 as Chile made the transition back toward social democracy under civilian rule. The FOSIS is designed to be a long-term program that strikes at the structural causes of poverty in ways that most SIFs do not. It is also largely independent of external funding sources. See Karin Stahl, "Anti-Poverty Programs: Making Structural Adjustment More Palatable," *NACLA Report on the Americas* 29, no. 6 (May-June 1996): 32-36.

53. Lawrence Summers, "The United States and the World Bank," speech delivered to the Overseas Development Council, published in *Treasury News*, 11 October 1994: 4.

54. Even if the World Bank reached Stage Eleven for cynical reasons—e.g., trying to forestall the political instability of social revolution or other forms of the expression of legitimate popular grievances with structural adjustment programs—Stage Eleven nevertheless remains an important step in the Bank's moral evolution.

55. Peirce quoted in Lawrence E. Cahoone, ed., *From Modernism to Postmodernism* (Oxford: Blackwell, 1996), 150.

56. James, *Essays in Pragmatism*, 155.

57. Robert Stephen Milne and Diane K. Mauzy, *Singapore: the Legacy of Lee Kuan Yew* (Boulder, Colo.: Westview Press, 1990), 114.

58. In the vein of advocating a broader and more authentic form of pragmatism, we direct the reader's attention to the work of John Dryzek, who makes the case of the primacy of ecological rationality. Dryzek writes, "The preservation and enhancement of the material and ecological basis of society is necessary not only for the functioning of societal forms such as economically, socially, legally, and politically rational structures, but also for action in pursuit of *any* value in the long term. The pursuit of such values is

predicated upon the avoidance of ecological catastrophe. Hence the preservation and promotion of the integrity of the ecological and material underpinning of society—ecological rationality—should take priority over competing forms of reason in collective choices with an impact upon that integrity." Dryzek, *Rational Ecology*, 58-59, italics in original.

59. The *Voices of the Poor* study, carried out by the World Bank at the end of the twentieth century, stands as an official endorsement of these principles and as an embrace of the Bank's moral evolution, especially as we outlined in Stages Six, Seven, and Ten. Although the book published as a result of this study carries a careful disclaimer that the book's findings, interpretations, and conclusions "should not be attributed in any manner to the World Bank, to its affiliated organizations, or to members of its Board of Executive Directors," the Bank's recognition of the importance of commissioning such a study to serve as background material for its annual development report speaks volumes. The book concludes with a consideration of what a commitment to "deep change" would entail. The authors speak of professional change ("a paradigm shift"), personal change, and institutional change. Narayan et al., *Voices of the Poor*, 288. It is this third category we wish to highlight. The authors write: "*Institutional* change is cultural and behavioral. To the extent that organizations reward domineering behaviors, they are antithetical to the sensitive, responsive and empowering approaches needed to give the needs and interests of poor people priority. These behaviors are dictated by the norms, rules, rewards, incentives and values implicit in organizations." Narayan et al., *Voices of the Poor*, 289, italics in original.

Epilogue

When Vanderbilt-trained economics professor Muhammad Yunus returned from the United States to his village in Bangladesh and observed the tremendous daily struggles of women who labored long hours every day and still were not able to assuage the entrenched poverty through which their families struggled, he knew something had to be done. He would come to know that none of the conventional wisdom in the late 1970s applied in this situation, either as an explanation for their continued poverty or as a solution to it. The women, who were weavers of bamboo stools, lacked sufficient money to buy their materials directly and so were reliant upon middlemen (*paikars*), who sold them their materials on credit and then bought the finished product at a pittance, leaving the women with, on average, a daily wage that was the equivalent of two cents. After talking extensively with the weavers, Yunus learned that there were forty-two people each working for approximately two pennies a day—because collectively they lacked capital amounting to 856 *taka*, the equivalent of twenty-one U.S. dollars. Some of the women needed only ten or twenty *taka*, and the greatest amount any one person needed was sixty-five *taka*. Not only was Yunus stunned to learn of this situation; he was deeply troubled. He said he felt "ashamed to be part of a society which could not make [twenty-one dollars] available to forty-two hard-working, skilled human beings so that they could make a decent living."[1] From his own funds, he gave them a loan of the money they collectively needed.

He then approached banks in search of loans so that the weavers would have a sustainable source of support. The banks flatly rejected his request as soon as they learned that the women could offer no collateral. Conventional wisdom, as dispensed by the banks and the U.S. Agency for International Development, called for the women to find wealthy patrons who would serve as guarantors of loans and for the interest rates charged for such loans to be thirty-six percent (rather than the thirteen percent Yunus had suggested), in order to cover the ostensibly greater risks associated with lending to those who held no property. Reflecting on this years later, in 1984, Yunus remarked, "The financial institutions' contention that they can deal only on the basis of collateral is merely a device to deceive the poor. To say that there can be no banking without collateral is like saying men will not be able to fly unless they have wings. . . . To suggest that human beings were incapable of devising any other form of banking except with the provision of collateral would be quite ridiculous."[2] He went on to demonstrate just how ridiculous it was by founding the Grameen Bank, which operated on a new set of principles, including solidarity, cooperation, and the pledge of mutual aid among groups of loan recipients, the vast majority of whom are women. By 1993, just ten years after the project had gotten underway in earnest, membership in the Grameen Bank had grown to 1.6 million borrowers, spread throughout 25,000 villages in Bangladesh; furthermore, Grameen employed approximately 11,000 people, and the loans they sanctioned (charging well under standard interest rates) generated enough interest income to pay all salaries.[3] The success and sustainability of the Grameen Bank have since been replicated in similar socially responsible microfinance projects all around the world.

In our estimation, the comment by Yunus highlights that very often, the principal obstacle to instituting greater social justice is the failure of human imagination, the failure to give human creativity its full due. We wholeheartedly agree with the sentiment expressed by Yunus, as well as with Paulo Freire, who wrote in his last published work: "As great as the conditioning power of the economy may be over our individual and social behavior, I cannot accept being completely passive before it. To the extent that we accept that the economy, or technology, or science, it doesn't matter what, exerts inescapable power over us, there is nothing left for us to do other than renounce our ability to think, to conjecture, to compare, to choose, to decide, to envision, to dream."[4] The closing down of imagination is, then, the renunciation of our very humanity.

Contributing to the failure of human imagination and to the widespread despair—common even among those who are convinced of the need for greater social justice—that springs from the belief that nothing can be done to change the design of our world in any substantive way is the lack of knowledge about projects all around the world that are doing exactly this: transforming the design of our world at local and regional levels. It is beyond the scope of this book to offer comment on or even begin to enumerate the vast array of such projects, but we certainly encourage interested readers to seek them out, for every progressive cause is helped by the inspiration of example. Although descriptions and images of such projects will not reach the eyes or ears of the majority of consumers of the current mainstream media, it is important to acknowledge that seeds of workable cultures—i.e., ones that do work to mobilize resources to meet needs—are being planted in all regions of the world, in many cases utilizing older cultural resources and melding them with new approaches set within the context of this historical moment.[5]

Our approach herein has been to offer a critique of the foundations of the global economy so that participants in these small-scale and larger projects aimed at poverty eradication, which are already underway, will be further empowered to effect deep change that can outlast the ill-fated attempts at social democracy that did not sufficiently strike at the root cause of the insecurity generated by the institutions of modernity. The story of Muhammad Yunus and the craft laborers whose plight was the impetus for the idea of the Grameen Bank illustrates the trumping by genuine ethics of the liberal ethics that are at the heart of the philosophical and institutional underpinnings of the global economy. Yunus owed no legal obligations to these women. He could have been a mere passerby, not giving a second glance as the *paikars*, exercising the freedom their access to property gave them, represented the cruel face of "the market" to these weavers of bamboo stools. Instead he was moved to take action by a sense of shame that fellow members of his community, despite all their toil, were left out in the cold. In the course of instituting the Grameen Bank, its organizers ended up acting on entirely redefined concepts of what "freedom" and "property" should mean in practice. The Grameen Bank encourages the responsible exercise of the rights and duties of property ownership and channels the benefits of property so that more people enjoy them. It facilitates communities' moving beyond the rules of a strictly commercial society based on contractual relationships between mutually indifferent buyers and sellers, toward a truly human society whose norms function to help ensure that everyone is cared for. And it encourages its participants to use their freedom to discern the right thing to do, to make the right choices, and to be faithful to their values and commitments. As such, we would consider this project an effort to subsidize de-alienation and to find ways of including its participants as co-creators of a community of care.

Many respond to earnest efforts at ethical construction—the seeking of greater compliance with extant standards based on genuine ethics, and at the same time, elevation of the ethical standards by which the economy is organized—by lifting high the banner of resignation, with its stultifying motto, "That's just the way things are." Yet, as Yunus and many thousands of others have understood, the world is as it is because we have made it so, and "the way things are" is not the way things have to be. To reiterate the belief with which we began this work, there is nothing in all of nature that prevents individuals and institutions from being guided by principles of cooperation and sharing, except: ourselves.

Notes

1. Yunus quoted in Alex Counts, *Give Us Credit* (New York: Times Books, 1996), 39.

2. Ibid.

3. Ibid., 1-11.

4. Paulo Freire, *Pedagogy of Indignation* (Boulder and London: Paradigm Publishers, 2004), 33.

5. In addition to various works mentioned in previous chapters, see also Paul Ekins, *A New World Order: Grassroots Movements for Global Change* (London: Routledge, 1992); Jeremy Seabrook, *Pioneers of Change: Experiments in Creating a Humane Society* (London: Zed Books; and Philadelphia: New Society Publishers, 1993); Anirudh Krishna, Norman Uphoff, and Milton J. Esman, eds., *Reasons for Hope: Instructive Experiences in Rural Development* (West Hartford, Conn.: Kumarian Press, 1997); and Frances Moore Lappé and Anna Lappé, *Hope's Edge: The Next Diet For A Small Planet* (New York: Jeremy P. Tarcher/Putnam, 2002).

Bibliography

Abers, Rebecca. "Learning Democratic Practice: Distributing Government Resources through Popular Participation in Porto Alegre, Brazil." Pp. 39-66 *in Cities for Citizens: planning and the rise of civil society in a global age*, edited by M. Douglass and J. Friedmann. Chichester, U.K.; and New York: J. Wiley, 1998.

———. *Inventing Local Democracy: grassroots politics in Brazil*. Boulder, Colo.: Lynne Rienner Publishers, 2000.

Aguirre, Manuel. *Esquema de la Doctrina Social Católica*. Caracas: Ediciones SIC, 1940.

Ahmad, Khurshid, ed. *Studies in Islamic Economics*. Delhi: Amar Prakashan, 1983.

Aimer, Peter. "The Strategy of Gradualism and the Swedish Wage-Earner Funds." *West European Politics* 3 (July 1985): 43-53.

Al-Faruqui, Isma'il R., and Abdullah Omar Nassef, eds. *Social and Natural Sciences: The Islamic Perspective*. Jeddah, Saudi Arabia: Hodder and Stoughton for King Abdulaziz University, 1981.

Alker, Jr., Hayward. *Rediscoveries and Reformulations*. Cambridge: Cambridge University Press, 1996.

Allen, William R. *Midnight Economist: Broadcast Essays III*. Los Angeles, Calif.: International Institute for Economic Research, 1982.

Althusser, Louis. *For Marx*. Translated by Ben Brewster. New York and London: Verso, 1996 (1965).

Alvarez Junco, José, and Adrian Shubert, eds. *Spanish History Since 1808*. London and New York: Arnold, 2000.

Anderson, Benedict. *Imagined Communities: Reflections on the Origin and Spread of Nationalism*. London and New York: Verso, 1983.

An-Nalim, Abdullahi Ahmed, ed. *Human Rights in Cross-Cultural Perspective: A Quest for Consensus*. Philadelphia: University of Philadelphia Press, 1992.

Anscombe, Elizabeth. *Times, Beginnings, and Causes*. London: Oxford University Press, 1975.

Aquinas, St. Thomas. *St. Thomas Aquinas on Charity*. Milwaukee, Wisc.: Marquette University Press, 1960.

———. *Summa Theologiae*. London: Blackfriars, 1975.

Arendt, Hannah. *The Human Condition*. Chicago: The University of Chicago Press, 1958.

———. "Lying in Politics: Reflections on the Pentagon Papers." Pp. 3-47 in *Crises of the Republic*. New York: Harcourt Brace Jovanovich, 1972.

Aristotle. *Nichomachean Ethics*. Translated by Martin Ostwald. Indianapolis, Ind.: Bobbs-Merrill Educational Publishing, 1962.

391

Arruda, Marcos. "A Creative Approach to Structural Adjustment: Towards a People-centred Development." Pp. 132-44 in *Beyond Bretton Woods: Alternatives to the Global Economic Order*, edited by John Cavanaugh, Daphne Wysham, and Marcos Arruda. London; and Boulder, Colo.: Pluto Press, 1994.

————. *External Debt: Brazil and the International Financial Crisis*. Translated by Peter Lenny. London; and Sterling, Va.: Pluto Press, 2000.

Arvelaiz, Maximilien and Temir Porras Ponceleon. "U.S. Pushing for a Coup d'Etat: Venezuela, Target of Opportunity." *Covert Action Quarterly*, no. 72 (Spring 2002): 12-17.

Axelrod, Robert. *The Evolution of Cooperation*. New York: Basic Books, 1984.

Bachelard, Gaston. *The New Scientific Spirit*. Translated by Arthur Goldhammer. Boston: Beacon Press, 1984 (1934).

Balzer, Marjorie Mandelstam, ed. *Shamanic Worlds: Rituals and Lore of Siberia and Central Asia*. Armonk, N.Y.; and London: North Castle Books, 1997.

Bani-Sadr, Abulhasan. *The Fundamental Principles and Precepts of Islamic Government*. Translated by Mohammad R. Ghanoonparvar. Lexington, Ky.: Mazda Publishers, 1981.

————. *Work and the Worker in Islam*. Translated by Hasan Mashhadi. Tehran: The Hamdami Foundation, 1981.

Barthes, Roland. *Mythologies*. Translated by Annette Lavers. New York: Hill and Wang, 1972 (1957).

Bartley, W.W., III. *The Collected Works of F.A. Hayek, Vol. 1: The Fatal Conceit, The Errors of Socialism*. Chicago and London: The University of Chicago Press, 1988.

Barton, Greg. "Islam in opposition? It's not that easy." *Inside Indonesia*, no. 52 (Oct.-Dec. 1997): 1-3.

Bartra, Roger. *La Jaula de la Melancolia; identidad y metamorfosis del mexicano*. Mexico City: Grijalbo, 1987.

Bates, Robert, and Anne Kruger, eds. *Political and Economic Interaction in Economic Policy Reform*. Cambridge, Mass.: Blackwell, 1993.

Bautista Urbaneja, Diego. *Pueblo y petróleo en la política venezolana del siglo XX*. Caracas: CEPET, 1992.

Bellah, Robert N., Richard Madsen, William M. Sullivan, Ann Swidler, and Steven M. Tipton. *Habits of the Heart: Individualism and Commitment in American Life*. Berkeley; Los Angeles; London: University of California Press, 1985.

Belloc, Hilaire. *The Catholic Church and the Principle of Private Property*. London: Catholic Truth Society, 1933.

————. *The Crisis of Civilization*. New York: Fordham University Press, 1937.

Bengelsdorf, Carollee. *The Problem of Democracy in Cuba: Between Vision & Reality*. New York and Oxford: Oxford University Press, 1994.

Bennett, William J. *The Book of Virtues: A Treasury of Great Moral Stories*. New York: Simon & Schuster, 2000.

Bennett, William J., John J. DiIulio, Jr., and John P. Walters. *Body Count: Moral Poverty—and How To Win America's War against Crime and Drugs*. New York: Simon & Schuster, 1996.

Benson, Peter L. *All Kids are Our Kids: What Communities Must Do to Raise Caring and Responsible Children and Adolescents*. San Francisco: Jossey-Bass, 1997.

Bernstein, Richard J. *The Restructuring of Social and Political Theory*. New York and London: Harcourt Brace Jovanovich, 1976.

Berry, Thomas. *The Dream of the Earth*. San Francisco: Sierra Club Books, 1988.

Betancourt, Rómulo. *Venezuela: Política y Petróleo*. Barcelona; Caracas; Mexico City: Editorial Seix Barral, S.A., 1979 (1956).

Bhaskar, Roy. *Scientific Realism and Human Emancipation*. London: Verso, 1986.

Bicchieri, Cristina. "Norms of Cooperation." *Ethics* 100 (1990): 838-61.

Bingham, Richard D., ed. *Managing Local Government: Public Administration in Practice*. Newbury Park, Calif.: Sage Publications, 1991.

Birdsall, Nancy, and John Williamson, with Brian Deese. *Delivering on Debt Relief: From IMF Gold to a New Aid Architecture*. Washington D.C., Institute for International Economics/Center for Global Development, 2002.

Bloch, Marc. "La lutte pour l'individualisme agraire dans la France du dix-huitieme siecle." *Annales d'histoire économique et sociale* 2 (July 1930): 329-83; and 2 (October 1930): 511-56.

Boff, Leonardo. *Eclesiogénesis: Las comunidades de base reinventan la Iglesia*. Santander, Spain: Editorial Sal Terrae, 1986.

Bond, George D. *The Buddhist Revival in Sri Lanka: Religious Tradition, Reinterpretation, and Response*. Columbia, S.C.: University of South Carolina Press, 1988.

Booth, Anne, and Peter McCawley, eds. *The Indonesian Economy during the Soeharto Era*. Kuala Lumpur; Oxford; New York; Melbourne: Oxford University Press, 1981.

Bosworth, Barry, and Alice Rivlin, eds. *The Swedish Economy*. Washington, D.C.: The Brookings Institution, 1987.

Bottomore, Tom, Laurence Harries, V.G. Kiernan, and Ralph Miliband, eds. *A Dictionary of Marxist Thought*. Cambridge, Mass.: Harvard University Press, 1983.

Boulding, Elise. *Building a Global Civic Culture: Education for an Interdependent World*. New York and London: Teachers College Press, 1988.

Boulding, Kenneth E. *The Image: Knowledge in Life and Society*. Ann Arbor, Mich.: University of Michigan Press, 1956.

Bourchier, David, and Vedi Hadiz, eds. *Indonesian Politics and Society: A Reader*. London: Routledge, 2002.

Bourdieu, Pierre. *Esquisse d'une theorie de la pratique*. Geneva: Droz, 1972.

———. *Outline of a Theory of Practice*. Translated by R. Nice. Cambridge: Cambridge University Press, 1977.

———. *The Logic of Practice*. Stanford, Calif.: Stanford University Press, 1990.

Bowles, Samuel. "What Markets Can—and Cannot—Do." *Challenge* (July-August 1991): 11-16.

Bowles, Samuel, and Herbert Gintis. *Schooling in Capitalist America: Educational Reform and the Contradictions of Economic Life*. New York: Basic Books, 1976.

———. *Democracy and Capitalism: Property, Community, and the Contradictions of Modern Social Thought*. New York: Basic Books, 1986.

Braudel, Fernand. *Civilization and Capitalism, 15th-18th Century, Vol. 1: The Structures of Everyday Life, The Limits of the Possible*. New York; Cambridge; Hagerstown, Md.; Philadelphia; San Francisco; London; Mexico City; São Paulo; Sydney: Harper & Row Publishers, 1979 (1967).

Bread for the World Institute. *Hunger in a Global Economy*. Silver Spring, Md.: Bread for the World Institute, 1997.

Brecher, Jeremy, and Tim Costello. *Global Village or Global Pillage: Economic Reconstruction from the Bottom Up*. Boston: South End Press, 1994.

Brecher, Jeremy, Tim Costello, and Brendan Smith. *Globalization from Below*. Cambridge, Mass.: South End Press, 2000.

Brehdahl, Maury E., Philip C. Abbott, and Michael R. Reed, eds. *Competitiveness in International Food Markets*. Boulder, Colo.; San Francisco; Oxford: Westview Press, 1994.

Breman, Jan, and Gunawan Wiradi. *Good Times and Bad Times in Java: Socio-economic dynamics in two villages towards the end of the 20th century*. Leiden, Neth.: KITLV Press, 2002.

Brody, David. *Workers in Industrial America: Essays on the 20th Century Struggle*. New York and Oxford: Oxford University Press, 1980.

———. *In Labor's Cause: Main Themes on the History of the American Worker*. New York and Oxford: Oxford University Press, 1993.

Budhoo, Davison. "IMF/World Bank Wreak Havoc on Third World." Pp. 20-23 in *50 Years is Enough: The Case Against the World Bank and the International Monetary Fund*, edited by Kevin Danaher. Boston: South End Press, 1994.

Bukey, Evan Burr. *Hitler's Austria: Popular Sentiment in the Nazi Era, 1938-1945*. Chapel Hill and London: The University of North Carolina Press, 2000.

Bunge, Mario. *Causality: The Place of the Causal Principle in Modern Science*. Cleveland, Ohio: World Publishing Co., 1963.

Burke, Peter. *History & Social Theory*. Ithaca, N.Y.: Cornell University Press, 1993.

Burkett, Paul, and Martin Hart-Landsberg. "East Asia and the Crisis in Development Theory." *Journal of Contemporary Asia* 28, no. 4 (1998): 435-56.

Caballero, Nestor, and Elia Schneider. *Huelepega, ley de la calle*. DVD. Directed by Elia Schneider. Caracas: Venezuela Unity Films, 1999.

Cahoone, Lawrence E., ed. *From Modernism to Postmodernism*. Oxford: Blackwell, 1996.

Calvo Hernando, Pedro. *Todos me dicen Felipe*. Barcelona: Plaza & Janes, 1987.

Camilleri, Joseph A., Kamal Malhotra, and Majid Tehranian, eds. *Reimagining the Future*. Bundoora Victoria, Australia: Politics Department, La Trobe University, 2000.

Caporeal, Linnda R., Robyn M. Dawes, John M. Orbell, and Alphons J.C. van de Kragt. "Selfishness Examined: Cooperation in the Absence of Egoistic Incentives." *Behavioral and Brain Sciences* 12 (1989): 683-739.

Carr, Raymond. *Spain, 1808-1975*. Oxford: Clarendon Press, 1982 (1966).

Carter, Stephen L. *Integrity*. New York: HarperPerennial, 1997.

———. *Civility: Manners, Morals, and the Etiquette of Democracy*. New York: HarperCollins, 1999.

Cassell, Philip, ed. *The Giddens Reader*. Stanford, Calif.: Stanford University Press, 1993.

Caufield, Catherine. *Masters of Illusion: the World Bank and the Poverty of Nations*. New York: Henry Holt and Company, 1996.

Centro de Estudios del Desarrollo (CENDES). *Estudio de diagnóstico para el plan maestro de ordenamiento territorial del area de la Faja Petrolifera de Orinoco*. Caracas: University of Venezuela, 1976.

Cerezo Galán, P. *Palabra en el tiempo: poesia y filosofia en Antonio Machado*. Madrid: Editorial Gredos, 1975.

Chagnon, Napoleon A. *Yanomamo: the Fierce People*. New York: Holt, Rinehart and Winston, 1968.

Chapra, M. 'Umar. *The Economic System of Islam*. Karachi: Department of Publications, University of Karachi, 1971.

Chomsky, Noam. *Aspects of the Theory of Syntax*. Cambridge, Mass.: MIT Press, 1965.

————. *Cartesian Linguistics: A Chapter in the History of Rationalist Thought*. New York and London: Harper & Row, 1966.

————. *Language and Responsibility*. Translated by John Viertel. New York: Pantheon Books, 1977.

————. *Deterring Democracy*. London: Verso, 1991.

Cobb, John B., Jr. *The Earthist Challenge to Economism*. New York: St. Martin's Press, 1999.

Cocks, R. C. J. *Sir Henry Maine: A Study in Victorian Jurisprudence*. Cambridge; New York; New Rochelle; Melbourne; Sydney: Cambridge University Press, 1988.

Cohen, Jeffrey H. *Cooperation and Community: Economy and Society in Oaxaca*. Austin, Tex.: University of Texas Press, 1999.

Cohen, Lizabeth. *Making a New Deal: Industrial Workers in Chicago, 1919-1939*. Cambridge; New York; Port Chester; Melbourne; Sydney: Cambridge University Press, 1990.

Collier, George A. *Socialists of Rural Andalusia: Unacknowledged Revolutionaries of the Second Republic*. Stanford, Calif.: Stanford University Press, 1987.

Collins, Joseph (with Frances Moore Lappé and Nick Allen). *What Difference Could a Revolution Make? Food and Farming in The New Nicaragua*. San Francisco: Institute for Food and Development Policy, 1982.

Colomer, Josep. *Game Theory and the Transition to Democracy: The Spanish Model*. Aldershot, U.K.: Edward Elgar Publishing, 1995.

Contreras, Manuel. *El PSOE en la II República: Organización e ideología*. Madrid: Centro de Investigaciones Sociológicas, 1981.

Coraggio, José Luis. "Economics and Politics in the Transition to Socialism: Reflections on the Nicaragua Experience." Pp. 143-70 in *Transition and Development: Problems of Third World Socialism*, edited by Richard R. Fagen, Carmen Diana Deere, and José Luis Coraggio. New York: Monthly Review Press, 1986.

————. *Territorios en transición: crítica a la planificación regional en América Latina*. Quito: Ciudad, 1987.

Coraggio, José Luis and Carmen Diana Deere, coordinators. *La transición difícil: La autodeterminación de los pequeños países periféricos*. Mexico City: Siglo Veintiuno, 1986.

Corcoran, Barbara. *Strike!* New York: Atheneum, 1983.

Coronil, Fernando. *The Magical State*. Chicago: University of Chicago Press, 1997.

Counts, Alex. *Give Us Credit*. New York: Times Books, 1996.

Cowie, Jefferson. *Capital Moves: RCA's 70-Year Quest for Cheap Labor*. Ithaca, N.Y. and London: Cornell University Press, 1999.

Craypo, Charles, and Bruce Nissen, eds. *Grand Designs: the Impact of Corporate Strategies on Workers, Unions and Communities*. Ithaca, N.Y.: ILR Press, 1993.

Cripps, Stafford. *The Struggle For Peace*. London: Victor Gollancz, 1936.

————. *Towards Christian Democracy*. New York: Philosophical Library, 1946.

Crisp, Brian F., Daniel H. Levine, and Juan Carlos Rey. "The Legitimacy Problem." Pp. 139-70 in *Venezuelan Democracy Under Stress*, edited by Jennifer McCoy, Andrés Serbin, William C. Smith, and Andrés Stambouli. New Brunswick, N.J.: Transaction Books, 1995.

Crouch, Harold. *The Army and Politics in Indonesia*. Rev. ed. Ithaca, N.Y.; and London: Cornell University Press, 1988.

Cyert, Richard M., and James G. March. *A Behavioral Theory of the Firm*. Englewood Cliffs, N.J.: Prentice-Hall, 1963.

Dahm, Bernhard. *Sukarno and the Struggle for Indonesian Independence.* Translated by Mary F. Somers Heidhues. Ithaca, N.Y.; and London: Cornell University Press, 1969.

Dahrendorf, Ralf. *After Social Democracy.* London: Liberal Publication Department, for The Unservile State Group [Unservile State Papers, No. 25], 1980.

Dahrendorf, Ralf, ed. *Europe's Economy in Crisis.* New York: Holmes & Meier, 1982.

Dalton, George, ed. *Primitive, Archaic and Modern Economies: Essays of Karl Polanyi.* Boston: Beacon Press, 1968.

Daly, Herman E. *Beyond Growth: The Economics of Sustainable Development.* Boston: Beacon, 1996.

Danaher, Kevin, ed. *50 Years is Enough: The Case Against the World Bank and the International Monetary Fund.* Boston: South End Press, 1994.

Davies, Wendy, and Paul Fouracre, eds. *Property and Power in the Early Middle Ages.* Cambridge; New York; Melbourne: Cambridge University Press, 1995.

Davis, Mike. *City of Quartz: Excavating the Future in Los Angeles.* New York: Vintage Books, 1992.

Dawkins, Richard. *The Selfish Gene.* Oxford: Oxford University Press, 1989.

Dawley, Alan. "Workers, Capital, and the State in the Twentieth Century." Pp. 152-202 in *Perspectives on American Labor History: The Problems of Synthesis*, edited by J. Carroll Moody and Alice Kessler-Harris. DeKalb, Ill.: Northern Illinois University Press, 1989.

De Bernis, Gérard Destanne. "Development or Pauperization?" Pp. 86-137 in *Poverty, Progress, and Development*, edited by Paul-Marc Henry. London: Kegan Paul, 1991.

De la Cierva, Ricardo. *Historia del Socialismo en España, 1879-1983.* Barcelona: Planeta, 1983.

Delgado, Christopher L., and Sidi Jammeh, eds. *The Political Economy of Senegal under Structural Adjustment.* New York: Praeger Publishers, 1991.

Derrida, Jacques. *Margins of Philosophy.* Translated by Alan Bass. Chicago: The University of Chicago Press, 1982.

———. *Specters of Marx: The State of the Debt, the Work of Mourning, and the New International.* London: Routledge, 1994.

Descartes, Rene. *Discours de la Methode pour bien conduire la raison et chercher la verite dans les sciences.* Paris: Fayard, 1986 (1637).

Desgupta, Partha, and Ismail Serageldin, eds. *Social Capital and Poor Communities.* Washington, D.C.: World Bank, 2000.

Dillman, Bradford L. *State and Private Sector in Algeria: The Politics of Rent-seeking and Failed Development.* Boulder, Colo.; and Oxford: Westview Press, 2000.

Dilthey, Wilhelm. *Introduction to the Human Sciences: An Attempt to Lay a Foundation for the Study of Society and History.* Translated by Ramon J. Betanzos. Detroit, Mich.: Wayne State University Press, 1988 (1923).

Dinwiddy, John R. *Bentham.* Oxford and New York: Oxford University Press, 1989.

Dooley, Arch R. et al. *Wage Administration and Worker Productivity.* New York; London; and Sydney: John Wiley & Sons, 1964.

Dormael, Armand van. *Bretton Woods: Birth of a Monetary System.* New York: Holmes & Meier Publications, 1978.

Dornbusch, Rudiger. *Latin American Trade Misinvoicing as an Instrument of Capital Flight and Duty Evasion: Motives, Evidence, and Macroeconomic Implications.*

Washington, D.C.: Inter-American Development Bank [Occasional Paper No. 3], 1990.

Dorr, Donal. *Option for the Poor: A Hundred Years of Vatican Social Teaching.* Maryknoll, N.Y.: Orbis, 1992.

Dorrien, Gary. *The Neoconservative Mind: Politics, Culture, and the War of Ideology.* Philadelphia: Temple University Press, 1993.

Drake, Paul W. *The Money Doctor in the Andes: The Kemmerer Missions, 1923-1933.* Durham, N.C.: Duke University Press, 1989.

———. "The Money Doctors: Foreign Advisers and Foreign Debts in Latin America." *NACLA Report on the Americas* 21, no. 3 (Nov.-Dec. 1997): 32-36.

Drucker, Peter F. *The End of Economic Man.* New York: The John Day Company, 1939.

Dryzek, John S. *Rational Ecology: Environment and Political Economy.* Oxford and New York: Basil Blackwell, 1987.

Dubofsky, Melvyn. *The State and Labor in Modern America.* Chapel Hill, N.C.; and London: The University of North Carolina Press, 1994.

Dumont, Louis. *From Mandeville to Marx: The Genesis and Triumph of Economic Ideology.* Chicago and London: The University of Chicago Press, 1977.

Durkheim, Emile. *The Division of Labor in Society.* Translated by George Simpson. New York: Macmillan, 1933 (1893).

———. *Suicide, a study in sociology.* Glencoe, Ill.: Free Press, 1951 (1897).

Dworkin, Andrea. *Pornography: Men Possessing Women.* New York: Perigee Books, 1979.

Edgren, Gösta, Karl-Olof Faxén, and Clas-Erik Odhner. *Wage Formation and the Economy.* London: George Allen and Unwin, 1973.

Effendy, Bahtiar. *Islam and the State: The transformation of Islamic political ideas and practices in Indonesia.* Singapore: Institute of Southeast Asian Studies, 2002.

Egan, Eileen. *Such a Vision of the Street: Mother Teresa—The Spirit and the Work.* New York: Doubleday, 1985.

Eisler, Riane. *The Chalice and the Blade: Our History, Our Future.* New York: Harper-Collins, 1987.

Ekins, Paul. *A New World Order: Grassroots Movements for Global Change.* London: Routledge, 1992.

Ekins, Paul, and Manfred Max-Neef. *Real-life Economics: Understanding Wealth Creation.* London and New York: Routledge, 1992.

Ellner, Steve. *From Guerrilla Defeat To Innovative Politics: Venezuela's* Movimiento al Socialismo. Durham, N.C.: Duke University Press, 1988.

———. "The Politics of Privatization." *NACLA Report on the Americas* 21, no. 3 (Nov.-Dec. 1997): 6-9.

Elorza, A. "Los primeros programas del PSOE (1879-1888)." *Estudios de Historia Social* 8-9 (1979):143-80.

Eng, Pierre van der. *Agricultural Growth in Indonesia: Productivity Change and Policy Impact since 1880.* New York: St. Martin's Press, 1996; and Houndmills, Basingstoke, Hampshire, U.K.; and London: Macmillan Press, 1996.

Escobar, Arturo. *Encountering Development: the Making and Unmaking of the Third World.* Princeton, N.J.: Princeton University Press, 1995.

Esposito, John L., and John O. Voll. "Khurshid Ahmad: Muslim Activist-Economist." *The Muslim World* 80, no. 1 (January 1990). Reprinted as Pp. 33-54 in *Islamic Resurgence: Challenges, Directions and Future Perspectives, A Roundtable with Prof.*

Khurshid Ahmad, edited by Ibrahim M. Abu-Rabi. Islamabad, Pakistan: Institute of Policy Studies, 1995.

Estes, Ralph W. *Accounting and Society.* Los Angeles: Melville Publishing Co., 1973.

———. *Tyranny of the Bottom Line: Why Corporations Make Good People Do Bad Things.* San Francisco: Berrett-Koehler Publishers, 1996.

Evans, Grant. *The Politics of Ritual and Remembrance: Laos Since 1975.* Honolulu: University of Hawaii Press, 1998.

Fehr, Ernst and Simon Gächter. "Cooperation and Punishment in Public Goods Experiments." *American Economic Review* 90, no. 4 (September 2000): 980-94.

Feith, Herbert. *The Decline of Constitutional Democracy in Indonesia.* Ithaca, N.Y.: Cornell University Press, 1962.

Feith, Herbert, and Lance Castles, eds. *Indonesian Political Thinking, 1945-1965.* Ithaca, N.Y.: Cornell University Press, 1970.

Ferraro, Curro. *Economía y explotación en la democracia Española.* Bilbao, Spain: ZYX, 1978.

Fleisher, Frederic. *The New Sweden: The Challenge of a Disciplined Democracy.* New York: David McKay Company, 1967.

Flood, Merrill M. "Some Experimental Games." *Management Science* 5 (1958): 5-26.

Flyvbjerg, Bent. *Making Social Science Matter: Why social inquiry fails and how it can succeed again.* Translated by Steven Sampson. Cambridge and New York: Cambridge University Press, 2001.

Forrester, Viviane. *L'Horreur Economique.* Paris: Fayard, 1996.

Foucault, Michel. *Discipline and Punish: the Birth of the Prison.* New York: Pantheon Books, 1977.

———. *The Order of Things: An Archaeology of the Human Sciences.* London: Routledge, 2001 (1970).

Fowler, Robert Booth. *The Greening of Protestant Thought.* Chapel Hill, N.C.; and London: The University of North Carolina Press, 1995.

Freire, Paulo. *Cultural Action for Freedom.* Cambridge, Mass.: Harvard Educational Review, 1988 (1970).

———. *The Pedagogy of the Oppressed.* New York: Continuum, 1989 (1970).

———. *The Pedagogy of Indignation.* Boulder and London: Paradigm Publishers, 2004.

Freud, Sigmund. *Jokes and Their Relation to the Unconscious.* New York: Norton, 1960.

Frieden, Jeffry. "Invested Interests: The Politics of National Economic Policies in a World of Global Finance." *International Organization* 45, no. 4 (Fall 1991): 425-51.

Friedman, Milton, with the Assistance of Rose D. Friedman. *Capitalism and Freedom.* Chicago and London: The University of Chicago Press, 1962.

Friedman, Milton. *Essays in Positive Economics.* Chicago: The University of Chicago Press, 1964.

Frolich, N., J.A. Oppenheimer, and O.R. Young. *Political Leadership and Collective Goods.* Princeton, N.J.: Princeton University Press, 1971.

Frost, Gerald, and Andrew Mchallam, eds. *In Search of Stability: Europe's Unfinished Revolution.* Westport, Conn.: Praeger Publishers, 1992.

Fukuyama, Francis. *Trust: Social Virtues and the Creation of Prosperity.* New York: The Free Press, 1995.

Fuller, R. Buckminster. *Utopia or Oblivion: The Prospects for Humanity.* Toronto and New York: Bantam Books, 1969.

Fumo, Claudia. *The World Bank's Partnership with Nongovernmental Organizations.* Washington, D.C.: World Bank, 1996.

Furniss, Norman, and Timothy Tilton. *The Case for the Welfare State: From Social Security to Social Equality.* Bloomington, Ind.; and London: Indiana University Press, 1977.

Galtung, Johan. *The True Worlds: A Transnational Perspective.* New York: The Free Press, 1980.

Gandhi, Mohandas K. *All Men Are Brothers.* New York: Continuum Publishing, 1990.

Ganz, David. "The ideology of sharing: apostolic community and ecclesiastical property in the early middle ages." Pp. 17-30 in *Property and Power in the Early Middle Ages,* edited by Wendy Davies and Paul Fouracre. Cambridge; New York; Melbourne: Cambridge University Press, 1995.

Gatlin, Joe. "Ministry vs. Fiscal Responsibility," *Habitat World* (April/May 2001): 2.

Geary, Patrick J. *Before France and Germany: The Creation and Transformation of the Merovingian World.* New York and Oxford: Oxford University Press, 1988.

Geertz, Clifford. *The Religion of Java.* Glencoe, Ill.: Free Press, 1960.

———. *Peddlers and Princes: Social Change and Economic Modernization in Two Indonesian Towns.* Chicago: The University of Chicago Press, 1963.

———. *Agricultural Involution, the process of ecological change in Indonesia.* Berkeley: University of California Press, 1963.

———. *The Social History of an Indonesian Town.* Cambridge, Mass.: MIT Press, 1965.

Geiger, Susan. *TANU Women. Gender and Culture in the Making of Tanganyikan Nationalism, 1955-1965.* Portsmouth, N.H.: Heinemann; Oxford: James Currey; Nairobi: E.A.E.P.; Dar es Salaam: Mkuki Na Nyota, 1997.

George, Henry. *Progress and Poverty.* New York: D. Appleton & Co., 1881.

Gereffi, Gary. "Rethinking Development Theory: Insights from East Asia and Latin America." Pp. 26-56 in *Comparative National Development: Society and Economy in the New Global Order,* edited by A. Douglas Kincaid and Alejandro Portes. Chapel Hill, N.C.; and London: The University of North Carolina Press, 1994.

Gerstle, Gary. *Working-class Americanism: The politics of labor in a textile city, 1914-1960.* Cambridge; New York; Port Chester; Melbourne; Sydney: Cambridge University Press, 1989.

Ghai, Dharam, ed. *The IMF and the South: The Social Impact of Crisis and Adjustment.* London: Zed Books, 1991.

Ghoshal, Baladas. *Indonesian Politics 1955-59: The Emergence of Guided Democracy.* Calcutta and New Delhi: K.P. Bagchi & Company, 1982.

Gibbon, Peter, Yusuf Bangura, and Arve Ofstad. *Authoritarianism, Democracy, and Adjustment: The Politics of Economic Reform in Africa.* Uppsala, Sweden: Scandinavian Institute of African Studies, 1992.

Giddens, Anthony. *The Class Structure of the Advanced Societies.* New York; Evanston, Ill.; San Francisco; London: Harper & Row, 1973.

———. *New Rules of Sociological Method.* New York: Harper & Row, 1976.

———. *A Contemporary Critique of Historical Materialism.* Berkeley: University of California Press, 1981.

———. *The Nation-State and Violence.* Vol. 2 of *A Contemporary Critique of Historical Materialism.* Berkeley: University of California Press, 1981.

———. *The Constitution of Society: outline of a theory of structuration.* Berkeley: University of California Press, 1984.

————. *The Third Way: The Renewal of Social Democracy*. Cambridge: Polity Press, 1998.

————. *The Third Way and its Critics*. Cambridge: Polity Press, 2000.

Gilligan, Carol. *In a Different Voice: Psychological Theory and Women's Development*. Cambridge, Mass.; and London: Harvard University Press, 1982.

Gilmour, David. *The Transformation of Spain: From Franco to the Constitutional Monarchy*. London; New York; Melbourne: Quartet Books, 1985.

Gimbutas, Marija. *The Gods and Goddesses of Old Europe, 7000 to 3500 BC: Myths, Legends, and Cult Images*. Berkeley and Los Angeles: University of California Press, 1974.

Ginsberg, Anthony. *South Africa's Future: From Crisis to Prosperity*. London: Macmillan, 1998.

Glaeser, Bernhard, ed. *The Green Revolution Revisited: Critique and Alternatives*. London: Allen and Unwin, 1987.

Godelier, Maurice. *Rationality and Irrationality in Economics*. Trans. Brian Pearce. New York and London: Monthly Review Press, 1972.

Goffman, Erving. *Behavior in Public Places: Notes on the Social Organization of Gatherings*. New York: Free Press of Glencoe, 1963.

————. *Interaction Ritual: Essays on Face-to-Face Behavior*. New York: Doubleday, 1967.

Gonzalez, Felipe. *Socialismo es Libertad*. Barcelona: Galba, 1978.

Gordon, Edward E. *Skill Wars: Winning the Battle for Productivity and Profit*. Boston: Butterworth-Heinemann, 2000.

Goulet, Denis. *Etica del desarrollo*. Montevideo: Instituto de Estudios Políticos para América Latina, 1965.

————. *The Cruel Choice: A New Concept in the Theory of Development*. New York: Atheneum, 1971.

————. *A New Moral Order: Development Ethics and Liberation Theology*. Maryknoll, N.Y.: Orbis Books, 1974.

————. *The Uncertain Promise: Value Conflicts in Technology Transfer*. New York: IDOC/North America, 1977.

Gramsci, Antonio. *The Modern Prince and Other Writings*. New York: International Publishers, 1959.

————. *Selections from the Prison Notebooks*. Translated by Quintin Hoare and Geoffrey Nowell Smith. New York: International Publishers, 1989.

Greider, William K. *Who Will Tell the People: The Betrayal of American Democracy*. New York: Touchstone Books, 1993.

————. *One World Ready or Not: The Manic Logic of Global Capitalism*. New York: Simon and Schuster, 1997.

Green, Duncan. *Silent Revolution: The Rise of Market Economics in Latin America*. New York: Monthly Review Press, 1996.

Guerra, Alfonso, et al., eds. *El futuro del socialismo*. Madrid: Editorial Sistema, 1986.

Gutiérrez, Gustavo. *A Theology of Liberation: History, Politics, and Salvation*. Maryknoll, N.Y.: Orbis Books, 1973 (1971).

————. *The Truth Shall Make You Free: Confrontations*. Translated by Matthew J. O'Connell. Maryknoll, N.Y.: Orbis Books, 1990 (1986).

Gutman, Herbert G. *Work, Culture & Society in Industrializing America: Essays in American Working-Class and Social History*. New York: Vintage Books, 1977.

Habermas, Jürgen. *Knowledge and Human Interests*. Translated by Jeremy J. Shapiro. Boston: Beacon Press, 1971 (1968).

———. *Communication and the Evolution of Society*. Boston: Beacon Press, 1979.

———. *Between Facts and Norms: Contributions to a Discourse Theory of Law and Democracy*. Cambridge, Mass.: MIT Press, 1996.

Hacohen, Malachi Haim. *Karl Popper: the Formative Years, 1902-1945: politics and philosophy in interwar Vienna*. Cambridge and New York: Cambridge University Press, 2000.

Hall, Stuart. "The great moving nowhere show." *Marxism Today* (November/December 1998): 9-14.

Hammond, J.L., and Barbara Hammond. *The Age of the Chartists, 1832-1854*. New York: A.M. Kelley, 1967.

Handelman, Howard, and Werner Baer, eds. *Paying the Costs of Austerity in Latin America*. Boulder, Colo.; and London: Westview Press, 1989.

Hardt, Michael, and Antonio Negri. *Empire*. Cambridge, Mass.: Harvard University Press, 2000.

Harre, Rom, and E.H. Madden. *Causal Powers: A Theory of Natural Necessity*. Totowa, N.J.: Rowman & Littlefield, 1975.

Harrison, Joseph. *The Spanish economy: From the Civil War to the European Community*. Cambridge; New York; and Melbourne: Cambridge University Press, 1995.

———. "Tackling national decadence: economic regenerationism in Spain after the colonial debacle." Pp. 55-67 in *Spain's 1898 Crisis: Regenerationism, modernism, post-colonialism*, edited by Joseph Harrison and Alan Hoyle. Manchester, U.K.; and New York: Manchester University Press, 2000.

Hartsock, Nancy. *Money, Sex and Power: Toward a Feminist Historical Materialism*. Boston: Northeastern University Press, 1985.

Harvey, David. *The Condition of Postmodernity: An Enquiry into the Origins of Cultural Change*. Cambridge, Mass.; and Oxford: Basil Blackwell, 1989.

Hasan-Rokem, Galit. "Communication with the Dead in Jewish Dream Culture." Pp. 213-32 in *Dream Cultures: Explorations in the Comparative History of Dreaming*, edited by David Shulman and Guy G. Stroumsa. New York and Oxford: Oxford University Press, 1999.

Hausmann, Ricardo. "Sobre la crisis económica venezolana." Pp. 87-113 in *América Latina, alternativas para la democracia*, edited by Juan Carlos Rey, Julia Barragán, and Ricardo Hausmann. Caracas: Monte Avila Editores, 1992.

Hayek, Friedrich A. von, ed. *Collectivist Economic Planning: Critical Studies on the Possibilities of Socialism*. London: Routledge & Kegan Paul, 1935.

Hayek, Friedrich A. von. *The Road to Serfdom*. Chicago: The University of Chicago Press, 1976 (1944).

———. *Law, Legislation, and Liberty: A new statement of the liberal principles of justice and political economy, Vol. 2, The Mirage of Social Justice*. Chicago and London: The University of Chicago Press, 1976.

Hazlitt, Henry. *The Failure of the "New Economics": An Analysis of the Keynesian Fallacies*. Princeton, N.J.; Toronto; London; New York: D. Van Nostrand Company, 1959.

Heilbroner, Robert L. *The Making of Economic Society*. Englewood Cliffs, N.J.: Prentice-Hall, 1962.

Henderson, Hazel. *Building a Win-Win World: Life Beyond Global Economic Warfare*. San Francisco: Berrett-Koehler Publishers, 1996.

————. *Beyond Globalization: Shaping a Sustainable Global Economy*. West Hartford, Conn.: Kumarian Press, 1999.

Henrich, Joseph, Robert Boyd, Samuel Bowles, Colin Camerer, Ernst Fehr, Herbert Gintis, and Richard McElreath. "In Search of *Homo Economicus*: Behavioral Experiments in 15 Small-Scale Societies." *American Economic Review* 91, no. 2 (May 2001): 73-78 .

Henry, Paul-Marc. *Poverty, Progress, and Development*. London: Kegan Paul, 1991.

Herman, Donald L. *Christian Democracy in Venezuela*. Chapel Hill, N.C.: University of North Carolina Press, 1980.

Herod, Andrew, ed. *Organizing the Landscape: Geographical Perspectives on Labor Unionism*. Minneapolis, Minn.: University of Minnesota Press, 1998.

Hicks, J.R. "A Neo-Austrian Growth Theory." *Economic Journal* 30, no. 318 (1970): 257-81.

————. *Capital and Time: A Neo-Austrian Theory*. Oxford: Oxford University Press, 1973.

Higgins, Benjamin. Foreword to Clifford Geertz, *Agricultural Involution: the process of ecological change in Indonesia*. Berkeley: University of California Press, 1963.

Hilferding, Rudolf. *Böhm-Bawerk's Criticism of Marx*. New York: A.M. Kelly, 1949.

Hill, Hal. *The Indonesian Economy*. Second ed. Cambridge: Cambridge University Press, 2000.

Hirst, Paul, and Grahame Thompson. *Globalization in Question: The International Economy and the Possibilities of Governance*. Second ed. Cambridge: Polity Press, 1999.

Hitchcock, Michael. *Islam and Identity in Eastern Indonesia*. Hull, U.K.: University of Hull Press, 1996.

Hockett, Charles Francis. *A Course in Modern Linguistics*. New York: The Macmillan Company, 1958.

Holland, Joe. *Social Analysis: Linking Faith with Justice*. Maryknoll, N.Y.: Orbis Books, 1983.

Hollis, Martin and Edward Nell. *Rational Economic Man*. London: Cambridge University Press, 1975.

Hooks, bell. *Ain't I A Woman: black women and feminism*. Boston: South End Press, 1981.

Hubbard, Barbara Marx. *The Hunger of Eve*. Harrisburg, Pa.: Stackpole Books, 1976.

Hutton, Will. *The revolution that never was: An assessment of Keynesian economics*. London and New York: Longman, 1986.

Ibn Taymiya, al-Shaykh-al-Imam Taqui al-Din Ahmad. *Public Duties in Islam: The Institution of the Hisba*. Edited by Khurshid Ahmad. Leicester, U.K.: The Islamic Foundation, 1982.

Iracheta Cenecorta, Alfonso X., and Martim Smolka, eds. *Los pobres de la ciudad y la tierra*. Zinacantepec, Mexico: El Colegio Mexiquense, 2000.

Isaak, Robert A. *Managing World Economic Change*. Third ed. Englewood Cliffs, N.J.: Prentice-Hall, 2000.

Iyer, Raghavan. *The Moral and Political Thought of Mahatma Gandhi*. Oxford: Oxford University Press, 1973.

Jacobs, Jane. *The Death and Life of Great American Cities*. New York: Random House, 1961.

————. *Systems of Survival: A Dialogue on the Moral Foundations of Commerce and Politics*. New York: Vintage Books, 1992.

James, William. *Essays in Pragmatism*. New York: Hafner Publishing Co., 1948.

Jameson, Kenneth P., and Charles K. Wilber, eds. *The Political Economy of Development and Underdevelopment*. New York: McGraw-Hill, 1996.

Jelavich, Barbara. *Modern Austria: Empire and Republic, 1815-1986*. Cambridge; London; New York; New Rochelle; Melbourne; Sydney: Cambridge University Press, 1987.

Johansson, Alf. *Löneutvecklingen och arbetslösheten*. Stockholm: Norstedt, 1934.

Juliá, Santos. "The Socialist era, 1982-1996." Pp. 331-44 in *Spanish History Since 1808*, edited by José Alvarez Junco and Adrian Shubert. London: Arnold, 2000.

Juliá, Santos, ed. *El socialismo en España*. Madrid: Editorial Pablo Iglesias, 1986.

Justinian. *Justinian's Institutes*. Translated by Peter Birks and Grant McLeod (with the Latin text of Paul Krueger). Ithaca, N.Y.: Cornell University Press, 1987.

Kahn, Lawrence M., and J. Keith Murnighan. "Conjecture, Uncertainty, and Cooperation in Prisoner's Dilemma Games." *Journal of Economic Behavior and Organization* 22 (1993): 91-117.

Kammer, Fred. *Doing Faith Justice: An Introduction to Catholic Social Thought*. New York: Paulist Press, 1991.

Kant, Immanuel. *Perpetual Peace*. New York: Columbia University Press, 1939.

———. *Critique of Pure Reason*. Translated by Norman Kemp Smith. London: Macmillan, 1964.

———. *Foundations of the Metaphysics of Morals*. Translated by Lewis White Beck. Indianapolis, Ind.: Bobbs-Merrill, 1976.

Karl, Terry Lynn. "Petroleum and Political Pacts: The Transition to Democracy in Venezuela." Pp. 196-219 in *Transitions from Authoritarian Rule: Latin America*, edited by Guillermo O'Donnell, Phillipe C. Schmitter, and Laurence Whitehead. Baltimore, Md.; and London: The Johns Hopkins University Press, 1986.

———. *The Paradox of Plenty: Oil Booms and Petro-States*. Berkeley; Los Angeles; London: University of California Press, 1997.

Katz, Jerrold J., and Paul M. Postal. *An Integrated Theory of Linguistic Descriptions*. Cambridge, Mass.: MIT Press, 1964.

Kaul, Inge, Isabelle Grunberg, and Marc Stern, eds. *Global Public Goods: Global Cooperation in the 21st Century*. New York and Oxford: Oxford University Press (published for UNDP), 1999.

Keating, W. Dennis. "The Dilemma of Old Urban Neighborhoods." *Washington University Journal of Law and Policy* 3 (2000): 699-708.

Kelly, Marjorie. *The Divine Right of Capital: Dethroning the Corporate Aristocracy*. San Francisco: Berrett-Koehler Publishers, 2001.

Kenny, Kevin. *Making Sense of the Molly Maguires*. New York and Oxford: Oxford University Press, 1993.

Kern, Robert W. *Red Years, Black Years: A Political History of Spanish Anarchism, 1911-1937*. Philadelphia: Institute for the Study of Human Issues, 1978.

Kerridge, Eric. *The Agricultural Revolution*. London: George Allen & Unwin, 1967.

Keynes, John Maynard. *The End of Laissez-Faire*. London: The Hogarth Press, 1926.

———. *The General Theory of Employment, Interest, and Money*. London: Macmillan, 1954.

King, Martin Luther, Jr. "A Comparison of the Conceptions of God in the Thinking of Paul Tillich and Henry Nelson Wieman." PhD diss., Boston University, 1955.

———. *Where Do We Go From Here: Chaos or Community?* New York: Harper and Row, 1967.

Kirzner, Israel. *The Economic Point of View*. Kansas City: Sheed and Ward, 1960.

Klant, Johannes J. *The Rules of the Game: the logical structure of economic theories.* Cambridge: Cambridge University Press, 1984.

Knauft, Bruce. "Culture and Cooperation in Human Evolution." Pp. 37-67 in *The Anthropology of Peace and Nonviolence*, edited by Leslie E. Sponsel and Thomas Gregor. Boulder, Colo.; and London: Lynne Rienner Publishers, 1994.

Kohlberg, Lawrence. "Stage and sequence: The cognitive-developmental approach to socialization." Pp. 347-480 in *Handbook of socialization theory and research*, edited by D.A. Goslin. Chicago: Rand McNally, 1969.

————. *Collected Papers on Moral Development and Moral Education*. Cambridge, Mass.: Moral Education Research Foundation, Harvard University, 1973.

Kondo, Tetsuo. "Some Notes on Rational Behavior, Normative Behavior, Moral Behavior, and Cooperation." *Journal of Conflict Resolution* 34 (1990): 495-530.

Kornai, Janos. *Anti-Equilibrium*. Amsterdam: North Holland Publishing Co., 1971.

Kornblith, Miriam, and Daniel H. Levine. "Venezuela: The Life and Times of the Party System." Pp. 37-71 in *Building Democratic Institutions: Party Systems in Latin America*, edited by Scott Mainwaring and Timothy R. Scully. Stanford, Calif.: Stanford University Press, 1995.

Korten, David C. *When Corporations Rule the World*. San Francisco: Berrett-Koehler Publishers; and West Hartford, Conn.: Kumarian Press, 1995.

————. *The Post-Corporate World: Life After Capitalism*. San Francisco: Berrett-Koehler Publishers; and West Hartford, Conn.: Kumarian Press, 1999.

Kreisky, Bruno. *Zwischen den Zeiten: Erinnerungen aus fünf Jahrzehnten*. Berlin: Siedler Verlag, 1986.

Krishna, Anirudh, Norman Uphoff, and Milton J. Esman, eds. *Reasons for Hope: Instructive Experiences in Rural Development*. West Hartford, Conn.: Kumarian Press, 1997.

Krueger, Anne. "The Political Economy of the Rent-Seeking Society." *American Economic Review* 64 (June 1974): 291-303.

Krueger, Frederick W., ed. *Christian Ecology, Being an Environmental Ethic for the Twenty-First Century: The Proceedings from the First North American Conference on Christianity and Ecology*. San Francisco: North American Conference on Christianity and Ecology, 1988.

Kuhn, Thomas. *The Structure of Scientific Revolutions*. Enlarged ed. Chicago: University of Chicago Press, 1970.

Kung, Hans, ed. *Yes to a Global Ethic*. New York: Continuum, 1996.

Lacey, Nicola. "Community in Legal Theory: Idea, Ideal, or Ideology?" *Studies in Law, Politics, and Society* 15 (1995): 105-46.

Lachman, Desmond, Adam Bennett, John H. Green, Robert Hagemann, and Ramana Ramaswany. *Challenges to the Swedish Welfare State*. Washington, D.C.: International Monetary Fund [IMF Occasional Paper No. 130, Sept. 1995], 1995.

Laclau, Ernesto, and Chantal Mouffe. *Hegemony and Socialist Strategy: Towards a Radical Democratic Politics*. London: Verso, 1985.

Lal, Deepak. "The Misconceptions of 'Development Economics.'" *Finance and Development* 22 (June 1985): 10-13.

Lancry, Pierre-Jean. "La Conception du Salaire chez Turgot." Pp. 101-32 in *Turgot, Economiste et Administrateur*, edited by C. Bordes and J. Morange. Paris: Presses Universitaires de France, 1982.

Lappé, Frances Moore, and Joseph Collins. *Food First: Beyond the Myth of Scarcity*. New York: Ballantine Books, 1978.

Lappé, Frances Moore, and Anna Lappé. *Hope's Edge: The Next Diet For A Small Planet*. New York: Jeremy P. Tarcher/ Putnam, 2002.

Lepowsky, Maria. *Fruit of the Motherland: Gender in an Egalitarian Society*. New York: Columbia University Press, 1993.

Leval, Gaston. *Collectives in Spain*. London: Freedom Press, 1945.

Levinas, Emmanuel. *Totality and Infinity*. Pittsburgh: Duquesne University Press, 1969.

Levine, Daniel H. *Conflict and Political Change in Venezuela*. Princeton, N.J.: Princeton University Press, 1973.

Lévy, Isaac Jack, and Rosemary Lévy Zumwalt. *Ritual Medical Lore of Sephardic Women: Sweetening the Spirits, Healing the Sick*. Urbana, Ill.; and Chicago: University of Illinois Press, 2002.

Lewis, John, Karl Polanyi, and Donald K. Kitchin, eds. *Christianity and the Social Revolution*. London: Victor Gollancz, 1935.

Lewis, Oscar *La Vida: A Puerto Rican Family in the Culture of Poverty—San Juan and New York*. New York: Random House, 1966.

Li, Wai-yee. "Dreams of Interpretation in Early Chinese Historical and Philosophical Writings." Pp. 17-42 in *Dream Cultures: Explorations in the Comparative History of Dreaming*, edited by David Shulman and Guy G. Stroumsa. New York and Oxford: Oxford University Press, 1999.

Lickona, Thomas, ed. *Moral Development and Behavior: Theory, Research, and Social Issues*. New York: Holt, Rinehart, and Winston, 1976.

Lida, Clara E. "Agrarian Anarchism in Andalusia: Documents of the *Mano Negra*." *International Review of Social History* 14 (1969): 315-52.

Lieuwen, Edwin. "The Politics of Energy in Venezuela." Pp. 189-225 in *Latin American Oil Companies and the Politics of Energy*, edited by John D. Wirth. Lincoln, Neb.: University of Nebraska Press, 1985.

Lindahl, Erik. *Penningpolitikens medel*. Lund, Sweden: Gleerup, 1930.

Lindbeck, Assar, Per Molander, Torsten Persson, Olof Petersson, Agnar Sandmo, Birgitta Swedenborg, and Niels Thygesen. *Turning Sweden Around*. Cambridge, Mass.; and London: MIT Press, 1994.

Lindblom, Charles E. *Politics and Markets*. New York: Basic Books, 1977.

———. "The Market as Prison." *Journal of Politics* 44, no. 2 (May 1982): 324-36.

Lipsitz, George. *The Possessive Investment in Whiteness: How White People Profit from Identity Politics*. Philadelphia: Temple University Press, 1998.

Lizot, Jacques. "Words in the Night: The Ceremonial Dialogue—One Expression of Peaceful Relationships Among the Yanomami." Pp. 213-40 in *The Anthropology of Peace and Nonviolence*, edited by Leslie E. Sponsel and Thomas Gregor. Boulder, Colo.; and London: Lynne Rienner Publishers, 1994.

López-Cordón, María Victoria. *La Revolución de 1868 y la Primera República*. Madrid: Siglo XXI, 1976.

López-Maya, Margarita, and Luis E. Lander. "A Military Populist Takes Venezuela." *NACLA Report on the Americas* 32, no. 5 (Mar.-Apr. 1999): 11-15.

Love, David A. "Shell Oil disregards human rights in Nigeria." *The Progressive*, 25 June 1998: 1-2.

Lundberg, Erik Filip. *Studies in the Theory of Economic Expansion*. New York: Augustus Kelly, 1964.

————. "The rise and fall of the Swedish economic model." Pp. 195-211 in *Europe's Economy in Crisis*, edited by Ralf Dahrendorf. New York: Holmes & Meier, 1982.

————. "The Rise and Fall of the Swedish Model." *Journal of Economic Literature* 23 (March 1985): 1-36.

————. *The Development of Swedish and Keynesian Macroeconomic Theory and its Impact on Economic Policy*. Cambridge: Cambridge University Press, 1996.

Lundberg, Erik, Rudolf Meidner, Gösta Rehn, and Krister Wickman. *Wages Policy Under Full Employment*. Translated and edited by Ralph Turvey. London: William Hodge and Company, 1952.

Luria, Alexander R. *Speech and the Regulation of Behavior*. New York: Liveright, 1961.

————. *Language and Cognition*. Edited by James V. Wertsch. New York; Chichester, U.K.; Brisbane; Toronto; Singapore: John Wiley & Sons, 1981.

Luthuli, Albert. *Let My People Go*. New York: New American Library, 1962.

Lux, Kenneth. *Adam Smith's Mistake: How a Moral Philosopher Invented Economics and Ended Morality*. Boston and London: Shambhala, 1990.

Luxemburg, Rosa. *The Accumulation of Capital*. Translated by Agnes Schwarzschild. London: Routledge and Kegan Paul, 1951.

MacAndrews, Colin. *Central Government and Local Development in Indonesia*. Singapore: Oxford University Press, 1986.

MacIntyre, Alasdair. *Against the Self-Images of the Age*. New York: Schocken Books, 1971.

MacLean, Paul D. *The Triune Brain in Evolution: Role in Paleocerebral Functions*. New York: Plenum Press, 1990.

Macy, Joanna. "In Indra's Net: Sarvodaya and Our Mutual Efforts for Peace." Pp. 170-81 in *The Path of Compassion: Writings on Socially Engaged Buddhism*, edited by Fred Eppsteiner. Berkeley: Parallax Press, 1988.

Magot, J. "New Report Slams Bank Dam Record." *BankCheck Quarterly* 10 (December 1994): 11.

Main, Alexander, Maximilien Arvelaiz, and Temir Porras-Ponceleon. "Virtual Reality: Real Coup." *Covert Action Quarterly*, no. 72 (Spring 2002): i, 5, 34, 40.

Maine, Sir Henry. *Ancient Law*. London: Murray, 1861.

Makhijani, Arjun. *From Global Capitalism to Economic Justice*. London: Zed Books, 1991.

Mance, Euclides André. *La rivoluzione delle reti: l'economia solidale per un'altra globalizzazione*. Bologna: EMI, 2003.

Mandeville, Bernard de. *The Fable of the Bees, or Private Vices, Publick Benefits.* Edited by Irwin Primer. New York: Capricorn Books, 1962 (1714).

Mangabeira Unger, Roberto. *Law in Modern Society: Toward a Criticism of Social Theory*. New York: Free Press, 1976.

Mansbridge, Jane J. "On the Relation of Altruism and Self-Interest." Pp. 133-43 in *Beyond Self-Interest*, edited by Jane J. Mansbridge. Chicago: University of Chicago Press, 1990.

Marcus, Steven. *Engels, Manchester and the Working Class*. New York: Norton, 1985.

Marcuse, Herbert. *One-Dimensional Man: Studies in the Ideology of Advanced Industrial Society*. Boston: Beacon Press, 1964.

Maritain, Jacques. *The Person and the Common Good*. South Bend, Ind.: The University of Notre Dame Press, 1973.

————. *The Degrees of Knowledge*. South Bend, Ind.: The University of Notre Dame Press, 1995.

Martin, Hans-Peter, and Harald Schumann. *The Global Trap: Globalization and the Assault on Democracy and Prosperity*. London: Zed Books, 1997.

Martz, John D. "Petroleum: the National and International Perspectives." Pp. 243-69 in *Venezuela: the Democratic Experience*, edited by John D. Martz and David J. Myers. Rev. ed. New York and London: Praeger Publishers, 1986 (1977).

————. *Acción Democrática: Evolution of a Modern Political Party in Venezuela*. Princeton, N.J.: Princeton University Press, 1966.

Martz, John D., and David J. Myers, eds. *Venezuela: the Democratic Experience*. New York and London: Praeger Publishers, 1986 (1977).

Marx, Karl. *Economic and Philosophical Manuscripts of 1844*. Moscow: Progress Publishers, 1959.

————. *Theories of Surplus Value*. New York: International Publishers, 1968.

————. *Capital: A Critique of Political Economy*. Reprinted as Vol. 50 of *Great Books of the Western World*, edited by Mortimer J. Adler. Chicago: Encyclopedia Britannica, 1990.

Marx, Karl, and Friedrich Engels. *The German Ideology, Part One*. Edited by C.J. Arthur. New York: International Publishers, 1988.

Mason, Edward S., and Robert E. Asher. *The World Bank Since Bretton Woods*. Washington, D.C.: The Brookings Institution, 1973.

Massey, Doreen. *Spatial Divisions of Labour: Social Structures and the Geography of Production*. London: Macmillan, 1984.

McAfee, Kathy. *Storm Signals: Structural Adjustment and Development Alternatives in the Caribbean*. Boston: Oxfam America, 1991.

McAllester Jones, Mary. *Gaston Bachelard, Subversive Humanist: Texts and Readings*. Madison, Wisc.; and London: University of Wisconsin Press, 1991.

McCarthy, George, and Royal Rhodes. *Eclipse of Justice: Ethics, Economics, and the Lost Traditions of American Catholicism*. Maryknoll, N.Y.: Orbis, 1992.

McCoy, Jennifer. "The Politics of Adjustment: Labor and the Venezuelan Debt Crisis." *Journal of Interamerican Studies and World Affairs* 28 (Winter 1986-87): 103-38.

McDonough, William, and Michael Braungart. *From Cradle to Cradle: Remaking the Way We Make Things*. San Francisco: Northpoint Press, 2002.

McKersie, R.B., and L.C. Hunter. *Pay, Productivity and Collective Bargaining*. London and Basingstoke, U.K.: Macmillan Press, 1973.

McNamara, Robert S. *The McNamara Years at the World Bank: Major Policy Addresses of Robert S. McNamara*. Baltimore, Md.; and London: The Johns Hopkins University Press, 1981.

Meidner, Rudolf. *Employee Investment Funds, an approach to collective capital formation*. London: George Allen & Unwin, 1978.

Merchant, Carolyn. *The Death of Nature: Women, Ecology, and the Scientific Revolution*. New York: Harper and Row, 1980.

Meredith, Martin. *Nelson Mandela: a biography*. New York: St. Martin's Press, 1998.

Middleton, Neil, and Phil O'Keefe. *Redefining Sustainable Development*. London: Pluto Press, 2001.

Milani, Brian. *Designing the Green Economy: The Postindustrial Alternative to Corporate Globalization*. Lanham, Md.; Boulder, Colo.; New York; and Oxford: Rowman & Littlefield, 2000.

Milinski, Manfred. "Cooperation Wins and Stays." *Nature* 364 (1993): 12-13.

Mill, John Stuart. *The Logic of the Moral Sciences*. London: Gerald Duckworth & Co., 1987.

Milne, Robert Stephen, and Diane K. Mauzy. *Singapore: the Legacy of Lee Kuan Yew*. Boulder, Colo.: Westview Press, 1990.

Mises, Ludwig von. *Socialism: An Economic and Sociological Analysis*. Translated by J. Kahane. New Haven, Conn.: Yale University Press, 1951.

Moltmann, Jurgen. *The Source of Life*. Philadelphia: Fortress Press, 1997.

Mommer, Dorothea. *El Estado Venezolano y la Industria Petrolera*. Caracas: Universidad Central de Venezuela, Facultad de Ciencias Económicas y Sociales, 1974.

Montgomery, Arthur. *How Sweden Overcame the Depression, 1930-1933*. Stockholm: Alb. Bonniers Boktryckeri, 1938.

Montgomery, David. *The Fall of the House of Labor: The Workplace, the state and American labor activism, 1865-1925*. Cambridge: Cambridge University Press, 1987.

Moral Sandoval, Enrique. *Pablo Iglesias, Escritos y Discursos, Antología Crítica*. Santiago de Compostela, Spain: Ediciones Salvora, 1984.

———. "El socialismo y la dictadura de Primo de Rivera." Pp. 191-212 in *El socialismo en España*, edited by Santos Juliá. Madrid: Pablo Iglesias, 1986.

Morato, Juan José. *Pablo Iglesias Posse, Educador de Muchedumbres*. Madrid and Barcelona: Espasa-Calpe, 1931.

Mouffe, Chantal, ed. *Dimensions of Radical Democracy: Pluralism, Citizenship, Community*. London: Verso, 1992.

Mounier, Emmanuel. *Personalism*. Translated by Philip Mairet. South Bend, Ind.: The University of Notre Dame Press, 1979.

Moxon-Browne, Edward. *Political Change in Spain*. London and New York: Routledge, 1989.

Murillo, Maria Victoria. *Labor Unions, Partisan Coalitions, and Market Reforms in Latin America*. New York and Cambridge: Cambridge University Press, 2001.

Myrdal, Gunnar. *Konjunkturer och offentlig hushållning*. Stockholm: Kooperativa Förbundet, 1933.

———. *The Political Element in the Development of Economic Theory*. Translated by Paul Streeten. London: Routledge & Kegal Paul, 1953.

———. *Beyond the Welfare State: economic planning and its international implications*. New Haven, Conn.: Yale University Press, 1960.

———. *Asian Drama*. Vol. 2. New York: Twentieth Century Fund and Pantheon Books, 1968.

———. *The Challenge of World Poverty: a world anti-poverty program in outline*. New York: Pantheon Books, 1970.

Nafziger, E. Wayne. *The Debt Crisis in Africa*. Baltimore, Md.; and London: The Johns Hopkins University Press, 1993.

Nagel, Ernest, and James R. Newman. *Gödel's Proof*. New York: New York University Press, 1958.

Narayan, Deepa, Robert Chambers, Meera K. Shah, and Patti Petesch. *Voices of the Poor: Crying Out for Change*. Oxford and New York: Oxford University Press, 2000.

Nash, Mary. "Towards a new moral order: National Catholicism, culture and gender." Pp. 289-302 in *Spanish History Since 1808*, edited by José Alvarez Junco and Adrian Shubert, eds. London: Arnold, 2000.

Nevins, Joseph. *Operation Gatekeeper: The Rise of the "Illegal Alien" and the Making of the U.S.-Mexico Boundary.* New York and London: Routledge, 2002.

Nietzsche, Friedrich W. *Twilight of the Idols Or, How to Philosophize With a Hammer.* Translated by Richard Polt. Indianapolis, Ind.: Hackett Publishing Co., 1997.

Nissen, Hans-Peter, and Bernard Mommer. *Adiós a la bonanza, crisis de la distribución del ingreso en Venezuela.* Caracas: ILDIS-CENDES, Editorial Nueva Sociedad, 1989.

Nitisastro, Widjojo. *The Socio-Economic Basis of the Indonesian State.* Ithaca, N.Y.: Modern Indonesia Project, Southeast Asia Program, Department of Far Eastern Studies, Cornell University, 1959.

Norberg-Hodge, Helena. *Ancient Futures: Learning from Ladakh.* San Francisco: Sierra Club Books, 1992.

Novak, Michael. *The Spirit of Democratic Capitalism.* New York: American Enterprise Institute, 1982.

———. *The Catholic Ethic and the Spirit of Capitalism.* New York: The Free Press, 1993.

Nowak, Martin A., and Karl Sigmund. "Tit for Tat in Heterogeneous Populations." *Nature* 355 (1992): 250-53.

———. "The Alternating Prisoner's Dilemma." *Journal of Theoretical Biology* 168 (1994): 219-26.

Nowak, Martin A., Karen M. Page, and Karl Sigmund. "Fairness versus Reason in the Ultimatum Game." *Science* 289 (September 8, 2000): 1773-75.

Nozick, Robert. *Anarchy, State, and Utopia.* New York: Basic Books, 1974.

Nutini, Hugo G., and Betty Bell. *Ritual Kinship: The Structure and Historical Development of the Compadrazgo System in Rural Tlaxcala.* Vol. 1. Princeton, N.J.: Princeton University Press, 1980.

Offe, Claus. *Strukturprobleme des kapitalistischen Staates.* Frankfurt: Suhrkump, 1972.

Ohlin, Bertil. "Some Notes on the Stockholm Theory of Savings and Investment—I." *Economic Journal* (March 1937): 53-69.

———. "Some Notes on the Stockholm Theory of Savings and Investment—II." *Economic Journal* (June 1937): 221-40.

Okogu, Bright Erakpoweri. *Africa and Economic Structural Adjustment: Case Studies of Ghana, Nigeria, and Zambia.* Vienna: OPEC Fund for International Development, 1992.

Ollman, Bertell. *Alienation.* Cambridge: Cambridge University Press, 1971.

Ong, Carah. "Ballistic Missile Defense: Shield or Sword." *Waging Peace: Newsletter of the Nuclear Age Peace Foundation* 11, no. 2 (Summer 2001): 6.

Onimode, Bade, ed. *The IMF, the World, and the African Debt.* Vol. 1. London: Zed Books, 1989.

Onishi, Norimitsu. "As Oil Riches Flow, Poor Village Cries Out." *New York Times,* 22 Dec. 2002: 1, 14-15.

Opland, Jeff. *Xhosa Oral Poetry: Aspects of a black South African tradition.* Cambridge; London; New York; New Rochelle; Melbourne; Sydney: Cambridge University Press, 1983.

Ortner, Sherry. "Anthropological Theory since the Sixties." *Comparative Studies in Society and History* 26, no. 1 (1984): 126-66.

Otteson, James R. "The Recurring 'Adam Smith Problem.'" *History of Philosophy Quarterly* 17, no. 1 (January 2000): 51-74.

Padilla Bolívar, Antonio. *El movimiento Socialista Español.* Barcelona: Planeta, 1977.

Parliament of the World's Religions, Karl-Josef Kuschel, and Hans Kung, eds. *A Global Ethic: The Declaration of the Parliament of the World's Religions*. New York: Continuum, 1994.

Patomäki, Heikki. *After International Relations: Critical Realism and the (Re)Construction of World Politics*. London: Routledge, 2001.

Patterson, Orlando. "The Last Sociologist." *New York Times*, 19 May 2002.

Payer, Cheryl. *The Debt Trap: the IMF and the Third World*. New York: Monthly Review Press, 1975.

———. *The World Bank: A Critical Analysis*. New York: Monthly Review Press, 1982.

———. *Lent and Lost: Foreign Credit and Third World Development*. London and New Jersey: Zed Books, 1991.

Payne, Stanley G. *Falange: A History of Spanish Fascism*. Stanford, Calif.: Stanford University Press, 1961.

———. *Fascism in Spain, 1923-1977*. Madison, Wisc.; and London: The University of Wisconsin Press, 1999.

Peirats, José. *Los Anarquistas en la crisis política española*. Madrid: Jucar, 1977.

Peirce, C.S. "How to Make our Ideas Clear." Reprinted as Pp. 102-08 in *From Modernism to Postmodernism*, edited by Lawrence E. Cahoone. Oxford: Blackwell, 1996 (1878).

Peires, J.B. *The House of Phalo: A History of the Xhosa People in the Days of Their Independence*. Berkeley; Los Angeles; London: University of California Press, 1982.

Pelinka, Anton. *Austria, Out of the Shadow of the Past*. Boulder, Colo.: Westview Press, 1998.

Pérez Baró, Albert. *30 meses de colectivismo en Cataluña (1936-1939)*. Barcelona: Editorial Ariel, 1974.

Pérez-Díaz, Víctor M. *The Return of Civil Society: The Emergence of Democratic Spain*. Cambridge, Mass.; and London: Harvard University Press, 1993.

Pesch, Heinrich. *Heinrich Pesch on Solidarist Economics: Excerpts from the Lehrbuch der Nationalökonomie*. Translated by Rupert J. Ederer. Lanham. Md.; New York; Oxford: University Press of America, 1984.

Petkoff, Teodoro. *Una Segunda Opinion*. Caracas: Grijalbo, 2000.

Piaget, Jean. *The Moral Judgment of the Child*. London: Trench, Trubner & Co., 1932.

Pietri, Arturo Uslar. *De una a otra Venezuela*. Caracas: Monte Avila Editores, 1972 (1946).

Pigeaud, Theodoor. *Java in the 14th Century*. 5 vols. The Hague: Martinus Nijoff, 1960-1963.

Pirie, N.W. *Food Resources, Conventional and Novel*. Baltimore, Md.: Penguin Books, 1969.

Plato. *The Republic*. Translated by B. Jowett. New York: The Modern Library, 1941.

Plon, Michel. *La théorie des jeux: une politique imaginaire*. Paris: Francois Maspero, 1976.

Polanyi, Karl. *The Great Transformation*. New York and Toronto: Rinehart & Company, 1944.

———. "The Economy as Instituted Process." Pp. 29-53 in *The Sociology of Economic Life*, edited by Mark Granovetter and Richard Swedberg. Boulder, Colo.; and Oxford: Westview Press, 1992.

Pontusson, Jonas. *The Limits of Social Democracy: investment politics in Sweden*. Ithaca, N.Y.; and London: Cornell University Press, 1992.

Popper, Karl. *The Open Society and its Enemies*. Princeton, N.J.: Princeton University Press, 1950.

————. *The Poverty of Historicism*. New York: Harper and Row, 1964.

Porter, Donald. *Managing Politics and Islam in Indonesia*. London: Routledge-Curzon, 2002.

Poundstone, William. *Prisoner's Dilemma*. New York: Doubleday, 1992.

Prawiro, Radius. *Indonesia's Struggle for Economic Development*. Kuala Lumpur: Oxford University Press, 1998.

Preston, Paul. "The Agrarian War in the South." Pp. 159-81 in *Revolution and War in Spain, 1931-1939*, edited by Paul Preston. London and New York: Methuen, 1984.

————. *The Triumph of Democracy in Spain*. London and New York: Methuen, 1986.

————. *The Coming of the Spanish Civil War: Reform, Reaction and Revolution in the Second Republic, 1931-1936*. London: Routledge, 1994.

Prévert, Jacques. *Paroles*. Paris: Gallimard, 1949.

Price, Robert M. *The Apartheid State in Crisis: Political Transformation in South Africa, 1975-1990*. New York and Oxford: Oxford University Press, 1991.

Przeworski, Adam. *Capitalism and Social Democracy*. Cambridge: Cambridge University Press, 1986.

Putnam, Robert D. *Bowling Alone: The Collapse and Revival of American Community*. New York: Simon & Schuster, 2000.

Quijano, Aníbal. "Modernidad, identidad y utopia en América Latina." Pp. 27-42 in *Modernidad y Universalismo*, edited by Edgardo Lander. Caracas: Editorial Nueva Sociedad, 1991.

Quinn, Daniel. *Beyond Civilization: Humanity's Next Great Adventure*. New York: Harmony Books, 1999.

Rabinow, Paul, and William M. Sullivan, eds. *Interpretive Social Science: A Reader*. Berkeley; Los Angeles; and London: University of California Press, 1979.

Raghavan, Chakravarthi. *Recolonization: GATT, the Uruguay Round, and the Third World*. Penang, Malaysia: Third World Network, 1990.

Rainwater, Catherine. *Dreams of Fiery Stars: The Transformations of Native American Fiction*. Philadelphia: University of Pennsylvania Press, 1999.

Randall, Laura. *The Political Economy of Venezuelan Oil*. New York; Westport, Conn.; London: Praeger Publishers, 1987.

Rapoport, Anatol. *Conflict in Man-Made Environment*. Harmondsworth, U.K.: Penguin, 1974.

————. *Game Theory as a Theory of Conflict Resolution*. Dordrecht, Neth.: Klüwer, 1974.

————. *Fights, Games, and Debates*. Ann Arbor, Mich.: University of Michigan Press, 1960.

Rawls, John. *A Theory of Justice*. Cambridge, Mass.: The Belknap Press of Harvard University Press, 1971.

Reagon, Bernice Johnson. "Coalition Politics: Turning the Century." Pp. 356-68 in *Home Girls: A Black Feminist Anthology*, edited by Barbara Smith. New York: Kitchen Table, Women of Color Press, 1983.

Redclift, Michael. *Sustainable Development: Examining the Contradictions*. London: Methuen, 1987.

Reder, Melvin W. *Economics: The Culture of a Controversial Science*. Chicago: University of Chicago Press, 1999.

Ricardo, David. *The Principles of Political Economy and Taxation.* London: J.M. Dent & Sons, 1965 (1821).

Rich, Bruce. *Mortgaging the Earth: The World Bank, Environmental Impoverishment, and the Crisis of Development.* Boston: Beacon Press, 1994.

Richards, Howard. *The Evaluation of Cultural Action.* London: Macmillan, 1985.

————. *Letters from Quebec.* San Francisco and London: International Scholars Press, 1996.

————. *Understanding the Global Economy.* Delhi: Maadhyam Books, 2000.

Richardson, Samuel. *The Works of Samuel Richardson.* Vol. 1. London: Henry Sotheran Co., 1933.

Ricklefs, M.C. *A History of Modern Indonesia since c. 1200.* Third ed. Houndmills, Basingstoke, Hampshire, U.K.: Palgrave, 2001.

Riesman, David, in collaboration with Reuel Denney and Nathan Glazer. *The Lonely Crowd: A Study of the Changing American Character.* New Haven, Conn.: Yale University Press, 1950.

Ríos, Fernando de los. *Escritos sobre democracia y socialismo.* Edited by Virgilio Zapatero. Madrid: Taurus Ediciones, 1974.

————. *El sentido humanista del socialismo.* Edited by Elías Díaz. Madrid: Editorial Castalia, 1976.

Robbins, Richard. *Global Problems and the Culture of Capitalism.* Boston: Allyn and Bacon, 1999.

Robinson, Joan. *An Essay on Marxian Economics.* London; Melbourne; Toronto: Mac-Millan, 1967 (1942).

Robison, Richard. *Indonesia: The Rise of Capital.* Sydney: Allen and Unwin, 1986.

————. "Politics and Markets in Indonesia's Post-oil Era." Pp. 29-63 in *The Political Economy of South-East Asia: An Introduction,* edited by Garry Rodan, Kevin Hewison, and Richard Robison. Melbourne: Oxford University Press, 1997.

————. "Indonesia: Crisis, Oligarchy, and Reform." Pp. 104-37 in *The Political Economy of South-East Asia: Conflicts, Crises, and Change,* edited by Garry Rodan, Kevin Hewison, and Richard Robison. Second ed. Melbourne; Oxford; New York: Oxford University Press, 2001.

Rodríguez, Miguel. "Public Sector Behavior in Venezuela." Pp. 236-48 in *The Public Sector and the Latin American Crisis,* edited by Felipe Larraín and Marcelo Selowsky. San Francisco: ICS Press, 1991.

Rorty, Richard. *Essays on Heidegger and others: Philosophical papers, Vol. 2.* Cambridge; New York; Port Chester; Melbourne; Sydney: Cambridge University Press, 1991.

Rosado, Antonio. *Tierra y Libertad: memorias de un campesino anarcosindicalista andaluz.* Barcelona: Editorial Crítica, 1979.

Roseberry, William. *Anthropologies and Histories: Essays in Culture, History, and Political Economy.* New Brunswick, N.J.: Rutgers University Press, 1989.

Rosenberg, John D., ed. *The Genius of John Ruskin: Selections from His Writings.* New York: George Braziller, 1963.

Rostow, Walt Whitman. *The Stages of Economic Growth: A Noncommunist Manifesto.* 3rd ed. New York: Cambridge University Press, 1990 (1960).

Rothstein, Bo. *Just institutions matter: The moral and political logic of the universal welfare state.* Cambridge; New York; Melbourne: Cambridge University Press, 1998.

Rousseau, Jean-Jacques. *La Nouvelle Héloïse, Lettres de deux amants*, in *Oeuvres Completes, Volume 2*. Paris: Gallimard (Bibliotheque de la Pleiade), 1961 (ca. 1755).

———. *Emile, or On Education*. Translated by Allan Bloom. New York: Basic Books, 1979 (1764).

———. *A Discourse on Inequality*. Translated by Maurice Cranston. Harmondsworth, Middlesex, U.K.: Penguin Books, 1984 (1755).

Rowley, Charles K., Robert D. Tollison, and Gordon Tullock. *The Political Economy of Rent-Seeking*. Boston; Dordrecht, Neth.; and Lancaster, U.K.: Kluwer Academic Publishers, 1988.

Rucker, Rudy. *Infinity and the Mind: The Science and Philosophy of the Infinite*. Princeton, N.J.: Princeton University Press, 2000.

Rusk, David. *Inside Game/Outside Game: Winning Strategies for Saving Urban America*. Washington, D.C.: The Brookings Institution, 1999.

Russell, Bertrand. *German Social Democracy*. New York: Simon and Schuster, 1965.

Ryner, J. Magnus. "Assessing SAP's Economic Policy in the 1980's: The 'Third Way,' the Swedish Model, and the Transition from Fordism to post-Fordism." *Economic and Industrial Democracy* 15, no. 3 (1994): 385-428.

———. "Maastricht Convergence in the Social Democratic Heartland: Sweden and Germany." *International Journal of Political Economy* 28, no. 2 (1998): 85-123.

———. *Capitalist Restructuring, Globalisation and the Third Way: Lessons from the Swedish Model*. London: Routledge, 2002.

Sacred Writings: The Qur'an. Translated by Ahmed Ali. Princeton, N.J.: Princeton University Press, 1984.

Sadleir, Randal. *Tanzania, Journey to Republic*. London and New York: The Radcliffe Press, 1999.

Saegert, Susan, J. Phillip Thompson, and Mark R. Warren, eds. *Social Capital and Poor Communities*. New York: Russell Sage Foundation, 2001.

Salazar-Carrillo, Jorge. *Oil in the Economic Development of Venezuela*. New York: Praeger, 1976.

Sampson, Anthony. *Mandela: the authorized biography*. New York: Alfred A. Knopf, 1999.

Samuelson, Paul. *Foundations of Economic Analysis*. Cambridge, Mass.; and London: Harvard University Press, 1947.

Sandelin, Bo, ed. *The History of Swedish Economic Thought*. London and New York: Routledge, 1991.

Sarasqueta, Anton. *De Franco a Felipe*. Barcelona: Plaza & Janes, 1984.

Sartre, Jean-Paul. *Being and Nothingness: An Essay on Phenomenological Ontology*. Translated by Hazel E. Barnes. New York: Washington Square Press, 1966 (1953).

———. *Critique of Dialectical Reason*. Translated by Alan Sheridan-Smith. Edited by Jonathan Rée. London: NLB, 1976 (1960).

Schöttler, Peter. "Mentalities, Ideologies, Discourses: On the 'Third Level' as a Theme in Socio-Historical Research." Pp. 72-115 in *The History of Everyday Life: Reconstructing Historical Experiences and Ways of Life*, edited by Alf Lüdtke. Translated by William Templer. Princeton, N.J.: Princeton University Press, 1995.

Schuck, Michael. *That They Be One: The Social Teachings of the Papal Encyclicals, 1740-1989*. Washington, D.C.: Georgetown University Press, 1991.

Schumacher. E. F. *Small is Beautiful: Economics as if People Mattered*. London: Blond & Briggs, 1973.

Schumpeter, Joseph. *History of Economic Analysis.* New York: Oxford University Press, 1954.

Schuyler, George W. *Hunger in a Land of Plenty.* Cambridge, Mass.: Schenkman Publishing Company, 1980.

Schwartz, Eli. *Trouble in Eden: A Comparison of the British and Swedish Economies.* New York: Praeger, 1980.

Schwarz, Adam. *A Nation in Waiting: Indonesia in the 1990s.* Boulder, Colo.; and San Francisco: Westview Press, 1994.

Schweitzer, Marjorie M. *American Indian Grandmothers: Traditions and Transitions.* Albuquerque, N. Mex.: University of New Mexico Press, 1999.

Scott, Joan Wallach. *Gender and the Politics of History.* New York: Columbia University Press, 1988.

Seabrook, Jeremy. *Pioneers of Change: Experiments in Creating a Humane Society.* London: Zed Books; and Philadelphia: New Society Publishers, 1993.

Searle, John. *Speech Acts.* Cambridge: Cambridge University Press, 1969.

Sefa Dei, George J. "Knowledge and Politics of Social Change: the implication of anti-racism." *British Journal of Sociology of Education* 20, no. 3 (1999): 395-409.

Sen, Amartya K. "Rational Fools: A Critique of the Behavioral Foundations of Economic Theory." *Philosophy and Public Affairs* 6, no. 4 (1977): 317-44.

———. *On Ethics and Economics.* Oxford: Basil Blackwell, 1987.

———. *On Economic Inequality.* Enlarged ed. Oxford: Clarendon Press, 1997.

Seton-Watson, Hugh. *Nations and States: An Enquiry into the Origins of Nations and the Politics of Nationalism.* Boulder, Colo.: Westview Press, 1977.

Share, Donald. *Dilemmas of Social Democracy: the Spanish Socialist Workers Party in the 1980s.* New York: Greenwood Press, 1981.

Sharp, Gene. *The Politics of Nonviolent Action.* Boston: Porter Sargent, 1973.

Shetty, Y.K., and Vernon M. Buehler, eds. *The Quest For Competitiveness: Lessons from America's Productivity and Quality Leaders.* New York; Westport, Conn.; and London: Quorum Books, 1991.

Shiva, Vandana. *Staying Alive: Women, Ecology and Survival in India.* New York: St. Martin's Press, 1989.

———. *The Violence of the Green Revolution.* London: Zed Books, 1991.

———. *Stolen Harvest: The Hijacking of the Global Food Supply.* Boston: South End Press, 1999.

Sigmund, Karl. *Games of Life: Explorations in Ecology, Evolution, and Behaviour.* Oxford: Oxford University Press, 1993.

Sigmund, Karl, Ernst Fehr, and Martin A. Nowak. "The Economics of Fair Play." *Scientific American* 286, no. 1 (January 2002): 83-87

Sigmund, Paul E. *Multinationals in Latin America: The Politics of Nationalization.* Madison, Wisc.: University of Wisconsin Press, 1980.

Singh, Bilveer. *Succession Politics in Indonesia: The 1998 Presidential Elections and the Fall of Suharto.* Houndmills, Basingstoke, Hampshire, U.K.; and London: Macmillan, 2000; and New York: St. Martin's Press, 2000.

Skarzynski, Witold von. *Adam Smith als Moralphilosoph und Schoepfer der Nationaloekonomie.* Berlin: Theobald Grieben, 1878.

Skidelsky, Robert. *John Maynard Keynes.* Vol. 2, *The Economist as Saviour, 1920-1939.* London: Macmillan, 1992.

Smith, Adam. *An Inquiry into the Nature and Causes of the Wealth of Nations.* New York: The Modern Library, 1937 (1776).

———. *The Theory of Moral Sentiments.* Edited by D.D. Raphael and A.L. Macfie. Oxford: Clarendon Press, 1976 (1759).

———. *Lectures on Justice, Police, Revenue and Arms.* New York: Augustus M. Kelley, 1964 (1896).

Smolka, Martim, and Fernanda Furtado, eds. *Recuperación de plusvalías en América Latina: alternativas para el desarrollo urbano.* Cambridge, Mass.: Lincoln Institute of Land Policy; and Santiago, Chile: Pontificia Universidad Católica de Chile, 2001.

Sniegocki, John Henry. "Catholic Social Teaching and the Third World." PhD diss., University of Notre Dame, 1999.

Soja, Edward. *Postmodern Geographies: The Reassertion of Space in Social Theory.* London: Verso, 1989.

Solo, Robert A. *The Philosophy of Science and Economics.* Armonk, N.Y.: M.E. Sharpe, 1991.

Sparr, Pamela, ed. *Mortgaging Women's Lives: Feminist Critiques of Structural Adjustment.* London: Zed Books, 1994.

Spinner, Helmut. *Popper und die Politik.* Berlin: Dietz, 1987.

Stahl, Karin. "Anti-Poverty Programs: Making Structural Adjustment More Palatable." *NACLA Report on the Americas* 29, no. 6 (May-June 1996): 32-36.

Stein, Peter, and Ingemar Dörfer. *The Death Knell of Social Democracy: Sweden's Dream Turns Sour.* London: Institute for European Defence and Strategic Studies, 1992.

Stirati, Antonella. *The Theory of Wages in Classical Economics: A Study of Adam Smith, David Ricardo and Their Contemporaries.* Aldershot, U.K.; and Brookfield, Vt.: Edward Elgar, 1994.

Stokes, Eric. *The English Utilitarians and India.* Oxford: Clarendon Press, 1959.

Stoller, Robert J. *Sexual Excitement: Dynamics of Erotic Life.* New York: Pantheon, 1979.

Stone, Diane, ed. *Banking on Knowledge: The Genesis of the Global Development Network.* London: Routledge, 2000.

Sukarno. *Toward Freedom and the Dignity of Man: A Collection of Five Speeches by President Sukarno of The Republic of Indonesia.* Djakarta: Department of Foreign Affairs, 1961.

Sully, Melanie A. *Continuity and Change in Austrian Socialism: The Eternal Quest for the Third Way.* Boulder, Colo.: East European Monographs; and New York: Columbia University Press, 1982.

Summers, Lawrence. "The United States and the World Bank." Speech delivered to the Overseas Development Council, published in *Treasury News*, 11 October 1994: 4.

Swanger, Joanna B. "Workers' Control and the Structural Trap of the Chilean Copper Nationalization, 1955-1973." Master's thesis, University of Texas at Austin, 1993.

Swift, Anthony. *Children for Social Change: education for citizenship of street and working children in Brazil.* Nottingham, U.K.: Educational Heretics Press, 1997.

Swimme, Brian, and Thomas Berry. *The Universe Story.* New York: HarperCollins, 1994.

Taylor, Charles. "Interpretation and the Sciences of Man." *Review of Metaphysics* 25 (1971): 3-51.

Taylor, Frederick Winslow. *Shop Management.* New York: Harper & Brothers, 1903.

———. *The Principles of Scientific Management.* New York: Harper & Brothers, 1911.

Tedlock, Barbara. "Sharing and Interpreting Dreams in Amerindian Nations." Pp. 87-103 in *Dream Cultures: Explorations in the Comparative History of Dreaming*, edited by David Shulman and Guy G. Stroumsa. New York and Oxford: Oxford University Press, 1999.

Teresa, Mother. *My Life for the Poor*. Edited by José Luis González-Balado and Janet N. Playfoot. San Francisco: Harper & Row, 1985.

Thevenin, Nicole-Edith. *Revisionnisme et philosophie de l'alienation*. Paris: Christian Bourgeois, 1977.

Tilton, Tim. *The Political Theory of Swedish Social Democracy: Through the Welfare State to Socialism*. Oxford: Clarendon Press, 1990.

Tinbergen, Jan. *Central Planning*. New Haven, Conn.; and London: Yale University Press, 1964.

———. *Economic Policy: Principles and Design*. Amsterdam: North-Holland Publishing Company, 1966 (1956).

———. *Shaping the World Economy: Suggestions for an International Economic Policy*. New York: The Twentieth Century Fund, 1962.

Toer, Pramoedya Ananta. *The Fugitive*. New York: W. Morrow & Co., 1990.

———. *Child of All Nations*. New York: W. Morrow & Co., 1993.

———. *House of Glass*. New York: W. Morrow & Co., 1996.

Tomlins, Christopher L. *The State and the Unions: Labor Relations, Law, and the Organized Labor Movement in America, 1880-1960*. Cambridge; London; New York; New Rochelle; Melbourne; Sydney: Cambridge University Press, 1985.

Tucker, Robert C., ed. *The Marx-Engels Reader*. Second ed. New York and London: W. W. Norton & Company, 1978.

Tugwell, Franklin. "Petroleum Policy and the Political Process." Pp. 237-54 in *Venezuela: The Democratic Experience*, edited by John D. Martz and David J. Myers. New York and London: Praeger Publishers, 1977.

Tuller, Lawrence. *Finance for Non-Financial Managers*. Holbrook, Mass.: Adams Media Corporation, 1977.

Tullock, Gordon. "The Welfare Costs of Tariffs, Monopolies and Theft." *Western Economic Journal* 5 (1967): 224-32.

Turnbull, Colin M. *The Mountain People*. New York: Simon and Schuster, 1972.

United Nations Development Programme. *Human Development Report 1998*. New York: Oxford University Press, 1998.

United States Catholic Conference. *A Justice Prayer Book with Biblical Reflections*. Washington, D.C.: United States Catholic Conference, 1998.

Vallenilla, Luis. *Oil: The Making of a New Economic Order, Venezuelan Oil and OPEC*. New York: McGraw-Hill Book Company, 1975.

Vanberg, Viktor J., and Roger D. Congleton. "Rationality, Morality, and Exit." *American Political Science Review* 86 (1992): 418-31.

Van Young, Eric. "Quetzalcóatl, King Ferdinand, and Ignacio Allende Go to the Seashore; or Messianism and Mystical Kingship in Mexico, 1800-1821." Pp. 109-27 in *The Independence of Mexico and the Creation of the New Nation*, edited by Jaime E. Rodríguez O. Los Angeles: UCLA Latin American Center Publications, 1989.

———. *The Other Rebellion: Popular Violence, Ideology, and the Mexican Struggle for Independence, 1810-1821*. Stanford, Calif.: Stanford University Press, 2001.

Vilas, Carlos. "Neoliberal Social Policy: Managing Poverty (Somehow)." *NACLA Report on the Americas* 29, no. 6 (May-June 1996): 16-25.

————. "Economic Restructuring, Neoliberal Reforms, and the Working Class in Latin America." Pp. 137-64 in *Capital, Power, and Inequality in Latin America*, edited by Sandor Halebsky and Richard Harris. Boulder, Colo.: Westview Press, 1995.

Voltaire. *Philosophical Dictionary*. Translated by Theodore Besterman. London: Penguin Books, 1984.

————. *Letters Concerning the English Nation* [also known as *Philosophical Letters*]. Translated by Nicholas Cronk. London: Oxford University Press, 1994 (1733).

Wallerstein, Immanuel. *The Modern World System*. 3 vols. San Diego, Calif.: Academic Press, 1989.

————. *Unthinking Social Science: The Limits of Nineteenth-Century Paradigms*. Cambridge: Polity Press, 1991.

Walsh, Michael, and Brian Davies, eds. *Proclaiming Justice and Peace: Papal Documents from Rerum Novarum through Centessimus Annus*. Mystic, Conn.: Twenty Third Publications, 1991.

Watson, Alan. *The Spirit of Roman Law*. Athens, Ga.; and London: University of Georgia Press, 1995.

Watson, Alan, ed. *The Digest of Justinian*. Philadelphia: University of Pennsylvania Press, 1985.

Weber, Max. *The Theory of Social and Economic Organization*. Translated by A.M. Henderson and Talcott Parsons. New York: Oxford University Press, 1947.

————. *The Protestant Ethic and the Spirit of Capitalism*. Translated by Talcott Parsons. New York: Charles Scribner's Sons, 1958.

Weintraub, Stanley. *Silent Night: The Remarkable 1914 Christmas Truce*. New York: The Free Press, 2001.

Wendt, Alexander. *Social Theory of International Politics*. Cambridge: Cambridge University Press, 1999.

Wermel, Michael T. *The Evolution of Classical Wage Theory*. New York: Columbia University Press, 1939.

Whalen, Carmen Teresa. *From Puerto Rico to Philadelphia: Puerto Rican Workers and Postwar Economics*. Philadelphia: Temple University Press, 2001.

Wieacker, Franz. *A History of Private Law in Europe*. Oxford: Clarendon Press, 1995.

Wilber, Charles K., and Kenneth Jameson. *An Inquiry into the Poverty of Economics*. Notre Dame: University of Notre Dame Press, 1983.

————. *Beyond Reaganomics: A Further Inquiry into the Poverty of Economics*. Notre Dame and London: University of Notre Dame Press, 1990.

Wilkinson, Richard G. *Unhealthy Societies: the Afflictions of Inequality*. London: Routledge, 1996.

Williams, J.R. "Religion, Ethics, and Development: An Analysis of the Sarvodaya Shramadana Movement of Sri Lanka." *Canadian Journal of Development Studies* 5, no. 1 (1984): 157-67.

Wilpert, Gregory. "Venezuelans Give Chávez Control of Constituent Assembly." *NACLA Report on the Americas* 33, no. 2 (Sept.-Oct. 1999): 45-46.

————. "Coup and Countercoup: An Eyewitness Account." *NACLA Report on the Americas* 35, no. 6 (May/June 2002): 2, 6, 55.

Wilson, William Julius. *When Work Disappears: The World of the New Urban Poor*. New York: Knopf, 1996.

Wink, Walter. *The Powers That Be: Theology for a New Millennium*. New York; London; Toronto; Sydney; Auckland: Doubleday, 1998.

————. *Engaging the Powers: Discernment and Resistance in a World of Domination.* Minneapolis, Minn.: Fortress Press, 1992.

Winters, Jeffrey A. *Power in Motion: Capital Mobility and the Indonesian State.* Ithaca, N.Y.: Cornell University Press, 1996.

Wirth, John, ed. *Latin American Oil Companies and the Politics of Energy.* Lincoln, Neb.: University of Nebraska Press, 1985.

Wittgenstein, Ludwig. *Philosophical Investigations.* Oxford: Basil Blackwell, 1958.

Wolfensohn, James D. "People and Development." Annual Meetings Address to the Board of Governors of the World Bank, Washington, D.C., 1 October 1996.

Wood, David, ed. *Derrida: A Critical Reader.* Oxford; Cambridge, Mass.: Blackwell, 1992.

Wood, Ian. *The Merovingian Kingdoms, 450-751.* London and New York: Longman Group, 1994.

————. "Teutsind, Witlaic and the history of Merovingian *precaria*." Pp. 31-52 in *Property and Power in the Early Middle Ages*, edited by Wendy Davies and Paul Fouracre. Cambridge; New York; Melbourne: Cambridge University Press, 1995.

Wright, Tony. *Socialisms: Old and New.* London and New York: Routledge, 1996.

Wrong, Michela. *In the Footsteps of Mr. Kurtz: Living on the Brink of Disaster in Mobutu's Congo.* New York: HarperCollins, 2001.

Young, Bruce. "The 1982 Elections and the Democratic Transition in Spain." Pp. 132-46 in *Democratic Politics in Spain: Spanish Politics after Franco*, edited by David S. Bell. London: Frances Pinter, 1983.

Yunus, Muhammad. "Redefining Development." Pp. ix-xiii in *50 Years is Enough: The Case Against the World Bank and the International Monetary Fund*, edited by Kevin Danaher. Boston: South End Press, 1994.

Zago, Angela. *La rebelión de Los Angeles.* Caracas: Fuentes Editores, 1992.

Ziegler, Rolf. "The Kula: Social Order, Barter, and Ceremonial Exchange." Pp. 141-68 in *Social Institutions: Their Emergence, Maintenance and Effects*, edited by Michael Hechter, Karl-Dieter Opp, and Reinhard Wippler. New York: Aldine de Gruyter, 1990.

Index

Africa. *See* Nigeria; South Africa; Tanzania

agape, 8, 9, 17, 87, 172, 174, 232, 305, 327, 336

Aguirre, Manuel, S.J., 327

Ahmad, Khurshid, 228, 250n9, 252n14

al-Faruqui, Isma'il, 228, 250n9

alienation, 316, 319–27, 331, 333. *See also* de-alienation

Alinsky, Saul, 329

Allende, Salvador, 332, 347n58

Althusser, Louis, 30, 61n23, 322

Amato, Amedeo, 121

Anderson, Benedict, 95n16

Annales school, 61n23, 168

An-Na'lim, Abdullah Ahmed, 228

anomie, 290, 311n8

Aquinas, St. Thomas, 172, 173, 174, 193, 228, 352, 357, 379n14

Arendt, Hannah, 94n16, 121, 138n6

Argentina, 143n36, 221

Aristotle, 31, 45, 54, 73, 84, 155, 228, 250n10, 271, 319, 351

Arruda, Marcos, 143–44n36; concept of "*economía solidaria*," 143–44n36

Asia. *See* Bangladesh; India; Indonesia; Japan; Malaysia; Pakistan; Philippines; Singapore; Sri Lanka; Thailand

Augustine, 228

Australia, 306

Austria, 181–206, 227; "Austrian Way," 182, 186, 189, 195, 204n18; failure of social democracy in, 185, 186–87; Freedom Party, 181, 184, 186, 187, 195, 203n1; Green Party, 181, 183, 193; neoliberal reforms in, 181, 183; People's Party, 184, 186, 187–88, 193, 204n12; principle of *Proporz*, 188; social democracy in, 185, 186–88, 195, 202; social democrats in, 183–84, 185, 189, 194; *Sozialistische Partei Osterreichs* (SPO), 181, 186, 187, 188, 192, 195, 203n3, 203n5; unemployment in, 203n3; *Versachlichung*, 187, 193

Averroes, 228, 251n10

Avicenna, 228, 251n10

Axelrod, Robert, 2, 3, 22–25, 37–38n41, 38n43

Bachelard, Gaston, 276, 283n33

Badawi, Mohamed Aboulkhair Zaki, 228

Bangladesh, 387

Bani-Sadr, Abulhasan, 228, 250n9

Barthes, Roland, 62n32, 266

Becker, Gary, 261, 280n8

Bellah, Robert, 291

Bello, Walden, 267

Belloc, Hilaire, 226, 228, 246n2

benevolence, Adam Smith's concept of, 15–18, 21, 36n33, 173, 174, 229, 334-35

Benjamin, Medea, 267

Bennett, William J., 309–10n5

Benson, Peter, 290, 305

Bentham, Jeremy, 137n2

Berry, Thomas, 205n24, 231, 253n15

Betancourt, Rómulo, 343n38

Black, Eugene, 358

Boulding, Elise, 205n24

Boulding, Kenneth, 205n24

Bourdieu, Pierre, 54, 55, 60n13, 63n47, 64n55, 93n3

Bowles, Samuel, 3, 32n3, 54, 122, 230
Brahe, Tycho, 300–301, 313n28
Branting, Hjalmar, 25, 39n48, 160,
    165, 170–71; on *uppfostran*, 171
Braudel, Fernand, 78–79n17
Brazil, 238, 344n42, 363, 364, 381n34
Brecher, Jeremy, 264. *See also*
    Globalization from Below
Buddhism, 172, 216, 221, 224n23, 231,
    232, 327, 350; in Ladakh region of
    India, 175–77
Budhoo, Davison, 371–72
Burkett, Paul, 302

Caldera, Rafael, 346n54
Calvin, Jean, 291
capital accumulation, 19, 32n3, 73–74,
    76, 87–88, 89, 91, 95n21, 218,
    274, 304, 305–6, 318, 356–57
capital, exit power of. *See* capital flight
capital flight, 32n3, 54, 79n18, 130,
    159, 160, 176, 198–99, 205n28,
    205–6n29, 227, 275; as crucial test
    for social democracy, 198; in
    Spain, 90
capitalism, 13, 14, 15, 18, 19, 20,
    27–31, 40–41n58, 50, 53, 77n3,
    112–13, 119–20, 161n7, 167, 175,
    187, 197, 216, 225–26, 227–28,
    229, 231, 263, 271–73, 274–75,
    285, 289, 293, 305, 333, 353–54,
    376; attempts to stabilize, 111 (*see
    also* Keynesian macroeconomic
    theory); constitutive rules of (*see*
    constitutive rules); failure of
    Keynesian macroeconomic
    management of, 49; instability of,
    101–2, 110, 111, 119, 120–21,
    300–301; as interruption of history
    of moral progress, 226–30, 286;
    Marx's ethical critique of, 73, 170,
    172, 335; as mutable, 54; radical
    critiques of, 316–19; as resistant to
    transformation, 50, 52. *See also*
    market economy
care ethic, 305, 306, 313n32
caritas, 17, 21, 174, 357, 379n14
Carter, Stephen L., 309–10n5

Chapra, M. 'Umar, 228, 250n9, 252n14
Chávez, Hugo, 332, 346–47nn55–57
Chile, 289, 364, 384n52
Chomsky, Noam, 16, 35–36n30,
    381n38; concepts of depth
    grammar and surface grammar,
    16, 35–36n30
Christendom, medieval, 13–14, 172–74
Christianity, 5–9, 13–14, 33n13, 216,
    231, 232, 299, 327; Christian
    critiques of capitalist economy,
    226, 246–47n2, 248–29n4
circulation, 315, 318, 322; primacy of,
    over production, 30–31, 274–75,
    315, 318; relation of, to
    production, 28–31, 87–88. *See
    also* exchange-value; production;
    use-value
class oppression, 51
class struggle, 317; limitations of
    concept of, 261–63, 280–81n9
Cobb, John B., Jr., 372, 383n50
Collins, Joseph, 32n3, 349
Colomer, Josep, 83–86, 94n15
commercial society, 27, 389
competition, 153, 163n22, 167,
    198–99, 334, 352; as obstacle to
    social democracy, 198–99,
    213–14, 315
Confucianism, 172
constitutive rules (of capitalism; of
    modernity), 31, 41n58, 45–47, 50,
    51, 52, 53, 54, 55–56, 57, 59n1,
    59n8, 60n14, 88, 92, 110, 112,
    119–20, 122–23, 124–25, 130,
    138n7, 147, 148, 150, 155, 158,
    159, 167, 175, 191, 199, 225,
    242–43, 259, 288, 295, 298,
    300–301, 308, 318, 321, 324, 361,
    372; Christian critiques of, 193; as
    historical cause, 57, 64n55, 288;
    Marxist critiques of, 193. *See also*
    cultural structures; norms
contracts, 17, 18, 139–40n16, 172, 225,
    227–28, 242–43, 249–50n7,
    254–55n39, 372, 389; as
    supplanting social bonds, 227–28

cooperation, ix–x, 1–31, 58, 59n8, 108, 110, 124, 171, 175, 176, 217, 223n17, 232, 239, 278–79, 329, 351, 388–89; in game theory, 37–38n41; lack of, 110–11, 117n26; and sharing, principles for, 217–18

cooperatives, 68, 89, 149, 171, 198, 216, 219–21, 305, 329, 333; in Indonesia, 240–41, 294; in Spain, 68, 89; in Sweden, 149

Coraggio, José Luis, 144n36; concept of *"economia solidaria,"* 144n36

Costello, Tim, 264. *See also Globalization from Below*

Cripps, Sir Stafford, 226, 246–47n2

cultural action, 1, 46, 108, 160, 163n33, 198

cultural hegemony, 160

cultural resources, 233–34, 253n22, 273, 276, 279, 302, 350, 388

cultural structures, 31, 45, 54, 59, 75, 76, 86, 111, 136, 153, 159, 244, 266, 286, 293, 315, 364; ethical construction of, 45 (*see also* ethical construction); of exchange, 88, 92; as historical cause, 48, 64n55, 360; humans as creators of, 168, 193, 196, 231, 253n15, 388–89. *See also* constitutive rules; norms

cultures of solidarity, 147, 160, 175–77, 243, 245, 251n11, 271, 280n6, 388

currency speculation, 176–77, 245

Darwinian generosity, 37–38n41

de-alienation, 174, 247–48n3, 319, 324, 325, 327–37, 339n6, 341nn25–26, 342n27, 342n36, 349–50; subsidizing, 315–16, 319, 334–37, 389

debt, 244, 364, 370–73, 374–75

debt forgiveness, 217, 244, 375. *See also* jubilee

democracy, ix, 76, 91–92, 143–44n36, 194, 195, 198, 199, 200–201, 219, 225–26, 226–27, 306, 319, 324, 337, 339n6, 367–68, 381n38

Denmark, 183

Derrida, Jacques, 168, 169, 175, 178n4, 179n15, 246n1; on Rousseau, 168, 169, 178n4

Descartes, Rene, 268–71, 288; influence of, upon economics, 268–71

development, economic, 118n28, 228, 235, 238, 248n3, 279, 308, 331, 354, 355–57, 368, 377n9, 378–79n11, 380n25

dharma, 21–22

dikaiosyne (justice), 4, 17

Dilthey, Wilhelm, 288, 309n4

direct action, 305

division of labor, 13, 34n22, 230

dominator societies, 6, 33n8

Dryzek, John, 384–85n58

Dumont, Louis, 173–74, 178–79n12

Durkheim, Emile, 290, 310–11n8, 319; concept of *"anomie,"* 290, 311n8

ecological sustainability, 108, 147, 160, 177, 223n19, 244, 293, 318, 384–85n58

ecology, 218, 225, 287, 319, 372, 374

economia solidaria, 143–44n36

economic rationality, 225, 227–28, 230, 231, 234–36, 251n12

economics, 2, 13, 15, 34–35n24, 46, 47, 48, 50, 53–54, 56, 111, 113, 125, 163n22, 172–74, 198, 227, 231, 267–71, 307, 308, 352–53; as arising historically with capitalist institutions, 125; assumptions regarding self-interest, 174, 216, 226, 229, 352; classical, 125–27, 128, 130, 168; as cultural structure, 231, 234, 293; and failure to meet needs, 111, 340n16, 352–53; false premises of, 300; force metaphors in, 53–54, 226, 269–70; inability of, to explain root causes of poverty, 124, 267–71; incorrect separation of, from ethics, 286, 289, 302,

305, 307; influence of Descartes upon, 268, 269–70; invention of, 173–74; need for reconsideration of, 173, 193, 198, 267–71, 286, 300–301, 307; as quasi-natural science, 53–54, 63n41, 226, 230, 286, 300–301, 305, 308, 322, 352, 388; unreliability of predictions of, 56, 270, 300–301

Edgren, Gösta, 153–55

Eisler, Riane, 6, 32–33n7, 187

Empire, 27–30

enchantment, 173, 327

Engels, Friedrich, 36n34, 137n2, 310n6, 320

Enlightenment, 10–12, 72, 255n39, 292

epistemic fallacy, 57

epistemology, 43–58, 64–65n57

Escobar, Arturo, 356, 363, 380n25

ethic of solidarity, 31, 144n36

ethical construction, 263, 288, 332, 334, 389; history as process of, 175, 226–27, 286, 353; philosophy of, 50, 51, 54, 57, 69, 86, 108, 109–10, 160, 168–69, 175, 182, 192, 197–98, 331

ethics, 1, 3, 12, 13, 15, 17, 18, 36n31, 36n33, 64–65n57, 108, 197, 217, 227, 228, 229, 232, 310n5, 319, 322, 389; of freedom, 120–21; restructuring of traditional, to facilitate capitalism, 16–18 (*see also* liberal ethics; middle-class values)

Europe. *See* Austria; Denmark; Germany; Holland; Norway; Spain; Sweden; Switzerland; United Kingdom

The Evolution of Cooperation, 22–25

exchange, logic of, 193, 351–54, 357, 358–61, 364–65, 372, 374, 376; failure of, to meet needs, 358–61; as logic of non-love, 351–53; need to supplement, 359–61, 365

exchange-value, 29, 30, 73, 87–88, 193, 268, 302, 304; distinction of, from use-value, 73–74, 268, 302,

304, 319–20. *See also* circulation; production; use-value

fascism, 93n6, 183, 191–92, 193–95, 200, 205n25

Faxén, Karl-Olof, 153–55

Fielding, Henry, 291

Fleisher, Frederic, 145

flexible accumulation, 91, 96n30

Flyvbjerg, Bent, 48, 54–56

folkshemmet, 101, 106

Fordism, 161n7

Forrester, Viviane, 353

Foucault, Michel, 28, 29, 40n57, 48, 50–51, 54, 55, 61n23, 63n34, 76, 121, 168, 246n1; *Discipline and Punish*, 50; on power, 50–51, 63n34, 76

Franco, Francisco, 82, 83, 84, 90, 91

free market capitalism, 14, 101, 108, 109, 111, 120, 127, 148, 149, 198, 229–30, 251n12, 293, 306, 371; Christian critiques of, 193, 226; unproven ability of, to provide general prosperity, 183

freedom, 9, 21–22, 31, 36n31, 120–22, 125, 126, 136, 153, 168, 175, 198, 225, 230, 233, 243, 254n39, 256n40, 300, 306, 328, 389; Gandhi's conception of, 21; as implying instability, 120, 300; in market economy, 108, 120, 230; reconceptualizing definition of, 31, 387–89; religious tempering of concept of, 233

Freire, Paulo, 108, 136, 143n35, 160, 163n33, 319, 325, 329, 342n27, 388; definition of "cultural action," 163n33

Freud, Sigmund, 289–90, 303, 310n7

Friedman, Milton, 142–43n33, 153, 163n22, 335

Fukuyama, Francis, 310n5

Fuller, R. Buckminster, 147, 162n11, 349

Galtung, Johan, 138–39n9, 221, 378n11; definition of "structural violence," 138–39n9

game theory, 22–25, 37–38n41, 39n45, 125; Prisoner's Dilemma, 37n41, 39n45; Tit For Tat, 24–25, 38n41; Ultimatum Game, 37n41

Gandhi, Mohandas, 2, 3, 21–22, 74, 216, 218, 264, 269, 320, 352, 357

Geertz, Clifford, 235, 279, 293–94, 296, 299

gender oppression, 51; under Franco dictatorship, 82, 93n6

George, Susan, 267

Germany, 149, 156, 183, 185, 210

Giddens, Anthony, 28, 32n2, 40–41n58, 59n1, 110, 261, 280–81n9; on class-divided societies, 110

Gilligan, Carol, 223n17, 305, 313n32; concept of "care ethic," 305, 313n32

Ginsberg, Anthony, 211–14, 215, 218–19, 221

Gintis, Herbert, 3, 32n3, 54, 122, 230

globalization, 1, 27, 116n9, 157, 181, 193, 210, 263, 264–67, 271–73, 274, 313n26; as arising from failure of social democracy, 274. *See also* capitalism; neoliberalism

Globalization from Below, 264–67

González, Felipe, 82, 89, 90, 96n26, 97n32

Goulet, Denis, 226, 248n3

government, relative impotence of, 148, 151, 159, 175, 243, 304; solution to impotence of, 305–6

Grameen Bank, 305, 359–60, 387–89

Gramsci, Antonio, 143n35, 160, 163–64n33, 232, 233, 242, 253n21, 288, 381n38; on "common sense," 143n35, 233, 242, 253n21, 288; on "cultural hegemony," 160, 164n33; distinction between "common sense" and "good sense," 253n21, 288; on "moral and intellectual reform," 160, 163n33, 232, 288

Great Depression, 101, 102, 103, 116n7, 128, 169, 201, 288

growth point, 136, 143n35, 305

Guatemala, 217, 374

Gutiérrez, Gustavo, 252n14, 357

Habermas, Jürgen, 48–50, 62n33, 275, 283n32, 329, 381n38; *Knowledge and Human Interests*, 48, 50, 62n33, 275

Habibie, B.J., 236, 253n24, 298

Habitat for Humanity, 216–18

Haider, Jörg, 181, 184, 186, 187, 195

Hammarskjöld, Dag, 99, 114n1, 136, 140n21, 184

Hansson, Per Albin, 101, 184, 325

Hardt, Michael, 2, 3, 27–30, 40n57

Hart-Landsberg, Martin, 302

Hartsock, Nancy, 48, 51–52, 53, 63n37

Harvey, David, 96–97n30, 141n24, 274

Hatta, Mohammad, 294, 295

Hayek, Friedrich von, 27, 40n56, 169; *The Road to Serfdom*, 169, 204n16

Hazlitt, Henry, 125–26, 127; criticism of Keynes, 125–26

Hegel, Georg Wilhelm Friedrich, 9, 73, 194, 352

Heidegger, Martin, 196, 319

Henninger, Josephine, 185

Hill, Hal, 242, 301

Hinduism, 172, 231, 256n39, 327

historiography, 48, 61n20, 61–62n23, 64n55, 83–85, 225, 244–45, 288, 322, 345n50, 360

Hitler, Adolf, 101, 128, 169, 183, 192, 194, 195, 199, 288

Holland, 14, 183, 352, 370

homelessness, 124, 325; as caused by property rights, 124

Hubbard, Barbara Marx, 174, 179n13

humans as creators of culture, 168, 193, 196, 232, 253n15, 388–89

Hume, David, 352

Iglesias, Pablo, 69–72, 74, 78n8, 78n11, 85, 95n18

IMF. *See* International Monetary Fund

imperialism, 27

India, 37n40, 172, 238, 362, 363, 364, 365, 369, 373; Ladakh region of, 175–77

Indonesia, 231–56, 257–83, 288–89, 293–302; alleviation of poverty in, 238; *Bappenas*, 235, 243; Communist Party, 258, 296; comparative advantage of, 235, 238; cooperatives in, 240–41, 294; corruption in, 238, 295, 307, 308; cultural resources of, 233–45, 275–79; economic crash of 1997, 242, 258, 265, 289, 300–302, 308; economic rationality in, 234–36; family ties in, 239–40; foreign debt of, 235; *gotong royong* (mutual aid), 294, 296; Guided Democracy, 296, 311–12n20; macroeconomic policies of, 241–42; military sector in, 237; nationalization in, 258; New Order, 297–98, 300, 304, 311n19; oil revenues of, 258; *Pancasila* ideology in, 278, 283n37, 300; *pembangunan* (development), 297–98, 300, 302, 303–04; policy of food self-sufficiency in, 276–77; poverty in, 288–89; public sector in, 237, 294; relationship with IMF, 235, 267; Roman-Dutch law in, 242; *seka*, 279; self-reliance of, 235; social democracy in, 294–96; social democratic constitution of, 236–38, 240–41, 244, 254n37; Suharto dictatorship, 237, 242, 258, 277, 288, 298, 300, 307, 370; Sukarno regime, 254n37, 258

inflation, 52, 106, 176, 275

institutional facts, 44–45, 47–48, 55, 86

International Monetary Fund (IMF), 221, 231, 235, 236, 237, 265, 267, 277, 332, 345n53, 346n54, 354, 370, 371–72, 373, 375, 382n39, 383n47. *See also* Structural Adjustment Programs

investment, 27, 89, 90, 91, 102, 126, 129, 155, 156, 157, 159, 176, 213–15, 216, 233, 244–45, 301, 305–6, 334, 336–37, 352, 361–62, 364; employee investment funds, 157–58, 165–66; profit motive and, 87, 215, 244–45, 305–6; strikes, 159, 160, 176, 360. *See also* capital flight; profit motive

iron law of wages, 100, 109, 110, 114–16n4, 147–48, 151–52, 175

Islam, 172, 216, 228, 229, 231, 232, 239, 250n9, 255n39, 293, 298–99, 312n25, 327, 350; Muslim critiques of liberal ethics of modernity, 228, 239, 250n9, 252n14, 254n28

Iyer, Raghavan, 21–22, 37n40

James, William, 375

Jameson, Kenneth P., 226, 247–48n3, 279

Japan, 156, 210

Jesus, 2, 3, 5–10, 13, 14, 17, 33n8, 57

jubilee, 335, 375

Judaism, 6, 216, 232, 299, 335, 375

just price, theory of, 172, 352

justice, 1, 4, 17, 19, 225, 287, 292, 319, 357, 388; orienting economy toward, 112, 217–18, 379n14, 388

Justinian, 254–56nn39–40

Kant, Immanuel, 18, 36n31, 45, 60n13, 62n31, 139n10, 255–56nn39–40, 271, 323; categorical imperative, 36n31, 323; *Foundations of the Metaphysics of Morals*, 36n31; idea of freedom, 255n39; ideal of autonomy, 49; *Perpetual Peace*, 45, 381n38

Kautsky, Karl, 320

Keynes, John Maynard, 101, 102, 103, 109, 110, 117n23, 123, 125, 128–30, 142n33, 145, 150, 170, 336, 358, 370, 371, 379n17; *General Theory*, 101, 117n23, 126, 128; on instability of capitalism, 109

Keynesian economic policies, 146, 161n8, 166; in Austria, 183; in

Sweden, 101–8, 110, 112, 123, 128–36, 148–60

Keynesian macroeconomic theory, 91, 96n29, 142n33, 150, 379n17; inability of, to sustain social democracy, 147–48, 274, 287. *See also* macroeconomics

King, Martin Luther, Jr., 357

kinship, 72, 121, 138n7, 174, 234, 240–41, 243

Kohl, Helmut, 91

Kohlberg, Lawrence, 223n17, 329

Korten, David C., 205n24

Kreisky, Bruno, 182–93, 204n11

Kropotkin, Peter, 264

Kuhn, Thomas, 300

Kung, Hans, 310n5

Laclau, Ernesto, 226–227, 230, 249n5; concept of radicalized liberalism, 226–27

Lappé, Frances Moore, 349

Lassalle, Ferdinand, 21, 36n34, 72, 114–15n4, 193

Latin America. *See* Argentina; Brazil; Chile; *economía solidaria*; Guatemala; liberation theology; Mexico; Sandinistas; Venezuela

Letters from Quebec, 2, 61n18, 62n31, 64n57, 205n25

liberal ethics, 36n31, 227, 228, 389; alternatives to, 175–77, 388–89; obstacles posed by, 147–48, 175, 389

liberation theology, 230, 249n4, 252n14, 357

Lindahl, Erik, 128

Lindblom, Charles, 243, 244

local initiative, 218

Locational Revolution, 257–59, 260, 263, 265, 267, 274–75, 277, 280n5

Locke, John, 18, 179n12

López-Cordón, Maria Victoria, 67

love ethic, 1, 17, 65n57, 273, 283n29, 352–53, 357–61, 372, 376; as key to social democracy, 273

love, logic of. *See* love ethic

Lundberg, Erik, 99, 101–3, 110, 111, 116n10, 117n17, 133, 140–41n21, 142n29, 142n32, 146, 166, 184; on the Swedish model, 101, 102, 146

Luther, Martin, 256n40, 291

Luthuli, Albert, 219

Luxemburg, Rosa, 29, 42n62, 264

macroeconomics, 100–101, 102–4, 106, 108, 110–13, 114n1, 121, 123, 128–29, 166; as frustrated by freedom, 121; invention of, 170; Keynes' rationale for, 128; as revolt against classical economics, 125; use of, to manage economy, 149. *See also* Keynesian macroeconomic theory

Maine, Sir Henry, 227, 249–50n7

Malaysia, 238, 297, 370

Malthus, Thomas, 115n4, 162n11

Mandel, Ernest, 315

Mandela, Nelson, 207–12, 216, 218, 220, 221

Mandeville, Bernard de, 173, 178–79n12

Marcuse, Herbert, 47, 48, 61n20, 326, 342nn29–30; concept of "technological rationality," 48, 49

Maritain, Jacques, 319

market, 18, 29, 31, 126, 168, 172, 226, 229–31, 275, 305, 306, 320–21, 341n18, 350, 351, 374; definition of, 120; ethical foundations of, 167, 225, 230, 254–55n39 (*see also* freedom; property); logic of, 214; pre-capitalist, 31

market economy, 108–9, 114n1, 247n2, 351, 353

Marx, Karl, 2, 3, 19–21, 27, 28–31, 36n34, 42n67, 46, 51–52, 72–74, 77n4, 87–88, 92, 95nn21–22, 99, 112, 115–16n4, 120, 123, 137n2, 170, 172, 190, 193, 194, 217, 231, 240, 243, 275, 300, 302, 304, 313n26, 315, 318, 319–26, 333, 334, 335; on alienation, 319–27, 335; *Capital*, 30, 46, 73, 74, 87,

123, 137n2, 172, 320, 321, 333;
critique of capitalism, 315; on de-
alienation, 316, 335; on distinction
between production and
circulation, 30–31, 87–88, 275,
318, 321–22; on exploitation, 87,
318; on expropriation, 333; on
family economy, 240; on freedom,
29; labor theory of value,
95nn21–22, 318, 340n10;
preference of, for science over
ethics, 231; principle of
production for use, 217; on
property, 29
Max-Neef, Manfred, 253n22
McNamara, Robert, 235, 358, 368–69,
372, 382n40
Medina, Pablo, 346n54
Meidner, Rudolf, 105, 132–36, 157,
160, 165–66, 174, 178n2. *See also*
Rehn-Meidner model
Mexico, 94n16, 224n22, 362, 363, 371
microcredit, 305, 388. *See also*
Grameen Bank
microeconomics, 103, 107, 108, 114n1,
128–29, 147
middle-class values, 285–87, 288,
289–93, 295, 296, 300–301, 303,
304–5, 307–8, 309–10n5, 310n6;
blindness of, 303–5; relationship
of, to capitalism, 292–93, 294,
303, 304; as virtue-truncated,
292–93, 298, 303. *See also* liberal
ethics
Mill, John Stuart, 200, 257, 280n3
Mises, Ludwig von, 27, 40n56, 233,
251n12
modern society; as arising in opposition
to medieval Christendom, 172–73;
birth of, 172; ethical foundations
of, 153; norms of exchange in,
153, 155
moksha, 37n40, 232, 253n17
Moller, Gustav, 184
money, 159, 168, 176, 198, 244,
251n12, 269, 293, 306, 322; as
"imperfect" means of organizing
cooperation and sharing, 217

money economy, versus subsistence
economy, 217
moral development, psychology of, 86,
186, 195, 197–98, 216,
222–23n17, 227; need for larger
role for, 195, 197–98
Morgenthau, Hans, 358
Mother Teresa, 2, 3, 25–27, 216
Mouffe, Chantal, 226–27, 230, 249n5;
concept of radicalized liberalism,
226–27
Mounier, Emmanuel, 319
Mussolini, Benito, 183, 189, 192, 195
Myrdal, Alva, 136, 184
Myrdal, Gunnar, 10, 99, 103, 114n2,
116n7, 116–17n13, 122, 128, 129,
131, 136, 143n34, 148–50, 155,
162nn12–13, 168, 169, 175,
178n2, 184, 249–50n7, 256n42;
Beyond the Welfare State, 148–50,
162n12; on "eighteenth-century
ideals," 99, 122, 175; on
instability of capitalism, 103,
116–17n13

Nasution, General, 297
nationalization, 89, 207, 220, 322, 333,
347–48nn58–59, 357; in
Indonesia, 258; in South Africa,
207, 208, 209, 210; in Spain, 89;
lack of, in Sweden, 139n11, 334;
as subject to market constraints,
333–34, 347–48nn58–59; in
Venezuela, 328, 333, 342n37;
versus investment, 207, 357
needs, x, 86, 108, 111, 119, 122, 124,
138n9, 159–60, 233, 244–45, 259,
275, 305, 318, 319–21,
340–41n16, 350, 351, 352, 356,
361, 372
Negri, Antonio, 2, 3, 27–30, 40n57
neoliberal economic policies, 90; in
Austria, 181, 183; in Spain,
90–91; in Sweden, 161–62n10,
175; in Venezuela, 331, 345n53,
346n54. *See also* neoliberalism
neoliberalism, 1, 142n33, 157,
161–62n10, 168, 192, 213–15,

219, 288, 334, 374; alternatives to premises of, 216–19; as arising from failure of social democracy, 334; premises of, 215; proposed solution of, to poverty, 215, 243–44

Netherlands. *See* Holland

New Zealand, 194, 306

Newton, Sir Isaac, 10, 46, 269, 276; *Principia Mathematica*, 46

Nicaraguan Revolution. *See* Sandinistas

Nietzsche, Friedrich, 122, 138n8

Nigeria, 238, 262, 281–82nn10–11

Nitisastro, Widjojo, 236–37, 240–42, 245

nonprofits, 216, 219–21, 305

nonviolence, 1, 201, 264, 319

Norberg-Hodge, Helena, 160, 175–77, 218

norms, 168, 231, 233, 300, 307, 319, 326–27, 328, 389; as causal, 225, 244–45, 288, 322, 360; of market culture, 190–91, 233, 300, 318; of solidarity, in traditional society, 174; reshaping of, 169, 192–93, 197–98, 231, 233, 244–45, 291, 304, 307, 319, 389 (*see also* ethical construction). *See also* constitutive rules; norms

Norway, 183, 315

Novak, Michael, 122–23, 139n10

Nyerere, Julius, 221, 224n23

Odhner, Clas-Erik, 153–55

Ollman, Bertell, 320, 322, 325, 341n23, 341n26

The Open Society and its Enemies. See Karl Popper

overproduction, 28, 102–3; as generic feature of capitalist macroeconomics, 102–3

Pakistan, 365

Pareto optimality, 230, 252n13

partnership societies, 6

Patomäki, Heikki, 48, 57

patriarchy, 8, 32nn7–8, 52, 187, 243

Payer, Cheryl, 370–71

peace, 287, 292, 319

Peirce, C.S., 234, 375

Pérez, Carlos Andrés, 345–46nn53–54

periodization, 360

Perón, Juan, 221, 332

Pesch, Heinrich, 226, 246n2

Philippines, 242, 366

Piaget, Jean, 45, 51

Pirie, N.W., 349

Piven, Frances Fox, 267

Plato, 2, 3–5, 13, 14, 17, 45, 51, 54, 59n6, 121, 194, 228, 229, 269, 288

Pol Pot, 288

Polanyi, Karl, 226, 227, 231, 247n2, 252n14, 279

polis, 4–5, 232

Pontusson, Jonas, 159

Pope John XXIII, 248n4

Pope Leo XIII, 248n4

Pope Pius XI, 248n4

Popper, Karl, 53, 163n22, 165, 167, 182, 184–86, 190–91, 194–202, 204nn16–17, 205n27, 319; concept of "interventionist state," 186, 204n16; definition of rational, 165, 199; influence of, upon mainstream social science, 186, 190, 194–202; *The Open Society*, 182, 185, 186, 194–96, 199–201, 204nn16–17

postmodernism, 28, 47, 168

post-structuralism, 168

poverty, 1, 104, 214, 233, 260–63, 300, 315–16, 319, 342n26, 349–50; as avoidable, 1, 259; causes of, 122, 124, 225, 259, 280n6; as default condition, 110; estimates of, globally, 118n28; in medieval Europe, 172; neoliberal prescriptions for, 215; problem of elimination of, 109, 116n4, 123, 243–44, 315–16, 318, 351; ways to overcome, 217–18, 221, 233, 244–45, 315–16, 318, 322, 334–37, 342n26, 349–50, 359–61, 387–89; World Bank's exacerbation of, 370–73; World

Bank's mission to eliminate, 368–69

power, 19, 50–51, 71, 75–76, 85, 89, 92, 154, 159, 189–91, 199, 220, 260–63, 264, 265–66, 274, 319, 329, 388; Gene Sharp's theory of, 265–66; versus rules, 50–51, 159, 190–91, 199, 220

pragmatism, 375–76

Prévert, Jacques, 172, 178n10

private property, 17, 293, 306–7, 333; Christian critiques of, 193. *See also* property

privatization, 213, 306

production, 29–30, 333–34; for exchange, 88–89, 170–71, 275; relationship to circulation, 29–30, 87–89, 275–76, 333–34; for use, 217, 275, 302-3, 305. *See also* circulation; exchange-value; use-value

profit, 152–55, 163n24, 176, 233, 275, 305–6, 318; functions of, 153

profit maximization, 90, 235, 275, 303, 352, 367; as cultural norm, 170, 198, 303. *See also* profit; profit motive

profit motive, 19, 73–74, 76, 79n18, 86–87, 88, 90–92, 192–93, 197–98, 217, 306, 318, 352, 366; as basic cultural structure, 88, 318; Christian critique of, 193; in Indonesia, 295; Muslim critique of, 252n14; need for breaking addiction to, 182, 184, 193, 197–98, 244, 275. *See also* profit; profit maximization

profit seeking, as vice, 155

proletariat. *See* working class

property, 18, 125, 136, 168, 175, 198, 225, 230, 242–43, 328, 333, 341–42n26, 352, 361, 372, 389; ethical and legal norms of, 153, 155, 225, 242–43, 254–55n39; as implying exclusion, 120, 303; owners, freedom of, 131, 159, 243

property rights, 17, 18, 21–22, 31, 36n31, 89, 109, 126, 131, 172,

220, 228, 233, 243, 245, 361; as cause of poverty, 124; as implying exclusion, 120, 122–23; "onion" theory of, 123, 156; religious tempering of concept of, 233

Przeworski, Adam, 90, 91, 96n29

Putnam, Robert, 309–10n5

Quijano, Aníbal, 341n25

Quinn, Daniel, 3, 32n3, 59n8, 223n19

racism, 29, 60n17, 207, 209, 219, 222n6

radicalism, 317–19, 340n9

Rapoport, Anatol, 23–25, 39n45

rational choice theory, 82, 83–85, 86, 93n3, 196, 270

Rawls, John, 324

Reagan, Ronald, 91

Reagon, Bernice Johnson, 340n9

Rehn, Gösta, 105, 132–36, 150–51. *See also* Rehn-Meidner model

Rehn-Meidner model, 132–36, 142n26, 142n31

reification, 341n18, 341n23

religion, 6–9, 10–12, 17–18, 25–26, 231–33, 276, 308, 319. *See also* *specific religions*

rents, 315, 318, 334–35, 338–39n1; use of, in subsidizing de-alienation, 334–35

rent-seeking, 338–39n1

repression, 154, 263–64, 289, 302

revolving fund, 218

Ricardo, David, 115n4, 335

Richards, Howard, 2, 3, 26, 43–44, 47, 51, 62n31, 143n35, 168, 205n25, 291, 342n36

Richardson, Samuel, 291–92

rights, 124. *See also* freedom; property rights

Robbins, Richard, 257–58, 261

Robinson, Joan, 95n22, 318, 340n10; critique of Marx's labor theory of value, 95n22

Robison, Richard, 241

Roman Empire, 11, 242. *See also* Justinian

Roman Law, 17, 18, 36n31, 125, 242–43, 254–56nn39–40; enumeration of principles of, 242–43

Roosevelt, Franklin D., 355

Rorty, Richard, 268

Rostow, Walt, 279, 377n9

Rousseau, Jean-Jacques, 168, 169, 178nn3–4, 268, 269

rules. *See* constitutive rules; power

Ruskin, John, 272, 283n28

Russell, Bertrand, 72–73, 78n16, 241, 246n1

Ryner, J. Magnus, 161n4, 161n7

Sampson, Anthony, 209, 210

Sandinistas, 32n3

sangha, 232, 253n17

Sartre, Jean-Paul, 115n4, 120, 137n4

Sarvodaya Shramadana, 221, 224n23

Sassen, Saskia, 267

Say, Jean Baptiste, 140n20

Say's Law, 128, 130, 140n20

Schumacher, E.F., 120

Schumpeter, Joseph, 115n4

Searle, John, 44, 45, 59n1; definition of institutional facts, 44; distinction between institutional facts and brute facts, 44–45

Sechi, Father Bruno, 122, 138n9; definition of "structural violence," 122, 138n9

self-interest, 13, 14, 30, 38n41, 120, 173–74, 197, 215, 220–21, 226, 228–29, 245, 320–21, 334, 335; as false premise of neoliberalism, 216; as unproven in game theory, 37–38n41

self-reliance, 220–21, 350, 367–68

Sen, Amartya, 232, 233, 306

shalom, 232

sharing, ix–x, 1–31, 58, 108, 124, 175, 176, 217, 232, 239, 278–79, 389; and cooperation, principles for, 217–18

Sharp, Gene, 265–66; theory of power, 265–66

Shintoism, 172

Shiva, Vandana, 267, 382n39

Singapore, 306, 319, 352, 375–76

Skarzynski, Witold von, 16, 18

Smith, Adam, 2, 3, 13–19, 21, 34nn21–22, 36n33, 112, 125, 139–40n16, 173, 174, 176, 228, 229, 230, 262, 275, 304, 320–21, 333, 334, 350, 352, 359–60; on benevolence, 15–18, 21, 36n33, 173, 174, 229, 334–35; on primacy of use over exchange, 275, 304, 320, 350; restructuring of traditional ethics to fit capitalism, 13, 16–18; on self-interest, 228–29, 320–21, 334; *The Theory of Moral Sentiments*, 15–16; *The Wealth of Nations*, 15–17, 125

Smith, Brendan, 264. *See also Globalization from Below*

social democracy, 1–2, 10, 30, 31, 50, 51, 86, 92, 103, 136, 137n1, 141n24, 159, 175, 183, 192, 197, 198, 221, 225–26, 233, 271–74, 306, 307, 316–17; advancing the construction of, 315, 318–19; as best attempt thus far at alleviating poverty, 2, 137n1, 306; British, 162n20; construction of, 233; as countercurrent to narrow economic rationality, 230; nineteenth-century definition of, 69, 241; nineteenth-century German, 72, 193, 241; obstacles to, 55, 82, 130, 286; philosophical weakness of, 230–31; reason for failure of, 334; Swedish, 99, 100, 104, 106, 123, 125, 146, 152, 153, 166–67, 333; twentieth-century European, 111

social science, critical, 49

social science, mainstream, 2–3, 46–47, 48, 53, 54, 62n33, 99, 157, 162n13, 185, 186–87, 189–202, 288; causality in, 56–57, 288; failures of, 46–47, 287; inadequate paradigms of, 167, 260–63, 287; influence of physics upon,

196–98; methodology of, 152, 182, 287; Popper's influence upon, 185–86, 189–97, 199–202. *See also* economics
social structure, 26, 123, 163n33, 244, 304
socialism, 25, 27, 74, 75, 76, 96n29, 161n7, 172, 226, 339n3; in Spain, 75; in Sweden, 170–71
Socrates, 4–5, 51, 74, 270, 320, 329
solidarity, 5, 16, 71, 72, 75, 121, 171, 199, 227, 228–29, 327–29, 374, 388; ancient ideologies of, 229; cultural structures of, 75; culture of, 70, 199
Solo, Robert A., 48, 53–54, 63n41
South Africa, 207–24; African National Congress (ANC), 207, 209–10, 211, 216, 219, 220; apartheid in, 207, 209, 219; dependence upon investment in, 210–11, 212, 219; economic interventionism, during apartheid, 222n6; Freedom Charter, 207–9, 217, 219, 224n22; investment in, 207, 209, 210–11, 219; grow-and-share policies in, 211, 219; loss of investor confidence in, during apartheid, 209–10, 211, 216; National Party, 207, 209, 222n6; nationalization in, 207, 208, 209, 210, 213; neoliberal prescriptions for, 211–15; resistance to apartheid, 209–10, 216; social democracy in, 208, 213; socialism in, 207, 208, 218; socioeconomic inequality in, 212; *South Africa's Future*, 211–14; tax policy in, 213; unemployment in, 212; Xhosa culture in, 218, 223–24n20
Soviet Union, 169, 211, 360
Spain, 67–80, 81–97, 149, 289; anarchism in, 67–68, 69, 74, 77nn4–5; anarcho-syndicalism in, 68, 77n5; capitalist development in, 67–68, 77n3; Civil War, 68, 75, 77–78n5, 81, 82; comparative advantage in, 91; economic crisis

in, 89; failure of socialism in, 75, 79–80n24; *Falange*, 82, 93n5; First Republic, 67; Franco dictatorship, 75, 82, 83, 84, 91; Moncloa Pacts, 89, 96n26; neoliberal economic reforms in, 90–91; organized labor in, 74, 75, 85, 89; *Partido Socialista Obrero de España* (PSOE), 69, 71–72, 75, 78nn13–14, 79nn20–21, 82, 89, 90, 91, 93n4, 95n24, 96n27; Primo de Rivera dictatorship, 70, 74–75, 79n20; self-reliance in, 91; socialism in, 67, 71, 74–75, 76; *Unión de Centro Democrático* (UCD), 82, 89, 90, 93n7; *Unión General de Trabajadores* (UGT), 78n8; unemployment in, 90, 96n27; working class in, 71, 75, 89. *See also* Felipe González; Pablo Iglesias
speculation. *See* currency speculation
Sri Lanka, 221, 224n23
Stalin, Joseph, 149, 169, 288
stewardship, 198, 220, 228, 245, 320, 328, 350
Stockholm School, 99, 103, 113, 114n1, 128, 129, 141n21, 146, 150, 170, 184; distinction of, from Marxism, 170
strike, 88, 154, 155, 158, 266; as relatively ineffectual, 266
Structural Adjustment Programs (SAPs), 370–73, 383n47
structural trap, 266, 267, 347n58
structural violence, 122, 138–39n9
structure. *See* cultural structures; social structure
Suharto, 237, 242, 258, 277, 298, 299, 302, 304, 307–08, 370
Sukarno, 254n37, 258, 288, 294–98, 304, 311–12n20, 312n24
Sukarnoputri, Megawati, 235, 267, 297, 298, 304
Sutowo, Ibnu, 260–61
Swanger, Joanna, 347n58
Sweden, 99–118, 119–44, 145–64, 165–79, 183, 184, 186, 227, 334,

356; attempt to maintain full employment in, 149–51, 161n8, 169; banking system in, 105; decline of exports in, 146; inflation in, 106; LO (trade union federation), 104, 105, 106, 117n19, 129, 160, 171; neoliberal reforms in, 161–62n10, 175; nontradable sector and tradable sector in, 103, 132–33; organized labor in, 151, 159; the planning illusion in, 148–52; profits in, 153–55, 156; reliance upon exports in, 169–70; SAF (employers' federation), 104, 106, 129; social democracy in, 146, 152, 153, 166–67 (*see also* Swedish social democracy); solidaristic wage policy in, 100, 116n6, 135; tax policy in, 105, 129, 132, 133–34, 156, 159–60; unemployment in, 147, 162n10. *See also* Swedish Illusion, Swedish model, Swedish social democracy

Swedish Illusion, 130–31, 145, 147, 148–60

Swedish model, 141n24, 147, 155, 158, 159; illusions of, 145, 147, 148–60

Swedish social democracy, 146, 152, 153, 166–67; consequences of success of, 146, 152; construction of, 169–71, 173, 174–75; failure of, 146–47; influence of, upon Bruno Kreisky, 184; influence of, upon Karl Popper, 204n17

Switzerland, 149, 183

system-changing reform, 182, 184–85, 186, 190–92, 198, 199, 220; versus system-immanent reform, 186, 204n11

Tanzania, 221, 224n23; nationalization in, 224n23; "Ujamaa," 221, 224n23

tax havens, 214

Taylor, Charles, 46–47, 50, 60n13, 60n17; concept of constitutive rules, 46

Taylor, Frederick, 141n23

Taylorism, 141n23

Thailand, 238

Thatcher, Margaret, 91, 211

The Theory of Moral Sentiments, 15–16

Tinbergen, Jan, 14, 19, 34–35n24

traditional societies, 138n7, 173, 227

Tribal Unity, 194, 196

trusteeship, 198, 218, 350

Turgot, Anne-Robert-Jacques, 115n4

underemployment, 158, 167, 300

Understanding the Global Economy, 47, 61n22

unemployment, 52, 54, 110, 127–28, 130, 195, 300, 325; causes of, 110; official calculation of rates of, 140n19; solutions for, 195; structural, 176, 300

United Kingdom, 188

United Nations, 210

United States, 77n4, 145, 149, 188, 213, 354, 360

uppfostran (upbringing), 171

use-value, 30, 252n14, 268, 302, 304–5, 319–21, 340–41n16, 350. *See also* circulation; exchange-value; production

value capture, 338n1

values, 6, 108, 227, 288, 291, 297, 300, 305. *See also* care ethic; cooperation; ethics; love ethic; middle-class values; sharing; solidarity; stewardship; trusteeship; virtue

Velasco Alvarado, Juan, 332

Venezuela, 315–48; *Acción Democrática* (AD), 316, 317, 331, 339n4, 339n7, 343n41; *Causa R*, 339n8, 346n54; Center for Development Studies (CENDES), 328, 331, 344n47, 347n57; Chávez administration, 332; *Comité de Organización Política*

Electoral Independiente (COPEI), 317, 327, 331, 339n4, 339n7; community development programs in, 328–30; *desarrollista* paradigm in, 330–32; economic crises in, 345n53, 346n54; IMF austerity measures in, 332, 345n53, 346n54; MARAVEN, 328–30, 335; *Movimiento al Socialismo* (MAS), 316, 339n5; nationalization in, 328, 333, 342n37; oil industry in, 318, 328–31, 333, 335, 342–43nn37–38, 344–45nn49–50; Pérez Jimenez dictatorship, 316; property rights in, 328; socialism in, 316; transformed conception of property in, 328; volunteerism in, 329–30

virtue, 4, 10, 17–18, 121, 227, 228, 269, 335–36

Voltaire, 2, 3, 10–12, 34n17

volunteerism, 218, 278, 290–91, 305, 329–30

Wallerstein, Immanuel, 61n18, 113, 118n28, 162n13, 168, 255n39, 274, 377n9

The Wealth of Nations, 15–17, 125.

Weber, Max, 78n15, 121, 168, 173, 227, 279, 294, 327; distinction between modern and traditional societies, 168, 173; on traditional societies, 121, 168, 173

Wendt, Alexander, 58

Wertrationalitat (value rationality), 173

Wesley, John, 291

White, Harry Dexter, 357–58

Wilber, Charles K., 226, 247–48n3, 279

Wilkinson, Richard G., 306

Williams, Roger, 291

Wink, Walter, 6, 33n8

Winters, Jeffrey, 257–59, 261, 280n5. *See also* Locational Revolution

Wittgenstein, Ludwig, 48, 50, 60n13, 167, 196, 288; *Rechtfertigung*, 167

Wolfensohn, James D., 373

working class, 29, 150, 170, 260, 286, 290, 310n6, 326, 361, 378n10; Austrian, 181; British, 14; Indonesian, 302; precariousness faced by, 158, 358–59; Spanish, 69, 75, 77, 90; as subject of history, 28, 29; Swedish, 105, 158, 171

World Bank, 55, 148, 152, 221, 231, 235, 237, 265, 301, 354–85; acceptance of elimination of poverty as mission of, 368–69, 382–83n42, 385n59; cooperation of, with NGOs, 373–74; creation of, 354–55, 357–58, 379n15; ethical regression of, 370–73, 374; existence of, as proof of limitations of private enterprise, 362; funding from, without reference to profit motive, 366; history of, as stages of moral progress, 361–75; ideology of development of, 355–56; legitimation of the public sector by, 366–67; loans by, 362–65, 367–68, 370–73, 374–75, 380nn28–29; as originally lacking moral compass, 354–56; Social Investment Fund, 384n52; soft loans from, 364–66; Structural Adjustment Programs (SAPs), 370–73

World Economic Forum, 210

World Trade Organization, 263, 265, 370

Yunus, Muhammad, 359–60, 387–89

zakat, 232, 245, 252n14, 253n17, 305

About the Authors

Howard Richards is Research Professor of Peace and Global Studies at Earlham College. He was the first lawyer for Cesar Chavez when Chavez began to organize the United Farm Workers in Delano, California; and also the first Western Region Vice President of Students for a Democratic Society in the 1960s. Among other works, Professor Richards is the author of *Life on a Small Planet, Apuntes de Filosofía, The Evaluation of Cultural Action, Ética y Economía, La ciencia social al servicio de la esperanza, Letters from Quebec: A Philosophy for Peace and Justice, Volumes I and II,* and *Understanding the Global Economy.*

Joanna Swanger is assistant professor of Border Studies and Resident Director of Earlham College's Border Studies Program, which explores globalization from the vantage point of the El Paso/Ciudad Juárez frontier. She specializes in Latin American and U.S. labor history and has written numerous articles on these topics.

Both authors are members of the Global Political Economy Commission of the International Peace Research Association, both have traveled and conducted research in many parts of the Americas—and Latin America in particular—and both are contributors to *Ciudades Educadoras,* a transnational project of building a network of cities devoted to economic solidarity and sustainable peace, which has its world headquarters in Barcelona and its American headquarters in Rosario, Argentina.